DATE DUE

SE 17 '97			

DEMCO 38-296

Law, magistracy and crime in Old Regime Paris, 1735–1789 is centered on the great Paris lawcourts, the Châtelet and Parlement, and their criminal defendants during the eighteenth century. This volume reconstructs the general system of royal criminal justice and much of the accompanying Old Regime political structure: the provenance, formation, authority, and ethos of the magistracy and its relations with the monarchy, the Church, the aristocracy, the bourgeois, and the plebeians. The doctrines and practices of punishment are examined, along with the jurisprudence of moral and criminal responsibility and the ideology and mechanics of royal pardon and commutation. The procedure for trial and judgment of defendants that was in force from 1670 to the Revolution is described and analyzed in detail. Three example cases illustrate the operations of the Châtelet and the Parlement.

Law, magistracy, and crime
in Old Regime Paris, 1735–1789

Law, magistracy, and crime in Old Regime Paris, 1735–1789

—

Volume 1
The system of criminal justice

RICHARD MOWERY ANDREWS

 **CAMBRIDGE**
UNIVERSITY PRESS

cate of the University of Cambridge

ngton Street, Cambridge CB2 1RP

lew York, NY 10011-4211, USA

kleigh, Victoria 3166, Australia

University Press 1994

First published 1994

Printed in the United States of America

Library of Congress Cataloging-in-Publication Data
Andrews, Richard Mowery.
Law, magistracy, and crime in Old Regime Paris, 1735–1789 /
Richard Mowery Andrews.
p.   cm.
Includes bibliographical references.
Contents: v. 1. The system of criminal justice.
ISBN 0–521–36169–9 (v. 1 : hc)
1. France. Parlement (Paris) – History. 2. Paris (France).
Châtelet – History. 3. Criminal courts – France – Paris – History.
4. Judgments, Criminal – France – Paris – History.   5. Criminal
justice, Administration of – France – Paris – History. 6. Punishment –
France – Paris – History.   I. Title.
KJV3747.A53   1992
345.44'36101'09 – dc20
[344.436105109]   92–4214
                                                                        CIP
A catalog record for this book is available from the British Library.

ISBN 0–521–36169–9 hardback

To the memory of my mother, Ruth Mowery Andrews,
and my grandparents, Gus Mowery and Ida Powell Mowery

Contents

Contents

Contents

Illustrations, charts, and tables

Figures

Maps

Illustrations, charts, and tables

Charts

The genealogical charts are of patrilineal descent by generations. Each generation is listed under a Roman numeral. Children are placed directly under father and mother according to the number of their generation. The dates of their birth and death follow their names. The name of the eldest son in each generation is sometimes given in italics, when that information is known. The offices held by each male, and the dates of the acquisition of period of tenure, are given after his name. The sign oo stands for marriage; it is followed by the marriage date and the family name of the bride or groom.

Tables

Preface

This work is devoted to the criminal justice of the Châtelet and Parlement of
Paris during the eighteenth century, from the early years of the reign of Louis
XV through the first year of the Revolution. The two volumes are one history,
in its two components: It is intended for all readers who are concerned with
issues of guilt, judgment, punishment, and mercy, who are curious about the
workings, crisis, and ending of a major legal and political culture and about
crime within the life of a great metropolis, as well as for students and scholars
of Old Regime France.

Volume 1 reconstructs the system of Old Regime criminal justice. That system existed from roughly 1670 to 1789 without major alterations. It governed
lawcourts throughout France, with only minor differences between regions and
jurisdictions. Its elements were court organization and jurisdictions, the constitution and composition of the royal magistracy, incrimination and criminal
responsibility, penology, royal pardon, the procedure for trial and judgment, and
the principles of jurisprudence that informed criminal justice.

Volume 2, *The Action of Criminal Justice*, recounts the operations of the system
in the criminal courts and at the punishment sites of the Châtelet and Parlement from 1735 to 1789. It is diachronic, tracing continuities and changes in
crimes, criminals, judgments, and punishments. Royal criminal statutes and
their jurisprudence were integral to the system. But for the sake of symmetry
between the two volumes, and of greater clarity in the second, they are discussed mainly in Volume 2. That volume is concentrated on the social worlds of
Parisian crime and criminals, evolutions in punishment, death sentences, and
executions, and, finally, on crises and creativities in criminal justice during the
final years of the Old Regime. The entire work concludes with a discussion of
the origins of Revolutionary criminal justice.

Law – criminal, civil, and administrative–was the foundation of the French
state from the late Middle Ages to the Revolution, and beyond. Kings ruled
through legislative acts, just as they created lawcourts and promulgated codes
for those who governed and judged in their names. Criminal justice was a terrain of confrontation on which all strata and classes of Parisian, and French,
society periodically encountered each other. Its punishments also provided the
foremost spectacle of secular authority in French urban civilization. Centered

xiii

on Paris, this work is also centered on the last and (in ways that will be described) most perfect era in the long history of royal criminal justice: 1735 to 1789. The legal system was constructed over many centuries. It reached its apogee of coherence in ideology, jurisprudence, organization, and enforcement in that era. During the last two decades before the Revolution, the system encountered pressures of a nature and volume that it could not withstand. Paris, the island and then city where the rule by law of French monarchs began, was also a principal arena for the final crisis of royal criminal justice.

The subject is vast and complex: the criminal law; crimes and criminals in a great metropolis and its hinterland; the magistrates of what were perhaps the two most important courts of the Old Regime, and their judgments. Some aspects of that history have been investigated by others to whose work I am indebted. Many aspects have remained unknown. This study is holistic in ambition, at once legal, political, and social. But it is without pretense to completeness or closure.

What began, in 1985, as a research venture into the Old Regime judicial background to authority in Revolutionary Paris soon became a much larger exploration, one that I trust also gives greater clarity to the protagonists, programs, and institutions of criminal and political justice during the period 1791 to 1795. I have wished to chart avenues for further and deeper inquiry by other historians, and to convey the excitement of discovery that I, hitherto a historian of the French Revolution and Revolutionary Paris, have experienced inside the world of the Old Regime. That world both generated and gave a problematic legacy to the Revolution.

Acknowledgments

The primary research for the two volumes and the writing of most of Volume 1 were accomplished during the five years that I served as senior Mellon Fellow at the Society of Fellows in the Humanities and as senior lecturer in the department of history at Columbia University. Those were superb environments for this study, a fact that has been particularly gratifying to someone who was first introduced to serious learning as a freshman in Columbia College. In a sense, this work completes a circle begun there long ago.

I owe special thanks to Fellows of the Society, at the Heyman Center for the Humanities, for sharing their creative scholarship and for giving critical attention to my efforts: to Dilwyn Knox, Mary Campbell, Gauri Viswanathan, Mark Rollins, Janet Johnson, Andrew Apter, Akeel Bilgrami, Franciscus Verellen, Martha Saxton. I thank faculty associates of the Society for their encouragement and criticisms: Eugene Rice, John Mundy, Marc Raeff, Steven Marcus, Richard Kuhns, Ainslee Embree, Barbara Stoler Miller, Theodore de Bary. Loretta Nassar, former Director of the Society, contributed a unique blend of warmth, intellectual acumen, and administrative support. By the variety of their humanistic knowledge and the quality of their collegiality, members of the Society of Fellows caused me to perceive ramifications of law, authority, and moral consciousness that I would have ignored otherwise.

The last of Volume 1 was written at the Center for the Humanities of Oregon State University: I thank Peter Copek, Director, and the members of the Center for their hospitality and interest, and for facilitating final computer presentation of the manuscript of Volume 1. That presentation was done with great skill by Eric Ackerson of Old Towne Computer in Corvallis. The rivers and forests of Oregon have given their special nourishment to spirit, body, and mind, including a bounty of salmon, steelhead, and rainbow trout – patiently researched and strenuously acquired. Another circle, one begun during boyhood on the Quachita River of Arkansas, has been completed.

Robert Paxton, Patrice Higonnet, Isser Woloch, Robert Allen, Colin Lucas, and Albert Hamscher gave penetrating reading and commentary to portions of the manuscript. Most of the ideas in Volume 1 were discussed with Carol Pixton, who also aided in transcribing several archival sources and in formatting tables and charts. I am grateful to Roger Blumberg, of the Heyman Center for

Acknowledgments

the Humanities, for contributing his mathematical expertise to unraveling the complexities of Old Regime penal judgment. Frank Smith, executive editor for history and social sciences at Cambridge University Press, gave skilled editorial counsel. Mme. Bourgoin, archivist of the French National Archives, and Whitney Bagnall, special collections librarian of the Columbia University Law Library, graciously and expertly assisted me in obtaining source materials. I also wish to thank the American Council of Learned Societies for a grant-in-aid of research for the summer of 1986.

Gregory Aldrich, Gregory Gleason, Douglas and Suzan Harper, John Gillis, Marion Truslow, Bruce Woodruff, David Berger, Jim Dingman, John Anderson, Bob Trippel, Helen Sether, and Ermal Griswold have been vitally sagacious, loyal, and sustaining friends. Finally, this work would never have been written without the love, and the abiding examples of personal fortitude, that were given by my parents.

Richard Mowery Andrews

Corvallis, Oregon
July 1991

Principal sources and abbreviations

Archives Nationales

AD III 6 to 17: printed sentences and judgments by Parisian tribunals, especially the Châtelet and Parlement, with notations by Thomas Gueulette, deputy prosecutor of the Châtelet (1735–89).

AD III 19: "Arrêts de Mort depuis le dernier décembre 1730 jusqu'en 1740 inclusivement" and "Arrêts de Mort depuis l'année 1741 jusqu'en l'année 1750 inclusivement." Ms. by Thomas Gueulette.

AD III 27b and 28: edicts, rulings, and instructions on criminal jurisprudence (eighteenth century).

AD III 31: ordinances and rulings on trial procedure and penalties (1730–89).

VI 73 to 537: royal letters of appointment to office for the judges of the Châtelet who served between 1735 and 1789.

X2a 1302, 1306, 1307: Parlement of Paris, criminal appeals chamber, registers of distribution of cases judged on appeal (September 1747 through November 1749; January 1785 through December 1789).

X2b 1334: Parlement of Paris, minutes of torture preliminary to execution and of executions (1750–78).

Inventory 449, U 995: Parlement of Paris; register of royal remissions and commutations of penalties (1704–1767).

Inventory 450, 10 ms. volumes: Parlement of Paris, alphabetical registers of all persons judged by the criminal appeals chamber (1700–90). These registers give the name, age, occupation, and domicile of the accused, the jurisdiction in first instance, the charge or accusation, sentence in first instance and its date, the date of appellate judgment by the Parlement, the exact appellate and final judgment(s). The following have been transcribed: names of persons judged on appeal from all courts (including the Châtelet) in the jurisdiction of the Parlement during the years 1736, 1762, 1787, and 1789; names of persons judged in first instance by the Châtelet and then on appeal by the Parlement, during the years 1748 and 1775; persons sentenced to prejudgment torture by the Parlement in the period 1735 to 1749; persons sentenced to death by the Parlement in the periods 1735 to 1749 and 1775 to 1789.

Y 1867 to 1869: Châtelet, dossiers of candidacy and reception for judges who served between 1735 and 1789.

Y 10050 to 10477: Châtelet, criminal chamber, transcripts of criminal trials and judgments, 1736–87. More than 150 cases have been examined from the years 1736, 1748–9, 1762, 1774–6, 1780–1, 1785–7.

Y 10510: Châtelet, register of deliberations and rulings of the criminal chamber (1755–89).

Y 10514, 10516, 10517, 10518, 10525, 10526, 10529, 10530: Châtelet, criminal chamber, registers of judgments (November 1747 through November 1749; January 1761 through June 1761; July 1761 through July 1762; August 1762 through January 1763; October 1774 through July 1775; July 1775 through October 1776; January 1785 through August 1786; September 1786 through December 1789).

Y 10648, 10649: Châtelet, registers of arrests and jailings (October 1785 through October 1786; March 1789 through March 1790).

Y 18794, 18795: Châtelet, registers of provostial arrests, jailings, and judgments (January 1764 through June 1780; July 1780 through January 1791).

Bibliothèque Nationale

S. P. Hardy. "Mes loisirs ou journal d'événements tels qu'ils parviennent à ma connoissance, commencant à l'année 1775." 6 ms. vols. Nouvelles acquisitions françaises, Fr. 6682–7.

Works of jurisprudence and collections of royal statutes are listed under "Abbreviations." The eighteenth-century jurists whose works are cited were all serving magistrates or barristers in important courts. They were both scholars and practitioners, and their works informed the curricula of the law faculties where magistrates were educated.

Abbreviations

The following abbreviations are used for works frequently cited in the notes. See also the list of Archives Nationales manuscripts, in the list of "Principal Sources,"

Amiot
: Amiot, Claude. "Procès criminels de la Chambre de la Tournelle du Parlement de Paris." 2 ms. vols. Paris, 1701–2. In A.N. U 942.

A.N.
: Archives Nationales de France.

Conférences
: *Procès-verbaux des conférences tenus par ordre du roi entre Messieurs les Commissaires du Conseil et Messieurs les Députés du Parlement*

	de Paris pour l'examen des Articles de l'Or-donnance civile du mois d'Avril 1667 et de l'Ordonnance criminelle du mois d'Août 1670. Louvain, 1700.
Delamare	Delamare, Nicolas. *Traité de la police.* 4 vols. Amsterdam, 1729.
Denisart	Denisart, Jean-Baptiste. *Collection de dé-cisions nouvelles et de notions relatives à la ju-risprudence actuelle.* 4 vols. Paris 1771.
Desmarquets	Desmarquets, Charles. *Nouveau stile du Châtelet de Paris et de toutes les jurisdictions ordinaires du royaume, tant en matière civile et criminelle que de police.* Paris, 1771.
Domat	Domat, Jean. "Le droit public." In *Les Loix civiles dans leur ordre naturel, suivies du droit public.* Luxembourg, 1702.
Ferrière	Ferrière, Claude-Joseph de. *Dictionnaire de droit et de pratique.* 2 vols. Paris, 1769.
Guide	Michel Antoine, Henri-François Buffet, Suzanne Clémençet, Ferréol de Ferry, Monique Langlois, Yvonne Lanhers, Jean-Paul Laurent, and Jacques Meurgey de Tupigny. *Guide des recherches dans les fonds judiciaires de l'ancien régime.* Paris: Imprim-erie Nationale, 1958.
Guyot	Guyot, Pierre-Jean-Jacques Guillaume, ed. *Répertoire universel et raisonné de juris-prudence civile, criminelle, canonique et béné-ficiale.* 17 vols. Paris, 1784–7.
Isambert	Isambert, Decrusy, and Jourdan, eds. *Re-cueil général des anciennes lois françaises, depuis l'an 420 jusqu'à la révolution de 1789.* 29 vols. Paris, 1821–33.
Jousse, *Nouveau commentaire*	Jousse, Daniel. *Nouveau commentaire sur l'ordonnance criminelle du mois d'août 1670, avec un abrégé de la justice criminelle.* 2 vols. Paris 1771.
Jousse, *Traité*	*Traité de la justice criminelle de France.* 4 vols. Paris, 1771.
Muyart, *Institutes*	Muyart de Vouglans, Pierre-François. *In-stitutes au droit criminel.* Paris, 1757.
Muyart, *Instruction*	*Instruction criminelle suivant les loix et or-donnances du royaume.* Paris, 1762.

Principal sources and abbreviations

Muyart, *Loix criminelles*	*Les loix criminelles de France dans leur ordre naturel.* Paris, 1783.
RHDFE	*Revue historique du droit français et étranger.*
Rousseaud	Du Rousseaud de la Combe, Guy. *Traité des matières criminelles.* Paris, 1769.
Serpillon	Serpillon, François. *Code criminel ou commentaire sur l'Ordonnance de 1670.* 4 vols. Lyons, 1767.
Soulatges	Soulatges, Jean-Antoine. *Traité des crimes.* 3 vols. Toulouse, 1762.

General introduction

A. The metropolis and its region

Eighteenth century Paris has been the most described of modern European cities. That historiographic plentitude derives largely from the fact that Paris was the original and then, during five years, leading arena for the Great Revolution. Most studies of the Old Regime city have been written in the shadow of that event, some with teleological constraints. This study draws upon that rich and broad literature, although its focus is concentrated. It investigates the city within the parameters of criminal justice, through the lens of judicial sources, over a long period. It therefore develops, necessarily, into an account of some of the forces that generated the Parisian and French Revolution, and that shaped much of criminal legislation in the years 1789 through 1791 and beyond.

The criminal law was national by the eighteenth century. In the capital and its highly populous region, the principles and efficacy of that law were tested more acutely and continuously than anywhere else in the realm. The city impacted on the law during the eighteenth century. Those who enforced, violated, or observed the law in Paris lived and acted within a great, complex, and criminogenic metropolis. Its forceful presence will unfold across the two volumes of this study.

The capital was porous, its circumference ill defined. During the seventeenth and eighteenth centuries, tree-lined boulevards (to the north) and crude embankments (to the south) replaced walls. At the *portes,* or gates, where the royal highways became city streets, there were only customs posts and guard stations. All the principal wagon and coach routes of France led to those streets, from the frontiers of the realm. Within a 200-mile radius, the network of roads converging on Paris was one of the most dense in Europe.[1] Most of the rivers of northern and eastern France flowed into the Seine, whose course connected Paris to the ocean via Rouen and Lè Havre. Those waters carried great

[1] See Paul Vidal de la Blache, *Tableau de la géographie de la France* (Paris, 1905), p. 379, and Guy Arbellot, "La grande mutation des routes de France au milieu de XVIIIe," *Annales: Economies, Sociétés, Civilisations,* 28 (1973): 765–91.

volumes of commodities and people to the fourteen ports of the city.[2] The Turgot–Bretez map of Paris (Map 1, frontis piece). dating from 1739, loyally por-
trayed a river filled with boats, of many sizes and cargoes, from the Porte de la
Rapée to the Isle des Cygnes.

The capital was the vortex for the most populous and agriculturally productive provinces of eighteenth-century France. The region especially vital to the
sustenance of the metropolis – to its nourishment in wheat, dairy products,
meat, legumes, and wines, as well as immigrant laborers, transport, and communications – was its own countryside, the inner region of the Ile-de-France.
For administrative purposes (particularly taxation), this area was defined by a
royal *élection* within a larger unit, the Generality of Paris. For judicial purposes,
the Paris region was divided into many *bailliages*, of which the Paris Châtelet
was the largest. The social reality was saturation, a *pays plein;* in the *election* of
Paris there were 442 parishes (not including those of the city), 47,685 house
holds, and probably a quarter-million inhabitants; in the Generality of Paris,
there were 2,103 parishes, 209,670 households, and more than 1 million villagers and townspeople.[3]

Abundance, poverty, and fears characterized the Paris region during the
eighteenth century. Most of the foodstuffs the countryside produced were destined for consumption in Paris, especially when harvests were bad. The farmers were mainly tenants with large families, working on small plots owned by
seigneurial landlords (many of whom resided in Paris). The inhabitants of its
market towns were inclined to riot over tax increases or against the export of
food in times of dearth, and to migrate elsewhere. Much of the land was Crown
property. Great royal forests and woodlands, reserved for Court hunts and for
high-grade timber exploitation, ringed the capital in every direction.[4] They are
graphically depicted on the Cassini and Jaillot maps of the Paris region (Map 2
and see Map 6). The primary and secondary roads linking the capital to France,
as well as the Seine, Marne, and Oise rivers, wound for long distances through
forests. There, brigandage and vagabondage were endemic, as was bitter contention between peasants and royal forest guards. The kings and *grands seigneurs*
of France hunted stags in woods – Senart, Armainville, Bondy, Rambouillet,
Marly, Montmorency, Saint-Germain – whose byways and recesses also served
as territories of depredation and refuge for gangs of highwaymen and smug-
glers, many of whom had once been soldiers in royal regiments or peasants on
seigneurial estates. People who could do so traveled those roads by daylight,
rather than at night, either armed or in groups. The entire Paris basin was
characterized by exchanges and itineraries, of all manner of commodities and

[2] Richard Cobb, *Paris and Its Provinces, 1792–1802* (London: Oxford University Press, 1975), pp.
59–86.
[3] Abbé Joseph Expilly, *Dictionnaire géographique, historique et politique des Gaules et de la France,* 6
Vols. (Paris, 1768), Vol. 5, p. 569. These figures are for 1767.
[4] For the enforcement of that royal monopoly, see Yves Gaultier, "La capitainerie royal des chasses
de la Varenne du Louvre, Grande Vénerie de France," in *Etudes d'histoire du droit parisien,* ed.
Françis Dumont (Paris: Presses Universitaires de France, 1970), pp. 13–158.

by members of all social classes.[5] Many of the itineraries led to trials in the metropolis, at the Châtelet and the Parlement of Paris.

Between 2 and 3 percent of the French population (or about 1 in 50 of the king's subjects), lived in the capital during the eighteenth century. Most of the city's people had been born elsewhere. Paris was simultaneously magnetic and imperious in its relations with the rest of the realm. An entire triumphalist literature described its potency, while ignoring its contradictions and brutalities.[6]

Since the High Middle Ages, Paris had been the first city of the French state, the principal locus for its constantly growing cadre of high officers in taxation, finance, military administration, and justice, and of the French Church, through the university and its auxiliary *collèges*, the seminaries, monasteries, convents, and their incomparable libraries. From the sixteenth century onward, it was also the capital of *savoir* in secular arts, letters, and science.[7] During the eighteenth century, Paris became one of the foremost commercial and manufacturing centers of the realm by the quantity and diversity of its enterprise.

At midcentury, there were approximately 40,000 master artisans and tradesmen in Paris; by 1789 there were perhaps 50,000. Marcel Reinhard estimated their social group (families) to number some 120,000 people at midcentury, a group far more numerous than the recognized elites of the city – clergy, officers of state, nobility. A large number of these master artisans and tradesmen belonged to the venerable "six great" craft guilds: drapers and haberdashers, hatters, fabric manufacturers, goldsmiths, grocers, wine merchants. Many others – notably masters in the building trades, publishers, printers, and bookbinders – had their own professional associations.[8] In 1790–1, each of some 3,800 masters was sufficiently capitalized to employ more than a few workers at wage. Only about 50 of the masters regularly employed more than 100 such workers; half (about 1,900) employed 5 to 20 workers at wages. Production was artisanal, not industrial, in character, but its cumulative volume and value were great; so was its aggregate labor force (male and female) of some 70,000. The most renowned and lucrative sectors of the Parisian economy were also those with the most enterprises and the largest work forces: building construction, decoration and furnishings; luxury craftsmanship; leather goods, fabrics and

---

[5] See especially Cobb, *Paris and Its Provinces*, pp. 40–56; Michel Philipnneau, *La vie rurale de la banlieue parisienne: Etude de géographie humaine* (Paris: Librairie Armand Colin, 1956).

[6] And in the genre of Expilly: " 'PARIS, Lutetia Parisiorum,' ville capitale de la province de l'Ile-de-France, du gouvernement de même nom, & de tout le royaume de France. Nommer cette ville, c'est dire en quelque sorte ce qu'elle est, puisqu'il n'est personne qui ne sache qu'elle passe avec raison pour la plus belle, la plus riche, la plus peuplée, la plus florissant, & pour l'une des plus grandes villes de l'Europe. On sait aussi qu'elle ne le cede à aucune ville du monde, soit par le nombre prodigieux de ses superbes batiments, soit par la sagesse de son gouvernement, soit par rapport aux sciences & aux autres arts qu'on y cultive, soit pour toutes les commodités, & les agréments qu'on y trouve, soit enfin par le commerce prodigieux qui s'y fait" (Expilly, *Dictionnaire*, vol. 5, p. 399).

[7] On those political, religious, and cultural infrastructures of power in Paris, see Pierre Chaunu, *La mort à Paris, XVIe, XVIIe et XVIIIe siècles* (Paris: Librairie Arthème Fayard, 1978), pp. 200–17.

[8] Marcel Reinhard, *Nouvelle histoire de Paris; La révolution, 1789–1799* (Paris: Librairie Hachette, 1971), p. 46.

Map 1. Paris: "Plan de Turgot" (1739). Commissioned by Michel-Etienne Turgot, provost of merchants of Paris and royal councillor of state; designed by Louis Bretez. Modern facsimile by Institut National Géographique.

Map 2. Paris region (c.1750) from the "Carte géométrique de la France" by Cassini de Thury. Modern facsimile by Institut National Géographique.

apparels, the "fashion of Paris." Tens of thousands of master artisans and tradesmen did not employ labor at wages: They either worked alone or remunerated their journeymen and apprentices (who were frequently also their sons, nephews, cousins, or in-laws) with food, lodging, craft training, and small coin.[9]

Since at least the mid-seventeenth century, the master artisanate had been excluded from political power in the city and from the formation of policy. Collectively, however, it retained greater social power than any other group in the metropolis (including royal administrators and magistrates), for it could command labor on a scale far beyond the capacity of any other.

The magnitude and prestige of production by Parisian craftsmen, manufacturers, and builders masked a raw and fierce labor economy; so too did the paternalist ideology of the artisanal guilds. Production was nonmechanized, labor-intensive, physically attritional, and often dangerous, even in the luxury crafts. Employment was insecure, seasonal, and vulnerable to rapid fluctuation in market demand. Those conditions were acute in the building and associated trades and in textile, fabric, leather, and clothing manufacturing which together formed the two largest employers of laborers in the Parisian economy. The work forces of construction enterprises often contracted by as much as one-half during the winter. In most trades, pay was by the *journée;* in textiles it was usually piece rate. For all but the skilled, privileged, and those working for family enterprises, pay was consistently low in relation to the cost of living (except for the price of bread and wine, within the laborer's reach in normal years). Strikes were illegal. Craft guilds were dominated by the more substantial *maîtres* and generally served the interests of employers. Masters lived in tense relations with their journeymen and apprentices: Corporatist solidarity alternated with bitter and sometimes violent conflict.[10] The very structure of production, with its easily fractured relations between those who deployed capital and those who sold their labor, was criminogenic. Most large- and median-scale commerce and subcontracting were transacted by bills of exchange and promissory notes, not by direct payment, so that opportunities for fraud and contrived bankruptcies were inherent to the system.

Most of the products of Paris were not exported; they were displayed, merchandised, and consumed in the metropolis and its region. The city offered a plethora of goods – expensive and cheap, new and used, sold, bartered, and stolen. The abundance of commodities, commercial transactions, and services concentrated (but quite unequally distributed) within Paris stimulated greed, competitiveness, and jealousy, sharpened class antagonisms, and gave myriad

---

[9] Documentation for this statement is employers' requests to the Treasury for small denominations of *assignats,* the paper currency introduced by the Revolutionary government with which to pay their workers. The documents listing these requests (A.N. F 30 115–60) form the most important source on the organization and geography of manufacturing in Paris at the close of the Old Regime. (For a list of the abbreviations used in these notes, see "Principal Sources" in the front matter.)

[10] See Michael Sonenscher, *Work and Wages; Natural Law, Politics and the Eighteenth-Century French Trades* (New York: Cambridge University Press, 1989).

occasions for theft, fraud, and violence. The impoverished were surrounded by wealth, and the affluent by poverty. Capital of France, Paris was equally the premier city of criminality. The records of the Châtelet suggest that in any given year between 1740 and 1790, 1 person in every 200 to 300 of the population was arrested and tried for a serious offense.

Accessibility and economic magnetism shaped the Old Regime metropolis. Paris continually expanded outward beyond its official limits; simultaneously, the population density of the inner city increased. The expansion did not dissipate the interior pressures and volatilities. From the early reign of Louis XV into the Revolution, the social geography of Paris changed, in ways that surpassed the control and threatened the authority of those who governed.

Eighteenth-century maps of the metropolis, from the pictorial masterpiece commissioned by Turgot in the 1730s to Verniquet's geometric representation in 1785–90, offer a stark contrast between a claustral, dense, and labyrinthine city *intra muros* and expansive, seemingly vacant faubourgs *extra muros*, immediately beyond the exterior boulevards of the Right and Left Banks. Solid ranks of buildings suddenly give way to rural flatlands or to bluffs divided into rectangular plots. Inner Paris was truly a labyrinth, of 903 streets.[11] But the starkness of contrast is deceptive. By midcentury, the farmlands and pastures of the faubourgs were already undergoing transformation. Around ecclesiastial establishments, along thoroughfares, then laterally along farm roads, they were being occupied: the northern, eastern, and southern by apartment buildings, ateliers, factories, shops, and taverns; the western by residences and shops that purveyed to the wealthy. By the 1780s, the social hierarchies, compactions, and tensions of the inner city were being re-created on main streets in the faubourgs Saint-Antoine, Temple, Saint-Martin, Montmartre, and Saint-Victor.

In 1702, the innermost parts of the faubourgs were administratively incorporated in to Paris, and the new limits encompassed an area of about 2,500 acres. In 1785 through 1787, new customs barriers enclosed most of the outer faubourgs and gave Paris an official area of 8,500 acres. The population rose from about 475,000 to 500,000 in 1715 to between 600,000 and 700,000 in 1789, an increase of some 35 percent over the span of only three generations.[12] During both periods, Paris had about twice the population of Lyons, the second-largest city of France. But that growth was distributed unevenly, both socially and spatially.

From the late 1760s to the eve of the Revolution, architects and building entrepreneurs created new, affluent, and monumental *quartiers* in the northwestern and western reaches of the city. Wide avenues, mansions with enclosed

---

[11] Expilly, *Dictionnaire*, vol. 5, p. 404.

[12] Daniel Roche, *Le peuple de Paris: Essai sur la culture populaire au XVIIIe siècle* (Paris: Editions Aubier Montagne, 1981), pp. 15, 19, 22. The population figures for Old Regime Paris, especially those generated during the eighteenth century, are estimates that were arrived at by several different methods of calculation. On those methods, see Roche, pp. 19–20. His book is an excellent study of popular life in Old Regime Paris, in its material dimensions and sensibilities.

gardens, spacious apartment buildings, expensive shops and luxury ateliers, neoclassical public edifices and squares replaced market gardens, pastures, and tenements in the faubourgs Saint-Honoré and Roule, on the Chaussé d'Antin and the rue de Richelieu, around the Place Vendôme, the Opéra, and the Tuileries Palace, along the regal and perfectly aligned expanse of the Champs-Elysées. On the Left Bank, the wealthy and aristocratic faubourg Saint-Germain expanded westward to the Invalides and the Ecole Militaire. On both banks of the Seine, the rich and empowered began to desert the constricted, swarming Quarters of the Halles, the River, the rues Saint-Denis, Saint-Martin, and Temple, the Marais, the Cité, and the University.[13] The poor were present throughout the city, even in the new *beaux quartiers*, and almost every Parisian street harbored bourgeois, with their wealth and enterprises. But a novel and durable social partition of space emerged during the second half of the century, along the rough boundary formed to the north by the Porte Montmartre and the rue Notre-Dame des Victoires and to the south by the rue de Tournon and the Luxembourg Palace. To the west of that boundary lay an elegant, aerated section inhabited by rentiers, financiers, and speculators, officers of state, old and new nobility, barristers, luxury craftsmen, lackeys, and servants. To the east lay the venerable deteriorated Quarters of central Paris and the nearby enclaves of the northern, eastern, and southeastern faubourgs, where the mass of population remained concentrated. That Paris – of narrow, packed streets, dank and sunless squares, alleyways and cul-de-sacs, high, recessive buildings with bulging façades; of ubiquitous stalls, shops, ateliers, and taverns; of lawcourts, *collèges*, and university faculties; of Gothic and Renaissance churches, monasteries, and convents; of cemeteries, refuse, and effluvia – was mainly an artifact of the period 1450–1650. That was the old city. It absorbed most of the 35-percent increase in population during the eighteenth century.[14] It remained, until the nineteenth century, the principal locus of metropolitan secular, ecclesiastical, and intellectual authority, and of capital, labor, crime, and riot. The maps exaggerated the contrast between "Ville" and "faubourgs," but they express a figurative truth.

[13] Louis Bergeron, "Croissance urbaine et société à Paris au 18e siècle," in *La ville au 18e siècle; Colloque d'Aix-en-Provence* (Aix-en-Provence: 1974), pp. 127–134; Alfred Destrez, *Le faubourg Saint-Honoré de Louis XIV au Second Empire* (Paris: Henri Lefebure, 1953); Yves Durand, "Répartition de la noblesse dans le quartiers de Paris," in *Contributions à l'histoire démographique de la Révolution française*, 2nd ser. (Paris: Commission d'Histoire Économique et Sociale de la Révolution Française, 1965), pp. 22–5; Jacques Hillairet, *Connaissance de Vieux-Paris vol. 2: Rive Gauche et les Iles*, 2 vols. (Paris: Editions Gonthier, 1963), pp. 224–70.

[14] In 1715 more than three-fourths of the total population of the city lived in the Quarters of central Paris (Alan Williams, *The Police of Paris, 1718–1789* [Baton Rouge: Louisiana State University Press, 1979], pp. 248–9). Some two-thirds lived there in 1793–4; 409,077 people, as against 212,454 in the faubourgs. At the end of the eighteenth century, central Paris occupied less than one-half the physical space of the city. See Reinhard, *Nouvelle histoire de Paris*, p. 414; Albert Soboul, *Les Sans-culottes parisiens en l'an II: Mouvement populaire et gouvernement révolutionnaire, 2 juin 1793 / 9 thermidor an II* (Paris: Clavreuil, 1958), pp. 1091–2; R. M. Andrews, "Paris of the Great Revolution; 1789–1796," in *People and Communities in the Western World*, 2 vols., ed. Gene Brucker (Homewood, Ill.: Dorsey, 1979), vol. 2, pp. 68–9.

General introduction

Central Paris had a spine, the portions of the rues Saint-Denis and Saint-Martin that ran from the respective *Portes* to the river, and their prolongations on the Left Bank by the rue du la Harpe – rue d'Enfer and the rue Saint-Jacques – rue du faubourg Saint-Jacques. The streets vertebral to that spine included the Quarters of the Halles, the Louvre, and the Palais-Royal, the Temple, Marais, Gréve, Saint-Paul, and Saint-Antoine, on the Right Bank, and Saint-André-des-Arts, Saint-Benoît, the Montagne Sainte-Genéviève, and the Place Maubert on the Left Bank. The entire area was involuted, but not closed. Each of its *quartiers* was open to satellite faubourgs through streets that radiated outward, and those streets flowed into the road network of which Paris was the heart.[15]

In the eighteenth century, central Paris was characterized by physical and human density and by socioeconomic compression. In its protean social variety, it was microcosmic of the entire metropolis and, by the provenance of its inhabitants, of the entire realm.

A distance of less than 2 miles separated the Porte Saint-Martin from the Church of Sainte-Genéviève at the southern limit of the Latin Quarter; a shorter distance separated the Place du Palais-Royal from the Porte Saint-Antoine. In 1789, close to 400,000 people lived in the space formed by those points. And yet large tracts of that space, and of the faubourgs, were barely inhabited. They were ecclesiastical preserves: churches, monasteries, and convents, with few residents, high walls, and vast cloisters. By the 1780s, more than 20,000 people – the population of an important provincial town – lived in the small hexagon formed by the Porte and rue du Temple, the rues des Gravilliers, Jean Robert, Saint-Martin, and the Porte Saint-Martin. They lived in about 1,500 buildings.[16] The Benedictine priory, church, and gardens of Saint-Martin-des-Champs occupied one-third of the hexagon. Only a few hundred clerics and their servants lived there, in an environment at once ethereal, hermetic, and vestigial.[17] Every parish of the exiguous city had such exclusionary areas, most of which had been established during the Middle Ages on land then peripheral to Paris.[18] The Church was the largest corporate landowner within the Old Regime metropolis.[19]

[15] For more detailed socioeconomic and topographical description of central Paris and the faubourgs at the end of the Old Regime, see the following by Richard Mowery Andrews: "Paris of the Great Revolution"; "Réflexions sur la Conjuration des Egaux," *Annales; Economies, Sociétés, Civilisations*, 29 (1974): 73–106; "Social Structures, Political Elites and Ideology in Revolutionary Paris, 1792–94: A critical evaluation of Albert Soboul's *Les Sans-culottes parisiens en l'an II*," *Journal of Social History* (1985): 71–112. See also Reinhard, *Nouvelle histoire de Paris;* Roche, *Le peuple de Paris.*

[16] Expilly, *Dictionnaire*, vol. 5, p. 401.

[17] Ibid., p. 493, and Pons-Augustin Alletz, *Le géographie parisien, ou le conducteur chronologique et historique des rues de Paris*, 2 vols. (Paris, 1769), vol. 2, p. 322.

[18] See Adrien Friedmann, *Paris, ses rues, ses paroisses du Moyen Age à la Révolution: Origine et évolution des circonscriptions paroissiales* (Paris: Plon, 1959), and Bernard Rouleau, *Le tracé des rues de Paris: Formation, typologie, fonctions* (Paris: CNRS, 1967).

[19] Reinhard, *Nouvelle histoire de Paris*, pp. 20–26, 404.

General introduction

In the late eighteenth century, there were on average 800 to 1,000 people for every 2.5 acres in central Paris, one of the highest population densities in Europe. At the core of Paris – on the Cité island, in the central market area (the Halles), around the rues des Arcis and Lombards, in the Marais and the Quarter of the Place de Grève, on the Montagne Sainte-Genéviève – the compaction was most acute. In the most venerable quarter of Paris, the Cité between the rue du la Barillière and the end of the rue du la Chanoinesse, some 10,000 people lived in the shadow of the Hotel-Dieu and Notre-Dame Cathedral. When the streets were not filled with traffic (for there were no sidewalks), it was possible to walk from the rue Saint-Denis to the town hall of Paris (the Hôtel de Ville) in under ten minutes and from the rue des Lombards to the river at the Quai Pelletier in about seven. More than 22,000 people lived there during the reign of Louis XVI. There were almost as many on the slopes of the Montagne Sainte-Genéviève, between the rue de l'Estrapade and the Place Maubert.[20]

Most inhabitants of central Paris, both long-term residents and migrants, lived either in slums or very near them. The desperately poor and the better-off dwelt in close, promiscuous, and frequently abrasive proximity to one another. At the end of the Old Regime, there were 128,000 residential rental properties for all of Paris, ranging in cost from more than 10,000 livres a year (0.1%) to between 40 and 200 livres a year (58%). The last category housed approximately 220,000 people: families in cramped, ill-heated, airless apartments of one or two rooms, in buildings with a single staircase and a courtyard commode; or individuals sharing one furnished room.[21] About 25,000 people lived in such *chambres garnies*. During the eighteenth century, Parisian landlords, rentiers, and contractors built relatively few residential buildings in central Paris. New construction was largely reserved for opulent quarters. Instead, they repaired or "renovated" old dwellings – to accommodate more tenants, by further partitioning of existing space. Housing deteriorated, but rents increased.[22]

Day and night, the world of the street gave temporary release from claustral lodgings, as from loneliness and poverty. The Parisian street was a public space inhabited. It was simultaneously cosmopolitan and primitive, convivial and abrasive, entertaining and threatening, replenishing and destructive of life. There were more than twenty times as many beer shops and wineshops, taverns, and *guingettes* on the streets and squares of Paris as there were public fountains for drawing water: more than 3,000 drinking places, or about 1 for every 200 Parisians. They were everywhere, but most concentrated in the old city. Popular and petty bourgeois sociabilities were centered in them, as were

---

[20] These are estimates, based on subtractions from the Revolutionary census data of 1793 through 1795. For that data, see Reinhard, *Nouvelle histoire de Paris*, pp. 176–7, and Soboul, *Les Sans-culottes parisiens en l'an II*, pp. 1091–2.

[21] Reinhard, *Nouvelle histoire de Paris*, pp. 42–3, 100–3.

[22] Roche, *Le peuple de Paris*, pp. 100–30.

love and sexuality, commerce, violence, larceny, and social protest.[23] Main streets and boulevards were studded with cheap theaters, dance halls, and gambling dens, prostitutes, open-air entertainers (storytellers, singers, and musicians, jugglers, puppeteers, acrobats, dancing goats, dogs, and bears), and vendors of everything from shaving water to magic lanterns and pornographic engravings.[24] The street was a world of slow and thick movement, where all social classes periodically mingled in various ways, from early in the morning to late at night, when the respectable, wary, or broke went home and the police emerged to impose their quiet and their order. The densities experienced were more comprehensive and frictional than the ratios of population to surface area can suggest.

No street in France was so replete with social trajectories and so thick with human, vehicular, and animal traffic as the narrow, curving rue Saint-Denis, from the Porte to the Châtelet and the river. Every dauphin of France entered Paris through that gate and descended the street to baptism at Notre-Dame. Each dead king left the city by that route on his way to interment in the royal basilica at Saint-Denis. Most of the elaborate religious processions that dominated the calendar and marked the seasons of the city wound along it. The Parisian economy breathed through the rue Saint-Denis. Heavy wagons rumbled over its stones day and night, moving to and from the provinces, bringing raw materials for Parisian manufacturers and carrying the products of those enterprises throughout France. Several of the city's largest road-transport and warehouse businesses were on or near this street: the Grand Cerf, the Croix-Blanche, the Aigle d'Or, and the Chariot d'Or (whose owner employed more than 100 drivers, stableboys, laborers, clerks, and servants in 1789).[25] The Royal Postal, Coach, and Transport service for the eastern provinces was based at the Grand Cerf. Shipping depots and their environs contained dozens of hostelries and inns for provincial and foreign merchants; transactions between them and their local Parisian counterparts amounted annually to millions of livres. Food for the metropolis – grain, flour, and meat from the Ile-de-France, Normandy, Flanders, and the Baltic regions; wine, fruit, vegetables, and dairy products from the rural *banlieue* – were transported each morning through the Porte to the Halles by hundreds of conveyances – wagons and carts, donkeys, baskets strapped to the backs of peasants. Each year thousands of immigrant laborers from the northern provinces entered Paris by the Porte Saint-Denis, found lodging in the furnished rooms of "sleep merchants," queued each morning on the Place de Grève in the hope of hire by masters of the building trades or clothing and accessories manufacturers (most of them located in the

---

[23] See Thomas Brennan, *Public Drinking and Popular Culture in Eighteenth-Century Paris* (Princeton: Princeton University Press, 1988).

[24] The most thorough work on the theaters and other popular entertainment is Robert M. Isherwood, *Farce and Fantasy: Popular Entertainment in Eighteenth-Century Paris* (New York: Oxford University Press, 1986).

[25] A.N. F30 137, doss. Chaillan and Abraham.

Quarters of Saint-Denis and Saint-Martin), filled the cheap wineshops of the neighborhood (more numerous there than in any other), and, when they slid into crime or rioting, were tried at the Châtelet and punished on the Grève or marched off in chains to penal labor at Marseilles or Brest. The lower portions of the rues Saint-Denis and Saint-Martin, and the area between them, had the highest concentration of slum lodgings, wineshops, poverty, prostitution, and criminality in Paris.

The splendid Notre-Dame bridge and its twin, the Pont-au-Change, were the main routes from the Right Bank to Notre-Dame Cathedral and the Palais de Justice, and, therefore, to and from the capital sites of ecclesiastical and secular authority in the Old Regime metropolis. Those bridges funneled directly and inescapably into the blockages, noise, filth, and carnality of the rues de la Planche-Mibraye, Arcis, Gèvres, and Pied-de-Boeuf.

That is surely the most stench-ridden place in the world. There, one finds a tribunal called the Grand-Châtelet, then dingy arches and the congestion of a dirty market, then the depository [the Paris morgue] for rotting corpses that are found in the River or murdered in the environs of the city. Add to that a prison, a meat market, a slaughter pen; it all forms a complete enclave, fouled, covered in mire, and set at the entry to the Pont-au-Change. . . . Do you wish to go from that bridge to the rue Saint-Denis? Carriages must detour by a narrow street with an open sewer; and near that sewer is the rue "Pied-de-Boeuf," which leads into small, fetid alleys that are soaked in animal blood, half of which rots into the pavement, while the other half flows into the River. A pestilential vapor covers the place, never dissipating, when one emerges onto the Pont Notre-Dame, in the rue du la Planche-Mibray, one is forced to hold one's breath and hurry past, so suffocating is the odor of these streets.[26]

The buildings and streets of that enclave were filled with prostitutes: "They prostitute themselves amidst the howls and pitiful bleating of slaughtered droves, blows of poleaxes, fumes of blood."[27]

The Quarter of the Place Dauphine, Quai des Orfèvres, and Quai des Morfondus was a unique, supremely elegant product of Renaissance wealth and ingenuity. It was planned, at the end of the sixteenth century, by Achille de Harley as a simultaneously aesthetic and commercial enterprise under the patronage of Henri IV, a genesis commemorated by that king's equestrian statue across from the apex of the Place Dauphine. It was completed in pure triangular form and solid masonry during the seventeenth century. That Quarter was the citadel of French craftsmanship in precious metals and stones, the home of the most accomplished artisans in the Parisian guild of *orfèvrerie-bijouterie-horlogerie*. More than 600 of those masters and journeymen lived and worked there at the close of the Old Regime.[28] They produced for a clientele which encompassed

---

[26] Louis Sébastien Mercier, *Le tableau de Paris*, 12 vols. (Amsterdam, 1783–8), vol. 5, pp. 101–2.
[27] Ibid., vol. 7, p. 8. Cf. Erica-Marie Benabou, *La prostitution et la police des moeurs au XVIIIe siècle*, (Paris: Librairie Académique Perrin, 1987), pp. 199–200.
[28] A.N. F 7 4803, register of *cartes de sûreté*, Pont-Neuf section, 1793–5.

every social group from the Court and the high nobility to the petty bourgeoisie. Their boutiques on the quays and within the Place Dauphine formed, in Mercier's phrase, a long cordon of silver divided into a hundred thousand separate pieces, "whose image, shimmering in the sun, dazzled those who contemplated it from across the river."[29] But the insularity of the Quarter was no more than architectural and economic, for the square and the quays opened directly onto the plebeian swarm of the Pont-Neuf. That wide bridge was less a thoroughfare than a permanent street bazaar, thronged with jugglers, musicians, and singers, soothsayers, ambulant vendors, "empirical" doctors and dentists, beggars, prostitutes, thieves, con men, and fences.

Saint-André-des-Arts and the Montagne Sainte-Geneviève had probably the most important concentration in Europe of university faculties, royal academies, *collèges*, publishers and bookshops, public and private libraries, savants and authors. That area, surfeited with intellectual distinction, was closely intertknit on the north and east with the river docks, the Place Maubert, the rue Mouffetard and the most primitive faubourg, Saint-Marcel. The economy of the river and the Faubourg Saint-Marcel was based on rough physical work with mineral, animal, and vegetable matter. One-fourth of the city's slaughter yards – where cattle and sheep were driven, penned, killed, drained, dressed, and sold in bulk – were concentrated in and around the Place-aux-Veaux. In 1789, fourteen of the forty-four breweries in Paris were in the Faubourg Saint-Marcel, the majority within its most densely inhabited area. The reeking waste was either transported in open carts to market-gardeners or discharged into the river, just upstream from the Latin Quarter. The bulk of the some 141,400,000 gallons of wine consumed annually by Parisians during the late Old Regime arrived at the Halle-au-Vin on the Quai Saint-Bernard. That quay also served as the storage place for masses of logs that were floated each spring down the Seine. They were manhandled from the river by hundreds of haulers, who had to fight slime and currents, and then stacked over a rat-infested expanse of mud and decay between the rue des Fossés Saint-Bernard and the rue de Seine. The largest and deepest stone quarries in the Paris region were not far to the south; many of the masters and laborers who worked them lived along the rues Mouffetard, Saint-Jacques, and Faubourg Saint-Jacques, near the university. The Bièvre stream bisected the region, less than a half-mile from the *collèges* of the Montagne Sainte-Geneviève, which educated the governing classes of the realm. This was one of the most polluted watercourses in France: Its banks were clustered with tanneries, starch and dye works, and laundries.[30] The pop-

---

[29] Mercier, *Le tableau de Paris*, vol. II, p. 224. And: "Tout l'or de Pérou vient aboutir à la Place Dauphine. . . . La 'cisélure' & 'guillochage' soumettent tous les bijoux de l'Europe à passer par ses mains. Il regne par la 'gravure' (ibid., Vol. 2, pp. 275–6).

[30] Haim Burstin, *Le Faubourg Saint-Marcel à l'époque révolutionnaire: Structure économique et composition sociale*, Bibliothèque d'histoire Révolutionnaire, ser. 3, no. 22 (Paris: Société des Etudes Robespierristes, 1983).

ulace of the Faubourg Saint-Marcel had the reputation of being the most impoverished, violent, and credulous in Paris.[31]

At each dawn, carts laden with corpses set out from the morgues of the Hôpital-Général and the Hôtel-Dieu. Led by a priest on foot, who slowly rang the bell of the dead, they wound their way through the Cité, the Latin Quarter, and the Faubourg Saint-Marcel to Clamart, a short distance east of the Bièvre. That was the pauper's cemetery for Paris.

> Here, there are neither pyramids, tombs, inscriptions, nor mausoleums. The place is naked. This soil, greasy from burials is where young surgeons come in the night, climbing the walls and carrying off cadavers to subject them to their inexperienced scalpels. Thus, after the death of the pauper he is still robbed of his body, and the strange dominion exercised over him does not end until he has lost the last traces of human resemblance.[32]

Intermediate to the social and cultural extremes of central Paris were the propertied and literate classes, in their full range from shopkeepers, artisans with a few apprentices and journeymen, clerks and scribes, to prosperous merchants, manufacturers, artists, and intellectuals, nobles, men of the law, and state officers. They were numerous and rooted throughout the old *quartiers*. Social segregation was commonly a matter of a distinction between closely grouped streets, adjacent apartment buildings, or even between the lower and upper stories within a single building. There was a typical configuration of habitat within individual buildings of the old city: shops on the ground floor, with a low *entresol* above; ateliers ringing the courtyard behind; relatively spacious and high-rent apartments on the first and second floors, often with a room for servants; cramped and cheaper apartments on the upper stories; a garret that was frequently divided into single rooms for the poor and transient. Such buildings replicated the social diversity that characterized life in the streets. Virtually every Quarter had hierarchies that ranged from opulence to misery.

The center was the most productive economic area of the metropolis during the eighteenth century. Only the Faubourg Saint-Antoine approached its importance. More than two-thirds of the enterprises that employed labor, including most of the larger ones, were situated in Paris *intra muros*. All types of merchants, contractors, manufacturing entrepreneurs, and master craftsmen lived there, most very near to their enterprises. So too did masses of the journeymen, apprentices, common and piece-rate workers whom they employed, and masses of those who animated the small street trades. Master-merchant entrepreneurs on the rues Saint-Martin, Saint-Denis, or Saint-Honoré lived

---

[31] "C'est le quartier où habite la populace de Paris, la plus pauvre, la plus remuante, & la plus indisciplinable. Il y a plus d'argent dans une seule maison du fauxbourg Saint-Honoré, que dans toute le fauxbourg Saint-Marcel . . . pris collectivement. . . . Ce sont des hommes réculés de trois siècles par rapport aux arts & aux moeurs regnantes" (Mercier, *Le tableau de Paris*, vol. 1, pp. 268–9).

[32] Ibid., vol. 2, pp. 233–4.

only a short distance from the tenements where their workers were lodged by sleep merchants, two and three to a room and a straw mattress.

The replenishment and growth of Paris, both Ville and *faubourgs*, occurred through immigration. During the eighteenth century, less than 50 percent of the population was native to the metropolis; by the 1780s, less than 40 percent. The proportion of immigrants to natives was high at most socioeconomic levels – from savants, artists and publicists, wealthy merchants and master craftsmen, to domestic servants and common laborers.[33] In the Quarter of the Porte Saint-Martin, only about 36 percent of the 368 masters of construction, craft, and manufacturing enterprises – who in 1790 employed approximately 4,000 workers – were natives of Paris. More than 70 percent of their workers were immigrants.[34] At the end of the Old Regime, almost 60 percent of the master jewelers, gold- and silversmiths, and watchmakers in and around the Place Dauphine (the aristocracy of Parisian luxury craftsmen) were immigrants. Most had come to Paris as young apprentices or journeymen, from towns in the central, northern, or eastern provinces or from Switzerland.[35]

From midcentury to the Revolution, between 7,000 and 14,000 provincials and foreigners immigrated annually to Paris.[36] Most of them walked to the capital, in long stages and relays, with pauses for work or begging. Patterns of displacement were relatively constant across the century, although the volume increased dramatically during the 1770s and 1780s. Provincial immigration may be conceived in concentric circles outward from Paris: The majority trekked from within a 200-mile radius – from Normandy, eastern Brittany, northern Poitou, Anjou, Maine, and Touraine, Berry, and the Orléanais, Limousin, Auvergne, Burgundy, the Bourbonnais and Nivernais, the Franche-Comté, Lorraine and western Alsace, Champagne, Picardy, Artois, and Flanders. Most of those provinces were under the jurisdiction of the Parlement

---

[33] Current knowledge of the provenance and social composition of immigration is based mainly on the study of identity cards and other census materials of the Revolutionary period and Old Regime marriage contracts and wills as well as judicial, prison, hospital, and military records. See especially Andrews, "Social Structures, Political Elites and Ideology in Revolutionary Paris," pp. 86, 90–1; Burstin, *Le Faubourg Saint-Marcel*, pp. 79–90, 116–32, 318–19; Adeline Daumard and François Furet, *Structures et relations sociales à Paris au milieu de XVIIIe siècle*, (Paris: Librairie Armand Colin, 1961), pp. 59–69; Marcel Reinhard, ed., *Contributions à l'histoire démographique de la Révolution française*, Commission d'Histoire Economique et Sociale de la Révolution, (Paris: CNRS, 1st ser. 1962; 2nd ser. 1965; 3rd ser. 1970), and Reinhard, *Nouvelle histoire de Paris: La Révolution*, pp. 117–19; Raymonde Monnier, *Le Faubourg Saint-Antoine (1789–1815)*, (Paris: Société des Etudes Robespierristes, 1981), pp. 27–34; Roche, *Le peuple de Paris*, pp. 23–32. For an excellent description of the forces that propelled emigrations from the mountain provinces to the cities, see Abel Poitrineau, *Remues d'mommes: Les migrations montagnardes en France, 17e–18e siècles*, (Paris: Aubier Montaigne, 1983).

[34] A.N. F 7 4795, register of *cartes de sûreté*, Gravilliers section, 1793–5, and F 30 133–5.

[35] A.N. F 7 4803, register of *cartes de sûreté*, Pont-Neuf section, 1793–5.

[36] Roche, *Le peuple de Paris*, p. 24. Foreigners were a small and stable element among long-term immigrants – about 5% during the eighteenth century. They were mostly artisans or male servants from Rhenish Germany, Switzerland, or the Austrian Netherlands; chimney sweeps or construction workers from Savoy; silk merchants or weavers from the Piedmont; or bankers, wholesale merchants, or financiers from Amsterdam, Geneva, Bern, or Brussels.

of Paris; they also formed the capital's main provisioning area for raw materials and foodstuffs. The highest number of immigrants arrived from the Seine basin and the Ile-de-France, that is, from a radius of less than 75 miles. The 200-mile radius comprised most of France north of the Loire River, the most urban, literate, wealthy, and administered region of the realm. But it also contained the greatest density of seigneurial landholdings, infeudated tenancies, population growth, and enclaves of poverty (especially in the mountains of Auvergne and the Limousin, the *bocages* and marshlands of western France, and the declining cottage-industry towns of Flanders, Artois, and Picardy). Emigration by the relatively skilled and literate was generally from small and median-sized towns, from walled *bourgs* that had markets, bailliage courts, craft guilds, and schools. A large proportion of the unskilled and illiterate originated in peasant villages. Overwhelmingly, among both social categories, these were movements of young, unmarried men and women, aged 15 to 25. They reflected the general population of France during the second half of the century: youthful and expectant of life.[37]

In 1790–1, the Committee on Mendicancy of the Constituent Assembly calculated that about 10 percent of the population of Paris was indigent: that is, so lacking in basic necessities as to require public assistance or confinement.[38] That was probably also the minimal percentage during most of the eighteenth century.[39] Demographic research on the years 1750 to 1790 suggests that at least 10 percent of the Parisian population was either freshly immigrant or migratory – domiciled in the city for less than one year. The two populations – indigents and recent immigrants or migrants – were not identical, but they did overlap broadly. Lower-class immigration swelled, from the 1760s into the Revolution. Those were peristaltic movements of plebeians away from the scarcities of overpopulated villages and towns, in all provinces north of the Loire River, to a metropolis in a cycle of economic and physical expansion. For many of them, the promise of Paris dissolved into bitter disillusionment.

"Immigration" connotes a distinct trajectory from an original environment to a new, and usually final, one. That describes most Parisian immigrants who became successful or who simply managed to survive in the laboring, craft, and small-trade economies of the city. They, however, were a minority among the legions of provincials who migrated to the metropolis during the eighteenth century. Most were men and women whose lives were a matter of fluctuations and improvisation. They circulated in and out of Paris, either sporadically or

[37] See the previously cited works on immigration. See also Jacques Dupaquier, "Sur la population française au XVIIe et au XVIIIe siècles," in *Revue Historique*, 92 (1968): 43–79, and "Les caractères originaux de l'histoire démographique française au XVIIIe siècle," *Revue d'Histoire Moderne et Contemporaine*, 23 (1976): 183–99; François Furet and Jacques Ozouf, *Lire et écrire; L'Alphabétisation des français de Calvin à Jules Ferry*, 2 vols. (Paris: Editions de Minuit, 1977).

[38] C. Bloch and A. Tuetey, *Procès-verbaux et rapports du Comité de Mendicité de la Constituante, 1790–91* (Paris, 1911), p. 769.

[39] Pierre Goubert, "Le monde des errants, mendiants et vagabonds à Paris et autour de Paris au 18e siècle," in *Clio parmi les hommes* (Paris: Mouton, 1976), pp. 265–78.

seasonally (according to the demands for labor in the building and textile trades, for domestic servants, or for harvesters in the provinces), disappeared and reappeared for long intervals and in different social modes. They permeated central Paris and most of the faubourgs.

Immigrants who assimilated to the city and became lasting Parisians usually came with at least the rudiments of skills. And most came as adolescents to a welcoming network of relatives from their natal *pays*, relatives already established in Parisian trades, who secured work and lodging for them. Those were chain migrations: multigenerational kinship groups of ferrous-metal workers from the Norman *bocage* and the Franche-Comté; wood-parquetry and inlay craftsmen from the Jura; cabinetmakers from Lorraine and Alsace; stonecutters and masons from Auvergne and the Limousin; weavers from Flanders and Picardy. They linked Parisian ateliers, shops, and construction sites with distant villages and towns, in a reciprocal flow of pedagogies, labor, and remittances. Such patronage was crucial to success: The extended family, formed of blood and marital ties, was the basic social unit of artisanal and commercial enterprises in eighteenth-century Paris.

Persons without skills and solidly implanted relatives were subject to the brutal vicissitudes of the urban market and a tragic, sordid subsistence economy. That economy entrapped a large proportion of the populace of Paris and its region. (Its criminal permutations form a major subject of Volume 2.) These immigrants lived by a combination of odd jobs, charity (whether through begging in the streets or from the Church and the Hôpital-Général), militia or regimental service (and desertion), concubinage or prostitution, scavenging, theft. They experienced frequent and furtive changes of domicile and incarcerations. The life required cunning, hardness, and for support, shifting, often illicit associations and dependencies formed in taverns, lodging houses, and on work sites.[40] Those men and women filled the criminal chambers of the Châtelet and the Parlement of Paris across the century. They were tried by royal magistrates who were, in great majority, second-, third-, or even fourth-generation Parisians.

At any given time, from the early reign of Louis XV to the Revolution, from 10,000 to 20,000 women of Paris gained their living, either fully or partially, by prostituting themselves. Most solicited openly, on the streets. They represented between 15 and 20 percent of the Parisian female population between the ages of 15 and 45. It is probable that fewer than one-third of them had been born in the city or its *banlieue*. Most had come to Paris originally to work as seamstresses, domestic servants, hairdressers, shop or tavern girls, street vendors, or singers.[41] Between 1723 and 1752, 30,078 men and boys were incarcerated, at least once, at Bicêtre (the men's prison) for begging or vagabondage –

---

[40] For descriptions of the plebeian subsistence economy, see Olwen Hufton, *The Poor of Eighteenth-Century France* (Oxford: Clarendon Press, 1974), and Christian Romon, "Le Monde des pauvres à Paris au XVIIIe siècle," *Annales: Economies, Sociétés, Civilisations*, 37 (1982): 729–63.

[41] Benabou, *La prostitution et la police des moeurs*, pp. 272, 328.

about 1,000 a year. Sixty-nine percent of them were not even natives of the Ile-de-France.[42]

The city attracted a population far larger than its economy and stratifications could legitimately sustain. Many of those in the labor reserve were doomed to parasitism, whereas their mass allowed employers to remunerate unskilled labor at minimal rates. People convicted of crimes in the provinces and banished from their communities by judicial sentence also gravitated to Paris, in search of anonymity and opportunity. An official Old Regime discourse blamed the immigrant and migrant for their own distress, and for the disorders of the city. Other, more perspicacious, minds looked into the metropolis and saw that it brutalized far more extensively than it civilized. They saw an environment that spawned pathologies. (Those voices of crisis, and their agendas, are heard in Volume 2.) Begging, vagabondage, and criminality were, in fact, as integral to the collective life of Old Regime Paris and its region as labor. In crucial respects, eighteenth-century Paris resembled New York or Los Angeles today.

When Mercier contemplated the city from one of the towers of Notre-Dame Cathedral in 1788, he marveled at the magnitude of its need for food, especially bread, the staple of popular diet: "Where are the guarantees for the subsistence of all these people, roosting on top of each other as they are? How do they oblige the inhabitants of vast countrysides to sow and till for them, to nourish them?"[43] He answered his question: "Paris sucks in provisions, and holds the entire realm hostage to its needs. There, one is insensitive to the calamities that periodically afflict the countryside and the provinces, because cries of need and dearth would be more dangerous in Paris than anywhere else, and would give a deadly and contagious example."[44]

To keep the supply and price of bread and other vital foodstuffs within reach of low and (for long periods) virtually stagnant popular incomes was the main preoccupation of those responsible for governing Paris during the eighteenth century. The politics of *subsistances* were a police matter, in three principal ways: (1) inspection and control of provisioning (quantity, quality, and transport) and pricing for the metropolis; (2) regulation of urban marketplaces, of stocking, selling, and buying; (3) discipline of public opinion and behavior. The last enterprise involved dispelling or repressing fears and rumors of dearth (whether true or false); preventing or prosecuting clandestine selling and hoarding, as well as popular attempts to seize foodstuffs or to force their sale below authorized prices ("la taxation populaire," in the parlance of the Old Regime and the Revolution). Since at least the sixteenth century the monarchy had assumed the role of ultimate guarantor for the provisioning of Paris, a role embodied in the eighteenth century by a multitude of laws and regulations, civil officials and magistrates, royally licensed merchants, millers, and shippers.

---

[42] Goubert, "Le monde des errants, mendiants et vagabonds," pp. 275–6.
[43] Mercier, *Le tableau de Paris*, vol. II, p. 6.
[44] Ibid., vol. 4, p. 202.

The collective task was extraordinarily intricate. The provisioning system, which reached into remote farmlands in most provinces of France and far beyond to the grain-producing regions of the Baltic, the Mediterranean, and North Africa and the fisheries of the North Atlantic, was constantly vulnerable to disruptions.[45] Both the popular and the propertied classes of Paris judged the performance of the state in that role more acutely than in any other of its roles. When dearth threatened and prices rose, they did not blame climate or bad harvests; they blamed the government, the merchants it licensed, along with the *grands seigneurs* and *gros fermiers* of rural France. They tended to regard themselves as hostages to rural France, and to the state.

Few Parisians starved to death during the eighteenth century. But a great many experienced the gnawing, low-level hunger of undernourishment. For tens of thousands, the margin of survival was very thin. That fact was registered in the popular fascination with eating and drinking, in the use of food as currency for sex, friendship, and military and criminal recruitment, in frequent migration, in everyday theft of foodstuffs, and in rioting.

In the view of the authorities, the threshold of disorder, even chaos, in Paris was chronically low. The very morphology of the city was propitious to crime and rioting. Ruptures in the fragile equilibriums between employment, wages, subsistence prices, and charitable resources; surges in immigration (as from 1740 to 1760 and 1770 to 1790); erosions of deference and discipline among the laboring classes; hostility to royal policies among the propertied and educated: Those were viewed as constant threats, periodically actualized in subversions and violence. The threats all materialized in the conjuncture of 1788–9.

For those who wielded authority in Old Regime France, especially in the cities, order depended on social boundaries and classifications. All subjects needed to be classifiable and accountable by estate, occupation, domicile, marital status, age, even province of origin. Those who escaped such classification became adventurers, or *gens sans aveu* – a broad and special legal category during the Old Regime and the Revolution. Transients and vagabonds were regarded as real or potential anarchs or criminals, not merely because they lived outside the support structure and restraints on behavior provided by stable employers, neighborhoods, parishes, and families, but also because their transience and anonymity meant that they were easily lost to official surveillance and discipline in its local jurisdictions. Anonymity signified a licence to prey; social motility signified fraud. The impoverishment that usually accompanied those conditions signified mendicancy, crime, and propensity to riot. In the mentality of authority, such people could corrupt otherwise hard-working and disciplined plebeians by the contagion of their close example. The anxiety of the empowered became acute when masses of lower-class transients permeated a

[45] The fundamental work on the politics of *subsistances* and the provisioning of Paris during the eighteenth century is by Steven L. Kaplan, *Bread, Politics and Political Economy in the Reign of Louis XV,* 2 vols. (The Hague: Nijhoff, 1976). See also Richard Cobb, *The Police and the People: French Popular Protest, 1789–1820* (Oxford: Clarendon Press, 1970), pp. 215–24.

city, when labor markets constricted, when social distinctions and roles became blurred, when theft, rioting, and defiance of authorities escalated – as happened in Paris during the final period of the Old Regime.

Eighteenth-century maps of the city – even the Turgot–Bretez, with its attention to detail and differences – offer an image distorted by the necessity for broad two- or even three-dimensional representation. Similarly, and despite their powers of observation, the great Old Regime chroniclers of Parisian life, such as Louis-Sébastien Mercier and Edine Rétif de la Bretonne, were captivated by the dramatic contrasts between *quartiers* and styles of life, by social extremes and stereotypes. In reality, there were multiple, shifting human topographies superimposed in depth on a narrow space: "all these people, roosting on top of each other." This study, centered on the world disclosed by the judicial archive, explores a dynamic and deeply layered Paris, a city of overlapping and mutually abrading microcommunities; fluid and often violent passages from private into public spheres of living, and vice versa; collective movements that temporarily obliterated hierarchical distinctions and physical boundaries; sudden, life-transforming encounters between the socially unequal; identities and occupations that were changed like clothing; complicities and antagonisms that were strange, concealed, and intense, a large heterodox variety of codes for behavior and strategies for survival or aggrandizement.

B. The judiciary within the city

The lawcourts: geography, powers, personnel

One might say that it was there before anything else was named. Paris was not yet called Paris. Then, it was hardly a palace, and justice was rendered in Latin. But it was there, between the two arms of the Seine, as it is today.[46]

This evocation of the Palais de Justice conveys the organic relations between justice, the city of Paris, and the state that were already close to millennial by the eighteenth century. The metropolis had grown outward, in expanding circles, from its original geographical nucleus on the Ile de la Cité, the nucleus formed by the royal palace of the early Capetians, and the first chambers and prison of the Palais de Justice. Notre-Dame Cathedral and the Sainte-Chapelle were later creations, respectively, of the twelfth and thirteenth centuries.[47] Royal authority also developed outward from that nucleus, to encompass first the Ile-de-France and then an entire realm. Those relations were expressed on the armorial crest of the City of Paris, which depicted a high-prowed, silver-

---

[46] Sylvie Péju, *Palais de Justice* (Paris: Editions du Seuil, 1987), p. 11.
[47] Hillairet, *Rive Gauche et les Iles*, pp. 78–81.

colored ship (symbol of wealth) under full sail on waves, amid golden fleurs-de-lis (symbol of the kings of France), on a red ground (color of Saint-Denis the Martyr, the patron saint of both the Crown and Paris).[48]

Sylvie Péju's evocation of the Palais also recalls the primordial importance of naming. For in France, as elsewhere, it was by a long history of naming that places, objects, and persons were brought into social and then political being, that law was created, that power was fashioned.

The eighteenth-century Palais de Justice was a vast ensemble that visually dominated both banks of the Seine from a great distance. Its facades and towers, on the high embankments of the Cité Island, were prominent from the hills that fringed the metropolis and rose above all but a few buildings on either side of the river. On the great Turgot–Bretez map of 1739 (see Maps 1 and 3), all the large arteries of the city flow to or from that island, as if to and from a heart and source. The monumentalism of the island, from Notre-Dame Cathedral to the Place Dauphine, is salient on that map. The images express both a statist esthetic and a political reality. Any geographical and political survey of judicial Paris must begin there.

The Palais de Justice housed sixteen of the twenty-two tribunals that dispensed criminal and civil justice in Old Regime Paris, including the Parlement of Paris. The other six were also sited within the Old City, on the Right Bank, close to the river and the island. The sixteen lawcourts within the Palais included four superior, or *sovereign*, courts with vast jurisdictions.

The Parlement of Paris was the oldest and most powerful of the French sovereign courts. Its jurisdiction encompassed almost one-third of the realm. The Parlement is a principal subject of this book, and its organization and powers are described in Part I, Chapter 2. The Chambre des Comptes was the superior court for surveillance and adjudication of all matters concerning the administration and accountancy of royal funds and the royal domain, as well as prosecution of financial abuses by officials charged with public funds. It also registered and verified all fiefs and privileges accorded by the king. The jurisdiction of the Chambre des Comptes of Paris embraced the Generalities of Paris, Soissons, Amiens, Chalons, Orléans, Bourges, Moulins, Poitiers, Limoges, Riom, Lyon, Bordeaux, Montauban, La Rochelle, and Tours. For purposes of rough fiscal administration and tax collection, France was divided into *Généralités*, of which there were thirty-four in 1789. The jurisdiction of the Chambre des Comptes of Paris embraced the Generalities of Paris, Soissons, Amiens, Chalons, Orléans, Bourges, Moulins, Poitiers, Limoges, Riom, Lyon, Bordeaux, Montauban, La Rochelle, and Tours.

A third sovereign court of Paris, the Cour des Aides, was the superior tax court. Its authority extended over the same provinces as that of the Parlement

---

[48] Roland Mousnier, *The Institutions of France under the Absolute Monarchy, 1598–1789*, 2 vols.; vol. 1: *Society and the State* (Chicago: University of Chicago Press, 1979), p. 580.

Map 3. Ile de la Cité (detail from Map 1).

of Paris (except Auvergne). It had civil and criminal appellate jurisdiction over the collection and evasion of royal taxes and those of the General Tax Farm (except the salt tax). It ruled on requests for fiscal exemptions and issued writs for the seizure of real property in payment of debts owed the Crown. It also decided cases involving disputed nobility and titles. The Generality of Paris was divided into twenty-one *élections*. An *élection* was the basic administrative and judicial unit for the assessment and collection of most royal taxes. The tribunal of the *élection* of Paris, a lower court, had primary jurisdiction over disputes and offenses concerning taxes in the metropolis and its *élection*, which comprised 442 parishes. This court was under the appellate jurisdiction of the Cour des Aides.

For most of France north of the Loire, the fourth sovereign court of Paris, the Cour des Monnaies, had superior and final jurisdiction in all civil, criminal, and administrative matters concerning the royal currency: minting, mint officials, assaying, gold- and silversmiths, the sale and purchase of gold and silver, crimes of false measure or adulteration of precious metal, debasement of the coinage, counterfeiting, and theft from the royal mints. The Cour des Monnaies was served by the tribunal of the general provost of monies, which had authority to arrest and judge, in first instance, those suspected of counterfeiting or of debasing the currency.

The Chambre des Requêtes de l'Hôtel du Roi was an antechamber to both the royal Council and the Parlement of Paris, and a judicial rival to the latter. In was composed of *maîtres des requêtes* (masters of requests), all of whom were former sovereign court magistrates; they served as deputies to the Chancellor of France and also as ex officio members of the royal Council. Their tribunal decided appeals to rulings by sovereign courts, special cases referred by the royal Council, and civil and criminal cases involving officers of the royal household, royal secretaries, and officers of various sovereign courts. (Their decisions could be appealed to the Parlement of Paris.)

The Chambre Souveraine des Décimes du Clergé of Paris, one of eight ecclesiastical courts in France, was composed principally of the archbishop of Paris, several bishops, and some clerical judges. It tried all cases pertaining to the *dîme*, or obligatory tithe portion of all harvests (including those on noble domains), which was the main source of Church revenue.

The administrative and judicial powers of the Bureau des Finances, Chambre du Domaine et du Trésor of the Generality of Paris (and its counterparts in the other Generalities of France) were wide, but many of its powers also overlapped with those of the *intendants* (executive administrators of provinces) and the various *chambres des comptes* and were taken over by them during the eighteenth century. The bureau administered the royal domain and buildings; collection of the salt tax; all fiefs held in the king's name; the maintenance of public roads and bridges, and of the streets of Paris. It served as either court of first instance or appeal in civil and criminal cases concerning those areas of administration within the Generality of Paris.

General introduction

The *Connétablie et Maréchaussée de France*, or Constabulary, was a supreme military court with broad authority. It was presided over by the grand provost, the superior of the thirty-three provincial *prévôts de maréchaussée* (provosts of constabulary), including those of the Generality of Paris and the Ile-de-France. This military tribunal in the Palais de Justice was the appeals court for sentences handed down by provincial military *courts*. Its decisions could be appealed to the Parlement of Paris. The thirty-three local constabulary tribunals were presided over by *prévôts* (provosts), all of whom were senior army officers, but staffed primarily by royal civil magistrates. These tribunals had civil and criminal jurisdiction over military discipline; disputes and crimes in which serving soldiers and officers of the royal army or militia were victims or aggressors; cases of robbery and murder on the highway outside of towns and cities; riot and rebellion against the authority of magistrates and military forces. In certain of these instances, the jurisdiction of provosts was preempted by royal civil courts or by Parlements.

The jurisdictional area of the Admiralty Court of Paris corresponded to that of the Parlement of Paris. It was the appellate court for civil cases involving fishing, riverine and maritime commerce, the construction and provisioning of ships, capture on the high seas, and minor crimes committed at sea, on rivers, or in ports and harbors. The cases were judged in first instance by nine local admiralty courts of France. When a maritime or riverine crime involved serious penalties, appellate judgment was by the Parlement of Paris.

The jurisdiction of the Paris Tribunal of Streams and Forests also paralleled that of the Parlement, and the tribunal was staffed in part by *parlementaires*. It had final jurisdiction over disputes and crimes involving ownership or use of streams, woodlands, or forests, resources that had been under the legal stewardship of the crown since the sixteenth century. The lower Tribunal of Streams and Forests for the immediate region of Paris judged those cases in first instance.

The Bailliage du Palais was a lower civil and criminal court with jurisdiction over only the interior of the Palais de Justice; appeals to its decisions in criminal cases were decided by the Parlement of Paris. The Chambre des Bâtiments tried matters concerning building construction and maintenance in Paris and Versailles, including fraud, depredations, and disputes between entrepreneurs and workers. It too was under the appellate jurisdiction of the Parlement of Paris. The Chambre de la Marée was a tribunal staffed by magistrates of the Parlement; it tried civil and criminal cases pertaining to the provisioning, transport, and sale of salt and freshwater fish for the city and faubourgs of Paris.

The building that housed the principal criminal and civil court of the metropolis – the Grand-Châtelet, or, by exact title, the Provostry, Vicomtry, and Presidial Seat of Paris – was virtually an extension of the Palais de Justice, for it was situated on the Seine directly across from the Quai de l'Horloge and the main towers of the Parlement of Paris. So too was the municipal tribunal, the Bureau de la Ville, in the Hôtel de Ville, across the Pont Notre-Dame from the

Cité. The Bureau de la Ville had jurisdiction over cases involving commercial offenses by Parisian merchants and offenses committed on the riverine ships and ports of Paris.

The tribunal of the Salt Warehouse, on the rue des Orfèvres near the Châtelet, tried cases involving infractions of the royal monopoly on the provisioning, buying, and selling of salt in Paris and its *banlieue;* its sentences could be appealed to the Cour des Aides. The Arsenal (on the Right Bank, across from the Ile-Saint-Louis) was the administrative headquarters for the Artillery of France. Until 1755, the bailliage tribunal at the Arsenal judged civil and criminal cases pertaining to the manufacturing of saltpeter and gunpowder, as well as contracts and work for the artillery arm; thereafter, the tribunal tried only cases involving crimes committed within the extensive confines of the Arsenal.

The Louvre Palace fronted the river, less than one-half mile west of the Palais de Justice. It housed the Grand Conseil, a sovereign court whose powers rivaled and, in some matters, surpassed those of the Parlement of Paris. Since its creation at the end of the fifteenth century, the Grand Conseil had served as a supreme court of appeal for the realm. It was empowered to register and publish royal legislative acts (especially when Parlements refused to do so); to decide jurisdictional contests between a Parlement and a lower court; and to decide among contradictory rulings by various Parlements. The Grand Conseil also had principal jurisdiction in cases pertaining to the privileges and property of the French Church. In addition, by royal order, criminal cases involving important individuals and corporations could be taken from other courts, including a Parlement, for trial and judgment by the Grand Conseil. The tribunal of the Varenne du Louvre enforced the royal monopoly over hunting rights (and authorization to hunt) in the forests in the close environs of Paris, focusing particularly on poaching, resistance to game wardens, and illicit fencing or construction in the royal woodlands. The Prévoté de l'Hôtel du Roi had exclusive jurisdiction over crimes committed in the confines or in the train of the royal Court (when the king traveled); in royal palaces, residences, and their grounds (Louvre, Tuileries, Luxembourg, Palais-Bourbon; Chancellery; Ecole Militaire; the chateaus of Vincennes, La Muette, and the Invalides, and the many royal chateaus in the environs of Paris). It had primary jurisdiction over civil disputes involving the provisioning of the Court and litigation against privileged merchants who supplied the Court. Its decisions could be appealed to the Grand Conseil.[49]

The multiplicity of lawcourts, created by French monarchs at different periods and for a variety of purposes, amounted to surfeit by the eighteenth cen-

---

[49] On those lawcourts, see *Guide;* Marcel Marion, *Dictionnaire des institutions de la France aux XVIIe et XVIIIe siècles* (Paris: Picard, 1984); Mousnier, *Institutions of France,* vol. 2: *The Organs of State and Society,* pp. 251–301. There are abundant, serial records of these courts for the sixteenth, seventeenth, and eighteenth centuries in the French National Archives. Only a fraction of them have been studied by historians. They are keys to deep and detailed social, economic, and political knowledge of early modern and Old Regime France.

tury. Their competencies overlapped and generated jurisdictional conflicts that
had to be arbitrated repeatedly by superior courts or by the Chancellor or the
royal Council. Surfeit also meant that all Parisians of the inner city lived in
proximity to the chambers of royal justice. All delictual actions, civil conten-
tions, and subjects of the king in the metropolis and its region were liable to
trial and sentencing in first instance (and most also on appeal) by at least one
Parisian court of law staffed by royal magistrates and operating according to
fixed procedural rules.

Paris was the premier judicial city of France, as measured not only by the
abundance of its lawcourts and the scope of their jurisdictions but also by the
number of judicial officers and their families who lived in the metropolis and
played a dominant role in its governance. In the mid-eighteenth century, there
was a total complement of 6,094 officers of justice for Paris, all but about 100
of them royal officers.[50] Their number was roughly the same at the close of the
Old Regime. The total complement was not far below that of the other great
institution of authority in Paris, the Church, which included three cathedral
chapters and fifty-two parishes, the university and *collèges*, some forty monastic
establishments, and more than one hundred convents. These institutions were
served by more than 8,000 ecclesiastics, of whom 3,500 were regular clergy.[51]
By the Abbé Joseph Expilly's calculation, Paris in 1767 had a population of
599,912. This meant that there was approximately 1 judicial officer for every
98 inhabitants of the metropolis.[52] If we allow each officer a family of 4, the
judiciary of Paris, as a social group, numbered some 24,300, forming about
4.5 percent of the city's population. These officers, unlike 10 to 20 percent of
the rest of the population of Paris, were not transients: They were a permanent
cadre of the city – professionally, socially, and culturally. Sixty percent of the
judicial officers belonged to great and powerful institutions: 2,170 of them
served the five sovereign courts, 1,494 in the Parlement of Paris. Another
1,573 were members of the Châtelet. Approximately 1,000 of the officers were
magistrates: royal judges, advocates, or prosecutors. In Paris, as throughout
France, they were the elite of the judiciary. There were almost as many magistrates in the metropolis as in the remainder of the vast jurisdiction of the Parlement of Paris, which embraced all, or part, of eighteen provinces. The
jurisdiction contained one hundred forty-two royal civil and criminal courts at
the bailliage and the presidial level in that many towns (other than Paris),
staffed by 1,035 magistrates who held primary judicial authority over more than
9 million subjects.[53] The majority of the remaining 5,000 Parisian officers of
justice were clerks, summons-servers, criers, guards, or police officers. The

---

[50] Expilly, *Dictionnaire*, vol. 5, p. 560 ("Récapitulation-générale des officiers des divers tribunaux
de justice, établis à Paris en 1767").
[51] Ibid., p. 515.
[52] Ibid., p. 401.
[53] Philip Dawson, *Provincial Magistrates and Revolutionary Politics in France, 1789–1795* (Cambridge, Mass.: Harvard University Press, 1972), pp. 350–4.

many clerks were essential to a legal system in which all judicial procedure was specified in writing and the particulars of each trial carefully recorded, and in which almost all decisions were circulated in print or announced publicly.

To the 6,094 judicial officers one might add the 518 barristers and 405 solicitors (as of 1767) who were licensed to plead in the Parlement and other Parisian courts,[54] whose roles are described in Chapter 1. There was a man of the law for every 85 inhabitants of Paris.

Royal magistrates were the true rulers of Old Regime Paris. They were so through the administrative and surveillance power of lawcourts (especially the Parlement of Paris), the authority of the Lieutenant Generalcy of Police in all aspects of collective urban life, and their prominence in the staffing of the city's municipal government.

The structure of the municipal government of Paris and the attributes of its officers had been defined by a royal ordinance of 1415, which remained technically in effect until 1789. The Bureau de la Ville, housed in the imposing Hôtel de Ville on the Place de Grève, was the core of the municipality. The bureau had originated in the medieval Company of Merchants of the River of Paris, and, as a remnant of its origins, the title of its chief officer remained *prévôt de marchands* (provost of merchants). The nomenclature reflected an era when guild masters and syndics truly governed the city. The provost was assisted by 4 *échevins* (executive officers), each of whom served for two years (with 2 elected each year) and 24 town councillors, appointed by him and the *échevins*. Their principal agents were the *quartiniers* of the sixteen municipal "quarters" of Paris (units distinct from the division of the city, in 1702, into twenty police Quarters), who had subdivisional agents under their authority to execute municipal ordinances. The Bureau de la Ville had numerous administrative personnel at the Hôtel de Ville but only small police forces. It set expenditures and let contracts for the construction and repair of bridges, ramparts, quays, fountains, and other works in Paris; set rates for municipal taxes; regulated refuse collection and disposal, house numbering, and street lighting; arranged public ceremonies; maintained the lists of inhabitants who were authorized to bear arms; ordered census taking (of many sorts) in the quarters; kept the official rolls listing the *bourgeois de Paris;* and supervised many other administrative tasks. The Bureau de la Ville was also a court of law, presided over by the provost of merchants. It arbitrated or tried commercial cases involving goods arriving by river at the ports of Paris, cases involving loans to the state that were secured by the municipality, and disputes over the use of the Seine. Those were impressive communal powers, but from the late seventeenth century to the Revolution most were displaced from independent Parisian notables to royal officers of justice.

Technically, the provost of merchants and his *échevins* were elected by a small assembly of notables from the *corporation* of the *bourgeois de Paris,* in an impres-

---

[54] Expilly, *Dictionnaire*, vol. 5, p. 540.

sive ceremony. To qualify for membership, a man had to have resided in the city, with his family and the bulk of his property, for at least one year; present a certificate from his parish priest attesting to regular church attendance; pay his municipal taxes in person; volunteer for service in the City Guard; and, most importantly, obtain certification as *bourgeois* from the local *quartinier,* who had the power of selection and exclusion. Only about 1 among 10 of the city's resident master craftsmen were admitted to the rolls of the *bourgeois de Paris* during the seventeenth and eighteenth centuries. The king had to approve elections to the Bureau de la Ville, and in fact he generally designated the provost of merchants beforehand to the electors. Although elected for a two-year term, that official could be reelected indefinitely if he enjoyed the royal favor. Between 1598 and 1715, there were 25 provosts of merchants, serving an average of four years each. Twenty-two of them had previously served as high judicial officers of the Crown, including 12 judges of the Parlement of Paris and 3 civil lieutenants of the Châtelet. After the provost of merchants, the most powerful officer at the Hôtel de Ville was the *procureur du roi et de la ville* (procurator for the king and the city); he was a professional magistrate, ostensibly appointed by the provost, but the office was actually purchased and hereditary; he dealt directly with the secretary of state for the king's household and served the king's interests in regard to Paris.[55] Of the 236 *échevins* of Paris between 1598 and 1715, at least 102 had previously been barristers or else judicial or administrative officers of state.[56] Fewer than half of the men who served as *échevins* between 1701 and 1789 were actually merchants or former merchants, or master artisans.[57] During the reign of Louis XVI (1774–89), two-thirds of all *échevins*, town councillors, and even *quartiniers* were men of the law, with barristers at the Parlement forming the majority among them.[58]

The Old Regime provost of merchants was no longer a merchant. The narrow rolls of the *bourgeois de Paris* were filled with the names of officers of state, barristers, notaries, wealthy wholesale merchants, entrepreneurs, and rentiers. At midcentury, there were approximately 40,000 tax-paying master artisans and tradesmen in Paris, of which only a few thousand employed significant numbers of skilled workers.[59] These artisans and tradesmen were the bedrock of the Parisian economy and its affluence, and they formed a substantial portion of the socially authentic *bourgeoisie* of Paris. At best, their interests were represented at the Hôtel de Ville by men either socially different or economically superior.

[55] On the organization and staffing of the Paris municipal government during the seventeenth and eighteenth centuries, see Mousnier, *Institutions of France,* vol. 1, pp. 574–90.
[56] Ibid., p. 588.
[57] My computation from A. Trudon des Ormes, "Notes sur les Prévôts des Marchands et échevins de la ville de Paris au XVIIIe siècle (1701–89)," in *Mémoires de la Société de l'Histoire de Paris et de l'Ile-de-France,* 38 (1911): 107–223.
[58] Mousnier, *Institutions of France,* vol. 1, p. 589.
[59] Reinhard, *Nouvelle histoire de Paris,* p. 46.

The *tribunal de commerce,* or commercial court, at the Hôtel de Ville was the only significant municipal entity that remained relatively autonomous during the eighteenth century. It was composed of a judge and four *consuls.* The consuls were elected each year by the various Parisian merchant guilds; the four consuls selected their presiding judge from among former consuls. These officers were senior and wealthy masters of their guilds, and thus representatives of the artisanal, manufacturing, and commercial society of Paris. In exercising their narrow sphere of legal authority, they were supervised by the provost of merchants and the Parlement of Paris. The commercial court tried cases involving disputes between Parisian merchants (or between merchants and notaries) concerning contracts, bills of exchange, partnerships, and debts, but only if the sums involved did not exceed 500 livres. Above that amount, the cases had to be brought as civil actions before a royal court, principally the Châtelet. In January 1716, a royal edict required the commercial tribunal to surrender jurisdiction over cases of fraudulent bankruptcy to royal courts.[60]

Policing

In April 1733, when it wanted cannons to fire in a public celebration, the Muncipality of Paris had to borrow ten from the governor of the military fortress at Vincennes, because none of the city's pieces would fire.[61] The municipal company of musketeers (les chevaliers de l'Arquebus), whose origins were in the fourteenth century, still existed, with a miniscule budget from the Hôtel de Ville. By the eighteenth century, however, this group was little more than a recreational society for affluent men (numbering 51 in 1762) who competed in marksmanship and marched in parades.[62] There was also a vestigial *bourgeois militia* of Paris. At midcentury, it consisted of some 50 officers, who bought expensive commissions from the king but had virtually no troops to command.[63] A genuine militia force of Parisians did exist from 1743 to the Revolution, but only as a standing reserve for the royal army. The complement was set at 5,000 and recruited by lottery from among unprivileged and poor residents of the city, under the auspices of the lieutenant general of police and the minister of war. These militiamen were commanded by retired army officers. In peacetime, they were assembled and drilled for one or two weeks a year. In wartime, they were used primarily to garrison fortifications and to secure communications in frontier regions.[64]

The only armed and uniformed force that remained under the direct authority of the Bureau de la Ville was the City Guard, which during the eighteenth

---

[60] Marion, *Dictionnaire,* p. 139; Mousnier, *Institutions of France,* vol. 1, pp. 583–4.
[61] Jean Chagniot, *Paris et l'armée au XVIIIe siècle: Etude politique et sociale* (Paris: Economica, 1985), p. 81.
[62] Ibid., pp. 81–3.
[63] Ibid., p. 84.
[64] Marion, *Dictionnaire,* pp. 376–9.

century, numbered three foot companies of 100 officers and men each. Membership in all ranks was purchased, after 1690, from the Crown, not the municipality. Most members of the Guard were small tradesmen who enjoyed various tax exemptions through membership and served at rather long intervals. Their duties were specialized and sporadic: guarding the Hôtel de Ville and its dignitaries; assisting in municipal tax collection; escorting riverine convoys of grain destined for Paris; guarding the stocks of grain and firewood near the quays; providing security during ceremonies. The Guard was not a general police force, although it could be mobilized (slowly) against rioters.[65]

The manufacturing and mercantile bourgeois of Paris were politically fragmented among their guilds, corporations, and parishes, where they were socially powerful and enjoyed important privileges. During the eighteenth century, they no longer governed, defended, or policed their city. Their traditional institutions of communal self-government and defense were reduced to ceremonial vestiges, much like the remnants of the old walls that had once protected the city.

There were two powerful police forces for Paris and its region. Both were state institutions, commanded by chief magistrates at the Châtelet under the ultimate authority of the Parlement of Paris and the royal Council.

Louis XIV created the Lieutenant Generalcy of Police in 1667, as the supreme agency for the judicial and administrative policing of the metropolis.[66] That creation coincided with the royal decision not to refortify Paris. The security of the capital henceforth depended on the army, at the frontiers, and on the police within. Its chief, appointed by the king, was formally titled *Lieutenant-général de la ville, prévôté et vicomté de Paris*. The jurisdiction of the lieutenant general of police corresponded to that of the Châtelet, of which he was a senior magistrate. He was also a member of the royal Council. He reported to, and received directives from, the secretary of state for the king's household. Between 1667 and 1789, 14 men held the office. Before their appointment (usually in early middle age), 13 had been career magistrates, 3 in presidial courts, 4 in the Grand Conseil or the Cour des Aides of Paris, and 6 in the Parlement of Paris. Several went on to a higher state office after their tenure as lieutenant general.[67]

In the course of the eighteenth century, the Lieutenant Generalcy was endowed with extensive powers, including the authority to issue ordinances, which led to rivalry with other administrations and judicial institutions. The Lieutenant Generalcy enforced city regulations concerning the some 140 Parisian artisanal and mercantile guilds; commerce in foodstuffs, drink, and fuel; censorship and the book trade; fairs, theaters, taverns, and other places of public entertainment; public morals and security in general; religious observance; sanitation; medicine; charity for the destitute; building construction; street il-

---

[65] Chagniot, *Paris et l'armée*, pp. 85–94.
[66] The following description of the lieutenant generalcy is based on Williams, *Police of Paris*.
[67] Ibid., pp. 296–303.

lumination and traffic control; and fire fighting. The agency supervised the royal lottery; recruited the city militia; policed army and navy personnel in the city (and arrested deserters), as well as all foreigners.

The lieutenant general presided over a police court at the Châtelet that held twice-weekly sessions during the eighteenth century. There, after inquiry and written report by police commissioners, he arbitrated minor disputes between individuals or urban corporations; judged infractions of regulations and petty delictual actions that were subject only to fines or mild penalties; and handled cases involving violations of public morals (prostitution, pimping, vagabondage, begging) that were subject to penalties of exposure in stocks, wearing the iron collar, banishment from Paris, or incarceration in the Hôpital-Général. This *chambre de police* dealt with more of the population than any other regular judicial session at the Châtelet. During most of the eighteenth century, the lieutenant general and his assistants pronounced an average of 100 verdicts a week.[68] The lieutenant general was also responsible for finding and arresting all those caught in flagrant delict, suspected or accused of serious crimes (*grand criminel*). Such suspects were then tried by the judges of the Châtelet, under the authority of either the criminal lieutenant of the Châtelet or the provost of constabulary, or by another court, depending on the nature or site of the offense.

The lieutenant general of police met twice monthly with the *premier président* (first president), and the general prosecutor of the Parlement of Paris, along with the provost of merchants. That permanent Assemblée de Police, chaired by the first president at his residence in the Palais de Justice, was the active core of political power in Old Regime Paris. Those four decided questions regarding administration of the city and the implementation of royal policy, as they arose.[69] Other officials and private individuals were frequently invited to discuss issues of special concern. The lieutenant general also chaired weekly meetings with the criminal lieutenant of the Châtelet, the provost of constabulary, and the commander of the Paris Guard that were devoted to matters of police and public security.

The total personnel either under the command or at the disposition of the lieutenant general of police numbered 3,114 at the close of the Old Regime, or 1 police agent for every 200 Parisians. Fully 1,891 police agents were engaged in criminal patrolling, inspection, or detective work. The main patrol forces of the city were the Watch (Guet) and the Guard (Garde). The Watch was a militia, composed of men who purchased their rank and served two out of every three nights each week. They numbered 152 until 1771, when half the company was incorporated into the more professional and salaried Guard of Paris.

[68] Ibid., p. 33.
[69] "Most legislation affecting Paris, whether it eventually appeared as a decree of the Parlement, as an ordinance of the 'bureau de ville,' or as a regulation from the hands of the lieutenant of police was, in fact, the work of men from each of these jurisdictions, acting together. Lines dividing the most important institutions in Paris were finally less significant in determining where authority and power lay than in deciding what legal form the exercise of both should take" (ibid., p. 178).

At the close of the Old Regime, the Guard numbered from 900 to 1,000 well-armed foot patrolmen and mounted troops, many of whom were veterans of the royal army. They were salaried and well disciplined. By day, they manned guard posts in the twenty administrative Quarters of the city and faubourgs; by night, they patrolled the streets and river quays in squads of 5 to 12. They were at the service of the police commissioners and police inspectors of the Quarters.

The 48 *commissaires-enquêteurs-examinateurs* (commissioner–investigator–examiners) of police for the twenty Quarters of Old Regime Paris were the elite of the judicial and administrative police. (The administrative Quarters in 1704 and 1749 are depicted on Maps 4 and 5.) Each Quarter had a resident commissioner; the largest and most populous had two or three. Like the magistrates, they were career state officers who purchased their offices, which were costly. Many of them, if not most, had had a legal education and experience as barristers or solicitors.[70] Between 1715 and 1780, 169 men served as police commissioners in the twenty Quarters of Paris. The average tenure was twelve years in a Quarter, but 69 of them served for more than twenty-one years.[71] Commissioners were under the authority of the civil lieutenant and the criminal lieutenant of the Châtelet (heads of the civil and criminal courts), as well as that of the lieutenant general of police. A police commissioner's duties, within his Quarter, almost replicated those of the lieutenant general of police within the entire metropolis. The commissioners arbitrated local civil disputes and initiated prosecution for infractions of ordinances. They received complaints of crimes and denunciations of suspected criminals and transmitted them in writing to the criminal lieutenant of the Châtelet. Commissioners were empowered to arrest, interrogate, and jail anyone caught committing a crime, and thus to begin the information-gathering phase of criminal inquiry and trial.[72]

The police commissioners were assisted by twenty police inspectors, one to each Quarter of the city. The inspectors were a specialized and quite active investigative cadre. They executed arrest warrants issued by the commissioners, the lieutenant general, or judges of the Châtelet. They also gathered information; inspected boarding-houses, taverns, gambling dens, and bordellos; penetrated illicit or criminal groups; tracked suspects; entrapped those suspected of prowling for criminal opportunities (especially at night); arrested beggars and vagabonds; and filed regular intelligence on the shadow world of real or incipient criminality, debauchery, disorder, and riot. Police inspectors employed, and variously used, some 300 to 400 informants. Some of these were regular employees (subinspectors or agents); many others were madams of bordellos,

---

[70] Steven L. Kaplan, "Note sur les commissaires de police de Paris au XVIIIe siècle," in *Revue d'Histoire Moderne et Contemporaine*, 28 (1981): 670.

[71] Ibid., pp. 682–3.

[72] The most vivid account of the powers and activities of the police commissioners is by Arlette Farge, *La vie fragile: Violence, pouvoirs et solidarités à Paris au XVIIIe siècle* (Paris: Hachette, 1986).

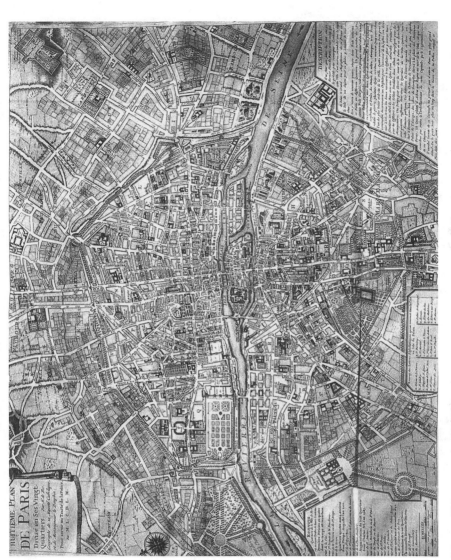

Map 4. "Huitième plan de Paris, divisé en ses vingt quartiers" by Nicolas Dela-mare, *Traité de la Police*, 3 vols. (Amsterdam, 1729), vol. 2.

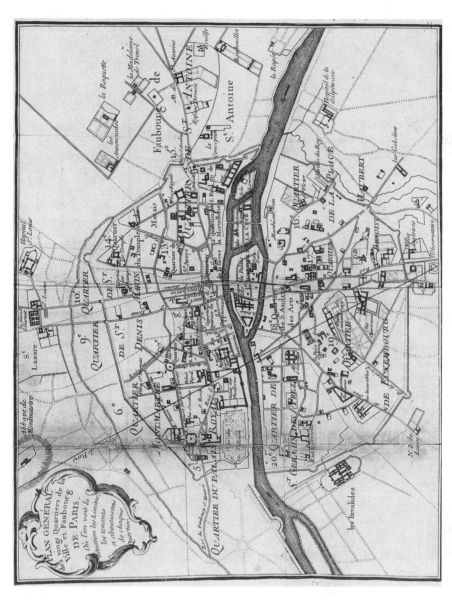

Map 5. "Plan général des vingt Quartiers de la Ville et Faubourg de Paris," from abbé Antonini, *Mémorial de Paris*, 2 vols. (Paris, 1749), vol. 2.

street pedlars, porters, domestic servants, retired soldiers, tavern-keepers, or former convicts.

The *prévôt-général de la connétablie et maréchaussée* (general provost of constabulary) of the Ile-de-France (always a retired army officer and a senior magistrate of the Châtelet), commanded a mounted company that numbered, during most of the eighteenth century, approximately 200. After 1778, a minimum of four years' service in the royal army was officially required for enlistment in that force; before then only about one-third of its members were veterans of the king's regiments. The Constabulary policed the roads of the Ile-de-France. In the environs of Paris, brigades (four or five cavaliers and an officer) were permanently stationed at Franconville, Saint-Denis, Nanterre, La Chapelle, Neuilly, Passy, Saint-Germain-en-Laye, Versailles, Sèvres, Bourg-la-Reine, Villejuif, Longjumeau, Choisy, Charenton, Vincennes, Pantin, Bondy, and Le Bourget. Within Paris, there were mounted or foot detachments of Constabulary of the Louvre Palace, the Invalides, on the rue Saint-Jacques, near the Portes Saint-Denis and Saint-Martin, and at stations along the ring of faubourgs and the customs barriers. This positioning enabled the mounted units to police all of the arterial routes that radiated from Paris to the rest of France. They ostensibly compensated, in depth of patrolling and speed of pursuit, for what they lacked in density of presence. Their main targets were beggars, vagabonds, people who were violating sentence of banishment from the city, highway robbers, military deserters, and marauding soldiers. The Constabuary of the Ile-de-France also gathered information and made arrests outside of Paris for the lieutenant general of police, as did the smaller constabulary of the general provost of monies. At time of crisis, those forces could be ordered to duty within the city. Beyond the inner Ile-de-France were the Constabulary brigades of the Generality of Paris.[73]

Because the armed police units of Paris were used primarily to prevent or repress crimes and isolated disorders and to protect persons and properties, they were dispersed in small squads throughout the city. In the years 1765 to 1770, there were forty-four stations from which patrolling was done by the Guard, the largest of the forces. Seventeen of the twenty administrative Quarters had at least one Guard detachment, and eleven Quarters had two or more: The aristocratic Faubourg Saint-Germain had six, the Quarters of the Louvre Palace four, and the Cité four. Those last fourteen detachments (152 officers and men) protected the rich, the titled, and the empowered. There were eight Guard stations on the exterior boulevards, at each of the main entries to Paris, from the Porte Saint-Antoine to the Barrière des Gobelins. Another fourteen were on the river, lifeline of the city's provisioning and stockpile area, from the Port de la Conférence, near Chaillot, to the Port de la Gare, well upstream from central Paris. There were only five stations for mounted Guards in the

---

[73] On the Constabulary, see Williams, *Police of Paris*, pp. 86–9; Clive Emsley, "La Maréchaussée à la fin de l'Ancien régime: Note sur la composition du corps," *Revue d'Histoire Moderne et Contemporaine*, 33 (1986): 622–44; and Chagniot, *Paris et l'armée*, pp. 105–7.

entire city, two in the northwest, one in the Faubourg Saint-Antoine, one on the rue de la Harpe in the Latin Quarter, and one on the rue du Bac in the Faubourg Saint-Germain. They were supplemented by a roving force of some eighty mounted Guards, who moved throughout the city during the night. Although the number of Parisian Guards (foot and mounted) on regular duty was steadily increased (from approximately 600 at midcentury to more than 1,000 in 1788–9), their grid had strange and dangerous gaps. There were no Guard posts or Watch stations for large areas of the densely populated, heavily plebeian Quarters that were foyers of crime and rioting during the eighteenth century: on the Right Bank, large areas of the faubourgs Saint-Antoine, Montmartre, and Poissonière, the Halles area, and the rues Saint-Denis and Saint-Martin; on the Left Bank, a major portion of the Faubourg Saint-Marcel.[74] Those areas were the sites of about two-thirds of the crimes of personal violence tried as petty crimes at the Châtelet and for almost two-thirds of the serious crimes tried as *grand criminel* at the Châtelet from 1765 to 1785.[75]

Guard detachments and Watch squads were present and visible, but they were stationed or patrolled in regular patterns, often at significant distances from each other, in a metropolis with labyrinthine streets and myriad squares and marketplaces. Ordinary crowds on streets or in marketplaces could metamorphose rapidly into angry, protesting gatherings that rapidly gained mass, energy, and direction. The police of Old Regime Paris were not regularly deployed to prevent or abort such movements; they usually had to confront them head-on. In 1750, 1775, 1788, and 1789, they were completedly overwhelmed. Sometimes they even lost during local confrontations with popular *attroupements*. Then the military had to be brought out.

The royal army was the final reserve force for the policing of Paris.[76] Two infantry regiments belonging to the king's military household, the French Guards and the first batallion of the Swiss Guards, were permanently garrisoned in or near Paris, except during military campaigns. That professional soldiery totaled 4,350 officers and men. Until the late 1770s, they were supplemented by the 350 cavalrymen of the Black Musketeers regiment, barracked on the rue de Charenton in the Faubourg Saint-Antoine. These forces served foremost as a deterrent against riot and insurgency, by their very presence, but in the course of the eighteenth century they were given other important duties in the everyday policing of the city.

---

[74] For the geography of policing, see Chagniot, *Paris et l'armée*, pp. 128–9, and Williams, *Police of Paris*, pp. 76–81.

[75] Arlette Farge and André Zysberg, "Les théâtres de la violence à Paris au XVIIIe siècle," *Annales: Economies, Sociétés, Civilisations*, 34 (1979): 1000, and Porphyre Petrovitch, "Recherches sur la criminalité à Paris dans la seconde moitié du XVIIIe siècle," in A. Abbiateci et al., *Crimes et criminalité en France, 17e–18e siècles* (Paris: Armand Colin, 1971), p. 248.

[76] The following description of the role of the army in the policing of Paris is based on Chagniot, *Paris et l'armée*, pp. 163–93.

Soldiers manned permanent guard posts, mainly in the faubourgs where they lived or were barracked or on the strategic, much trafficked Pont-Neuf, from which several detachments did regular nightly patrolling (especially after 1776). Those well-armed patrol squads totaled 168 men on a normal night. Their first responsibility was military policing (rousting soldiers out of cabarets and *guingettes* after curfew and getting them off the street), but they also had standing orders to assist the local police when asked. They did permanent guard duty in royal establishments such as the Invalides, Louvre, Tuileries, Arsenal, and Ecole Militaire and patrolled the Opéra, the Comédie-Française and the Comédie-Italienne; and the annual Saint-Germain and Saint-Laurent trade fairs. When dearth or disturbances threatened, the French Guards and the Swiss Guards protected the main marketplaces, the river ports, the offices and excise barriers of the General Tax Farm, and the Royal Bank. They also marched in state ceremonial events in the city.

After the 350 Black Musketeers were permanently withdrawn from Paris in 1776–7, there was no longer a concentrated, well-trained cavalry force that could deter or break up riotous assemblies by forming a wall of horses or charging with drawn sabers. The mounted units of the Paris Guard were dispersed throughout the city, and in any case they were less intimidating to Parisians than the Musketeers had been. After 1776, the government had to depend on lethal force – the bayonets and the volley fire of Guards infantry – to stop riots once they got beyond police control. Horses and sabers injured and wounded; bayonets and musket balls killed.

Soldiers could not legally jail civilians whom they arrested, even if someone caught committing a crime had assaulted them. The soldiers were required to put civilians directly into the custody of Guard or Watch squads. Those had, in turn, to bring the arrested person before the local police commissioner, who alone was authorized to order jailing and begin a judicial inquiry. Although the French Guards and the Swiss Guards received their orders in the king's name from the minister of war or the royal Council, rather than from the lieutenant general of police, they were legally accountable to the Parlement of Paris for their execution of all orders concerning civilians, just as were the police of t'.e Lieutenant Generalcy of Police and the Constabulary. Soldiers and police of all ranks could be, and occasionally were, indicted by the Parlement for use of excessive force, arbitrary arrest, or illegal jailing of civilians. In consequence, military commanders in Paris behaved cautiously during the early stages of riots in 1750, 1775, 1788, and July 1789 from fear of judicial censure or prosecution.

Old Regime criminal law, enforced in Paris principally by the Châtelet and Parlement, was conservative in the matter of collective disturbances, out of respect for the right to assemble and process, in a civilization where public gatherings and ceremonies, formal and informal, secular and religious, were integral to collective life. Most royal legislation against popular *attroupements* penalized only those in which weapons were brandished, officers of justice were assaulted, or violence, looting, or property damage had occurred. The law was otherwise silent and permissive. Generally, the Parlement and royal Council explicitly interdicted such movements in and around Paris only after they had become riotous and violent. The law concentrated on selective judicial punishment – not forceful prevention – of collective disorders. Punishment of rioters, like that of ordinary criminals, occurred only after lengthy formal trial and sentencing by a lawcourt (a trial that also involved scrutiny of the actions of the police and military), well after disorders had spent themselves, and after distinguishing the causes and leaders or instigators of the riot and the specific acts of violence committed. Such punishment was always selective, never general.

The reluctance of military officers and the Lieutenant Generalcy to use deadly force against criminals and rioters, and the reluctance of the Châtelet and the Parlement to countenance the use of such force, derived partly from one of the monarchy's great civil accomplishments: the general disarming of Parisians during the last century of the Old Regime. This disarming was accomplished by repeated and comprehensive royal edicts that restricted the sale, purchase, ownership, or bearing of firearms, daggers, or swords in the metropolis and indeed throughout the realm.

The state's legal offensive against the carrying of weapons by private persons was begun early in the sixteenth century. Its beneficent purpose was stated by Francis I in the preamble to the edict of May 1539: "We wish to ensure that all of our subjects equally live in reverence and fear of divine and human justice, that without weapons each may consider and comport himself in his home and elsewhere as securely as if he were armed, and to prevent our good and loyal subjects, who are accustomed to live in peace and tranquility, from being injured by the evil, wicked, and incorrigible who carry weapons."[77] The offensive was pursued energetically by Louis XIV in the aftermath of the armed Parisian *frondes* of 1648–52. A royal declaration of December 1660 outlawed the carrying of firearms or swords in Paris by anyone other than police officers or soldiers on duty, judicial officers, officers of the royal household, and nobles. The declaration also banned the manufacture, sale, purchase, or use of daggers, bayonets, or pocket pistols by all persons throughout the realm (except bayonets for soldiers in service), under penalties ranging from a fine or confiscation to corporal punishment.[78] In March 1728, sword canes, spiked staffs, or any other "secret and hidden offensive weapons" (such as those interdicted in 1660) were outlawed, under severe penalties against manufacturers, sellers, owners, or bearers (six months in prison for the latter). This law established state control

---

[77] Isambert, vol. 12, p. 557. This edict outlawed the wearing of armor or carrying of weapons (either concealed or openly), alone or in company, with or without disguises, in towns, villages, forests, or on roads, by all persons (including nobles) except soldiers or officers of justice in service, under penalty of "confiscation of body and properties."

[78] Ibid., vol. 17, pp. 387–92.

over gunsmiths and makers of edged weapons and led to police inspection of their shops and account books.[79] A declaration of August 1737 forbade the soldiers of the French or Swiss Guards to carry swords or other weapons at night, except in their quarters or guard posts or when on patrols, without individual written authorization from their captain. They were also forbidden to assemble or promenade, when off duty, during the day with their swords in groups of more than four, under penalty of three years' galley servitude.[80] Subsequent royal edicts and police ordinances specifically outlawed the carrying of firearms or of edged or pointed weapons, in Paris by servants and artisans.[81] Those edicts were paralleled by increasingly refined and severe penal laws against dueling. Legislation against the bearing and use of weapons, especially firearms, was rigorously enforced by the Lieutenant Generalcy and the criminal courts. The use of such weapons in any crime meant a more severe sentence for the offender, often the death sentence. The long-term efficacy of the legislation is revealed by the fact that most violent robberies in and around the Old Regime metropolis were committed with knives or bludgeons, or at most pistols. It is also revealed in the major violent riots of the eighteenth century. In 1725, 1750, 1775, and 1788, protesting or insurgent Parisians had only paving stones, tools, or clubs with which to confront well-armed forces of order. The *journées* of July 12 through July 14, 1789, had great impact because the insurgent population managed to arm itself by breaking into the arsenal of the Royal Military Hospital at the Invalides and securing thousands of muskets. That unprecedented action, and the ensuing defection of the French Guards to the insurgency, precipitately reversed the relations of force that had obtained for more than one hundred years between Parisians and the state. It ended a royal monopoly of lethal force that had been carefully and incrementally forged over centuries.

The principal official ceremonies in Old Regime Paris, and thus displays of authority, were monarchical or ecclesiastical, not municipal. The most highly visible armed forces that paraded in public executions, celebrations of military victories, royal marriages, births of dauphins, coronations, entries, peace treaties, for the annual *fêtes* of Sainte-Geneviève, Saint-Louis, Saint-Jean, the Assumption, and commemorations of the liberations of Paris in 1346 and 1594 were the Guardsmen and the regimented companies of the Lieutenant Generalcy. Every spring the king reviewed the regiments of the royal household (including both the French and the Swiss Guards) on the Sablons Plain near Paris. Those were vivid and sonorous demonstrations of disciplined force, grandeur, and sovereignty. Parisians of all classes flocked to them, whereas few attended the contests of the *Chevaliers de l'Arquebus*.

The power of the Lieutenant Generalcy in the administration and policing of the city; the active supervisory authority of the Parlement of Paris over all aspects of its governance; the subordination of the military and police to civil,

[79] Ibid., vol. 21, pp. 311–12.
[80] Ibid., pp. 30–3.
[81] November 1776 (ibid., vol. 24, pp. 94–5); May 1784 (ibid., vol. 27, pp. 410–12).

essentially judicial, authority; the staffing and virtual absorption of the municipality at the Hôtel de Ville by royal magistrates, barristers, and royally designated provosts; the general disarming of the city: Those crafted developments politically transformed the capital of France from a fortified, communal, and largely self-governing entity into a royal and bureaucratic city. The possessive pronoun in the royal formula "Our good City of Paris" was accurate: That transformation was a major achievement of the Old Regime monarchy. Ironically, it was accomplished in less than one hundred years, between the 1660s and the 1750s, when the kings of France no longer resided in Paris but at Versailles. The result was a metropolis fastidiously – even excessively – administered, regulated, and ordered by competing organs of the monarchy. But their dominion was not truly alien: The personnel of the organs of state – from the police agents, soldiers of the Guards regiments (except the Swiss Guards), and summons-servers at the Châtelet to the magistrates of the various lower courts and sovereign courts – were also Parisians, most by birth, all by life-residence and personal identity. They were, simultaneously, agents of the Crown and privileged inhabitants of the metropolis.

All the various organizations that policed the city were the agents and subordinates of judicial authority, accountable to it for their actions. Statutes and ordinances restrictively defined police powers of coercion, arrest, and jailing. Old Regime Paris was ruled by law, not by force; it was ruled principally by a system of criminal and civil justice, animated by the magistrates. By the eighteenth century, the vital elements of the system were common to the rest of France.

Eighteenth-century Parisians lived continually in the presence of royal authority, even though the Court was at Versailles and the king rarely visited the city. In consequence, royal authority and prestige – represented by the king's magistrates, administrators, provosts, police, and soldiers – was exposed, tested, scrutinized, and judged by the people of Paris during every crisis of order and every escalation of crime within the city. The justice dispensed at the Châtelet and at the Parlement was highly visible, because those courts had foremost criminal jurisdiction over the metropolis and because their judgments were announced and executed publicly. When a crisis of order or a dissension over policy led the Parlement of Paris to oppose the will and actions of the royal ministers or the Lieutenant General of Police, as occurred with increasing frequency and intensity from the 1760s to 1788–9, authority in the metropolis was split. During the same decades, both the propertied classes of the city and members of the judiciary perceived a drastic escalation of popular criminality and indiscipline. The anxiety produced by this perception led many to question the very system of royal criminal law and to imagine a new, more efficient and expeditive system of power and "justice." That perception and its outcome are principal subjects of Volume 2.

The culture of the state, an essentially legal and national culture, was more highly developed among Parisians than anywhere else in France, except the

Court at Versailles. That fact would become manifest during the death throes of the Old Regime. The very language and categories in which most adversarial reformist projects were cast during the 1780s (including the Parisian *cahiers de doléances* of 1789), as well as the prominent and often imperious role that Parisians assumed in shaping state policies and staffing state bureaucracies, from the summer of 1789 to the fall of 1794, emanated from that long formation.

C. The judiciary within the state

The large and intricately organized judicial community whose authority permeated Old Regime Paris was the product of a lengthy political development, one begun by French kings and their Chancellors during the late middle ages and that embraced the entire realm by the end of the seventeenth century. As an important part of that general development, the judicial world of Paris was a magnified image of urban France in the eighteenth century.

To this Christian people subject to me, and to the end that the entire Christian people of God's Church shall preserve for all time true peace according to the desire of all, I promise in the name of Jesus Christ:

Item: To forbid all conditions and ranks of persons to commit any and all crimes and iniquities;

Item: To instruct all judges to use equity and mercy, to the end that a clement and merciful God will grant me and you his Mercy,

Item: I shall make every effort, and in good faith, to eliminate from my land and from any jurisdiction subject to me all persons denominated heretics by the Church.

All these things said above I solemnly swear.[82]

This was the Coronation Oath, sworn to publicly in Reims Cathedral – before an assembly of Peers of the realm, prelates of the Gallican Church, and representatives of the French Estates – by every French monarch from Louis XI in 1462 to Louis XVI in 1774. Although royal jurists insisted that this oath was not a contract between the king and the people, it did express a consistent purpose of the Valois and Bourbon monarchs to construct and maintain a system of rule by criminal, civil, and ecclesiastical law for the kingdom of France, a system of justice enforced by royally delegated and regulated magistrates. That purpose was fully achieved by the eighteenth century; its instrument was a vast corpus of royal ordinances, statutes, and edicts that defined all aspects of justice, public finance, provincial administration, and religious orthodoxy; its agents were the tens of thousands of families, or dynasties, who formed the world of professional royal officialdom. That was an urban world. Officials resided in towns and cities, where the organs of government were sited. Yet their collective authority reached into the most remote corners of rural France, extending to all subjects of the Crown, including the most venerable aristocratic families on their seigneurial lands. That authority was backed by force. In Jan-

---

[82] Ibid., vol. 9, p. 458.

uary 1466, Louis XI decreed that henceforth all judgments and rulings by all Parlements of France were to be put into effect, against any and all resistance, with the use of armed force if necessary.[83] During the sixteenth century, that provision was extended to all royal courts and administrations. Only the king, acting, in practice, through the Chancellor of France, the royal Council, or the Grand Conseil, could legally countermand the actions of his agents.

In both contemporary definition and in reality, there were three hierarchies in Old Regime France. The first was the hierarchy of social orders, or Estates (clergy, nobility, and below these all others). The second was the hierarchy of wealth or economic class, which often confounded and subverted the primary hierarchy of orders. The third was the hierarchy of royal officialdom, of governance. This last hierarchy transcended and selectively absorbed the first two: It could make a bourgeois the political superior of a noble, and then ennoble him; it endowed laymen with vocations that rivaled those of the clergy in moral and political importance; it made men from merely affluent families the superiors, in both prestige and power, of the monumentally rich; it encinctured its members, even the lowest, with the unique and divine magic of royal sovereignty.

Only kings created and bestowed offices of state. An October 1467 edict of Louis XI guaranteed life tenure to every royal officer of justice, unless he resigned or was convicted in a court of law of malfeasance in office or dereliction of duty. It defined their collectivity in the following terms: "in our officers consists, under our authority, the direction of the means by which the public welfare of our realm is policed and preserved; they are the essential ministers of that public welfare, as members of the body of which we are the head."[84] By the late seventeenth century, most of the supreme governing personnel of France – chancellors, ministers, and secretaries of state – were chosen from the ranks of the royal magistracy. Those men were products of legal culture and legal experience. All of them had acquired some direct knowledge of the popular and the small-propertied classes by serving as judges or prosecutors in criminal and civil courts.

The most powerful, comprehensive elite in Old Regime France was not the nobility but those who held judicial or executive offices of state. By the eighteenth century, that elite had come to resemble a caste. After 1644, entire categories of superior magisterial and administrative offices conferred hereditary nobility on their holders, and thus created nobles. The seigneurial and military nobility of France neither created those offices nor controlled access to them. A noble family that did not serve the state in civil offices or military commissions was cut off from power and prestige and threatened in its identity. In 1698, the threat was conveyed subtly by Louis Pierre d'Hozier, master of genealogy and *juge d'armes* to Louis XIV, when he stated the purpose of the official *Armorial général de la France:*

---

[83] Ibid., vol. 10, pp. 528–9.
[84] Ibid., pp. 541–2.

To assemble in a public monument all that is relevant to the nobility, to distinguish true nobles from usurpers of title, to denote, as much as is possible, the beginning of each noble family, to follow its progress and growth, in a word, to ascertain its past, present, and future condition, so that, whatever mishap should occur, no noble should lose a Title that he had inherited from his paternity, or earned by his virtues, *and so that the Prince may know those of his subjects upon whose loyalty and services he may continue to count most particularly* [italics mine].[85]

In 1778, the number of proprietary civil offices of state throughout France was officially, and conservatively, estimated to be 50,969.[86] They included the entire royal judiciary and the administrations for taxation, finance, war, the royal domain, and the royal household.

In 1515, at the beginning of the reign of Francis I, there were no more than 5,000 career officers of state. In only 263 years the state had grown tenfold, whereas the population of the realm had increased by less than one-third, from 16 million to 26 million.[87] In 1778, nearly one-half of the offices were judicial, in courts similar to those that I have described for Paris. There was a proprietary and professional royal officer of justice for about every 1,000 people in the total population of eighteenth-century France.

Government by holders of proprietary, or "venal," offices was a system created legislatively by the kings of France. Its origins and history up to the mid-seventeenth century have been traced by Roland Mousnier.[88] From the fifteenth century onward, when kings created offices of state they sold them to men who met the specific formal qualifications for those offices. That was a contractual arrangement. In principle, the monarchy could repurchase and then resell an office, but in practice it rarely did so. The officer received a small annual salary (*gages*), calculated as a fixed percentage of the price of the office, various emoluments attached to the office, including valuable tax exemptions. Before 1604, an officeholder could sell his office to another man, resign in favor of his son or a blood relative, or bequeath it to one of his heirs. If he did any of these things, either he or the recipient had to pay the Crown a large fee, usually one-fourth the assessed value of the office. The buyer or recipient then had to prove that he had the necessary qualifications, receive formal royal appointment to the office (and pay requisite fees for that *provision*), and be accepted by the institutional company (court or administration) to which the office was attached. If the officeholder did not sell, or resign in favor of someone else, forty days before he died in office, the full ownership reverted to the Crown, and the office could then be resold at royal will. In fact, however, the legal de-

[85] Louis Pierre d'Hozier and Antoine Marie d'Hozier de Sérigny, *Armorial général de la France*, 7 vols. (Paris, 1738–68), vol. 1, p. viii. Italics mine.

[86] William Doyle, "The Price of Offices in Pre-Revolutionary France," *Historical Journal*, 27 (1984): 832.

[87] Chaunu, *La mort à Paris*, p. 201.

[88] Roland Mousnier, *La vénalité des offices sous Henri IV et Louis XIII*, (Paris: Presses Universitaires de France, 1971). There is a more succinct description in his *Institutions of France*, vol. 2, pp. 27–53.

vices of resignation and transfer allowed offices to be made familial patrimony, and thus dynastic, long before their hereditary transmission was officially authorized in 1604. A December 1604 edict of Henri IV annulled the forty-days clause and instituted a special annual fee, the *droit annuel*, set at one-sixtieth the assessed value of an office, and a resignation fee of one-eighth the assessed value; officers who paid those fees could transmit their offices directly to their heirs as family patrimony. If the officer died in office, ownership passed to his paternal family, his widow, or his heirs. After 1604, offices were defined in civil law as hereditary, or lineal, property.

The relationship between the monarchy and these officeholders was symbiotic. The Crown obtained both a vocational governing class to enforce its laws and a regular inflow of revenue from the exercise, resale, and inheritance of offices; officialdom gained the security of life (later patrimonial) tenure. During the Old Regime, the symbiosis operated at virtually all levels of government, from ambulant tax collectors in remote *élections* and summons-servers in rural bailliages to treasurers of Generalities and presidents of Parlements.

The royal purpose of creating a professional judiciary and administration was achieved only because from the fifteenth through the eighteenth centuries, there was an indispensable willingness to invest and serve in civil offices among families of the Third Estate, and even the Second Estate, throughout France. Most civil offices were relatively expensive. Few magisterial offices generated significant revenue for their proprietors, although all did include valuable exemptions from royal taxes. Judicial officers were barred by royal laws from engaging in commerce or manufacturing.[89] Despite those strictures, from the sixteenth century onward large and median family capital flowed steadily from private banking, trade, and manufacturing (where many fortunes were built during the Old Regime) into royal offices. Once placed there, this capital gradually lost its dynamism. Those choices led to dramatic social and economic changes for the bourgeois of early modern and Old Regime France. The French legalistic state developed because of their choices. Its history cannot be grasped only through institutions; those institutions were composed of families and their vocations.

From the mid-sixteenth to the late seventeenth century, Chancellors of France, *parlementaires*, and royal jurists elaborated civil laws that served to encourage and preserve family dynasticism in state service. Those laws, binding on all social groups throughout France, superseded many local customs and traditional Church canons regarding marriage, procreation, and inheritance. They were crafted to protect the parental authority, lineage property, and succession rights that maintained families in royal officialdom.[90]

---

[89] Explicitly by the December 1701 edict of Louis XIV, which did authorize nobles who were not judicial officers to engage in wholesale and maritime trade (Isambert, vol. 20, pp. 400–2).

[90] For discussion of the political import of the civil legislation, see Sarah Hanley, "Engendering the State: Family Formation and State Building in Early Modern France," in *French Historical Studies*, 16 (1989): 4–27.

Since marriages are the seminary of States, the source and origin of civil society, and the foundation of families that compose commonwealths, which provide the principles for their discipline, and within which the natural reverence of children for their parents is the bond for the legitimate obedience of subjects toward their sovereign, the kings preceding us have deemed it worthy of their attention to legislate the public order, external decency, integrity, and dignity of marriage.[91]

Royal legislation refashioned marriage into an act simultaneously public and familial, under the jurisdiction of the criminal law enforced by royal magistrates. The refashioning began with Henri II's edict of February 1556; it was essentially completed with the declaration of Louis XIII in 1639.

Marriages were to be contractual arrangements made by the elders of families, not decisions by sons and daughters. No promise of marriage could be notarized without the presence and endorsing signature of the parents or legal guardian. Men and women under the age of 25, even widows, who married without the formal, written, and certified consent of their fathers and mothers (or legal guardian, if the parents were deceased) were ineligible for any dower payment, donation, or inheritance; so too were their progeny. Such disinheritance was obligatory; it did not depend on parents or guardian. Men over 30 and women over 25 who married without parental consent could be disinherited by their families.[92] Elopement, even by mutual agreement, was redefined as the capital crime of *rapt de seduction*, or abduction. Even if the parents of the couple consented (or acquiesced) after the fact of clandestine marriage, and pregnancy or childbirth, the criminal event stood, and the marriage was voided. The children that issued from such a marriage were bastards, without any rights of inheritance.[93] The statutory penalty for the crime of abduction was death, without possibility of royal pardon – even if the suborned or abducted "victim" alleged that she or he had willingly agreed to the marriage.[94] A man who persuaded a young woman to leave home or to marry him against the will of her parents faced the noose or, if he was noble, the beheading sword. Clerics who married couples without the written and witnessed consent of their parents

---

[91] Preamble to the November 1639 declaration on marriage (Isambert, vol. 16, p. 520).

[92] 1579 Ordinance of Blois, Articles 41–4 (Isambert, vol, 14, p. 392); 1639 declaraltion, Article 2 (Isambert, vol. 16, p. 522).

[93] "Voulons, suivant les saints décrets et constitutions canoniques, tels mariages faits avec ceux qui auront ravi et enlevé lesdites veuves, fils et filles, être déclarez nuls et de nul effet et valeur, comme non valablement, ni légitimement contractez; sans que par le temps, consentement des personnes ravies, leurs parens et tuteurs prêtez avant ou aprés lesdits prétendus mariages, ils puissent être validez ou confirmez: et que les enfans qui viendront desdits mariages soient et demeurent bâtards et illégitimes, indignes de toutes successions directes et collatérales qui leur pourroient échoir: ensemble les parens qui auroient assisté, donné conseil, aide ou retraite, ou prêté consentement ausdits prétendus mariages et leurs heirs à toujours incapables de pouvoir succéder directement ou indirectement ausdites veuves, fils ou filles: et desquelles successions au dit cas, nous les avons privés et déclarés indignes, sans que lesdits enfans puissent être légitimés, ni lesdits parens réhabilitez pour recueillir lesdits biens. Et si aucuns lettres étoient impêtrées nous importunité ou autrement, défendons à nos juges d'y avoir auçun égard" (1629 ordinance, Article 169 [Isambert, vol. 16, pp. 273–4]).

[94] Ibid., and 1579 Ordinance of Blois, Article 41 (Isambert, vol. 14, p. 391).

could be indicted as accomplices to abduction, as could all who aided or participated in such marriages. The penalties for such complicity ranged from servitude in the galleys to death. Those cases were removed from the authority of ecclesiastical tribunals and placed exclusively under the jurisdiction of royal courts.

Children who issued from concubinage, or even from marriage between a man in the last period of life and his kept woman, were ineligible for any inheritance. That man's property legally reverted to his family or passed to his children by earlier marriage.[95] Widows with children, if they remarried "foolishly to persons beneath their social condition," could not make communal-property arrangements with those partners or bequests to them, nor could they sell any of their inheritance or dower properties; those were to be reserved for their children by previous (and socially respectable) marriage or else revert to their families.[96] A 1697 edict authorized parents to disinherit widowed daughters over 25 who remarried without their consent, even to men of equal or superior social condition.[97]

The consent textually required by these laws was that of the father and mother, if both were alive. Royal legislation subjugated sons and daughters to parental, and thus familial – not simply patriarchal – authority.

Legal marriage based on parental consent, or the contractual alliance of two families, was also a public and sacramental event, performed exclusively by priests. Forthcoming marriages had to be announced in the parish church well before the ceremony, on at least three separate saint's days. At least four witnesses other than the parents had to be present at the wedding. Anyone who gave false witness about a marriage contract or ceremony might be sentenced to galley servitude (men) or banishment from the jurisdiction for at least nine years (women). The couple had to be residents of the parish ("true and ordinary parishioners"); if one or both were not, the priest had to receive permission to marry them from the bishop or archbishop of the diocese. The event had to be fully registered by the priest. By the mid-seventeenth century, marriages that did not conform to these rules were defined as clandestine, devoid of both legitimacy and heritage.[98] Parish priests, curates, or vicars were obliged by law to keep registers of all marriages, baptisms, and burials and to deposit those documents with the local royal court within two months after

---

[95] 1639 ordinance, Article 6 (Isambert, vol. 16, p. 524); edict of March 1697, Article 8 (Isambert, vol. 20, p. 291).

[96] 1579 Ordinance of Blois, Article 182 (Isambert, vol. 14, pp. 423–4). Article 145 of the 1629 ordinance went farther: Widows who remarried beneath their condition were automatically deprived of the dower portion from the previous marriage; it reverted to their family (Isambert, vol. 21, p. 267).

[97] Isambert, vol. 20, p. 290.

[98] 1579 Ordinance of Blois, Article 40 (Isambert, vol. 14, p. 392); 1629 ordinance, Article 39 (Isambert, vol. 16, p. 234); 1639 declaration, Articles 1 and 5 (ibid., vol. 16, p. 522); edicts of March and June 1697 (Isambert, vol. 20, pp. 287–91, 292–5).

the end of each calendar year. The registers became civil and statist records. They were used to verify date of birth (and thus the inheritance rights of eldest children), the legitimacy of marriages and children, and to police abortion and infanticide.[99]

That legislation, centered on parental authority and public transparency, favored dynasticism in profession and stable conveyance of lineage property from generation to generation. In the Paris region and much of northern France, from the sixteenth century to the Revolution, the legislation was enforced within the matrix described by Sarah Hanley:

Marriages were constructed financially from blood lines; inheritance followed suit. The new couple constructed a household by incorporating investments allocated by respective families. The husband brought an estate share and reserved a dower portion for the future widow. The wife brought a dowry, and the husband had the usufruct over the interest but could not dissipate the principal. The community property was shared by husband and wife as partners, but the lineage property ("propres") remained linked to the family of origin until the birth of children to whom it would later descend. Should either spouse die without issue, the lineage portion of the deceased person's property (usually a significant sum) ascended back to the bloodline of origin.[100]

Arranged marriages kept progeny under the discipline of their families and allowed the formation of large, endogamous kinship groups. Both forces were vital to the existence of royal officialdom.

Offices were classified in civil law as "immovable property" (similar to real estate) and subclassified, like all other forms of immovable property, into two categories: *acquêts*, or property acquired by a person during his own lifetime with his own capital; and *propres*, or lineage property that he had inherited or received in "endowment" from his own family at the time of his marriage or as dowry from the bride's family. *Acquêts* were personal property that could be sold, given away, or bequeathed in a will by the owner. *Propres* had to be transmitted as inheritance to children; if there were no children, this property reverted to the family from whence it came, and thus remained perpetually in the lineage. Even before the December 1604 edict, there were subtle means by which offices could be held in trust for male children not yet of age or passed to collateral male heirs as lineage property. After 1604 and the institution of the *droit annuel*, offices became full *propres*, or lineage property. Women could not hold office, but in the absence of a male heir a woman could inherit an office and then assign it. A woman could also bring property in office as part of her dowry in marriage. Furthermore, "Venality allowed complete separation of the office from the family without loss of the investment if there were no suitable male heir; or, as one often sees in the history of great robe families, the office

---

[99] 1579 Ordinance of Blois, Article 181 (Isambert, vol. 14, p. 423).
[100] "Hanley, Engendering the State," p. 12.

49

was transferred to a collateral line when the direct male descendant was an infant, was incompetent, or was unwilling."[101] Those legal devices were contrived to ensure the smooth transmission of family vocations – not merely individual careers – of official service to state and commonwealth from each generation to the next. They were effective, as will be shown for the magistrates of the eighteenth-century Châtelet and the Parlement of Paris.

Venal-hereditary officialdom, with magistracy at its core, was a distinct historical stage in the development of the state and public authority in France. It supplanted that combination of royal favorites and commissioners, ducal protégés and clients, urban plutocrats, and local feudal oligarchies that had wielded lay authority in medieval France. It was supplanted by the combination of bureaucracy and electoral democracy that has constituted authority since the Revolution. But the rule of venal-hereditary officialdom laid the foundations for modern French bureaucratic government, for it developed and legated the intellectual culture and techniques of career service to the state and commonweal. It was the original source for the prestige that careers within *la fonction publique* have enjoyed among the middle classes of modern France.

The creativity of venal-hereditary officialdom reached beyond political culture. From the sixteenth century to the Revolution, the exercise of magistracy and high civil administration required formal humanistic and legal education – the education that is described in Chapter 6.[102] Families that chose those vocations gave such education to their sons, feeding them into the high culture of the *collèges* and universities. It is therefore not fortuitous that most eminent figures of French letters, philosophy and science, between 1550 and 1789, came from a patrimony of royal officialdom. Their ranks include La Boétie, Montaigne, Bodin, Hotman, Scarron, Pascal, Descartes, Malebranche, Racine, Corneille, Boileau, La Fontaine, La Bruyère, Marivaux, Montesquieu, d'Alembert, and Voltaire. Few members of the intellectual elite came from families and formative environments of the military mobility or the mercantile bourgeoisie, and even fewer from the artisanate or the landowning peasantry. From the sixteenth century to the Revolution, magistrates and other royal civil officers formed much of polite and cultivated society in Paris and the provinces. They were patrons of Renaissance humanism, and they became a principal audience for the great doctrinal controversies of the French Reformation and Counter-Reformation. They were key participants in the literary and scientific acade-

---

[101] Ralph E. Geisey, "Rules of Inheritance and Strategies of Mobility in Prerevolutionary France," *American Historical Review*, 82 (1977): 282–3. This is the most penetrating modern study of royal office as heritable property in Old Regime France. See also his "State-building in Early Modern France: The Role of Royal Officialdom," *Journal of Modern History*, 55 (1983): 190–9.

[102] That requirement proceeded from a royal design, stated by Francis I in the January 1522 edict that created the office of criminal lieutenant for every bailliage court, seneschalcy court, and provostial court of France: "et auxquels offices nous pourvoirons, orès et cy après de gens notables, suffisans et expérimentez" (Isambert, vol. 12, pp. 197–8).

mies, *sociétés de pensée*, and *salons* that developed throughout urban France during the eighteenth century and that formed the cultural infrastructure of the Enlightenment. Royal magistrates were both the chief progenitors of the 1789 Revolution and among the leading architects of a new polity. They are central protagonists in this study.

PART I

Themistocracy

Introduction: Meanings

"Themistocracy" has two meanings in this work: (1) the system of rule of law, criminal, civil, and administrative, in Old Regime France; (2) a socio-political group, the men and their families who embodied and animated that system. Subsequent parts explore the structure and action of the criminal law. In Part I, I concentrate on themistocrats, particularly on the magistrates of the Châtelet and the Parlement of Paris. In ways that will be described, those were the two most powerful and creative lawcourts of the metropolis and, perhaps, of the realm.

The French themistocracy included the entire royal judiciary. Judges, royal prosecutors, and royal advocates of both the lower and the superior courts were endowed by the monarchy with supreme authority over the rest of judicial personnel. These three groups of officers were the magistrates, and it is principally to them that I refer as "the themistocracy." Throughout France, judges had the greatest authority among the three categories of magistrates. They supervised and conducted all the operations of their courts: arbitrations; investigations and trials; sentencing. In the criminal chambers, they exclusively possessed the power of life and death. Judges of superior, or sovereign, courts had the authority to interpret the law. Royal prosecutors and royal advocates, recording secretaries, barristers, solicitors, police commissioners and agents of the *Maréchaussée*, and the legions of lesser personnel attached to the courts were their professional associates, but not their peers in power.

What was the authority of judges in law? What were the cost, revenues, and privileges of their offices? What were their duties, and how was the performance of duty organized? What were their social origins, and the patterns of their character formation, recruitment, and careers? What were the elements of their solidarity? What were their relations with commoners, aristocrats, and kings? What was their corporate ideology, even personality? Those questions are the substance of Part I. To answer them is to describe the vocation and socio-political being of themistocracy. I shall juxtapose that description with general principles of the criminal law, and then address an ultimate question: Was themistocracy in eighteenth-century France essentially the rule of an oligarchy, through the instrumentality of the law; the rule of law through the agency of its magisterial servants; or a holistic fusion of the two, and thus an authentic political culture?

55

The Châtelet of Paris

A. The jurisdiction

The jurisdiction of the Châtelet encompassed the city and faubourgs of Paris, several bailliage courts of the inner Ile-de-France (Brie-Comte-Robert, Corbeil, Vincennes, Choisy-le-Roi, Versailles, Saint-Germain-en-Laye, Meudon) and scores of seigneurial courts.[1] The *prévôt de Maréchaussée* (provost of Constabulary) at the Châtelet had wider jurisdiction, over roads, thoroughfares, and vagabonds throughout the inner Ile-de-France. The entire jurisdiction covered mostly the territory of the *élection* of Paris (see Map 6). The lesser courts of the region, whether royal or seigneurial, were accurately designated, in a 1698 map of the jurisdiction, as "filles de Châtelet." The Châtelet was one of the original sixty bailliage courts of France that Henri II had elevated, in 1552, to the rank of presidial court, thereby empowering them to render final judgment in a wide range of civil cases, either in first instance or on appeal. But in contrast to the other presidial courts, the Châtelet had civil and criminal authority over a population that never numbered less than three-quarters of a million during the eighteenth century. At the close of the Old Regime, that population probably exceeded 1 million.[2] By both demography and the actual volume of cases tried and judged, the Châtelet was therefore the chief presidial court of France. It was also preeminent by virtue of the social variety and complexity of those cases, for they included all forms of rural and urban litigation and crime. That unique scale of authority and responsibility was the basis for Delamare's encomium to the Châtelet judges:

The dignity of this Tribunal, premier of all the ordinary courts of the Realm, and the eminent qualities of its Magistrates have always attracted candidates of distinguished merit to form its Council. The great number and importance of the legal matters

---

[1] But it did not include the interior and grounds of the king's properties in Paris: the Louvre, Tuileries, Luxembourg, and Palais-Bourbon, the Chancellery, the chateaus of Vincennes and La Muette, the Invalides Hospital, and the Ecole Militaire. They were policed by their governors under the jurisdiction of the provost of the Hôtel du Roi.

[2] The population, both domiciled and migrant, of Paris and its faubourgs was between 550,000 and 650,000 during most of our period. That of the exterior jurisdiction was officially 293,222 in the 1780s. "Population du Parlement de Paris divisée suivant les jurisdictions qui y ressortissent" (ms.), 1780s, A.N. D 1 V *bis*, 47.

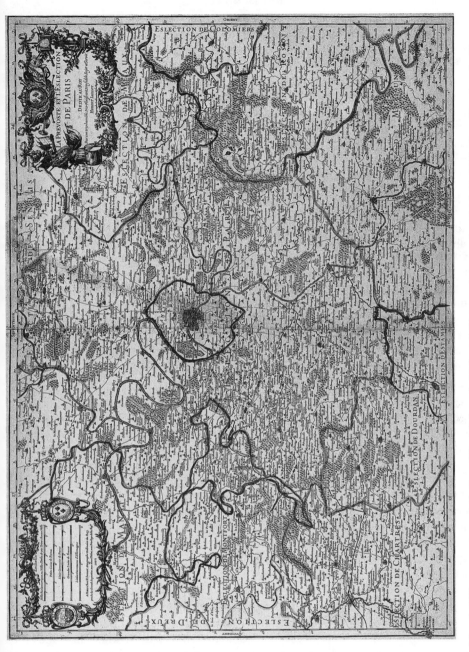

Map 6. "The provostry and *élection* of Paris" (1727), Hubert Jaillot, royal geographer, in A.N. NN 38-3. (Reprinted with permission of the French National Archives.)

transacted, which originate, are instructed and judged there, continually increase the knowledge acquired by judges before their entry to the Company. One may justly say of this Company that it is one of the most knowledgeable among the entire judiciary of France and a veritable Seminary of Magistrates. Judges leave the Company only to enter the highest offices of the Robe, where they always serve brilliantly.[3]

´B. The organization of the court

The internal organization of the Châtelet was complex. There were five main chambers during the eighteenth century: (1) the Civil Parquet (*le parc civil*); (2) the Civil Chamber (*la chambre civile*); (3) the Presidial Chamber (*le présidial*); (4) the Council Chamber (*le chambre du conseil*); (5) the Criminal Chamber (*la chambre criminelle*).

The Civil Parquet met Tuesday through Saturday. It published all acts required by law to be published, such as royal edicts, the rulings of sovereign courts, and announcements of auctions, wills and testaments, and entails of estates. It heard and often judged cases involving clerical benefices and property subject to royal authority; litigation over inheritance; property disputes between married couples or between families over dowries; suits for separation of common property or for interdiction permitting someone to dispose freely of money or property; disputes between masters and servants, or between notaries or solicitors and their clients; and suits over seals and inventories of properties. For most of those cases, the Parquet session was divided into an audience, for hearing and pleading, and a closed session for deliberation.

The Civil Chamber sat on Wednesday and Saturday. It tried in first instance and rendered final judgment on the following types of cases, if the money value involved did not exceed 1,000 livres: nonpayment of rent; suits for the distrainment of goods and money; disputes occasioned by the sale of subsistence commodities, such as grain, flour, bread, wine, meat, or firewood; disputes between retail merchants over commercial transactions (if there was no written contract); disputes over the repair of buildings; appointment of guardians or trustees for property; suits involving wages and remunerations for servants, workers, schoolmasters, physicians, and apothecaries.

The Presidial Chamber met four days a week. It heard and decided verbal appeals from sentences rendered by lower courts in the Châtelet's jurisdiction on all civil cases, when the sum assessed against the appellant did not exceed 1,000 livres.

The Council Chamber judged all civil cases that required full trial by written procedure (which normally was begun or completed in the Civil Parquet). The Council Chamber tried most cases that came to Civil Chamber when the value involved exceeded 1,000 livres, and most other litigation over real property. The Council Chamber also decided jurisdiction in criminal cases, thus classifying them, after questioning the accused. The questioning was essentially to deter-

---

[3] Delamare, vol. 1, p. 213.

mine whether the case was subject to provostial or presidial trial and judgment, without appeal of sentence, or if it was subject to ordinary trial and judgment, with mandatory appeal of sentence to final decision by the Parlement. General assemblies of all magistrates of the Châtelet, the reception of delegates from other courts or from the Chancellery, and the examination and reception of new magistrates were customarily held in the great chamber where the Council met.

Criminal chamber sessions were held Tuesday through Saturday. All criminal cases were tried and judged there, in three basic categories (which are given detailed description in Parts II and III). *Petit criminel,* or petty crimes, were cases of insults, slander, assaults, or brawling that were subject to fines or damages, not to publicly defaming or physical punishments, and that did not require trial by the full written procedure of the 1670 criminal ordinance. Cases that were provostial or presidial in character, whether by the nature of the defendant (such as vagabonds or soldiers outside their barracks) or by the nature of the crime (such as burglary or highway robbery) were judged there, in last resort or without appeal of the verdict to the Parlement. *Grand criminel* were cases of serious crimes, subject to harsh penalties, but in which verdicts were automatically appealed to final decision by the Parlement of Paris. For magistrates, this was the most arduous of the five chambers. This was so because of the strictness and complexity of the procedure that had to be followed for trials in *grand criminel* (including provostial and presidial cases), the sheer quantity of cases, the penal gravity of most, as well as the moral and political consequences of executing sentences. This was also the highest chamber in the royal priority of justice, the one whose decisions were scrutinized most closely by the Parlement of Paris and the Chancellor of France.[4]

C. The officers and their duties

The immense labor of classification, trial, and judgment within the chambers of the eighteenth-century Châtelet was accomplished by only four superior magistrates, the *lieutenants,* and fifty-six judges, or *conseillers* (whose number was increased to sixty-four in 1774).[5] They were directly assisted by four *avocats du roi* (royal advocates) and a *procureur du roi* (chief prosecutor) who had eight deputies. The four advocates represented royal interests and argued points of law primarily in civil and administrative cases. Their pleadings were made verbally before judges. The *procureur du roi* was the public prosecutor. His presentations were written. These officers and their deputies were proprietary and had the status of magistrates. The supporting staff for the Châtelet magistrates

---

[4] On the activity of the chambers and the secondary sessions of the Châtelet, see the royal edict of January 1685, in Isambert, vol. 19, pp. 472–80; Guyot, vol. 3, pp. 321–4; Yvonne Lanhers, "Châtelet," in *Guide,* pp. 163–220.

[5] On the duties of those officers, cee Guyot, vol. 10, pp. 557–72, and E. Laurain, "Essai sur les présidiaux," *RHDFE,* 19 (1895), pt. 2, pp. 273–87, 289–95.

was large, numbering more than 1,000 barristers, solicitors, recording clerks, summons-servers, proctors, notaries, police commissioners, and inspectors, but their roles were all variously ancillary to the tasks that magistrates had to accomplish personally.[6]

The *Lieutenant civil* (civil lieutenant) was the supreme magistrate of the Châtelet, and he had the most onerous duties. His was one of the most expensive magisterial offices in France. From 1684 until the Revolution, the official price was 400,000 livres. He presided over all general assemblies of the Châtelet and represented its interests to the king, Chancellor, and Parlement. He was responsible for the allocation and distribution of most civil cases within the Châtelet. He was presiding judge of both the Civil Parquet and the Civil Chamber. In the Civil Chamber, he personally heard and decided cases, assisted only by a king's advocate. In addition, he was responsible for reviewing and ruling on all requests for civil summons, for distrainment of property or money, for the appointment of a guardians and trustees for a minor or invalid, and for the postponement of civil trials. He also had responsibility for inquiring into any evidence of criminal behavior, such as fraudulent or collusive bankruptcy, or forgery, or bribery, that emerged from civil cases.

The civil lieutenant's privileges were commensurate with his authority. He could concurrently own, in addition to the civil lieutenant's office, magisterial office in another sovereign court. Whenever he visited the Parlement, his arrival was announced by the crier, and the chief usher at the Palais de Justice escorted him up the grand interior staircase when he entered and accompanied him down when he departed. In processions, he led the Châtelet dignitaries; in ceremonies he took precedence over the treasurers of Generalities and provinces. At the episcopal palace, he sat next in precedence to bishops and grand vicars. He easily obtained audience with the Chancellor of France.

The *Lieutenant criminal* (criminal lieutenant), second-highest officer of the Châtelet, presided over all sessions of the Council Chamber in which jurisdiction in criminal cases was decided and was responsible for all operations of the Criminal Chamber. Twice weekly, on Tuesday and Friday, he personally heard and judged complaints or accusations concerning less serious crimes (*petit criminel*). He supervised the development of all cases of serious crime (*grand criminel*). During the early phase ("preparatory instruction") of virtually every such case, he personally questioned the defendants and heard witnesses. (That amounted to dozens of cases each month.) He then usually nominated a judge for the "definitive instruction" of the case. The criminal lieutenant presided during the judgment of defendants in the Criminal Chamber and voted on sentence.

The two *Lieutenants particuliers* (particular lieutenants) alternated in presiding over the Presidial Chamber and the civil audiences of the Council Cham-

---

[6] Expilly, *Dictionnaire*, vol. 5, p. 543. The 605 barristers of the Parlement could also plead at the Châtelet.

ber, each serving for one month at a time. Each of them also personally instructed a number of trials. They generally assisted the civil and criminal lieutenants and replaced them when absent.

The duties of the fifty-six (later sixty-four) judges of the Châtelet were regulated by a royal edict of January 1685, which remained in force until the Châtelet was abolished in 1790. Those duties were segmented and were performed according to an unvarying sequence. The company of judges was organized into four separate groups, or *colonnes* (columns). Each column usually consisted of fourteen judges, with two or three additional emeriti, or "honorary," judges,[7] who still elected to serve. Each column was balanced in terms of the ages and longevity of service of its judges. Every judge belonged to a distinct column. The columns rotated in service among four chambers of the court during the judicial year. Each column (and judge) served for a month at a time, successively in the Criminal Chamber, the Civil Parquet, the Presidial Chamber, and the Council Chamber. By this system, every judge served for three months of every judicial year in each of the four chambers. (For column assignments and rotation in 1762, see Table 1.1.) All judges of a column alternated in the role of conducting cases and "reporting" on them (recommending sentence) in the chambers where trial followed full written procedure. In each of the four chambers, decision on sentence was by majority vote among the deliberating judges, not by the will of the lieutenants.

The system of rotation was ingenious. It virtually guaranteed corporate equality and solidarity in the exercise of justice, for it made specialization by individual judges impossible. Each performed the same duties as his colleagues and developed, over time, the same experience, knowledge, and general competence in civil, criminal, and administrative law. Some were inevitably more intelligent, attentive, and learned, and therefore more influential, than others, but none possessed a monopoly of expertise in any area of the law or was otherwise professionally indispensable to the Châtelet. None could become a narrow technician, and none judged alone.

[7] After twenty years of service, a judge was entitled to petition the civil lieutenant for *droit de vétérance*, or honorary status. If the civil lieutenant and company of judges approved, the petition was usually granted by the Chancellery. Honorary status allowed the judge to sell his office and remain active on the bench without receiving any salary, fees, or emoluments. He could participate in deliberations and vote on verdict in civil and criminal cases, but he could not instruct or report cases. "Les Magistrats vétérans ne peuvent ni instruire ni rapporter une affaire; ils n'ont que le droit de concourir par leurs suffrages au jugemens qui se forment à la pluralité des voix. On ne leur donne d'allieurs ni gages, ni épices, ni emolumens. Mais ils conservent tous les honneurs & touts les privilèges attachés au charges dont ils se sont démis" (P. J. P. Guyot, *Traité des droits, fonctions, franchises, exemptions, prérogatives et privilèges annéxes en France à chaque Dignité, à chaque Office & à chaque Etat, soit Civil, soit Militaire, soit Ecclesiastique*, 4 vols. [Paris, 1787–8], vol 4, p. 23. There were an average of seven honorary judges in the Châtelet at any time between 1735 and 1789. They were distributed among the four columns. Their service filled the frequently long intervals between the departure of a judge and his replacement, helping to ensure continuity in jurisprudence and practice within the court, and they compensated for the inexperience of the unusually large proportion of young judges during the 1780s. Honorary judges were also numerous in the Parlement and most presidial courts.

Table 1.1. *Châtelet: rotation of service by columns, 1762*

First column

Girard (1706)	Marotte du Coudray (1743)
de Montault (1720)	Lejuge (1748)
Léonard de Malpeines (1726)	Béville (1753)
Pitouin (1738)	Petit de la Honville (1758)
Roger de Bonlieu (1739)	Souchet (1761)
Sauvage (1741)	Rossignol, honorary (1701)

Service: *Criminal*, January, May, September; *Civil Parquet*, February, June, October; *Presidial*, March, July, November; *Council*, April, August, December.

Second column

Hazon (1706)	Sulpice d'Albret (1743)
Loys (1720)	Nau de Saint-Marc (1750)
Auvray (1727)	Duval (1753)
Brussel de Sancy (1738)	Roger de la Presle (1758)
Quillet (1739)	Boucher, honorary (1722)
Dupont (1742)	

Service: *Criminal*, April, August, December; *Civil Parquet*, May, September, January; *Presidial*, June, October, February; *Council*, July, November, March.

Third column

Couvreur (1718)	Pelletier (1744)
Pillet (1726)	Millon (1750)
Pezié (1732)	Phélippes de la Marnière (1753)
Davesne de Fontaine (1738)	Huerne (1759)
de Villiers (1740)	Maréchal, honorary (1736)
Dufresnoy (1743)	

Service: *Criminal*, March, July, November; *Civil Parquet*, April, August, December; *Presidial*, May, September, January; *Council*, June, October, February.

Fourth column

Lugat (1719)	Villiers de la Noue (1743)
Benoît (1726)	Testard du Lys (1746)
Fosseyeux (1737)	Nouët de Montanglos (1752)
Carpentier (1738)	Batissier (1758)
Avril (1740)	Montglos (1759)
	Josson, honorary (1741)

Service: *Criminal*, February, June, October; *Civil Parquet*, March, July, November; *Presidial*, April, August, December; *Council*, May, September, January.

The following was therefore the calendar of service for the Criminal Chamber in 1762:

January	first column	July	third column
February	fourth column	August	second column
March	third column	September	first column
April	second column	October	fourth column
May	first column	November	third column
June	fourth column	December	second column

Note: The date after each name is that of entry into the Châtelet.

Source: Almanach royal (Paris, 1762), pp. 291–5.

The only formal differentiation among the judges was seniority, a result of experience. The *doyen*, or most senior judge in a chamber, consulted with the presiding lieutenant on the distribution of cases for instruction and judgment and replaced him when necessary. The most senior judges also conducted the inquiries into the qualifications of each candidate for a judgeship in the Châtelet. In order to be eligible to vote on verdict in a criminal case where sentence could not be appealed, a judge had to have served for at least two years. To vote in all other criminal cases, he had to be at least 25 years old. But in May 1713 the Crown authorized lieutenants (and presidents of sovereign courts) to select reporting judges from men under 25, stipulating, however, that they could vote only on the cases for which they reported.[8] Either during his first two years or until he was 25, a judge of the Châtelet or the Parlement was in a quasi-formal apprenticeship. He was a youth, and youthfulness was an inferior, undesirable condition in the civilization of Old Regime France. To be young was to be incomplete and variously subaltern, an object of "dressage" in family, society, and profession. But, among judges, equality in formal competence began at a relatively low threshold of experience. All attained seniority by remaining in service. Formal equality of responsibility, power, and privilege among Châtelet judges was based on this general equality of practice.

In the Châtelet, as in all royal presidial and bailliage courts, the company of judges was at the summit of a rigid internal hierarchy, but within itself the company was almost perfectly democratic. Their corporation was characterized by mutual dependence and respect, feelings of solidarity with other officials and courts, co-optation of new members, and decision by majority opinion in all deliberations. Since all of the Châtelet judges were proprietors of their offices, performed the same duties, shared the same privileges and rewards, and had received an identical professional education, it was virtually impossible for any group of them to create professional dominion over the others, whether individually or collectively. Professional democracy transcended and attenuated social distinctions between judges of the Châtelet, distinctions of Estate (nobles and commoners) and of economic class (gradations in family wealth). It accommodated divergences of opinion in judgment of civil and criminal cases, while producing an ideology wherein "judge" and "magistrate" were singular, not plural, entities.

The fundamental power of all Old Regime judges consisted in their monopoly of the authority to try and punish. But the price of that power in the Châtelet was extraordinary personal labor, both intellectual and physical. The judicial calendar of Old Regime France was dominated by the religious calendar. There

---

[8] "Si nous voulions bien leur permettre de rapporter des procès et d'y opiner, parce que la nécessité où ils se trouveroit par là d'examiner et discuter tout un procès pour pouvoir en rendre compte, et donner leurs suffrages, les accoutumeroit de bonne heure au travail et les empechêroit même de se dissiper . . . que parce que s'il leur échappoit quelque chose, les conseillers préposés pour les assister lors de leur rapport, ne manqueroit pas de s'en apercevoir et de le relever" (royal declaration of 20 May 1713, in Isambert, vol. 20, pp. 602–3).

were no court sessions on Sunday. In addition, the Châtelet, Parlement, and other courts of Paris observed thirty-one holidays, of which twenty-eight were religious. Although the judicial year was officially 282 days, that year was further abbreviated by a six-week vacation, lasting from September 9 to the Monday preceding the feast of Saint Simon and Saint Jude (October 28). During those six weeks, the Châtelet and Parlement were staffed by reduced complements of judges who sat only a few days a week in each chamber. The vast collective labor of the Châtelet was therefore compressed into a judicial year of some 250 days.[9] That labor was organized imperatively and conducted according to intricate civil and criminal procedural codes. The schedules of judges during the 250 days were relentless.

Châtelet judges spent between one-third and one-half of their total professional hours on criminal affairs, deciding jurisdiction in the Council Chamber, trying cases in the Criminal Chamber. There, and in contrast to the Civil Parquet, they were assisted only by the royal prosecutor and his deputies, whose roles were secondary to theirs. Since defendants and plaintiffs could not have legal counsel, except in a few types of criminal cases, judges were not aided (or hindered) by the energies and arguments of barristers. They alone were responsible for deciding all points of fact, and all points of law, in the cases before them. The volume of crimes, and of trials, steadily increased between 1735 and 1789, but the system of trial and judgment remained constant.

During the year 1764, the judges in the Council Chamber heard accusations against almost 200 individuals who had been arrested and charged by the Constabulary. They decided whether there were grounds for trial, and if so, whether the case was provostial in nature (and thus subject to trial without appeal) or required full trial in the criminal chamber, with right of appeal. There was almost one such case per day of the session.[10] During the twelve months of 1762, the Criminal Chamber handed down provisional or final judgment on more than 600 defendants in cases of *grand criminel*, an average of 55 decisions in each month of fewer than twenty session days. Each of those individual judgments was the advanced, or last, stage of a long inquiry that in many cases had spanned months. An average of five judges, in addition to the criminal lieutenant, decided sentence in each such cases; one of them was the reporting judge who had usually conducted the criminal inquiry for the case from its early stages.[11] At least seven judges heard each case for which sentence could not be appealed to the Parlement. Every judge conducted several criminal inquiries (or instruction of cases) during the judicial year, beyond his regular service on the bench of each of the four chambers. The workday of Châtelet magistrates lasted from early morning to late evening, first at court or in the interrogation rooms of the Châtelet prison, and later at their homes reading dossiers. Per-

[9] *Almanach royal*, 1749 (pp. 274–5) and 1782 (pp. 390–1).
[10] Register of arraignments of those arrested by the *maréchaussée* (1764), A.N. Y 18794.
[11] Register of judgments in cases of *grand criminel* (1762), A.N. Y 10517–10518.

sonal asceticism and efficacy in performing professional duties were corporately required of them, and obtained from them.

D. Costs and rewards of office

Among Châtelet magistrates, as with the collectivity of the royal magistracy, "venality" of office signified the opposite of its modern connotation. Their families had purchased for them an office that meant a career of exacting, consuming, and quite poorly remunerated labor. That purchase and its career were a sacrifice of money, not a lucrative investment.

The maximum price for most magisterial offices had been fixed by royal edicts at various times during the seventeenth and eighteenth centuries. The actual prices, usually below those ceilings, were largely determined by fluctuation in demand for a given office. Demand was shaped by an intricate combination of elements: whether or not an office ennobled its occupant and (potentially) his family; its honorific standing, authority, and remunerations; the volume and difficulty of the work required; its availability or accessibility. Illustrious, ennobling, and powerful offices, such as a judgeship in the Parlement of Paris – which were highly dynastic, thus barely accessible, and only moderately remunerative – had a lower market price than certain more accessible, remunerative, but less prestigious offices. A judgeship in a sovereign court that demanded highly technical competence and sustained work, such as one in the Chambre des Comptes, the Cour des Aides, or the Cour des Monnaies, attracted a restricted and stable demand. The requirements, both formal and informal, for admission to high magisterial offices were exacting. They were known to every retiring seller and potential buyer, and they limited demand for such offices. Wealth alone could not buy a judgeship. Between 1700 and midcentury, the prices of judgeships in most of the great Parisian courts declined; they then either stabilized or began to rise, until the Revolution (Table 1.2).[12] The devaluative trend over much of the eighteenth century encouraged both individual life tenures and family dynasticism in office, and thus promoted corporate stability within the Paris courts. During most of the century, it was virtually impossible to speculate economically on the purchase of high themis-

[12] This information is drawn from several sources: François Bluche, *Les magistrats du Parlement de Paris au XVIIIe siècle (1715–1771)* (Paris: University of Besançon, 1960), pp. 164–7; "Les magistrats des cours parisiennes au XVIIIe siècle: Hiérarchie et situation sociale," *RHDFE*, 52 (1974): 93; "Les magistrats de la Cour des Monnaies de Paris au XVIIIe siècle (1715–1790)," *Annales Littéraires de l'Université de Besançon*, 81 (1966): 19; "Les magistrats du Grand Conseil au XVIIIe siècle (1690–1791)," in Annales Littéraires de l'Université de Besançon, 82 (1966): 22; Guy d'Árvisenet,"L'office de conseiller à la Cour des Aides de Paris au XVIIIe siècle," *RHDFE*, 33 (1955): 539; Philippe Rosset, "Les conseillers du Châtelet de Paris de la fin du XVIIe siècle: Etude d'histoire sociale," *Paris et L'Ile-de-France, Mémoires des Sociétés Historiques et Archéologiques de Paris et de L'Ile-de-France*, pt. 2, no. 22, (1971): 255–56. For general discussion of office prices and their fluctuations during the eighteenth century, see especially George V. Taylor, "Noncapitalist Wealth and the Origins of the French Revolution," *American Historical Review*, 72 (1967): 469–96, and Doyle, "Price of Offices."

Table 1.2. *Prices for office of judge in main Paris courts (livres)*

Year	Châtelet	Parlement	Grand Counseil	Chambre des Comptes	Cour des Aides	Cour des Monnaies
1700	27,000	100,000	70,000	45,000		
1710–15	25,000	90,000				
1720–5		83,000	44,000		59,000	
1730–5	15,000	42,000				
1740–2	8,000	55,000				
1748–50	7,000	40,000	30,000	50,000	40,000	32,000
1757		50,000				
1771–2	16,000	50,000				
1775–8			25,000			36,000

Sources: Data constructed from François Bluche, *Les magistrats du Parlement de Paris au XXIIIe siècle (1715–1771)*, *Annales Littéraires de l'Université de Besançon* (Paris: University of Besançon, 1960), pp. 164–7: "Les magistrats des cours parisiennes au XVIIe siècle: Hiérarchie et situation sociale," *RHDFE*, 52 (1974): 93; "Les magistrats de la Cour des Monnaies de Paris au XVIIIe siècle (1715–1790)," *Annales Littéraires de l'Université de Besançon*, vol. 81 (1966), p. 19; "Les magistrats du Grand Conseil au XVIIIe siècle (1690–1791), *Annales Littéraires de l'Université de Besançon*, vol. 82 (1966), p. 22; Guy d'Arvisenet, "L'office de conseiller à la Cour des Aides de Paris au XVIIIe siècle," *RHDFE*, 33 (1955): 539; Philippe Rosset, "Les conseillers du Châtelet de Paris de la fin du XVIIe siècle: Etude d'histoire sociale," in *Paris et L'Ile-de-France, Mémoires des Sociétés Historiques et Archéologiques de Paris et de L'Ile-de-France*, no. 22, pt. 2, (1971), pp. 255–6.

tocratic office, whereas it was consistently possible to do so, and lucratively, with offices in public finance administration.

During the eighteenth century, the *livre tournois* was roughly equivalent to 25 French francs of the 1990s, or $3.50. Therefore, a judgeship in the Parlement of Paris that cost 40,000 livres in roughly 1750 was worth about 1 million francs, or $143,000, in the currency of the 1990s. Châtelet judgeships were inexpensive by comparison with those in the sovereign courts of Paris, but 15,000 livres, or even 8,000 livres, was a vast sum in comparison with the income of most commoners in Paris during the eighteenth century, and very substantial in relation to most bourgeois patrimonies. Early in the century, an unskilled Parisian laborer who managed to work 250 days a year earned an average of 230 livres a year; in the 1780s, he earned 320 livres a year. Therefore he was not likely to earn 8,000 livres in a lifetime. From 1775 to 1790, the average total worth at decease of Parisian artisans, other than master craftsmen, was 1,776 livres, in all forms of property. (Only about 4 percent of that property was money.)[13] A study of Parisian marriage contracts concluded in 1749 reveals that

[13] Roche, *Le peuple de Paris*, pp. 76, 87.

among 560 master craftsmen and merchants, 429 received, from their parents
and in dowry, money and property worth 5,000 livres or less. Among the 63
grooms in the liberal professions (barristers, solicitors, physicians, architects,
savants, artists), only 25 received more than 15,000 livres.[14] One can conclude
that for all but those families in the highest tiers of eighteenth-century Parisian
wealth, to purchase an office for 15,000 livres was to make a major and lasting
commitment of patrimonial capital.

Purchase of the magisterial office from the retiring incumbent (or from
his family, if he had died in office) was the first expenditure required. After
purchasing the office, every aspiring magistrate had to obtain a royal letter
of appointment to it before he could formally apply to the company of magistrates for admission. Getting such a letter of appointment entailed paying
substantial fees to the Crown, including the *huitième denier,* an amount equal to
one-eighth the official price of the office; the *marc d'or,* set at about 1,000 livres
for a Châtelet judgeship; and between 100 and 150 livres for parchment and
seal. The royal letter of appointment was a formulaic and grandiloquent
document. (See the letter for Augustin Testard du Lys appointing him to
the bench of the Châtelet in the appendix to part I.) But it did not complete,
or even guarantee, investiture. The candidate still had to apply for admission
to the company of judges and undergo their inquiry. They alone formally admitted him to the office. After being admitted to office, the new judge paid
the court a customary *pot de vin* of some 500 livres. To retain the office as
lineage property, and to prevent its reversion to the Crown should the incumbent die in office, a supplementary annual due (the *droit annuel,* termed colloquially the *paulette*) had to be paid: It was a fixed one-sixtieth of the office
price. After Louis XV accorded ennobling status to Châtelet judgeships in
1768, entrants who were not already fully noble in estate had to pay an additional *marc d'or de noblesse,* of between 1,500 and 2,500 livres, to obtain letters
of appointment.

In return, from the Crown, the candidate who had been accepted by the
Châtelet received an annual salary (*gages*) amounting to approximately 3 percent
of the purchase price of his office. If the price of the office was 15,000 livres,
the salary was 450, or roughly only one and one-half times the annual income
of an unskilled Parisian laborer. The judge would have had to serve for thirty-
three years simply to earn back the sum his family had originally paid. If one
subtracts the annual dues of 250 livres he had to pay from the 450 livres he received each year, the actual salary was only 200 livres a year. That salary cost the
Crown very little. The fees paid at the time of appointment, on a price of 15,000
livres, easily totaled 3,000 livres; therefore in effect the Crown was merely paying back to the magistrate each year the sum that his family had originally dis-
bursed to the Treasury. It did so during the first ten years of his crucially
important services. If he served a career tenure of thirty years, his service cost

---

[14] Daumard and Furet, *Structures et relations sociales à Paris,* pp. 18–19.

the Crown only 6,000 livres. The cycle began again when our Châtelet judge or his family sold the office.

Judges gained some additional revenue from judicial fees (colloquially known as *épices*), which were carefully assessed, collected, and paid out by special officers of the court at fixed rates. Although no comprehensive study of the financing of justice (or of judicial fees) in the eighteenth-century Parisian courts has been made, there are numerous indications that judges in presidial courts and Parlements received scant income from such fees. In August 1665 the Parlement of Paris issued, for all courts in its jurisdiction, a ruling whose two hundred articles set forth all judicial acts, civil and criminal, for which fees could be demanded from litigants or plaintiffs. The ruling also set the rate for each fee and prescribed the procedure for dividing fees among judges. The ruling was confirmed and its main provisions extended to all courts of France by a royal edict of 1673. The ruling and its rates were not revised for more than one hundred years, despite general inflation.

In criminal cases, only the lieutenant or the reporting judge was entitled to a fee. An instructing judge could claim 7 livres for inspecting the scene of a crime but nothing for other procedural acts. The panel of judges that decided jurisdiction and rendered sentence in criminal cases was not entitled to fees for those duties. The fines that were usually assessed on a defendant convicted of a serious crime or on a plaintiff or litigant whose charges were judged unfounded were mostly less than 200 livres. Those sums were collected (when they could be collected, in money or belongings) as the "king's commissions" and used principally to defray the costs of arrest, detention, or trial; only a small portion was divided among lieutenants and judges.[15]

Civil litigation was the source of most fees received by judges. Only those cases that had to follow full written procedure were subject to fees. The civil lieutenants of the Châtelet, and their counterparts in other presidial and bailliage courts, had first choice of instructing or reporting a civil case. The fees generated by such a case were divided as follows: approximately one-half to the reporting judge (who was often also the instructing judge), and the remainder to be divided among the judges who had decided the case. Judges' personal income from fees seems to have been small during the eighteenth century. The presidial court of Poitiers had a large bench (twenty-five to forty judges in active service) and a large jurisdiction, over a population that numbered 343,437 at the close of the Old Regime. In those respects, it resembled the Châtelet. Each of the Poitiers judges received an average of between 150 and 250 livres a year in fees during the century.[16] That was probably also the range for eighteenth-century Châtelet judges. The average for a judge of the Parlement

---

[15] Jousse, *Traité*, vol. 2, pp. 812–13, 826–37.
[16] Dawson, *Provincial Magistrates*, pp. 82–3; "Population du Parlement de Paris divisée suivant les jurisdictions qui y ressortisssent" (A.N. D 1 V *bis* 47).

of Paris was only from 250 to 450 livres annually, despite their huge caseload, for appellate judgment of civil and criminal cases generated fewer fees than judgment in first instance.[17]

By strictly economic calculations, the labor of virtually every royal judge in Old Regime France was exploited labor; indeed, in terms of utility, it was perhaps the most exploited form of labor in the civilization. Their "product" was considered to be of supreme value, for it was no less than the preservation of social, economic, religious, and political order. The system of venality was originally designed to provide the monarchy with a dedicated, professional magistracy at little direct cost to the Treasury. The design succeeded because the motivation of magisterial families was not pecuniary. For those families, magisterial careers were, in material terms, an expensive consequence of capital, not a source of capital. In psychological terms, those careers were a socially prestigious and morally exalted vocation. Magistrates participated, officially and directly, in the fundamental powers of both kingship and priesthood, protecting social peace, dispensing justice, discovering and punishing evil. No other laymen of France did so, officially and directly. The judges' uniform symbolically expressed that dual participation: scarlet robe (a royal color) for plenary sessions and ceremonies; black robe (clerical hue) for chamber sessions and prisons.

The authority and exclusiveness of the vocation formed its principal reward. It was buttressed by privileges, several of which were economically significant. Magistrates of the Châtelet and Parlement were exempted from the *taille* (the most costly direct tax); the impost on salt, and other urban excise taxes; duties on the sale or purchase of seigneurial property; taxes on the grain and wine produced on their estates; the obligation to billet soldiers; and Watch or Guard duty. They were entitled to import food and other produce from their estates or farms for household consumption in Paris without paying customs duties and, discreetly, to sell some of those commodities to factors for resale in Parisian markets.[18] Those privileges were a permanent economic incentive for them to acquire and husband rural properties.

E. Tenures in judgeships

Some 275 men served as judges of the Châtelet between 1735 and 1789. My sample concentrates on those who composed the bench in the years 1735, 1762, and 1789. They numbered 130, or 47 percent of the approximate total. They may be considered statistically representative of the whole, for two rea-

---

[17] Bluche, *Les magistrats du Parlement de Paris*, pp. 168–70. See also Albert N. Hamscher, *The Parlement of Paris after the Fronde, 1653–73* (Pittsburgh: University of Pittsburgh Press, 1976), pp. 166–8, 180, 184.
[18] Delamare, vol. 1, pp. 213–14; Mousnier, *Institutions of France*, vol. 2, p. 343.

sons: (1) they numbered almost one-half of the 275 judges; (2) they incarnated the Châtelet bench at the beginning, middle point, and end of our fifty-five–year period,[19] and are thus diachronically representative of the total.

Two royal ordinances, of April 1679 and August 1682, required that every candidate for a royal judgeship hold the degree of *license* in law (obtained by three years of formal study and examination in a university law faculty) and two years of practical study at the bar of a Parlement. The educational requirement was enforced, but the second requirement was not fully enforced, since candidacy was, in fact, permitted after only one year of inscription at the bar. After 1683, the minimum regulation age for judges was supposed to be 25, but the Crown systematically granted exemptions from this requirement to candidates for judgeships when the other conditions were satisfied.[20] Most Châtelet judges entered the court with such exemptions, and the average age at reception, among 103 of the 130 judges of 1735, 1762, and 1789, was 23. Admission to the company at that age occurred after six to eight years of humanistic education in a *collège;* followed by two to three years of legal study in a university and a year or less at the bar.

By comparison with the officer corps of the army and with the priesthood, this was a late age for beginning a career. The seeming precocity in a vocation so complex and politically important was based on assumptions shared by the Crown and the themistocracy. Judges were to be recruited, not simply as individuals or because of their institutional education but as sons of a patrimony and products of a moral indoctrination begun in infancy. They would learn the *métier* of judge within the court, through emulation of their elders in the collegial practice of justice.

For the great majority of them, the office was a full career, spanning more than twenty years. Length of tenure is known for 65 of the 93 judges who formed the bench in the years 1735 and 1762 (see Table 1.3). Only 4 of them served for fewer than ten years and at least 2 of those left for judgeships in

---

[19] They have been identified nominatively from the *Almanach royal* for 1735–6, 1762–3, and 1789–90. The composition of the bench has also been determined for 1748, 1775, 1780, and 1785 from the almanacs. There are two functional sources on the 130 judges. Their letters of royal appointment (*lettres de provision d'office*) to Châtelet judgeships state baptismal date and parish, date of appointment, the name of the departing judge from whom they purchased the office, fees paid for appointment, and often the offices held by their fathers or elders. The letters for 104 of the 130 have been found and examined. They are in chronological sequence from the 1690s to 1789, in the following cartons of A.N. V 1: 73, 85, 108, 169, 174, 230, 231, 235, 266, 269, 272, 276, 288, 297, 301, 314, 323, 327, 335, 339, 362, 374, 378, 396, 400, 411, 430, 454, 458, 484, 490, 499, 503, 515, 519, 524, 529, 533, 537. Cartons Y 1867, 1868, and 1869 contain the dossiers of "moral inquiry," recommendations, and admission to Châtelet judgeships for candidates who obtained a letter of appointment and who met the requirements of the court. Dossiers for 112 of the 130 have been consulted. They include almost all among the 130 who entered the Châtelet after 1718. The lieutenants and chief prosecutors are described in Chapter 3.

[20] On royal requirements and royal exemptions, see Rosset, "Les conseillers du Châtelet de Paris," pt. 1, pp. 207–13.

Table 1.3. *Tenures of Châtelet judges: bench years 1735 and 1762*

Bench year	Judge's family name	Appointment year	Age	Exit year	Exit age	Years of tenure
1735	Bruant des Carrières	1692	24	1745	78	54
1735	de Manneville	1693	24	1738	69	45
1735	Héron	1693	25	1746	78	53
1735	de la Vergne	1693	26	1740	73	47
1735	Tarrade	1695	23	1750	78	55
1735	Barangue	1695		1743		48
1735	de Berny	1696		1739		43
1735	Desnotz	1705	25	1740	60	35
1735	Drouard	1705	23	1750	67	45
1735/1762	Girard	1706	22	1766	82	60
1735	Noüet de Montanglois	1706	31	1752	76	45
1735	Fagnier de Monslambert	1706	23	1737	54	31
1735	Hamelin	1706	22	1740	56	34
1735	Josse	1707	23	1743	59	36
1735	Lérat	1713		1737		23
1735	Lebeuf	1718	25	1750	57	32
1735/1762	Couvreur	1718	28	1775	84	56
1735	Boutet	1718	23	1758	62	40
1735/1762	Lugat	1719		1762		43
1735/1762	de Montault	1720	22	1762	64	42
1735/1762	Loys	1720	27	1762	69	42
1735	Boucher	1722	22	1746	46	24
1735	Besset de la Chapelle	1725		1740		15
1735	Le Petit	1725		1740		13
1735	Filleul	1726	20	1738	32	12
1735/1762	Pillet	1726	21	1778	73	52

Table 1.3. (cont.)

Bench year	Judge's family name	Appointment year	Age	Exit year	Exit age	Years of tenure
1735/1762	Léonard de Malpeines	1726	26	1762	62	36
1735/1762	Benoît	1726	40	1762	76	36
1735/1762	Auvray	1727	24	1762	59	35
1735	Davoust	1728	21	1752	45	24
1735	de Largillière	1729		1743		14
1735	Granjean de la Croix	1729	27	1756	54	27
1735	Bouquet	1732	22	1738	28	6
1735	Langlois	1733	22	1738	27	5
1735	Nérot	1734	22	1742	30	8
1735	Frécot	1734	20	1739	25	5
1735	Maréchal	1734	22	1753	40	18
1735/1762	Pezié	1735	33	1762	60	27
1735	Chouart de Magny	1735	19	1746	30	11
1735	Roger Grozier de Montheuchet	1735	22	1757	40	22
1762/1789	Fosseyeux	1737				48 plus
1762/1789	Davesne de Fontaine	1738	23		74	47 plus
1762	Pitouin	1738	25		62 plus	37 plus
1762	Brussel de Sancy	1738	20		57 plus	37 plus
1762	Roger Groizier de Bonlieu	1739		1782		43
1762	Quillet	1739		1781		42
1762	de Villiers	1740	28	1752	41	12
1762/1789	Avril	1740		1789–90		49–50
1762	Dufresnoy	1743	25	1783	67 plus	42 plus
1762/1789	de Villiers de la Noue	1743	23	1783	63–64	40–41
1762	Marotte Ducoudray	1743		1783		40
1762	de Sulpice d'Albert	1743	26	1767	50	24

1762/1789	Pelletier	1744	28	1789–90	74–75	45–46
1762	Nau de Saint-Marc	1750	25	1763	38	13
1762/1789	Millon	1750	27	1783–84	60–61	33–34
1762	Noüet d'Ormoy de Montanglos	1752		1780		
1762/1789	Duval	1753	21	1789–90	57–58	36–37
1762	de Salles Béville	1753	23	1789–90	59–60	36–37
1762/1789	Phélippes de la Marnière	1754	18	1789–90	53–54	34–35
1762	Batissier	1758	21	1788	51–52	30–31
1762	Roger Grozier de la Presle	1758	25	1778	45	20
1762	Huerne	1759	25		41 plus	16 plus
1762	Gasteau de la Chatrière	1762	22	1779	39	17
1762	Leroy d'Herval	1762	29	1787	54	25

Sources: Almanach royal (Paris, 1735–6, 1762–3, 1789–90), and the letters of provision and dossiers, A.N., cited in note 19 to this chapter.

Table 1.4. *Tenures of Châtelet judges: bench year 1789*

Judge's family name	Appointment year	Age	Years of tenure
Bouron des Clayes	1766	21	23
Chuppin	1768		21
Lemoine	1769		20
Michaux	1771	22	18
Judde de Neuville	1771	24	18
Boucher d'Argis	1771	20	17
de Gouve de Vitry	1772	22	17
Legros de St. Germain	1772	20	17
Dupuy	1775	21	14
Dubois	1775	20	14
Destouches	1777	24	12
Laiourcé	1777	26	12
Mutel	1778	25	10
Garnier	1778	21	11
Vanin	1778	20	1
Silvestre	1779	21	10
Baron	1779		9
Baron des Fontaines	1780	22	9
Nau	1780	24	9
Nau de Champlouis	1780	21	9
Vanin de Courville	1780	21	9
Martin de St. Martin	1780	27	9
Quatremère de Roissy	1781		8
Silvestre de Chanteloup	1781	20	8
Chapelain des Brosseron	1783	17	6
Vieillot	1784	24	5
Solle	1784	20	5
Trochereau	1784	24	5
Maussion	1784	19	5
Duval	1784	21	5
Geffroy	1784	21	5
Goupy	1784	24	5
de la Garde du Marest	1784	32	5
Le Marié d'Aubigny	1784	20	5
Rouhette	1785	18	4
Denois de Fontchevreuil	1786	22	3
Maupetit	1786	24	3
De Pétigny	1787	20	2
Henry	1787	20	2
de la Hupraye	1787	22	2
Chabaud	1787	21	2
Des Maisons	1787	19	2
Clavier	1788	25	2
Delahaye	1788	22	1

Table 1.4. *(cont.)*

Judge's family name	Appointment year	Age	Years of tenure
Grillon des Chapelles	1788	19	1
Boivin de Blancmure	1788	31	1
Delarche	1788	19	−1
Camet de la Bonnardìere	1789	19	−1
Marquet de Montbreton	1789	19	−1
Try	1789	34	−1
Michau de Montblin	1789	18	−1
Jarry	1789	31	−1
Bourjot	1789	20	−1
Chrétien de Poly	1789	20	−1
de la Borne de Ménildon	1789	18	−1

Sources: See source note to Table 1.3.

sovereign courts.[21] Twenty-six of the 97 remained on the bench for more than forty years. The average tenure was thirty-three years: That was a professional lifetime. There were, however, several epic tenures of more than fifty years and numerous venerable judges who died in office. Normatively long tenures gave the Châtelet a high level of judicial expertise, of corporate prowess in the knowledge and practice of jurisprudence. Serial examination of criminal cases tried by the Châtelet suggests that at least ten years were required for a judge to become experienced and expert in criminal justice. In ten years he would have confronted, at least once, virtually every type of crime and defendant and every major issue of procedure and penology. Judges whose range of experience spanned at least fifteen years formed a near majority of the Châtelet bench during most of the period between 1735 and 1789 (see Tables 1.4 and 1.5). After twenty years, a judge would possess an encyclopedic mental archive of juristic, technical, and social knowledge in civil and criminal matters.

[21] Auguste Langlois became a judge of the Parlement of Paris, where he served until his death in 1756 (A.N. Y 1867; François Bluche, "L'origine des magistrats du Parlement de Paris au XVIIIe siècle (1715–1771): Dictionnaire généalogique," in *Mémoires de la Fédération des Sociétés Historiques et Archéologiques de Paris et de L'Ile-de-France*, 5–6 (1956): 238). Jacques Frécot went to a judgeship in the Grand Conseil (1739); he served there for fifty-two years, until the end of that court in 1791 (A.N. Y 1867; Bluche, "Les magistrats du Grand Conseil," p. 81.

Table 1.5. *Years on bench of Châtelet judges, 1735–1789*

Year	5 or less	6-10	11-20	21-30	31-40	41+	Total Judges	Av. Years
1735	9	13	10	9	3	4	48	17
1748	13	12	9	10	2	3	49	15
1762	9	4	11	11	4	6	45	20
1775	24	11	13	4	11	1	64	14
1785	22	13	8	6	3	6	58	13
1789	21	11	13	4	4	5	58	14

Note: These figures do not include the honorary judges (an average of 7) in service during the period; all of them had served for more than twenty years.

Sources: See source note to Table 1.3.

2

The Parlement of Paris

A. The jurisdiction

The Parlement of Paris was the most venerable and the most powerful court in France. A full delineation of its powers – over administrative, charitable, and educational institutions, in the settlement of disputes between organs of state, in civil and ecclesiastical litigation and controversies, and in the drafting of royal legislation and the creation of jurisprudence – is beyond the limits of a study centered on criminal justice and has been provided by others.[1] The Parlement of Paris played a greater role in the development of criminal law and justice, within and even beyond the confines of royal statutes, than any other institution in France, except for the Chancellor and the monarch in council. But there is no thorough study of the actual work accomplished by any chamber of the Parlement of Paris during the eighteenth century, and thus no adequate history of the Parlement as a court of law. Virtually all scholarship on the Old Regime Parlement of Paris has been prosopographical, political, or narrowly judicial, focusing on the social composition of the court, its conflicts with the Crown, the episcopacy, and other major institutions, or on its judgments of specific types of crimes and criminals. That is ironic, for Parlement was, first and foremost, a supreme court of civil, criminal, and administrative law: This was its quotidian being. The splendid volume and quality of the surviving court records, from each of the Parlement's main chambers, seems to have deterred historians instead of attracting them. Much is known of the *parlementaires*, but little of the Parlement of Paris as a lawcourt.

The civil and criminal jurisdiction of the Parlement of Paris was vast. (It is displayed on Maps 7 and 8 and on Table 2.1.) It encompassed more than one-third of territorial France: The Ile-de-France, Picardy, Champagne, the Orléanais, Touraine, Maine, Anjou, Berry, Bourbonnais, Poitou, Aunis, Marche, Auvergne, Lyonnais, and portions of Burgundy, Normandy, and Lorraine. The Parlement was the appellate (appeals) court for the Châtelet and also for 138

---

[1] The most complete description is by Monique Langlois, "Parlement de Paris," in *Guide*, pp. 65–160. See also Albert N. Hamscher, *The Parlement of Paris after the Fronde, 1653–1673;* J. H. Shennan, *The Parlement of Paris* (Ithaca: Cornell University Press, 1968); Bailey Stone, *The Parlement of Paris, 1774–1789* (Chapel Hill: University of North Carolina Press, 1981).

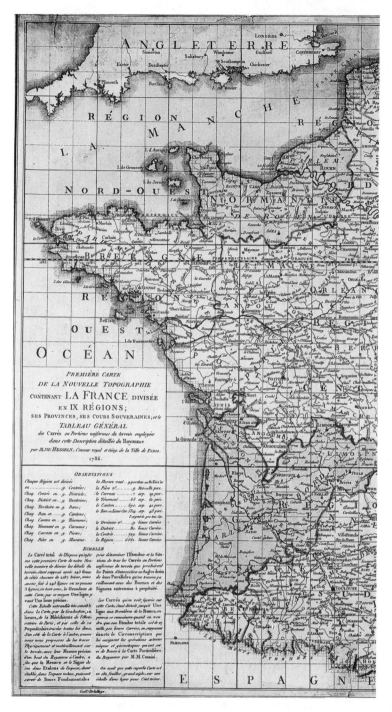

Map 7. France: jurisdictions of the Parlements (1786), Hesselin, geographer for the City of Paris, in A.N. NN 192-41. (Reprinted with permission of the French National Archives.)

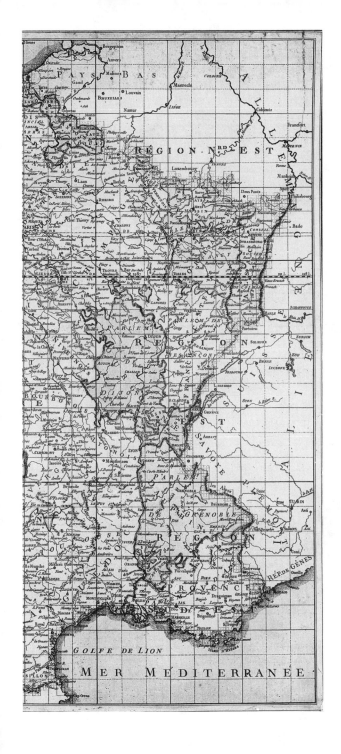

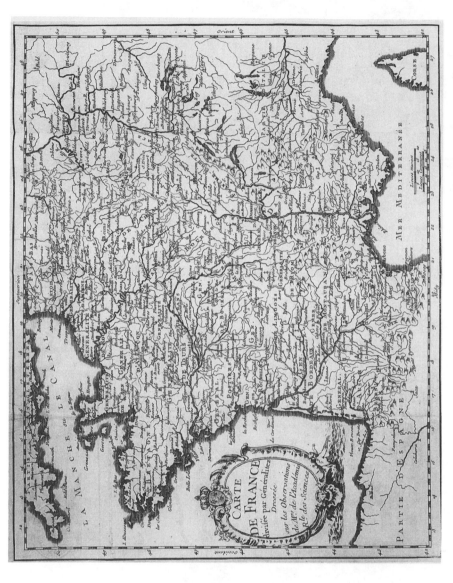

Map 8. France: the territories of the Generalities (1749), from Antonini, *Mémorial de Paris*, vol. 2.

other bailliage, seneschalcy, and presidial courts and their jurisdictional populations (Table 2.1).[2] In the 1780s, it was therefore the supreme court for a population of about 9.75 million, a population greater than that of contemporary England and Wales combined.

Civil cases in which the value of the claim exceeded 1,000 livres could be, and frequently were, appealed beyond the presidial courts to the Parlement. The Criminal Ordinance of 1670 mandated appellate decision by a Parlement in all cases of *grand criminel* that were tried by a subaltern (or even a presidial) court within the Parlement's jurisdiction. Only cases subject to provostial judgment were excepted from appeal. For all others, appellate decision was necessary, regardless of the verdict rendered by the lower court. Defendants and the full documentation of their original trials were transported to the Parlement of Paris for final hearing, review, and judgment by its Criminal Chamber, the Tournelle. The Parlement of Paris was also the tribunal of first instance, in civil and criminal matters, for prominent personages and leading institutions.

B. The court: organization and personnel

The Parlement of Paris was the citadel of written procedure in French justice, which is why its archives are among the most extensive of any Old Regime institution. The written procedure, and the huge volume of cases adjudicated by the Parlement, required tremendous labor from magistrates and their supporting staffs, and an intricate division of that labor. The Parlement of Paris was organized hierarchically into four principal sections, or chambers, all housed in the Palais de Justice.

The Grand-Chambre was the oldest and supreme chamber of the Parlement. It heard and tried, in first and final instance, all civil cases that involved the royal domain or the royal household; the princes or peers of France; officers of the Parlement and the Chambre des Comptes; the Hôtel-Dieu or the University of Paris as corporations; litigation concerning royal nomination of bishops or archbishops or royal administration of diocesan properties and revenue when such offices were vacant (the Crown's *droit de régale*); cases of high treason; and, in joint session with the criminal appeals chamber, all criminal accusations against high officers of the Crown, servitors of the royal household, knights of chivalric orders, magistrates of the Parlement and Chambre des Comptes, clerics, "*gentilshommes*" (men who were at least fourth-generation noble), royal secretaries of the chancelleries, and officers of justice from courts within the jurisdiction of the Parlement. This was jurisdiction over the most

---

[2] Data were constructed from two manuscripts, "Etat des bailliages et sièges royaux ressortissans nuëment au Parlement de Paris" and "Population du Parlement de Paris divisée suivant les Jurisdiction qui y ressortissent"(A.N. D 1 V *bis* 47), prepared by the Ministry of Finance under Necker during the late 1770s and early 1780s.

Table 2.1. *Provincial subaltern courts in jurisdiction of Parlement of Paris*

Generality	Seneschalcy court	Bailliage court	Other	Presidial court	Population
Amiens				Abbeville	70,048
Amiens				Amiens	234,087
La Rochelle				Angers	251,732
La Rochelle				Angoulême	95,134
Amiens		Ardres			1,872
Riom		Aurillac			78,650
Paris				Auxerre	128,486
Lorraine		Bar			81,900
Paris		Bar-sur-Seine			14,300
Tours	Baugé				47,918
Orléans		Beaugency			39,208
Tours	Beaufort				19,500
Paris		Beaumont-sur-Oise			10,452
Amiens				Beauvais	67,288
Limoges			Bellac		2,912
Alençon			Bellême		54,522
Orléans				Blois	142,608
Orléans			Bois-commun		6,110
Amiens	Boulogne				55,666
Lyons		Bourg-Argental			27,352
Bourges				Bourges	109,028
Amiens			Calais		26,962
Châlons				Châlons-sur-Marne	58,292
Orléans				Chartres	96,233
Tours	Château-du-Loir				42,146
Tours				Château-Gontier	33,046

	Généralité	Population
Châteauneuf-en-Thimer	Alençon	29,195
Château-Regnard	Orléans	8,086
Châteauroux	Bourges	111,670
Château-Thierry	Soissons	41,772
Châtellerault	Poitiers	30,949
Châtillon-sur-Indre	Poitiers	20,020
Châtillon-sur-Marne	Châlons	20,358
Chaumont-en-Bassigny	Châlons	162,084
Chaumont-en-Vexin	Rouen	16,380
Chauny	Soissons	25,208
Chinon	Tours	66,664
Civray	Poitiers	53,556
Clermont-en-Argonne	Metz	20,318
Clermont-en-Beauvaisi	Amiens	40,892
Clermont-Montferrand	Riom	135,192
Cognac	La Rochelle	13,665
Compiègne	Paris	17,700
Concressault	Bourges	27,534
Creil	Paris	2,080
Crépy-en-Valois	Soissons	20,786
Cusset	Moulins	12,428
Dorat	Limoges	2,839
Dourdan	Orléans	7,462
Dunkerque	Lille	39,920
Dun-le-Roi	Bourges	31,772
Epernay	Champagne	40,046
Etampes	Paris	19,916
Fîmes	Châlons	4,498
Fontenay-le-Comte	Poitiers	91,103
Gien	Orléans	12,922

Table 2.1. (cont.)

Generality	Seneschalcy court	Bailliage court	Other	Presidial court	Population
Moulins				Guerêt	165,162
Soissons		Guise			82,610
Amiens		Ham			1,248
Orléans		Janville			8,086
Bourges		Issoudun			88,540
Tours				La Flêche	66,146
Nancy		La Marche			28,184
Tours		Langeais			6,240
Châlons				Langres	85,046
Soissons				Laôn	114,728
La Rochelle				La Rochelle	88,834
Tours		Laval			63,726
Tours				Le Mans	343,950
Tours		Loches			44,382
Orléans		Lorris			10,322
Tours		Loudun			13,348
Poitiers			Lusignan		12,957
Lyons				Lyons	299,561
Rouen		Magny-en-Vexin			16,848
Paris				Mantes	20,570
Dijon				Mâcon	138,372
Tours		Mamers			26,312
Soissons		Marle			1,602
Paris				Meaux	73,892
Bourges		Mehun			12,376
Paris				Melun	63,102

Généralité				Population
Paris		Meudon		2,730
Paris		Meulan		13,260
Riom		Montagut		10,764
Orléans			Montargis	69,056
Lyons		Montbrison		73,762
Amiens		Montdidier		61,204
Paris		Montfort-l'Amaury		193,206
Tours		Montdoubleau		7,400
Poitiers	Montmorillon			140,673
Amiens		Montreuil-sur-Mer		15,990
Tours		Montrichard		3,692
Paris		Moret		14,820
Alençon		Mortagne		29,458
Moulins			Moulins	281,386
Paris		Nemours		41,626
Orléans		Neuville-aux-Loges		3,038
Moulins		Nevers		4,030
Poitiers	Niort			17,461
Paris		Nogent-sur-Seine		?
Soissons		Noyon		22,984
Orléans			Orléans	151,942
Amiens		Péronne		78,754
Poitiers			Poitiers	343,437
Paris		Pontoise		23,634
Paris			Provins	27,820
Châlons			Rheims	426,984
Riom			Riom	591,014
La Rochelle		Rochefort		20,126
Orléans		Romorantin		29,978
Amiens		Roye		19,604

Table 2.1. (*cont.*)

Generality	Seneschalcy court	Bailliage court	Other	Presidial court	Population
Châlons		St.-Dizier			11,258
Riom		St.-Flour			19,214
Poitiers		St.-Maxiant			36,615
Moulins				St.-Pierre-le-Moutier	229,112
Amiens		St.-Quentin			50,648
Châlons		Ste.-Ménéhould			116,324
Tours	Saumur				112,024
Paris				Senlis	33,514
Paris				Sens	112,294
Châlons		Sezanne			43,940
Soissons				Soissons	76,162
Orléans		Sully			572
Tours				Tours	171,574
Châlons				Troyes	129,480
Orléans		Vendôme			64,792
Paris		Versailles			56,576
Riom			Vic-en-Carlades		22,126
Bourges		Vierzon			8,658
Lyons		Villefranche			119,532
Paris		Villeneuve-le-Roi			12,090
Soissons		Villers-Coterêts			18,122
Orléans		Vitry-aux-Loges			2,080
Châlons				Vitry-le-François	38,376

Poitiers				33,623
Orléans				54
Orléans				8,684
	Vouvant-Chatelleraix			
	Yenville			
	Yevre-le-Châtel			
Total: 8	Total: 80	Total: 10	Total: 40	Total: 9,045,888

Courts are grouped under their appropriate designation and then listed alphabetically. (To locate on map 8, look in the Generality in which court was located.) Population given for each court is that of its jurisdiction in the 1770s, not of its seat. The table omits three Parisian courts that were under the direct appeals jurisdiction of Parlement: the Châtelet, the small bailliage court of the Arsenal, and the bailliage court of the Palais de Justice (an antechamber of the Parlement that judged offenses committed in the buildings or grounds of the Palais). Some lesser royal courts within the jurisdictions of the presidial courts are also omitted (although their populations are included). The presidial courts judged civil cases on appeal from those courts, but not criminal cases, which were judged on appeal by the Parlement.

Data constructed from two manuscripts, "Etat des bailliages et sièges royaux ressortissans nuëment au Parlement de Paris" and "Population du Parlement de Paris divisée suivant les Jurisdictions qui y ressortissent," A.N. D IV *bis*, 47.

powerful elites and corporations of France. The Grand-Chambre also received; debated; and published or else amended and "remonstrated" (objected to) royal edicts. It issued rulings (*arrêtés*) on contested or ambiguous points of law, which were binding on the courts within its jurisdiction, and thus created jurisprudence. The Chancellor of France, the Princes, Dukes, and Peers, the archbishop of Paris and the abbot of Cluny, and four masters of petitions were *ex officio* members of the Grand-Chambre. It was staffed by the *Prémier Président* (first president), the supreme magistrate of the Parlement; 9 *présidents à mortier;* 21 regular lay judges (25 after 1756); 12 ecclesiastical judges; and some 40 honorary judges (including the presidents of the two lower chambers of the Parlement, the Chambre des Enquêtes and the Chambre des Requêtes). Plenary sessions of the entire Parlement met in the hall of the Grand-Chambre, and there also the king personally addressed the court in *lits de justice.* Accession to membership in the Grand-Chambre was by seniority among the judges of the lower chambers; the requirement was twenty-five years' service in either.

The Chambre des Enquêtes formed the second tier in the hierarchy of the Parlement. It judged civil cases on appeal from subaltern courts (except those reserved for the Grand-Chambre) and equally voluminous appeals in *petit criminel* from those courts. It also instructed, and occasionally judged in first instance, cases referred by either the Grand-Chambre or the royal Council. Before 1756 it was composed of five sections, each with 3 presidents, a complement of 30 to 32 regular lay judges, and at least 1 ecclesiastical judge. By royal edicts of 1756 and 1757, the Enquêtes was reduced in size to three sections, each with 2 presidents and 33 judges, 2 of whom had to be clerics.[3] The five, and then three, sections of the Enquêtes were equal in authority, status, and method of calculating seniority. Serving there was a long and thorough appren-

---

[3] This was done in retaliation for *parlementaire* opposition to royal and episcopal orders that the last sacrament be refused to Jansenists. The judges of the suppressed fourth and fifth chambers of the Enquêtes were not forced from office, although Louis XV had desired their removal as a demonstration of his sovereignty over the Parlement. Faced with a mass resignation of *grand-chambriers* and *enquêteurs*, and protests from provincial Parlements, the Crown backed down: The most senior of the *enquêteurs* were promoted to a temporarily enlarged Grand-Chambre and the others were absorbed by the first three chambers. As judges retired, the three chambers gradually arrived at the regulation total of 69 judges (Shennan, *Parlement of Paris,* pp. 310–11). The great confrontation between Crown and Parlement came in 1771. Chancellor Maupeou and Louis XV suspended the entire Parlement and exiled its members from Paris. The Grand Conseil was given several of its powers in administrative law, and several presidial courts were made into *grands bailliages* with power of final judgment over civil and criminal cases. All magisterial offices were made appointive, not venal. The Châtelet, in solidarity with the Parlement, refused its new status as *grand bailliage,* and the number of its judgeships was drastically reduced. There was extensive themistocratic opposition to these measures, supported by publicists. The Maupeou reform failed. Shortly after Louis XVI's accession in 1774, he restored the old judicial and *parlementaire* order. In terms of the administration of justice, the Maupeou reform was a brief interlude in the history of the Parlement and Châtelet. But it was of major importance in exacerbating conflict between the themistocracy and the Crown. On the Maupeou reforms, see Lucien Laugier, *Un ministère réformateur sous Louis XV: Le triumvirat (1770–1774)* (Paris: La Pensée Universelle, 1975).

ticeship for the Grand-Chambre, since the *Enquêteurs* judged a wide variety of civil cases, and dealt with numerous cases of *petit criminel* and *grand criminel* during their regular tours of duty in the criminal appeals chamber.

The Chambre des Requêtes heard and judged in first instance civil cases in which men who possessed the right of *committimus* were involved as plaintiffs or defendants. *Committimus* was the right to plead one's cause before a Parlement; it was either granted by royal letter or attached to an office. It was enjoyed by the dignitaries and high officials enumerated earlier who were tried in criminal matters by the Grand-Chambre. They could also appeal judgments by the Requêtes to final decision of the Grand-Chambre. There were two sections of the Requêtes, each, before 1771, with 2 presidents and 10 to 12 judges; after the restoration of the Parlement in 1774, there was only one section, with 2 presidents and 13 judges. Few judges passed an entire career in the Requêtes. A judge who obtained initial office there customarily passed to the Enquêtes when a vacancy opened in one of its sections and served there until he died in office, retired, or entered the Grand-Chambre by seniority.

Three mutations occurred simultaneously when a judge of the Grand-Chambre retired from regular service, sold his office, or died. First, he was replaced by the most senior judge in the lower chambers. Second, every judge in those chambers moved up one place in seniority. Third, the vacancy created (usually in the Enquêtes) was filled by the entering judge (now the most junior) to whom the retired or deceased *grand-chambrier* had sold or bequeathed his office. An average of 90 new judges entered the Parlement in each decade of the eighteenth century. More than one-half of them were the grandsons, sons, nephews, or brothers of *parlementaires*.

The criminal appeals chamber, or Tournelle, met in a round tower of the Palais de Justice on the Quai de l'Horloge. The tower was connected directly with the Conciergérie prison. A contemporary explains, "It is called the Tournelle because judges from other chambers serve there only by turns, so that the practice of convicting people and sentencing them to death does not ruin the natural gentleness of judges and make them inhumane."[4]

The criminal appeals chambers of French Parlements formed the summit of Old Regime criminal justice. From 1670 to 1790, most defendants in cases of *grand criminel*, throughout their jurisdictions, were definitively judged in the Tournelles. Most had first been convicted by a lower court. Life or death, freedom or incarceration, honor or dishonor were decided in Tournelles. To make such decisions was officially and morally the supreme duty of *parlementaires*. Judges and deputy prosecutors in Tournelles were responsible – to the general prosecutor of the Parlement, the Chancellor of France, and ultimately to the king – for discerning and censuring flaws in the original trials reviewed on appeal. If the flaws were serious, *parlementaires* were expected to recommend

---

[4] Ferrière, vol. 2, p. 289.

sanctions against the lower-court magistrates involved and to order retrial of the case. That was the official means by which judicial discipline was enforced on subaltern courts.

Judges of the Tournelles were obliged to examine thoroughly the procedural documentation of original trials that came before them. The Paris Tournelle sat three, sometimes four, days a week (usually Wednesday, Friday, and Saturday), except for the many religious holidays. Intervals between sessions were necessary so that judges, especially those charged with reporting cases, could study the documentation. In consequence, the chamber met for only about 140 sessions during a calendar year. It was staffed by some 66 judges each year, including the 5 most junior *présidents à mortier* from the Grand-Chambre, who served all year; all of the regular lay *grand-chambriers*, who served by rotation in two groups, each group for six months; 2 judges from each section of the Enquêtes (before 1756; 3 thereafter), who served in the Tournelle for three months, then rotated back to the Enquêtes and were replaced by another group of 9 or 10. Ecclesiastical judges did not serve in the Tournelle. Although 66 judges staffed the criminal chamber during every judicial year, only 25 or 26 of them were in service at any one time. Each case, and the fate of each defendant, were decided by majority vote among a panel of 10 judges. Ten judges per defendant, among the complement of 26, meant that every judge of the Tournelle was engaged in its collective labor. A single day-long session often meant at least five cases, each with several complicitous defendants all of whom had to be, and were, individuated in hearing and judgment.

The most intellectually demanding and time-consuming task was reporting cases to the bench. Reporting judges either volunteered or were selected by the *présidents à mortier*. All but a few of the 26 judges performed this duty, some more often than others. Reporting was the principal means by which young judges were introduced to the practice of criminal jurisprudence. Each reporting judge received his case dossier a few days before trial was scheduled. At the trial, after final hearing of the defendant by the bench and reading of the prosecutor's written recommendation, the reporter verbally summarized the full documentation of the case, pointed out any errors or dubieties in the original procedure and judgment, and, if there were none, recommended verdict. In practice, his summary was more important than his recommendation. The *grand-chambriers* gave continuity to the jurisprudence of the Tournelle and had the greater weight in its decisions. As we shall see, the rules for deciding verdicts slightly favored the opinions of those most senior in a panel of judges. But for all of them, service in the Tournelle – an intellectual, moral, and physical treadmill – was a large part of the price for their grand authority, privileges, and dignity.

The first president, chief executive officer of the Parlement of Paris, was appointed by the king. The office of first president of the Parlement was held in dynastic succession by a few families from the late sixteenth century onward.

Like the civil lieutenant at the Châtelet, the first president convened and presided over plenary sessions of the entire court, conducted the deliberations of the Grand-Chambre, generally represented the Parlement, and was a principal interlocutor of the Chancellor and the royal Council. He worked closely, but often in tension, with the *Procureur-Général* (general prosecutor) and the *Avocat-Général* (king's advocate) of the Parlement; the latter two officers were direct representatives of the royal interest, whereas the first president stood for the Parlement as a corporation. His office required great skill in both jurisprudence and diplomacy. Within the Parlement, the first president, the *présidents à mortier,* and the presidents of the Cour des Enquêtes and the Cour des Requêtes had supervisory authority: They set the agendas and allocated tasks in their chambers, presided at the judgment of cases, and generally ensured that the protocol and procedures of the Parlement were observed. Their apparel was distinctive and splendid: a scarlet robe adorned with braid and ermine, and a black velvet mortarboard hat trimmed with gold lace. Their offices were fabulously expensive. At midcentury, a presidency in the Enquêtes cost almost 200,000 livres, a presidency *à mortier* in the Grand-Chambre more than 500,000 livres.[5]

Presidents of the Parlement were socially august, and dynastic, beyond the generality of *parlementaires*, but they did not transcend the *conseillers* of their chambers in actual judgmental authority. The *présidents à mortier* of the Tournelle made up the docket of sessions with the chief recording secretary, distributed cases for reporting, and presided at trial. They seldom reported cases, but they did vote on verdict. The vote of every other judge on the panel, including the younger *enquêteurs*, was officially equal to that of the *président à mortier.* His was merely one among ten votes, and could be less influential than the vote of a *grand-chambrier* more senior in experience. Judging defendants and litigants was the most important duty of judges, whatever their rank. In Parlements and subaltern royal courts, that duty was accomplished democratically.

The general prosecutor of the Parlement was the principal "king's man" in the court, serving even more directly than the first president as the voice of the king and the Chancellor. Like the first president, he could purchase office only on royal appointment. He corresponded with the Chancellor and prepared written briefs in civil, criminal, and administrative cases that involved the royal interest. All royal prosecutors in subaltern courts of the jurisdiction were technically under his supervision. He was public prosecutor in all criminal cases judged by the Grand-Chambre in first instance or on appeal, and he could initiate those cases. He or his deputies reviewed appeals cases for the Tournelle and recommended sentence before the reporting judges, but they did not vote on verdict. He was responsible for ensuring the execution of all

[5] Bluche, "Les magistrats des cours parisiennes au XVIIIe siècle," p. 92.

judgments by the Parlement. The inspection and direction of prison and *hôpital-général* administrations was one of his chief duties, and he officially committed to asylums people deemed criminally insane. He gave his opinion on pleas for royal pardon by defendants convicted of capital offenses.

Although the general prosecutor and his deputies had great influence over adjudication, they did not have the power of judicial decision. That was the monopoly of judges, in the Parlement and every royal court.[6] The company of Parlement judges (between 1735 and 1789, an average complement of 22 presidents, 163 regular lay judges, 19 ecclesiastical judges, and some 40 honorary judges) had enormous responsibilities. Their supporting officers numbered more than 1,200, of which some 600 were barristers.[7]

C. Tenures in judgeships

The average age at entry to office among the men who served as judges of the Parlement between 1715 and 1771 was 22.[8] Many were young dynasts who entered the Enquêtes or Requêtes at 18 or 19; few entered over the age of 26. They could not voice their opinions in the Tournelle, except as reporters of cases, until they attained the age of 25 and had two years of experience in the Enquêtes and Requêtes. A *parlementaire* developed professional knowledge and sagacity only through many years of service; these were not bestowed along with a *license* in law. Since the Parlement of Paris was the cynosure of the themistocracy, judges rarely left the court, except for high offices such as a mastership of petitions (of which there were only 80), an intendancy, or a ministerial position. The great majority of *parlementaires* spent very long lives on its bench. There were two contemporary generational stereotypes of the *parlementaire:* an arrogant and immature youth, invested with an authority far beyond his capacities; and a very old man, enfeebled by age, yet encrusted in office. Both types existed in the Parlement and were highly visible to Parisians when the court processed ceremonially. But they were minorities.

We may compare the magistracy of the Parlement in two sample years, 1748 and in 1787, by general composition and seniority. The court in 1748 was characteristic of the Parlement during the period 1735 to 1771, and the court in 1787 for the period 1775 to 1789. We can thus assess the collective experience of wielding intricate procedures, in a mass of legally, socially, and politically varied cases, among the *parlementaires* of those years, in the Enquêtes, Grand-Chambre, or Tournelle.

In 1748, the five subchambers of the Enquêtes were composed of 157 judges, with the years of experience summarized in the table:

[6] The preceding summary of the Parlement's organization is based on Langlois, "Parlement de Paris"; Shennan, *Parlement of Paris*, pp. 9–85; and Mousnier, *Institutions of France*, vol. 2, pp. 302–11.

[7] Expilly, *Dictionnaire*, vol. 5, p. 532.

[8] Bluche, *Les magistrats du Parlement de Paris*, pp. 57–8.

		Years			No. of judges
5 or less	6–10	11–20	21–30	31–40	
First chamber	10	5	8	7	1	31
Second chamber	10	4	8	7	2	31
Third chamber	9	12	8	5	0	34
Fourth chamber	7	6	8	5	4	30
Fifth chamber	5	9	12	4	1	30
Totals	41 (26%)	36 (23%)	44 (28%)	28 (18%)	8 (5%)	157

This was supposedly the "junior" chamber of the Parlement made up of younger members, but in fact only one-fourth of its judges were novices with five or fewer years of experience. More than one-half had served for longer than ten years, and more than one-third for at least twenty years. The average in the Enquêtes was approximately fifteen years' experience on the bench, just as among the Châtelet judges in a given year. Fifty-three of the 157 judges eventually rose by seniority to the Grand-Chambre, most of them after thirty to thirty-five years in the Enquêtes. Sixty-one remained in the Enquêtes for tenures of at least twenty-five years or until they died in office. Eleven acquired a presidency in the Parlement, and another 10 became masters of Petitions (of whom 7 were eventually appointed intendant of Generalities or provinces). Only 6 of the 157 left the Enquêtes for another court or for high administrative office. Eighty percent of the 157 served their entire career in the Parlement, but about one-half did so in the Enquêtes. In 1748, about one-fourth of the judges in the Enquêtes had served for more than the quarter-century required for admission to the Grand-Chambre. The essential reasons for the maturity that reigned in the Enquêtes were the small number of positions in the Grand-Chambre compared with the number of judges in the Enquêtes, and the vocational longevity of the *grand-chambriers*.

As for the Grand-Chambre, in 1748 there were 21 regular lay *grand-chambriers*. None had entered the senior chamber after only twenty-five years in the Enquêtes: Ten had served there for between twenty-six and thirty years, and 11 had served for between thirty-one and thirty-five years. Most had served a long, active tenure within the Grand-Chambre, 10 for more than twenty years, 6 for ten to twenty years, and only 5 for less than six years. Only 4 judges of the Grand-Chambre chose semiretirement to honorary status. At least 11 died in active service, 5 between the ages of 62 and 72, 3 between the ages of 73 and 80, and 3 over 80. Etienne Le Mée was unusual: Born in 1681, he entered the Enquêtes in 1711 and the Grand-Chambre in 1742; he remained in active service as judge and as *doyen* of the Parlement until his death in 1775, at the age of 94, having outlived his own father by sixty-four years.

Despite their tenacity in service, the majority of *grand-chambriers*, in any given year of the period 1735 to 1771, were between the ages of 55 and 65, and therefore were not dramatically older than the majority of judges in the Enquêtes.

In the 1780s, the judges of the Parlement were substantially younger than in preceding decades, a fact most clearly visible in the Enquêtes:

	Years					No. of judges
	5 or less	6–10	11–20	21–30	31–40	
First chamber	11	7	5	0	0	23
Second chamber	10	8	6	0	0	24
Third chamber	10	8	6	0	0	24
Total	37 (52%)	20 (28%)	14 (20%)	0	0	71

In 1787, there were 27 active lay *grand-chambriers*. Four had served in the Parlement for more than forty years, 5 for thirty-one to forty years, and 5 for twenty-five to thirty years. Thirteen had served for twenty to twenty-four years and had entered the Grand-Chambre exempted from the rule of twenty-five years in the Enquêtes. The majority were between the ages of 45 and 60.[9]

Between January 3 and December 20, 1748, the Tournelle of the Parlement of Paris judged almost 400 *grand criminel* defendants, in 256 separate cases. Of the 66 judges of the Tournelle, 56 (85%) reported at least one case; so did at least 18 of the 21 *grand-chambriers* and at least 30 of the *enquêteurs*. (The age and experience of the judges reporting on cases in the Tournelle in 1748 are presented in Table 2.2.)[10] Only 10 had five years or less of experience; 25 of them had fifteen or more. In 1748, the average years of service among the ostensibly junior judges in the Enquêtes was twelve years; in 1787, it was ten years.

[9] The composition of the Enquêtes and Grand-Chambre in 1748 and 1787 has been determined from *Almanach royal*, 1749 (pp. 175–90) and 1788 (pp. 301–17), and Bluche, "L'origine des magistrats du Parlement de Paris."

[10] The composition of the "Tournelle" in 1748 and 1787 is drawn from the manuscript "Registre du greffe criminel," A.N. X2a 1302 (1748) and 1306 (1787). These docket registers of the "Tournelle" give, in sequence, the last name of the reporting judge, the names of the defendants, the court of first judgment, and its sentence. The *Almanachs royal* for 1749 and 1788, and Bluche, "L'origine des magistrats du Parlement de Paris," have been used to identify the reporting judges by chamber, age, and years of service. "Uncertain" on Tables 2.2 and 2.3 means that there was more than one active judge of that family name in the Grand'Chambre or Enquêtes during that year. For example, in the "Tournelle" of 1748 there were two Montullés: Jean-Baptiste-François I, "grand'chambrier" who had entered the Parlement in 1706; and his son, Jean-Baptiste-François II, who had entered the fifth chamber of Enquêtes in 1741 (Bluche, "L'origine des magistrats du Parlement de Paris," p. 319). It is probable that each reported some of the 31 cases under their name. In calculating years of experience in the Parlement up to 1748 or 1787, only the lowest of more than one figure has been counted (e.g., for the Montullés, 7 not 42).

Table 2.2. *The Tournelle in 1748: age and experience of reporting judges*

Enquêtes and Chamber	Grand'Chambre	Uncertain	Age	Years of experience	Cases
(1st) Le Mercier de la Rivière			29	1	3
(1st) Le Nain			23	2	7
(2nd) Amyot de la Barre			20	2	2
(3rd) Bérulle			23	3	5
(4th) Glatigny				3	1
		Coste		3 or 45	2
		Lamoignon		4 or 18	9
(1st) Laverdy de Nizeret			25	5	8
		Boutin		5 or 28	25
		Bragelonge		5 or 30	2
(3rd) Pinterel de Neufchâtel				6	1
		Montullé		7 or 42	31
(2nd) Bellanger d'Essenlis			28	7	2
(2nd) Clément de Feillet			33	7	16
		Lattaignant		7 or 45	3
(5th) La Coré			28	7	9
(1st) Verduc de Soisy				8	2
(4th) Taboureau des Réaux			30	8	5
		Roussel		9 or 13	5
		Rolland		9, 22, or 41	4
(2nd) Piarron de Chamousset			29	9	1
(3rd) Boula de Montgodefroy				9	4
(5th) Saget			32	10	8
(4th) Bèze de la Belouse			35	10	1
(1st) Dubois d'Anisy			31	11	9
(1st) Noblet de Romery			32	11	6

Table 2.2. (cont.)

Enquêtes and Chamber	Grand'Chambre	Uncertain	Age	Years of experience	Cases
(5th) Trublet de Nermont			36	12	3
(5th) Douet de Vichy			31	12	1
	Le Peletier de Rosambo (Pres.)			13	4
(2nd) Bèze de Lys			35	13	3
(4th) Huguet de Sémonville			40	15	1
		Delpech		15 or 19	2
(3rd) Lossendière				17	2
(5th) Foucault de Magny			42	17	1
(1st) Maissat			40	17	4
(4th) Chalmette				23	3
(3rd) Le Maistre de St.-Péravy			53	25	1
(5th) Le Riche de Cheveigné			53	28	1
(3rd) L'Evesque de Gravelle			49	28	4
(2nd) Barré				28	1
	de Blair		61	29	2
	Barraly		53	29	1
(4th) Anjorrant				30	1
		Hénin		31 or 39	1
	Thomé		58	35	1
	Pajot de Malzac		60	37	4
	Le Mée		67	37	2
	Louvencourt		61	38	1
	Rulault			39	4
	Tubeuf		64	40	2
	Benoise de Mareille		62	40	11
	Fermé		62	40	2

Severt	42	9
Lambelin	42	7
Pinon de Quincy	44	4
Simonnet	51	2

Total: 31	*Total:* 15	*Total:* 10	*Average:* 41	*Average:* 18	*Total:* 256

"Uncertain" means that there was more than one active judge of that family name in the Grand'Chambre or Enquêtes in that year. For example, in the Tournelle of 1748 there were two Montullés: Jean-Baptiste-François I, *grand-chambrier*, who had entered the Parlement in 1706, and his son Jean-Baptiste-Francois II, who had entered the fifth chamber of the Enquêtes in 1741 (Bluche, "L'Origine des magistrats du Parlement de Paris," p. 319). It is probable that each reported some of the thirty-one cases listed under his name. In calculating years of experience in the Parlement up to 1748 or 1787, only the lowest of more than one figure has been counted (i.e., for the Montullés, seven rather than forty-two).

The composition of the Tournelle bench in 1748 and 1787 is drawn from the manuscript "Registre du greffe criminel," A.N. X 2a 1302 (1748) and 1306 (1787). These docket registers of the Tournelle give, in sequence, the last name of the reporting judge, the names of the defendants, and the court of first judgment and its sentence. The *Almanachs royal* for 1749 and 1788, and Bluche, "L'origine des magistrats du Parlement de Paris," have been used to identify the reporting judges by chamber, age, and years of service.

In 1787, the 66 judges of the Tournelle rendered final verdict on almost 850 defendants, in 522 separate cases. (See Table 2.3 for their age and experience.) Twenty-two of the 25 *grand-chambriers* reported at more than 40 percent of all cases tried. Novice judges remained a small minority in the Tournelle, despite the general youthfulness of the Enquêtes bench. Only 8 of the 36 *enquêteurs* selected for the Tournelle in 1787 were from the group of 37 with less than six years' experience. Each quarter, the presidents of the subchambers of the Enquêtes chose the 3 judges from among their own number for service in the Tournelle, and they chose groups that were balanced in experience. The average number of years served by the judges of the Tournelle was almost the same in 1787 as in 1748.

The youthful age at which men entered the Parlement, combined with advancement by seniority, had positive systemic effects that are often ignored. It guaranteed that judges reached their intellectual and professional maturity (after fifteen to twenty years' service) while they were still in their prime, 35 to 45 years old, with many years remaining before old age and the onset of its debilities, and that there was no generational abyss between the judges of the Enquêtes and those of the Grand-Chambre. It guaranteed an equilibrium of generations within the Tournelle, but one in which mature and experienced judges had greatest voice.

The rationality and rectitude of the judgments rendered in both the criminal chamber of the Châtelet and the Tournelle of the Parlement, within the context of eighteenth-century criminal law and jurisprudence, is a central issue addressed in subsequent chapters of this work. But the general professional maturity of those judges, up to the final years of the Old Regime, is beyond question. So too was their general dedication to the duties of office.

Magistrates were economically dependent on their families, rather than on the state, for the capital with which to purchase office and to maintain themselves in office. Their financial security was ensured, successively by stipend before marriage, parental or kinship endowment (and bridal dowry) at marriage, and finally inheritance. During the seventeenth and eighteenth centuries, it was axiomatic that those families had to possess solid affluence.

That was regarded as necessary to protect magistrates from corruption in office, to spare them material anxiety and the temptation of material pursuits, and to free them for their professional duty: "Poverty darkens the mind, dulls sensibility, diminishes authority, and threatens integrity."[11] This pragmatic, relatively modern attitude toward affluence was diametrically opposite to any radical Christian idealization of poverty. The wealth of Parisian themistocratic families consisted principally in real property, both urban and rural; the monetary value, but not the revenue, of offices; long-term state bonds and private annuities; and valuables such as household furnishings, gold and silver plate, jewelry, and objets d'art. Precious objects were not collected for essentially

[11] Delamare, vol. 1, p. 238.

Table 2.3. *The Tournelle in 1787: age and experience of reporting judges*

Enquêtes and Chamber	Grand' Chambre	Uncertain	Age	Years of experience	Cases
(3rd) Goislard de Monsabert				2	9
(1st) Boullanger de Rivery				2	13
		Lambert		3 or 5	44
(1st) Desmé de Chavigny				3	18
(?) Villiers de la Berge				3	3
(1st) Perré de la Viltraux				3	1
(2nd) Le Chanteur				3	2
(2nd) Duchesne				5	2
(3rd) Devin de Fontenay				6	12
(2nd) Talon				6	2
(1st) Lenoir de Vilmilan				7	45
(2nd) Leclerc de Lesseville				8	5
(?) Malartic				8	6
		Duport		9 or 38	27
(1st) Bourrée de Courberon				9	3
(1st) La Bletonnière				9	11
(3rd) Robert				9	5
(2nd) Molé de Champlatreux				9	3
(2nd) Anjorrant				9	3
(3rd) Boula de Savigny				9	1
(3rd) Morel de Vindé				9	1
(1st) Brisson				9	1
(3rd) Guenier de Romagnat				10	6
(3rd) Boula de Colombier				11	1
(1st) Brochant d'Anthilly				12	4
(1st) Gars de Courcelles				12	7

Table 2.3. (cont.)

Enquêtes and Chamber	Grand' Chambre	Uncertain	Age	Years of experience	Cases
(1st) Duval d'Eprémesnil				12	9
(3rd) Favières				12	2
(1st) Noblet			44	17	4
(2nd) Ferrand			36	18	25
(3rd) Hanmer-Claybrooke				18	1
(2nd) Oursin des Bures				19	8
(2nd) Desponty de Ste. Avoye			39	19	6
(3rd) Dudoyer			59	19	4
	Camus de Pontcarré		40	20	14
(3rd) Clément de Givry			41	20	4
	Clément de Blavette		42	20	1
	Chuppin		43	20	13
	Clément d'Etoges		39	21	2
(3rd) Masson de Vernon				21	23
	Langlois de Pommeuse		43	21	9
	Le Riche de Chevelgné		44	21	4
	Outremont		67	21	11
	Serre de St. Roman		41	22	5
	L'Escalopier			24	1
	Bruant des Carrières		46	25	16
	Amelot de Châteauneuf			27	11
	Marquette de Mareuil		66	28	3
	Dionis du Séjour		53	29	21
	Pasquier de Coulans		51	29	16
	Robert de St. Vincent		62	29	1
	Nouêt		58	39	2

Dupuis de Marcé		62	39	9
Frédy		66	40	15
Glatigny			42	9
Titon			43	5
Lefèvre d'Ormesson		69	46	12
Boula de Montgodefroy			48	21
Total: 22	Total: 2		Average: 17	Total: 522

Total: 34

Sources: See source note to Table 2.2.

sumptuary reasons; they were hoarded, and occasionally pledged, exchanged, or sold, as negotiable capital, a surrogate for money. There was a characteristic type of themistocratic fortune, consisting of proprietary, not venture, capital, and a great variety of scale within the type. The value of the capital of a typical Châtelet family ranged from less than .25 million livres to nearly 1 million livres; that of *parlementaires* varied from less than .25 million livres to several million livres. Such fortunes generated stable but often unspectacular annual incomes, derived primarily from rents, agrarian dues, and the interest on annuities, and bonds. The average annual income ranged from 15,000 to 50,000 livres among Châtelet families and from 25,000 to 150,000 livres among the *parlementaires*. This capital had to be carefully managed and legated from one generation to the next.[12]

It is against the high cost of a judgeship and of a magistrate's vocation, costs only partially defrayed by privileges, and the intense labor required of judges that one must set the royal edicts that banned magistrates from participating in any kind of mercantile activity.[13] That ban was generally respected, particularly by magistrates of the Châtelet and the Parlement of Paris. It demarcated the themistocracy from most of the French bourgeoisie, and even from much of the nonmagisterial nobility, who were authorized to participate in wholesale and maritime trade. It obliged the families that chose magistracy to renounce commerce and manufacturing and the opportunity they offered for large profits, just as it forced conservative and proprietary economic behavior on families within the magistracy. Once a Parisian or provincial family entered the themistocracy, it generally remained there, or in royal civil administration, for the rest of its existence during the Old Regime. The ban defined themistocracy as a sacrifice, an honor, and a calling – the true meanings of vocation. It also served to distinguish, as much as law and custom can distinguish, themistocrats from those whom they judged. Most of their professional lives were spent in hearing, trying, judging, and punishing those motivated by either avarice or need, in civil and criminal justice. The magistrates were insulated from both of those conditions.

[12] Rosset, "Les conseillers du Châtelet," pt. 2, pp. 233–302, and Bluche, *Les magistrats du Parlement de Paris*, pp. 143–241.
[13] The most important was in December 1701 (Isambert, vol. 20, pp. 400–2).

3

Themistocrats

When the judges of the Châtelet or the Parlement of Paris recruited a new colleague, they almost invariably co-opted a young and inexperienced man. The entity selected through his person was essentially his family; a candidate was less the embodiment of a self than of a social patrimony. Patrimony consisted primarily in the activities (thus capital), reputation, and professional history of a family, and secondarily in those of the kinship group to which the family belonged through marriages. Only some forms of patrimony were suitable. Most candidates for a judgeship had been chosen and prepared by their elders for a themistocratic or administrative career long before they were offered to the scrutiny of a court. For that reason, the agency of family was as decisive in creating judges as the selection rules of the company of judges. Each successful candidacy represented a convergence between choices and accomplishments by preceding generations of the candidate's family and the sociopolitical exigencies of a judicial institution. The terms for that convergence were both precise and durable across the seventeenth and eighteenth centuries.

A. The magistrates of the Châtelet: socioprofessional origins and development

The judges

It has been possible to determine the socioprofessional paths and patrimonies that led to and from the eighteenth-century Châtelet themistocracy for 65 of the 130 judges who composed the bench in the years 1735, 1762, and 1789, and for 16 of the 19 lieutenants and prosecutors of the Châtelet between 1735 and 1789.[1] Their numbers and their distribution over a long period make them broadly representative of the Châtelet bench during the entire century.

[1] The following prosopography is based on the letters of provision in A.N. V 1 73–537, the dossiers of reception in Y 1867–1869, and the printed sources cited in the notes. The printed sources are mainly compendia listing the personnel of the other Parisian courts, municipal officers, superior royal administrators, the royal secretaries in the Grand Chancellery, and the French nobility. They form a relatively complete guide to the families of the judges who were either fully or incipiently noble among the 130. They were 37% of that total. It is possible to determine noble or

Only 3 of the 65 judges entered the Châtelet from an immediate patrimony of commerce (see Table 3.1), and those three did so early in our period, at the end of the seventeenth century. Among the 130 judges on the Châtelet bench in 1735, 1762, and 1789, I have found no other sons of merchants. The eighteenth-century Châtelet matched the Parlement of Paris in social exclusiveness as regards that vast segment of Parisian bourgeois. Two of those three families had developed important official attributes that palliated their mercantile character, in the generations preceding the admission of their sons to the Châtelet. Judge Etienne de Berny's father and grandfather were cloth merchants. But his great-grandfather had been mayor of Amiens at the end of the sixteenth century, and his father had retired from active commerce to become judge–consul of the clothiers' guild of Paris and a royal secretary (1695) before Etienne became a candidate for the Châtelet.[2] Pierre Héron was the descendant of at least five generations of Parisian cloth merchants, apothecaries, and wholesale grocers. But his father, grandfather, and great-grandfather had been judge–consuls, and thus dynastic members of Parisian municipal government, during most of the seventeenth century. One of his uncles had become judge of the Cour des Aides in 1668 and married a daughter of the Faverolles, a powerful family of the Chambre des Comptes with members in the Châtelet during the seventeenth century.[3]

There were 4 judges from a patrimony of medicine or architecture (DesMaisons, Geoffroy, Goupy, Tarade). Their fathers were professionally distinguished and enjoyed royal appointments. Etienne-Louis Geoffroy was a physician and professor in the medical faculty of the University of Paris. He also purchased a

bourgeois condition for every judge who entered the Châtelet between 1770 and 1789, from the letters of *provision* in A.N. V 1 and Robert De Roton, *Les arrêts du Grand Conseil portant dispense du marc d'or de la noblesse* (Paris: 1951). Non-noble entrants during that period were required to pay the *marc d'or d'anoblissement.* Royal letters of appointment, especially the letters before 1770, did not usually describe the father or elders of the postulant judge unless the family was notable in state service. Our information on the family histories of bourgeois judges of the Châtelet (1735–89) is considerable, but it is more random than on their ennobled colleagues. Many other Châtelet judges who are not among the 65 described here were probably the sons of judicial and administrative officers. Their family names occur frequently on the lists of various officials and barristers in the royal almanacs during the eighteenth century. For example, Pierre-Nicolas-Joseph Lejuge served in the Châtelet from 1748 to after 1762; and another Lejuge was judge of the Chambre des Comptes from 1713 to at least 1750 (*Almanach royal*, 1750, p. 194). The two men's domiciles were virtually adjacent, respectively in the rue des Barres and the rue des Prêtres-Saint-Paul, but I do not know their filiation, if any. I have been cautious in social identification. What follows is an approach to the eighteenth-century Châtelet magistracy. Their full social, economic, and cultural history remains to be written, primarily from notarial records, other family papers, and genealogical archives.

[2] *Annuaire de la noblesse*, 37 (1881): 359–60; Bluche, "L'origine des magistrats du Parlement de Paris," pp. 84–5; M. G. Denière, *La jurisdiction consulaire de Paris (1563–1792)*, (Paris, 1872), pp. 520–1.

[3] Pierre Héron's son became a judge of the Parlement of Paris, and his daughter was married to Louis-Achille Dionis du Séjour, judge of the Cour des Aides (1724–90) (Bluche, "L'origine des magistrats du Parlement de Paris," pp. 213–14; Rosset, "Les conseillers du Châtelet de Paris," pt. 2, p. 265; Christine Favre-Lejeune, *Les secrétaires du roi de la Grande Chancellerie de France: Dictionnaire biographique et généalogique (1672–1789)*, 2 vols. [Paris: Sedapols, 1986] (vol. 1, pp. 480–1).

Table 3.1 *Social origins of 65 Châtelet judges*

Judge	Tenure years	Noble	Father's occupation or offices
de Berny, Etienne	1696–1739	Inc.	Cloth merchant; royal secretary
de la Vergne, Abel-Pierre	1693–1740	No	Merchant
Héron, Pierre	1693–1747	No	Cloth merchant; judge consul
Geoffroy, Etienne-Mathieu	1784–9	Inc.	Physician; professor of medicine; royal secretary
Tarade, Jean-Luc-Odile	1695–c. 1750	Inc.	Royal architect and builder; royal secretary
DesMaisons, Charles-Pierre	1787–9	Yes	Royal architect, member-Royal Academy
Goupy, Guillaume-Louis-Nicolas	1784–9	Inc.	Royal architect and builder; royal secretary
Chapelain des Brosserons, Jacques-Marie	1783–9	Inc.	First clerk of "parties casuelles," Chancellery; royal secretary
Davesne de Fontaine, Pierre-René	1738–85	Yes	Royal secretary
Delahaye, Etienne-Gabriel	1788–89	Inc.	Royal secretary
Frécot, Jacques	1735–39	Inc.	Banker; clerk in Chancellery; royal secretary
Girard, Jacques-Claude	1706–66	Inc.	Controller, Chancellery of Dauphiné; royal secretary
Lebeuf, Robert-Edmé	1718–c. 1750	Inc.	Royal secretary
Lérat, Louis-Pierre	1713–38	Inc.	Royal secretary
Batissier, Claude	1758–88	Yes	Treasurer, Generality of Paris
Bruant des Carrières, Claude	1692–1746	No	Principal agent, Superintendent of Finance (Nicolas Fouquet)
Choart de Magny, Louis	1735–c. 1746	Yes	General receiver, Generality of Bordeaux
de Sulpice d'Albert, André-Louis	1743–67	?	Commissioner of war; controller of Church *dîmes*
de Villiers, Jacques-Etienne	1740–52	Inc.	Secretary in intendancies of Tours and Paris; clerk to general controller of finance; royal secretary
Dupuy, André-Julien	1775–89	Yes	Treasurer, Generality of Riom
Grillon des Chapelles, Amador-Jean	1787–9	Inc.	Receiver of annuities on excise taxes; royal secretary
Langlois, Auguste	1734–38	Yes	General receiver, Generality of Montauban; royal secretary

Table 3.1 (cont.)

Judge	Tenure years	Noble	Father's occupation or offices
Marquet de Montbreton, Jacques	1788–9	Yes	General receiver, Generalities of Rouen and Grenoble
Nérot, Moïse-Augustin	1734–42	Inc.	General receiver for royal domains, Generalities of Caen and Rouen; royal secretary
Besset de la Chapelle-Million, Nicolas-Pierre	1725–c. 1740	Yes	Judge, Parlement of Lorraine; secretary to Royal Naval Council
Boucher d'Argis, André-Jean	1771–89	Yes	Judge, Superior Council of Dombes
Boucher, Jacques	1722–45	Inc.	Judge, Châtelet; royal secretary
Bouquet, Jean-François	1732–38	Yes	Judge, Hôtel-de-Ville (Paris); "échevin"
Chrétien de Poly, Jean-Prosper	1789	Yes	Judge, Cour des Aides
Couvreur, Etienne	1718–c. 1770	?	Judge, Châtelet
de la Huproye, Antoine-Edmé	1787–9	Yes	Judge, finance tribunal, "élection" of Orléans; royal secretary
de Manneville, Victor	1693–1738	No	Judge, bailliage of Boulogne
de Villiers de la Noue, Prudent	1743–83	Yes	Judge, Parlement of Dauphiné; royal secretary
Delarche, Jean-Henry-Alexandre	1788–9	Yes	Judge, Superior Council of Pondichery; judge, Grand Conseil
Fagnier de Monslambert, François	1706–37	Yes	Judge, Châtelet
Hamelin, Claude-Sylvain	1706–c. 1740	?	Judge, Châtelet
Maussion, Thomas-Antoine-Jean	1784–9	Yes	Judge, Grand Conseil
Michau de Montblin, Jacques-Hypolite	1789	Yes	Judge, Parlement of Paris
Noüet d'Ormoy de Montanglos, Louis	1752–c. 1780	No	Judge, Châtelet
Chuppin, Jean-Nicolas	1768–89	Yes	Deputy prosecutor, Parlement of Paris; general treasurer of "marc d'or," Chancellery
de Gouve de Vitry, Jean-Charles	1772–89	Inc.	General prosecutor, Cour des Monnaies
Destouches, Claude-Nicolas	1777–89	Yes	Magistrate, Cour des Aides
Le Marié d'Aubigny, Jean-Baptiste	1784–9	Yes	General advocate, Chambre des Comptes

LeRoy d'Herval, Joseph	1762–89	Yes	Deputy prosecutor, Parlement of Paris
Henry, Alexandre-Denis	1787–9	Yes	Principal recording secretary, Chambre des Comptes; royal secretary
Nau de Champlouis, Claude-Thomas	1780–9	Yes	Principal recording secretary, Parlement of Paris
Nau Pierre	1780–89	Yes	Principal recording secretary, Parlement of Paris
Pelletier, Charles-Louis-Guillaume	1744–89	Yes	Auditor, Chambre des Comptes
Phélippes de la Marnière, Daniel-Louis	1754–89	?	Auditor, Châtelet; president, barristers of Parlement of Paris
Auvray, Louis	1727–62	No	Notary, Châtelet
Bouron des Clayes, François-Hilaire	1766–89	Yes	Notary, Châtelet; royal secretary
Boutet, Henri-Gabriel	1718–58	Yes	Notary, Châtelet; "échevin," Paris
Brussel de Sancy, Augustin-Charles	1738–c. 1775	Yes	Notary, Châtelet; royal secretary
Desnotz, Jean	1705–c. 1740	Inc.	Notary, Châtelet, "échevin," Paris; royal secretary
Jarry, Jean-Michel	1788–9	Inc.	Notary, Châtelet; royal secretary
Silvestre de Chanteloup, Aubin-Jean	1781–9	No	Notary, Châtelet
Silvestre, Jacques-Abraham	1779–89	No	Notary, Châtelet
Granjean de la Croix, Robert-François	1729–56	Inc.	Solicitor, Châtelet; royal secretary
Barangue, Pierre-Antoine	1695–1743	Inc.	Barrister, Parlement of Paris; royal secretary
Lalourcé, Charlemagne	1778–89	No	Barrister, Parlement of Paris
Noüet de Montanglos, Louis	1706–52	No	Barrister, Parlement of Paris
Rouhette, Jean-François-Marie	1785–9	Yes	President, barrister of Parlement of Paris
Duval, François-Alexis	1784–9	?	Judicial officer, Paris (court unknown)
Mutel, Hubert-Jean	1778–89	No	Police commissioner, Châtelet
de Salles Béville, François	1753–89	?	President, finance tribunal, Generality of Orléans

Abbreviations: Inc.–Judge was incipiently but not fully noble when he entered Châtelet, because father had not yet held an ennobling office long enough to have attained hereditary nobility. *Yes/No*–Judge's family had/had not acquired hereditary nobility before he assumed office. *Sources:* Letters of provision in A.N. VI 73–537; the dossiers of reception in Y 1867–1869; and the printed sources cited in the notes.

royal secretaryship in 1766.[4] Jean-Luc-Odile Tarade (tenure, 1695–c.1750) descended from a fifteenth-century notary for the seigeneurial domain of Cérisay in Normandy. His grandfather and father were royal architects and building contractors; his father purchased a royal secretaryship in 1690. One of Jean-Luc-Odile's uncles, a protégé of Vauban's, was superintendent of fortifications for the cities of Dôle, Fribourg, Belfort, and Strasbourg during the 1680s and 1690s; he was ennobled for his service to the Crown in 1687.[5] Pierre DesMaisons had been ennobled for artistic merit in 1769, was a member of the Royal Academy of Architecture, and in 1779 was commissioned to rebuild a portion of the cathedral of Saint-Denis.[6] Claude-Martin Goupy (father of Guillaume-Louis-Nicholas Goupy, tenure 1784–9), was the son and grandson of master stonemasons and had been a master mason himself for many years. But during the 1760s, he gained appointment as building contractor to the prince of Condé and then to the king. In 1769, he purchased a seigniory at Meaux and, ten years later, a royal secretaryship and its nobility.[7] His son was the only judge among these 65 whose father had once been an artisan.

Seven judges (Chapelain des Brosserons through Lérat, on Table 3.1) were sons of Chancellery officers, all of whom were royal secretaries. At least two of those fathers were principally bankers.[8] The antecedents of at least three of the seven judges belonged to the social world of wholesale trade, the counting-house, and the atelier:

Judge	Grandfather (gf) / great-grandfather (ggf)
Chapelain des Brosserons	gf Charles-François (1692–1764): household officer of duke of Orléans; ggf Pierre (d. 1701): Parisian wine merchant (and son of tanner)[9]
Davesne de Fontaine	gf Pierre: building contractor and royal secretary (1693)[10]
Frécot	gf Daniel: "bourgeois of Abbéville" and collector of the *taille* at Auvilliers (Picardy)[11]

Ten of our 65 Châtelet judges (Batissier through Nérot, on Table 3.1) were sons of royal tax or financial administration officers. Eight of those officers were in the highest tiers of the fiscal pyramid, serving as treasurers or general

[4] A.N. V 1 515; Favre-Lejeune, *Les secrétaires du roi*, vol. 1, pp. 614–15.
[5] Henri Woëlmont de Brumagne, *Notices généalogiques*, 9 vols. (Paris, 1923–35), vol. 5, pp. 979–87.
[6] A.N. V 1 529; Anatole Granges de Surgères, *Répertoire historique et biographique de la "Gazette de France"* (Paris, 1902–6), vol. 2, p. 200.
[7] A.N. Y 1869; Favre-Lejeune, *Les secretaires du roi*, vol. 1, pp. 645–6.
[8] Charles-Pierre Chapelain was a banker who became a financial agent to the duke of Orléans and then first secretary of *parties casuelles* in the Chancellery (Favre-Lejeune, *Les secrétaires du roi*, vol. 1, p. 337). Jacques I Frécot was also a Paris banker before he acquired his Chancellery clerkship and royal secretaryship (Bluche, *Les magistrats du Parlement de Paris*, pp. 85–6).
[9] Favre-Lejeune, *Les sécretaires du roi*, vol. 1, pp. 337–8.
[10] Henri Jouglas de Morenas, *Grand armorial de France*, 7 vols. (Paris, 1934–52), vol. 1, p. 301.
[11] Bluche, *Les magistrats du Parlement de Paris*, pp. 85–6.

receivers for entire Generalities or as principal secretaries or controllers in the central administration. Royal financial administration, the only other segment of officialdom comparable to the judiciary in numbers and power, engendered and nourished magisterial vocation. Antecedents are known for five judges from this patrimony:

Bruant	**gf** provincial bailliage magistrate; **ggf** same[12]
de Villiers, Jacques	**gf** Martin: Parisian merchant[13]
Grillon des Chapelles	**gf** cloth merchant, then receiver of the *taille* at Chateauroux[14]
Langlois	**gf** Pierre (d. 1698): "bourgeois de Paris" and administrator of les Halles[15]
Marquet de Montbreton	**gf** Maurice: resin manufacturer and merchant at Bordeaux and Paris, contractor for military hospitals; **ggf** resin-maker near Bordeaux[16]

The most common path of ascent was from commerce to venal-hereditary fiscal office, and thence to magistracy. But many such families retained fiscal offices after placing sons in the themistocracy, as a means of financing those judicial vocations.[17]

The history of the Choart family, as revealed by their patrilineal genealogy from the fifteenth century to the end of the Old Regime, is a paradigm of dynastic versatility within royal officialdom (see Chart 3.1). They were one of the few families of the eighteenth-century Châtelet (or Parlement of Paris) to have been socially rooted in Paris by the early fifteenth century. During the second

[12] Bluche, "L'origine de magistrats du Parlement du Paris," p. 114.

[13] A.N. Y 1867; V 1 323; Favre-Lejeune, *Les secrétaires du roi*, vol. 2, p. 1303; J. F. Bosher, *French Finances, 1770–1795: From Business to Bureaucracy* (Cambridge: Cambridge University Press, 1970), pp. 52, 59, 293.

[14] A.N. Y 1869; V 1 533; Favre-Lejeune, *Les secrétaires du roi*, vol. 1, pp. 655–6.

[15] There were two major branches of this family during the eighteenth century; both descended from Pierre, the seventeenth-century Parisian bourgeois. The scion of the senior line, Pierre Langlois de la Fortelle (1657–1719), purchased the general receivership of finance for the province of Champagne and a royal secretaryship (1695). He sold the finance office for first a judgeship (1698) and then a presidency in the Chambre des Comptes, where he served until his death. His sons and grandsons were judges of the Parlement of Paris and the Chambre des Comptes until the Revolution. The scion of the cadet line, Phillipe Langlois de la Pommeuse (1661–1734), acquired the general receivership of finance in the Generality of Montauban and a royal secretaryship in 1702. He had two sons. Louis-Charles was judge of the Châtelet from about 1730 to 1734, and then judge of the Grand Conseil from 1737 until his death in about 1770. The younger son, Auguste Langlois, served as judge of the Châtelet from 1734 to 1736 and then acquired a judgeship in the Parlement of Paris. Sons of both made careers in the Parlement and Grand Conseil. For the two Langlois of the cadet line, the Châtelet was a *lieu de passage* between finance officialdom and the supreme themistocracy. It was so for several other eighteenth-century families (A.N. Y 1867; Favre-Lejeune, *Les secrétaires du roi*, vol. 2, pp. 784–5; Bluche, "L'origine des magistrats du Parlement de Paris," pp. 238–9).

[16] A.N. Y 1869; V 1 537; Bluche, "L'origine des magistrats du Parlement du Paris," pp. 299–300; Bosher, *French Finances*, p. 332.

[17] That progression and practice will be illustrated by the case of the Maussion family and its clan allies in Chapter 5.

Chart 3.1. *Choart genealogy*

I	II	III	IV	V	VI	VII	VIII	IX

Jean I Choart (d. c.1440): royal prosecutor, Châtelet

Jean II Choart (d. c.1490): seigneur of Epinay
near St. Denis; civil lieutenant, Châtelet

Charles I Choart (d. c.1520): seigneur of La Borde, Magny,
St. Loup, Buzenval, regions of the Oise and Marne; royal provost of Pontoise

Charles II Choart de Magny (1513–62): provost of Pontoise

Nicolas Choart de Magny (1550–1615): judge,
Chambre des Comptes (1581–1614)

Gabriel I Choart des Brosses and Magny (b. c.1597, d. 1687):
treasurer of war in Burgundy; treasurer royal bridges and roads.
Generality of Paris; councillor of state

Gabriel II Choart de Magny (1646–1713): treasurer royal bridges
and roads; general treasurer, fortifications of France

Louis Choart de Magny I (1687–1751): general receiver of
finance, Generality of Bordeaux

Louis Choart de Magny II (1715–1790s): judge,
Châtelet (1735–41); general receiver of
finance, Generality of Bordeaux (1741–90)

Bénigne Choart des Brosses (1721–c.1790):
judge, Châtelet (1742–7); judge, Parlement of
Paris (1747–89)

Bénigne II Choart de Crécy: judge, Parlement
de Paris (1789–90)

Gabriel Choart de Cornillon (b. c.1728): judge, Chambre des Comptes (1754–62); president, Cour des Aides

Jean-Baptiste-Louis Choart de Cornillon: judge, then president, Cour des Aides (1780–90)

Jean Choart de Fontanelle: judge, Chambre des Comptes (1785–90)

Sources: Bluche, "L'origine des magistrats du Parlement de Paris," pp. 132–33; Henri Coustant d'Yanville, *Chambre des Comptes de Paris* (Paris, 1866), pp. 636, 673, 911; A Trudon des Ormes, "L'état civil des citoyens nobles de Paris en 1789," in *Mémoires de la Société de l'Histoire de Paris et de l'Ile de France*, 26 [1899]: 280–1).

half of the fifteenth century, a period of intense agrarian crisis and depression consequent on the Hundred Years' War, the Choarts acquired seigneurial domains in the Paris region. Because of those fiefs, they were officially recognized as noble in the sixteenth century. For five generations (Jean I to Nicolas), the senior and principal line had magisterial vocations in the Châtelet, at Pontoise, and then in the Chambre des Comptes of Paris. For the next three generations, the Choarts were primarily royal treasurers and general receivers. Those offices generated considerable revenue for their occupants. Then, beginning with Louis Choart de Magny in the eighth generation, the family achieved a duality of high-level fiscal offices and sovereign court judgeships that lasted until the Revolution. Within each of these historical stages, sons succeeded fathers in principal offices. The Choarts remained Parisian and in close proximity to the *loci* of royal power during those four hundred years.[18] By eighteenth-century standards, they were "old" aristocracy (dating from the sixteenth century). But their essential venerability was in royal officialdom.

The dominant bloc among Châtelet judges was formed by sons of judicial officers. They accounted for 41 of the 65 Châtelet judges whose family background has been traced, or 63 percent. Their fathers had held a range of offices in the middle and upper ranks in the hierarchy of the robe; there were no low-status careers such as clerks or summons-servers, and only one solicitor, among them. Their fathers were, in great majority, Parisian magistrates. This configuration expressed the dynamic roles of the Châtelet as a corporate intersection of great and lesser, but rising, judicial families and as a crucible where the superior judiciary of Paris was formed.

Of the 41 sons of the judiciary, 16 were the sons of judges. Seven such fathers were judges in the sovereign courts of Paris or the provinces, 5 were Châtelet judges, and 4 were in lesser tribunals. Five of the 41 were sons of royal advocates or prosecutors in sovereign courts (Parlement of Paris, Chambre des Comptes, or Cour des Monnaies). Five were sons of principal clerks, auditors, or other magistrates in Parisian sovereign courts. Thus, 26 of the 41 Châtelet judges were progeny of magistrates who held high judicial offices, most of which were ennobling. At least 15 were sons of members of the *grand robe*. Another 14 were sons of career notaries or proctors of the Châtelet or career barristers of the Parlement of Paris.

The notaries of the Châtelet formed a large, powerful, and wealthy corporation of 113 during the seventeenth and eighteenth centuries. Their offices

---

[18] Louis I and Louis II Choart had their primary residences in Paris, during their tenures as general receivers for Bordeaux. In 1742, Louis II Choart de Magny (Châtelet, 1735–41) married the daughter of Louis Bronod, Châtelet notary (1719–65) and royal secretary (1731). They had two daughters who were married in perfectly endogamous fashion. One wed the son of François-Joseph Harvoin, receiver of the *taille* for the Generality of Paris, then general receiver at Alençon and Tours. Adrienne, the youngest, was married to Charles-Frédéric Godard d'Aucour, also general receiver for the Generality of Alençon. Their son, Adrien, became a count of the empire (1809), prefect of the Seine-et-Marne, and then member of the Napoleonic Council of State (Favre-Lejeune, *Les secrétaires du roi*, vol. 1, pp. 293–92, 633–4; vol. 2, pp. 687–8).

were venal, hereditary, and heavily dynastic in composition. They served as official Parisian agents, accountants, and holders of property and capital transactions for individuals, families, and businesses. They managed dowries, wills and testaments, divisions of inheritance. Their general duties and powers combined those of a modern civil lawyer, a portfolio manager, and the trust officer of a bank. They enjoyed the lucrative privilege of being authorized to practice throughout France. Handsomely remunerated by commissions and retainerships, they amassed capital and frequently served as bankers. Among all of the professional groups of Old Regime Paris, only judges in the major courts possessed a knowledge of property values and the flow of private capital equal to theirs. That knowledge meant money, when it was converted into investment advice for clients. Their clientele (and thus web of patronage), access to economic intelligence, their affluence, and their propensity to self-ennoblement by purchase of royal secretaryships were strong foundations for themistocratic vocations among their descendants. Châtelet notaries belonged to the civic elite of Paris, consistently providing a large number of *échevins* for the administration of the city.[19]

The barristers of the Parlement of Paris were a privileged group of advocates, licensed to plead civil and criminal cases in the sovereign courts and Châtelet of Paris. They numbered 605 in the late eighteenth century. Most judges, royal prosecutors, and advocates in Old Regime Paris had initially been members of their official corporation, the Order of Barristers. Its supreme officer was the president, or *batonnier.* The order was self-selecting and self-regulating. The work of barristers was intellectually and professionally demanding and enjoyed great prestige within the French judiciary. They were entitled to plead cases, both verbally and in writing, directly before judges, whereas *procureurs* (proctors and solicitors) could only prepare written briefs. The barristers, like the notaries, provided about one-third of the *échevins* of Paris during the eighteenth century.[20]

It has been possible to reconstruct the paternal lineage for 23 of the 41 Châtelet judges who were sons of judicial officers. Three of these sons were fourth generation in the magistracy. François-Hilaire Bouron des Clayes (tenure, 1766–89) was descended from two consecutive generations of Châtelet notaries and royal secretaries. His great-grandfather had been prosecutor of the presidial court at Reims.[21] Jean-Claude Boucher, the great-grandfather of another of the 41, André-Jean Boucher d'Argis (tenure, 1772–89), was a barrister at Lyons and later served as judge in the superior court of Dombes during most of the seventeenth century. His son Gaspard (grandfather of the Châtelet Boucher d'Argis) was also a barrister at Lyons and acquired the seigneury of

---

[19] F. Foiret, *Une corporation parisienne pendant la Révolution: Les notaires* (Paris: Champion, 1912), pp. 1–24.

[20] Michael P. Fitzsimmons, *The Parisian Order of Barristers and the French Revolution* (Cambridge, Mass.: Harvard University Press, 1987), pp. 1–32.

[21] A.N. Y 1868; V 1 430; Favre-Lejeune, *Les secrétaires du roi*, vol. 1, pp. 271–2.

Argis in the Bresse. Gaspard's son, Antoine-Gaspard, became a barrister in Paris, a judge of the superior court of Dombes, and finally an *échevin* of Paris (1767–8). Antoine-Gaspard also collaborated with Diderot on the Great Encyclopedia and wrote treatises on jurisprudence.[22] The Michau de Montblin were also a provincial family in the seventeenth century. The great-grandfather of Jacques-Hypolitte Michau (tenure, 1789–90) was a judge of the Grand Conseil (1690–1750), but he had been born at Bruz in 1668, the son of a local tax collector for the Estates of Brittany.[23]

Eight judges were the third consecutive generation in the magistracy:

Barangue	**gf** Pierre (b. 1644): proctor, Châtelet; **ggf** Parisian tailor[24]
de Manneville	**gf** François: barrister at Boulogne[25]
Desnotz	**gf** Jean: notary, Châtelet[26]
de Villiers de la Noue	**gf** Prudent III: judge and commissioner in *élection* of Sézanne; **ggf** Prudent II: *échevin*, Sézanne[27]
Hamelin	**gf** Josse: judge, *élection* of Paris; then Cour des Aides[28]
LeMarié-d'Aubigny	**gf** Jerôme (d. 1763): judge, Chambre des Comptes; **ggf** Jean-Baptiste (1660–1742): general receiver of finance in Picardy; royal secretary[29]
Maussion	**gf** Thomas-Urbain (1696–1758): judge, Grand Conseil; **ggf** Thomas (1663–1744): general receiver of finance, Generality of Alençon; royal secretary[30]
Nouët de Montanglos	**gf** Guy (1670–1746): barrister, Parlement of Paris[31]

[22] A.N. Y 1868; V 1 454; Roton, *Les arrêts du Grand Conseil*, p. 15; M. Prévost and R. d'Amat, *Dictionnaire de biographie française*, 18 vols.; (Paris, 1932–88), vol. 6, pp. 1213–15.

[23] A.N. V 1 537; Bluche, "L'origine des magistrats du Parlement de Paris," pp. 313–14; Bosher, *French Finances*, pp. 332–3.

[24] Rosset, "Les conseillers du Châtelet," pt. 1, pp. 265, 273; Favre-Lejeune, *Les secrétaires du roi*, vol. 1, p. 164.

[25] A.N. V 1 85; Rosset, "Les conseillers du Châtelet," pt. 1, p. 235; pt. 2, p. 255; Woëlmont de Brumagne, *Notices généalogiques*, vol. 3, pp. 440–3.

[26] A.N. V 1 169; *Annuaire de la noblesse*, 62 (1906): 270. Germain-Marquis, a brother of the Châtelet Desnotz, was judge in the Chambre des Comptes (1716–59); he was succeeded by his son (1759), who served there until 1790.

[27] A.N. Y 1867; V 1 355, 503; Jouglas de Morenas, *Grand armorial*, vol. 6, p. 478.

[28] A.N. V 1 174; Bluche, "Le personnel de l'Election de Paris (1715–91)," in *Paris et L'Ile-de-France, Mémoires*, 26–7 (1978): 357; Rosset, "Les conseillers du Châtelet," pt. 2, p. 234. Claude-Sylvain Hamelin's uncle was also a judge of the Cour des Aides.

[29] A.N. Y 1869; V 1 515; Roton, *Les arrêts du Grand Conseil*, pp. 129–30; Favre-Lejeune, *Les secrétaires du roi*, vol. 2, pp. 849–50. The earliest known ancestor was Jacques LeMarié, household military officer of Anne of Austria, wife of Louis XIII.

[30] See Chapter 5.

[31] A.N. V 1 174; Bluche, "L'origine des magistrats du Parlement de Paris," p. 314.

Twelve of the 41 sons of judges were the second consecutive generation in the judiciary. What had their grandfathers and great-grandfathers been?

Besset de la Chapelle-Millon	**gf** Henri: general controller of royal buildings, arts, and manufactures, then inspector of *beaux-arts* and historian; **ggf** François, *seigneur* of la Chapelle-Millon and military officer[32]
Boucher, Jacques	**gf** Charles: Parisian cloth merchant; **ggf** Claude (d. 1705): Parisian cloth merchant[33]
Brussel de Sancy	**gf** Nicolas: Parisian merchant and *échevin*[34]
Chrétien de Poly	**gf** Jean-François (d. 1743): Parisian cloth merchant[35]
Chuppin	**gf** Charles: officer, Chancellery, keeper of the rolls of office; **ggf** Nicolas: general treasurer of *marc d'or* in the Chancellery (son of Parisian silk merchant)[36]
de la Hurproye	**gf** guardian of the seals in mastership of royal watercourses and forests at Troyes[37]
Henry	**gf** Parisian merchant[38]
Jarry	**gf** Richard: Parisian goldsmith[39]
LeRoy d'Herval	**gf** René: officer of royal household[40]
Nau de Champlouis	**ggf** Jacques: treasurer of war in Burgundy[41]
Nau, Pierre	**ggf** treasurer of war in Burgundy
Pelletier	**gf** Antoine: Parisian banker and director of East Indies Company, royal secretary; **ggf** "bourgeois de Paris"[42]

---

[32] A.N. Y 1867; F. A. A. de La Chesnaye-Desbois, *Dictionnaire de la noblesse*, (Paris, 1863–76), vol. 3, pp. 75–7; Prévost and d'Amat, *Dictionnaire*, vol. 6, p. 321. This was one of the few Châtelet families whose nobility was of pre-1500 seigneurial origin. The Bessets were from Languedoc. Henri I gravitated to the Court and Paris during the reign of Louis XIII. The Châtelet Besset had paternal relatives in the Chambre des Comptes during the eighteenth century.

[33] A.N. Y 1867; Favre-Lejeune, *Les secrétaires du roi*, vol. 1, pp. 252–3.

[34] A.N. Y 1867; V 1 314; Favre-Lejeune, *Les secrétaires du roi*, vol. 1, p. 302. The Châtelet Brussel's uncle was a judge of the Chambre des Comptes during the first half of the eighteenth century.

[35] A.N. Y 1869; V 1 537; Favre-Lejeune, *Les secrétaires du roi*, vol. 1, p. 367–8.

[36] See Chapter 5.

[37] A.N. Y 1869; V 1 529; Favre-Lejeune, *Les secrétaires du roi*, vol. 1, p. 442.

[38] A.N. Y 1869; V 1 529; Roton, *Les arrêts du Grand Conseil*, p. 441; Favre-Lejeune, *Les secrétaires du roi*, vol. 2, p. 700.

[39] A.N. V 1 537; Favre-Lejeune, *Les secrétaires du roi*, vol. 2, p. 730.

[40] A.N. Y 1868; V 1 411; Bluche, "L'origine des magistrats du Parlement de Paris," p. 278.

[41] The two Naus were brothers, both received in 1780. A.N. Y 1869; V 1 499; Bluche, "L'origine des magistrats du Parlement de Paris," p. 325; Jouglas de Morenas, *Grand armorial*, vol. 5, p. 146.

[42] A.N. Y 1867; V 1 339; Coustant, *Chambre des Comptes*, p. 829; Favre-Lejeune, *Les secrétaires du roi*, vol. 2, p. 1060.

The remote social provenance of the 41 judges whose families were dynastic in the magistracy is manifest: Their ancestors had been in wholesale commerce (especially the cloth trade), private finance or royal finance, provincial or royal household administration. During the sixteenth and seventeenth centuries their families had bifurcated, in either the senior or cadet line with one branch moving toward the themistocracy. The bifurcations were choices that had become sustained and successful vocations for three or four generations before the late eighteenth century. This evolution excluded commerce and private finance as careers in the themistocratic lineage, and was therefore a financial renunciation. But it did not exclude collateral careers in royal administration (especially royal financial and tax administration), for many of these families also had sons and in-laws in such administrative offices until the Revolution.

The de Villiers de la Noue exemplify a slow but obstinate rise, over several generations, from various provincial offices, in the sixteenth and seventeenth centuries to the Parisian themistocracy in the eighteenth century (see Chart 3.2). Their rise was similar to that of several other Châtelet families (and of many more in the Parlement of Paris). The de Villiers de la Noue were a family from Champagne, based in Sézanne, that combined financial, judicial, and administrative offices during the five generations that preceded Prudent IV, a family of local notabilities. In the fifth generation, they became allied by marriage with the Camusats of Troyes, a family whose condition and future resembled their own. The Camusats were merchants and *échevins* during the sixteenth and seventeenth centuries. François Camusat purchased a royal secretaryship and its nobility in 1709; his descendants became magistrates of the financial district of Troyes and then of the Chambre des Comptes in Paris.[43] Prudent-Joseph de Villiers de la Noue and his brother Louis-François were the first generation of the de Villiers to have careers in the Parisian themistocracy; they did so from the base of their father's position in the Parlement of Dauphiné. Prudent-Joseph's daughter married a judge of the Chambre des Comptes. Louis-François' son succeeded him in the Parlement of Paris, after a magisterial apprenticeship (1781–4) in the Châtelet.[44]

The 65 Châtelet judges of 1735 to 1789 came from fifty-eight distinct families. None of those families was in professional decline when its son entered the Châtelet. The families fall into two groups: those rising to or within the judiciary and administration, and those already established in sovereign courts or superior administrative offices and whose sons (often cadets) served a judicial apprenticeship at the Châtelet before acceding to such higher positions, usually by dynasticism. Socially, the fifty-eight families were a rather wide but clearly delimited spectrum that ranged from those with several generations of

[43] Favre-Lejeune, *Les secrétaires du roi*, vol. 1, p. 311.

[44] A.N. V 1 335, 503; Bluche, "L'origine des magistrats du Parlement de Paris," pp. 409–10; Coustant, *Chambre des Comptes*, p. 913; Jouglas de Morenas, *Grand armorial*, vol. 6, p. 478; Roton, *Les arrêts du Grand Conseil*, p. 366.

high royal offices, and thus of hereditary nobility, to those recent to officialdom and thus of bourgeois heritage.

More than half of the judges of the Parlement of Paris and the Chambre des Comptes between 1715 and 1790 were dynastic members of their respective courts: that is, fathers, sons, uncles, nephews, or brothers of other judges in those courts. In contrast, dynasticism was not prevalent in the eighteenth-century Châtelet. Of the 65 whose family history we know, 5 were sons who succeeded their fathers as career Châtelet judges.[45] There were also seven pairs of brothers.[46] Together, 19 men constituted less than one-third of 65, or 15 percent, of 130 judges.

For most individual judges, the Châtelet was a career. But for many families, the Châtelet was a generational stage in the rise to supreme magistracy or high administration. In 1735 and 1762, 77 judges composed the bench of the Châtelet. We have prosopographical information on 34 of them. The careers of 13 of their sons are represented on Table 3.2. The only known military officers among these sons were the 2 sons of Jean-Luc-Odile Tarade. Seven of the 13 sons became career judges in sovereign courts.[47]

The executive officers

The 19 men who served as executive officers (lieutenants and royal prosecutors) of the Châtelet between 1735 and 1789 (Table 3.3) shared the general social characteristics of the judges. But their levels of patrimonial achievement were distinctly higher than the norm among judges, commensurate with their professional rank and responsibilities. So too was the practice of father–son dynasticism, as illustrated by the Argouges (1710–66); the Lecontes (1700–35), the Lenoirs (1718–65), and the Moreaus (1713–80).[48]

The office of civil lieutenant, highest in the Châtelet, was held from 1710 to 1746 by Jerôme d'Argouges de Fleury and from 1746 to 1766 by his son,

---

[45] Fagnier de Monslambert (1706–37); Claude-Sylvain Hamelin (1706–c.1740); Etienne Couvreur (1718–75); Jacques Boucher (1722–45); Louis Nouët d'Ormoy (1752–c.1779).

[46] Louis-Charles Langlois de Guérard (c.1729–34) and Auguste Langlois de Ressy (1734–6); Auguste Louis Choart de Magny (1735–41) and Bénigne Choart des Brosses (1742–7); Pierre-Blaise Roger Grozier (1735–58) and Louis Roger Grozier (1758–78); Pierre Nau (1780–9) and Claude-Thomas Nau de Champlouis (1780–9); Antoine-Jean Vanin (1778–89) and Charles-Simon Vanin de Courville (1780–9); Jacques-Abraham Silvestre (1779–89) and Aubin-Jean Silvestre de Chanteloup (1781–9).

[47] The actual proportion of Châtelet sons who achieved a position in sovereign court or superior administration was undoubtedly higher. Several Châtelet judges had only daughters (e.g., Prudent de Villiers and Louis Choart) or had no surviving children (e.g., Barangue and Frécot), and there is no adequate prosopographical source on the Cour des Aides of Paris. Some sons probably became judges of the Parlements at Rouen and Metz.

[48] The lieutenant generals of police are not included in this description. There are summary biographies of them in Williams, *Police of Paris*, pp. 297–303. Their family histories closely resembled those of the other lieutenants.

Chart 3.2. *De Villiers (la Berge and la Noue) genealogy*

I	II	III	IV	V	VI	VII	VIII	IX
François I de Villiers (fifteenth century): domainal landlord in Champagne								
	Jacques de Villiers: royal treasurer, province of Champagne (1509)							
		François II de Villiers: deputy, Third Estate of Champagne to Estates-General (1560), oo Marie-Thérèse de Camusat						
			Prudent I de Villiers de la Berge: magistrate in bailliage of Sézanne; master of petitions to Queen Marguerite of Valois					
				Prudent II de Villiers de la Berge: *échevin* of Sézanne (1661), personally ennobled by that office				
					Prudent III de Villiers de la Berge: judge, finance tribunal for *élection* of Sézanne			
						Prudent IV de Villiers de la Berge: judge, Parlement of Dauphiné, hereditary nobility recognized by royal letter (1737)		
							Prudent-Joseph de Villiers de la Noue (b. 1720, d. ?): judge, Châtelet (1743–84)	
								Catherine-Marguérite de Villiers oo Augustin-Louis Lambert Deschamps de Morel: judge, Chambre des Comptes (1761–90)

Louis-François de Villiers de la Berge (b. 1728, d.?):
deputy prosecutor, Parlement of Paris (1749–70); judge,
Parlement of Paris (1770–84)

Prudent V de Villiers de la Berge (b. 1761, d. ?): judge,
Châtelet (1781–4); judge, Parlement of Paris (1784–90)

Sources: A.N. V 1 335, 503; Bluche, "L'origine des magistrats du Parlement de Paris," pp. 409–10; Coustant, *Chambre des Comptes*, p. 913; Jouglas de Morenas, *Grand Armorial*, vol. 6, p. 478; Roton, *Les arrêts du Grand Conseil*, p. 366.

Table 3.2. *Offices held by sons of 13 Châtelet judges: bench years 1735 and 1762*

Sons	Noble	Offices
Boucher, Jacques	Yes	Judge, Châtelet (1722–45)
Boucher, Nicolas	Yes	Judge, Chambre des Comptes
de Manneville, Hector-François	Yes	Judge, Châtelet; judge, Parlement of Paris (1740–67)
de Manneville, Gabriel-Simon	Yes	Judge, Grand Conseil (1737–72); judge, Cour des Aides (1774–90)
Fagnier de Monslambert, Michel	Yes	Judge, Cour des Aides (1748–75); Master of Petitions (1775–?)
Nouët d'Ormoy de Montanglos, Louis	No	Judge, Châtelet
Bruant des Carrières, Jean	Yes	Judge, Chambres des Comptes (1727–86)
de Villiers du Terrage, Marc-Etienne	Yes	Principal clerk, Finance Ministry
Langlois, Auguste-Henri	Yes	Judge, Parlement of Paris (1766–?)
Davesne de Fontaine, Achille-Pierre	Yes	Judge, Chambre des Comptes (1765–90)
Héron, Pierre-Marc	Yes	Judge, Parlement of Paris (1740–c.70)
Tarade, Francois-Gabriel	Yes	Lieutenant-colonel of cavalry; military governor Montdidier and Péronne
Tarade, Sébastien	Yes	Captain of Fontbauzard Dragoon Regiment

Abbreviations: Yes–Judge's family had acquired hereditary nobility before he assumed office.
Sources: See source note to Table 3.1.

Table 3.3. *Social origins of Châtelet executive officers, 1735–1789*

Magistrate	Office	Tenure	Noble	Father's office
Argouges de Fleury, Jérome	Civil lieutenant	1710–46	Yes	Judge, Parlement of Paris; master of petitions; councillor of state
Argouges de Fleury, Alexandre-François	Civil lieutenant	1746–66	Yes	Civil lieutenant
Angran d'Alleray, Denis-François	Civil lieutenant	1774–89	Yes	Judge, Cour des Aides; intendant of commerce, royal council
Leconte des Graviers, Claude-François	Criminal lieutenant	1734–35	Yes	Criminal lieutenant
Nègre, Gabriel-François	Criminal lieutenant	1735–51	Yes	Proctor, Parlement of Paris
de Sartine, Antoine-Raymond Jean	Criminal lieutenant	1755–59	Yes	Finance officer to King Philip V of Spain; intendant of Catalonia
Lenoir, Jean-Charles-Pierre	Criminal lieutenant	1759–65	Yes	Particular lieutenant
Testard du Lys, Augustin	Criminal lieutenant	1765–74	?	?
Bachois de Villefort, Charles-Simon	Criminal lieutenant	1774–89	Yes	Judge, Cour des Monnaies
Lenoir, Jean-Charles-Joseph	Particular lieutenant	1718–54	Yes	Silk merchant; cashier of East Indies Company; royal secretary
Lenoir, Jean-Charles-Pierre	Particular lieutenant	1754–59	Yes	Particular lieutenant
Chardon, Daniel-Marc-Antoine	Particular lieutenant	1760–68	Yes	Judge, Cour des Aides
Petit de la Honville, Armand-Jean	Particular lieutenant	1768–89	Yes	Judge, Cour des Aides
Guerey de Voisins, Etienne-Louis	Particular lieutenant	1730–64	?	?
Dupont, Etienne-Claude	Particular lieutenant	1764–89	?	?
Bellanger, Angélique-Charles	Particular lieutenant	1785–9	Yes	Notary, Châtelet; royal secretary
Moreau, François	Royal prosecutor	1713–41	Yes	Judge, Parlement of Paris
Moreau,	Royal prosecutor	1741–80	Yes	Royal prosecutor, Châtelet
de Flandre de Brunville, François-Antoine	Royal prosecutor	1780–9	Yes	Financier; auditor, General Tax Farm; royal secretary

Abbreviations: Yes–judge's family had acquired hereditary nobility before he assumed office; ?–estate unknown.
Sources: See source note to Table 3.1.

Alexandre-François-Jérôme (see Chart 3.3). Bluche described the Argouges as follows:

A house of chivalric origin and indisputably the most venerable of the noble families that served in the Parlement of Paris during the reign of Louis XV; it originated in lower Normandy, where its nobility has been certified since 1223. . . . It formed several branches brilliantly successful in the episcopacy, high military rank, the Order of Malta, the royal Council, the first presidency of the Parlement of Brittany.[49]

Jérôme d'Argouges had left a dynastic judgeship in the Parlement of Paris to become civil lieutenant of the Châtelet, and his son left the civil lieutenancy, after a long tenure, for membership in the royal Council. That elder sons of a great and wealthy family, one solidly rooted in the Parlement of Paris and royal Council by the second half of seventeenth century and to whom various high offices in the judiciary and administration were available, chose to serve as civil lieutenant is testimony to the political and professional importance of the Châtelet as an institution. The Argouges were succeeded by Jean-François Dufour de Villeneuve. Son of a magistrate in Auvergne, he began his judicial career in 1735 as lieutenant general of the presidial court of Clermont-Ferrand. He rose rapidly: master of petitions (1744); president of the Grand Conseil (1747–60); intendant of Burgundy (1760–6); civil lieutenant of the Châtelet (1766–74). Denis-François Angran d'Alleray was the last civil lieutenant of the Châtelet. In 1774, he left the office of general prosecutor in the Grand Conseil for the civil lieutenancy and served there until 1790. During the three generations

[49] "L'origine des magistrats du Parlement de Paris," pp. 66–7; Michel Antoine, *Le gouvernement et l'administration sous Louix XV: Dictionnaire biographique* (Paris: CNRS, 1978), pp. 9–10. The Argouges emerged politically beyond the confines of Normandy quite suddenly at the end of the sixteenth century, in the generation of Charles, baron of Rânes. That was the period when many great families of the eighteenth-century Parlement of Paris and royal Council had also emerged from provincial notability to statist vocations. But the Argouges were of the comparatively few families of early feudal nobility that made the transition to statist nobility of the Old Regime. From at least the late twelfth century to the mid-sixteenth century, they had accumulated an impressive stock of seigneurial properties and wealth: the domains of Gratot, Thaon, Quietteville, Boussigny, Gouville, Annebecq, and Rânes (all in the present *départements* of Calvados, the Manche, and the Orne). Since at least the mid-thirteenth century, they had also held various royal commissions: guards of ports, fortress captain at Caen and Vire, recruiters of soldiery for the kings of France. They remained loyal to the kings of France during the English occupation of Normandy and were rewarded. The accumulated wealth and royal favor were sufficient for Charles d'Argouges and his wife Marie-Madelaine Clausse de Fleury (the daughter of a grand master of waters and forests) to purchase the rank of *maréchal de camp* (equivalent to a general) for one son and a judgeship in the Grand Conseil for the other. The barony of Rânes was elevated to the rank of a marquisate by Louis XIV in 1672 (generation of Nicolas d'Argouges). It included several fiefs, in four parishes. During the last quarter of the seventeenth century, the annual revenue from that domain was 30,000 livres (Louis Duval, *Etat de la Generalité d'Alençon sous Louis XIV* [Paris, 1890], p. 159.) As the genealogy of the two branches that issued from Charles in the late sixteenth century reveals, one branch remained military (yet rooted in Normandy and the military governorship of Alençon) until the end of the Old Regime and its extinction in the male line, whereas the other remained magisterial and essentially Parisian, with only one exception.

Chart 3.3. *Argouges genealogy*

I	II	III	IV	V	VI
				Rânes branch	

Charles d'Argouges, baron of Rânes (b. 1570, d. ?): gentleman of the royal household

    Michel d'Argouges de Rânes (1612–1701): *maréchal de camp*, royal army

    Henry d'Argouges, baron of Rânes (b. ?, d. ?): governor and grand bailiff of Alençon

        Nicolas I d'Argouges, chevalier of Rânes (b. ?, d. ?): captain in French Guards regiment, invalided from wounds at siege of Maestricht (1673)

        Nicolas II d'Argouges, marquis of Rânes (b. 1635, killed in battle of Seckengen, 1678): captain in French Guards regiment; grand bailiff of Alençon; colonel-general of dragoons; lieutenant general of the army (1677)

            Michel d'Argouges de Gratot (b. ?, d. 1752): royal page; lieutenant general, bailliage of Caen

            Louis d'Argouges, marquis of Rânes (b. 1669, d. 1748): musketeer; lieutenant, Royal Dragoon regiment; captain, Bertoncelles Dragoons; brigadier and then *maréchal de camp*; military governor of Alençon

                Louis-François d'Argouges, count of Rânes (b. 1712 [Paris], d. 1767 [Normandy]): military governor of Alençon

Chart 3.3. *(cont.)*

Rânes branch

I	II	III	IV	V	VI
					Nicolas-Louis d'Argouges, baron of La Ferté-Macé (b. 1712, d. 1774 [Paris], twin of Louis-François): cornet of dragoons; chevalier of Saint-Louis; lieutenant-colonel of Chapt Dragoons
					Joachim d'Argouges (b. 1727, d. 1741 [Metz]): cornet, Languedoc Dragoon regiment
				Louis-Charles d'Argouges, marquis of Rânes (b. 1704, d. 1767 [Rânes]): commander of d'Argouges Dragoons; maréchal de camp of the army	
					Charles-Pierre-François d'Argouges, baron of Rânes (b. 1751 [Paris], d. ?): mestre de camp, Languedoc Dragoon regiment
					no male heir

d'Achères / Fleury branch

I	II	III	IV	V
Charles d'Argouges, baron of Rânes (b. c.1570, d. ?)				
	Jacques-François d'Argouges de Fleury (b. c.1625, d. 1695 [Versailles]): judge, Grand Conseil; first president, Parlement of Brittany (1661); councillor of state			

Florent d'Argouges, baron of Plessis (b. 1647, d. 1719 [Paris]): master of petitions, Hôtel-du-Roi; intendant of generalities of Moulins and Dijon; councillor of state

Michel-Pierre d'Argouges (b. 1685 [Paris], d. 1731 [Périgueux]); doctor of theology; abbot of Notre-Dame de Jouy-la-Brie; Bishop of Périgueux; ecclesiastical councillor of state

Jean-Pierre d'Argouges de Fleury, marquis (b. 1647 [Paris], d. 1731 [Paris]): judge, Parlement of Paris; chancellor of Order of Saint-Lazare; master of petitions; councillor of state

Louis-Henri d'Argouges de Fleury (b. 1689 [Paris], d. 1770 [Paris]): captain Artois Cavalry; *maréchal de camp*; lieutenant general of the army and commandant of cavalry

Jérôme d'Argouges de Fleury (b. 1682, d. 1767 [Paris]: judge, Parlement of Paris (1704); master of petitions (1710); civil lieutenant, Châtelet (1710–46); councillor of state

Alexandre-François-Jérôme d'Argouges de Fleury (b. 1718 [Paris], d. 1782 [Paris]): judge, Parlement of Paris (1741); master of petitions (1746); civil lieutenant, Châtelet (1746–66); councillor of state

Sources: Michel Antoine, *Le gouvernement et l'administration sous Louis XV: Dictionnaire biographique* [Paris: Centre National de la Recherche Scientifique, 1978], pp. 9–10; Bluche, "L'origine des magistrats du Parlement de Paris," pp. 66–67; Woëlmont de Brumagne, *Notices généalogiques*, vol. 6, pp. 25–33).

that preceded Denis-François, the Angrans had colonized the Parlements of Lorraine and Paris, the Cour des Aides, and the Chambre des Comptes (Chart 3.4).[50]

Lineages have been reconstructed for 10 of the 14 Châtelet criminal lieutenants, particular lieutenants, and prosecutors:

Leconte des Graviers	**gf** judge, Cour des Aides
	ggf controller of domains, City of Paris
	gggf *échevin* of Paris[51]
Sartine	**gf** wholesale merchant at Lyon
	ggf wholesale merchant at Lyon[52]
Lenoir, J.-C.-P.	**gf** silk merchant on rue Saint-Denis, Paris; royal secretary (1709); cashier, East Indies Company

[50] Bluche, "L'origine des magistrats du Parlement de Paris," pp. 62–3; Bluche, "Les magistrats du Grand Conseil," pp. 45–6; Antoine, *Le gouvernement*, p. 8; Coustant, *Chambre des Comptes*, pp. 693, 739, 903. The Angrans were one of the major Jansenist families of the seventeenth-century Parisian judiciary. Louis Angran (the grandfather of Denis-François, civil lieutenant) was educated at Port-Royal and became a patron and protector of Arnauld and Nicole. Several of the Angran daughters and wives continued the patronage of Jansenist predicators into the early eighteenth century, during the period of anathema and persecution (Prévost and d'Amat, *Dictionnaire*, vol. 2, pp. 1234–5).

[51] The Leconte family was unusual by its venerability in the Parisian elite. The early sixteenth-century patriarch was Charles Leconte, "master carpenter to the king" (Francis I). Two of his sons served as *échevins* of Paris, one of them (Jean) for three periods between 1578 and 1594. For many years Jean Leconte also held the royal appointment as supervisor of the Paris fish market: "Les vendeurs de poisson de mer étaient des agents speciaux, dont le service avait beucoup d'analogie avec celui dont sont aujourd'hui chargeés les facteurs sur les marchés en gros. Ils opéraient la vente de la denrée, qui devait tout passer par leurs mains; ils payaient comptant les mareyeurs; ils veillaient à la bonne qualité et à la bonne livraison de la marchandise, ainsi qu'à la stricte exécution des règlements édictés par l'autorité. . . . Ces postes, auxquels était attribuée une redevance basée sur les quantités de poisson vendues, étaient lucratifs et recherchés" (A.d'Affry de la Monnoye, *Les jetons de l'échevinage parisiens* [Paris, 1878], p. 42). He died in 1613. The family was ennobled by *échevinage* and enriched by the fish market. Early in the seventeenth century, the Lecontes entered the sovereign courts, where they served until at least the mid-eighteenth century. Claude Leconte, auditor of the Chambre des Comptes (1666–1709), had two sons. The eldest, Augustin I Lecomte, judge of the Cour des Aides (1702), married into the Bragelonges, one of the most powerful families in the Parlement of Paris. Their son Claude-François entered the Parlement. The cadet, Nicolas, served as criminal lieutenant from about 1700 to 1725 and was succeeded by his son, Claude-François-Nicolas. The subsequent generation of the two branches became cavalry officers, as did their sons until the Revolution. The continuity within this energetic versatility was royal service: from a carpenter and fish-market overseer to the king, to magistrates, to regimental officers (A.N. V 1 259, Y 1867; Nicolas Viton de Saint-Allais, *Nobiliaire universel de France*, [Paris, 1872–6], vol. 1, pp. 22–4; Bluche, "L'origine des magistrats du Parlement de Paris," p. 251; D'Affry de la Monnoye, *Les jetons*, pp. 41–2).

[52] A.N. V 1 370; Jacques Michel, *Du Paris de Louis XV à la Marine de Louis XVI: L'oeuvre de Monsieur de Sartine*, 2 vols. (Paris: Editions de l'Erudit, 1983), vol. 1, pp. 11–12, 151. This was an old family of the mercantile bourgeoisie of Lyon that had built its fortune in the wholesale food and spice trade during the late sixteenth and early seventeenth centuries. Sartine's father rose from trade to merchant banking and investment in royal financial administration. Because of that activity, he was appointed financial counselor to Phillip V, the first Bourbon king of Spain.

Themistocrats

	ggf Parisian cloth merchant[53]
Chardon	gf barrister, Parlement of Paris, and president of the Order of Barristers (1699)
	ggf cloth merchant at Tours and Paris[54]
Petit de la Honville	gf judge, Grand Conseil[55]
Bellanger	gf barrister, Parlement of Paris[56]
de Flandre de Brunville	gf household officer of duchess of Burgundy; financier[57]

From a common ancestry of seventeenth-century cloth merchants, the Moreau family developed into one of the most ramified dynasties of the eighteenth-century Parlement of Paris (see Chart 3.5). The Moreaus dominated the office of royal prosecutor in the Châtelet from the reign of Louis XIV to the eve of the Revolution (father to son, from 1713 to 1780). When we examine that development genealogically, we find that from 1709 to 1790 at least 9 Moreaus served as judges of the Parlement.[58] These 9 spanned only three generations, but in all variants of consanguinal relationship and succession. Three of the 9 subsequently became councillors of state, intendants of Generalities or provinces, ministers of state, or presidents of the Grand Conseil and Chambre des Comptes. The Moreaus were unique within the Châtelet, and almost unique within the Parlement of Paris, by the generational rapidity of their rise and the scale of their themistocratic dynasticism. In regard to scale, their uniqueness was also a model for other and lesser families dedicated to the judiciary. Dynasticism was the logical perfection of venal-hereditary officialdom. And it could compress time: Through concentrating progeny and resources on the Parlement of Paris, the Moreaus attained within three generations the professional summits occupied by the Argouges de Fleury. By the mid-eighteenth century, the two families were virtually political equals, although the Argouges were then fifteenth-generation noble and the Moreaus only third-generation.

---

[53] The Lenoirs were one of the great mercantile families of seventeenth-century Paris; their wealth and patronage were increased by Jean-Charles Lenoir's office and partnership in the East Indies Company. He was the father of Jean-Charles-Joseph (particular lieutenant, 1718–54). During the eighteenth century, the Lenoirs were closely allied with families of the royal General Tax Farm. Their ennoblement dated from Jean-Charles's royal secretaryship in 1709, Jean-Charles-Pierre Lenoir had a brilliant career after the criminal lieutenantcy: master of petitions (1765–8); president of the Grand Conseil (1768–74); lieutenant general of Police (1774–5, 1776–85); councillor of state (1785–9) (A.N. V 1 370, Y 1868; Antoine, *Le gouvernement*, p. 165; Favre-Lejeune, *Les secrétaires du roi*, vol. 2, pp. 861–4).

[54] The grandfather, Daniel, was a barrister highly regarded for his erudition and his skill in pleading. Daniel-Marc-Antoine left the particular lieutenantcy for the position of intendant of Corsica in 1768 (he had served as interim intendant of Saint-Lucia in 1763–4). After 1771, he occupied various high offices in naval administration (Antoine, *Le gouvernement*, pp. 62–3; Prévost and d'Amat, *Dictionnaire*, vol. 8, pp. 488–90).

[55] A.N. V 1 396, Y 10510, fol. 19; Bluche, "Les magistrats du Grand Conseil," p. 126.

[56] Favre-Lejeune, *Les secrétaires du roi*, vol. 1, p. 188; Roton, *Les arrêts du Grand Conseil*, p. 393.

[57] Favre-Lejeune, *Les secrétaires du roi*, vol. 1, p. 555.

[58] Bluche, "L'origine des magistrats du Parlement de Paris," pp. 319–21; Antoine, *Le gouvernement*, pp. 189–90; Favre-Lejeune, *Les secrétaires du roi*, vol. 2, pp. 983–4.

Chart 3.4. *Angran genealogy (de Fontpertuis and d'Alleray)*

I	II	III	IV
Euverte Angran I de Fontpertuis (b. c.1581, d. 1661): principal clerk for petitions, Hôtel-du-Roi; principal receiver of deposits, Cour des Aides; royal secretary (1634)			
	Jacques Angran de Fontpertuis (1618–74): viscount of Fontpertuis; judge, Parlement of Lorraine (Metz)		
		Louis-Augustin Angran (1669–1747): bailiff and captain of Sologne	
			Louis Angran de Fontpertuis (1719–84): judge, Parlement of Paris (1740); removed from office in 1741 by his family and placed in Saint-Lazare by *lettre de cachet*, for debauchery and profligacy
	Pierre Angran de Fontpertuis-Lailly (b. c.1620, d. ?): royal secretary; judge, Chambre des Comptes (1641–56)		
		Euverte Angran II de Fontpertuis-Lailly (b. c.1650, d. 1714): judge, Chambre des Comptes (1677–1714)	
			Pierre-Euverte Angran de Fontpertuis-Lailly (b. c.1685, d. 1762): judge, Chambre des comptes (1714–62)
	Louis Angran de Fontpertuis-Lailly (1623–1706): judge, Parlement of Lorraine		
		Louis-Euverte Angran d'Alleray (1678–1733): judge, Cour des Aides; master of petitions; intendant of commerce in royal Council	

Louis-Alexandre Angran d'Alleray (b. 1713, d. c.1780): judge, Parlement of Paris (1735–71)

Denis-François Angran d'Alleray (1716–94): judge, Parlement of Paris (1735); general prosecutor, Grand Conseil (1746–74); civil lieutenant, Châtelet (1774–90)

Sources: Antoine, *Le gouvernement*, p. 8; Bluche, "L'origine des magistrats du Parlement de Paris," pp. 62–3; Bluche, "Les magistrats du Grand Conseil," pp. 45–6; Coustant, *Chambre des Comptes*, pp. 693, 739, 903.

Chart 3.5. *The Moreau family: dynasticism and endogamy*

I	II	III	IV
Jean I Moreau (b. ?, d. ?): Parisian cloth merchant			
	Pierre Moreau (b. ?, d. 1725): cloth merchant; royal secretary (1708); general treasurer, Invalides Royal Military Hospital		
	oo Marie Charron (daughter of Parisian cloth merchant)		
		Pierre-Jacques Moreau de Nassigny (1689–1768): judge, Parlement of Paris (1709–65)	
		oo Claude-Antoinette d'Amoressan de Nassigny (daughter of judge, Parlement of Paris)	
			Jean-Louis Moreau de Beaumont (1715–85): judge, Parlement of Paris (1736–45); master of petitions; president, Grand Conseil (1745–47); intendant, Generality of Poitiers, then the provinces of Franche-Comté and Flanders (1747–56); intendant of finances (1756–65); councillor of state (1765–85)
			oo Marie-Françoise Grimod de la Reynière (daughter of a General Tax Farmer); children?
			Claude-François Moreau de Nassigny (1717–39): vicar of Notre-Dame of Paris; ecclesiastical judge, Parlement of Paris (1738)
		Jean Moreau de Séchelles (1690–1760): judge, Parlement of Paris (1719–27); master of petitions (1719); intendant of Hainault (1727–33/43); councillor of state (1742); intendant of Flanders (1743–54)	

oo Marie-Anne d'Amoressan de Pressigny (sister of Claude–Antoinette above, daughter of judge, Parlement of Paris)

François Moreau de Beauplan (b. ?, d. 1733): judge, Parlement of Paris (1715–33); married?

Jean II Moreau (b. ?, d. ?): Parisian cloth merchant; controller in Grand Chancellery (1706)

oo 1. Marguérite Nicéron, daughter of Parisian wholesale grocer. 2. Anne Gault, daughter of Parisian merchant

François Moreau (1686–1754): judge, Parlement of Paris (1710–13); royal prosecutor, Châtelet (1713–41)

oo Anne-Françoise Robert (daughter, judge, Parlement of Paris)

—— Moreau (b. ?, d. ?): royal prosecutor, Châtelet (1741–80)

married?

Gabriel-François Moreau de Vignolles (b. ?, d. ?): vicar, Notre–Dame of Paris; ecclesiastical judge, Parlement of Paris (1747–58); bishop of Vence (1758–?)

Chart 3.5. *(cont.)*

I	II	III	IV
		Jean-Baptiste Moreau de Saint-Just (b.1695, d. ?): judge, Parlement of Paris (1718–54)	
		oo Marie-Catherine Coignet (daughter; judge, Parlement of Paris)	
			François-Jean-Baptiste Moreau d'Etrelles (1727–62): judge, Parlement of Paris (1747–60); master of petitions; president, Chambre des Comptes (1760–2)

Sources: Antoine, *Le gouvernement*, pp. 189–90; Bluche, "L'origine des magistrats du Parlement de Paris," pp. 319–21; Favre-Lejeune, *Les secrétaires du roi*, vol. 2, pp. 983–4. Boldface denotes the two Moreaus who were royal prosecutors at the Châtelet.

Marriages and kinship

Almost all Châtelet judges and executive officers were married between the ages of 27 and 32, after five to ten years of professional activity. Those were marriages arranged by parents, alliances that perpetuated royal officialdom, especially the cohesion of the magistracy. A marriage was one of the most important and calculated events in the life of a themistocratic or administrative family. It linked two patrimonies (biologically, materially, and politically), and two professional futures. The marriage of a Châtelet themistocrat reflected both his father's vocation, and rank in that vocation, and his own situation as a judge in a major court. Most marriages were at relative endogamy of vocation and parity of rank between paternal families. Châtelet judges who were the sons of middle- or high-ranking magistrates or administrators usually married daughters of middle- or high-ranking magistrates or administrators.[59] (This emerges clearly from a comparison of the data in Tables 3.1, 3.3, and 3.4.) When hypergamy occurred (as it did, infrequently), it was usually of the bride, not of the Châtelet groom. The genealogy of the Moreaus dramatically illustrates the strength of the endogamy principle in choice of marriage partner.

Judicial or administrative patrimony, at and above the level of the Châtelet, married only rarely with commercial patrimony.[60] The notion that rich merchant

---

[59] The marital history of the Davesnes de Fontaine illustrates this practice over four generations. Pierre-René Davesne de Fontaine served a life tenure in the Châtelet (1738–85). His grandfather, Pierre Davesne, had probably begun as an artisan in the building trades of Paris. He married Suzanne Colas, the daughter of a *bourgeois de Paris* who was probably also a master artisan. Pierre rose to the entrepreneurial status and wealth of a building contractor and purchased a royal secretaryship in 1693. He transmitted the secretaryship and a seigneurial estate to his son Jean, "écuyer et seigneur de Fontaine." Jean married Renée Amiot, the daughter of a *parlementaire* family that had been ennobled in the mid-seventeenth century by a royal secretaryship. Their son, Pierre-René of the Châtelet, the first generation in the magistracy, married Louise-Marguérite Lebègue. She was the daughter of Achille Lebègue, a senior barrister of the Parlement of Paris and a royal secretary; a Lebègue had been judge of the Châtelet in the seventeenth century. In 1765, their eldest son, Achille-Pierre, was placed in a judgeship at the Chambre des Comptes, where the Amiots had influence. As a sovereign court judge, Achille-Pierre married (1770) into a comparable family of officialdom: Charlotte Lecoulteux was the daughter of a treasurer of the Generality of Paris and the sister of a judge in the Chambre des Comptes. In four generations, the Davesnes transformed themselves from artisans into superior themistocrats; their marriages were crucial elements in that transformation (A.N. V 1 314, Y 1867; François Bluche, "Les officiers du Bureau des Finances à Paris au XVIIIe siècle," *Bulletin de la Société de l'Histoire de Paris et de l'Ile de France*, 97 (1970): 147–215, 191; Coustant, *Chambre des Comptes*, p. 738; Favre-Lejeune, *Les secrétaires du roi*, vol. 2, p. 802, 819–22; Jouglas de Morenas, *Grand armorial*, vol. 1, p. 301; Trudon des Ormes, "L'état civil," pp. 261, 320.

[60] The following were notable rare exceptions to this rule. Denis-François Angran d'Alleray married Marie-Geneviève-Charlotte Darlus (1742). Her father was a wealthy tax farmer and royal secretary, but the family was still close to trade. Her grandfather, uncles, and cousins were wine merchants, although purveyors to the Court and to the duke of Orléans (Favre-Lejeune, *Les secrétaires du roi*, vol. 1, pp. 421–2). François Fagnier de Monslambert (judge, 1706–37) was son of a Châtelet judge and the grandson of a royal secretary and clerk in the office of royal domains. He was married to Marie Darbouin, also the daughter of a wine merchant and royal secretary (Favre-Lejeune, *Les secrétaires du roi*, vol. 1, pp. 418–19; Roton, *Les arrêts du Grand Conseil*, p. 117).

Table 3.4. *Marriages of Châtelet judges, lieutenants, and prosecutors: offices held by father-in-law*

Officer	Noble	Wife's name	Nobility	Father-in-law's occupation or offices
de Manneville, Victor	No	Marie-Louise Favée	?	Merchant, general receiver "Hôtel-Dieu" of Paris
de Villiers de la Noue, Prudent	Yes	Françoise-Marie Grégoire	Yes	Civil and criminal Lieutenant, Limoges presidial; royal secretary
Fagnier de Monslambert, François	Yes	Marie Darboulin	Inc.	Wine merchant and purveyor to the Crown; royal secretary
Hamelin, Claude-Silvain	?	Fare Tiercelet	Inc.	Royal secretary
Maussion, Thomas-Antoine-Jean	Yes	Marie-Jean Bertoult d'Hautecloque	Yes	Marquis, officer of royal guards
Nau de Champlouis, Claude-Thomas	Yes	. . . Langlois de la Fortelle	Yes	Judge, Parlement of Paris, President Chambre des Comptes
Bruant des Carrières, Claude	No	Thérèse de Faverolles	Yes	Judge, Chambre des Comptes
Chouart de Magny, Louis	Yes	Claude-Louise Bronod	Inc.	Notary Châtelet; royal secretary
de Villiers, Jacques-Etienne	Inc.	Florence Mustelier	Inc.	Royal secretary
Langlois, Auguste	Yes	Marie-Madelaine de Blair	Yes	Judge, Parlement of Paris
Davesne de Fontaine, Pierre René	Yes	Louise-Marguérite LeBegue	Yes	Barrister, Parlement of Paris; royal secretary
Frécot, Jacques	Inc.	Angélique-Marie Huché	Inc.	Wholesale merchant & royal secretary

Name	Spouse			Occupation
Héron, Pierre	Marie LeBé	No	No	Judge, bailliage of Troyes
Judde de Neuville, Antoine-Louis	Madelaine-Agathe Pietre	?	Yes	Deputy prosecutor, Parlement of Paris
Hazon, Michel-Jean-Baptiste	Madelaine-Charlotte LeCouteulx	No	Inc.	Wholesale merchant and banker; royal secretary
Argouges, Jérôme	Marie-Françoise de Creil de Bournezeau	Yes	Yes	Judge, Parlement of Paris; intendant of La Rochelle and Metz; Councillor of State
Argouges, Alexandre-François	Marguérite-Françoise Lefebvre de la Faluère	Yes	Yes	Judge, Parlement of Paris; Grand Master Waters and Forests, Ile-de-France
Angran d'Alleray, Denis-François	Marie-Angélique Darlus	Yes	Yes	Royal secretary and General Tax Farmer
Leconte, Claude-Nicolas	. . . Bonneau	Yes	Yes	Financier; royal secretary; governor of Châteauneuf-en-Thimerais
Sartine, Antoine-Raymond-Jean	Marie-Anne Hardy du Plessis	Yes	Yes	Captain of Foix Infantry Regiment; royal secretary
Lenoir, Jean-Charles-Joseph	Marie-Anne Lenoir de Cindré	Inc.	Inc.	Royal secretary and General Tax Farmer
Lenoir, Jean-Charles-Pierre	Marie-Nicole Denis	Yes	?	Principal clerk, Royal Council of Finance
Chardon, Daniel-Marc-Antoine	Louise-Nicole Dufresne de Villeneuve	Yes	Yes	Treasurer, Generality of Caen

Table 3.4. (cont.)

Officer	Noble	Wife's name	Nobility	Father-in-law's occupation or offices
Bellanger, Angélique-Charles	Yes	. . . Saintard	Inc.	Royal secretary; director East Indies Company
Moreau, François	Yes	Anne-Francoise Robert	Yes	Judge, Parlement of Paris
de Flandre de Brunville, François-Antoine	Yes	Angélique-Marie des Vaux	Inc.	Royal secretary; accountant for "gages," Parlement of Flanders

Abbreviations: Inc.—judge was incipiently but not fully noble when he entered Châtelet, because father had not held office long enough to have attained hereditary nobility. *Yes*—judge's family had acquired hereditary nobility before he assumed office. *No*—judge was not noble at entry; ?—estate unknown.

Sources: See source note to Table 3.1.

families easily married their daughters upward into the themistocracy, and thereby bought entry to its ranks, is a myth. And only 2 of the 26 Châtelet magistrates whose marriages have been determined were wed to daughters of the sword nobility: Sartine (into the Hardy du Plessis) and Thomas-Antoine-Jean Maussion (into the Bertoult d'Hautecloque). This is striking, for 17 of these 26 Châtelet magistrates were fully noble at birth, and most of the 17 were at least third-generation aristocrats.

Every officer of the Châtelet belonged to three families: paternal, maternal, and marital. Through each of those families he also belonged to an extensive kinship group, one comprised of many other families linked by blood and marriage. Kinship groups were the political integuments of themistocracy in Old Regime France. They were communities of solidarity, patronage, and promotion that bonded the personnel and families of discrete institutions and linked those institutions as in a web. It has been possible to trace the kin families to which 34 judges, lieutenants, and prosecutors of the Châtelet belonged by the marriages of their grandfathers, fathers, uncles, brothers, and sisters (see Table 3.5).[61] At least one-third of the 65 judges were cousins by marriage. More extensive and finely meshed prosopographical research (in notarial records at the Archives Nationales and genealogical charts at the Bibliothèque Nationale) would undoubtedly reveal a more inclusive network of kinship within the Châtelet, and between the Châtelet and the sovereign courts of Paris. The network would probably resemble the linkages between *parlementaires* evoked by Bluche: "If one could represent the genealogical trees of these eighteenth-century magistrates in their full development, limbs, boughs, and foliage would be interlaced as in a virgin forest."[62]

The principal force that determined the social composition of the Châtelet themistocracy during the eighteenth century was endogeny (growth from within), or the self-replication of royal officialdom. It is manifest in recruitment for the bench and executive offices, marriage alliances, and kinship. Within a severely endogenous politics of recruitment, strongest preference was accorded to the sons and grandsons of members of the middle and upper ranks of the judiciary. Families that were alien to royal officialdom, however great their wealth, had only the most narrow access to the Châtelet themistocracy. At least 12 of the 65 Châtelet judges in our sample years were bourgeois at the beginning of their careers, but only 3 of those 12 (Berny, Héron, and Vergne) were the sons of merchants. By contrast, vocational families of the judiciary, whether bourgeois or noble, and including families with limited economic means, had broad access. Money could buy nobility in eighteenth-century France. It could not buy a judgeship in the Châtelet or, as we shall see, in the Parlement. The fundamental requirement was a patrimony of career service within institutions of governance. The eighteenth-century Châtelet was a meritocracy of families.

---

[61] This information is random in the aforementioned sources; it is therefore both suggestive and incomplete on clans.

[62] Bluche, *Les magistrats du Parlement de Paris*, p. 126.

Themistocracy

Table 3.5. *Kinship of Châtelet magistrates*

Magistrate	Affiliated families
Judges	
Besset de la Chapelle	**gf** Dangois (Parlement of Paris); **f** *Chardon*
Bouron des Clayes	**f** Beaufort (Chambre des Comptes; royal secretary)
Brussel de Sancy	**gf** *Lenoir;* **f** Tournais (tax receiver)
Chapelain	**f** Collet (barrister, Parlement of Paris)
Chuppin	**f** *Hazon*; **s** *Maussion*
Davesne de Fontaine	**f** Amiot (Parlement of Paris and Chambre des Comptes)
Desnotz	**gf** *Héron*
Grillon des Chapelles	**f** Delarue (payer of annuities on Royal bonds)
Héron	**gf** *Chuppin* (and Parlement of Paris) **f** *Boucher* (and Parlement of Paris) **u** Faverolles (Chambre des Comptes)
Jarry	**f** Brisset (clerk, Royal Council); **s** LeMarchand (judge Cour des Aides)
Langlois	**gf** Humbert (chief magistrate at Ste. Ménehould) **f** Sandrier (royal secretary, general receiver finance, Generality of Limoges) **b** Touzard (principal receiver of salt tax, Paris)
LeMarié d'Aubigny	**gf** Perrotin de Barmont (treasurers, Generalities of Paris and Bourges; treasurers and general controllers, Navy and Fortifications)
Manneville	**f** DuFlos (barrister, Parlement of Paris)
Michau de Montblin	**f** de Cotte (president, Parlement of Paris)
Pelletier	**f** *Lenoir*
Silvestre and Silvestre de Chanteloup	**f** *Judde*
Villiers du Terrage	**f** Barbotin (royal secretary)
Executive officers	
Argouges (Jerôme)	**f** Lepeletier de Morfontaine (judges and presidents, Parlement of Paris) **u** Duvau (general receiver finance, Generality of Tours; general treasurer, Queen's household)

Angran	**f** Dunoyer (Treasurer, Generalities of Montauban and Paris) **b** Verthamon (judges, Parlement of Paris)
Flandre de Brunville	**s** du Cluzel de la Chabrerie (master of petitions, intendant, Generality of Tours)
Leconte, Claude-Nicolas	**f** Lottin (master of petitions, Hôtel-du-Roi) **u** Bragelonge (judges and presidents, Parlement of Paris) **s** de Brétignières (judges, Parlement of Paris)
Lenoir, Jean-Charles-Joseph	**f** Danse (cloth merchants, Beauvais and Paris)
Lenoir, Jean-Charles-Pierre	**f** Lenoir de Cindré (general receivers and Tax Farm official)

Abbreviations: **b** – brother; **f** – father; **gf** – grandfather; **u** – uncle; **s** – sister.
Italic name indicates Châtelet family.
Sources: See source note to Table 3.1.

It was also an expansive crucible. It absorbed men from families of the lesser judiciary and administration and made them colleagues of the sons of great magisterial and administrative families. It provided the experience and credentials needed for entry into sovereign courts or high administration by a subsequent generation.

The socioprofessional origins of the Châtelet judges and executive officers of the eighteenth century almost duplicate those that Philippe Rosset has described for the Châtelet judges who served between 1660 and 1700. Rosset counted as Chancellery officers all royal secretaries, regardless of their other, active offices and professions (except those of the superior judiciary). I have not done so. The 10.7 percent of 1735 to 1789 (Table 3.6) are those with no offices known other than the secretaryship or Chancellery. The total percentage of royal secretaries among the 65 is 37 percent. That increase over the seventeenth century probably reflects the considerable expansion in the number of secretaryships between 1680 and 1720. Rosset did not enumerate patrilineages (grandfathers and great-grandfathers) as I have done whenever possible. But he found three main types of social ancestry for his 150 judges: the judiciary, far back into the sixteenth century; royal financial administration offices, usually in the provinces; and commerce and manufacturing, usually at least three generations removed from the Châtelet judge. Marital politics among the judges of the period 1660 to 1700 were essentially the same as during the eighteenth century. Rosset identified the bridal families of 52 of the 210 judges; 47 were of the judiciary or royal administration. Not one judge, noble or bourgeois, among the 52 married a daughter of military paternity. In one-third of the marriages, the professions and rank of father and father-in-law were identical.[63]

---

[63] "Les conseillers du Châtelet" (pt. 1, pp. 259–74). Rosset gathered socioprofessional information on the fathers of 150 of the 210 judges who served between 1660 and 1700. His results are compared with mine in Table 3.6.

Table 3.6. *Professions of fathers of Châtelet judges, bench 1660–1700 and 1735–1789 (%)*

	1660–1700	1735–1789
Superior judiciary (sovereign court magistrate)	28.0	26.0
Median or lesser judiciary	18.6	37.0
Chancellery officer (including 37 royal secretaries)	25.5	10.7
Royal finance and tax administration	9.4	15.3
Merchants	4.6	4.6

Source: Data for 1660–1700 from Philippe Rosset, "Le conseilliers du Châtelet de Paris de la fin du XVIIe siècle: étude d'histoire sociale," in *Paris et l'l'le-de-France: Mémoires des Sociétés historiques et archéologiques de Paris et de l'l'le-de-France*, pt. 1, pp. 259–74. My figures are from sources within the source note of Table 3.1 and in the many footnotes.

The comparison reveals an obdurate stability and cohesion in recruitment that lasted from at least 1660 to 1789. One wonders when the pattern began.

Before 1600, the ancestors of many, if not most, eighteenth-century Châtelet judges and executive officers had been provincial. These families gravitated to Paris during the seventeenth century, as merchants, attorneys, or clerks to ducal or princely families or as minor judicial or administrative officers. They began their ascent during the great expansion of state offices that characterized the reigns of Henri IV, Louis XIII, and Louis XIV. The very magnetism of royal office that drew them to the city prescribed their evolution once there. By the late seventeenth century, their implantation in the metropolis was deep but socially narrow, achieved primarily through officialdom. From at least that period onward, they were far more closely related by marriage, culture, and material interest to similar families of Parisian officialdom than to their cousins who had remained in the provinces. In these respects, the judges of the Châtelet did not differ substantially from those of the eighteenth-century Parlement of Paris, as will be demonstrated in some detail. The familial development of most *parlementaires* had begun earlier, starting with professional emigration to Paris in the sixteenth century, implantation in the Parisian judiciary or Paris-based royal administration during one period, 1550 to 1650, and older and more substantial vocation by 1700.[64] Most of the eighteenth-century Châtelet families were still in process of mutation, still advancing toward the consummate establishment, in the city and the themistocracy, attained by the *parlementaires*. Like the *parlementaires*, they put behind them more than a geography.

[64] See Bluche, *Les magistrats du Parlement de Paris.*

Of those 41 sons of judicial officers among our 65 judges, only 4 had a grandfather who was a merchant or manufacturer; of the 10 sons of finance officials, another 4 had such a grandfather; of the 7 from the Chancellery, only 1 son had this heritage. Of the 13 executive officers whose lineages are known, only 4 (Lenoir, Sartine, and the two Moreaus) had a mercantile grandfather or great-grandfather. Fifty-eight of the 65 judges, and at least 10 of the 19 lieutenants and prosecutors, were three or more patrilineal generations distant from trade or commodity production. Three generations is almost the span of a century. From the vantage point of a 20-year-old aspirant to the Châtelet in the eighteenth century, who was the son and grandson of magistrates or administrators, three generations back in time to a merchant great-grandfather was a past that probably still existed in family memory but was socially long dead.

The primary social identity and mobility of an Old Regime family existed through its patrilineage. So too did its capital, which was accumulated and passed on from father to sons in accordance with strict inheritance laws. Although some Châtelet judges, like Pierre Héron and the two Bouchers, had cousins who were engaged in commerce, most of the profits of that commerce remained within the merchant lineage. By law, the bulk of family capital had to be handed down, in each generation, from fathers of merchants to sons of merchants, except for the dowry portion given to daughters. Although merchants could loan capital, at a low rate of interest, to their magisterial cousins, a magisterial family with a collateral branch in trade remained distinct from that branch, socially and economically.

For these reasons (in addition to those soon to be considered), the fact that approximately 63 percent of the eighteenth-century Châtelet judges were legally commoners or, more exactly, bourgeois, is of little significance. Just like their noble colleagues, they belonged to a vocational and endogenous group that was distinct from the living mass of the French bourgeoisie, distanced from commerce, commodity production, and the quest for profits. Their very presence in the Châtelet resulted from a renunciation of those activities by their elders or ancestors. In a society of nobles, bourgeois, and plebeians, they belonged to a separate entity: hereditary magistracy and governance.

Relations with the Third Estate

In French urban civilization, from at least the sixteenth century to the Revolution, the artisanate was the main progenitive class for both mercantile and manufacturing enterprise. *Négociants,* or wholesale merchants dealing in commodities, were usually descendants of the few master artisans who had amassed significant capital through craft skill, effective supervision of their journeymen and apprentices, retail merchandising of their product from ateliers and small shops, work on commission for affluent clients, and sub-contracting with other artisans. Wholesale cloth merchants commonly descended from master silk-weavers, or linen- and woolen-makers; building contractors and ar-

chitects from stonemasons, carpenters, and parquetry-makers; large-scale purveyors of precious stones and jewelry from goldsmiths, gem-cutters, and
jewelers. Manufacturers, or *fabricants*, were usually successful master artisans
who employed large work forces and produced in quantity, often in association
with merchants. Artisans labored; *négociants* and *fabricants* commanded labor
and commercialized its product. They were a small elite in a populous universe
of craftsmen and tradesmen. *Négociants* and *fabricants* provided the executives
in the corporate organization of production and commerce, serving as judge–
consuls of their guilds, representatives on the Municipal Council of Paris, and
échevins of Paris. In those capacities, they belonged to the governing structure of
urban France and collaborated with representatives from the judiciary. From
those capacities, they could envision a possibility of magisterial careers for their
grandsons (usually after placing their sons in Chancellery secretaryships, financial administration, the notariat or the profession of barrister). Artisans and
shopkeepers could not realistically envision that possibility.

Simple master artisans and tradesmen were the largest single social group
within the urban propertied classes of Old Regime France. Artisans and
tradesmen numbered over 60,000 in Paris at the close of the period.[65] In
seventeenth- and eighteenth-century Paris, they were the majority among victims of property crimes, a large portion of the defendants in criminal cases, and
a large proportion of the litigants in civil actions before the Châtelet. The
themistocracy of eighteenth-century Paris had no social connections or affinities with the surrounding universe of ateliers and shops. Its patrimony, capital,
existence, and identity differed radically from that universe. The professional
relations of magistrates, whether bourgeois or noble, to artisans and tradesmen
were determined by the civil and criminal law, just as the property they defended was property as defined in law. In judicial practice, those relations were
neither hostile nor partisan. They were as formal and ideational in character as
magistrates' relations to plebeians.

Despite their socioprofessional insularity, the high judiciary of magistrates
and barristers enjoyed great authority and prestige among merchants, rentiers,
and members of the liberal professions, the principal groups of the bourgeoisie
from which the themistocracy had historically evolved. This was revealed conclusively in 1789, when the Third Estate chose its deputies to the Estates-
General. Themistocrats and barristers were chosen, by electoral assemblies
throughout France, out of all proportion to their actual numbers within the
propertied groups of the Third Estate. In Paris, 11,716 voters, in sixty primary
assemblies, chose the 407 electors of the metropolitan Third Estate, who in
turn selected from their midst the Parisian commoners' representatives to the
Estates-General.[66] More than half of the 20 deputies and 20 substitutes chosen

[65] Reinhard, *Nouvelle histoire de Paris*, pp. 45–61.
[66] Approximately 30,000 adult male Parisians, domiciled in the city and who paid a head tax of 6
livres or more, were eligible to vote in primary assemblies. Some 40% (11,716) of them did so.
The largest abstaining group within the 30,000 were artisans and tradesmen. The largest single

were of the judiciary: 15 barristers (all but 2 from the Parlement of Paris); 3 notaries; 2 proctors; and 2 judges of the Châtelet. The percentages of magistrates and barristers chosen as deputies were even higher in the provinces. Throughout France, some 46,200 electors (of which the majority were merchants and landowners) chose 585 deputies to represent the Third Estate at Versailles.[67] Twenty-nine percent of the 585 were magistrates (lieutenants, provosts, judges, king's prosecutors or advocates), of which the great majority served in royal bailliage, presidial, or sovereign courts or finance tribunals. One in 5 of the 585 deputies was a royal magistrate. Thirty-one percent were barristers, proctors, or notaries; of these barristers "au Parlements" were the most numerous group. A further 10 percent belonged to administrative or municipal officialdom. Only 12 percent of the 585 were merchants. Nine percent were simply landowning rentiers or independent farmers. Five percent were of the liberal professions (mostly medical doctors and savants). Less than 1 percent each were military officers or manufacturers, although there were hundreds of bourgeois officers in the army and tens of thousands of masters of commodity production in the France of 1789.[68] To a remarkable degree (39% of all Third Estate deputies), the peasants and artisans of France found themselves "rep-

---

group (172) among the 407 electors were men of the law. See François Furet, "Les élections de 1789 à Paris, le Tiers État et la naissance d'une classe dirigéante," in *De l'Ancien Régime à la Révolution française: Recherches et perspectives* (Göttingen: 1978), p. 199.

[67] Ran Halévi, "The Monarchy and the Elections of 1789," *Journal of Modern History*, 60 (suppl.), (1988): S75–S97. In the provinces, the peasants that did participate in primary assemblies were filtered out in the selection of the electors that chose deputies, as were members of the artisanate in the major cities.

[68] My computation from Armand Brette, *Les constituants: Liste des députés et des suppléants élus à l'Assemblée constituante de 1789* (Paris, 1897). Langres, in southern Champagne, was a town of some 9,000 in 1789 and the seat of an electoral bailliage for the Estates-General. It is the subject of a fine social and political history by Georges Viard, *Tradition et lumières au pays de Diderot: Langres au XVIIIe siècle* (Langres: Société Historique et Archéologique de Langres, 1985). During the eighteenth century, if not long before, the civic and much of the propertied elite of the town was formed principally by the 66 officers of thirteen distinct judicial and administrative bodies (including a presidial court with 29 magistrates and two tax courts with 16); the 54 secretaries and process-servers who assisted them; and some 68 barristers, proctors, and notaries. They and their families accounted for almost 10% of the population in 1789. In addition, there were 237 bourgeois rentiers; 139 merchants (of which a minority were wholesalers); 766 *gens de métiers*, or artisans, organized into twenty-four guild corporations; and about 64 farmers, who resided in, or on the fringes of, town. Magistrates, administrators, and barristers accounted for about 12–15% of the propertied adult male population of the Third Estate at Langres in 1789. But they accounted for all of the seven deputies and substitutes to the Estates-General (of which 4 were royal magistrates). That election, which proceeded expeditiously and harmoniously in its two stages, reflected a long-term political reality, not a revolutionary configuration of power. Since at least the late seventeenth century, magistrates and barristers had largely controlled municipal government at Langres (the offices of mayor and *échevin*), and entry to their ranks was the ambition of most local mercantile families. "Sur tous les plans, 'Messiers du présidial' tenaient à Langres le haut du pavé. Ils en avaient pleinement conscience. . . . Cette solidarité conduisait finalement à l'accaparement des responsabilités et du pouvoir: détenteurs d'une part importante des richesses langroises, les robins et leurs fils occupaient une place prépondérante à l'hôtel de ville ou au chapitre de la cathédrale et tenaient la plupart des leviers du commande. De plus, c'était en grande partie par leur intermédiaire que la ville assurait son emprise sur les campagnes environnantes" (Viard, 225–6). The election for the Third Estate at Langres in

resented," in 1789, at Versailles by officers of state who had exercised political authority over them for centuries. In their socioprofessional being, the 585 Third Estate deputies to the Estates-General of 1789 were virtually avatars of the 187 deputies from that estate to the Estates-General of 1614–15. The only significant change was the higher proportion of barristers in 1789. In 1614–15 the 187 deputies included 121 royal officials, nearly all of them magistrates of the "bailliages" and the "sénéchaussés"; with the addition of municipal officials the total reaches 139 out of 187; with the officials of the provincial estates, 147; with the lawyers (whose profession brought them into contact with the office-holders and who almost to a man aspired to office), the figure rises to 177 out of 187. For the rest there were two "merchants" and one "laboureur," that is a well-to-do peasant who owned a plough team.[69]

Royal officialdom combined with the legal profession (a combination that was numerically and politically dominated by magistrates and barristers) accounted for 70 percent of the bourgeois deputies in the Constituent Assembly (1789–91), and for 410, or more than one-third, of all deputies in the assembly. For themistocrats and barristers to have been chosen so systematically by the other constituent social groups of their Estate to be representatives and protagonists of the Estate in the forthcoming great confrontations with the monarchy, nobility, and clergy signifies that for the middle and upper tiers of the French bourgeoisie, the judiciary remained endowed with an intellectual – even an honorific – supremacy. This collective selection by the propertied classes of the Third Estate, in its rural and urban electoral assemblies in 1789, reaffirmed the ancient prestige of themistocracy within the Third Estate, a prestige so powerfully expressed in 1614. But it also created the first legislative near-majority of the Revolution: the solid bloc of bourgeois judicial and administrative deputies with which most noble themistocrat deputies would ally in the Constituent Assembly.

B. Robe nobility

Origins and meaning

The point of departure for examining themistocrats as nobles is the fact that the development of the robe nobility, or the legal and hereditary ennoblement of men and their families through career tenure in high magisterial and administrative office, occurred late in the long histories of the French monarchy, magistracy, and nobility. As a hereditary (and thus authentic) nobility, the nobility of the robe existed for only 146 years, from 1644 to 1790. Before the royal edict of July 1644, no magisterial office in any sovereign court conferred no-

1789, and its social foundations, were probably typical of those in most French towns. Here, as elsewhere, merchants and landowners chose as their representatives themistocrats, royal administrators, and practitioners of the law.

[69] Roland Mousnier, "The Development of Monarchical Institutions and Society in France," in *Louis XIV and Absolutism*, ed. Ragnhild Hatton (Columbus, Ohio: Ohio State University Press, 1976), p. 39.

bility on its incumbent. The creation of the *noblesse de robe* was a long process, occurring in two distinct stages: (1) The gradual extension to the high magistracy and administration of specific privileges that were characteristic of the nobility, primarily by the Valois kings (Louis XII to Henry III) during the fifteenth and sixteenth centuries; (2) full, hereditary ennoblement through office, by legislation of the Bourbon monarchs and their regents from 1644 to 1719.[70]

There were significant differences between the two stages of entitlements. The privileges granted by kings to high officers of justice, in specific edicts from at least the late fourteenth century to 1644, were essentially economic rather than honorific. The grants were pragmatic: They encouraged families to enter and remain in the magistracy by compensating them for the exercise of offices that were costly to get but poorly remunerated. The privileges were attached to the person and immediate family of the serving or retired magistrate and could not be handed down to his posterity.[71] Various sixteenth- and early seventeenth-century *parlementaires* and jurists argued that the accumulated privileges of high magistrates (most of which were also the same privileges enjoyed by nobles) and the great importance to king and realm of their service conferred nobility on them.[72] But those claims were neither validated by the Valois kings nor recognized by most nobles. The themistocracy remained common in estate until the seventeenth century, except for individual families that were ennobled by royal letter, by various other offices, or by long ownership of seigneurial domains.[73] The transition in the social status of sovereign court magistrates began with Henry IV's (imprecisely worded) edict of March 1600:

[70] The fundamental work on this subject is by François Bluche and Pierre Durye, "L'anoblissement par charges avant 1789," in *Les cahiers nobles*, nos. 23 (vol. 1) and 24 (vol. 2), 1962.

[71] They were the privileges described in Chapter 1. The magistrates of most Parisian sovereign courts had been made beneficiaries of those privileges by 1570, some of them long before then. The privileges could amount to thousands of livres per annum for a sovereign court family during the sixteenth century and afterwards, especially if it owned rural estates. The privileges remained intrinsic to high magisterial office until the Revolution. See Jean-Richard Bloch, *L'anoblissement en France au temps de François Ier: Essai d'une définition de la condition juridique et sociale de la noblesse au début du XVIe siècle* (Paris, Felix Alcan 1934), pp. 87–95. By exempting magistrates from military obligations, both personal and monetary, royal legislation made a significant distinction between them and the lay nobility, for the latter were subject to those obligations. Hereditarily ennobled magisterial families retained their military exemption after 1644, which contributed to their inferiority in the eyes of the sword aristocracy.

[72] The arguments are presented in Bloch, *L'anoblissement*, pp. 75–81, 87–92.

[73] Few themistocrats seem to have been ennobled by royal letter (which granted full and hereditary nobility). During the long reign of Francis I (1515–47), only 183 *lettres de noblesse* were issued, including a mere fourteen to magistrates and another dozen to financial administration officers of the Crown (Bloch, *L'anoblissement*, pp. 154–90). Most went to wealthy rentiers, military commanders, and officers of royal and ducal households (including servants). Before 1600 there were few ennobling offices of state. The following were the principal ones: Chancellor of France; the four secretaryships of state; masterships of petitions to the royal Council; the chief offices in the royal household; secretary and other key offices in the Grand Chancellery; presidents of sovereign courts who were appointed to the royal Privy Council; and provincial governors (ibid., p. 76). From 1485 onward, royal secretaryships and other offices in the Grand Chancellery, of which there were at least 120 in 1500, conferred hereditary nobility after twenty years or death in office (Bluche and Durye, "L'anoblissement," vol. 2, pp. 7–8). Before the seventeenth century, the most accessible ennobling office was the *échevinage*, in sixteen towns and

We forbid all persons to assume the title of *ecuyer* or to insinuate themselves into the *corps* of the nobility who are not descended from an ancestor and father having exercised the profession of arms or served the public in some honorable office, such as those which by law and custom of the realm give a beginning of nobility to posterity, without ever having committed an action that is base and derogative of the condition of nobility.[74]

A half-century elapsed before that pronouncement became a legal, and thus a political and social, actuality. The robe nobility was brought into full and precise existence by Cardinal Mazarin and then Louis XIV. Principal offices in all superior courts of France were made hereditarily ennobling, in either the first degree (after twenty years' service or death in office) or the second degree (gradually, by father and son each serving for twenty years or until death in office).[75] As with the French nobility in general, the "heredity" passed exclusively in patrilineage, from a father to his sons and daughters. Since the late Middle Ages there had been robe families that had belonged to the Second

cities of France. There were usually four *échevins*, or chief administrative officers, in each of those municipalities; each incumbent served for only two years but could be reelected. Consistently, most of them were merchants, rentiers, magistrates, barristers, or notaries. In 1371, Charles V granted hereditary nobility in the first degree to those who served as *échevins* of Paris. The grant was revoked in 1577 by Henri III; by his edict, only fathers and sons whose service in the office totaled twenty years gained hereditary nobility. Hereditary nobility for *échevins* of Paris was restored by Louis XIV in 1706, and the restoration seems to have been applied retroactively to families of the seventeenth-century *échevinage* (Guyot, vol. 6, pp. 601–2); Bluche and Durye, "L'anoblissement," vol. 1, p. 33). Over the long period 1400 to 1789, more families were probably ennobled through *échevinage* than by any other means; seigneurial aristocrats contemptuously referred to them as "nobles of the town-hall bell." Ennoblement of *échevins* testifies to the importance attached by the kings of France to urban wealth and political support. Finally, bourgeois could legally purchase seigneurial properties, but the Ordinance of Blois (1579) ruled that purchase, or even long-term ownership, of seigneurial domains would no longer confer nobility and its privileges: "Les roturiers et non nobles, achetant fiefs nobles, ne seront pour ce annoblis, ni mis au rang & dégré des nobles, de quelque revenu & valeur que solent les fiefs par eux acquis" (in Ferrière, vol. 2, p. 230). Such families henceforth required royal confirmation of their nobility; if they could produce no other documentation of their claim to nobility, the confirmation was usually refused. During the fifteenth and sixteenth centuries, most judges of the Parlement of Paris were bourgeois in family origin and remained commoners in formal Estate (Shennan, *Parlement of Paris*, pp. 110–11).

[74] Quoted from Bluche and Durye, "L'anoblissement," vol. 2, p. 15.

[75] The degree of hereditary nobility granted shifted back and forth between first and second degree, between 1644 and 1719, for the principal officers of the sovereign courts of Paris (president, judges, royal prosecutors and advocates, deputy prosecutors, and chief recording secretaries) as follows: Parlement (first degree, 1644–69; second degree, 1669–90; first degree, c. 1690–1790); Grand Conseil (first degree, 1644–69; second degree, 1669–1717; first degree, 1717–90); Chambre des Comptes (first degree, 1645–69; second degree, 1669–91; first degree, 1691–1790); Cour des Aides (first degree, 1645–69; second degree, 1669–91; first degree, 1691–1790); Cour des Monnaies (first degree, 1719–90). However, the same offices in many provincial sovereign courts were made hereditarily ennobling in the second degree (after two generations). The Parlements of Normandy (Rouen) and Languedoc (Toulouse); the Chambres des Comptes at Aix-en-Provence, Montepellier, and Nantes; and the Cours des Aides at Caen, Clermont-Ferrand, Montauban, and Rouen all remained in that condition until their abolition early in the Revolution (Bluche and Durye, "L'anoblissement II," vol. 1, pp. 22–30). These royal shifts between first- and second-degree ennoblement of high-robe officers could easily have caused venerable families of the military aristocracy to regard all those ennoblements as arbitrary, incoherent, even fantastic.

Estate, but only after 1644 was there a robe nobility. The Crown and its genealogists made the ennobling edicts de facto retroactive: Seventeenth- and eighteenth-century families with an ancestor who had served a career tenure in a sovereign court were deemed to have been ennobled by that ancestral service, even if it had occurred long before 1644, and the generational degree of their nobility was counted from the time of the original service.[76] The ennobling legislation accomplished a social transformation within the state, and created a major dissonance within the French nobility.

Louis XIV transposed the upper institutional ranks of the themistocracy (and much of high civil administration) from the Third Estate to the Second Estate. In principle, the change greatly widened access for themistocrats to supreme offices – those of secretary, or minister of state, or councillor – for which noblemen were traditionally preferred. By formally ennobling sovereign court magistrates, the king assured them that in future no executive offices would be denied them because of their estate – that theoretically, all such offices would be within reach of their progeny. Henceforth, the themistocracy as a professional group straddled the two estates and was a major conduit from the third to the second. This signified a general honorific promotion of themistocracy, one that enhanced its distinctiveness from the aggregate estates of commoners and aristocrats. When a magistrate and his family rose high in the profession, they automatically changed estate, whether they had sought to or not, while remaining themistocratic in all essential respects. For that reason, ennoblement was not a profound social change for them.

Magisterial offices in sovereign courts had been the venal and, in many cases, dynastic property of families long before they were made ennobling, just as the duties of magistrates and the internal organization of their courts were defined long before that honorific endowment. Hereditary ennoblement confirmed, slightly increased, and (most importantly) guaranteed in perpetuity of lineage all the material privileges that most sovereign court magistrates had enjoyed before 1644. Nobility was, therefore, a handsome attribute newly bestowed on old, firmly established, essentially self-regulating institutions and their professional culture. That novelty caused other aristocrats to contest the nobility of robe nobles. But there is also strong evidence that nobiliary status remained marginal to the abiding professional identity, recruitment, and existence of all but a few high-ranking themistocrats.

Nobles of the Châtelet

Châtelet judgeships did not ennoble until 1768. By royal decrees of May and August of that year, the Châtelet offices of civil and criminal lieutenant were granted first-degree hereditary nobility (after twenty years' service or death in office). The offices of royal prosecutor, deputy prosecutor, advocate, and judge of the Châtelet were to confer personal nobility after ten years' service but he-

---

[76] Bluche, *Les magistrats du Parlement de Paris*, p. 134.

reditary nobility would be achieved only at the conclusion of forty years' service or with death in office after twenty years. The terms of ennoblement were made retroactive for the officers serving in 1768. The royal purpose was to encourage life tenure and, probably, dynasticism in office.[77] But the elevation of the Châtelet to an ennobling institution in 1768 did not substantially alter the social recruitment of its themistocracy or attract bourgeois candidates. All but possibly 3 of the 16 lieutenants who served between 1735 and 1789 were already fully noble when they took office. The 3 royal prosecutors who served between 1713 and 1789 had been noblemen from birth or childhood. Forty-eight (37%) of the 130 Châtelet judges in the period 1735 to 1789 were already noble, either fully (29) or incipiently (19), when they entered the court.[78] About 30 percent of judges on the bench in 1735 had been full or incipient nobles at entry; so were some 40 percent of judges on the bench in 1789. The hereditary ennoblement offered by a Châtelet judgeship (forty years' service, or death in office after twenty years) could not have enticed bourgeois families that were driven by ambition for aristocratic status, for other and more easily attainable offices gave far more rapid access to hereditary nobility; such families neither sought nor were sought by the Châtelet magistracy. It was of no interest to those that were noble.

The declared purpose of the 1768 edicts (to promote life tenure) was certainly redundant, and possibly self-defeating. Twenty-six noblemen, several of them second- or third-generation in the robe nobility, served on the bench in either 1735 or 1762. Fourteen of them served tenures of more than thirty-one years; 5 labored for twenty to thirty years; 4 worked for eight to nineteen years; and only 3 served short terms of seven years or less. More significantly, the tenures of their bourgeois colleagues were essentially the same: Twenty-six of the bourgeois judges served for more than thirty-one years; 9 for twenty to thirty years; 61 for eight to nineteen years; and none for less than eight years. Thus, 54 percent of noble judges served for more than thirty-one years, until they died or retired in old age, as did 63 percent of bourgeois judges. From at least 1660 to 1768, therefore, most bourgeois magistrates of the Châtelet devoted their lifetimes to the court without any prospect of ennoblement. One

---

[77] "Rien ne pouvant être plus convenable au bien de notre service en notre Châtelet de Paris, que d'y conserver un nombre d'anciens officiers capables de maintenir une saine jurisprudence & de former les jeunes officiers, il nous a paru qu'un des meilleurs moyens d'y parvenir ètoit d'accorder la noblesse à ceux des officiers dudit siège, qu'un long exercice de leurs fonctions rendroit susceptible de cette faveur. Une telle distinction . . . attachera de plus en plus lesdits officiers à leur siège, & encouragera les autres à suivre leurs exemples, par l'assurance qu'ils auront d'obtenir la noblesse personele après un temps fixe, & de parvenir à la noblesse personele héréditaire en persévérant dans l'exercise des mêmes fonctions. Nous donnerons en même temps aux principaux & aux anciens officiers de nôtre Châtelet une juste récompense de leurs services, & au principal siège de justice d'entre nos bailliages, au tribunal ordinaire de notre capital, un témoignage autentique de notre singulière protection" (edict of August 1768, from Guyot, vol. 3, p. 322). See also Bluche, "Les magistrats des cours parisiennes," p. 91.

[78] Philippe Rosset estimated that 46% of Châtelet judges who served between 1660 and 1700 were fully or incipiently noble ("Les conseillers du Châtelet," pt. 1, p. 242).

may doubt that their successors after 1768 were motivated to long service by that prospect.[79]

A significant change in the Châtelet themistocracy did occur during the period 1770 to 1789. Its nature was not social, nor is it possible to gauge the influence, if any, of the ennobling decrees of 1768 on that change. Across the eighteenth century, young sons of Parisian robe-noble families were placed in Châtelet judgeships to serve a highly instructive practical and jurisprudential apprenticeship until a sovereign court office became available for them, usually through dynastic preferment. These young nobles were always present, in limited numbers. Approximately 5 such transient judges entered or left the Châtelet during each decade before 1770.[80] In 1774, the Châtelet bench was expanded from fifty-six to sixty-four judgeships. These offices were in demand: Between January 1770 and December 1788, 35 to 40 transients acquired and then relinquished Châtelet judgeships, most of them after less than five years' service. Almost all of them were replaced with novice judges soon after their departure. The rate of transience and replacement in these years was at least 50 percent greater than during any nineteen-year period between 1720 and 1770. The demand caused many vastly experienced, older judges to sell their offices and retire sooner than they would otherwise have done. At least 24 of the transients (or themistocratic apprentices) were young nobles from families of high magistracy or administration, and at least 16 of them left the Châtelet to succeed elders or kin in sovereign courts or superior administration.[81] There was probably a surfeit of robe nobility by the 1770s, in comparison with the number of high offices available to them. Fourteen other judges of noble themistocratic patrimony entered during this period and were still on the bench in 1789. Their proportion was not unusual within the eighteenth-century Châtelet. In sum, the Châtelet of 1789 was only marginally more nobiliary in its makeup than it had been in 1762 or 1735 (if one discounts those judges ennobled retroactively by the 1768 decrees), and the socioprofessional origins of its judges remained fundamentally the same. Yet the high rate of transience between 1770 and 1788, by comparison with the decades preceding 1770, had a new professional consequence whose importance transcended social continuity. During the great crisis period of criminal justice and the judicial system, 1785 to 1788, there was an unprecedentedly large number of young and novice judges, with fewer than seven years' experience. They made up 45 percent of the total in 1789. That last, youthful generation of the Châtelet, nobles and bourgeois, was

---

[79] A company of magistrates gained greater social prestige when their court was elevated by the king to ennobling status, and thus possessed greater theoretical appropriateness for nobles and attractiveness for bourgeois. But it is not clear that such promotion significantly affected the social recruitment or length of tenure in most courts.

[80] Between 1730 and 1770, the following high-robe families were among their number: Le Nain, Lefèvre d'Ormesson, Lepelletier, Gilbert de Voisins, Voyer d'Argenson, de Paule d'Aguesseau, Turgot (A.N. Y 1867, 1868).

[81] Documented from A.N. Y 1869 and Roton, *Les arrêts du Grand Conseil.*

more versed in the literature of the Enlightenment than in the intricacies of the Great Criminal Ordinance.

Nobility was not sought by judges once they had begun careers in the Châtelet, although it was readily available in the form of royal secretaryships to those with family or kinship capital. Among the some 55 bourgeois judges (of the 130) who served during the period 1735 to 1768, only Victor de Manneville and Louis Auvray purchased a secretaryship, and thus nobility. Perhaps the authority, privileges, and prestige of the Châtelet themistocracy were sufficient distinction for most of them. The Nouëts, father and son, served in succession from 1706 to at least 1775. They were a branch of an affluent family that belonged, during the eighteenth century, to a kinship group that included families of great wealth. Their genealogical chart (Chart 3.6) reveals those matrices, as well as the fact that the Châtelet Nouëts remained bourgeois, within a close family and large group of high-robe nobility. In all probability they did so voluntarily. After 1768, Louis Nouët d'Ormoy de Montanglos was ennobled retroactively, and automatically, for his long service.[82]

Most families of noble Châtelet themistocrats were recent to the Second Estate. Eight of the 16 lieutenants and prosecutors whose estate is known were second-generation noblemen, 3 were third-generation, 1 was fourth-generation and 1 was fifth-generation. Only the Argouges were feudal nobility. Twenty-eight of the 48 judges were second-generation noblemen (including those incipiently noble at entry to office), 8 were third-generation, and only 4 were fourth-generation, or *noblesse de race*. Two judges (Choart de Magny and Besset de la Chapelle) were of lineage nobility dating from before 1600.[83] The only descendants of military nobility among these 63 magistrates were the two Argouges and Besset de la Chapelle. At least 15 of the 48 noble judges were born

---

82 The Nouëts were originally from Maine, where they belonged to the judiciary and the Church during the late sixteenth and early seventeenth centuries. Their implantation in Paris was achieved by Claude (1634–99), who had a distinguished career as barrister of the Parlement. The senior branch during the eighteenth century (Guy Nouët and his descendants) became noble through a royal secretaryship purchased in 1707; the cadet branch did not buy nobility until the 1760s. The middle line, the Nouëts of the Châtelet, remained bourgeois until the 1768 edicts. Their cousins by marriage – Bruant, Boisgibault, and Ferrand – were rich robe nobles. The first two were second-degree noble, the third was seventh-degree. One wonders what significance the distinctions between bourgeois and noble and between degrees of nobility had inside this dynasty of the robe and administration. The Nouëts and their kinsmen were unitary in profession but mixed in estate. That situation was not uncommon within themistocratic families, because of the vicissitudes of ennobling offices and because nobility was transmitted only from fathers to sons and daughters. Thus, many robe nobles had judicial or administrative brothers, nephews, and cousins who were bourgeois.

83 "Second-generation" noble means that the man in question was the son of an *anobli*, a father who had acquired personal nobility through office or by other means but had not yet acquired hereditary nobility for his sons. After the father served the required tenure or died in ennobling office, the son then became a "first-generation" hereditary noble. Even before that, the son enjoyed all privileges of nobility and was conventionally regarded as noble. A "third-generation" noble was the grandson of an *anobli*. The sources for the figures in the text are the sources cited in Chapter 3 for the socioprofessional origins of Châtelet judges. Forty-nine of the 69 noble judges of the Châtelet between 1660 and 1700 were second- or third-generation noble; only 4 were fifth- or sixth-generation noble (Rosset, "Les conseillers du Châtelet," pt. 1, p. 245).

Chart 3.6. *The Nouët family*

I	II	III	IV
Claude Nouët (b. 1634, d. 1699 Paris): barrister Parlement of Paris oo Jeanne de Massac (daughter barrister Parlement of Paris)	Guy Nouët (b. c.1670, d. c.1746 Paris): president, barristers Parlement of Paris; royal secretary, 1707; oo Cathérine Chrestien	Nicole Nouët oo 1723 Marie-Joseph Berthelot (judge, Parlement of Paris)	
		Jean-Jacques Nouët (b. 1697 [Paris], d. 1746 [Paris]): judge Parlement of Paris, 1719–46; oo 1729 Elisabeth Bruant des Carrières (daughter judge Châtelet)	Nicole II Nouët oo 1750 Jacques Charpentier de Boisgibault (Grand Master of Waters and Forests, then president Cour des Aides)
			Elisabeth-Cathérine Nouët oo Michel-Antoine Ferrand (judge, Parlement of Paris)
			Claude-Guy Nouët (b. 1729, d. ?): succeeded father as judge, Parlement of Paris, 1748–at least 1771
	Louis Nouët de Montanglos (b. 1675 [Paris], d. c.1755): judge Châtelet, 1706–52, wife unknown	Louis Nouët d'Ormoy de Montanglos (b. c.1725 [Paris], d. ?): succeeded father as judge, Châtelet, 1752–at least 1775)	

Chart 3.6. (cont.)

I	II	III	IV
		Jacques Nouët (b. 1670s, d. ?): proctor, Parlement of Paris; oo Elisabeth Sergent	
			Etienne Nouët (b. 1715 [Paris], d. ?): general treasurer Naval Invalid Hospitals; secretary of the registry, Royal Treasury; royal secretary, 1767; wife unknown
			Antoine-Etienne Nouët (b. c.1750, d. ?): succeeded father as general treasurer Naval Invalid Hospitals, seigneur d'Andreze, Haute-Lages, and Tranzy; oo 1786 Denise-Charlotte Salernes (daughter general tax farmer)

Sources: Annuaire de la noblesse, vol. 79, 1930, p. 53; Bluche, "L'origine des magistrats du Parlement de Paris," pp. 86, 114, 174; Coustant, Chambre des Comptes, p. 729; Favre-Lejeune, Les secrétaires du roi, vol. 1, pp. 206–7; Woëlmont de Brumagne, Notices généalogiques, vol. 6, p. 244.

into bourgeois estate; the ennoblement of their families had been commenced by their fathers after their birth. Most of the noble families of the Châtelet were still rising within the themistocracy. Their nobility was both a consequence and a furtherance of professional accomplishments. But the socioprofessional patrimonies of most noble lieutenants, prosecutors, and judges of the Châtelet fundamentally resembled those of most of their bourgeois colleagues, whether in 1735 or 1789. The notable distinctions between aristocratic and bourgeois magistrates were differences in their fathers' seniority or rank within royal administration or the judiciary and perhaps differences in wealth. The nobility of 12 judges originated in the high magisterial or administrative offices held by their fathers or grandfathers, who had been the treasurers of Generalities, magistrates of sovereign courts, or *échevins* of Paris. Royal secretaryships in the Grand Chancellery (Paris) were the source for the nobility, either incipient or full, of some 30 Châtelet judges, and thus for almost two-thirds of those who were noble. All but a few of the fathers or paternal elders of these judges had exercised active professions or offices (some of which were ennobling) concurrently with their Chancellery secretaryships. In that, and most other respects, these Châtelet judges conformed to the general pattern of men and families ennobled by royal secretaryships between 1672 and 1789.

The secretaryships in the Grand Chancellery of Paris and in the twenty provincial chancelleries of France were possibly the most spectacular, but certainly the most numerous, of ennobling offices in Old Regime France.[84] The purchaser immediately acquired the material and other privileges of personal nobility. When he had served for twenty years or died in office, he gained even more than hereditary and transmissible nobility. He automatically acquired *noblesse de race*, or the retroactive ennoblement of the three preceding generations of his paternal ancestors, no matter what their occupations had been. No other office ennobled both posterity and the dead. In 1672, there were 240 secretaryships in the Grand Chancellery. Sixty additional were created in 1691, and the number was finally stabilized at 300, from 1727 to the end of the chancelleries in 1790. Between the years 1672 and 1789, 2,050 men (belonging to 1,737 families) purchased or inherited those offices: four-fifths of the office-holders (or 1,646) were commoners when they acquired the office; 303 were incipiently noble (and thus gained either accelerated ennoblement or *noblesse de race*); 111, or 5 percent, were fully noble.[85] Even more purchased or inherited the some 500 secretaryships in the twenty provincial chancelleries.

Originally the job of the secretaries had been to prepare, sign, and send the writs of justice and pardon that emanated from chancelleries. By the late seventeenth century, however, most of that work was done by professional clerks,

---

[84] The following description is drawn from Favre-Lejeune, *Les sécretaires du roi*, and David D. Bien, "The 'Secrétaires de Roi:' Absolutism, Corps, and Privilege under the Ancien Régime," in *De l'Ancien Régime à la Révolution française: Recherches et perspectives* (Göttingen: Vandenhaeck & Ruprecht, 1978), pp. 153–68.

[85] Favre-Lejeune, *Les secrétaires du roi*, pp. 13, 39.

and the secretaryship had become principally a sinecure that allowed other professional activity. A secretaryship in the Grand Chancellery was extremely expensive, costing 44,000 livres in 1672, 70,000 livres in 1704, 90,000 livres in 1731, and 120,000 livres in 1780.[86] A secretaryship required few formal qualifications and little work. The plutocratic and sinecuristic character of the office, and the putative *noblesse de race* of its holders, made it an easy object of derision for contemporaries: The ridiculously and contemptibly pretentious Monsieur Jourdain, of Molière's *Le bourgeois gentilhomme*, was a royal secretary. But the office had deeper realities.

One-third of the 2,050 secretaries who served in the Grand Chancellery between 1672 and 1789 came from the judiciary: 120 from the high robe (but only 30 from Parisian sovereign courts); 395 from the middle or lower robe, mainly bailliage, presidial, or tax courts (of which 78 were Châtelet notaries and 185 were barristers of Parlements). Another 31 percent were from finance officialdom, of which the majority were receivers, treasurers, or tax farmers. Bankers, wholesale merchants, shippers, or master artisans and manufacturers accounted for 15 percent of the royal secretaries, although their proportion increased over the century. Another 12 percent were various rentiers or men of the arts and the liberal professions (including Jean Racine, Jean-Baptiste Lully, and Baron d'Holbach). Only 6 percent were military officers.[87] A secretaryship was a favorite way to manage a professional *montée à Paris* for those with wealth and ambition. Sixty-seven percent of the secretaries in the Grand Chancellery were natives of the provinces, and about half of them spent their mature careers in Paris. Men bought a secretaryship late in their careers: The average age at acquisition was 46, and the average tenure was sixteen years. A large number died in office. Most secretaries of the period 1672 to 1789 (64% of the total) were mature judicial or administrative men, well established in their careers, who sought the advantages of chancellery office and its ennoblement for their progeny. There was high turnover of secretaryships: During the fifteen years 1774 to 1789, 266 men became secretaries within the company of 300 at the Grand Chancellery.[88] Although there was a high rate of marital endogamy among royal secretaries, there was little dynasticism, for we find that 85 percent of the 2,050 secretaries (or their families) sold, and thus relinquished, their office after one generation.

Chancelleries were attached to sovereign courts. Royal secretaries were therefore both high Crown officers and colleagues of the superior themistocracy, with a unique opportunity to cultivate social and professional relations with the latter. The office was an ideal placement for families that had capital and

---

[86] Ibid., p. 35. By comparison, the prices of the office of judge in the Parlement of Paris: 1682, 100,000 livres; 1701, 83,000 livres; 1731, 41,500 livres; 1771, 50,000 livres (Bluche, *Les magistrats du Parlement de Paris*, p. 167).

[87] Ibid., pp. 74–5.

[88] David D. Bien, "La réaction aristocratique avant 1789: L'Exemple de l'armée," *Annales: Economies, Sociétés, Civilisations*, 29 (1974): 46.

high professional ambitions in magistracy and administration. The preponderance of career royal officials among the secretaries suggests an essentially professional rather than social motivation behind the acquisition of secretaryships. So too, does the presence of bankers, *négociants*, forge-masters, and magnates of craft guilds, since these were the upper strata of the French bourgeoisie, many of them quasi-official, serving as judge–consuls, *échevins*, or merchants enjoying the monopoly of a royal charter. Most of the external recruitment of the higher royal magistracy and administration was from those social groups. For them, tenure as royal secretary formed an excellent bridge between private finance or commerce and public administration, as well as a patrimonial credential to support the candidacy of subsequent generations for magistracy.[89] Most of the 1,737 families of the Grand Chancellery did use secretaryships for professional aggrandizement, many of them with great success. Between 1672 and 1789, 152 sons and 110 grandsons of secretaries entered the Parlement, Chambre des Comptes, Cour des Aides, or Grand Conseil of Paris; 131 masters of petitions and intendants were the sons or grandsons of royal secretaries.[90] The advantages of the office were not merely social and professional.

The economic relationship between the monarchy and the royal secretaries was symbiotic. We may take as our example a secretaryship that might have been bought from the Crown in 1704, for 70,000 livres. The purchaser would receive about 3,000 livres a year from the Crown in salary (*gages*), or return on his purchase. If he died, after an average tenure of sixteen years, the Crown only had to pay back 48,000 livres of the purchase price; not until after twenty-three years would it have had to reimburse the full 70,000 livres. The Treasury had therefore in effect received a superb long-term loan at virtually no interest. If the incumbent or his family sold the office, the Treasury collected a few thousand more livres in transmittal fees and *droit annuel* from the new secretary. Royal secretaries were also subjected periodically to what were described as "salary increases." These were actually new, large capital sums levied on their company as a whole, which were to be reimbursed to them individually, and piecemeal, in the form of higher annual salaries over the years. The main pretext of this royal practice was the constantly growing purchase value of the office. In response to these ministerial pressures, with royal approval the company of secretaries contracted for loans from private investors, which the company then used to make large loans to the state. The secretaries profited, in the long term, from these ventures. In addition to salary, a secretary received from 1,000 to 2,000 livres a year in fees and emoluments and from investments made by the company. Since the value of his office continually appreciated, when he or his family sold, after twenty years, they gained from one-fourth to one-third over the amount originally paid for the office, considerably more than the interest

---

[89] Favre-Lejeune, *Les secrétaires du roi*, p. 84.
[90] Ibid., p. 87.

paid on most private loans and annuities. The office of royal secretary was also good collateral for a private loan or for installment purchase of another, more demanding office. The royal secretaryship was, in sum, an investment that profited the purchaser while aggrandizing his family materially, socially, and professionally, over subsequent generations. For ambitious bourgeois, it signified more than a *savonette à vilain*, because it conferred far more than nobiliary identity. That is why it was so desirable to rising families of the themistocracy. Nearly 50 percent of the aristocratic families that provided magistrates for the Parlement of Paris between 1715 and 1771 had originally acquired nobility through a royal secretaryship, most of them in the sixteenth or seventeenth century.[91]

C. The *parlementaires:* socioprofessional origins and development

Modern representations

The Parlement of Paris was the most politically assertive and aristocratic in composition of the Parisian courts during the eighteenth century. Those two qualities have preoccupied all modern historians of the institution, largely because the Parlement led the successful defiance of royal absolutism and reform that resulted in the convening of the Assembly of Notables in 1787 and of the Estates-General in 1789. The defiance has usually been explained, fully or partially, as an "aristocratic reaction" against ministerial authoritarianism. The aristocratic surface of the Parlement was indeed brilliant, and it has almost blinded modern historians of the institution.

In his massive social history of the eighteenth-century *parlementaires*, François Bluche became fascinated by the permutations of their nobility.[92] He did not, however, study these officials in their everyday exercise of judicial authority, their concrete vocation, their voices as judges, and thus their existence as themistocrats. Had Bluche done so, it is likely that his conception of them would have been different, and far less nobiliary in its cast. Bailey Stone, the most recent and most comprehensive political historian of the late eighteenth-century Parlement of Paris, has recounted the *parlementaires'* long struggle against the reformist policies of the late Old Regime monarchy and their general defense of corporatist order and privileges, but, like Bluche, Stone reduced their identity, mentality, and behavior to an aristocratic model.[93] The reduction is all the more curious since there is no evidence that there was an operational

---

[91] Bluche, *Les magistrats du Parlement de Paris*, p. 90.

[92] There were a total of 303 serving magistrates of the Parlement in 1715: 81.5% were fully noble at entry; 9.2% were incipiently noble; 4.8% were bourgeois. In 1771, the proportions were as follows, among 288 magistrates: 81% fully noble; 9% incipiently noble; 10% bourgeois. In 1789, the proportion of bourgeois remained 10% (ibid., pp. 77–85).

[93] Bailey Stone, *Parlement of Paris, 1774–1789*, and *The French Parlements and the Crisis of the Old Regime* (Chapel Hill: University of North Carolina Press, 1986).

quota, either formal or informal, for bourgeois in the eighteenth-century Parlement of Paris (or in the Grand Conseil, Chambre des Comptes, Cour des Aides, Cour des Monnaies, or Châtelet), or any specifically nobiliary exclusiveness.[94] Bluche, Stone, and other historians have read social outcome as social intention. They have not proceeded from the fact that the *parlementaires* were, above all else and self-consciously, professional and dynastic magistrates, the *summum* of themistocracy.

Lineages and vocation

In order to understand the socioprofessional constitution of the *parlementaires* historically, through their familial origins and development and thus their evolution as themistocrats, I have selected all of the judges who entered the Parlement of Paris in the decade 1760 to 1770.[95] In all important respects, those 95 young men formed a microcosm of the 951 magistrates and 590 families that composed the Parlement from 1715 to 1771, as Bluche has described them. (See Table 3.7.)

Offices or professions are known for the fathers of 89 of the 95 young judges (col. *E*, Table 3.7):

	N	%
Judge or magistrate, Parlement of Paris	36	40
Judge or magistrate, other sovereign court of Paris	15	17
Judge or magistrate, provincial sovereign court	2	2
Officer of other provincial court	4	4
Barrister	3	3
Superior finance administrator	10	11
Superior administrator of war	6	7
Other officer of royal administration	3	3
Military or naval officer	7	8
Banker or private financier	2	2

Sixty-six percent of the entrants were sons of the judiciary; another 18 percent were sons of royal administrators. These proportions resemble those among the Châtelet judges. But there are important differences. The dominant bloc among the young *parlementaires* of 1760 to 1770 was formed by the 36 (40%) who had followed their fathers into the Parlement of Paris. That bloc was reinforced by the 15 young men whose fathers were magistrates in other sovereign

[94] The only articulated social prejudice in recruitment Bluche found among *parlementaires* was directed against sons of financiers and wholesale merchants. That prejudice was against an activity presumed to be usurious and motivated by greed, not against an estate or social class (*Les magistrats du Parlement de Paris*, pp. 77–81).

[95] The source for the following analysis is Bluche's genealogical dictionary, "L'origine des magistrats du Parlement de Paris au XVIIIe siècle," supplemented by Favre-Lejeune, *Les secrétaires du roi*.

Table 3.7. *Entering judges, Parlement of Paris, 1760–1770*

A	B	C	D	E	F
*+Amelot de Châteauneuf, D. -J.	1760		6	Army colonel	c
*+Anjorrant, Cl. E.	1762	28	8	Judge, Parlement of Paris	gf, b
Aubin de Planoy, Ch. -L.	1762		3	Judge, Parlement of Paris	
Barbier d'Increville, J. -B. -R.	1768	26	no	Judge, presidial court Vitry	
*+Barillon de Morangis, A. -M.	1761	25	9	Judge, Parlement of Paris	gf
Berthelot de la Villeurnoy, C. -H.	1768	19	10	Officer of engineers	
*Bignon, J. -F.	1766	19	5	General advocate, Grand Conseil, Council of State	pu
Blondel, A. -L.	1765	18	no		
Bonnaire de Forges, A. -Ch.	1761	21	4	General prosecutor, Grand Conseil	
Bougainville, N. -L. de	1765	47	2	Royal secretary	
Boula de Nanteuil, A. -F.	1767	19	4	Judge, Parlement of Paris	b
Bourgevin de Vialart, Ch. -M.	1763		4	Commissioner of war	
Bourgevin de Vialart, Ch. -P.	1769	28	4	Commissioner of war	b
*Brétignières, A. -C. -R. de	1765	20	5	Judge, Parlement of Paris	
Brochant de Villiers, A. -J.	1767	22	3	Judge, Parlement of Paris	
Bruant des Carrières, J. -B.	1763	22	2	Judge, Chambre des Comptes	
Cachet de Montezan, L. de	1765	19	6	President, Parlement of Dombes	
*+Camus de Pontcarré de Viarmes, L. -J.	1767	20	8	Judge, Parlement of Paris	b
*+Camus de Pontcarré de Viarmes, L. -F.	1764	18	8	Judge, Parlement of Paris	u
Caze de la Bove, G. -L. de	1762	22	7	Judge, Parlement of Paris	
Chardon, D. -M. -A.	1765	35	2	Judge, Cour des Aides	
Charpentier, A. -P. -A.	1765	22	no		
Chuppin, C. -J. -N.	1767	23	4	Deputy prosecutor, Parlement of Paris	
Clément d'Étoges, A. -A.	1766	20	4	Judge, Parlement of Paris	gf
Clément de Blavette, A. -A.	1767	22	4	Judge, Chambre des Comptes	u,c
Clément de Givry, A. -L.	1768	22	4	Judge, Parlement of Paris	b
Cordier de Launay, L. -G. -R.	1769	23	5	Judge, Parlement of Paris	
Coupard de la Bloterie, M. -J.	1768	21	3	General receiver, royal domains, Generality of Tours	
Desmé du Buisson, J. -P.	1765		inc.	Captain of fusillers, royal secretary	
Desponty du Fresnoy, A.	1768	20	4	Lieutenant, French Guards	
Dompierre d'Hornoy, A. -M.	1763	21	2	Judge, Chambre des Comptes	
Du Jouhannel de Jenzac, J. -B.	1770	23	inc.	Royal prosecutor, tax court, Generality of Riom	
Du Trousset of d'Héricourt, B. -J.	1765	21	5	General commissioner, Navy	u
Dudoyer de Vauventriers, E. -H.	1768	40	3	Judge, Chambre des Comptes	
+Dupré de Saint-Maur, A. -P.	1761		7	Judge, Parlement of Paris	c
Ferrand, A. -F. -Cl.	1769	18	8	Judge, Parlement of Paris	mu
Flandre de Brunville, F. -A. de	1766	21	inc.	Tax farmer; royal secretary	
Forien de Saint-Juire, T. -F. -G.	1765	49	2	Mayor of Poitiers; treasurer of war	
Fourmestraux de Briffeuille, I. -J. de	1767	26	3	Treasurer, Generality of Lille	

G	H	I	J
	Royal letter, 1580	Fish merchant, bourgeois Orléans early 1500s	6
Judge, Parlement of Paris	Parlement of Paris, 1520s	Seigneurial landlord, 1400s	6
	Royal secretaryship, 1704	Royal secretary; clerk to Minister of war Louvois	2
		Barrister, late 1600s	3
	Royal secretaryship, 1530s	Apothecary, Issoire, 1400s	7
	Seigeneurial 1400s	Seigneurial landlord, early 1400s	0
	General advocate, Parlement of Paris, 1620	Barrister, late 1500s	5
	Chambre des Comptes, 1661	Merchant, Le Mans, late 1500s	3
	Royal secretaryship, 1742	Deputy prosecutor, Châtelet, early 1600s	3
Lieutenant General of Police, Paris	Royal secretaryship, 1705	Wine-grower, Vierzon, early 1660s	3
	Paymastership, household cavalry, 1600s	Royal prosecutor, Admiralty Court, late 1500s	5
	Paymastership, household cavalry, 1600s	Royal prosecutor, Admiralty Court, late 1500s	5
	Parlement of Normandy, early 1600s	Barrister, Rouen, mid-1500s	6
	Cour des Monnaies, 1703	Merchant, judge-consul Paris, early 1600s	2
Royal prosecutor, Châtelet	Chambres des Comptes, 1727	Clerk to Finance Minister Fouquet, mid 1600s	3
President, Chambre des Comptes, Dijon	Princely letter, 1620	Magistrate, Parlement of Dombes, early 1600s	4
	"Echevinage" at Lyon, 1541	Mayor, Auxonne, late 1400s	8
President, Parlement of Provence	"Echevinage" at Lyon, 1541	Mayor, Auxonne, late 1400s	8
	Chambre des Comptes, Montpellier, 1597	Tax collector for Dauphiné, early 1500s	5
	Cour des Aides, 1720	Barrister, Parlement of Paris	3
Treasurer, Tours	Royal secretaryship, 1699	Silk merchant, Paris, mid-1600s	3
Judge, Chambre des Comptes	Royal letter, 1711	Apothecary, Arles, mid-1600s	3
Judge, Parlement of Paris	Royal letter, 1711	Apothecary, Arles, mid-1600s	3
	Royal letter, 1711	Apothecary, Arles, mid-1600s	3
	Royal secretaryship, 1607	Royal valet, 1500s	5
	Royal secretaryship, 1728	Tax officer; royal secretary	2
	Royal secretaryship, 1753	Captain of fusilliers	0
	Royal secretaryship, 1680	Shoemaker, Paris, late 1500s	3
Judge, Parlement of Paris	Chambre des Comptes, 1744	"Echevin" and mayor, Abbeville, mid-1600s	3
	Office, Finance Tribunal, 1737	Royal finance officer, Riom	1
General advocate, Montpellier	Royal secretaryship, 1655	Criminal lieut. bailliage Saint-Quentin	4
	Royal secretaryship, 1708	Commissioner of war	2
	Royal secretaryship, early 1500s	Seigneurial lord late 1400s	6
President, Parlement of Paris	Royal letter, 1574	Physician to the king, mid-1500s	6
	Royal secretaryship, 1750	Household officer, duchess of Burgandy, 1600s	2
	Mayorial office, 1722	Tax collector and mayor, Poitiers	1
	Finance office, 1718	Merchant, Lille, early 1500s	3

A	B	C	D	E	F
Fréteau de Saint-Just, E. -M.	1764	19	4	Judge, Chambre des Comptes	
Fumeron de la Berlière, L. de	1770	22	3	Commissioner of war	
Gaillifet, L. -F. -A. de	1768	20	9	President, Parlement of Provence	
Gars de Frémainville, A. -L. -A. de	1762		4	Judge, Parlement of Paris	
*Goujon de Thuisy, J. -G. -E. de	1769	21	8	Judge, Parlement of Paris	pu, mu
Gueau de Gravelle de Reverseau, J. -H. -I	1761	22	2	Barrister, Parlement of Paris	
Guerrier de Bezance, P. -F. -B.	1763	26	8	Judge, presidial court, Clermont-Ferrand	
Guillaume de Chavaudon, L. -M. -N.	1762		3	Judge, Parlement of Paris	gu,c
Guillemeau de Fréval, C. -F.	1765	20	5	Judge, Grand Conseil	
Hanmer-Claybrooke, A. -A. -J. de	1769		5	Military officer	
Hocquart de Mony, L. -Cl. -F.	1763	22	8	General treasurer, artillery of France	c
*Joly de Fleury de Brionne, A. -G. -M.	1767	21	5	General prosecutor, Parlement of Paris	pu,c,b
* + L'Escalopier, A. -J. -F. de	1763		7	Judge, Parlement of Paris	gf
La Bourdonnaye de Blossac, A. -C. -M.	1767	23	13	Judge, Parlement of Paris	mu
La Guillaumie, J. N. II de	1760	20	4	Judge, Parlement of Paris	gf,u,c
La Porte de Meslay, J. -B. -F. de	1766	23	4	Judge, Parlement of Paris	
Lambert des Champs de Morel, J. -B. -L.	1763		4	Judge, Chambre des Comptes	c
Langois de Pommeuse, A. -H.	1766	23	4	Judge, Parlement of Paris	u,c
* + Le Fèvre d'Ormesson de Noiseau, A. -I.	1770	17	7	Judge, Parlement of Paris	u,c
* + Le Fèvre d'Ormesson, H. -F. de Paule	1768	17	7	Judge, Parlement of Paris	pu,mu,c
Le Jay, A. -C. -L.	1766	29	7		
*Le Peletier de Rosambo, L. V.	1765	18	6	President, Parlement of Paris	gf,u,c
* + Le Rebours de Saint-Mard, J. -B. -A.	1767	21	7	President, Parlement of Paris	gf
Le Riche du Perché de Cheveigné, F. -A.	1766	46	3	Judge, Parlement of Paris	mu
* + Malon de Bercy, M. -E. -C. de	1766	21	11	Judge, Parlement of Paris	c
Marquet, J. -M.	1767	21	3	General receiver taxes, Generality of Lyon	
Masson de Meslay, J. -P.	1763	21	3	President, Chambre des Comptes	
Masson de Vernon, J. -A.	1767	19	3	Merchant West Indies Co.; royal secretary	1st c
Maulnorry, C. -B. de	1766	19	4	Barrister	u
*Maupeou, C. -V. -R. de	1767		7	President, Parlement of Paris; Chancellor	b
*Maupeou, R. -A. -A. de	1764	18	7	President, Parlement of Paris; Chancellor	gf,gu,c
Mauperché de Fontenay, A. de	1767		8	Deputy prosecutor, Parlement of Paris	
Mégret de Sérilly, A. -J. -F.	1768	22	3	Judge, Parlement of Paris; Intendant	
Meulan d'Ablois, M. -P. -C. de	1762	23	4	General receiver of taxes, Generalities of Riom and Paris	
Michau de Montblin, H. -L. -J.	1760		4	Judge, Grand Conseil; Intendant	u
* + Montholon, N. de	1761	25	7	Naval officer	1st c
* + Nicolaÿ, A. -C. -M. de	1767	20	9	President, Chambre des Comptes	u
Noblet, A. -T.	1770	27	4	Chief recorder, Chambre des Comptes	
Oursin, J. P.	1765	21	3	General receiver of taxes, Generality of Caen	b
Oursin de Bures, J. -B. -L.	1770	22	3	General receiver of taxes, Generality of Caen	b

G	H	I	J
Judge, Parlement of Paris	Royal secretaryship, 1662	Royal secretary	2
	Royal Secretaryship, 1705	Bourgeois, Poitiers, mid-1600s	2
	Seigneurial fiefs, 1400s	Seigneurial landlord, late 1400s	4
	Royal secretaryship, 1676	Tanner, Meulan, early 1600s	3
	Royal letter, 1523	Merchant and "échevin," Reims, 1400s	7
	Royal secretaryship, 1737	Magistrate, "élection" of Chartres	3
	Municipal office, Toulouse, 1522	Bourgeois, Toulouse	4
Judge, Parlement of Paris	Royal letter, 1704	Municipal judge, Troyes, mid-1500s	5
	Royal secretaryship, 1636	Royal physician, late 1500s	4
		Seigneur and chevalier, early 1600s	1
Tax farmer	1536	Provost, Ste.-Menehould, early 1500s	5
Intendant	Parlement of Brittany, 1629	Barrister, Parlement of Burgundy, late 1400s	7
	"Echevinage" Paris; judiciary, 1500s	Merchant, Paris, early 1500s	7
Judge, Parlement of Paris	Seigeneurial fiefs, 1427	Seigneurial landlord, early 1400s	5
	Royal secretaryship, 1652	Barrister, Parlement of Paris, early 1600s	4
	Royal secretaryship, 1671	Apothecary to kin, early 1600s	4
	Chambre des Comptes, 1632	Prosecutor, Admiralty court, late 1500s	4
Judge, Parlement of Paris	Royal secretaryship, 1680	Deposits clerk, Palais de Justice	4
Intendant	Royal secretaryship, 1598	Prosecutor, Parlement of Paris, late 1400s	7
Judge, Parlement of Paris	Royal secretaryship, 1568	Proctor, Parlement of Paris, late 1400s	7
	Royal secretaryship, 1543	Judge, Chambre des Comptes, mid-1500s	1
Minister of state	Royal secretaryship, 1637	Bailliage officer and syndic, Le Mans, late 1400s	8
General advocate, Cour des Aides	Seigneurial fiefs, early 1500s	Barrister, Parlement of Paris, early 1500s	6
	Finance office, 1700	Valet to the queen, mid-1600s	3
	Royal letter, 1468	Seigneurial landlord	8
	Royal letter, 1742	Resin merchant, Bordeaux and Paris	1
Tax farmer	Royal secretaryship, 1724	Merchant, Orléans, late 1500s	3
	Royal secretaryship, 1724	Merchant, Orléans, late 1500s	1
	Chambre des Comptes, Nevers, 1628	Bourgeois, Nevers, early 1500s	5
	Royal letter, 1586	Notary, Châtelet, mid-1500s	7
Judge, Parlement of Paris	Royal letter, 1586	Notary, Châtelet, mid-1500s	7
	Royal letter, 1498	Seigneurial landlord, Ile-de-France	1
General of the Army	Royal secretaryship, 1719	Mayor, St.-Quentin, early 1600s	4
	Royal secretaryship, 1668	Valet to Louis XIII, early 1600s	3
President, Parlement of Paris	Royal secretaryship, 1671	Tax collector, Brittany, late 1600s	3
General prosecutor, St. Domingo	Judicial offices, mid-1500s	General advocate, Parlement of Paris	5
President, Parlement of Paris	Parlement of Toulouse, 1491	Seigneurial landlord and magistrate	8
	Royal secretaryship, 1651	Tax collector, Brittany, mid-1600s	3
	Royal secretaryship, 1705	Seigneurial landlord, Normandy, early 1600s	2
	Royal secretaryship, 1705	Seigneurial landlord, Normandy, early 1600s	2

A	B	C	D	E	F
Outremont, A. -F. d'	1766	20	2	Barrister; secretary to duke of Lorraine	
Pernon, L. -C.	1766	23	3		
Phélippes de la Houssaye, A. -L.	1765	26	3	Army general, governor of Maubeuge	
Radix, J. -L.	1762		3		
Richard de Neusy, C. -M. -B.	1763	26	no		
Ricouart d'Hérouville, A. -B. -J.	1763		4	Maritime Intendant of Flanders	
Roslin d'Ivry, J. -M.	1768	19	3	General tax farmer	
Royer, H. -J.	1768	29	no	Chief magistrate, seneschalcy court, Arles	
Selle, C. -F. de	1769	20	3	Judge, Parlement of Paris	
Serre de Saint-Romain, J. de	1765		6	Judge, Chambre des Comptes	
Talon, J. -B.	1762		no	Judge, bailliage court, Châlons	c
Tandeau de Marsac, G.	1766	29	inc.	Treasurer, Generality of Limoges	mu
Tavernier de Boulogne, J. -B.	1770	21	3	General receiver of taxes, Generality of Poitiers	c
Thévenin de Tanlay, É. -J. -B.	1770	21	5	Judge, Parlement of Paris	c
Thomé, F. -P.	1762		4	General treasurer, galley fleet	u,c
Vin de Galande, J. -B.	1765	20	inc.	Banker; royal secretary, Paris	

Key to column headings: A, family name (* patrilineal ancestor in Parlement before 1700; + before 1600); *B,* entry year; *C,* age at entry; *D,* degree or generation of entrant's nobility; *E,* principal office or profession of father; *F,* consanguine or close marital relatives in Parlement during years preceding or at time of entry; *G,* main office or profession of entrant's father-in-law; *H,* source and beginning date of family's ennoblement; *I,* office or occupation of earliest known ancestor; *J,* number of generations in entrant's patrilineage that preceded him in judicial, administrative, or municipal offices of state.

courts of Paris (most of whom had close relatives in the Parlement). Only 4 of the 95 young judges were sons of royal secretaries (as against 26 of 130 young judges in the Châtelet). But thirty-seven (41%) of the ninety distinct patrilineal families had originally been ennobled by a royal secretaryship, a proportion not greatly different from the 62 percent of Châtelet judges, in the period 1735 to 1789, whose full or incipient nobility derived from a secretaryship. And in contradiction to the legend of aristocratic exclusiveness in recruitment for the Parlement, there were fewer sons of military and naval officers (and thus of the sword nobility) than there were sons who were either bourgeois (6) or only incipiently noble (5) when they entered the Parlement.

In addition to the 36 young judges who were sons of *parlementaires*, at least 10 had uncles or brothers in the Court when they entered (col. *F,* Table 3.7). Another 7 had close cousins in the Parlement. If one combines these groups of entering judges, with close relatives on the bench, the internal dynastic component in recruitment for the years 1760 to 1770 rises to 53 (or 59.5%) of 89

G	H	I	J
	Royal letter, 1759	Barrister	1
	Royal secretaryship, c. 1711; Cours des Monnaies, Lyon	President, Cour des Monnaies, Lyon	1
	Seigneurial and military, 1600s	Chevalier, royal commandant, Mézières, 1600s	0
	Royal secretaryship, 1724	Merchant, Lyons, late 1600s	1
Military officer	Royal secretaryship, early 1600s	Accountant, military provisioning, early 1600s	3
	Royal secretaryship, 1736	Collector of excise taxes, Poitou, late 1600s	3
		Barrister, Arles, early 1700s	2
Naval officer	Royal secretaryship, 1741	Household finance officer to duke of Chartres	2
General tax farmer	Seigneurial fiefs, 1500s	Seigneurial landlord, Languedoc, late 1400s	4
		Magistrate, Rosières (Picardy), mid-1500s	5
	Finance office, 1743	Lieutenant of police, St.-Vienne (Marche), 1600s	2
	Royal secretaryship, 1731	Judge, "élection" in Picardy, early 1600s	3
	Royal letter, 1652	Mayor, La Rochelle, late 1500s	4
	"Echevinage," Lyons, 1661	Merchant, Romans, early 1600s	4
	Royal secretaryship, 1760	Grocer, judge-consul, Paris, early 1600s	3

(*Notes to Table 3.7, cont.*) In column *F*, the abbreviations are *b*–brother; *c*–cousin; *gf*–grandfather; *gu*–granduncle; *mu*–maternal uncle; *pu*–paternal uncle; *u*–uncle. In column I, "same" means same as in column H.
Principal sources: Antoine, *Le gouvernement;* François Bluche, "L'origine des magistrats du Parlement de Paris au XVIIIe siècle"; Favre-Lejeune, *Les secrétaires du roi.*

entering judges. There were, in fact, only forty-two authentic vacancies – that is, forty-two positions that were not in dynastic preferment – among the ninety-five official vacancies on the junior bench of the Parlement between 1760 and 1770. Ten of those genuine vacancies were filled by sons of judges or other magistrates in the Grand Conseil, Chambre des Comptes, and Cour des Aides – that is, by sons of men who were almost the professional peers of the *parlementaires.* When the *parlementaires* recruited from the judiciary, but outside their own consanguinal and marital ranks, then, they preferred the sons of other sovereign court themistocrats, not sons of the middle or lesser robe. Another twelve positions were filled by sons of high-ranking royal administrators, the bureaucratic counterparts of sovereign court judges. Both of these patterns are evidence of *professional* exclusiveness, not aristocratic exclusiveness.

Twenty of the vacant judgeships (about one-fifth of the total) were obtained by young men who had no discernible close relatives in the Parlement and whose families did not belong to the superior ranks of the judiciary or administration. The fathers of 7 new judges were military or naval officers. (Their families are examined on pp. 168–9.) Four fathers were tax farmers, wholesale merchants, or bankers (and all of them were also either royal secretaries or descendants of royal secretaries). One was a provincial treasurer of war. Four were magistrates or judges in important provincial courts or finance courts; only two fathers were barristers. Three of the 6 young men from the middle robe were noble, but the families of most had served in officialdom for two or more generations before they obtained a judgeship in the Parlement: These were distinct promotions. But, paradoxically, those promotions of "new men" are comprehensible in terms of *parlementaire* dynasticism. A presidial judge at Vitry or Clermont-Ferrand, a royal prosecutor at Arles or in the finance tribunal at Riom, a barrister of the Parlement: Such judicial officers replicated earlier generations in the families that had become dynastic in the Parlement by the eighteenth century, as will soon be demonstrated. When a retiring dynast of the Parlement (whose sons were already placed) sold his office to the son of a presidial judge at Vitry, he very likely sold to a young man who professionally resembled his own grandfather or an earlier ancestor. The "new men" would actually have been familiar types, for dynasticism conveyed memory.[96] When they elevated those new men, the *parlementaires* both honored family memory and strengthened the future of professional dynasticism by rejuvenation.

The marriage of these young judges (col. *G*, Table 3.7), usually within seven years of entry to the Parlement, almost duplicated their own socioprofessional origins, and thus perpetuated claustral dynasticism. Thirty of their marriages can be analyzed socioprofessionally. Nineteen of the judges were sons of sovereign court judges, and they married daughters of sovereign court judges. Another 3 were sons of sovereign court judges, and they married daughters of high-ranking administrators. Reputable families of the middle or lower ranks of the judiciary or administration had little chance of gaining entry to the Parlement of Paris by marriage, for *parlementaires* did not marry the daughters of such families. Those families were not alone in that relative exclusion for only 3 of the 30 young judges married the daughters of military or naval families. The rarity of such marriages paralleled the rarity of such patrimony among Parlement judges. On this institutional terrain, as in the Châtelet, there was no unity of robe and sword.

The solidarity that is manifest in the recruitment of *parlementaires* (manifest through patrimonies and marriages) is not that of aristocrats; it is the corporate

---

[96] It is probable that orally transmitted memories of ancestors reached far back in themistocratic families, independently of genealogies and other documentation. It is also probable that grandparents were the decisive agents in the transmission of memory. My study of themistocratic families during the seventeenth and eighteenth centuries suggests that grandfathers commonly survived through the adolescence of their grandsons and lived in close proximity to them, often in commensal family households. Thus, the young would have known of their great-grandfathers and, in many cases, of their great-great-grandfathers through the oral agency of grandparents. That long memory, which could span almost two centuries and was undoubtedly a complex mixture of lies, legends, and facts, was vested in each present generation.

solidarity of vocational kinsmen or peers. When recruitment was not dynastic, it expressed the preference of those at the pinnacle of the themistocracy for candidates whose patrimonies were vested, and proven, in offices and responsibilities that bore comparison with the Parlement of Paris, and thus for sons of the supreme judiciary and administration. The barrier to admission that is visible was not any requirement of nobility; it was the requirement that the majority of aspirants come from a patrimony in high magistracy or administration. Such patrimony incidentally meant, in all but a few cases, an aspirant who was noble, but that barrier also excluded many potential candidates who were noble.[97]

The pattern of recruitment for the Parlement of Paris was remarkably stable from 1653 to 1789. We consistently find a father–son dynastic staffing of 30 to

[97] Hamscher, *Parlement of Paris after the Fronde,* carefully examined the 208 judges who entered the Parlement of Paris between 1653 and 1673. Fifty-eight (28%) were sons of judges or magistrates of the Parlement. Forty-three (21%) were sons of masters of petitions, councillors, or secretaries of state, and all but a few of those high officials had been *parlementaires.* Therefore, the father–son dynastic component of recruitment was in the range of 40–45%, as between 1760 and 1770. Thirty-nine (19%) were sons of magistrates in other Parisian sovereign courts, and many of them undoubtedly had close relatives in the Parlement before they entered. Another 7 were sons of provincial *parlementaires.* Thus, 71% were sons of sovereign court magistrates. Dynasticism in recruitment (grandsons, sons, brothers, nephews, first cousins) was probably 50–60%, as in the years 1760 to 1770. Thirty-five percent of the 208 were grandsons of sovereign court magistrates. For there to have been such high percentages of entrants from dynastic families of the high robe in the period 1653 to 1673, there had to have been basic continuity in recruitment for the Parlement stretching back at least two generations before the 1650s, or to at least 1600, and thus well before offices in Parisian sovereign courts became ennobling. As for sons of the sword nobility: "Family background in the sword was a mere 2.4%, thus calling into question a seventeenth-century application of Bluche's thesis of professional interaction between robe and sword" (ibid., p. 42). But, as the Parlement between 1760 and 1770 reveals, Bluche's own prosopographical evidence contradicts his thesis that there was such interaction during the late Old Regime. Some 20% of the 208 young judges studied by Hamscher came from patrimonies outside sovereign court magistracy or superior royal administration, slightly higher than the percentage of "new men" between 1760 and 1770. All but a few of them were commoners or incipient nobles from families of the middle ranks of the judiciary and administration. Hamscher correctly read their promotion as the expression of robe professionalism both within the Parlement and among the promoted families. Many more such men were admitted than sons or merchants, bankers, or military officers, as between 1760 and 1770. Hamscher's prosopography suggests that the ennoblement of *parlementaire* offices in 1644 had little effect on recruitment for those offices. The only significant difference in recruitment for the Parlement in the years 1653 to 1673 and 1760 to 1770 was not in social provenance. It was the fact that during the former period 67 (32%) entering judges had served in other offices, usually for less than seven years: The majority of them came from other Parlements and sovereign courts (29) or from the Châtelet (15). Many of them probably belonged to *parlementaire* families, although that was not computed by Hamscher. He did identify the fathers-in-law of 165 of the 208 judges of the earlier period: Fifty-six percent married daughters of sovereign court magistrates, and more than half of them married the daughters of *parlementaires.* Most of the remainder married daughters of superior royal administrators or officers of judiciary. Only 7 (4.2%) of these 165 young judges married daughters of the military aristocracy (ibid., pp. 32–53). Here again, the continuity with late eighteenth-century *parlementaire* behavior is striking. Stone (*Parlement of Paris, 1774–1789*) gave summary descriptions of the 71 lay judges who entered the Parlement during the last sixteen years of the Old Regime: Twenty-seven (38%) were from *parlementaire* lineages; 28 (39%) were from families in other sovereign courts or high royal administration; 8 (11%) were sons of other judicial or administrative fathers (most of whom were bourgeois); another 8 were either sons of military officers or came from families that were primarily military (Stone, *Parlement*, p. 30).

40 percent. This meant an actual patrilineal dynastic composition among the judges of well over 50 percent, since many sons served concurrently with their fathers. We also find a 20 to 25 percent prehension on recruitment by families in other sovereign courts. Thus 50 to 65 percent of vacancies were reserved, by the high and ennobled robe, for sons of the high and ennobled robe, and the great majority of the remaining 35 to 50 percent of vacancies were reserved for sons of either high administration or the middle ranks of the judiciary. Most of the few remaining vacancies were awarded to candidates from the lesser robe and administration.[98] Such recruitment was both other – and far more politically consequential – than nobiliary monopoly. It promoted the self-preservation of a nearly autonomous professional caste, one capable of defining itself both in qualified affinity with its subordinate colleagues – the middle ranks of the judiciary and administration – and in contradistinction to the rest of the French aristocracy, to the bourgeoisie of manufacturing, commerce, and banking, even to the monarchy itself and its ministers of state.

The histories of these *parlementaire* families, of their rise and then convergence (or mutual selection) in the Parlement of Paris, are histories of vocation, not of nobility. In most cases, nobility was no more than a late product, or epiphenomenon, of vocation. The family histories that preceded the young judges of 1760 to 1770 illuminate that professional truth of the Parlement of Paris.

Patrilineage in royal officialdom, or the number of generations of an entrant's family that preceded him in vocations of judiciary or administration is given for 92 of these 95 judges (col. *J* Table 3.6). The total number of such elders or ancestors is 372. Four generations was the average number of predecessors in royal officialdom among the 92 young judges; that is equivalent in years to more than a century. But that average is insufficiently expressive.

---

[98] In these crucial respects, the eighteenth-century Parlement was not unique among the sovereign courts of Paris. The Grand Conseil was the second court of Paris in authority and prestige. By Bluche's estimate, some 65% of the judges who served on the Grand Conseil between 1690 and 1791 were fully or incipiently noble when they entered office. But the main patterns of professional recruitment for the Grand Conseil resembled those for the Châtelet and the Parlement, despite the higher proportion of nobles than in the former court and the lower proportion than in the latter. I have examined the 86 judges who entered the court from 1760 to 1790, from Bluche's compendium, "Les magistrats du Grand Conseil au XVIIe siècle (1690–1791)." Fifteen percent were sons, nephews, or brothers of Grand Conseil judges; a further 13% were sons, nephews, or brothers of magistrates in other sovereign courts (mostly Parisian). The component of family and corporate dynasticism was therefore at least 28%. They accounted for about half of all noble judges among the 86. Of the remaining 62 judges, slightly more than half were sons of barristers of the Parlement of Paris or of magistrates in the Châtelet, provincial bailliage courts, and finance tribunals. Most of the remainder were sons of finance officers, many of whom had been ennobled by a royal secretaryship. Thus, most of the nobles were scions of magisterial families and most of the commoners were also sons of the judiciary, who would become noble through career service in the Grand Conseil. Exclusions, if they occurred, were socially dualistic: They affected bourgeois whose patrimony was not professionally suitable or distinguished, and nobles without patrimony in themistocracy or high administration. These criteria of selection were far more precise, vivid, and exclusionary than criteria of estate.

Ancestors in officialdom	Entering judges	
	N	%
0	3	3
1	10	11
2–3	36	39
4–6	30	33
7 or more	13	14

As many of these judges had 7 or more lineal predecessors in civil offices, and thus a vocational heritage of more than two hundred years, as had only 1 such ancestor or none at all. Forty-three (or 47%) of the 92 were at least the fifth patrilineal generation of their families in officialdom, and 24 of the remaining 49 judges were the fourth generation. All but a few of these men belonged to families that had devoted themselves originally to the judicial robe and the administrative pen between the late fifteenth and early seventeenth centuries and that had remained constant in state offices (most of them venal-hereditary) until the end of the Old Regime.

The data reveal some decisive relations between early patrilineal career, hereditary ennoblement of the family, and subsequent vocations of descendants. I have calculated the origin of nobility and degree (or generations) of nobility possessed by the descendant judges of 1760 to 1770 (cols. *H* and *D*, Table 3.7). In doing so, I use the rule employed by Bluche, which is the same rule employed by the royal genealogists of the late seventeenth and eighteenth centuries: If an ancestor had served a sufficient tenure in an office that was endowed with ennobling stature after 1644, the hereditary nobility of his patrilineal descendants is dated from that tenure, even if the office was not ennobling when held by the ancestor. (The nobiliary status of almost all of these *parlementaire* families had in fact been investigated and certified by royal genealogists.)

Only 10 of the earliest known ancestors (col. I, Table 3.7) were primarily seigneurial landlords, in the fifteenth and sixteenth centuries. Six ancestors were granted noble title before 1579 for possession of seigneurial fiefs or by royal letter of ennoblement; 3 were ennobled by offices of state or military service. Six of these originally seigneurial families chose and sustained magisterial or administrative vocations. The La Bourdonnayes de Bloissac, in Brittany, were probably the oldest of these families: Their aristocratic title had been certified as early as 1427. Their professions were primarily regional and military until the mid-seventeenth century. From then on, during the five generations that preceded Anne-Charles-Marie (1762), they were continuously judges and presidents of either the Parlement of Brittany or the Parlement of Paris, closely resembling the Argouges de Fleury of the Parlement and Châtelet. The Anjorrants, seigneurs in Berry, entered the Parlement in 1520 and remained there for eight successive generations before Claude-Euloge in 1762. The Duprès de Saint-Maur gained retroactive nobility through a royal secretaryship and judgeship in the Chambre des Comptes of Paris early in the sixteenth century and remained judges in the Chambre des Comptes and the Parlement for seven subsequent generations. The Malons de Bercy were ennobled in 1468 by seigneurial fiefs near Vendôme and service to the Crown. In the early sixteenth century, the family entered the Parlement of Paris. Subsequently, during the seven generations that preceded Maximilien-Emmanuel (1766), they were magistrates of the Parlements of Paris, Brittany, and Lorraine and of the Grand Conseil. The Oursins were seigneurs in western Normandy for at least two generations before they became royal secretaries and general receivers of taxes at La Rochelle and then Caen, early in the eighteenth century. They were financial administrators for two generations before the young brothers entered the Parlement in 1765 and 1770. The Serres de Saint-Roman were seigneurial (in Languedoc) for six generations, until Etienne (father of Jacques, 1766) became judge of the Chambre des Comptes in 1744. The Gallifets, of Dauphiné, were provincial nobles from 1487, but between 1614 and the 1780s, 3 of them were judges of the Parlement of Provence.

Only three of the ten old (or at least originally) seigneurial families had an essentially military, rather than magisterial or administrative, patrilineage. For two hundred years, the Berthelots were principally army officers, but the father of Charles-Honorine (1768) also served as a diplomatic agent of the Crown, in Italy, during the Seven Years' War. The Mauperchés of the Ile-de-France were dynastic officers of the Royal Guard since the mid-sixteenth century; however, the father of Auguste (1767) was deputy prosecutor of the Parlement (1733–71). Anne-Léon Phélippes de la Houssaye (1765) was the only one of these scions whose patrilineage seems to have been purely military, but we find that his maternal grandfather, Louis-François Simonnet, had been a judge of the Parlement from 1729 to 1754.

All but two or three of the ten originally seigneurial or *chevaleresque* families had moved into magisterial or administrative vocations, in at least one branch, long before their descendant entered the Parlement of Paris between 1760 and 1770. Ironically, 3 of the remaining 5 judges who were the sons of noble military or naval officers belonged to families that were primarily magisterial or administrative in vocation. Denis-Jean Amelot de Châteauneuf (1760) descended from a fish merchant at Orléans. The grandson of that merchant was a barrister who was ennobled for administrative services and then became president of the Parlement of Paris in 1586. Following him, for three successive generations until the father of Denis-Jean (1760), the Amelots were judges of the Parlement and the Grand Conseil and intendants of provinces. Aphrodise Desponty du Fresnoy (1768) was the son of a lieutenant in the French Guards regiment, but the preceding three generations of his lineage had been Parisian magistrates and financial administrators. The father of Nicolas de Montholon (1761) was a naval officer, yet all of his patrilineal ancestors back to the early sixteenth century had been judges of the Parlement or Châtelet. Amelot, Desponty, and Montholon were cases of return to a long family tradition of magisterial service after the hiatus of a paternal military career.

Thus, when one examines the judges whose distant family origins or source of nobility was seigneurial and, more immediately, those whose fathers were noble officers of the army or navy, one mainly finds lineages of magistracy and civil administration, not lineages of the sword. The Berthelots, Phélippes de la Houssaye, and Hanmer-Claybrookes were the only families of strictly military patrilineage among the ninety. The last were relative parvenus: They were English royalists who emigrated to France during Cromwell's protectorate, and the first of them to enter the French army (the Boufflers-Walloon regiment) was the father of Antoine-Albert (1769). There were only two sons of authentic sword-noble families (the Berthelots and Phélippes); they were as rare among the judges of 1760 to 1770 as the two sons of bankers.

Sixteen of the earliest known ancestors of the entering judges were merchants, artisans, or apothecaries, between the late 1400s and early 1600s, 11 of them in provincial towns; 2 others were simply provincial bourgeois (probably rentiers). Nine were barristers, solicitors, or notaries, of which 6 were Parisian. This group of twenty-seven families resemble the root families of most Châtelet themistocrats. Sons or grandsons of most of these ancestors were placed in royal or municipal offices. They were ennobled (during the sixteenth or seventeenth century) by those offices, by purchase of a royal secretaryship, or by royal letter for services rendered to the Crown. All persevered in officialdom until the end of the Old Regime.

Two families are particularly representative of the other Parlement of Paris families. The Brochants were one of the newest to officialdom of these twenty-seven families. Mathurin, the ancestor, was a cloth merchant and judge–consul of Paris in 1639. His son succeeded him as merchant and consul, but his grandson was placed in a judgeship of the Cour des Monnaies and ennobled by twenty years' service. The latter's son and his grandson (André-Joachim, 1767) were both judges of the Parlement. The Barillons de Morangis were venerable in officialdom. Pierre was a bourgeois apothecary at Issoire (Auvergne) at the end of the fifteenth century. His son was sent to Paris, as secretary to Chancellor Du Prat (who was also a native of Issoire), and this son bought a royal secretaryship in 1534. All but one of the five subsequent paternal generations of the family were judges of the Chambre des Comptes or Parlement of Paris. The most significant difference between the Brochants and the Barillons was in chronology, not in social origin or substantive development. The most superficial difference between them was degree of nobility during the 1760s: third-generation, for André-Joachim Brochant; ninth-generation, for Antoine-Marie de Barillon.

The earliest known ancestors, in thirty-four of the eighty-seven families (col. I, Table 3.7), were officers in the magistracy (16), tax administration (7), municipal government (7), and war provisioning or central royal administration (4).

How many generations did those families spend in officialdom before they attained positions that ultimately ennobled?

One generation	14 families
Two generations	10 families
Three generations	5 families
Four generations	3 families

Fourteen families, we see, attained such a position, or hereditary ennoblement by a royal secretaryship, during the first generation in officialdom, but eighteen families did so only after two to four generations in civil offices. For the majority of these thirty-two families (as for most of the other fifty-five) the path to aristocracy was a long, multi-generational path of vocation, and one that these families all continued to travel after they became noble.

There were eighty-one noble families. The source of ennoblement is known for eighty of the eighty-one (col. *H*, Table 3.7): a royal secretaryship (37); judicial office (16, and most retroactive); royal or princely letter (12); ownership of seigneurial fiefs (6); financial or other administrative office (3); other (1). The largest number of families, thirty-seven, were ennobled by a royal secretaryship, as with the noble families in the Châtelet. Sixteen of these royal secretaries were the first known generation of their lineages to hold state office, but they had exercised some office for several years before they purchased the secretaryship. Fourteen other Parlement of Paris families that were ennobled by a secretaryship had held state or municipal offices for one to three generations before the generation of purchase. Only seven of the thirty-seven ancestors who purchased a secretaryship were merchants, landlords, servants, or officers of great households who bought directly into nobility without any visible heritage in officialdom. The acquisition of a royal secretaryship and its hereditary nobility was therefore no *savonette à vilain*, or usurpation of *honneur*, for thirty of the thirty-seven families in this category, for they either were currently or had long been engaged in highly respected and demanding careers of service to the state. If one adds these thirty families to the twenty-four families immediately or retroactively ennobled by judicial, financial, or municipal office, one obtains fifty-four of eighty-one families (67%) that acquired hereditary nobility in the course of vocations in civil officialdom.[99]

Several of the families that were ennobled by royal or princely letter had developed important professional credentials before their social elevation. Benoît Cachet was deputy prosecutor of the Parlement of Dombes before he was ennobled in 1620. Julien Clément was royal physician and member of the Academy of Surgery when he was ennobled by Louis XIV in 1711. Jean Ferrand was

---

[99] That was also the dominant pattern within the Chambre des Comptes of Paris. Between January 1771 and January 1787, 102 judges entered that court; 62 (61%) were fully noble. The nobility of only 8 was seigneurial or military in origin. The families of 49 had been ennobled through judicial, administrative, or Chancellery office (Bluche, "Les magistrats des cours parisiennes au XVIIIe siècle," pp. 94–7).

personal physician to Charles IX when he was ennobled in 1574. The Thévenins had been mayors of La Rochelle and masters of the royal mint at Poitiers before they were ennobled by letter in 1652.

Some of the grandest and most gilded families of the eighteenth-century French aristocracy were indeed represented among the young men who entered the Parlement between 1760 and 1770: the Barillons de Morangis, the Lefèvres d'Ormesson, the Lepeletiers de Rosambo, the Maupeous, and the Nicolays. These families had been continuously dynastic in the Parlement and other sovereign courts of Paris since the sixteenth century, or for about one hundred years before that service ennobled. Nicolays had served as first presidents of the Chambre des Comptes in unbroken succession from 1506 to the Revolution.[100] It was from the base of themistocratic dynasticism that these families provided, during the seventeenth and eighteenth centuries, councillors of state, intendants (of Generalities, finance, and commerce), ambassadors, controllers general of finance, and Chancellors of France. By the 1760s, each family was at least sixth-generation noble, with a pedigree equaling those of many contemporary families of the sword aristocracy.

Yet despite their aristocratic luster, those families were not radically distinct from the *parlementaire* families that were only the second or third generation in sovereign courts, not even from many families of the Châtelet. They were merely among the most senior on a temporal continuum of themistocratic families. Most of the more junior *parlementaire* families on that continuum could eventually have attained the degree of nobiliary seniority the older families enjoyed in the 1760s, had the unforeseeable Revolution not supervened. And each of the great *parlementaire* lineages had once been socially modest commoners. Originally they were provincial, like at least thirty-five of the other eighty-two families and the majority of Châtelet families.[101]

[100] The rise and consolidation of the Nicolays are eloquently described by George Huppert in *"Les bourgeois gentilshommes": An Essay on the Definition of Elites in Renaissance France* (Chicago: University of Chicago Press, 1977), pp. 131–8. The scale of dynasticism among high-robe families is not revealed by strictly patrilineal genealogies. It is revealed in Françoise Mosser's larger presentation of the Lefèvres d'Ormesson. Six generations separated Henry-François de Paule Lefèvre (1768) and his first cousin Anne-Louis-François de Paule Lefèvre (1770) from their patrilineal ancestor Jean (d. 1530), who was a prosecutor in the Parlement of Paris. Those six generations included 28 adult males. Fourteen were magistrates of the Parlement of Paris, and another 6 of the Chambre des Comptes or Grand Conseil. Three were ecclesiastics, 2 of them during the seventeenth century. Two were treasurers of France. Only 1 was an army officer (Françoise Mosser, *Les intendants des finances au XVIIIe siècle: Les Lefèvre d'Ormesson et le "département des Impositions" (1715–1777)*, [Geneva: Droz, 1978], p. 254).

[101] One wonders who preceded the "earliest known ancestors" – the provincial apothecaries, tradesmen, rentiers, solicitors, or tax collectors listed in Table 3.7 – of these and other eighteenth-century *parlementaires*. The deep social ancestry of many was probably in the late medieval peasantry. Jean Jacquart has described the multisecular trajectories of such fortunate lineages, from their rural origins: "Au prix de beaucoup de travail et d'économies, en cumulant toutes les occasions de gagner quelques deniers, un maneouvrier peut tenter de prendre une petite location, d'acheter quelques terres, de parvenir à détenir l'attelage qui marquera son entrée dans le groupe des exploitants 'à charrue.' Les choses sont plus aisées au niveau de ceux-ci. . . . Il a pu économiser, arrondir sa ferme ou sa métairie de quelques baux supplé-

To most twentieth-century, middle-class historians, the social complexion of the late eighteenth-century Parlement of Paris appears dazzlingly aristocratic. Indeed, many of the new judges in 1760 to 1770 were at least fifth-generation nobles. The reasons for that situation are simple. Their lineages had remained devoted to themistocracy and administration after gaining nobility (either immediately or retroactively) in earlier centuries and had maintained dynastic prehension in the Parlement or other sovereign courts of Paris. Their nobility was indubitable by every Old Regime official standard; but it was also intensely parochial.

Nobiliary pedigree is an abstract entity: It signifies a cold fact of genealogy, a passive condition of the person, or a mystique of *race*. Dynastic continuity in vocation, on the other hand, is not an abstraction: It is an active experience of life. It is true that the sixth- or seventh-degree nobleman of the Parlement of Paris was, technically, a *noble de race*. He shared that vague category with thousands of other Frenchmen and women with whom he shared little else. But he was indubitably, and concretely, a themistocrat by *race*, whose elders had destined and formed him since birth for that role, just as they themselves had been destined and formed. And he shared that quality with thousands of themistocrats, in Paris and throughout France, whose families were old in the magistracy but recent to the Second Estate.

After 1644, dynastic recruitment for the high courts of Old Regime France was necessarily a recruitment principally of men fully or incipiently noble, because those courts ennobled their magistrates. Such recruitment expressed and ensured professional continuity, not nobiliary exclusiveness. The court as a corporation only partially decided the recruitment of dynasts, and the king had least control over their selection. Dynasts were selected primarily by the families that colonized the court and thus determined much of its composition over generational time. Familialism may in fact be understood professionally as a perfection of themistocracy. If we can think beyond the modern prejudice against nepotism, the son or nephew of a *parlementaire* or other sovereign court judge was likely to enter the Parlement of Paris with greater knowledge of his duties and preparation for his tasks than any other candidate, for he had been nurtured by elders whose careers were spent in sovereign courts. That nurtur-

mentaires. Quant au gros fermier, il a mieux 'fait son profit' grâce à l'éventail des possibilités offertes par l'élargissement du marché. Un de ses fils va 'aux écoles,' se frote d'un peu de droit chez le procureur ou le tabellion et entame ainsi pour le lignage une lente ascension social dont a de multiples et illustres exemples: laboureur, procureur, avocat auprès d'une juridiction inférieure puis d'une cour plus importante. Le petit-fils ou l'arrière-petit-fils couronnera le tout par l'acquisiton d'une charge de judicature modeste. En quatre ou cinq générations, avec un peu de chance, beaucoup de patience et d'économies, un beau mariage ou bon moment, le descendant du paysan siègera sur les fleurs de lys de quelque cour souveraine. Inutile de dire que la chose n'est pas fréquent" (*François Ier* [Paris: Fayard, 1981], pp. 59–60). Far more than luck was needed to produce that outcome. Jacquart invites us to imagine the calculation, self-discipline, frugality and sheer tenacity that virtually every generation of such a lineage had to practice at each stage of the long progression from rural laborers or tenant farmers to sovereign court themistocrats.

ance (whose forms are examined in Chapter 5), not social pedigree, was the reason for his preferment by the court.

To enumerate the percentages of commoners and nobles among the entrants to the superior magistracy during the eighteenth century, as historians so often have done, is implicitly, and fallaciously, to regard those broad conditions as both professionally significant and stable in meaning. A noble family of finance or administrative officialdom underwent a professional and social mutation when its son entered a Parlement: Its professional being and community expanded, or ultimately changed; and it was aggrandized in prestige. Every bourgeois who gained office in a sovereign court began immediately to change in social identity, for his office ennobled. That fact was known to every member of a sovereign court. In the person of our hypothetical bourgeois, however, the seller of office and his colleagues did not select a bourgeois per se. They promoted a family of officialdom whose candidate–son gave promise of professional quality. His noble sons would have a dynastic claim on office in that or a comparable court.

Those who assume that the attainment of nobility was the consuming ambition of bourgeois families within officialdom ignore or evade some central facts of the Old Regime.[102] Until July 1644, even high magisterial and administrative offices did not confer nobility, but we know that since at least the fifteenth century many thousands of bourgeois families had devoted themselves to the royal judiciary and administration without any promise of ennoblement. In addition, we know that few such families left officialdom after attaining nobility. A family that had achieved hereditary nobility by magisterial or administrative office was perfectly free to retire from office without losing the title and privileges of nobility. It could sell the office for money, and thereby divest itself of tasks that required expensive educations, demanded time and energy, and produced little revenue. The family could then invest the money in land, state bonds, or royal-charter companies and live well as seigneurial landlords and rentiers. It could also place sons in the officer corps of the army, instead of the judiciary or administration. But we find that few of the ennobled seventeenth- and eighteenth-century families of the robe and pen made this choice. Instead, they remained in magistracy or administration, generation after generation. The consuming ambition of those families therefore cannot have been sheer aristocracy. Their collective behavior suggests ambitions more substantial than title. Aristocracy conferred static privileges and general prestige; but only service in high offices of state conferred – simultaneously – authority, prestige, and privileges. That service gave a family membership – through work, marriages, and kinship affiliations with professionally comparable families – in a large, brilliant, and mutually sustaining community of the empowered and the ennobled, generation after generation.

[102] This assumption can be found in most general descriptions of Old Regime French civilization.

173

4

A Fourth Estate: the uniqueness of the themistocracy

A. The problem

We should now ask an expansive question, on a broad canvas: Can the noblemen of the Châtelet and the Parlement of Paris, or those of the entire Old Regime French themistocracy, be socially and politically comprehended, and accurately described, as "aristocrats"? The ostensible answer would be yes, by the simple facts that they belonged to a distinct juridical Estate and shared in its privileges, and most historians have given that answer. But such a description, if it is not to be purely abstract, would require more than passive, inherited, or even purchased identity. It would require strong evidence of affinities and reciprocities with aristocrats who were not of the themistocracy or royal officialdom, or, at the very least, strong evidence of greater solidarity with them than with any collectivity of commoners.

Affinities and solidarity cannot be presumed, or deduced from "objective material interests." Clearly, robe nobles and sword nobles did have certain objective material interests in common: aristocratic privileges, seigneurialism, proprietary offices or commissions. But objective material interests are those that a scholar can discern and to which he or she attaches importance. They may therefore be descriptively true without having been productive of solidarity among those whom they describe. For example, a robe noble may have been attached to his social status, seigneurial estates, and ownership of office without translating that attachment into any active solidarity or community with the sword nobility, especially since he shared the attributes of seigneurialism and proprietary office with a great many bourgeois of eighteenth-century France. The only objective interest shared exclusively by robe nobles and sword nobles was nobility itself.

The titles and privileges of French nobility were categorical and did not depend on source of ennoblement, seniority, or function. Nobility meant hereditary enjoyment of the privileges that I have described, by transmission in the paternal line. It also meant, in principle, heightened obligation to king and realm. The French aristocracy cannot accurately be divided, at any period of its history, into an ancient *noblesse de race* and a parvenu nobility of recent creation. The membership of the aristocracy, and thus its familial composition, evolved continually, from the Middle Ages to the Revolution. Most families survived in noble estate for no more than two hundred years. Beyond six or seven generations, they either became extinct in the male line or derogated title (usually by economic failure). As certain families declined and vanished from aristocracy, other families rose to replace them. In the France of 1789, only 8,500 families (33%) of some 26,000 aristocratic families had noble origins that antedated 1600; only 942 (3.7%) of the total had proof of nobility before 1400.[1] The principal sources of ennoblement also evolved: During the Middle Ages it derived from ownership of seigneurial fiefs, personal service to princely and ducal families, and military command, but from the late seventeenth century onward it derived largely from a multiplicity of royal and municipal civil offices. By the late sixteenth century, a basic principle concerning nobility had been established in law and general consciousness: Only the king could create new nobles.[2] The modern French aristocracy (1600–1789) was created primarily from the transformation of bourgeois into nobles through their purchase and career exercise of ennobling civil offices.[3] During the eighteenth century alone, more than 5,000 families acquired nobility in that manner, or about 20 percent of the total of noble families in 1789.[4]

In the long duration, *noblesse* retained three generic criteria, which could be satisfied by a variety of families and roles: (1) noble lineage; (2) distinguished

---

[1] Guy Chaussinand-Nogaret, *The French Nobility in the Eighteenth Century* (Cambridge: Cambridge University Press, 1985), p. 30.

[2] Pierre Goubert, *L'Ancien Régime* (Paris, Armand Colin 1969), 2 vols., vol. I, p. 170. A name with a particule did not signify nobility, just as ownership of seigneurial fiefs did not confer nobility after 1579. When a seventeenth- or eighteenth-century bourgeois purchased domainal property, he commonly added the name of the site to his family name. The result could be sonorous. Antoine-Edouard Le Gros de Saint-Germain and Pierre-Athanase Denois de Fontchevreuil, judges of the Châtelet, were both commoners. Their colleague, Jean-Henri-Alexandre Delarche, was at least third-generation noble (A.N. V 1 458, 524, 533).

[3] That principle of ennoblement was stated aggressively by Louis XIV, in the preamble to a 1696 edict: "Si la noble extraction et l'antiquité de la race qui donnent tant de distinction parmi les hommes, *n'est que le présent d'une fortune aveugle*, [italics mine] le titre et la source de la noblesse est un présent du prince qui sait récompenser avec choix les services importants que les sujets rendent à leur patrie. Ces services, si dignes de la reconnaissance des souverains, ne se rendent pas toujours les armes à la main; le zèle se signale des plus d'une manière" (quoted from Bluche, *Les magistrats du Parlement de Paris*, p. 103). "Venerability of line" as nothing more than "the gift of blind chance": This was defense of the new robe nobility against the disdain of the older seigenurial and military aristocracy. A comprehensive study of the royal politics of ennoblement, from the Middle Ages to 1789, has not been written, but it seems that the kings of France had, almost consistently, a pragmatic, even opportunistic, conception of ennoblement and nobility. Whatever forms of personal service and political or financial support they deemed to be especially vital to the state in a given period, and securely obtainable by ennoblement, they defined as nobiliary in character: *bellators* in the Middle Ages, then household retainers, executives of state, municipal oligarchs, financiers, superior magistrates and administrators, distinguished artists, savants, physicians, and inventors. Kings, the legal source of nobility, seem to have been the least affected by the mystique of nobility among all members of French civilization. Their politics of selective, pragmatic ennoblement had a coldly modernistic quality.

[4] Chaussinand-Nogaret, *French Nobility*, p. 28. As many as half of them had probably gained nobility through either a royal secretaryship or the *échevinage*.

service to monarch and realm; (3) a magnanimous and honorable life-style.[5] More than a juridical condition and its privileges, nobility therefore was also less than a caste. Although it required the performance of certain duties and adherence to a particular social code, it was formally open to bourgeois who had the capacity for high royal service. The wealth, education, and connections that permitted the entry of a bourgeois family into ennobling office usually permitted that family to live "magnanimously" (*vivre noblement*). That family acquired noble lineage with the simple passage of time, if it continued to live "honorably," cultivate patrimony, accumulate capital, and produce valid male heirs. In the fourth generation, it automatically became *noble de race*.[6]

The late eighteenth-century French aristocracy was highly populous (at least 120,000 persons, or about 1 in every 200 in the population of France). The aristocracy was dispersed throughout the country, spread among various professions (the Church, the army and navy, the royal magistracy and administration, universities and academies, even maritime and colonial trade) in prominent towns and on isolated domains. It lacked any general corporate organization. Only in a few provinces (such as Artois, Languedoc, and Brittany) were there assemblies of the nobility that met regularly. The pluralism of the French aristocracy was in fact the source of disunity and antagonism within its ranks. In the minds of some nobles – especially those of old, seigneurial *race* – true nobility was transjuridical, immaterial, beyond even royal creation or recognition. It was, in the phrase of Pierre Goubert, the "corps mystique et passionné de la noblesse," wherein honor and prowess were supposedly conveyed through ge-

---

[5] " 'Nobles': sont ceux qui ont le titre de noblesse sur l'ancienneté de leur race, & pour avoir toujours vécu noblement, ou qu'ils sont dûement annoblis par le Prince. . . . Le Noble est une personne distinguée, ou par la vertue de ses ancêtres, ou par la faveur du Prince. Les premiers sont les nobles de race; & les autres sont ceux à qui le Roi a par grace spéciale accordé les Lettres de noblesse, ou qui possedent des charges qui annoblissent. Nobles d'office, c'est-a-dire, devenues nobles par les provisions que le Roi leur a accordées d'Offices, qui annoblissent par rapport à la noblesse de leur fonction" (Ferrière, vol. 2, pp. 229–30). Cardinal Bernis, descendant of late medieval seigneurial and military nobles in Languedoc, who was minister of foreign affairs to Louis XV, defined the characteristics of "true and high nobility" in terms that were pluralistic but centered on distinguished service: "La profession militaire ou législative, premier attribut de la noblesse; l'ancienneté de la race, second attribut; l'illustration acquise, soit par la grandeur des emplois exercés, soit par la grandeur des alliances contractées, troisième attribut; le pouvoir et la domination sur quelque partie de l'Etat, quatrième attribut; enfin la pureté de la noblesse qui consiste dans la descendance des pères et des mères véritablement nobles, et l'authenticité de la noblesse, qui doit étre prouvée principalment par l'opinion publique, par l'histoire et plus particulièrement par des actes de famille non suspects, sont les attributs nécessaires et essentiels de la véritable et grande noblesse" (*Mémoires et lettres de François-Joachim de Pierre, Cardinal de Bernis (1715–1758)*, 2 vols., ed. Frédéric Masson [Paris, 1878], vol. 1, p. 127). In a more personal passage, he referred to sheer venerability of noble lineage with irony, "J'ai su toute ma vie mieux qu'un autre apprécier le mérite fortuite de la naissance," thus echoing the language of Louis XIV in 1696 (p. 2).

[6] By Henri III's declaration of May 1583, four generations of nobility bestowed *noblesse de race* on a noble family and entitled its males to the denomination "gentilhomme," in addition to that of "écuyer" or "chevalier" (Mousnier, *Institutions of France*, vol. 1, p. 127). Four generations measured about one hundred years in the life of a family, a long time in terms of society, but not genetically.

netic purity.[7] In the minds of many other nobles, nobility was far more prosaic: a socioeconomic means to professional ends, or a contractual and permanent reward (both material and honorific) for lifetimes of exacting and important service to the state. The classic, juridical definitions according to which the aristocracy was one and distinct (the idiom of the Old Regime, so dear to the writers of modern textbooks, to Marxian dogmatists, and to historians affected by *la nostalgie du blazon*), by the late seventeenth century had became archaic and superficial at best.

The aristocracy of Old Regime France was probably as widely and deeply variegated, both in mode of life and in self-consciousness, as the bourgeoisie. It certainly manifested far less solidarity and cohesion. "Nobility was a club which every wealthy man felt entitled, indeed obliged, to join. Not all nobles, by any means, were rich, but sooner or later all the rich ended up noble."[8] The second of the two statements cannot be true. The heterogeneity of the eighteenth-century French aristocracy, and the increase in ennoblements of bourgeois between 1715 and 1789, have led several historians to conclude fallaciously that nobility was, in fact and not merely in theory, quite accessible to talented and affluent bourgeois. In reality, nobility was accessible only to those bourgeois who could do one of the following things: (1) gain an ennobling themistocratic or administrative office; (2) purchase a royal secretaryship; (3) secure election to the *échevinage*, in one of the nineteen major towns where that office ennobled; or (4) win a royal letter of ennoblement for distinguished achievement in military service, the arts or letters, science, technology, or commerce and manufactures. Let us examine each of these avenues to nobility more closely.

Access to civil offices that ennobled was not easily obtained. It was severely limited, not only by the fixed number of such offices (about 2,500 for all of France) but by the prevalence of dynasticism within them. There were legions of bourgeois barristers and notaries in the orbits of the sovereign courts who had no real chance of acquiring a magisterial office in those courts, just as there were legions of middle-ranking fiscal and administrative officials who had no real chance of becoming treasurer of a Generality. Although there were more than 50,000 venal-hereditary offices of state, the 2,500 of them that ennobled were the property of families, not individuals, and men from nondynastic families had little chance at them. The acquisition of one of the 800 royal secretaryships was made a rare event by the tremendous cost of the purchase price. As for the *échevinage*, in major towns and cities, the number of industrious, respectable, and prosperous bourgeois who were eligible to be *échevin* exceeded

---

[7] Goubert, *L'Ancien Régime*, vol. 1, p. 171.

[8] William Doyle, *The Oxford History of the French Revolution* (Oxford: Clarendon Press, 1989), p. 28. Other works affirm the same propositions: Chaussinand-Nogaret, *French Nobility;* François Furet, *Interpreting the French Revolution* (Cambridge: Cambridge University Press, 1981); Simon Schama, *Citizens: A Chronicle of the French Revolution* (New York: Knopf, 1989).

by thousands the number chosen for that office during the eighteenth century.[9] A royal letter also was difficult to obtain. From 1700 to 1790, approximately 1,000 men (and their progeny), were ennobled directly by royal letter for personal merit or services: That is an average of only 11 men per annum for all of France. The careers of the 476 *anoblis* whose letters were registered in the Cour des Aides of Paris between 1712 and 1787 have been examined by Chaussinand-Nogaret, who found 76 servitors and favorites of the Court, 76 professional soldiers, 52 lower-court magistrates, 40 royal officeholders, 22 mayors or municipal officers, 50 merchants, 35 medical doctors, 22 artists and intellectuals, and 15 barristers.[10] Across those seventy-five years, a total of only 122 merchants, physicians, barristers, artists, and intellectuals were meritoriously ennobled – at a rate of 1 or 2 per annum. Their small proportion among the ennobled did increase after 1760, but royal preferment remained traditional: Those chosen were still usually courtiers, soldiers, or administrators, just as during the reign of Francis I. So too did the stigmas: There were only 50 merchants and 17 financiers among the 476 *anoblis*.

The number of bourgeois may have increased twofold in France between 1715 and 1789, for that was a period of accelerating commercial, manufacturing, and agricultural expansion. In relation to the growing population of merchants, luxury craftsmen, landowners, savants, writers, notaries, barristers, and administrators who possessed the basic qualifications for ennoblement – talent, education, affluence, and a record of personal and family service to the economy, polity, or culture of France – there was in fact a constriction of access to nobility during the eighteenth century. Men from that population became leading voices of antiaristocratic sentiment, before and during the Revolution. There was also a crucial split within the French nobility during the century, one that can be measured in the behavior of those at its highest strata.

B. Alterity

Among elites in Old Regime France, marriage, as we have observed, was a contractual social arrangement between families, not a decision by a young man

---

[9] Between 1701 and 1789, a total of 172 men served as *échevins* of Paris; professions are known for 130 of them. Seventy were of the judiciary: 16 magistrates, 24 barristers of the Parlement and 30 notaries of the Châtelet. Nine others were from royal administration. Four were professors or royal apothecary–surgeons. Forty-seven were merchants or master artisans. Even if all of those whose professions are unknown (42) were in fact merchants, the result would be only 89 merchants ennobled by the *échevinage*, in eighty-nine years. Computed from A. Trudon des Ormes, "Notes sur les prévots des marchands et échevins de la ville de Paris au XVIIIe siècle (1701–1789)." The master merchants among the artisanate of Paris numbered close to 5,000 at the end of the Old Regime. The 24 barristers of the Parlement who gained nobility from the *échevinage* in the period 1701 to 1789 belonged to a corporation that numbered from 575 to 600 in any given year of the century. The Lyons *échevinage* was similar, both in its social configuration and in the small number of bourgeois that it ennobled during the eighteenth century. See Maurice Garden, *Lyon et les Lyonnais au XVIIIe siècle* (Paris: Société d'Edition "les Belles-lettres," 1970), pp. 495–506.

[10] Chaussinand-Nogaret, *French Nobility,* pp. 33–5.

and a young woman. It was also the most elemental form of social bonding and social closure. Where that bonding did not occur between socioprofessional groups, there was alterity between them, despite all other appearances of unity – whether legal, nomenclatural, symbolic, or sumptuary.

The intendants of Generalities and provinces formed the highest cadre of civil governance in Old Regime France. Only secretaries of state and ministers of state surpassed them in authority, and most of those secretaries and ministers were themselves selected from among intendants. Intendants of generalities and provinces were appointed by the king, selected exclusively from among the eight-five masters of petitions who served the royal Council and the chancelleries. Intendants were ex officio members of the Council. Since, by formal requirement, all masters of petitions had to have served as sovereign court magistrates, intendants were clearly themistocrats, by experience and early career.

Masterships of petitions were venal-hereditary, highly dynastic offices. Between 1674 and 1742, the price of such a mastership varied between 80,000 and 180,000 livres; in 1752, it was fixed at 100,000 livres.[11] Between 1700 and 1789, approximately 180 men served as intendants. Most belonged to extremely wealthy families and owned large seigneurial estates. The majority were at least third-generation noble. Almost half of the 180 were *noblesse de race*. In the years 1710 to 1712 and 1749 to 1751, 60 men held the office (most of them also serving for several years before and after the sample periods). They represent two generations of intendants and the high *noblesse de robe*. Their socioprofessional origins have been traced (Table 4.1).[12]

The 60 intendants were essentially Parisian. Thirty-six came from the Parlement of Paris, 7 from the Grand Conseil, and 3 from the Cour des Aides; that is, 46 of the 60 had been Parisian sovereign court officials. The group was predominantly composed of former *parlementaires*. And it was intensely dynastic: At least 20 of the 60 were sons of intendants, and another 6 were sons of masters of petitions. Twenty-five of the 36 former Parlement of Paris officials among the intendants were sons of serving or former magistrates in that court, and they included many of its most senior lineages. Ten others were sons of magistrates in other sovereign courts, and 7 were sons of high-ranking civil or fiscal officers. Three were sons of merchants who had purchased royal secretaryships. There was no son of a military officer among the 60. And their fathers had married endogamously: 16 to daughters of magistrates; 10 to those of masters of petitions or intendants; 9 to those of civil or finance administrators; 5 to those of merchants or financiers; and only 2 to daughters of the *noblesse d'épée*. Collectively, these intendants' marriages were an accentuation of that

---

[11] Vivian Gruder, *The Royal Provincial Intendants: A Governing Elite in Eighteenth-century France* (Ithaca: Cornell University Press, 1968), pp. 61–2. This is the most complete study of the eighteenth-century intendants.
[12] Data have been constructed from Gruder, ibid., pp. 246–52; Antoine, *Le gouvernement;* and Favre-Lejeune, *Les secrétaires du roi.*

Table 4.1. Socioprofessional origins of the 60 intendants of generalities or provinces, 1710–1712 and 1749–1751

A	B	C	D	E	F	G	H
Aligre de Boislandry, E. J-F.-M. d'	1717–57	Judge, Parl. Paris	Pres. Parl. Paris	President, Cham. des Comptes, Normandy	Master of petitions	40	38
Aubert de Tourny, L.-U.	1695–1760	Judge, Grand Conseil	Pres. Cham. des Comptes, Normandy	Royal advocate, bailliage Vernon, royal sec.	General receiver, royal domains, Brittany	26	
Barberie de Saint-Contest, D.-C.	1668–1730	Judge, Parl. Paris	Intendant	Judge, Parl. Paris	Pres., Parl. Paris	32	30
Barentin, C.-A.-H. de	1703–62	Judge, Parl. Paris	Intendant	Master of petitions	Intendant	21	18
Barrillon d'Amoncourt, A.	1671–1741	Judge, Parl. Paris	Intendant		General tax farmer	23	18
Bauyn d'Angervilliers, N.-P.	1675–1740	Judge, Parl. Paris	Finance officer, royal household	Officer, French Guards regiment	Judge, Cham. des Comptes Paris	19	
Beauharnois, F. de	1665–1746		Manorial lord, Orléanais	Judge, Cham. des Comptes, Blois			
Bernage, L. de	1663–1737	Judge, Grand Conseil	Judge, Grand Conseil	Judge, Parl. Normandy	General controller, postal service	23	
Bernage de Vaux, J.-L. de	1716–80	Judge, Parl. Languedoc	Intendant	General controller, postal service	Wholesale merchant, royal sec.	33	
Bertier de Sauvigny, L.-J. de	1709–88	Judge, Parl. Paris	Pres., Parl. Paris	Finance commissioner to king of Spain	General tax farmer	27	20
Bertin de Bellisle, H.-L.-J.-B.	1720–92	Judge, Grand Conseil	Master of petitions	Minister of state	Did not marry		
Bignon de Blanzy, A.- R.	1666–1724	General advocate, Cour des Aides, Paris	General advocate, Parl. Paris		Royal sec., guardian of royal Treasury	25	
Blair de Boisemont, L-G. de	1716–78	Judge, Parl. Paris	Judge, Parl. Paris	Judge, Parl. Paris	Royal sec., banker	39	19
Boucher d'Orsay, C.	1675–1730	Judge, Parl. Paris	Provost of merchants, Paris			27	
Camus de Pontcarré de Viarme, J.-B.-E.	1702–75	Judge, Parl. Paris	First president, Parl. Normandy	Master of petitions		29	19
Caze de la Bove, G.-H. de	1711–50	Judge, Parl. Paris	General tax farmer	Royal prosecutor, seneschalcy Aix-en-Provence	Controller-general of finance	26	17
Chaumont de la Galaizière, A.-M.	1697–1783	Judge, Parl. Metz	Wholesale merchant, royal sec.	Merchant	President, Parl. Metz	27	16
Chaumont de la Millière, J.-L.	1711–56	Judge, Parl. Paris	Wholesale merchant, royal sec.	Merchant	General receiver, Gen. Châlons	34	15
Chauvelin de Beauséjour, B.	1673–1755	Judge, Parl. Paris	Master of petitions		Financier, royal sec.	28	
Chauvelin de Beauséjour, J.-B.	1701–67	Judge, Parl. Paris	Intendant	Financier, royal sec.	General Receiver, Gen. La Rochelle	28	15
Creil de Bournezeau, J.-F. de	1684–1761	Judge, Parl. Paris	Intendant	Royal councillor	Intendant	24	19
Dodart, D.	1679–1736	Judge, Parl. Paris	Judge, Parl. Paris		Barrister, Parl. Paris	24	20
Doujat, J-C.	1653–1726	Judge, Parl. Metz	Judge, Parl. Paris		Royal household officer, royal sec.	33	
Ferrand de Villemilain, F.-A.	1657–1731	Particular lieutenant, Châtelet	Particular lieutenant, Châtelet		Royal herald-at-arms	29	
Foullé de Martargis, E.-H.-A.	1678–1736	General advocate, Hôtel-du-Roi	Master of petitions	Master of petitions	President, Grand Conseil	22	

(A)	(B)	(C)	(D)	(E)	(F)	(G)	(H)
[…]ouiois de la Tour, C.-J.-B. des	1715–1802	Judge, Parl. Provence	Intendant	President, Parl. Paris		33	17
Joly de Fleury de la Valette, J.-F.	1718–1802	Judge, Parl. Paris	General prosecutor, Parl. Paris	Treasurer, Gen. Orléans		66	63
Jubert de Bouville, L.-G.	1645–1720	General advocate, Cour des Aides, Paris	Intendant	Intendant		19	
La Bourdonnaye, L.-F. de	1702–79	Judge, Parl. Brittany	Intendant	Infantry colonel, marquis		23	
La Bourdonnaye, Y.-M. de	1653–1726	Judge, Parl. Brittany	Judge, Parl. Brittany	Intendant		35	17
La Bourdonnaye de Blossac, P.-M. de	1716–1800	Judge, Parl. Paris	Pres., Parl. Brittany	Intendant		24	
La Briffe, P.-A. de	1678–1740	Judge, Parl. Paris	Intendant	General receiver, Flanders		25	22
La Briffe des Ferrières, L.-A. de	1705–52	Judge, Parl. Burgundy	Intendant	General tax farmer		31	17
Lallemant de Lévignen, L.-F.	1686–1767	Judge, Grand Conseil	General receiver, Gen. Soissons	General receiver, Gen. Amiens		27	
Lamoignon de Basville, N. de	1648–1724	Judge, Parl. Paris	President, Parl. Paris	Military officer, marquis		24	
Lamoignon de Courson, U.-G. de	1674–1742	Judge, Parl. Paris	Intendant	Intendant		21	
La Porte	Did not marry						
Le Guerchois, P.-H.	1670–1740	Judge, Parl. Normandy	General prosecutor, Parl. Normandy	Royal councillor		30	
LePelletier de la Houssaye, F.	1663–1723	Judge, Parl. Paris	Master of petitions	President, Grand Conseil		24	23
L'Escalopier, C.-C. de	1671–1753	Judge, Parl. Paris	Royal secretary	Treasurer, Gen. Lyons		43	
L'Escalopier, G.-C. de	1706–92	Judge, Parl. Paris	Treasurer, Gen. Lyons	Intendant		21	
Maignard de Bernières, C.-E.	1667–1717	Judge, Grand Conseil	President, Parl. Normandy			30	
Mégret de Sérilly, J.-N.	1702–52	General advocate, Cour des Aides, Paris	General receiver, Gen. Riom, royal sec.; Magistrate, tax court, Noyon	General prosecutor, Parl. Paris		44	42
Méliand, A.-F.	1670–1747	Judge, Parl. Paris	Royal sec.	Intendant		27	19
Méliand, C.-B.	1703–68	Judge, Parl. Paris	Royal sec.	Commissioner of war, royal sec.		23	16
Moreau de Beaumont, J.-L.	1715–85	Judge, Parl. Paris	President, Parl. Paris	General tax farmer		28	18
Moreau de Séchelles, J.	1690–1760	Judge, Parl. Metz	Merchant, royal sec.	Judge, Parl. Paris		22	
Peyrac de Moras, F.	1718–71	Master of petitions	Financier, royal secretary	Intendant		21	
Pineau de Lucé, J.	1709–64	Judge, Parl. Paris	Royal prosecutor, presidial court, Le Mans	General tax farmer, royal sec.		34	15
Quentin de Richebourg, C.-B.	1673–1733	Master of petitions	Intendant	Master of petitions		24	
Rossignol, B.-R.	1697–1754	Judge, Parl. Paris	President, Cham. des Comptes, Paris	Judge, Parl. Paris		31	
Roujault, N.-E.	1662–1723	Judge, Parl. Paris	Judge, Cham. des Comptes, Paris; Director, East India Company, royal sec.	General tax farmer, royal sec.		31	18
Savalette de Magnanville, C.-P.	1713–97	Judge, Parl. Paris	Commissioner of war	Military officer, governor of Bourg, marquis			

Key to column headings: (*A*) name; (*B*) lifetime; (*C*) original sovereign court and office; (*D*) father's principal office; (*E*) maternal grandfather's principal office; (*F*) father-in-law's principal office; (*G*) age at marriage; (*H*) bride's age at marriage.

Sources: Data constructed from Antoine, *Le gouvernement*; Favre-Lejeune, *Les secrétaires du roi*; and Gruder, *Provincial Intendants*, pp. 246–52.

strategy: 12 to daughters of intendants or masters of petitions; 11 to those of sovereign court magistrates; 20 to those of civil or finance administrators (of which 13 were to daughters of general tax farmers, treasurers, or general receivers for Generalities); 3 to those of military officers; and 2 to servitors at Court. There were only 5 alliances with the *noblesse d'épée* within a total of 96 marriages of intendants and their fathers. Each of these magnate families had attained perfect maturity as robe-and-pen nobles, a maturity from which lateral metamorphoses into military or Court aristocrats were possible.

They refused the metamorphoses. That is visible in the third generation, among the sons and daughters of intendants (Table 4.2).[13] The families maintained their eldest sons – the principal heirs of lineal property and agents of continuity – in vocations of the robe and pen, and they married them within that universe. Most of the fathers-in-law listed in Table 4.1 as having careers in administration were masters of petitions, and thus former magistrates. Some families (seven of fifteen) gave at least one cadet son to the army, but most of those sons were subsequently married to daughters of the civil nobility. Few if any such sons founded a military dynasty.[14]

Intendants married most of their daughters (15 of the 26 who were wed) to comparable families of the robe and pen. They gave almost as many daughters to the Church (5) as to the military aristocracy (6). And one wonders how many of those 6 daughters were wed to officers whose families had some robe connections in the preceding generation. The general strategy in the marriage of daughters was an exchange of large dowries between families of the civil nobility, not the building, via dowries, of bridges to the sword nobility. One consequence of the strategy was that a majority of the 60 intendants were cousins of other intendants.

Let us compare the 60 intendants to a group which occupied a similarly august rank in the military hierarchy of France. The families of 40 high-ranking military officers who served ex officio on the royal Council between 1715 and

---

[13] Genealogical information on that generation, drawn from La Chesnaye des Bois, *Dictionnaire de la noblesse*, and Woëlmont de Brumage, *Notices généalogiques*, is more indicative than complete. Both sources have more detailed information on old seigneurial and military families than on those ennobled after 1600.

[14] They conform to Roland Mousnier's general observation: "Though the world of the gown sent some of its younger sons into the world of the sword, it is important to note that the eldest sons as a rule remained 'robins' [magistrates] and that, also as a rule, the younger sons failed to rise very high either in the ranks of the army and navy or in their 'quality' as 'gentilshommes' and did not really create families belonging to the 'noblesse d'épée.' A few families from the world of the gown did become transformed into families of the 'grande noblesse d'épée,' but these were few and far between" (*Institutions of France*, vol. 1, p. 161). The 233 general tax farmers (1726–91) made similar choices for their sons. The great majority of tax farmers, and thus their progeny, were noble and extremely rich. They placed two-thirds of their eldest sons and one-third of cadets in high public finance offices, establishing 37% of the former and 18% of the latter as their successors in the General Tax Farm. The majority of the remainder found positions in sovereign courts. Only 20% of their sons were placed in the officer corps; 5.5% of eldest sons and 27.5% of cadets became officers (Yves Durand, *Les fermiers généraux au XVIIIe siècle* [Paris: Presses Universitaires de France, 1971], p. 375).

Table 4.2. *Children of intendants*

Name of intendant	Number	Intendancy	Magistracy	Administration	Army	Navy	Church	Court	Manor
Aubert de Tourny	2	s1			s2(M)				
Barberie de Saint-Contest	2	s1(Ad)s2							
Barentin	2		s1				s2		
Barillon d'Armoncourt	1		s(Ma)						
Bauyn d'Angervilliers	1		d						
Bernage	2		s1		s2				
Bignon de Blanzy	4	s1	s2 d1 d2						
Camus de Pontcarré	5		s1 s2		d1				d2 d3
Caze de la Bove	7	s1		s2(Ad) d1	s3 d2				d3
Chaumont de la Galaizière	1	s(Ad)							
Chaumont de la Millière	1			s					
Chauvelin de Beauséjour, J.B.	6	s1(Ad)		d1	s3(M)		s2 s4 d		
Creil de Bournezeau	1				d				
Ferrand de Villemilain	1				d				
Jubert de Bouville	7			s1(Ad) d1	s2 s3	s4	s5 d2		
La Briffe	6	s1(Ad)	d3		s2		s3 d2	d1	d
La Briffe des Ferrières	3		s1(Ad) d		s2				
Lamoignon de Beauville	1			s2 d4					
Lamoignon de Courson	6		s1(M) d1 d3				d2		
Lefèvre d'Ormesson	4	s1	s2(M) d1				d2		
L'Escalopier, C.-C.	3	s1(M)	s2		s3(M)				

Table 4.2. (cont.)

Name of intendant	Number	Intendancy	Magistracy	Administration	Army	Navy	Church	Court	Manor
Maignard de Bernières	1				s(A)				
Méliand, A.-F.	1			d					
Méliand, C.-B.	1				d				
Quentin de Richebourg	2		s1 s2						
Roujault	1		d						

Note: Number of children includes only those who survived to adulthood.

Abbreviations: *S1*–first son; *s2*–second son, etc. Abbreviations in parentheses refer to professional background of family into which intendant's child married; *A*–army; *Ad*–administration; *C*–royal court; *M*–magistracy; *Ma*–manorial (or scion who handled family estates and affairs and had no other profession).

Source: Data constructed from La Chesnaye des Bois, *Dictionnaire de la noblesse*, and Woëlmont de Brumage, *Notices généalogiques*.

1774 practiced even more strict dynasticism and endogamy (Table 4.3).[15] Those officers came from all provinces and were a representative cross-section of the grand *noblesse d'épée* of late seventeenth- and eighteenth-century France. They were ex officio members of the Council because of their high positions in the army, the military governance of provinces and fortifications, and the diplomatic corps. Several became secretaries or ministers of state for war or for foreign affairs. Virtually all belonged to old-lineage military aristocracy. Most had been commissioned originally, and had served for several years, in their father's regiment, and those were primarily the elite cavalry and infantry regiments, whose prestige within the army was comparable to that of Parlements within the themistocracy: the Picardy, Auvergne, Roussillon, Franche-Comté, and Navarre infantry regiments; the King's Guards and the Queen's Guards Regiments, the French Guards and Swiss Guards, the Black Musketeers and Gray Musketeers, the Royal Household Cavalry ("Maison du Roi"), and the ducal regiments of dragoons and *cuirassiers*. Several of these officers succeeded their fathers in high command or military governorships.

Only two (Jacques Bazin and Charles-Louis Fouquet) of the 40 military councillors were sons of civil nobles. Thirty-six were sons of professional officers, and 2 of titled seigneurial nobles without formal careers. Professions of maternal grandfathers are known for 33 of the 40: army (21); navy (1); seigneurial lord (3); civil or ministerial official (5); magistrate (3); servitor at Court (1). The duke of Charost was the maternal grandson of Nicolas Fouquet, superintendent of finance during the 1650s. The duke of Saint-Aignan's maternal grandfather was Jean-Baptiste Colbert, Louis XIV's greatest minister. The Gassions, maternal family of the baron of Montesquiou, were high-ranking military officers and magistrates in service to Henri IV.

As with the intendants, the marital pattern of fathers was replicated among sons. Thirty-six of the 40 military councillors married, 22 of them to brides from the *noblesse d'épée*. Three married into titled manorial families, and 2 into those of ducal servitors. Four married daughters of recently ennobled, and probably rich, administrators of finance and war provisioning. Only 4 married daughters of magistrates. Four of the 40 military councillors did not marry, and another 4 were childless. Twenty-one of the remaining thirty-two couples produced a total of 94 children whose careers or marriages have been determined. Most of those 94 progeny were married between 1730 and 1760, and their marriages reveal the persistence of professional and marital exclusiveness in that third generation (Table 4.4).[16] Thirty-seven of the 51 sons succeeded their fathers in the army; 7 were given to the Church (and became bishops, canons, or abbots); another 3 were placed in the naval officer corps. Not one was placed in the magistracy or civil administration. Twenty-one of the 27 sons whose

---

[15] Data on these officers were constructed from Antoine, *Le gouvernement;* La Chesnaye des Bois, *Dictionnaire;* and Woëlmont de Brumagne, *Notices généalogiques.*

[16] Data on marriages were constructed from La Chesnaye des Bois, *Dictionnaire*, and Woëlmont de Brumagne, *Notices généaologiques.*

Table 4.3. *Military councillors of state, 1715–1774*

Name and title	Highest military rank and date	Father's rank or office
Emmanuel-Armand de Vignerod du Plessis de Richelieu, duke of Aiguillion (1720–88)	Lieutenant general (1758); secretary of state for foreign affairs	Cavalry colonel
Antoine-Louis de Pardaillan de Gondrin, duke of Antin (1665–1736)	Lieutenant general (1702); governor Orléanais	Marquis of Montespan
Henry-Joseph Bouchard d'Esparbès de Lussan, marquis of Aubeterre (1714–88)	Brigadier general (1748); ambassador	Captain in royal Household regiment
François, count of Baschi (1701–77)	Musketeer officer (1719); ambassador	Cavalry captain
Jacques Bazin de Bezons (1646–1733)	Field marshal (1709)	Intendant of Languedoc
Charles-Louis Foucquet, duke of Belle-Isle (1684–1761)	Field marshal (1741); secretary of state for war	Marquis of Belle-Isle
Armand de Béthune, duke of Charost (1663–1747)	Lieutenant general (1702); governor Calais	Lieutenant general; governor, Calais, Picardy
Paul-Francois de Béthune-Charost (1682–1759)	Lieutenant general (1734); governor Calais	Lieutenant general; governor, Calais
Armand-Charles de Gontaut, duke of Biron (1663–1756)	Field marshal (1734)	Cavalry captain
Jean-Louis d'Usson, marquis of Bonnac (1674–1738)	Cavalry brigadier (1719); ambassador	Cavalry captain
Louis-Bufile de Brancas de Forcalquier, marquis of Céreste (1672–1750)	Lieutenant general (1710); ambassador	Marquis of Céreste
Louis-Bufile-Toussaint de Brancas, count of Céreste (1697–1754)	Captain of royal Horse Guards (1729); ambassador	Marquis of Céreste
Jean de Montboissier-Beaufort, count of Canillac (1681–1729)	Lieutenant general (1710); governor Amiens	Cavalry captain
Louis de Clermont, count of Cheverny (1645–1722)	Governor Provins; baillif Besançon and Dole	Brigadier general
Etienne-François, count of Stainville and duke of Choiseul (1719–85)	Lieutenant general (1759); secretary of state for war	Lieutenant royal Guards; ambassador
Charles-François de Vintimille, count Du Luc (1653–1740)	Captain of galleys (1680); ambassador	Brigadier general
Antoine Coeffier-Ruzé, marquis of Effiat (1639–1719)	Cavalry captain; governor of Montargis	Governor, Lower Auvergne
Victor-Marie, duke of Estrées (1660–1737)	Lieutenant general, naval army (1684); minister of state	Vice admiral and field marshal; viceroy, Canada
Louis-Charles Le Tellier, duke of Estrées (1695–1771)	Field marshal (1757); minister of state	Colonel, queen's Guards regiment
Gabriel-Jacques de Salignac, marquis of Fénélon (1688–k.i.a. 1746)	Lieutenant general (1738); ambassador	Infantry lieutenant colonel
Antoine de Gramont, duke of Guiche (1671–1725)	Field marshal (1724); governor Navarre and Béarn	Cavalry colonel; governor, Navarre and Béarn; ambassador
Henry d'Harcourt, duke of Harcourt (1654–1718)	Field marshal (1703); ambassador	Lieutenant general, government of Lower Normandy
Louis de Cardevac, marquis of Havrincourt (1707–67)	Lieutenant general (1758); ambassador	Cavalry colonel; governor Hesdin
Nicolas du Blé, marquis of Huxelles (1652–1730)	Field marshal (1703); minister of state	Lieutenant general

Maternal grandfather	Father-in-law's rank or office	Marriage age	Bride's age
Brigadier general	Colonel of dragoons; ambassador	20	14
	Governor, Saintonge and Angoumois	23	17
	Brigadier general; lieutenant-general of Anjou	24	18
	General treasurer, Royal mint	39	28
	Royal secretary; grand audencier, Chancellery	48	
Military officer	Brigadier general	27	
Superintendant of finance	Governor, Hainault and Tournay	17	14
Constable of France	Judge, Parlement of Metz	27	
Lieutenant general	Brigadier general	23	
Officer, Swiss Guards regiment	Field marshal	41	
Lord of St. Didier	Brigadier general	24	17
Lord of St. Didier	Did not marry		
President, seneschalcy court, Clermont-Ferrand	Particular lieutenant, Châtelet	16	
Captain, "gendarmes du Roi"	Infantry colonel; governor, Blois and Chambord	35	28
Military officer	Lieutenant general	31	15
Captain of galley fleet; ambassador	Marquis of La Marthe	21	
Brigadier general	Brigadier general	21	
Royal secretary	Field marshal	38	
Military officer	Marquis of Champagne-Vilaines	44	
Lieutenant general	First president, Parlement of Paris	33	24
Field marshal	Field marshal; viceroy Catalonia	16	15
Royal secretary	Colonel	33	
Military officer	Ambassador	30	20
Governor, Verdun	Did not marry		

Table 4.3. *(cont.)*

Name and title	Highest military rank and date	Father's rank or office
Claude-Louis d'Espinchal, marquis of Massiac (1686–1770)	Lieutenant general naval army (1756); secretary of state for navy	Navy engineer
Pierre d'Artagnan, baron of Montesquiou (c. 1645–1725)	Field marshal (1709); commander Brittany, Languedoc, Provence	Major; commander, Bayonne
Louis-François, marquis of Monteynard (1713–91)	Lieutenant general (1759); secretary of state for war	Marquis of Monteynard
Adrien-Maurice, duke of Noailles (1678–1766)	Field marshal (1734); minister of state	Field marshal; viceroy, Catalonia
Pierre-Paul, marquis of Ossun (1713–88)	Lieutenant general (1780); minister of state	Infantry captain
César-Gabriel de Choiseul-Chevigny, duke of Praslin (1712–85)	Lieutenant general (1748); secretary of state for foreign affairs, na	Cavalry colonel
Roger Brûlart de Sillery, marquis of Puyzieulx (1640–1719)	Lieutenant general (1696); ambassador	Colonel
Louis Philogène Brûlart de Sillery, marquis of Puyzieulx (1702–70)	Brigadier general (1734); minister of state	Infantry colonel; governor; Epernay and Huningue
Charles de Rohan, prince of Soubise (1715–87)	Lieutenant general (1748); governor Flanders and Hainault	Duke of Rohan-Soubise; captain, royal Guard
Paul-Hypolite de Beauvillier, duke of Saint-Aignan (1684–1776)	Lieutenant general (1738); ambassador; governor Burgundy	Cavalry colonel; ambassador; governor, Burgundy
Louis de Rouvroy, duke of Saint-Simon (1677–1755)	Cavalry colonel (1693); ambassador	First gentleman of the Royal chamber; governor, Blaye
Jean-Baptiste de Johanne, count of Saumery (1665–1738)	Officer of royal Guard (1695); commander, region of Blois	Brigadier general; governor, Blois & Chambord
Jacques-Joseph Vipart, marquis of Silly (1671–1727)	Lieutenant general (1718); commander, Normandy	Infantry colonel
Camille d'Hostun, duke of Tallard (1652–1728)	Field marshal (1703); ambassador; governor, Franche-Comté	Brigadier general; commander, region of Lyons
Claude-Louis-Hector, duke of Villars (1653–1734)	Field marshal (1702); governor, Provence; minister of state	Lieutenant general; councillor of state
François de Neufville, duke of Villeroy (1644–1730)	Field marshal (1693)	Field marshal; governor, Lyon

Source: Data constructed from Antoine, *Le gouvernement*; La Chesnaye des Bois, *Dictionnaire;* and Woëlmont de Brumagne, *Notices généalogiques.*

marriages are known married within the army (17), the Court (2), or the manorial aristocracy (2). Six were married to daughters of magistrates or civil administrators. Five of them were cadet sons. Thirteen of the 16 only sons or eldest sons were married to daughters of military or manorial noblemen. Only one of the 45 daughters was a spinster. Eight were given to the Church. Twenty-seven of the 36 daughters who did marry were wed to military officers, and only 3 to robe or administrative families. The others were given to titled seigneurial families.

These two highest and parallel, strata in the aristocracy of service – intendants of Generalities and provinces, and military councillors – collaborated in

Maternal grandfather	Father-in-law's rank or office	Marriage age	Bride's age
	Commissioner of the Navy	73	61
President, Superior Court of Béarn	Unknown		
	Marquis; seneschal, Beaucaire and Nîmes	40	19
Military officer	Count; governor Cognac and Aigues-Mortes	20	14
Captain, royal Guards regiment	Royal prosecutor, Parlement of Languedoc	36	
Captain, Duke of Orléans' Guard Company	Marquis of Villaines	20	15
Peer of France; governor Poitou	Lieutenant general	28	
Judge, Chambre des Comptes, Paris	Cavalry colonel; governor, Lower Languedoc	20	15
Constable of France	General; grand chamberlain of France	19	12
Controller general of Finance; secretary of state	Cavalry colonel	23	16
Lieutenant general; governor of Béarn	Field marshal; governor, Lorraine	18	17
Treasurer of war	Commissioner of war	23	
	Did not marry		
Brigadier general	Count of Viriville-La Tivolière; governor, Montélimar	25	
First gentleman of the royal chamber	Secretary, duke of Orléans, ambassador	49	
Lieutenant general; governor Dauphiné	Councillor, duke of Orléans	18	

the governance of France, often with great tension. They encountered each other occasionally at Court and processed together on ceremonial occasions, but they kept a fundamental distance. Only three (6%) of the 53 intendants in our sample whose marriages are known allied with the sword aristocracy; only 4 (9%) of the 36 military councillors of state who married allied with the high-robe nobility. None of the intendants of the periods 1710 to 1712 and 1749 to 1751, or their fathers, married the daughter of a military councillor of state. The only military councillor to marry into the family of an intendant was the count of Canillac, who wed the daughter of François-Antoine Ferrand in 1697. Among the 51 sons of military councillors whose marriages are known (Table

Table 4.4. *Children of military councillors of state*

Title of councillor	Number	Army	Navy	Church	Administration	Magistracy Court	Manor
Duke of Antin	4	s1(A) s2		s4			s3 (M)
Count of Baschi	4	s1(Ma) d3					d1 d2
Bazin	7	s1(Ma) s3 d1 d2		s2 d3			d4
Duke of Biron	13	s1(A) s4(A) s6(A) ds 2-7		s3 s5 d1			s2
Marquis of Bonnac	8	s1(C) s2 s3 d2 d3		s4			d1
Duke of Charost	3	s1(M) s2(M) s3					
Duke of Béthune-Charost	6	s3(A) d1 d2		s2 d1			s1(A)
Marquis of Brancas	7	s1(A) s3(C) d1 d4	s2	d2 d3			
Count Du Luc	2	s(A)				d	
Marquis of Fénelon	4	s1(A)			d2 d3		d1
Duke of Guiche	4	s1 (A) s2(A) d1 d2					
Duke of Harcourt	8	s1(A) s2 s4(A) s5(Ad) d2		d1			d1
Marquis of Havrincourt	3	s1 s2					
Marquis of Ossun	1	s(A)					
Marquis of Puyzieulx	4	s1 d1-3					
Marquis of Puyzieulx	1	d					
Prince of Soubise	2	d1 d2					
Duke of Saint-Aignan	9	s1(M) s2 s5 d3 d4	s3	s4 d1 d2			
Duke of Saint-Simon	3	s1(A) s2(M) d					
Count of Saumery	3	s3	s2				s1
Duke of Tallard	3	s1(A) s2 d					

Note: Number of children includes only those who survived to adulthood.

Abbreviations: s1–first son; d1–first daughter, etc. Abbreviations in parentheses refer to professional background of family into which military councillor's child married: *A*–army; *Ad*–administration; *C*–royal court; *M*–magistracy; *Ma*–manorial (or scion who handled family estates and affairs and had no other profession.)

Source: Data constructed from La Chesnaye des Bois, *Dictionnaire de la noblesse*, and Woëlmont de Brumagne, *Notices généalogiques*.

4.4), only 2 were wed to daughters of intendants: the eldest son of the duke of Saint-Aignan to the daughter of Creil de Bournezeau (1738), and the cadet son of the duke of Saint-Simon to Bauyn d'Angervilliers' daughter (1733).

Familial choices, repeated over generations, created these patterns. An elite family of Old Regime France was defined, in all crucial respects, by patrilineage. Vocation, offices or commissions, real property, and most movable property, and title (in the case of noble families) all passed principally from father to sons. Therefore, the marrying of sons was of far more consequence to a family than that of daughters. Through the career placement and the marriage of its sons, particularly the eldest, a family either confirmed and enhanced its vocation or began to change in vocation and identity. The army and the themistocracy were each dominated by a system of patronage that operated essentially within kinship groups, and thus depended heavily on the formation of powerful kinship networks through marriages. When a family that was rising or consolidating within the themistocracy married a son to a daughter of the *noblesse d'épée*, it "wasted" that son, in a political sense. Alliance with a family of sword nobility could not professionally aggrandize the themistocratic family or its son in his career, and it could only rarely bring a substantial dowry. The same was true for military families. They could gain only capital from marrying their sons to daughters of the *noblesse de robe*, although many of them needed that capital to finance expensive commissions in the army and the style of life incumbent on officers in elite regiments.

Comparison of the marital politics of intendants and military councillors of state therefore yields the same results as prosopography of the eighteenth-century Parisian themistocracy in the Châtelet and Parlement. Both reveal a wide split between the two main segments of the French aristocracy, from the mid-seventeenth century to the Revolution. The robe and the sword touched socially, but they rarely blended. This was true even in their respective highest ranks. Each displayed fundamental elements of caste behavior: dynasticism in vocation, especially among eldest sons, and endogamy in marriage, particularly of sons.[17] Such behavior nourished the antagonism that La Bruyère remarked with consternation in 1694:

The nobility risks its life for the security of the state and the glory of the sovereign; the magistrate discharges the prince of much of the burden of judging his people. These two duties are equally sublime, and of equally marvelous utility; men are hardly capable of greater things than these, and I do not know from what source the robe and the sword have drawn their mutual contempt.[18]

[17] These patterns contradict Franklin Ford's thesis of fusion between robe and sword during the eighteenth century (*Robe and Sword: The Regrouping of the French Aristocracy after Louis XIV* [Cambridge, Mass.: Harvard University Press, 1953]) and Chaussinand-Nogaret's refinements of that thesis (*French Nobility*).

[18] Translated from "Les caractères ou les moeurs de ce siècle," in *Oeuvres complètes de La Bruyère*, ed. Julien Benda (Paris: Bibliothèque de la Pléiade, 1951), pp. 260–1. For numerous expressions of that mutual contempt, from the mid-sixteenth to the mid-seventeenth century, see Davis Bitton, *The French Nobility in Crisis, 1560–1640* (Stanford: Stanford University Press, 1969).

La Bruyère's implicit question contains a key element of its answer, for he perceived the radically different character, requirements, and corporate mentality of the two vocations, and their rivalry for preeminent consideration from king and realm. The rivalry was probably inevitable, precisely because the two groups were distinct and yet accomplished the greatest and most highly respected tasks in French lay civilization.

Whenever a group identifies itself essentially by its vocation and profession, and not by its ancestry, class, or Estate, it assumes exclusive and exacting criteria of value. It must judge itself, be judged by others, and judge them in turn by performance, by efficacy and merit in the tasks of vocation. It develops arcana and arrogance of vocation. Vocational identity fragments large social aggregates or classes, in consciousness and in fact; it then recomposes them in new combinations of affinities, aversions, and rivalries. The French monarchy subtly forced such invidious criteria of value, and of self-valuation, on civil officialdom and on the military nobility of France.

In consequence of vocation, the robe nobility and the bourgeoisie were separated by further divides from most of the military and seigneurial nobility. Sons of the robe nobility received lengthy humanistic education in the *collèges* and legal education in the universities between the ages of 11 and 20, before they began their careers. In contrast, most sword nobles received a commission in a regiment between the ages of 14 and 17, where they began to learn the profession on the drill ground and "at the cannon's mouth." Men of the high robe were elites of an urban civilization. They were bound, for most of their lives, to the close precincts of town houses, family and kin, salons, academies, and court chambers. Men of the sword were primarily elites of an agrarian civilization. When they were not on their estates, they lived nomadically, in garrisons throughout France or on campaign in the war zones of Europe. They were men of violence. They lived in intimate acquaintance with wounds, killing, and death. And they procreated more abundantly than families of the robe: Military councillors of state had an average of 4.3 children (see Table 4.4), intendants an average of 2.8 (see Table 4.2).[19]

To functional, material, and psychological differences between robe and sword must be added the fact that the robe wielded authority over the sword, in the most serious and direct manner. Magistrates, both bourgeois and noble, of superior courts judged nobles in civil and criminal cases.[20] The magistrates

---

[19] Several of the military councillors of state had been wounded repeatedly, during their career on the battlefield, some as senior commander. The count of Canillac endured multiple wounds leading the Black Musketeers at Ramillies (1706) and Malplaquet (1709). The marquis of Fenélon was killed, as lieutenant general commanding at the Battle of Raucoux (1746). And the toll was high among the sons of the 40 councillors during the War of the Austrian Succession and the Seven Years' War; many were killed or severely wounded, leading their regiments and brigades from in front. The threat of losing sons in war was probably the main reason why military families produced more children than themistocratic families.

[20] Some of them did more than judge. In certain regions of France, particularly during the sixteenth and seventeenth centuries, families of judiciary and administration used the civil law to dispossess sword-noble families. Faced with declining revenues from seigneurial estates and

were empowered and bound to try, judge, and sentence aristocratic offenders against the criminal law, including duelists. Even the commanders and officers of garrisons in towns were subject to royal civil and criminal laws enforced by the magistrates of those towns, except during wartime sieges. When a criminal complaint was brought against a regimental aristocrat by a commoner, the officer was tried by a local royal court or a Parlement, not by a military tribunal. If a civil complaint was lodged against them, many aristocrats enjoyed the privilege of trial by a presidial court, with right of appeal to a Parlement. If charged with a crime, they could request trial by a Parlement. Those privileges distinguished them from most commoners, but they also subordinated the sword aristocracy to the authority of the high robe. That authority went even beyond legal judgment and discreet punishment. Any nobleman convicted by a Parlement of a crime that carried "defaming" penalty (as did most offenses in *grand criminel*) lost personal nobility and its privileges, unless a royal pardon was forthcoming. By the authority and provisions of the criminal law, magistrates could condemn a sword noble to death by public execution and supervise that execution.

C. Antagonisms

The military nobility had no remotely comparable authority over the themistocracy; royal legislation had seen to that since the sixteenth century. It had only powers of social and professional exclusion, the powers collectively exercised in 1781 and 1789. The most blatant "aristocratic reaction" in late Old Regime France was that of the sword against the robe and the administrative pen.

In the late Old Regime, there were a total of about 8,000 officers' commissions (if we include all officer ranks) in the army. Commissions for all but the very highest ranks were venal and costly.[21] During the years 1713 to 1789, the

their tenancies, and with high expenditure for military service during protracted wars, numerous old noble families went deeply into debt. In repayment, and either to avoid lawsuits or in consequence of them, they were forced to alienate domains. Local royal magistrates and administrators (bourgeois and *anoblis*), *échevins*, barristers, and notaries were often their principal creditors – and eventually the new owners of those domains. A noble family whose major (and usually modest) resources were alienated was faced with social ruin if it did not receive a substantial royal pension (and few did); it lost the economic capacity to live, serve, and marry nobly, and after one or two generations it disappeared from the nobility. Typically, its place was eventually taken by the rising creditor family that already possessed or would acquire ennoblement by offices. In Picardy, from the late sixteenth century to the early eighteenth, the scale of those proceedings amounted to a social revolution in ownership of domanial properties. See Pierre Deyon, *Amiens, capitale provinciale: Etude sur la société urbaine au 17e siècle* (The Hague: Mouton, 1967), pp. 265–83, 323–38, and Pierre Goubert, *Beauvais et le beauvaisis de 1600 à 1730: Contribution à l'histoire sociale de la France du XVIIe siècle* (Paris: S.E.V.P.E.N., 1960), pp. 206–22, 321–42.

[21] The price of the colonelcy of a regiment exceeded the price of a judgeship in the Parlement of Paris between 1714 and 1776: 55,000–75,000 livres for the twelve oldest infantry regiments, 30,000–40,000 livres for the others; 100,000–120,000 livres for elite cavalry regiments, 50,000 livres for most of the others. A lieutenancy of infantry cost 1,000–2,000 livres, but the officer needed at least that sum in annual income, beyond salary, to meet expenses (François Bluche,

officers led a professional army that numbered between 200,000 and 350,000 men. Themistocracy was honorable, but during the eighteenth century the ancient calling of military leadership and those who paid its "blood tax" remained preeminent within the large social universe of *honneur* and among the external groups that were spectators to that universe. In May 1781, the count of Ségur, the minister of war, and the Military Council (composed of senior generals) promulgated the famous ordinance that required at least four generations of nobility, or *noblesse de race*, for every candidate to a lieutenantcy (the obligatory entering rank) in the infantry and cavalry regiments of the army. The only exception subsequently allowed was for sons of career military officers. The Ségur Ordinance was approved in council by Louis XVI.

David Bien has conclusively demonstrated that this carefully drafted and well-enforced rule was not intended to exclude bourgeois from the officer corps but to exclude the robe and civil nobility.[22] At any given period between 1740 and 1781, only about 5 percent of army officers were commoners. The great mass of the officer corps had been noble since at least the reign of Louis XIV. The army was the largest nobiliary institution in Old Regime France, and it offered only the most narrow – even derisory – avenues for the ennoblement of officers: appointment to the senior ranks of *maréchal de camp* or lieutenant general (but only 5% of the 1,748 men who served as officers in those ranks between 1750 and 1789 were commoners at the time of their appointment); personal and nontransmissible nobility as *chevalier de Saint-Louis* for those who served thirty years, of which twenty had to be in the rank of captain; or hereditary ennoblement of family after three consecutive patrilineal generations had served as officers (which amounted to a maximum of two hundred families, between 1750 and 1789). Social ascent, in the sense of moving from common to noble estate, therefore was virtually impossible within the army or navy. That carefully maintained fact (long antecedent to the Ségur Ordinance) nourished a uniquely aristocratic consciousness among the families of the officer corps. By absolute contrast, there were almost 4,000 immediately or gradually ennobling civil offices during the second half of the century, or almost half the total of commissions in the army. There were at least 6,000 distinct families of robe and civil nobility, virtually all of whom had bourgeois elders or ancestors and continued to collaborate professionally with bourgeois. They were in general far more affluent than the majority of the *noblesse d'épée*.[23] The volume of

La vie quotidienne de la noblesse au XVIIIe siècle [Paris: Hachette, 1973], pp. 134–50). Bluche conjectured that nearly the total wealth of most provincial sword families was devoted to maintaining sons in the vocation of officer.

22 The following discussion of the Ségur Ordinance and the army is drawn from two of Bien's essays: "La réaction aristocratique avant 1789," pp. 23–48, 505–34, and "The Army in the French Enlightenment: Reform, Reaction and Revolution," in *Past and Present*, 85 (1979): 68–98.

23 That is revealed for Paris by Daniel Roche's reconstruction of nobiliary fortunes in the Marais Quarter in the years 1750 to 1755, from notarial records ("Recherches sur la noblesse parisienne au milieu du XVIIIe siècle: La noblesse du Marais," in *Actes du Quatre-vingt-sixième Congrès National des Sociétés Savantes* [Paris, 1961], pp. 541–78). Half of the magistrates of the

ennoblements by office did increase during the century, especially through royal secretaryships.

The Ségur Ordinance was crafted intelligently and successfully to exclude the great majority of the robe and civil nobility from the officer corps, for as of 1780 about three-fourths of such families had fewer than four generations of nobility, whereas the mass of the sword aristocracy were *noblesse de race*.[24] Robe families, and their numerous sons, were a theoretical menace to the monopoly of the army by the dynastic sword nobility: They had the demographic and economic capacity to absorb the officer corps and thereby eventually to confiscate the vocation and prestige of the sword nobility. That specter dominated the vision of the military establishment. But they were able to imagine such a specter only because they had long regarded the *noblesse de robe* as alien, inferior, and predatory on their profession. The ordinance was not essentially a response to

Parlement of Paris and the Chambre des Comptes, and very many from the other sovereign courts and the Châtelet, resided in that Quarter. Most of the sword-noble families who resided there were quite superior in rank and wealth to their provincial counterparts. The robe nobles of the Quarter were generally wealthier than the sword families, and the respective sources of wealth differed. The sword fortune was narrow and comparatively static; it consisted primarily in agrarian seigneurial properties and their revenues, and in military commissions. Robe property was more diverse and productive of revenue: urban real estate and its rents comprised 57% of real property, as against 43% in rural holdings; offices of state comprised 30% of total fortune; bonds, annuities, and loans to organs of state and to individuals, combined with possessions, precious objects, and money comprised 30–40% of total fortune. In scale and composition, the wealth of noble themistocrats in the mid-eighteenth century Marais closely resembled that of bourgeois and noble themistocrats in the Châtelet during the period 1660 to 1700 (see Rosset, "Les conseillers du Châtelet," pt. 25, pp. 233–302). It would have differed in kind and exceeded by far the wealth of the majority of provincial noble families whose vocations were military. For Orléans and its region, see Georges Lefebvre, *Etudes orléanaises: Contribution a l'étude des structures sociales à la fin du XVIIIe siècle*, 2 vols. (Paris: Commission d'Histoire Economique et Sociale de la Révolution, 1962), vol. 1, pp. 164–200; for the region of Amiens, see Deyon, *Amiens*, pp. 265–92. Economic inequality seems to have been almost as great within the nobility as within the Third Estate. On the basis of assessments for the *capitation* tax, Chaussinand-Nogaret (*French Nobility*, p. 53) estimated that the majority of themistocratic nobles throughout France received 10,000 to 50,000 livres in annual income, making them among the wealthiest 15% of the nobility. Such a family could raise 50,000 livres for a regimental colonelcy if it was determined to do so. He found that 60% of all eighteenth-century noble families had incomes of less than 4,000 livres per annum. They included the *hobereaux*, who consistently provided the army with the great majority of its officers below the rank of lieutenant colonel. Those men led squadrons, companies, and battalions, and they sustained most of the wounds, mutilations, and fatalities suffered by the officer corps during the long and bloody wars of the eighteenth century. Contempt and animosity for the robe was probably most intense among that large, impecunious, and sacrificial group of the French nobility. The Ségur Ordinance was intended to protect their hold on the officer corps.

24 Much of the noble themistocracy of the great Parisian courts was excluded by the four-generation requirement. Bluche determined pedigree for all fully noble judges who entered the sovereign courts of Paris between January 1771 and January 1787: 67 *parlementaires*, of which 34 were second- or third-degree noble; 63 in the Chambre des Comptes, 42 of second- or third-degree nobility; 17 in the Cour des Aides, 11 of second- or third-degree nobility; 11 in the Grand Conseil, 6 of second- or third-degree nobility ("Les magistrats des cours parisiennes au XVIIIe siècle," p. 97). Half of those 194 young robe aristocrats were formally barred from the officer corps of the army by the ordinance. For the full scale of exclusion of robe nobles throughout France, see Bien's calculations in "La réaction aristocratique." The authors of the ordinance clearly had some accurate knowledge of the robe nobility.

an actuality or a manifest threat, for during the eighteenth century, only about 15 percent of the commissions in the officer corps were purchased by sons of the robe, and the men involved were a mere fraction of the total number of those sons. The robe and pen nobility did not covet regimental commissions, but it did use the officer corps as honorable placement for excess sons and for those not suited to careers in the magistracy or administration.[25] The ordinance was produced by an act of imagination, an aggressive crystallization of traditional antagonisms, resentments, and repudiations. It was preemptive exclusion of *enfants de fortune* in favor of *enfants d'honneur,* according to the language of its authors.

The ordinance was motivated by more than social disdain and the tendentious pretext that amateurish, incompetent officers from robe families were largely responsible for French defeats in the Seven Years' War. Its explicit rationale was simultaneously cultural and professional. Eighteenth-century warfare required officers to train their troops in robotic discipline; to lead them expertly under fire, in intricate and rapidly altered tactical formations; to command from in front and in obedience to complex orders from superiors. The métier of officer required more than courage; it required self-abnegation, collective uniformity of mind and behavior, personal constancy, and frequent exertion in war and peace. Ségur and his generals believed that specialized instruction in military *collèges* and within regiments did not suffice to create an officer. They believed that the essential process that formed an officer was psychological, a formation that required special moral education, inculcating devotion to duty and fear of failure, and that these qualities could only be imparted from infancy by a military family and patrimony.[26] The argument of the sword nobility was not essentially genetic; it was a behavioralist argument, used

---

[25] Most commissions in the army, up to the rank of lieutenant colonel, were far less expensive than most offices in sovereign courts or high administration. Themistocratic families had a financial incentive to place one or more cadet sons in the officer corps. By doing so, they could save most of their capital for maintaining elder sons in magistracy or administration and also for handsomely dowering their daughters in marriages to other robe families. In such cases, the cadet son who was given to a regiment was thus honorably sacrificed by his parents so that the themistocratic vocation of the family could be securely perpetuated or expanded.

[26] See Bien, "La réaction aristocratique," pp. 522–3, 530. Yet Bien also conveys the violently contemptuous descriptions of robe nobles by officers in high military circles during the period of the ordinance, as men who have usurped nobility with money, who are debilitated by sedentary work, intellectual pursuits and luxury, greedy for honors, and incapable of the profession of arms. These charges echo an old adversary literature. Those stereotypic moral images seem more revealing of the motives behind the ordinance than the strictly professional considerations emphasized by Bien. However, the images were probably false, in large measure. Eighteenth-century sons of the magistracy were imbued from childhood with an ethos of service to king and commonweal, an ethos of duty that will be examined in Chapter 5. Most were taught to ride, fence, and shoot. They were well nourished. Most probably equaled the scions of sword-noble families in moral and physical strength and in basic capacity to face the rigors of military life. Contempt and fear commingled in the ordinance. The fear may have proceeded from a perception of the robe's capacities, with that perception then being concealed or rationalized as incapacity. The Ségur law was, in sum, a late and acute manifestation of the hostility to the robe and pen that was widespread among the dynastic sword nobility during the seventeenth and

by an exclusive, highly dynastic socioprofessional caste, one that also considered itself to be the only true nobility of France. Their implicit conviction was that magistracy and administration, however high the offices, were inferior, essentially bourgeois, forms of service to the realm, which did not prepare youth for military leadership.

Ironically, although the themistocracy also believed that family and environment had primary importance in shaping young men for its own vocation, the noble themistocracy had long since quietly reciprocated the disdain of the military elite. It rarely offered its most important vocational resource, eldest sons, to the army; it rarely married them outside civil officialdom; and it even more rarely welcomed sons of military families as candidates for themistocracy. Still, the robe aristocracy received the fait accompli of the Ségur Ordinance as a humiliating insult. It was tantamount to denying the nobility that they had acquired through long, expensive, and exacting familial service to the state.[27]

From another perspective, the Ségur Ordinance was merely a continuation of the long-term royal policy of encouraging vocationalism in state service, for it simultaneously protected those families whose traditional profession was arms and confined families of the civil nobility to careers of the robe and pen.

D. The revelation of 1789

The last and most consequential offensive of the sword against the robe was in the assemblies of the nobility that met throughout France during the first months of 1789 to elect deputies to the Estates-General. Some 26,000 aristocrats – most of the adult male nobility of France – attended the assemblies of the Second Estate to choose the commissioners who would draft the nobiliary *cahiers* and to elect their representatives to the Estates-General.[28] From 20 to 25 percent of those noblemen belonged to the magistracy, chancelleries, or civil

eighteenth centuries. According to Mousnier, "The world of the gown remained a world apart and distinct, despised by the men of the sword, for whom it consisted of 'bourgeois.' " (*Institutions of France*, vol. 1, p. 161).

[27] Beyond the attitudes and actions of the high military establishment, the writings of some officers, and the genealogies of a few thousand military families, the officer corps of the royal army remains the least known of all the important socioprofessional groups of Old Regime France – materially and psychologically. Few historians, even specialists in the seventeenth and eighteenth centuries, have studied that group from archival or other primary sources. Such research, which would require the combining of social, economic, and military historiography, could be broadly illuminating of Old Regime civilization. An excellent beginning would be to select one infantry regiment and one cavalry regiment and reconstruct the provenance, careers, experiences and attitudes of their officers from 1715 to the Revolution.

[28] Halévi "The Monarchy and the Elections of 1789," p. S87. By a royal declaration of January 24, 1789, *anoblis* and those incipiently noble were excluded from the assemblies of the Second Estate. All those who had "full and transmissible" nobility were eligible; this included second-generation nobles, or the sons of those ennobled in first degree by offices, and those who had served for twenty years in succession to their fathers in offices that ennobled gradually. Long before 1789, the great majority of ennoblements were in the first degree. About three-fourths of the entire robe and civil nobility were eligible to vote.

administration. But of the 288 noble deputies finally elected to represent the Second Estate, only 26 (or 9%) were themistocrats: 22 *parlementaires*, 2 judges of other sovereign courts, and 2 judges of presidial courts. Those 22 *parlementaires* were the only themistocrats from among the more than 1,000 noble themistocrats who had voted in the assemblies, many of them in rural or secondary bailliages. One can imagine their dismay at this outcome when they first gathered in the hall of the nobility at Versailles. In that 1789 election, discrimination against high-ranking royal administrators was even more thorough. Among the thousands of noble electors from such offices or families, only 3 such men, or 1 percent, were chosen to be deputies. The robe and pen nobility did not only compose almost one-quarter of the entire French aristocracy; it was also the most politically experienced segment. Its members were present in more than one-third of electoral assemblies, yet it formed a bare 10 percent of deputies. In the electoral assemblies of the Second Estate, there clearly had been an extensive, almost general repudiation of the robe and pen by the other aristocracy of France.

This occurred even in Paris and its region, which had been the political citadel of the noble themistocracy since at least the sixteenth century. Of the quota of 10 noble deputies and 10 substitutes selected to represent the city and faubourgs of Paris, 14 were high-ranking military officers or seigneurial nobles with old titles.[29] Only 6 were themistocrats: Achille-Pierre Dionis du Séjour, Adrien Duport, Louis-Michel Lepeletier de Saint-Fargeau, Charles-Louis Huguet de Semonville, Abel-François Malartic de Fondat, all judges of the Parlement of Paris, and François de Montholon, general prosecutor of the Chambre des Comptes.[30]

[29] The fourteen were: Joseph-Alexandre, viscount of Ségur, colonel of the Hainault Light Cavalry (and son of Minister of War Ségur); Stanislas-Marie-Adélaïde, count of Clerment-Tonnerre, colonel of the Royal Navarre regiment; Louis-Alexandre, duke of La Rochefoucauld, *maréchal de camp;* Trophiem-Gérard, count of Lally-Tolendal, former captain of heavy calvalry; Aiméry-Louis-Roger, count of Rochechouärt, *maréchal de camp* and military governor of the Orléanais; Hugues-Thibault, marquis of Luzignem, commander of the Flanders Infantry regiment; Charles-Philibert-Marie, count of Lévis-Mirepoix, colonel of the Marshal Turenne Infantry regiment; Anne-Pierre, marquis of Montesquiou-Fezensac, *maréchal de camp;* François, marquis of Beauharnois, colonel of a dragoon regiment; Louis-Marie-Céleste d'Aumont de Villequier, duke of Piennes, colonel of the Franche-Comté Light Cavalry regiment; Joseph, count Archambaut de Talleyrand-Périgord and marquis of Rosny, colonel of the Alsace Light Cavalry regiment; Hilarion-Paul-François du Puget, count of Barbantane, colonel of the Aunis Infantry regiment; Jean-Baptiste-Cyrus de Timbrune, viscount of Valence, colonel of the Chartres Dragoon regiment; Alexandre-Louis-Auguste de Rohan-Chabot, prince of Léon, colonel of the Royal Piedmont Infantry regiment (Brette, *Les constituants*, pp. 4–7).

[30] Ibid. Nobles could vote in the bailliages of either their primary or secondary residence. About 4,000 adult male and officially resident nobles were eligible to vote in the assembly for the Paris *ville et faubourgs* (Charles L. Chassin, *Les élections et les cahiers de Paris en 1789*, 4 vols. [Paris, 1888], vol. 2, pp. 247–8). Only some 910 did so. The majority of the 4,000 voted in provincial assemblies. In 1789, there were at least 1,500 Parisian nobles of the robe and administration; a large number of them voted *extra muros*, in the bailliages where they owned secondary, manorial residences (throughout the Ile-de-France and adjacent regions) and where competition for influence was expected to be less intense. All but a minuscule number of those who did so in the hope of being elected deputy were disappointed. But a higher proportion of military and seign-

Table 4.5. *Professions of 910 nobles voting in Paris, 1789*

Group	Number	% of total
Magistrate, Parlement of Paris	56	6.0
Magistrate, Châtelet	23	2.5
Magistrate, other courts	112	12.0
Barrister or notary	17	2.0
Royal administrative, municipal, or household official	131	14.0
Military or naval officer	234	26.0
Seigneur without stated profession (chevalier, baron, viscount, count, marquis, duke)	337	37.0
Others	4	0.4

Source: Computed from Brette, *Les constituants*; Chassin *Les élections et les cahiers*; A. Trudon des Ormes, "L'Etat civil des citoyens nobles de Paris en 1789," in *Mémoires de la société de l'Histoire de Paris et de l'Ile-de-France*, 26 (1899): 255–369.

Among the nobles who voted in Paris, magistrates and royal administrators outnumbered sword nobles by almost 100 (322, as against 234); they were resoundingly defeated by them in the election of deputies (Table 4.5). The royal administrators included many masters of requests, intendants, grand masters of waters and forests, councillors of state, treasurers and general receivers of Generalities – men and offices closely affiliated with the magistracy. Not one of them was elected to the Estates-General from Paris. And there were dozens of great robe lineages, *noblesse de race*, among the magisterial electors, such as the d'Aguesseaus, Nicolays, and Duprès de Saint-Maur. Among them, only Lepeletier and Montholon were chosen. The bloc that decided the election of Parisian deputies consisted of the 337 seigneurial nobles (of which there were more viscounts, counts, and marquises than simple chevaliers), most of whom had military filiations and loyalties. Their political solidarity was with the sword, against the robe and pen. The outcome was general symmetry between the composition of the assembly and the composition of the deputation: 36.5 percent of electors were of the robe or administrative pen, and 30 percent of deputies; 63 percent of electors were of the sword or seigneurial title, and 70 percent of deputies. This evident voting by blocs was an ancient and well-established factional division, translated into the politics of 1789.

eurial nobles chose to vote in Paris, instead of in country bailliages. By that choice, and their solidarity, they dominated the nobiliary assembly of Paris. The socioprofessional distribution of the 910 voters of Paris is presented in Table 4.5. Data computed from Trudon des Ormes, "L'état civil des citoyens nobles de Paris en 1789."

Fully 71 percent of noble deputies to the Estates-General from all of France were retired or serving officers of the army (195) or navy (11); most were regimental colonels or general officers. Another 19 percent were domainal aristocrats from the provinces, without stated profession, a group that meshed socially and politically with the sword nobility.[31] There were twice as many local seigneurs as there were themistocratic and administrative nobles among the deputies. Sword nobles outnumbered robe and pen nobles by 8 to 1 in the Assembly at Versailles.

Military and seigneurial nobles had closed ranks throughout France in refusing to delegate their representation, and thus their political embodiment and voice, to themistocrats and high administrators.[32] In fact, the composition of the Second Estate's deputation at Versailles in 1789 strikingly resembles its composition at the Estates-General of 1614–15, long before the robe nobility had come into existence.[33] In 1789, the sword nobles politically confiscated the Second Estate. This final schism within the aristocracy and defeat of the robe

[31] Computed from Brette, *Les constituants.* There was discrimination against robe nobles in the assemblies of most cities that were seats of Parlements or other superior courts. Both deputies from Colmar (Alsace) were military nobles. Only 1 of the 4 from Arras (Artois) was a magistrate. Six of the 7 deputies from the bailliages of Besançon, Amont-Vesoul, Lons-le-Saulnier, and Dôle were military nobles; the only themistocrat was the president of the Parlement of Franche-Comté. The solitary deputy from Douai, seat of the Parlement of Flanders, was a marquis and domainal lord. Seven of the 8 deputies from Dauphiné were either military officers or seigneurial aristocrats, whereas 8 of the 12 deputies from the Third Estate of that province were either magistrates or barristers. Both deputies from Nancy were *maréchaux de camp*, as were the 2 from Metz. One deputy from Toulouse was a president of the Parlement of Languedoc; the other 3 were military or domainal nobles (ibid., pp. 4–5, 140, 128–32, 135, 182–3, 155–6, 112, 151). Hundreds of noble themistocrats and administrators – magistrates in Parlements, Chambres des Comptes, Cours des Aides, presidial courts, chancelleries, and finance offices – resided in each of those cities and their environs. The nobility of France voted in some 375 bailliage assemblies; nobles of the robe and pen would have been present in at least one-third of them.

[32] In his memoirs and letters to his wife, the marquis of Ferrières, deputy from the Saumurois, stated fears and resentments that were probably common among the old provincial nobility in 1788–9 and underlay the elections. He claimed that at the time of the elections for the Estates-General, he was convinced that both the high robe and the elites of the Third Estate had hegemonic projects: "Chaque corps, chaque individu avait ses vues; le parlement espérait s'accroître de tout ce que les Etats généraux ôteraient au roi; la haute noblesse secouer le joug ministériel, auquel l'avait soumise le cardinal de Richelieu; les capitalistes et les rentiers voulaient assurer leurs créances, et faire de la dette du roi une dette de l'Etat. . . . Le parlement de Paris tendait par une marche lente, mais constamment suivie, à se constituer, à l'exemple du parlement d'Angleterre, représentant de la nation. La position fâcheuse du gouvernement l'invitait à profiter de la circonstance; et quelle immense autorité eût acquise le parlements s'il eût réussi dans ses ambiteux desseins! Les charges devenues un patrimoine de famille auraient fait, des membres qui le composaient, de véritables souverains héréditaires, d'autant plus puissants qu'à l'avantage d'être colégislateurs avec le monarque, ils auraient joint le droit redoutable de prononcer sans appel de la propriété et de la vie des citoyens. . . . Les Français attachés à l'ancienne constitution de l'empire, craignirent qu'on ne voulût porter atteinte à l'essence même de la monarchie. Les nobles de province rejetaient absolument les grands seigneurs. Ils trafiqueraient, disaient-ils, des intérêts de la noblesse" (*Mémoires du marquis de Ferrières*, in *Mémoires sur les assemblées parlementaires de la Révolution*, ed. M. de Lescure [Paris, 1880], pp. 4, 9). His own election resulted from a kind of intrigue, a caucus formed by seigneurial aristocrats who lived in the locality who shared his attitudes and who persuaded him to stand for election at Saumur.

[33] Mousnier, "Development of Monarchical Institutions and Society in France," pp. 38–9.

nobility was the ultimate expression of the attitudes behind the Ségur Ordinance, and it brought to consummation the latent, ancient antagonism that La Bruyère had described in 1694.

The year 1789 was a moment of decisive revelation, and resolution, for the noble themistocracy. For more than a century their collective situation had been liminal. Professionally, although they belonged to a group primarily composed of men who were bourgeois in formal estate, they themselves were not bourgeois. Juridically and socially, they were aristocrats, but they were treated as inferior or alien by most other aristocrats. Politically, they were officers of state, but they were frequently in an adversarial relationship to the king and his ministers, never more so than during the 1780s. In a sense, repudiation by their own estate in 1789, on the eve of the decisive contest with monarchical absolutism, forced the robe nobles to be nothing more nor less than what they had always been: professional men of law. Those who were elected to the Estates-General had the opportunity to become legislators, or ultimate men of law. They possessed inimitable skills for that task.

In the National Assembly of 1789–91, most of the robe-noble deputies allied with bourgeois themistocrats and barristers who had been elected to represent the Third Estate. Several robe-noble deputies rapidly assumed leadership roles within the alliance. That alliance had deep and coherent historical foundations.[34] Together, with the support mainly of liberal deputies from the lower clergy and an energetic radical minority of military-seigneurial nobles, robe nobles and bourgeois men of the law legislatively abolished the three Estates and replaced them with "citizenship." That citizenship was neither uniform nor

---

[34] Etienne Pasquier, third-generation *parlementaire* of Paris in the 1780s and future Chancellor of France under the July Monarchy, described one cohesive element of the alliance, the prestige that *parlementaire* families traditionally enjoyed among the local magistracy of the regions where they owned domainal properties and sojourned during judicial vacations: "On avait souvent recours à leur influence; les membres des nombreuses juridictions inférieures étaient fort empressés à leur apporter leurs hommages; tout contribuait à leur assurer, quand ils savaient s'en rendre dignes, l'existence la plus honorable et la plus enviée. Mes ancêtres avaient tout fait pour la mériter, aussi avaient-ils dans la ville du Mans, dans les environs de leur résidence, de nombreux amis, choisis parmi tout ce que la province renfermait de plus distingué. Le Mans, qui était loin d'être une ville importante, renfermait cependant de grandes ressources de société; dans la noblesse, dans la magistrature, dans la haute bourgeoisie et les propriétaires fonciers, il y avait des hommes de mérite, instruits, distingués, des femmes spirituelles, agréables, aimant le plaisir, inspirant ce goût à tout ce qui les entourait" (*Mémoires du Chancellier Pasquier*, ed. M. le duc d'Audiffret-Pasquier [Paris, 1894], pp. 7–8). But the closest friends and most frequent guests of the Pasquiers in their chateau at Tubeuf were colleagues, the Lamoignons and Berryers of the Parlement and royal Council. By his account, the only military nobles with whom the Pasquiers exchanged visits were the commander and officers of the Le Mans garrison regiment, a ducal regiment of dragoons; most of those officers had some connections at Court and in Parisian society (ibid., pp. 9–12). In giving counsel, hospitality, and patronage to the magistracy of presidial, bailliage, and tax courts in and around Le Mans, the Pasquiers were expressing loyalty to their vocation and to their origins. Their seventeenth-century ancestors were judges of the salt tribunal of Paris, *échevins* (the source of their nobility), and particular lieutenants of the Châtelet (Bluche, "L'origine des magistrats du Parlement de Paris," pp. 339–40). The electoral district of Le Mans sent 10 Third Estate deputies to the Estates-General. Seven of them were magistrates of the type described by Pasquier (Brette, *Les constituants*, pp. 71–2).

egalitarian. It was divided into men who enjoyed full political rights ("active" and "eligible" citizens) by virtue of owning property or capital, and those without property ("passive" citizens) who were accorded the full protection of the laws and most of the rights listed in the famous Declaration of 1789, but not the right to vote or to hold public office. This new principle of identity and empowerment amalgamated nobles and bourgeois into a single propertied and political class, while distinguishing all members of that class from the plebeians of France. In fashioning that synthesis and its boundaries, the Assembly moved beyond, yet also completed, the multisecular policy of the monarchy – the policy of bloating and diluting the nobility by incremental ennoblement of the enterprising and the affluent. The Revolutionary principle of public "careers open to talent" was not, therefore, a radical leap of social and political imagination; it was a new mutation of the old, and still extant, reality of public careers open to families of merit. Like merit during the Old Regime, citizenship in the Revolution of 1789 to 1791 was both exclusionary and inclusionary.

The bloc of "constituants" who most tenaciously resisted those innovations was composed primarily of provincial and old-lineage nobles from the army and the Church. They were incarnations of the same aristocracy that, for two hundred years, had refused to accept the meritocratic ennoblement of commoners. Those deputies became the original cadre of counterrevolution, and after 1791 many of them emigrated.

The behavior of the themistocratic deputies to the National Assembly, their rapid collective evolution from defenders of corporate order to legislators of citizenship and representative institutions, still requires explanation, as does their authorship of a revolutionary and structural transformation of French justice. (That explanation is attempted, at least partially, in Volume 2 of this work.) Ironically, their revolutionary politics, from 1789 to 1791, vindicated the sense of alterity, the suspicions and hostility, with which most of the sword nobility had long viewed the men of the robe.

Had the late Old Regime aristocracy thought of itself as a unitary community, it would have acted in solidarity. And had it done so, the 1789 Revolution could never have developed in the manner that it did. The main propellant within the legislative Revolution of 1789 to 1791 was not a militant bourgeoisie, but rather an alliance of interests and ideology between noble themistocrats and men from the traditionally highest tiers of the Third Estate, the men from the judiciary and administration who comprised 70 percent of Third Estate deputies. The latter incarnated the numerous and accomplished commoner elites of France for whom ennoblement had become a virtual impossibility during the preceding decades. Only the abolition of nobility could open the way for a new equilibrium between civic dedication and ambition, professional expertise, meritorious service to the nation, property, empowerment and prestige.

For all its radical consequence, their alliance reflected an old regime, not a new social configuration of power. There was a statist bourgeoisie and a statist nobility in eighteenth-century France; both were composed of those entrenched in officialdom, men who controlled the judiciary and financial administration, and their auxiliaries in the practice of law. They had existed in deep affinity – political, social, and cultural – since at least the seventeenth century.[35] They were the main, and successful, opponents of monarchical attempts at absolutist reform during the eighteenth century. The traditional privileges they defended during the Old Regime were general corporatist rights and powers (including the authority of craft guilds and parishes, as well as the legislative participation of the Parlements), and thus general principles of public order that were established in law, not narrowly aristocratic privileges. During the 1770s and 1780s, they successfully resisted pressure from rural and military nobles to gain new administrative and legislative powers by reviving the neo-feudal provincial assemblies, which would have diminished the authority of royal intendants, Parlements, and municipal oligarchies. For much of the century, the major political antagonists of the themistocracy were nobles: royal ministers, a large segment of the episcopacy, and the provincial and military aristocracy.[36]

Other than common Estate, no actual community bound together, during the seventeenth and eighteenth centuries, a bourgeois judge of the Châtelet or any presidial court (whose paternal and maternal families had probably belonged to royal officialdom for two or three generations) with a master artisan, even one sufficiently affluent to employ many journeymen and apprentices. The judge enjoyed the material privileges of magistracy (which included most of those at-

---

[35] And they had done so as colleagues within sovereign courts, contrary to the myth that those courts were aristocratic preserves. The number of magistrates that entered the fifteen Chambres des Comptes, Cour des Aides, and Cour des Monnaies of France during the period 1774 to 1789 was 589. Fully 391, or 66%, of them were either bourgeois or only incipiently noble in social condition at entry. During the same period, 680 magistrates entered the sixteen Parlements; 129 (19%) were bourgeois or incipiently noble. There is no evidence that these proportions of bourgeois to nobles in sovereign courts were unique to the late Old Regime (Bien, "La réaction aristocratique," pp. 508, 511). Nobles and commoners were also colleagues in lower courts, which did not ennoble their officers. In 1789, 40% of the lieutenantcies in the presidial courts of France were held by noblemen. Fifty-five percent of the magistrates in the large presidial court at Lyon were noblemen. Of the 110 magistrates in the eight seneschalcy courts of Languedoc, 15 were noblemen. In the lesser bailliage courts of Burgundy, 6% of magistrates were nobles (Dawson, *Provincial Magistrates*, pp. 72–5). The concluding observations of Philippe Rosset on the Châtelet judges of the late seventeenth century were true for their successors, and for the judges of most sovereign and presidial courts of France during the eighteenth century: "Quotidiennement ou presque, pendant environ les deux tiers de l'année, le fils du marchand côtoie le fils du maître des requêtes ou du conseiller d'Etat. Au même tribunal, nobles et roturiers confondus rendent la justice de concert. . . . Qui plus est, tous ces hommes coexistent sans paraître s'exclure en fonctions de critères juridiques ou sociaux. . . . Au total, on assiste à un étonnant brassage qui se poursuit pendant au moins un demi-siècle sans que nous paraisse rompu un non moins étonnant équilibre entre les diverse catégories sociales qui s'y trouvent impliquées" ("Les conseillers du Châtelet," pt. 2, p. 195).

[36] The most comprehensive accounts of themistocratic opposition to royal attacks on corporate privileges are in Laugier, *Un ministère réformateur sous Louis XV*, hostile to the themistocracy, and Stone, *The French Parlements and the Crisis of the Old Regime*, favorable to the themistocracy. For magistrates' opposition to political claims by sword and seigneurial nobles and their prosecution of military officers who verbally or physically abused men of the robe, see Stone, ibid., pp. 188–207, and "Robe against Sword: The Parlement of Paris and the French Aristocracy, 1774–1789," *French Historical Studies*, 9 (1975): 278–303.

tached to nobility); the artisan had quite inferior privileges. The artisan lived by working with his hands (if only in supervising and demonstrating) and by merchandising his product, activities that were both forbidden and alien to the judge. There was no parity between the two, for the judge exercised judicial authority over the artisan. The judge's distant ancestors may have been artisans, just as the artisan might well have hoped that his descendants would become royal magistrates. They may have encountered each other, occasionally and ritualistically, on a parish council or in a municipal ceremony, but they lived and worked within hermetically separate worlds.

Similarly, no actual community bound an aristocratic judge of the Châtelet or Parlement, whose grandfather or great-grandfather had been ennobled by civil office and whose socioprofessional milieu was Parisian officialdom (an intellectually curious and cosmopolitan world of salons, academies, and freemasonry lodges) to a typical aristocratic regimental officer in the Ile-de-France, whose nobility was of seigneurial origin or had been acquired from generations of service on the drill ground and battlefield and whose social milieus were provincial rural estates, garrison towns, and military camps. The regimental officer lived an intensely physical life, a kinesis of the body, in and for violence. His calling was death – his own or that of the enemy. The aristocratic judge lived intellectively; judging and punishing the violent, and thereby protecting life, were among his principal tasks. These two types of aristocracy were no less distinct, socially and culturally, than the bourgeois judge and the rich artisan.

There was, however, a manifest community of interest between the bourgeois magistrate and the noble magistrate, one that they experienced daily. They had received the same education. Both were likely to own domainal farmland and (unlike the average regimental officer) urban real estate as well as state bonds. Their shared vocation also meant common economic interests. And both were likely to be wealthier than the regimental aristocrat.

Together, in the Estates-General of 1789, noble and commoner themistocrats assumed the role of politically representing the general interests of all of French civil society. Their presumption was not unique to that moment: As interpreters and enforcers of law for all of French civil society, themistocrats had for centuries considered themselves uniquely invested with a representational capacity.

We are led to conclude that noble themistocrats in Old Regime France were no more social appendages of aristocracy than bourgeois themistocrats were social appendages of the bourgeoisie. Themistocracy was practically, and de facto, a separate Estate. In the 1570s, Michel de Montaigne perceived that development. "In addition to the three old estates – the Church, the Nobility, and the People," he wrote, there is also

a fourth estate, composed of those who conduct trials. . . . This estate, having the custody of the laws and thus sovereign authority over property and lives, forms a body distinct from that of the nobility, with the result that there are two highly contrary sets of laws, that of honor and that of justice. . . . By the code of arms, he who suffers an insult without avenging himself is degraded in honor and nobility; by civil law, he who avenges the insult incurs capital penalty (whoever appeals to the law for redress of an offense to honor is dishonored, and whoever does not do so is punished by the law). Of these two bodies [nobility and magistracy], so different yet each responsible to the monarch, one has peace as its charge, the other war; one has gain, the other honor; one has knowledge, the other virtue; one has the word, the other action; one has justice, the other valor; one has reason, the other force.[37]

The "fourth estate" existed professionally, and thus politically, through the universality of the royal civil and criminal law that it enforced. Estates and their subgroups were all subject to that law and to the jurisdiction of its magistrates. In consequence, themistocracy transcended, in identity and power, all three Estates. The transcendence was also social in nature, by the fact that during the seventeenth and eighteenth centuries themistocracy was primarily self-reproducing through professional endogamy and ultimately through dynasticism. Let us now turn to the mechanics of that self-reproduction.

[37] *Essais*, bk. 1, chap. 23, ed. Alexandre Micha (Paris: Garnier-Flammarion, 1969), 2 vols.; vol. 1, pp. 164–5.

5

Themistocratic family and kinship: the Maussions and their allies

I have selected one family and its kinship group for close examination, to determine how a family moved from modest provincial office into the grand magistracy of Paris and maintained itself there, and to reveal how a leading themistocratic dynasty of the eighteenth century was formed. The Maussions and their allies are emblematic of many families of Châtelet and Parlement of Paris judges in the period 1735 to 1789. Their history illuminates principal routes to and from superior judgeships, strategies for magisterial success, and connections between the Parisian themistocracy and other elites of government and society.

Genealogical charts tracing the Maussion family and the five principal families with which they allied by marriage in their male line between 1700 and 1784 serve as the spine to the following narrative of political ascent and consolidation. The five generations of the Maussion family that are traced span almost two hundred years.[1] Pierre Maussion was an adolescent in the France of Louis XIII, Richelieu, and the Thirty Years' War. Thomas-Antoine-Jean Maussion, his great-great-grandson and Châtelet judge from 1784 to 1790, witnessed the final dethronement of the Bourbon dynasty by the insurrection of July 1830, at the age of 64, from the vantage of the Chamber of Deputies.

The Maussions were not merely objects of an institutional history; they were also the agents of their own ascent, by the choices, stratagems, and alliances that we shall examine. They resembled the majority of dynastic families in the eighteenth-century sovereign courts of Paris and the minority of socially and politically distinguished families in the Chatelet. They also resembled, in major socioprofessional respects, nearly one-fourth of the entire French nobility on the eve of the Revolution.

---

[1] In addition to the sources cited in the source note to Chart 5.1 and in subsequent footnotes, I have examined selected notarial records of the Maussion family in the "Minutier central" of the French National Archives: the marriage contract of Thomas-Urbain Maussion de Candé and Jeanne-Elisabeth Rillart de Fontenay (1726), LXVII 404; the inventory of Thomas Maussion's estate after his death and the division of that estate among his heirs (1744), LXXVII 223. Daniel Dessert, *Argent, pouvoir et société au Grand Siècle* (Paris: Fayard, 1984) has been especially valuable for political, institutional, and economic contexts.

Themistocratic family and kinship

A. The rise of Thomas Maussion

Pierre Maussion, our generational point of departure, was bailiff of a rural court in the Maine (Chart 5.1). Brûlon was a large village on the plain of the Beauce, some 20 miles west of Le Mans. Its population, in 1689, consisted of 228 households.[2] His court was probably seigneurial, but it was in the jurisdiction of the royal bailliage court at Le Mans. Late in his career, Pierre Maussion gained the more considerable office of seneschal, or chief bailliage officer, in Champagne.

Thomas was chosen among five sons for a judicial or administrative career. He was sent to Paris and the law faculty. In 1692, as a 29-year-old Parisian barrister, he began the most decisive social mutation of the Maussion family that occurred in any generation during the seventeenth and eighteenth centuries. That year (which coincided with his father's death and his receiving his inheritance), he married Simone Garciau. She was the daughter of a senior Parisian barrister who had died a few years earlier. Her maternal uncle and guardian, Léon-Urbain Aubert, gave her in marriage and paid her dowry. The Garciaus were extremely well connected. The witnesses to the marriage contract, and thus patrons of the alliance, were Gabriel Garciau, barrister; Ange Garciau, priest; Gabriel Lenoir, barrister of the Parlement of Paris (a member of a branch of the mercantile and then magisterial Lenoirs); André Burgault, deputy prosecutor of the Parlement; Christophe de la Lire, Châtelet judge; Charles Boucher, receiver general for the royal domains in the Generality of Caen; Pierre LePetit, barrister of the Parlement and royal secretary; François Letellier, *écuyer* (minor nobleman) and son of an administrator of the Hôpital-Géneral. Her dowry was small, only 2,000 livres and a modest portion of her father's property. That is not surprising, for she had numerous siblings, and Thomas Maussion was himself still a potential, not yet an actuality. Through this marriage Thomas Maussion entered a rapidly rising group of financiers, magistrates, and royal administrators. At the center of the circle that sponsored the marriage, there were two powerful figures: Pierre Rollée and Léon-Urbain Aubert.

Simone Garciau's sister, Louise, was married to Pierre Rollée, who thus became the brother-in-law of Thomas Maussion. Rollée was receiver of the *taille* for the *élections* of Andeleys, Alençon, and Caen (from the 1690s), then royal secretary (1702). In 1707 he succeeded his clansman Léon-Urbain Aubert as receiver general for the Generality of Caen. In 1716, the net value of his fortune was almost 1 million livres.[3]

Léon-Urbain Aubert (1646–1726) had probably selected Thomas Maussion for marriage to his niece. Aubert's *montée à Paris* had been in the 1660s, from

---

[2] René Plessix, *Paroisses et communes de France: Dictionnaire d'histoire administrative et démographique, Sarthe* (Paris: CNRS, 1983), p. 122.

[3] On the Rollées, see Dessert, *Argent et pouvoir,* pp. 141, 685; Favre-Lejeune, *Les secrétaires de roi,* vol. 2, pp. 1173–4.

Chart 5.1. *The Maussion family*

I	II	III	IV	V
Pierre Maussion (b. ?, d. 1692): bailiff of Brûlon near Le Mans, Maine; seneschal in Champagne oo Renée Nadreau, seven children:				
	Adam Maussion (priest)			
	Jean Maussion (succeeded father as seneschal in Champagne)			
	Charles Maussion (medical doctor)			
	Urbaine Maussion			
	Renée Maussion (nun)			
	Urbain Maussion (priest)			
	Thomas Maussion (b. 1663 [Brûlons], d. 1744 [Paris]): barrister, Parlement of Paris; general receiver of taxes, Generality of Alençon (1696); royal secretary (1704–24); ennobled by the secretaryship, purchased seigneurial domain of Candé near Laval, Maine oo 1. Simone **Garciau**, three children. 2. Marie-Anne Charron, no children.			
			Thomas-Urbain Maussion de Candé (1696–1758 [Paris]): judge, Grand Conseil (1719–58) oo Jeanne-Elisabeth **Rillart de Fontenay** (1726), four children:	
				Charles-Marthe Maussion (b. 1730, d. ?): lieutenant, Auvergne infantry regiment Elisabeth-Jeanne Maussion

Louis Maussion de Candé (1731–1779 [Paris]): judge, Parlement of Paris (1751–79)
oo Antoinette-Geneviève **Chuppin** (1767), three children:

    Antoine-Charles Maussion de Candé (b. 1769, d. ?)
    Etienne-Thomas Maussion (b. 1772, d. ?)
    Antoinette-Cathérine Maussion (b. 1773, d. ?)

Thomas-Urbain Maussion de la Folletière (1732–95): succeeded father as judge, Grand Conseil (to 1774); judge, Cour des Aides (1775–91)
oo Cathérine **Thévenin de Tanlay** (1763), five children:

    Thomas-Antoine-Jean Maussion de la Folletière (b. 1764, d. ?): judge, Châtelet (1784–90)
    oo Marie-Jeanne Bertoult d'Hauteclocque (1795), four children

    Louis-Urbain Maussion de St. Vertus (b. 1766, d. ?)
    Louise-Cathérine Maussion (b. 1770s, d. ?)
    Thomas-Jean Maussion (b. ?, d. ?)
    Thomas-Urbain II Maussion (b. ?, d. ?)

Pierre-Jacques Maussion (b. 1700, d. ?): captain, Piedmont infantry regiment

Etienne-Charles Maussion de la Courtaujay (1705–1773 [Paris]): succeeded father as general receiver at Alençon, 1732
oo Marie-Thérèse **Bergeret** (1734), four children:

Chart 5.1. (cont.)

I	II	III	IV	V
			Etienne-Thomas Maussion de la Courtaujay (1750–94); judge, Châtelet (1768–73); judge, Parlement of Paris (1773); judge, Grand Conseil (1774); master of petitions, Chancellery (1775–87); intendant, Generality of Rouen (1787–9)	
			oo **Jeanne Perrin de Cypierre** (1784)	
			Antoine-Pierre Maussion (b. ?, d. 1778): succeeded father as general receiver, Alençon (1773)	
			Marie-Charlotte Maussion de la Courtaujay (b. ?, d. ?)	
			Marie-Geneviève Maussion de la Courtaujay (b. ?, d. ?)	

Sources: A.N. Y 1869, doss. Thomas-Antoine-Jean Maussion; Bluche; Bluche, "L'origine des magistrats du Parlement de Paris," p. 305; Bluche, "Les magistrats du Grand Conseil," pp. 113–14; Alexandre Daigre, ed., *Armorial général et universel d'Hozier: Recueil de Généalogies dressés de mis au jour par L'Institut Héraldique*, 3 vols., Paris, 1907–12, vol. 3, no pagination (this is the official genealogy certified by the d'Hoziers during the eighteenth century, with supplementary documentation from family notarial papers); Favre-Lejeune, *Les secrétaires du roi*, vol. 2, pp. 948–9; Woëlmont de Brumagne, *Notices généalogiques*, vol. 1 (p. 354), vol. 3 (pp. 18–19, 196–8, 715), vol. 6 (pp. 181–2).

the environs of Angers, where his father was a bailliage magistrate, as Pierre Maussion had been. Aubert earned a law degree and a clerkship to a barrister of the Parlement, much like Thomas Maussion twenty years later. During the 1680s he was taken into the employ of Louis Phélypeaux, count of Pontchartrain, and he rose within the entourage of Pontchartrain, who became successively secretary of state for the navy, for the royal domains, general controller of finance, and Chancellor of France. Aubert's first official commission for Pontchartrain was the financial administration of several royal properties in the Generality of Moulins. He excelled at this and was appointed intendant of that Generality (1678). Through proficiency, acquisition of capital, and ministerial influence, Aubert acquired the general receivership of Caen in 1694. He sold that office to Rollée in 1707 to become president of the Chambre des Comptes of Normandy, where he served from 1708 until his death in 1726. From the 1680s to his death, he was a major investor and speculator in royal finances. In 1682, Aubert had purchased a royal secretaryship and its nobility, and he acquired at least three seigniories during the following years. In 1698, he bought the large domain of Tourny in Normandy. In 1702 (the year that Aubert's nobility became hereditary from the royal secretaryship), Chancellor Pontchartrain arranged for that domain to be elevated to the status of a marquisate. Within thirty years, Léon-Urbain Aubert had changed from a young bourgeois of Anjou and Paris into the marquis of Tourny and the president of a sovereign court. His son and grandson became members of the administrative elite of eighteenth-century France, as intendants and royal councillors.[4]

Léon-Urbain Aubert became Thomas Maussion's most powerful kinsman and mentor.[5] Maussion, Aubert, and Rollée were linked by regional affinity. They were *gens de pays* from the Maine and Anjou who politically coalesced in Paris.[6] In the young Maussion, Pierre Rollée and Léon-Urbain Aubert could have seen a reflection of their own origins and early lives. Rollée's father and grandfather had been minor provincial officers, controllers of the salt tax at Château-Gontier (near Angers), and he had begun his Parisian career as a barrister of the Parlement. Léon-Urbain Aubert's original trajectory was from the

---

[4] His son (Louis-Urbain, 1695–1760) was successively judge of the Châtelet (1714–19), of the Grand Conseil (1719), master of petitions (1719–30), and intendant of the Generality of Limoges (1730–43) and of the Generality of Bordeaux (1743–57). His grandson (Claude-Louis, 1722–60) was royal advocate of the Châtelet (1742–5), judge of the Parlement of Paris (1745–6), general advocate of the Grand Conseil (1746–55); he then succeeded Louis-Urbain as master of petitions and intendant of Bordeaux (Antoine, *Le gouvernement*, pp. 12–13; Favre-Lejeune, *Les secrétaires du roi*, vol. 1, pp. 146–7; Woëlmont de Brumagne, *Notices généalogiques*, vol. 3, p. 286). On the financial career of Léon-Urbain, founder of this statist dynasty, see Dessert, *Argent et pouvoir*, p. 523.

[5] Between 1696 and 1708, he included Maussion in several contracts to make high-interest loans to the state and to obtain leases on royal and ducal domains (Dessert, *Argent et pouvoir*, pp. 644–5).

[6] Aubert and Rollée may well have been related before the Garciau nexus; some of Rollée's older cousins, paternal and maternal, were magistrates in or near Angers. That was the natal society of Léon-Urbain Aubert.

Chart 5.2.*Phélypeaux genealogy*

I	II	III	IV

Raymond Phélypeaux (b. ?, d. 1553): bourgeois of Blois, co-seigneur of La Vrillière

  Louis Phélypeaux (b. ?, d. ?): judge, presidial court of Blois, seigneur of La Vrillière and La Cave

    Raymond II Phélypeaux (1560–1629): royal secretary (1590–1619); treasurer; councillor and secretary of state, ennobled by the royal secretaryship

    Paul Phélypeaux (1569–1621); royal secretary (1592–1621); secretary of state (1610), ennobled by offices; seigneur of Pontchartrain

      Louis II Phélypeaux de Pontchartrain (b. ?, d. 1685): president, Chambre des Comptes of Paris (1650)

        Louis III Phélypeaux de Pontchartrain (1643–1727): judge, Parlement of Paris (1661–77); president, Parlement of Brittany (1677–87); intendant of finance (1689); secretary of state for the navy (1690–99); Chancellor of France (1699–1714)

Sources: Antoine, *Le gouvernement,* pp. 202–3; Bluche, "L'origine des magistrats du Parlement de Paris," pp. 345–6; Favre-Lejeune, *Les secrétaires du roi,* vol. 2, pp. 1074–6; Mousnier, *Institutions of France,* vol. 1, pp. 55–8.

household of an Anjou magistrate to the Paris law faculty, and thence to the service of Phélypeaux de Pontchartrain.

As their genealogy (Chart 5.2) reveals, the rise of the Phélypeaux, from the mid-sixteenth century to the 1690s, prefigured the familial rise of the Auberts and then the Maussions. "Le grand Pontchartrain," one of Louis XIV's most powerful ministers of state, was a robe noble three generations distant from bourgeois Estate and provincial magistracy. The young Léon-Urbain Aubert, whom he recruited during the 1680s, socially reincarnated Phélypeaux de Pontchartrain's own great-grandfather, and thus his own family's origins in royal officialdom. The Phélypeaux were from the west of France, Blois and its environs, and they may have been distant kin to the Auberts. Intermarriage across large regions was frequent among families of provincial magistracy during the sixteenth and seventeenth centuries.[7]

In 1696, Thomas Maussion purchased the office of receiver general of direct taxes for the Generality of Alençon (adjacent to the Generality of Caen). The price of that office was 220,000 livres.[8] Léon-Urbain Aubert's influence was

[7] See Pierre Goubert, "Les officiers royaux des Présidiaux, Bailliages et Elections dans la société française du XVIIe siècle," *XVII Siècle,* 42–3 (1959): 54–75.
[8] Dessert, *Argent et pouvoir,* p. 148.

probably decisive in that acquisition. Eight years later, in 1704, Thomas Maussion purchased a royal secretaryship for approximately 70,000 livres.[9] That enormous sum was provided by loans from the clan nucleus of Rollée–Aubert and patrons of the Garciau marriage. Those loans were an excellent long-term investment, for general receiverships were among the most durably remunerative offices in Old Regime France.[10]

Twenty-four of the thirty-four Generalities of eighteenth-century France were *pays d'élection*, where direct taxes on income and property were collected, and their litigation adjudicated, by royal officials rather than by commissioners of provincial estates. There were two general receivers for each of those twenty-four Generalities. These were venal-hereditary officers who served in alternate years. Each had his own royal contracts, accounts, coffers, and clerks. Each was responsible for the collection and transport to Paris of the monies from direct taxes, principally the *taille* (based on assessed income and property), the *vingtième* (a lesser tax similar to the *taille*), and the *capitation* (levied in fixed sums on families and households according to their socio-professional group).[11] Direct taxes were the source of between one-third and one-half of the monarchical state's revenue during the eighteenth century.[12] They were assessed each fiscal year by the royal Finance Council and the controller general for each Generality and *élection*. The general receiver who served incumbent for that year contracted with the council to remit the sum assessed before the end of fifteen months, normally in monthly installments. The *receveurs particuliers* (particular receivers) of the *élections* (second-tier offices in the fiscal bureaucracy) were also contractually bound to remit what they collected to him within stipulated periods. Parish collectors, who remitted to particular receivers, were at the base of the fiscal pyramid. The *taille* and *capitation* were stable taxes, for the sums assessed on Generalities and *élections* by the royal Council were not substantially increased during most of the eighteenth century, nor were they dramatically onerous for the mass of *taillables*.

The chronic royal problem during the eighteenth century was not evasion of or resistance to direct taxes. It was logistical: the ponderousness of the process and the delays in the collection and transporting of monies to provincial capitals and thence to the Treasury offices in Paris. Often the full tax revenue assessed for a Generality in a given year did not arrive for expenditure until eighteen months to two years after the beginning of that fiscal year (usually February).

---

[9] That was the average price in 1704, according to Favre-Lejeune, *Les secrétaires du roi*, vol. 1, p. 35.

[10] The following discussion of the office of receiver general of direct taxes during the seventeenth and eighteenth centuries is based mainly on Bosher, *French Finances*, pp. 67–125; Dessert, *Argent et pouvoir*, pp. 27–67; and Mosser, *Les intendants des finances au XVIIIe siècle*.

[11] For details on direct taxes, see Marcel Marion, *Les impôts directs sous l'Ancien Régime* (Paris, 1910).

[12] Michel Morineau, "Budgets de l'Etat et gestion des finances royales en France aux dix-huitième siècle," *Revue Historique*, 264 (1980): 314–15.

The French monarchy was therefore chronically in debt and faced recurrent short-term crises of payment.

Receivers general were obliged to keep detailed accounts of their collections and remittances, and their account ledgers were regularly and meticulously inspected by the treasurer–president of the finance tribunal in each Generality, the royal Finance Council, and the Chambre des Comptes of the province. The receiver general's office was legally defined as security for the propriety and efficacy of their administration; it could be confiscated by the state (along with their personal property) if their delays in remitting (and thus indebtedness to the state) became cumulative and dangerous. Such confiscations were frequent during the reign of Louis XIV. Since the reign of Francis I, receivers general had been subject to capital penalties if convicted of fraud or embezzlement of tax monies. Rule-governed and scrutinized, these officers had also to perform an exacting labor of inspection, supervision, accountancy, and judicial intervention during their tenure. But, unlike magistrates, they were not forbidden to invest in private finance or engage in commerce. They were also allowed to speculate, in the short term, with the monies they received within a fifteen-month period, so long as their accounts were cleared at the end of that period. The very structure of the royal fiscal system, and the chronic shortage of Treasury funds, encouraged them to speculate on the collateral of their offices.

Receivers general were remunerated as follows. They received from the Crown 5 percent per annum of the purchase price of the office (as *gages*, or salary); 2 percent of that amount for operating expenses; and 3–4 percent of the total sum that they collected and remitted under contract in a fiscal year. Three or 4 percent of some 2,000,000 livres was a considerable profit; but that profit could be multiplied: "As taxes were collected at a slow and variable rate throughout the fiscal year, and sometimes even after it had passed, convenience dictated a system of advances that could permit the government to spend money before it had actually been collected, and, at best, as soon as its collection had been authorized."[13]

Receivers general were encouraged by finance ministers and the royal Council to act as bankers to the state, to advance money from their own stock of capital at the beginning of their fiscal year (before collection had occurred), even to advance money during the alternate years when they did not serve. Such an advance (known as *rescription*) was negotiated as a short-term loan, at an interest of between 7 and 10 percent (instead of the 3- to 4-percent commission on remittances). Interest payments began as soon as the *rescription* was made; the principal was repaid within two years from tax monies deposited in the Treasury. Virtually all receivers general practiced *rescriptions*, usually, even in alternate years. To do so, they required a substantial portfolio of private capital to advance. It was not difficult for them to build those portfolios, given the force of kinship solidarities, conjoined with the magnetic attractiveness of their office

---

[13] Bosher, *French Finances*, p. 93.

to legions of prospective investors.[14] Because they managed great sums of money that were subject to strict accounting, general receivers could develop private credit and the capacity to act as bankers. Most of them were simultaneously short-term creditors in public finance and long-term debtors in private finance.

Alençon was a densely populated and moderately prosperous Generality. Its nine *élections* included western Normandy and the upper Maine. At the end of the seventeenth century, Alençon had a total population of 444,817, dispersed in 1,315 towns, villages, and parishes and 9,567 hamlets. The majority of *taillables* lived in villages and hamlets. The *taille* assessed and collected for 1696 in Alençon was 1,278,256 livres; by 1738, it had been increased to only 2,015,000 livres. During those forty-two years, the *capitation* oscillated between 430,000 and 600,000 livres.[15]

One may average these figures to begin a conservative estimate of Thomas Maussion's revenue from his thirty-seven years as receiver general (1696–1733). The average sum collected annually from the Generality in *taille* and *capitation* was 2,161,628 livres. Maussion served (biannually) as receiver general for eighteen of those thirty-seven years. Almost 39 million livres passed through his office in eighteen years. At 3.5-percent commission, his total commission for those years would have been 1,365,000 livres, or 36,892 livres annually. His *gages* were 11,000 livres, and his expense allowance 2,200 livres. Thomas Maussion's total annual revenue from office (without *rescriptions*), over forty-two years, would therefore have been approximately 50,000 livres. In theory, within ten years he could have repaid the purchase price of his general receivership. But an analysis of the composition of Maussion's fortune in 1716 reveals that the riches suggested by these sums were largely theoretical, or passive. The breakdown is as follows: land worth 116,806 livres (or 4.9%); buildings worth 58,581 livres (or 2.5%); offices of receiver general and royal secretary worth 411,722 livres, (or 17.3%); liquid capital, 1,789,426 livres, (or 75.3%); debts, 1,961,388 livres; net fortune 415,147 livres.[16] Since 1696,

[14] "Dans le petit monde des gens d'argent, l'importance des receveurs généraux des finances (ou des trésoriers généraux des états) est considérable. . . . Par leurs fonctions, ils se trouvent au contact de la masse des imposés et, par conséquent, en prise directe sur la masse monétaire du royaume. C'est dire combien ils se revelent les plus aptes à utiliser les liquidités du pays, avantage énorme dans un système financier où le métal semble la dimension de toute chose. L'intérêt principal d'une charge de receveur général ne se situe pas dans son rapport apparent (gages et taxations), relativement rémunérateur, mais dans les possibilités très larges de crédit et de financement que procure l'exploitation directe de l'impôt. . . . Il appartient au petit nombre de ceux qui bénéficient d'un répondant permanent, l'impôt direct; il s'avère donc un débiteur des plus sûrs et, par conséquent, il trouve toujours aisément des prêteurs qui s'engagent volontiers . . . ses côtés. On lui fait des avances d'autant plus facilement qu'on est persuadé de sa solvabilité à toute épreuve" (Dessert, *Argent et pouvoir,* p. 46). And that office remained highly dynastic until the end of the Old Regime. Michel Brugière examined some fifty of the receivers general who served during the 1770s and 1780s. Twenty-three succeeded a father, uncle, or brothers ("Louis XVI's Receivers-General and their Successors," *French History,* I (1987): 251).

[15] This information is drawn from Duval, *Etat de la Généralité d'Alençon sous Louis XIV,* pp. 94–8.
[16] Dessert, *Argent et pouvoir,* p. 140.

he had expended, or was still expending, more than 175,000 livres on real property.

The very large debt (after twenty years in office) strongly indicates that Maussion was still incrementally repaying the capital he owed for the purchase of his offices and, more importantly, that he did practice *rescriptions*, but with a portfolio that was still being developed. He was still repaying private loans that allowed him to advance money to the Treasury at high interest rates.

This financial profile was typical of most first-generation high fiscal officers of the Crown, as they have been described by Dessert, Wacquet, and Bosher. Maussion's debt was large, but it was primarily long-term and not pressing. To create a stock of 1 million livres to use for making advances to the Treasury (at 7–10% interest) an officer had to garner private investments. There were two universal methods for doing this: taking out long-term loans, which required repayment of both interest and principal; or selling *rentes*, or annuities, investments in which investors received interest but surrendered the principal.

Legally and technically, a *rente* was not a loan; it was an investment, with an agreed, fixed return. This was the most common form of raising money in the society of fiscal officers and magistrates. A *rente* had two great advantages over a loan. It circumvented the legal restrictions on interest rates or usury, since repayment of principal did not have to occur. It was contractual and entirely legal, and there were at least twenty distinct forms, in law, of private *rentes* during the Old Regime.[17] The most common was the annuity at fixed payment, whose most frequent variant was a life annuity. Receivers general were in an excellent position to attract such investments. One may illustrate the procedure. A merchant, aged 40, agreed to invest 50,000 livres in the portfolio of Thomas Maussion, receiver general, in exchange for a life annuity (*rente viagère*) paying 5 percent of 50,000 livres per annum. Once the contract was signed, the 50,000 livres was placed in Maussion's coffers, either in the full amount or in a few large installments within a short period. The merchant received an annuity of 2,500 livres a year (5%) on his investment. If he died at the age of 65, he (or rather, his heirs) had earned 62,500 livres, or a profit of 12,500 livres (25%) on the original investment: A life annuity could be redeemed. At the time of contract, it was customary for the parties to stipulate one or both of the following: Should the investor die before he received a total of 50,000 livres in annual payment, the creditor would either pay the balance to his heirs or would continue the annuity on their behalf to an agreed term. The investor could also request return of the balance, but only after the expiration of a certain (usually long) period and by giving notice well in advance. Through such agreements, investment in a *rente* was capital technically, but not actually, alienated. What did Thomas Maussion realize from this hypothetical transaction? If Maussion advanced the 50,000 livres to the Treasury for only twenty of those twenty-five

[17] See the *Encyclopédie, ou dictionnaire raisonné des Sciences, des Arts et des Métiers*, 28 (1780) pt. 2, pp. 315–20. On *rente*, see also Marion, *Dictionnaire*, pp. 481–5.

years, at a minimal *rescription* of 8 percent, he in fact advanced 1 million livres, from which he received 80,000 livres in interest. And he received back the 50,000 livres from the Crown every one to two years after he advanced it. Thus, over twenty years he received 4,000 livres each year in interest from the Crown on the 50,000 livres, from which he paid an annuity to the merchant of 2,500 livres. The interest received on *rescriptions* figured in his *portefeuille* along with the 50,000 livres. The amount of annuity remaining to be paid on the sum of 50,000 livres figured in his debt.

Maussion's stock of capital was formed of many such annuity contracts and a smaller number of long-term loans.[18] Men who, like Maussion, did not enter fiscal office with substantial private capital normally required many years of careful accumulation to build a fortune from the office or to realize the speculative possibilities of advances, for to do so they had to liquidate annuities and pay off debts. At the time of his death in 1744, his net fortune had climbed to 876,500 livres; about one-third of that sum was in real property. He had handled some 39 million livres during his tenure as receiver general. Ironically, the durable and solid portion of Thomas Maussion's worth in 1716 and in 1744 consisted in real property and in the capital value and fixed remuneration of his offices, not in what he made through monetary speculation. The full speculative value of the office was probably realized during the tenure of Thomas Maussion's cadet son, Etienne, to whom it was transmitted (with portfolio and debts) in 1733. Etienne held the office until his death in 1773, when it was transmitted to his cadet son, Antoine-Pierre.

In 1724, Thomas Maussion sold his royal secretaryship for approximately 100,000 livres. He had held it for twenty years, exactly the time requisite for hereditary ennoblement. In that year, his sons became hereditary aristocrats. Since the early 1700s he had been purchasing seigneurial estates, the most important of which was Candé, in Anjou.[19] Candé was 42 miles southwest of Brûlon, his natal village. It became the patronymic estate of the Maussions in their senior line.

B. Kinship, property, and consolidation in power

Thomas-Urbain Maussion, the eldest son of Thomas Maussion, was married in 1726 to Jeanne-Elisabeth Rillart de Fontenay (alliance I, Chart 5.3). In the marriage contract, Thomas Maussion legated the following property to his son: full ownership of the Grand Conseil judgeship that Thomas-Urbain had re-

---

[18] This is revealed by the inventory of his estate after his death in 1744 (A.N. "Minutier Central," LXXVII 223).

[19] It was some 20 miles northwest of Angers. The extensive *terre* at Candé belonged to the princes of Condé from 1633 to 1764. It consisted of a barony, six *chatellenies*, and about forty seigneurial estates (at least one of which Maussion probably purchased from the Condés) (Célestin Port, *Dictionnaire historique, géographique et biographique du Maine-et-Loire* 3 vols. [Paris, 1878] vol. 1, pp. 546–7).

Chart 5.3.*Maussion alliance I: Rillart de Fontenay*

I	II	III

Jacques Rillart (1625 [Paris]–1692 [Paris]): notary,
Châtelet (1647–72); royal secretary (1676–92), ennobled
by the secretaryship

oo Louise Lallement, four children:

        Agnès Rillart (b. ?, d. ?) oo (1671) Jacques Sandrier
        (first secretary to Secretary of State Pontchartrain; gen-
        eral receiver of taxes, Generality of Limoges)

        Mathieu-Jacques Rillart (1655–1736): royal master of wa-
        ters and forests
        oo Elisabeth Le Clerc, one child:

                Claude Rillart de Verneuil (b. ?, d. ?): lieutenant-general
                of the Vermandois
                oo Marie-Françoise de Blois

        Louis-Hubert Rillart de Fontenay (1664–1736): *maître*,
        Hotel du Roi
        wife's name unknown, one child:

                Jeanne-Elisabeth Rillart de Fontenay (wife of
                Thomas-Urbain Maussion de Candé)

        Jean Rillart (b. ?, d. 1707): payer of annuities on royal
        bonds
        oo Elisabeth Le Veau, one child:

                Louis-Hubert Rillart de Fontenay II (1680–1759): grand
                master of waters and forests of the Guyenne (1707–13);
                general receiver of finances, Flanders and Hainault;
                maître, Hotel du Roi
                oo Marie-Geneviève Soudrier de Nictry

Sources: Favre-Lejeune, *Les secrétaires du roi*, vol. 2, pp. 1154–5; Jean-Claude Wac-quet, *Les grands maîtres des Eaux et Forêts de France de 1689 à la Révolution* (Geneva: Droz, 1978), p. 401.

ceived in 1719 (at a price of approximately 40,000 livres); the seigneurial es-tates of Candé, La Folletière, and La Borde (Generality of Alençon) and Hau-dumière (near Blois). But he reserved usufruct of those estates, in exchange for an annual payment of 6,000 livres. And he promised to give Thomas-Urbain an annual loan of 2,000 livres a year, at 2-percent interest. Thomas-Urbain Maussion thus entered marriage endowed with the property of his judgeship, title to the principal family estates, and an annual revenue of approximately 8,000 livres, in addition to the revenues of his judgeship. The Rillart dowry amounted to at least 150,000 livres.[20] Her father was a Court fiscal officer (master of the royal household), and her cousin (Louis-Hubert) was successively grand master of waters and forests for the province of Guyenne (1707–13) and receiver general of direct taxes for Flanders and Hainault (1713–c.1750).[21] For the Maussions in 1726, this marriage would have signified financial consolidation.

The second son was commissioned in the Piedmont Infantry regiment, one of the oldest in the royal army. In 1732, Thomas Maussion retired and dynastically transmitted his general receivership to the cadet, Etienne (who also received the seigneury of La Courteaujay, near Paris). Etienne was married to Marie-Thérèse Bergeret in 1734 (alliance II, Chart 5.4). Her dowry was 150,000 livres. Thomas Maussion endowed Etienne with 50,000 livres.

The Bergerets accumulated great wealth during the eighteenth century. The fortune was created primarily by Pierre-François Bergeret (father of Marie-Thérèse), from his long tenure as collector for the General Tax Farm. When he died in 1771, he left an estate valued at 8,044,944 livres.[22] Jean-François Bergeret, his son and the brother-in-law of Etienne-Charles Maussion, served as secretary of finance in the royal Council (1748–84). Thus, in the third generation the Maussions obtained by marriage a new patron in the royal Council

---

[20] Its core was formed by numerous long-term *rentes* plus ownership of two Parisian town-houses, one on the Quai Bourbon and the other on the Ile-Saint-Louis (A.N., "Minutier Central," LXVII, 404).

[21] On the Rillarts, see Favre-Lejeune, *Les secrétaires du roi*, vol. 2, 1154–5; Jean-Claude Wacquet, *Les grands maîtres des Eaux et Fôrets de France de 1689 à la Révolution* (Geneva: Droz, 1978), p. 401.

[22] He was a relative and protégé of the banking family of Paris-Duverney. Yves Durand reconstructed the estate at decease of thirty-five tax farmers who died during the period 1732 to 1789. The average value of their estates was 3,321,034 livres. That of Pierre-François Bergeret de Frouville was among the largest. Only .43% (or 35,134 livres) was in gold, jewelry, or silver plate; about 5% in offices; and more than 50% in state bonds and private loans. Several of the loans were to the high nobility (the prince of Conti, 730,000 livres; the chevalier of Luxembourg, 250,000 livres; the duke and duchess of Duras, more than 500,000 livres; the marshal–duke of Richelieu, 150,000 livres). Many others were to magistrates and administrators (among them, the Chaumonts de la Galaizière and the Hazons, who were related to the Maussions). Most of the private loans were at a resoundingly usurious interest rate of 20%. He remained a private banker to nobility and officialdom long after resigning his commission as tax farmer. He also speculated in Parisian and provincial real estate. His properties in Paris were in the burgeoning western Quarters of the city, in or near the faubourg Saint-Honoré: two buildings on the Place des Victoires (worth 120,000 livres each); one on the rue de Richelieu (150,000 livres); one on the rue Neuve-des-Capuchines (154,000 livres); one on the Croix-des-Petits-Champs (60,000 livres); in all, a total of 604,000 livres in urban rental properties. He also owned seigneurial domains and farms in the Ile-de-France (notably the monumental chateau of Nointel, purchased from the prince of Conti), and in Languedoc, near Montauban (the chateau and fief of Nègrepélisse, bought for 372,000 livres in 1751). Land and buildings accounted for almost one-third of his estate. Yet Pierre-François Bergeret lived for much of his life in a rather modest *hôtel* on the rue Saint-Antoine, near the offices of the General Tax Farm. That choice, and the almost complete absence of gold, jewelry, precious objects, and personal adornments in his inventory, suggest an economics of familial aggrandizement, not of personal consumption (Durand, *Les Fermiers Généraux*, pp. 132–4, 138, 141, 146, 162, 451, 453, 469).

Chart 5.4. *Maussion alliance II: Bergeret*

I	II	III	IV
Pierre-Alexandre Bergeret (c. 1650–1716): attendant to the dauphin, gentleman of the royal falconry oo Marie Jamen, seven children:	three daughters three sons, officers of the army *Pierre-François Bergeret de Frouville* (b. 1683 [Paris], d. 1771 [Paris]): barrister, Parlement of Paris; treasurer of war; general director of military food procurement; tax farmer (1721–57); royal secretary (1722–71); ennobled by the secretaryship oo Claude-Anne de la Roche (1710), five children:	**Marie-Thérèse Bergeret** (c. 1714–1778) wife of Etienne Maussion de la Courtaujay Marie-Suzanne Bergeret (b. 1717, d. ?) oo Louis-Jacques Hocquart (general treasurer, artillery of France) Anne-Justine Bergeret (b. 1720, d. 1741) oo (1740) Charles Péan de Mosnac (judge, Chambre des Comptes) *Pierre-Jacques Onesime Bergeret de Grancourt* (b. 1715, d. 1785): general receiver of finances, Montauban (1741–85); general treasurer, Order of St. Louis oo Marguérite Richard de la Bretèche (1751), one child

Pierre-Jacques Bergeret de Grancourt (b. 1741, d.
1810): succeeded father as general receiver of finance,
Montauban, (1785–90)
wife unknown

Jean-François Bergeret de Frouville (b. 1719, d. 1783):
barrister, Parlement of Paris; royal secretary (1748); secretary, Council of State (1748–84)
oo Elisabeth Delahaye des Fossés (1749), three children:

Aimée-Charlotte Bergeret (b. 1751, d. 1840), mar.
cousin Louis-Hyacinthe Hocquart (1770)

Antoine-Salomon Bergeret (b. 1755, d. 1840): officer
Royal-Lorraine cavalry regiment, disinherited for marriage without permission

Adélaide-Etienne Bergeret (b. 1765, d. ?): royal secretary
(1783); succeeded father as secretary, Council of State
(1784)

Sources: Durand, Les Fermiers Généraux; Favre-Lejeune, Les secrétaires du roi, vol. 1, pp. 192–5.

in addition to the Auberts de Tourny. The Maussions also became dynastically Parisian in that generation.

When Thomas Maussion died in 1744 (at the age of 81), his estate, capital valued at 876,500 livres, was divided among his sons. Thomas-Urbain received the eldest son's legal one-half of the total estate; this amounted to the seigneuries with which he had been endowed in 1726 and more than 100,000 livres in other assets. Full title to La Courteaujay went to Etienne, along with ownership of the general receivership at Alençon. Pierre-Jacques of the Piedmont Infantry Regiment apparently received cash and annuities. Beyond expenditures on his household and for the hospitality and charity expected of high officeholders, Thomas Maussion had invested a lifetime of profits from his general receivership chiefly in patrimony for his sons, in the durable form of real property and offices. Each subsequent patriarch of the family would do the same.

The Maussion men of the fourth generation were principally themistocrats of the Parlement of Paris, Grand Conseil, Cour des Aides, and Châtelet. They married into families that resembled them in origin, evolution, and degree of nobility. They practiced strict corporate endogamy: There were no more marriages to daughters of financiers.[23]

The Chuppins (alliance III, Chart 5.5) were a venerable Parisian family, the only such family in the Maussion kinship group. By the late sixteenth century, the Chuppins were established cloth merchants in the city. During the seventeenth century, they entered the municipal elite of Paris: Jean I (the brother of Nicolas I on Chart 5.4) was a municipal councillor in 1630 and an *échevin* from 1639 to 1641. His son, Jean II, was placed in the judiciary as a Châtelet notary and was elected *échevin* of Paris for 1684 to 1686. Jean's brothers were Pierre and Nicolas II (on Chart 3.4). In their generation, which came to maturity during the last quarter of the seventeenth century, both branches of the family left commerce and municipal government for high administrative and magisterial vocations.

From the 1690s to at least the 1760s, the Chuppins were positioned at the very institutional core of officialdom. As treasurers of the *marc d'or* and keepers

---

[23] This socioprofessional evolution of the Maussions was reflected in their Parisian domiciles. Thomas had lived all of his Parisian career on the rue du Hazard, a small enclave of the Faubourg St.-Honoré between the rues Ste.-Anne and St.-Roch. This was a developing but peripheral Quarter during the early eighteenth century. His eldest son (Thomas-Urbain I) also resided there until at least 1750, in the same house. Thomas Maussion's cadet son, Etienne, resided on the Place des Victoires, near the palatial *hôtel* owned by his father-in-law, Pierre Bergeret. Etienne's son (Etienne-Thomas) lived on the rue Neuve-des-Mathurins, a fashionable and affluent portion of the Faubourg St.-Honoré where many private and public financiers lived in the eighteenth century. The Marais was the favorite residential Quarter for the Parisian themistocracy and the old (pre-seventeenth century) noble families of the city. It was where Louis Maussion de Candé (of the Parlement of Paris) chose to live. He purchased the sumptuous Hôtel Talard, on the rue des Enfants-Rouges (a segment of the present rue des Archives). His brother, Thomas-Urbain Maussion de la Folletière (Grand Conseil and Cour des Aides), shared the residence, as did the latter's son during his tenure as Châtelet judge (*Almanach royal*, 1720 [pp. 93, 99], 1750 [pp. 167, 364], 1765 [p. 218], 1782 [pp. 237, 327], 1789 [p. 388]).

of the rolls and accounts of royal offices in the Grand Chancellery, they were, in effect, skilled geographers of state institutions and careers: experts on the prices, privileges, fiscal exemptions, revenues, competencies, and composition of all venal offices of state, as well as overseers of all appointments to those offices. The *marc d'or* (the fee paid to the king for every venal appointment) varied from more than 3,000 livres (for a presidency in the Parlement of Paris) to some 40 livres (for the post of process-servers). It was collected and deposited by two general treasurers for all of France. Their offices had a highly stable value of 500,000 livres during the reigns of Louis XIV and Louis XV. The treasurers received 2.5 percent of all payments of the *marc d'or.* As keepers of the roles and accounts, the Chuppins were primary liaison between the Chancellery and the Chambre des Comptes of Paris.[24] Such men possessed incomparable knowledge of financial markets, status, and kinship structures within the entire hierarchy of officialdom. The Chuppins held those offices for three generations. In their fourth generation, that of Antoinette-Geneviève's marriage to Louis Maussion de Candé, the Chuppins left the Chancellery for the Châtelet and the Parlement of Paris.[25]

During the eighteenth century, the Thévenins (alliance IV, Chart 5.6) were a three-generation dynastic family of the Parlement of Paris. When Cathérine Thévenin de Tanlay was married to Thomas-Urbain II Maussion de la Folletière in 1763, she was contracted with the second generation of the Maussions in the Parlement and the Grand Conseil.[26] The couple's lavish spring wedding, in the Church of Saint-Nicolas-des-Champs, occurred one hundred years after the birth of Thomas-Urbain II's grandfather, Thomas Maussion, at Brûlon in 1663. The Thévenins were distinguished *parlementaires.* But like the Auberts de Tourny (and the Maussions, in a more modest fashion), their fortune had been created in the late seventeenth century by elders who were simultaneously private financiers and fiscal officers.[27]

The last Maussion alliance before the Revolution was to a family that had provided sovereign court judges (Parlement of Burgundy and Grand Conseil) since at least 1725 and an intendant since 1760.[28] Through his marriage to

---

[24] See Mousnier, *Institutions of France*, vol. 2, p. 207, on those offices.

[25] On the Chuppins, see d'Affry, *Les jetons*, pp. 197–8, 269–70; Bluche, "L'origine des magistrats du Parlement de Paris," p. 135; Favre-Lejeune, *Les secrétaires du roi*, vol. 1, pp. 369–70; A.N. Y 1868, doss. C.-J.-N. Chuppin.

[26] And she brought the following dowry to that marriage: 80,000 livres from her father and mother; 110,000 from her great-aunt; and 60,000 from her maternal uncle. In 1763, these 250,000 livres could have purchased four judgeships in the Parlement of Paris.

[27] These were Jean I and his brother Jean II. Like Aubert de Tourny, they were financial protégés and associates of Chancellor Pontchartrain. They invested at great profit in the fiscal administration of various royal and ducal domains, the collection of excise taxes, military procurement, and loans to the Treasury. Like the Auberts, once the original fortune had been consolidated the family left finance for magistracy (Dessert, *Argent et pouvoir*, pp. 97–8, 320, 381, 695).

[28] On the Perrins de Cypierre, see Antoine, *Le gouvernement*, p. 200; Bluche, "Les magistrats du Grand Conseil," p. 125.

Chart 5.5. *Maussion alliance III: Chuppin*

I	II	III	IV	V

Nicolas Chuppin (b. ?; d. ?): silk merchant, bourgeois of Paris

wife unknown, two children known:

Pierre Chuppin (1654 [Paris]–1710 [Paris]): notary, Châtelet (1680–1710); royal secretary (1700–10); marriage and children unknown

Nicolas Chuppin (1636 [Paris]–1713 [Paris]): *échevin* of Paris (1687–89); controller and then general treasurer *marc d'or* (1690); royal secretary (1699–1713); ennobled (by *échevinage*)
oo Nicole-Angélique Voysin (1663), three children:

Angélique Chuppin (b. ?; d. ?): oo Louis-François Moufle (general treasurer, *marc d'or*)

Nicolas-Augustin Chuppin (b. ?; d. ?): succeeded father as general treasurer, *marc d'or* (1700–20)
oo Marguérite LeCouteulx (1705), children unknown

Charles Chuppin de Cherey (b. 1684, d. ?): officer of the Grand Chancellery, keeper of the roles of office
oo Marie Yerrier (1711), one child:

Charles-Nicolas Chuppin (1712 [Paris]–?): deputy prosecutor, Parlement of Paris (1737–42); general treasurer, *marc d'or* (1743); succeeded father as keeper of roles of office in Grand Chancellery (to 1765)
oo Marie-Sophie Hazon (1742), four children:

224

Marie-Charlotte Chuppin (b. 1743, d. ?) oo
Claude-Charles Tourolles (general receiver for royal domains, Generality of Rouen)

Antoinette-Genéviève Chuppin (wife of Louis Maussion de Candé)

Charles-Jean-Nicolas Chuppin (b. 1744, d. ?): judge, Châtelet (1764–7); judge, Parlement of Paris (1767–71)

Jean-Nicolas Chuppin (b. 1740s, d. ?): judge, Châtelet (1768–90)

Sources: A.N. Y 1868, doss. C.-J.-N. Chuppin; d'Affry, *Les jetons*, pp. 197–8; Bluche, "L'origine des magistrats du Parlement de Paris," p. 135; Favre-Lejeune, *Les secrétaires du roi*, vol. 1, pp. 369–70.

Chart 5.6. *Maussion alliance IV: Thévenin de Tanlay*

I	II	III	IV	V	VI

Samuel Thévenin (b. ?, d. ?): master of the royal mint at Poitiers, ennobled by letter, 1652
oo Judith Groussault, one child known:

    Pierre Thévenin (b. ?, d. c.1700): captain–major La Fère regiment
    oo Jeanne de la Chaize, two children:

        Jean I Thévenin, marquis of Tanlay (b. 1647, d. 1708 [Paris]): financier; royal secretary (1694–1708)
        oo Esther Oreils (1672), one son:

            Jean II Thévenin de Coursan and Tanlay (b. ?, d. c.1710): judge, Parlement of Paris (1708); master of petitions, Grand Chancellery
            oo Louise de Jassaud (1700), three children:

                Jeanne-Louise Thévenin (b. ?, d. ?) oo Jean de la Faurie (1726), president, Cour des Aides

                Anne Thévenin (b. ?, d. 1738) oo Charles de Jessaud (1730), cousin (royal secretary, member of Royal Order of the Holy Spirit)

                Jean-Louis Thévenin de Tanlay (b. 1708, d. 1711): upon his death, the marquisate of Tanlay passed to the cadet line

        Jean-Claude Thévenin (b. c1663, d. 1729 [Paris]): chief clerk, Parlement of Bordeaux (1696); royal secretary (1699–1729)
        oo Jeanne des Palmes (1706), three children:

Jeanne (b. ?, d. 1738) oo René Guerault de Golyère (gentleman of the duke of Orléans' household)

Marc-Claude (b. 1711, d. ?): gentleman of the king's household (1738)

Jean-Thévenin III de Tanlay (b. 1707, d. ?): judge, Parlement of Paris (1731–51); honorary to 1771 oo Cathérine Joly (1740), five children:

    Jean IV Thévenin de Tanlay (b. 1741, d. ?): royal musketeer

    Cathérine Thévenin de Tanlay (b. 1742, d. 1796), wife of Thomas-Urbain Maussion de la Folletière

    Jean-Charles Thévenin de Tanlay (b. 1743, d. ?)

    Pierre Thévenin de Tanlay (b. 1744, d. ?)

    Etienne-Jean-Benoît Thévenin de Tanlay (b. 1749, d. 1802): judge, Parlement of Paris oo Bénigne Esprit

Sources: Bluche, "L'origine des magistrats du Parlement de Paris," p. 397; Favre-Lejeune, *Les secrétaires du roi*, vol. 2, pp. 1250–3; Woëlmont de Brumagne, *Notices généalogiques*, vol. 4, pp. 987–9.

Chart 5.7. *Maussion alliance V: Perrin de Cypierre*

I	II	III
Joseph-Louis Perrin de Cypierre (b. 1699 [Dijon], d. 1730 [Dijon]): judge, Parlement of Burgundy (1725–30) oo Charlotte Milain, one child known		
	Jean-François-Claude Perrin de Cypierre (b. 1727 [Dijon], d. 1790): judge, Grand Conseil (1746); president, Grand Conseil (1758–60); intendant, Generality of Orléans (1760–87); councillor of state (1789) oo Marie-Florimonde Parat de Montgeron (1752), one child known	
		Jeanne-Antoinette Perrin de Cypierre (wife of Etienne-Thomas Maussion de la Courtaujay)

Sources: Antoine, *Le gouvernement*, p. 200; Bluche, "Les magistrats du Grand Conseil," p. 125.

Jeanne Perrin de Cypierre (alliance V, Chart 5.7) in 1784, Etienne-Thomas Maussion de la Courtaujay gained appointment as intendant of the Generality of Rouen in 1787. In him the Maussions reached close to the summit of the hierarchy of royal administration. They enjoyed the distinction for only two years. In March 1794, the Revolutionary Tribunal tried and condemned Etienne-Thomas Maussion as a counterrevolutionary. He was executed on the Paris guillotine.

Tracing the actions and experiences of the other Maussions and their kinsmen after 1789 is beyond the scope of this work and its sources. But from 1790 onward, they all confronted a novel reality: the abolition and replacement of the system upon which their rise and collective existence had been based for more than 150 years, magisterial and administrative vocation through proprietary, dynastic officeholding. The Maussions and their allies exemplified the wealthy, privileged, and powerful robe and civil nobility of France on the eve of the Revolution.

Between 1726 and 1784, the Maussions formed an extensive kinship group with five other families, by the marriages in their male line. We can estimate that by the 1780s the combined financial resources of that kinship group must have been several million livres. The salient characteristic of the clan was the general symmetry of its families – their similarity to each other – not their social or professional differences. The Maussions shared social roots with their allies. The acknowledged patriarchal ancestors in five of these genealogies had been diligent bourgeois, minor judicial or administrative officers of the Crown during the early or mid-seventeenth century. The remote and hidden ancestors, in the fifteenth and sixteenth centuries, had quite possibly been tradesmen, artisans, or even peasants.[29] Five of the six families were originally provincial: Maine (Maussions), Ile-de-France (Rillarts), Burgundy (Bergerets and Perrins), Aunis (Thévenins). They became Parisian during the late seventeenth or early eighteenth century. They were ennobled during the reign of Louis XIV, all but two (the Thévenins and Chuppins) by a royal secretaryship. Their steady vertical progressions within the hierarchy of officialdom were similar, and all but two of the families concentrated sons and resources at the highest levels of the themistocracy during the second half of the century. The egregious speculations of Pierre-François Bergeret and Jean I Thévenin were unique within both their own families and the kinship group. Those two created fortunes, but the economic behavior of their descendants and the other scions of the group was more respectably and incrementally acquisitive.

Not one of these families gave a son to the Church during the eighteenth century, nor do the sources reveal that any of their daughters was placed in a conventual order. Refusal of ecclesiastical vocations was also general among the families of eighteenth-century Châtelet judges.[30] The group's involvement with the sword nobility was marginal. The Maussions purchased military commissions and careers for only two of their eleven sons between 1700 and 1788; the Bergerets for four of nine sons (three of them at the beginning of the century, before the family had risen in civil officialdom); the Thévenins for one of seven.[31] The Chuppins and Rillarts seem to have been exclusively civil in vocation. Only seven of thirty-nine sons from these five ennobled families were placed in the army during the eighteenth century, even though, until the Ségur Ordinance of 1781, regimental careers were available to all of these families. Nor did they give their eighteenth-century daughters in marriage to families of

---

[29] Official genealogies of Old Regime French elites are incomplete social history, for they nearly always begin with the first socially respectable ancestor. One suspects that the Chuppins were shop tradesmen before they became cloth merchants, and weavers before they became tradesmen.

[30] Precisely how general was this refusal among the top ranks of the magistracy of France during the eighteenth century? The question merits research. Magisterial families seem to have given sons and daughters to the Church with considerable frequency during the seventeenth century. The rarity of that commitment after 1700 may have been a long and decisive prelude to the political conflicts between magistracy and episcopacy that developed during the second half of the eighteenth century, conflicts that finally matured to aggressive anticlericalism among much of the pre-Revolutionary themistocracy.

[31] Because we do not know why those sons were placed in regiments instead of civil offices, we cannot simply assume that it was a matter of recently ennobled families desiring to assimilate symbolically to the most venerable of aristocratic vocations. In addition to considerations discussed previously, it may also have been a matter of personal temperament. Not all sons would have been tractable to the intellectually demanding, highly disciplined, and sedentary career of judge. The officer corps of the army was an ideal placement for sons who were not temperamentally and intellectually suited to magistracy or administration and who were physically energetic.

the sword nobility. They married their young women into families of magistracy and royal administration.[32]

Magistry and high-level administration were the collective vocations of these families. They dynastically transmitted their principal offices from generation to generation. Those offices of state composed the bulk of their material, moral, and social capital. And that capital was massive by the second half of the eighteenth century. Between 1750 and 1790, twenty men from this group of six families held thirty-two different high offices of state, either concurrently or in succession. Sixteen of the offices were judgeships, twelve in Parisian sovereign courts and four in the Châtelet. Five were intendancies or positions in the royal Council.

Those principal offices of state were not sinecures: They demanded a concentrated and intricate labor involving analysis, decision making, and supervision of execution, and an attention to detail that could not be delegated to subordinates. Property in office meant a lifetime of subjugation to the formal responsibilities of office.

The late seventeenth or early eighteenth century ennobled patriarchs of these families (Thomas Maussion, Jacques Rillart, Pierre-François Bergeret, Nicolas II Chuppin, Jean I Thévenin, Joseph-Louis Perrin) had converted the bulk of their money into rentier capital: state bonds; annuities (both public and private); loans at fixed interest; land; and offices. Among the Maussions and analogous families of the themistocracy, the economic dynamic was conversion of money into fixed capital, not of capital into money: the polar opposite of a capitalist dynamic.

[32] The Thévenins, Rillarts, Chuppins, and Bergerets had fifteen daughters during the eighteenth century; all but one married magistrates or civil administrators. The Maussions produced five daughters between 1700 and 1789. At least two of them were married before the Revolution, one into a family of magistracy and high administration, the other into the *noblesse d'épée*. In 1758, Marie-Geneviève Maussion de la Courtaujay was wed to Antoine-Pierre de Chaumont, marquis of La Galaizière. Despite the resounding title, he was the grandson of a wholesale merchant of Namur and royal secretary. His father was successively judge of the Parlement of Metz, intendant of the Generality of Soissons, and councillor of state. Antoine-Pierre was judge of the Parlement of Paris, master of petitions, and (at the time of his marriage) intendant of Lorraine and Barrois (Antoine, *Le gouvernement*, pp. 63–4; Woëlmont de Brumagne, *Notices généalogiques*, vol. 3, pp. 196–8). Marie-Charlotte Maussion de la Courtaujay was married in 1763 to Jean-Thérèse-Louis-Joseph Beaumont, marquis of Autichamp. His family had been noble since the fifteenth century, and its vocation was military. She may have been the only woman of the Maussion family to have married into the sword nobility during the eighteenth century. Jean, marquis of Autichamp, was successively an officer of a royal household cavalry regiment, aide-de-camp to the marshal–duke of Broglie, chevalier of St. Louis during the Seven Years' War, and governor of the fortress of Longwy. He emigrated with his wife and children in the entourage of the prince of Condé in July 1789. His counterrevolutionary military career was epic. He commanded a force in the Catholic and Royal Army of the Vendée in 1793–4. In 1797, after the defeat of this army, he entered the Russian service and became commander of a Guards cavalry regiment, general inspector of cavalry, and then lieutenant general. Marie-Charlotte probably died in Russia. Beaumont returned to France with the Bourbons in 1815 and was appointed governor of the military division that included Paris. In July 1830, at the age of 92, he was serving as governor of the Louvre Palace and led its unsuccessful defense against the insurgents – a spectacle that Thomas-Antoine-Jean Maussion observed distantly, from the Chamber of Deputies (Woëlmont de Brumagne, *Notices généalogiques*, vol. 3, 18–19).

The total capital held by Thomas Maussion's mature sons was probably several times the amount of his estate at decease, but little of that family capital appears to have been monetary or liquid. It consisted primarily in the sale value (quite large) and annual revenue (modest) of judicial offices; long-term annuities; and immovable property. Most of their revenue was a steady but small return on large investments. Paradoxically, dowries were one of their principal sources of liquid capital, but they had to reciprocate. (In this respect, the Maussions were biologically fortunate; they had only five daughters, as against fourteen sons, during the eighteenth century.) Although they systematically accumulated real property, both rural and urban, they hoarded most of it. In short, this was retentive investment or proprietary accumulation. They did not accumulate for the purpose of a luxurious life-style, emancipation from work, or even confirmation of noble status.

To suppose that *anoblis* of the robe and administration such as the Maussions and their allies bought seigneurial domains and other farmlands out of a need to emulate the classic model of aristocracy, and therefore out of a "status anxiety," is to dematerialize agrarian property, to construe it as symbol. The relations that require examination were the ones that obtained between landownership and office, not between landownership and aristocracy. The former relations were primarily economic.

Thomas Maussion purchased at least seven rural properties; three (Candé, La Folletière, and La Courtaujay) were substantial estates. Jean I Thévenin purchased a marquisate, a barony (Thorey, near Semur-en-Auxerrois), and eight other seigniories, mostly in Burgundy. Pierre-François Bergeret acquired at least a dozen estates and kept most of them for his family. Those patriarchs were the first generation of their families to hold high royal office, and they planned for the future of their lineages. They needed to endow their sons with property that had durable and growing capital value and that also generated annual revenue. In the French economy of the seventeenth and eighteenth centuries, large-scale domains – with woodlands, mills, pastures, orchards, and tenant farms that produced a variety of grains, hides, and wines, seigneurial dues and labor exacted from those farmers, and tax exemptions – were virtually the only form of property that combined those attributes. If the manor house is to be construed as symbol, it was most genuinely symbolic of that economic value and power, not of nobiliary identity. The market value of most agrarian domains steadily appreciated during the eighteenth century. Such investment was both eminently secure and profitable in the long term, in contrast to the high risk of investment in overseas and colonial trade. Real property was also the strongest collateral for loans and for the creation of private *rentes*. It could be mortgaged or leased out for money, exchanged, used as security for installment purchase of offices, or parceled out among heirs. Landownership on a significant scale provided a themistocratic family of Paris (or any French judicial city) with an abundance of tax-exempt food and wine (regularly transported by peasants of the domains) for its own consumption and for entertaining. It ensured the solvency of that family in the long duration. Landownership, both agrarian and urban, was a collective discipline. Of all forms of property, it was the most securely and bindingly transmissible to heirs, for it was legally the most difficult to squander. The goal of the Maussions and their counterparts was to create a permanent, granitic bloc of capital in land, rural and urban, upon which to found capital in office.

The investment behavior of the Maussion clan was altogether typical of the themistocracy. Land was a major element in the capital holdings of most seventeenth- and eighteenth-century *parlementaires* of Paris, Châtelet judges, and magistrates of those provincial courts that have been archivally examined.[33] In 1767, the *élection* of Paris (not including the city itself) comprised 442 parishes, with 47,685 households. It was fertile and expensive countryside, at the geographical heart of the Ile-de-France.[34] By the end of the seventeenth cèntury, if not well before, the bulk of the land in the *élection* that was not royal or ecclesiastical domain was owned in full or in part by Parisian bourgeois and nobles. Much of the land had once been owned by the peasant families who worked it. Many of the new owners were magistrates.[35] Ownership of most of the larger seigneurial estates in the region (and throughout the Generality) conferred the right to dispense civil and criminal justice, in first instance, to inhabitants of the estate (subject to the limitations that are discussed in Part III). In 1719, there were 166 such large seigniories in the *élection*. They were owned as follows: by the Crown and princes of the blood (49); the Church (27); magistrates of Parisian courts (39); other noble families (51). High royal officers (councillors and secretaries of state, intendants) accounted for many of the 51 in the last group. Families of the Parisian themistocracy owned some one-third of all the large nonroyal and nonecclesiastical domains in the close rural outlands of the city by the early eighteenth century.[36] Only 1 in 8 of those 166 estates was owned by a family of the sword nobility, always the family of a general or field marshal. A *parlementaire* family that inspected its estate in this region or passed a judicial vacation there was most likely to find itself riding, hunting, or dining in the company of the magisterial and administrative families with which it worked and shared conviviality in Paris.

When themistocratic families did not spend money on land and offices or on the sociability and charity required of superior officeholders, they spent it on

---

[33] In addition to the previously cited works of Bluche, Hamscher, Waquet, Rosset, Deyon, Doyle, and Roche, see Robert Forster, *Merchants, Landlords, Magistrates: The Depont Family in Eighteenth-Century France* (Baltimore: Johns Hopkins University Press, 1980). The judges of bailliage, presidial, and tax courts acquired detailed knowledge of current and prospective property values in their jurisdictions through the exercise of their offices in civil and fiscal litigation and could therefore invest on the basis of solid intelligence. See Goubert, "Les officiers royaux," pp. 54–75.

[34] Expilly, *Dictionnaire*, vol. 5, p. 569.

[35] Marc Venard, *Bourgeois et paysans au XVIIe siècle: Recherche sur le rôle des bourgeois parisiens dans la vie agricole au Sud de Paris au XVIIe siècle* (Paris: SEVPEN, 1957).

[36] This tabulation is from A. M. de Boislisle, ed., *Mémoires des intendants sur l'état des Généralités, dressés pour l'instruction du duc de Bourgogne*, vol. 1: *Mémoire de la Généralité de Paris* (Paris, 1881), pp. 205–11.

marital endowments to their sons or in dowries to their daughters for the purpose of kinship expansion. Kinsmen were their principal source of patronage for offices, and thus a principal source of their moral and material patrimony. Judicial offices could be purchased with installment payments spread over long periods, if the seller consented. Recommendations from kinsmen who were highly placed in the judiciary or administration could obtain that consent. They acted as social collateral for the installment buyer, and sometimes as a source of loans for purchase of office. Thomas Maussion's career was launched in that manner, and the initial breakthrough of the Maussions into the themistocracy occurred in that manner. The marquis of Salaberry may have personally known Thomas Maussion before he agreed to sell his judgeship in the Grand Conseil on installments to Thomas-Urbain Maussion in 1719, but he was undoubtedly acquainted with the Auberts de Tourny through the Chambre des Comptes of Normandy, the Grand Conseil, and Parisian elite society.[37] The process of kinship expansion was circular: the desirability in marriage of a family did not depend only on the offices and capital it possessed; it also depended on the perceived quality of its preceding marriage alliances, and thus of its kinship group. Kinsmen, even distant, were also latent monetary capital, for they were a vast source of loans at a moderate rate of interest, and of *rentes*. The Maussions not only were members of a large primary kinship group: Through the collateral marriages of their five allied families, they also belonged to a great constellation of some twenty-six dynastic magisterial and governing families by the late eighteenth century.

Office was the steel thread in the economic fabric of the Maussions and their allies. Landed property, bonds and annuities, dowries and marriage alliances, even collections of precious objects, were acquired and manipulated to the end of obtaining and exercising state offices. Such offices were never relinquished. They were only changed – sold to purchase higher offices of state. High judicial offices, unlike fiscal offices, were strangely, even paradoxically, immaterial in character. They were costly, but they generated little income; they demanded an ascesis of labor, but also a noble and expensive style of life from their holders. In order to finance the purchase and exercise of offices, the Maussions and most of their allied families were deeply involved economically

---

[37] Charles-François d'Irumberry, marquis of Salaberry, sold his judgeship in the Grand Conseil to succeed his father as president of the Chambre des Comptes. His sale of office to Thomas-Urbain Maussion in 1719 was a classic instance of promotion of a new family by an established themistocratic family. See Bluche, *Les magistrats du Grand Conseil*, p. 136; *L'origine des magistrats du Parlement de Paris*, pp. 384–5. The Maussions had traveled a vast political and social distance by 1784, the year in which Thomas-Antoine-Jean Maussion de la Folletière entered the Châtelet. His two principal references were close associates of his elders, at least one of whom was also a collateral relative. Auguste-Henry Langlois de Pommeuse, judge of the Parlement of Paris, was a friend and colleague of his uncle (Louis Maussion de Candé) and a kinsman of the Maussions through marriage to the Chuppins. Jean-Baptiste Sollier de Charmon, judge of the Cour des Aides, was a colleague of his father (Thomas-Urbain Maussion de la Folletière). Sollier's nephew (Guy-Marie) had entered the Châtelet in 1783 (A.N. Y 1869; Roton, *Les arrêts du Grand Conseil*, pp. 341, 439).

in both the royal fiscal system and the system of seigneurial landownership and privilege – two of the most traditional and generally unpopular elements of eighteenth-century French civilization.

As these families ascended and converged within officialdom, their marriages became increasingly endogamous, in professional terms. None of the Maussion marriages were hypergamic, except possibly the Garciau alliance in 1692. Their marriages were at approximate parity of status. One is struck by the homogeneity or affinity of the Maussions, Rillarts, Chuppins, Thévenins, and Perrins at their times of juncture. Each family was almost a socioprofessional mirror of the other, a mirror of achievements and ambitions. For each family of this large group, marriages were a strategy for consolidating identity, vocation, and wealth and for gradual, collective ascent within the hierarchy of power. That strategy of consolidation and gradualism is manifest even in the biology of their marriages.

Between the mid-seventeenth century and 1789, the Maussions, Rillarts, Bergerets, Chuppins, and Thévenins had twenty-six marriages in their male lines for which we know the number of surviving children:

Maussion		Rillart	
Generation	*No. of children*	*Generation*	*No. of children*
I	7	I	4
II	3	IIa	1
IIIa	4	IIb	1
IIIb	4	IIc	1
IVa	3		
IVb	4		
IVc	2		
	Avg. 4		Avg. 1.75

Bergeret		Chuppin	
Generation	*No. of children*	*Generation*	*No. of children*
I	7	I	2
II	5	II	3
IIIa	1	IIIa	1
IIIb	3	IIIb	4
	Avg. 4		Avg. 2.5

Thévenin	
Generation	*No. of children*
I	1 (known)
II	2
IIIa	1
IIIb	1
IV	3
V	5
	Avg. 3

The average number of children from these twenty-six marriages was three. This was distinctive, in a nation whose global average of surviving children per marriage was four to five during the eighteenth century. These magisterial couples wed at ages of fecundity and remained married until they were parted by death. The age at marriage is known for seventeen of the twenty-six men, who were, respectively aged 24 (1); 25 to 30 (8); 31 to 35 (4); 36 to 40 (2); over 40 (1). Most of their brides were aged between 18 and 23. The longevity of husbands and wives was considerable. One may assume that the incidence of miscarriage and infant mortality among these couples was lower than the eighteenth-century norm, for their general quality of life (economic, medical, and nutritional) was among the best in France. Most of their children were born at intervals of three to seven or more years. These patterns suggest regular periods of willed sexual abstinence or unconsummated erotic play – methods of birth control.

The seventeenth-century "first-generation" patriarchs of the Maussions, Bergerets, and Rillarts were prolific. Succeeding generations of those and the other families chose not to be. When each family attained high, costly, and arduous offices of state (in the second or third generation), they exercised restraint in procreation. Children were expensive for families of superior officialdom. They had to be educated for a vocation of public service or (if females) substantially dowered. After education, the sons had to be placed in offices that were equivalent or superior to the position already occupied by the father. The age for purchase of offices for sons was 20 to 25; for dowering and marriage of daughters, it was 18 to 23. That was a powerful incentive for conception at lengthy intervals. Civil and customary law of Paris and the Ile-de-France required that two-thirds of the nobiliary paternal estate be willed to the eldest son, if there was only one other heir, and that he receive one-half if there were two or more other heirs. The remaining one-third or one-half was parceled out equally among the other children. Parceling threatened any excess of sons and daughters, and their own progeny, with penury and then derogation of status. Nobility was indeed collective, by paternal descent; but to be noble, one had to live "nobly," and that life was expensive, even for those disposed to austerity. The fewer the children, the greater the nurturance, wealth, and power to distribute among all of them.

Here one glimpses the profile of the modern family, planned and nuclear. But each of these discrete families belonged to a ramified group. Their planning contained no element of sentimental individualism; it was directed at the social and political aggrandizement of a long posterity, of a dynasty. It expressed discipline. Parents and elders selected the marriage partner, just as they imposed the vocation. The rules of procreation were also imposed and inculcated.[38]

[38] Familial and sexual discipline were made all the more proximate and enduring by the fact of commensal households, in which the new couple lived for most of their lives in the home of the husband's father and mother. That was the practice of the eighteenth-century Maussions in their

The system of public authority and the system of family were a unified whole. The Maussions and their allies succeeded because they were able to conserve that unity within their collective lives. The long-term rewards for this behavior were manifest, to them as to us: authority, prestige, affluence, and a possibility of access to the highest offices of state.[39] Their behavior proceeded from a cast of mind that was calculating, meticulous, and rule-governed. Among these families, the imperium of private destiny formed a whole with the imperium of public destiny. It was as if each member were taught: "You are to conduct your life for the sake of those of our lineage who are not yet born."

C. Caste

Modern historians commonly use the broad concepts of "Estate" (or order) and "socioeconomic class" in describing Old Regime French society. "Profession" has been recognized, more recently and accurately, as a major organizing and differentiating principle within eighteenth-century France. But few historians are willing to use the concept of "caste" for understanding any large group in

senior lines: Thomas Maussion, Thomas-Urbain I, and his wife, on the rue du Hazard; Louis Maussion de Candé and his children, his cadet brother Thomas-Urbain Maussion de la Folletière and his wife, and the latter's son Thomas-Antoine-Jean, in the Hôtel Talard. Commensal households of this sort were common among families of the high magistracy and administration during the seventeenth and eighteenth centuries; they sometimes grouped three generations of patrilineage. As for the conjugal couple, "Il vit a ses pièces à part. Il vit en principe à part, mais il vit dans la maison. . . . Il va sans dire que les rélations [with the patriarch of household and his wife] étaient quotidiennes et peuvent pas ne pas l'être et par conséquent l'influence de la famille de procréation continue à s'exercer. La famille de procréation continue à agir comme famille d'orientation et pèse sur les jeunes" (Roland Mousnier, *La Famille, l'enfant, et l'éducation en France et en Grande-Bretagne du XVIe au XVIIIe siècle* [Paris: Cours de Sorbonne, 1975], p. 59).

[39] Louis XIV was the first king who systematically chose *anoblis* of the robe as secretaries and ministers of state. He thereby accomplished a social alteration in the supreme government of France, of which the Maussions and their collective eighteenth-century analogs were beneficiaries: "It is abundantly clear that in Louis XIV's reign it is not the bourgeoisie, but the nobility of the robe, which arrived at the summit of power. At the level of the highest positions in government and the state, representatives chosen from this social group were permitted to integrate with and become the equal of the highest nobility of the realm; from this time onward, their status was so high that they dominated the Second Estate. Louis XIV did not thrust the 'bourgeois' into power; but he used his authority to make government service equal in prestige to antiquity of lineage. By putting his ministers of the robe nobility on an equal footing with dukes, he gave the civil service a hitherto unheard-of importance and removed the inferiority hitherto imputed to it. The history of the great offices of government in the eighteenth century shows the continuance of Louis XIV's policy and demonstrates, despite a few anomalies, that the royal service was from now on unified: the kingdom needed administrators as much as soldiers" (François Bluche, "The Social Origins of the Secretaries of State under Louis XIV, 1661–1715," in Hatton, *Louis XIV and Absolutism*, pp. 96–7). Louis III Phélypeaux, count of Pontchartrain and Chancellor of France, personified the men from ennobled robe and administrative families who were placed in great offices of state by Louis XIV. In personal terms, the Pontchartrain–Aubert–Maussion transmission was a living example of the general and long-term continuity in governance that is described by Bluche in the passage just quoted.

that society. This concept is regarded as specifically Asian, or Hindu, in meaning and reality, and inapplicable to Western European social history.

Members of the eighteenth-century French themistocracy were neither Hindus nor anthropologists. They did not understand and describe themselves as members of a caste. They were not Marxian social scientists either, and did not identify themselves in terms of class. "Estate" and "profession" had meaning for them. But those categories of identity were in tension, even contradiction, during the eighteenth century. Did an *anobli* of the robe, or his magisterial progeny, belong essentially to the aristocracy or to the royal judiciary? His nobility derived only from personal statist function, a civil function, or from shallow descendance in such function. He had no venerability of lineage (or "*sang pur*"), no military ancestry, and he did not bear arms. In the collective vision of the military-seigneurial aristocracy, the *robin* remained essentially bourgeois and alien. As noble magistrate or civil administrator, at the rank of sovereign court judge or general receiver for an entire Generality, he still belonged to a group that was overwhelmingly common in its social composition. He worked with professional colleagues and subordinates who were bourgeois, or even less. Estates and professions were highly diffuse and confusing realities during the eighteenth century. The extreme variety in seniority, rank, prestige, wealth, lifestyle, and occupations within the populous French aristocracy was virtually equaled by that within the royal judiciary (which ranged from jailers, summons-servers, and solicitors in small-town courts to old dynasties of *parlementaires* in major cities). A judge of the Parlement of Paris or Grand Conseil knew that he was a man of the law, but he had no social affinity with the clerks and proctors of his own court. He was also a member of the French nobility, but his relations with families of old seigneurial and military title were remote and tenuous. How did he, and his family, create indispensable primary-group bonds, and therefore both self-definition and sustaining community?

The six families of the Maussion group suggest an answer to that question. They forged and perpetuated identity and community by dynastic continuance in offices and by practicing strict marital endogamy, in each generation, choosing marriage partners by the principle of parity of professional rank within the royal administration and judiciary. After they acquired ennobling offices, they did not marry either bourgeois families of magistracy and administration or noble families of the sword. They had formal external relations with the former and the latter but virtually no kinship bonding with either. Theirs was a marital behavior of dual closure: exclusion of military and court nobles, and exclusion of professional inferiors. Estate, class, and profession do not describe that behavior. It may, however, be defined as caste behavior:

The cultural rules of caste behavior establish a dichotomy in the total field of social relationships – political, economic and ritual relations are external, kinship relations are exclusively internal. In the "orthodox" ideal type of caste structure this distinction is quite clear and follows directly from the three caste traits of endogamy, hierarchy and occupational specialization.[40]

Caste may be defined as a small and named group of persons characterized by endogamy, hereditary membership, and a specific style of life which sometimes includes the pursuit by tradition of a particular occupation and is usually associated with a more or less distinct ritual status in a hierarchical system.[41]

The Maussions and their five allied families practiced caste dynasticism and endogamy from at least the 1690s to 1790. By doing so, they simultaneously avoided any taint of derogation (or "pollution") in either profession or estate and ensured a continual rise in socioprofessional status. Caste behavior allowed them to concentrate their primary familial and kinship resources (inheritance, dowries, reciprocities) on themistocratic and administrative vocations. It perfected their professionalism. With each generation, and each marriage at parity, the group became both more venerable in nobility and more powerful in profession. Through a politics of caste, they became *noblesse de race* (fourth-generation noble) and entrenched within the Parlement of Paris, Grand Conseil, Cour des Aides, and Châtelet by the eve of the Revolution.

Caste was their coherence. What began for the Maussions as social fortuity – their encounter with the Auberts in the Maine or at Paris – rapidly became, and then remained, a social determinism. The determinism operated within two grand matrices established by royal law early in the seventeenth century: hereditary officeholding and near-absolute parental authority over the selection of marriage partners. Rules of caste, distinct yet uncodified, developed within those matrices; they governed the marital choices of the Maussions and their allies, and ultimately their common socioprofessional rise. Those rules did not preclude professionally and socially harmonious relations or friendship with, and patronage of, bourgeois colleagues in the judiciary and administration. Nor did they prevent economic and ceremonial exchanges with aristocrats of the army and seigniories, or occasional placement of a son in a regiment. They did preclude bonding and fusion.

When they deposited their documentation in support of noble title with the royal genealogist Charles d'Hozier, the Maussions claimed an ancestor who had followed Francis I into his Spanish captivity after the battle of Pavia (1525). The claim was not certified by d'Hozier, but the Maussions were granted the heraldic device "Wholeheartedly loyal." At the center of their coat of arms was a large, and densely limbed poplar tree growing from a mound of silver. That plutocratic image was utterly appropriate.

---

[40] Edmund Leach, "What Should We Mean by Caste?" in *Aspects of Caste in South India, Ceylon and North-West Pakistan* (Cambridge: Cambridge University Press, 1960), p. 8.

[41] André Béteille, *Caste, Class and Power: Changing Patterns of Stratification in a Tanjore Village* (Berkeley and Los Angeles: University of California Press, 1971), p. 46. I owe these references and introduction to the concept of caste to Andrew Apter, of the Columbia University Society of Fellows and the Department of Anthropology, University of Chicago.

The Maussions collected taxes and rendered justice in the name of the king, according to procedures mandated by kings. In the Grand Conseil and Parlement of Paris, they sat on high-backed benches that were upholstered in purple velvet embroidered with the fleur-de-lis. But what could have been the relations between the Maussions and the kings of France whom they officially served: Louis XIV, Louis XV, and Louis XVI? None of the Maussions, and few of their kinsmen, were personally empowered by a king. Even Léon-Urbain Aubert, who was probably the closest in proximity to the Court among all of them, was a protégé of Pontchartrain, not of Louis XIV. By the agency of Pontchartrain, he initially received a commission, then offices. Thomas Maussion was Aubert's protégé. The Maussions and their kinsmen were all empowered by the acquisition of magisterial and administrative offices. Genuine royal delegation of authority had long since been to those offices, not to the persons of officers. Kings formulaically ratified accession to office with a letter of appointment, after the formal requirements for officeholding had been satisfied. Therefore, the key to understanding the power of the Maussions and their counterparts, and thus their relations to the reigning monarch, lies in the means by which they acquired office. And there were only three: (1) capital, for purchasing office from the departing officer or his family; (2) formal qualifications, objective and discernable; (3) corporate patronage and co-optation. Their individual relations to statist corporations were therefore immediate and vital. Their relations to the king were mechanical and abstract. This was true of the entire magistracy of France.

Magistrates were subservient to the civil and criminal law. Most of that law had indeed originated in royal decisions, expressed as edicts and codes (that were actually drafted, however, by former magistrates serving on royal councils). But once an edict or code was registered by the Parlements and then passed into law, jurisprudence, and practice, it became an objective entity. It was enforced as law, not as the will of a particular monarch (who, by the eighteenth century, was in most cases long since dead). Office and law both survived and transcended kings during the Old Regime.

The manifest primary loyalty of the Maussions, and their colleagues in the themistocracy, was to a system of rule, not to kings. They had no more, and no less, than a long-term, mutually binding contract with the institution of monarchy. Contract neither requires nor engenders sentiment. By the terms of the contract, the Maussions and their thousands of colleagues were, to a great extent, economically independent of the monarchy. They securely owned their offices as transmissible property. And they owned land, which is to say that they owned the principal means of production and source of capital in the French economy.

Within this system of rule, there was virtually no possibility for the development of royalist ideology, either as personal fealty to a monarch or as belief in absolute royal authority. Royalist ideology – or the doctrine that the king could legislate or decide policy innovatively, autonomously, at will – could exist at Court, among appointed secretaries and ministers of state and, perhaps, intendants, but not within the official and active body of the state.[42]

[42] The pomp and symbolism of the great royal processions, in which Parisian magistrates formed a cortege and rendered homage to the king, rather pathetically masked the concrete relations that obtained between those kings and those magistrates during the seventeenth and eighteenth centuries. To read the symbolism of ceremonies as describing real power relations is naïve. More generally, much of political ceremony in modern Europe seems nondescriptive: It is either obligatory, inertially repetitive, and performed without discernable instrumental calculation, or it is the contrivance of fictional, not actual, sociopolitical relationships, whether the fictions are archaic or utopian in character. To treat ceremonies as "thick description" of a society or polity in a given period is to risk being entrapped by obfuscation. Such fashionable hermeneutics cannot replace primary research on social and political relations.

6

Professional culture

Dynasticism and caste endogamy were not the only means by which the Old Regime themistocracy forged solidarities, replicated itself, and replenished its ranks. It was also constituted and preserved by a professional culture: intellectual; communal; affective; and moral. That culture formed the young.

A. Education

There was a generic education common to eighteenth-century *collèges*, despite varieties of emphasis among them and limited pedagogic innovation during the last two decades of the Old Regime. That education imparted a remarkably uniform intellectual molding.

After six years studying the humanities in a *collège de pleine exercice*, no one but the dullest scholar could have emerged from the rhetoric class who was not an extremely competent Latinist. To borrow a contemporary educational concept in the teaching of languages, the seventeenth- and eighteenth-century student was subject to a process of total immersion. For at least four hours a day throughout their adolescence future members of the liberal professional elite studied the language and literature of Ancient Rome, often to the exclusion of everything else. They did so too in such a manner than by the end of the course they could not only read and write Latin fluently but speak the language as well. They were to all intents and purposes (in the class-room at any rate) children of Rome rather than France, who spoke and composed in the grand Ciceronian manner and knew the history of the late Republic and Augustan era in far greater detail than that of their own recent past. In this respect the educational experience of Richelieu and Robespierre was indistinguishable.[1]

In the capital and its region, there were ten *collèges de plein exercice* that boarded students. All were attached to the University of Paris. They were the institutions that educated most future members of the Parisian themistocracy during the seventeenth and eighteenth centuries. Those *collèges* most favored by families of the Parlement and Châtelet were Louis-le-Grand, Navarre, Beauvais, Harcourt, and Juilly. Instruction by the *collèges* – six years of humanities

---

[1] L. W. B. Brockliss, *French Higher Education in the Seventeenth and Eighteenth Centuries: A Cultural History* (Oxford: Clarendon Press, 1987), p. 178. Most of the following discussion of education in the humanities, philosophy, and law is drawn from this comprehensive work.

followed by two of philosophy, culminating in the Master of Arts degree – was propaedeutic, and virtually prerequisite, to the professional study of the *sciences* – law, theology, and medicine – in a university faculty.

Except for the teaching of French composition in *collèges* and of French law in the university, the language of instruction and examination was Latin. The civil and spiritual governing elite of France was intellectually formed, or remolded during childhood and youth, by an occult language and system of thought.[2] That experience distinguished it from all other social groups, even from most of the nobility whose vocation was military.

Students normally entered the *collège* between the age of 10 and 12. Life there was strictly regimented and intensely communal, even for *externes*, who lived in lodgings or at home. Students were controlled by professors who were mostly clerics. There was chapel each morning, weekly sermons, communal dining, and generally at least four hours of classes every day except Sunday. The eighteenth-century *collège* imposed an education in close and disciplined sociability and in Catholic doctrine and devotion (whether Jesuit or Jansenist in orientation), along with a rigid shaping of the mind. Students were examined orally and in writing at the end of each year; the results determined whether they could move into the following class or would have to repeat. Latin was the core of the curriculum, from the initial year (the "sixth form") to the final year (the "first form"). The use of French was permitted in Latin class only during the first two years, to explain grammar and syntax; thereafter, only Latin was spoken. The first four years were devoted to mastering grammar, syntax, and vocabulary; the final two were concentrated on composition in prose and verse. The goal of humanistic education was a student who could think, read, write, and speak Latin fluently, in the manner of the great classical authors. They were also taught to read and write classical Greek, as the seminal language of Christian theology and European philosophy. That instruction was accorded less attention than Latin, however, and declined during the eighteenth century.

The French language and its literature were a secondary subject, but these grew in emphasis during the eighteenth century because of the standardization imposed by the Academy and the fact that French replaced Latin as the language of publication in high culture and the sciences from the late seventeenth century onward. In the sixth through the fourth form, the elements of the French language were taught principally with Latin as the medium of instruc-

---

[2] In the words of Walter J. Ong, "Insulated from the earliest life of childhood where language has its deepest psychic roots, a first language to none of its users, pronounced across Europe in often mutually unintelligible ways but always written the same way, Learned Latin was a striking exemplification of the power of writing for isolating discourse and of the unparalleled productivity of such isolation. . . . Learned Latin effects even greater objectivity by establishing knowledge in a medium insulated from the emotion-charged depths of one's mother tongue, thus reducing interference from the human lifeworld and making possible the exquisitely abstract world of medieval scholasticism and of the new mathematical modern science which followed on the scholastic experience" (*Orality and Literacy: The Technologizing of the World* [London: Methuen, 1982], pp. 113–14). To medieval scholasticism and mathematical modern science of the seventeenth century, one can add early modern jurisprudence.

tion, pairing conjugation of Latin verbs with the same in French, giving Latin derivations of French nouns, and acquiring Latin punctuation and syntax as bases for French prose style. Only after midcentury did Parisian *collèges* develop French as a five-year course that integrated grammar, composition, rhetorical exercises, and literary analysis. But that course still remained modeled on parallel, and more intense, instruction in Latin and the culture of classical Rome. By that method, even the native language of the young was purged of its demotic, spontaneous qualities and transmuted into the austere, formal, latinate French of the Academy. That was the French of the Court, chancelleries, seminaries, and lawcourts.

Selected passages from classical, canonic texts were the main vehicles for linguistic and moral instruction. In Greek, eighteenth-century professors favored Aesop, Demosthenes, Homer, Xenophon, Lucian, and the Gospels or Acts from the New Testament. In French, they preferred the classics of the *grand siècle:* The Fables of La Fontaine, the *Characters* of La Bruyère, and especially works by the great clerics Bossuet, Fléchier, Bourdaloue, and Massillon. The array of Latin authors studied was much wider. In included all literary genres and was arranged in order of increasing difficulty over the six years: in the sixth and fifth form, Cicero's *Litterae familiares*, Ovid's *Tristia*, the *Fables* of Phaedrus, the *Histories* of Cornelius Nepo; in the fourth and third, Cicero's *De officiis* (On public office) and *De amicitia*, Ovid's *Metamorphoses*, Terence's *Adelphi*, the *Eclogues* or *Georgics* of Virgil, and two of the Roman historians (Caesar, Sallust, Justin, or Quintus Curtius). The second and first forms studied rhetoric and poetics. Cicero's orations were main texts, along with the histories of Livy and Tacitus; instruction in poetics was crowned with Virgil's *Aeneid* and expurgated versions of Horace's *Odes*.

Professors explicated texts, emphasizing grammar, style, the logical progression of ideas, historical, mythological, or geographical referents, and ethical meaning. Their lectures alternated with oral classroom exercises by students: declension of verbs; translation; debates on questions set by professors; extempore speeches and verses on themes from the classical work and in the mode of its author. Written exercises (*devoirs*) were required almost every night. In the sixth through third forms, they ranged from copying texts (a mnemonic device also used to teach orthography), short essays on a theme assigned from the text under study to translating parts of that text into French. During the final two years, students wrote longer prose or verse pieces on assigned subjects: descriptions of historical or mythological events; panegyrics on great men; essays on Christian or political themes, such as the evils of luxury, the virtues of work or public service, the divine source of monarchy, or veneration of parents and elders. In many *collèges*, written exercises were graded and then made into competitive (and often humiliating) experiences: Students were obliged to read all or part of their *devoirs* to the class; as *correction*, the essays were criticized systematically and mercilessly by other students (usually the most accomplished) and the professor.

Eloquent and elegant performance, especially in public speaking, was a primary goal of the education. It was served by periodic performance of plays, to which parents and local notables were invited. Students displayed their declamatory skill by performing Latin or French tragedies, or occasionally comedies. During the eighteenth century, plays declined in favor of public oratorical exercises: "pleadings" of cases from antiquity, debates on set propositions, or question-and-answer competitions. Prizes were awarded publicly to the outstanding performers.

Composition in Latin and French prose and verse – the *summum* of the six years – was taught essentially as rhetoric. Old Regime *collèges* had a uniform conception of rhetoric. It was the art of persuasion, both rational and emotive, according to the five-part sequence – *inventio, dispositio, elocutio, memoria, pronunciatio* – set forth in Cicero's *De oratore.*

Each part concerned a special skill that the successful orator would need. The first taught the art of finding the requisite evidential material to win the hearts and minds of the audience; it dealt with the *loci communes* that could be used to sustain an argument, and the human passions and national *mores* that the orator would need to cultivate or not offend. The second concerned the way in which a speech should be structured; it identified the three oratorical genres (adulatory, forensic, and deliberative), isolated the major internal divisions of any speech (the exordium, *narratio*, etc.) and suggested the kind of evidence to be used in each. Next, under *elocutio* the student was introduced to the various rhetorical devices that could turn an ordinary discourse into an elegant one and bring the audience pleasure. Finally, the sections on memory and pronunciation were devoted to the study of oratory in action. They dealt with the problem of speaking from notes or learning a speech and the style of delivery: which stance to take up, which gesture or expression to use.[3]

In classical Greece and Rome, rhetoric had originally been an improvised oral art. It was transformed by Aristotle and Cicero into a canon of prose wherein orality remained but was subsumed by writing, encased in literature. As taught in humanistic *collèges* from the sixteenth to the nineteenth century, rhetoric was a dogmatic and agonistic form for both writing (thus publishing) and speaking – in Latin as well as in French. As written argumentation, it was universally understood and excellent for communication among the educated. It was applicable to a great variety of subject matters and allowed the evolution of distinctive styles. But the use of rhetoric as speech among individuals was a closed world, reserved for those who possessed the stock of referential knowledge and who knew the grammatical and logical rules. Thus, an ancient, emotively colored, oral form of communication finally became, in early modern and Old Regime France (and Europe), a repudiation of ordinary, living oral culture and a literary-philosophical dogma that expressed social distance and political transcendence.[4] Such rhetoric provided the basic structure for French legal argumentation, as deployed by Old Regime jurists in their writings, barristers in

---

[3] Brockliss, *French Higher Education*, pp. 128–9.   [4] See Ong, *Orality and Literacy*, pp. 108–66.

pleadings, and prosecutors in their trial summaries and recommendations of sentence. It was virtually as alien to the speech and thought patterns of the popular classes as rap is to academic and official language in the contemporary United States.

From their remolding by belles lettres, future magistrates passed into a higher realm of abstraction, devoting one or two years to philosophy, which was divided into logic, ethics, physics, and metaphysics. Logic and ethics received greatest emphasis within the curriculum. Logic was the science of reasoning, essential to all subsequent study in university faculties. Ethics was propaedeutic to the study and practice of law.[5]

The scholastic method of instruction in philosophy prevailed during the eighteenth century. In lecturing, professors divided their subject matter into "problems." Each problem was then customarily reduced to one or more "questions," to which arguments and counterarguments were adduced until resolution or synthesis was generated.

The logic course was based on Aristotle's monumental *Organon*, in its full sequence, from the *Categories* of mental activity (apprehension or perception, judgment, and ratiocination) to the rules for correct reasoning and for the acquisition of knowledge, or *scientia*. Greatest emphasis was given to syllogistic reasoning (as analyzed in the *Prior Analytics* and *Posterior Analytics*); syllogistic argument from axioms and causes was deemed the method for obtaining certain (as against conjectural or sophistic) knowledge. The *Art de penser*, by the Cartesian (and Jansenist) logicians Antoine Arnauld and Pierre Nicole, was included in the course by many eighteenth-century professors and studied by their pupils. That approach shifted emphasis away from the Aristotelian and Thomist pedagogy of mental categories and of illustrating logic by questions from metaphysics and theology to other issues: skepticism of sense experience and judgment, and a more rigorous focus on conceptual logic and criteria of certainty, as they are presented in the Descartes's *Discourse on Method*. Although most professors attempted to conciliate Aristotelian–Thomist with Cartesian canons of logic, the latter gained in authority during the eighteenth century. Methodical doubt of appearances, of judgment from sense experience, and of axiomatic propositions were introduced as the path to truth. Students were led to essentially Cartesian rules of reasoning:

First, nothing was to be proposed as an axiom that was not perfectly clear. Secondly, when proving a relatively obscure proposition, nothing was to be advanced except definitions, axioms, and propositions already demonstrated. Thirdly, in passing from primary to secondary truths the argument should always move through a series of connected, intermediate and truthful propositions; no short cuts should be made. Finally, in every stage of an argument a premium should be placed on clarity. The aim was to produce a demonstration that would read like a mathematical proof.[6]

---

[5] For a full discussion of philosophy in the *collèges*, see Brockliss, *French Higher Education*, pp. 185–227.

[6] Ibid., p. 204.

Rigor in evaluation of evidence was central to that method. Logic professors influenced by Cartesianism, and who were teaching future magistrates, addressed issues of testimony in the determination of truth. Testimony required skepticism. It consisted of unproven propositions received by the senses of the investigator. It had to be analyzed according to source and bias; quantity; plausibility in terms of what is already securely proven; clarity; coherence. That was the cast of mind within modern French natural science and jurisprudence of the eighteenth century.

The course in general ethics was essentially a marriage of Aristotelian and Catholic (Thomist) moral philosophy. Its principal text was Aristotle's *Ethics*. Students were led to the Aristotelian conclusion that the highest purpose and happiness of humankind were the pursuit of the good. That good was defined as an active, charitable, and social life of virtue, not one of contemplative withdrawal. Divine grace had endowed even postlapsarian humankind with reason, free will, and the capacity for the cardinal (and Aristotelian) intellectual virtues of knowledge, science, wisdom, and prudence, as well as the virtues of the will – justice, temperance, and fortitude. The antithetical forces were the passions, lodged in the body and inflecting on the will: pride, greed, concupiscence, jealousy. When educated, open to divine revelation and grace, informed by piety and humility, and conditioned by the sacraments, the intellect could lead the will, and thus the self, to virtue, although not perfectly. The virtuous life corresponded to the maximum good, and thus purpose, of humankind in its fallen condition. That life was the preparation of the soul for perfect grace and redemption after it departed the body. The thrust of this synthesis of Aristotelian natural law and Catholic divine law was toward individual fulfillment and salvation, achieved through pious intention, observance of the sacraments, and moral striving within a Christian commonwealth and its obligations. That was the orthodox moral philosophy of the French Counter-Reformation, although its activism and relative optimism were discretely contested by eighteenth-century Jansenists, who emphasized the fragility and transience of virtue within the world and the body and the limited freedom of individual will.

After the Ordinance of Blois of Louis XII (1498), all lieutenants and judges of royal bailliage courts had to possess the *licence* in law from a university law faculty.[7] That degree was required of all barristers, and thus of all candidates for magisterial office (except clerics). It became a necessity for all superior civil officers of the Crown.[8] Legal education in Old Regime France had been standardized and regulated by edicts of Louis XIV that were binding on law faculties and students throughout the realm.[9] The purpose was to impose on those

---

[7] Article 48, Isambert, vol. 11, p. 347.

[8] On the constituency of legal education, see Richard Kagan, "Law Students and Legal Careers in Eighteenth-Century France," *Past and Present*, 68 (1975): 38–72.

[9] Edicts of April 1679 (Isambert, vol. 19, pp. 195–202); August 1682 (ibid., pp. 401–6); and January 1700 (ibid., vol. 20, pp. 349–53).

whose profession would be justice "the necessity of learning the principles of jurisprudence, as much from canons of the Church and Roman laws, as from French law."[10]

Two years were required for the baccalaureate in law, and three for the *licence*. In order that study of humanities and philosophy not be cut short, the minimum age for admission to a law faculty was 17 (although candidates could be exempted from the age requirement by the Crown, for a fee). Attendance at lectures was policed. Students had to sign a register four times a year. Attendance notebooks were distributed for signing in the classrooms every three months, and they were filed with the *parquet* of the local Parlement. Every *licence* granted by a law faculty had to receive the approval of the general advocates and prosecutors of the region's Parlement; those magistrates were forbidden to grant approval without verifying the candidate's matriculation and attendance from registers and notebooks. Formal instruction was by the authoritarian method of lectures (usually lasting an hour and a half), as in the *collèges*. Students were required to attend at least two lectures each day of the university term over the three years and to transcribe them, in at least rudimentary form. Each student had to represent the transcriptions to the secretariat of the faculty before applying for a degree. Besides attending the *cours magistraux*, students could get private tutoring in the homes of professors or *docteurs agrégés* for additional fees. They could also circumvent regular attendance by obtaining lecture notes from other students and by getting complaisant professors to mark them as present when they had not been. The entire curriculum was directed toward general examinations at the end of the second and third years.

The first two years were devoted primarily to the study of Roman law (known as *le droit civil*), and secondarily to canon law. The 1700 edict prescribed the sequence of instruction and the texts. In the first year, they studied Justinian's *Institutes* of Roman law with an examination. In the second year the texts were the *Code* (judicial decisions by emperors preceding Justinian), lessons from the *Digest* (a collection of commentaries by Roman jurists), and selections from the *Decretals* (a thirteenth-century compilation of Church law), with further examination for the degree of bachelor of law. The third year was devoted principally to the study of French law, with an additional course elected in either Roman or canon law. There was a final, oral examination in French law, and the student also had to present written theses or propositions, and defend them before a faculty jury, at the end of the third year. Instruction and examination in French law were in the vernacular.

The study of Roman law, the foundation of the curriculum, was the long prelude to the study of French law. Roman law allegedly formed a logical system of justice in the matters of rights, property, contract, obligation, culpability, and penal liability, as well as in questions of persons, things, and actions. It was ju-

---

[10] Preamble to the 1679 edict (Isambert, vol. 20, p. 196).

risprudence that trained the mind in legal reasoning, much as *collège* instruction in Latin grammar and composition was presumed to discipline and shape native intelligence. The principles of Roman law were also taught as a supplemental authority to French customary law. Roman law was statist in its sources and nature, and its study subtly prepared students for courses in French law that concentrated on major royal ordinances, not on varieties of civil customs.

The third-year course in French jurisprudence was the cynosure of legal education. The Crown appointed each professor of French law, from among three candidates nominated to the Chancellor by the general advocates and prosecutors of the Parlement of Paris. The candidate had to be licentiate in law and to have served as a barrister or magistrate for at least ten years, "assiduously and successfully." Thus, the course was taught by experienced practitioners who were also schooled in jurisprudence. They were assisted by a fixed number of *docteurs agrégés* (preceptors with the doctorate in law) in each faculty, who served in examinations and gave private tutorials. Professors of French law were allowed wide latitude in selecting their subject matter. The texts most preferred for intensive exegisis, in the faculty of the University of Paris and elsewhere during the eighteenth century, were the Gallican Concordant of 1516 (which regulated the relations between the monarchy, the French Church, and the papacy); the 1695 ordinance of ecclesiastical authority; the comprehensive 1579 Ordinance of Blois; the 1667 Civil Ordinance; the 1670 Criminal Ordinance; and the civil ordinances of Chancellor d'Aguesseau.[11] Generally, professors concentrated on no more than two of these pillars of French law during a given year. They wrote, and occasionally published, their lectures. Professors commonly used both the works of major jurists (from Damhoudère and Loysel in the sixteenth century to Pothier, Jousse, Serpillon, and Muyart in the eighteenth) and collections of rulings by Parlements as major sources in explicating French statutes and customs.[12] The law faculties did not comprehensively instruct future barristers and magistrates in French positive law – civil, criminal, customary, or ecclesiastical. They introduced them to the principles of French jurisprudence through selective analysis of broad themes. A judge's operational knowledge of law was expected to come from his service as a clerk at the bar and then as a novice royal magistrate. That was consonant with general Old Regime cultural practice. Formal education was meant to shape the mind, not to fill it with knowledge. Expertise came from practice of a profession and from emulation of expert colleagues.

A fourfold method of exegisis was used by most Old Regime professors of Roman, canon, and French law. The exegesis focused on (1) historical examination of the intentions or purposes of those who authored the specific law under study; (2) description of the origin and early development of the issues addressed by that law (which often meant philological analysis); (3) examination

---

[11] Brockliss, *French Higher Education*, p. 279; Christian Chêne, *L'enseignement du droit français en pays de droit écrit (1679–1793)* (Geneva: Droz, 1982), pp. 166–7.

[12] Chêne, *L'enseignement du droit français*, pp. 252–8.

of how that legal issue or problem was treated in other systems (e.g., comparing a Roman law to a roughly corresponding canon or French law); (4) justification, or demonstrating the rational utility of the law studied and its accordance with principles of natural and divine law. The pedagogy was simultaneously erudite, analytic, and conservative. It served to legitimate and to intellectually conciliate the classical Roman heritage, Catholic doctrine, and the principal institutions of the French polity.[13]

Law faculty graduates whose *licences* were certified by the *parquet* of the Parlement were qualified to take the oath of barrister. Barristers were numerous. About 646 students matriculated each term at the law faculty of the University of Paris in the years 1770 to 1778.[14] The twenty-two law faculties of France produced about 1,000 licentiates each year during the eighteenth century.[15] Articles 16 and 17 of the 1679 edict set forth the requirements for progressing from the taking of the barrister's oath to judicial office: "Certificates of matriculation for the required number of years in law faculties, letters attesting the status of bachelor and licentiate and the oath of barrister, and certificates of attendance for two years in audiences of courts or tribunals in the jurisdiction of residence will be attached to the seal of all [royal] letters of appointment to judicial offices."[16] Two years' attendance at pleadings in sovereign or other royal courts and practical instruction by barristers was mandated so that licentiates would gain experience of the law before holding office. However, the Crown and the courts often granted waivers of that requirement to those who had purchased a judgeship, allowing them to petition for office after only a year's or even six months' attendance at the bar. Most judges of the Parlement of Paris, and many of the Châtelet, received such dispensations.[17] Most were sons of the *métier,* who had been guided toward it from childhood.

Legal education was regulated by royal legislation, and *collèges* were staffed principally by clerics. But Parlements had tutelary authority over the *collèges* and universities in their jurisdictions, including the power to nominate faculty, approve curricula, supervise instruction, and enforce degree requirements. The superior themistocracy of France policed its own intellectual replication by those institutions.

B. Community

The *collège,* the law faculty, and the bar were indispensable preparations for admission to themistocracy. But admission was not secured either by scholastic success or by royal appointment. It was secured through either dynastic succession or co-optation by a departing judge, and then formal acceptance by the company of judges.

[13] Brockliss, *French Higher Education,* pp. 277–334.
[14] Fitzsimmons, *Parisian Order of Barristers,* p. 4.
[15] Brockliss, *French Higher Education,* pp. 36–7. [16] Isambert, vol. 19, p. 200.
[17] Bluche, *Les magistrats du Parlement de Paris,* pp. 60–1; Rosset, "Les conseillers du Châtelet," pt. 1, pp. 213–14; A.N.Y 1868–1869.

To exercise this public authority, it is not sufficient to have the appointment of the Prince or Lord; it is also necessary to have the "capacities" required for the Office of Judge. Those requisite capacities are of three kinds: those concerning the person of the judge, such as religion, morals, science, and competent age; those concerning the formalities that must precede and accompany admission to office, or the inquiry into the life and morals of the candidate and the examination on the Law that he must undergo; the oath that he must swear before the judge who presides at his admission to the company.[18]

Every Old Regime judge had to be formally scrutinized, approved, and received by the court in which he had purchased office, and for which he had acquired royal appointment, before he could exercise office. That court determined his "capacities" for office by employing a mandatory procedure that had several phases. The procedure followed by the Châtelet was essentially the same as in all royal bailliage and sovereign courts.

An aspirant to the Châtelet applied for admission in a letter to the civil lieutenant. He included his royal letter of appointment to the office; receipts showing he had paid the purchase price and fees; his baptismal certificate; and a waiver of the age or kinship requirements, if he had received such. The civil lieutenant appointed a senior judge to monitor the candidacy. After the senior judge had verified the form and completeness of the documentation, he forwarded the dossier to the royal prosecutor. The prosecutor then selected "witnesses," or references, of known honor and "quality" to be heard on the religious devotion, morals, character, and intellectual ability of the candidate, usually with advice from judges who knew the candidate's (or his family's) associates and friends. Candidates were forbidden to nominate their own references to the prosecutor, but they or their elders could suggest names to judges of the court, who could then nominate to the prosecutor. One referral was always a priest, usually from the candidate's residential parish. The remaining two or three were lay persons well acquainted with the candidate. Consanguinal kin and direct in-laws could not act as references. The references were summoned to appear in the Council Chamber of the Châtelet at an appointed time to give *dépositions*, or recommendations. These hearings were the *information* on the candidate. They were conducted by the senior judge who monitored the candidacy. Each reference was heard separately and confidentially. All of his statements were transcribed and then attested to by signature. The text of the inquiry was sent to the prosecutor. If the recommendations affirmed that the candidate had the moral and intellectual qualifications required of a Châtelet judge, the prosecutor authorized the examination of the candidate in law.

The examination was conducted by one of the lieutenants of the Châtelet and by two of the most senior judges (who could not be the candidate's kinsmen or references). Its form had been established by a 1546 decree of the Parlement of Paris, which was amplified and generalized to all royal bailliage courts in an edict of the same year. He was first asked to give verbal commentary on a spe-

---

[18] Muyart, *Loix criminelles*, p. 479.

cific law that had been assigned to him three days earlier. Next the chief examiner produced three compendious volumes, one of Roman law, one of canon law, and one of royal ordinances. In succession, the examiner opened each of those tomes at random ("à la fortuité ouverte de chacun livre") on the candidate's table. Each time, the candidate had to explicate the passage open before him. This was an extemporary verbal commentary on a canonic written text, much in the manner of the *collèges* and legal education. It tested more than knowledge; a skillful performance required facility in the fusion of literary and oral expression. If the performance was successful, the lieutenants decreed his admission.

Soon after he passed the examination, he was administered the oath of office and formally installed in his column of service, by a simple but solemn ceremony that involved the entire company of judges. The essence of that ceremony was the oath:

To render justice loyally and well to the poor as to the rich, without acceptance from or exception of any person because of familial relation or friendship, to preserve and observe the laws, customs, and ordinances of the Realm, to be a good and loyal subject and servitor of the King, to keep secret the deliberations of the Company, and, in all things, to act as a good and wise councillor.

The sequence of the oath was a hierarchy in loyalties: first to justice; then to "laws, customs, and ordinances"; then to the king; then to the company. This was an oath of public office, not of personal fealty. Only from the moment of oath and installation did the novice judge enjoy the authority, rank, and privileges of office. His co-optation was completed.[19] His practical apprenticeship in the duties of themistocracy began.

The inquiries into the moral and personal capacities of candidates for Châtelet judgeships eloquently convey general themistocratic ideals. Inquiries were, in fact, ceremonies of normative self-definition and self-celebration by a great corporation. The recommendations on which they were based served to restate the magisterial ideal for both the reference and his interlocutors in the Châtelet. The virtues sought from candidates by the Châtelet, and described by references, were the virtues cherished by the company of judges. The secrecy of the hearings excluded all but magistrates, royal officials, and others of rank and

---

[19] On the preceding, see the following: the royal edicts and ordinances of 1546, 1560, and 1579, in Muyart, *Loix criminelles*, pp. 483–4; Delamare, vol. 1, p. 184; Rosset, "Les conseillers du Châtelet," pt. 1, pp. 214–17. The edict of January 1700 omitted canon law from the examination and emphasized French jurisprudence: "Voulons . . . que tous les officiers qui seront reçus en nos cours et siéges soient interrogés sur nos ordonnances, sur les coutumes et sur les autres parties de la jurisprudence française, aussi bien que sur le droit civil" (Isambert, vol. 20, p. 350). Examination records for individual candidates either were not kept or have not survived in the archives of the Châtelet. All of those installed in office had obviously met the standards of their examiners. The procedure for aspirants to judgeships in Parlements was basically the same, with some variants; see Bluche, *Les magistrats du Parlement de Paris*, pp. 55–6, 61–2. By the inquiries and examinations, courts enjoyed sovereign power in selecting their judges. However, that power had been delegated to them by the monarchy in the sixteenth-century edicts that defined the selection procedure.

authority from the selection of a judge, and thus from the values and affinities that determined the acceptability of a candidate. Secrecy encouraged candor, and the reputation of the reference was also at stake in these statements under oath. The ethos that emerges from these hundreds of voices may be considered a "pure" ideology, for it was neither a mask or propaganda directed at a public, nor collective self-delusion. It was an intimate system of belief, a subjectivity, that both reflected the ethical ideals taught in the *collège* and corresponded to the duties and tasks of the themistocracy. Finally, a major purpose of the inquiry was to instruct the young candidate, and remind the corporation, that simple purchase of and appointment to office did not signify either the right to exercise the authority of office or the freedom to exercise as one chose. The inquiry affirmed that the judge's authority in office depended on his performance of duties, while ascertaining whether the candidate gave such promise.[20]

Between 1718 and 1789, 287 laymen gave 306 recommendations for 112 of the 130 men who composed the Châtelet bench in 1735, 1762, and 1789.[21] The professional distribution of the men who served as references reveals that corporate endogamy dominated in these inquiries on candidates, just as it dominated in the provenances of candidates. As the accompanying graphs (Figures 6.1 through 6.4) indicate, 75 percent of all references, during the period 1718 to 1789, were judges, royal advocates or prosecutors, notaries, barristers, court recorders, or solicitors; 48 percent were judges in Parisian courts. More significantly, 48 (or 43%) of the 112 candidates were recommended by at least one sovereign court judge; 37 (33%) of the total were recommended by at least one Châtelet judge. Another 10 to 15 percent of the references were middle-ranking or high-ranking officers of the royal tax or finance administration; this is proportionate to the number of candidates with that patrimony.

The identities of lay references disclose a rough ethnography of the Paris to which Châtelet families belonged. Recommendations came from long and close knowledge of the candidate and his family, from a web of "knowing" (and thus of solidarities and reciprocities) that reveals the intimate community of the Châtelet magistracy. That community was both narrow and finely meshed. The great majority of its members were of magisterial and administrative official-dom, in a limited number of institutions (mostly Parisian), many clans, and several generations of the same or related families. Within these sociovocational confines, there was occasional versatility in affiliation: Joseph LeRoy d'Herval

---

[20] "La dignité, l'autorité, les droits & les privilèges des officiers ne leur sont donnés qu'à cause du service qu'ils doivent au public; ainsi le devoir général de tous officiers et de rendre ce service en s'acquittant bien de leurs fonctions. Ce devoir général et commun à tous officiers les oblige à se considérer dans leurs charges, comme y étant placés de la main de Dieu pour y remplir les devoirs particuliers . . . de telle sorte qu'ils comprennent que leurs charges les obligent à ces fonctions & qu'ils sont destinés par leur ministère à les remplir toutes" (Domat, p. 122).

[21] Dossiers of inquiry and reception are lacking for 18 of our 130 judges in A.N. Y 1867–1869. A total of 88 ecclesiastics supplied recommendations for the 112. They were principally rectors, canons, curates, or simple priests of the candidate's parish of catechism, residence, or particular devotion, or occasionally clerics who had tutored candidates in religion or canon law. Uniformly, they certified a piety that consisted, at least, in observance of the sacraments.

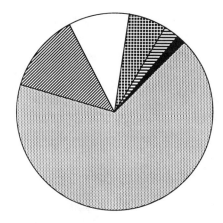

▦ Judge	67.1%
▨ Royal secretary	12.7%
▢ Other officer	10.1%
⊞ Barrister	6.3%
⊟ Finance bureau officer	2.5%
∎ Merchant	1.3%

Figure 6.1. Châtelet bench in 1735: professions of references. The 53 judges, or 67.1% of all references, belonged to the following courts: Châtelet (17); Parlement of Paris (14); Chambre des Comptes (10); Cour des Aides (6); Grand Conseil (4); Cour des Monnaies (1); Finance Bureau of the Generality of Paris (1). The "other officers" of the Crown (10.1%) were the following: lieutenant general of Constabulary; officer of Gendarmérie; naval officer; treasurer, Generality of Paris, treasurer; Office of Bridges and Roads; and *échevin* of Paris. The one merchant was Jean Levé, draper, who testified for Jean-François Bouquet in 1732. (A.N. Y 1867–1868).

(noble son of a deputy prosecutor in the Parlement of Paris) was recommended by a chief recorder of the Cour des Aides, a commissioner of military provisioning, and a receiver of customs taxes for the city of Paris, all of whom had known his family since before he was born.[22] Jean-François Rouhette (son of the president of the Order of Barristers) was recommended by a judge of the Admiralty Court, a judge of the Chambre des Comptes, and the lieutenant general of the Arsenal Court.[23] The patterns of association between Châtelet families and their references were simultaneously professional, social, and even spatial (for many were fellow parishioners). The majority of the 112 young men were recommended by the colleagues (and often kinsmen) of their elders, men who had observed their personal maturation to candidacy for the Châtelet. Between one-fourth and one-third were recommended by at least one generational peer and friend (who was often a socioprofessional superior); these references were mostly young magistrates or administrators who had known the candidates in *collège*, the law faculty, or the Parisian bar. And one may reasonably assume that in many, if not most, cases the references for an individual candidate were acquainted with each other through their joint relations with that candidate's family. Recommendations overarched distinctions between common and noble estate, but they rarely overarched distinctions of profession

[22] A.N. Y 1868.   [23] A.N. Y 1869.

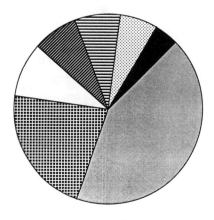

Judge	42.9%
Barrister	22.1%
Other officer	9.1%
Royal secretary	7.8%
Finance bureau officer	7.8%
Prosecutor, clerk	6.5%
Other	3.9%

Figure 6.2. Châtelet bench in 1762: professions of references. The 33 judges, or 42.9% of all references, belonged to the following courts: Châtelet (12); Chambre des Comptes (8); Cour des Aides (5); Parlement of Paris (4); Cour des Monnaies (1); Grand Conseil (1); Grenier à sel (1): Admiralty Court (1). The other royal officers (9.1%) were: a retired naval officer; an administrator of the Hôtel-Dieu of Paris; a lieutenant of the Maréchaussée; a royal censor of jurisprudence; a general inspector of the navy; a commissioner of war. The "others" (3.9%) simply designated themselves as *écuyer* or *seigneur.* (A.N. Y 1867–1868).

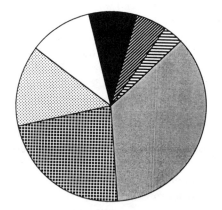

Judge	36.0%
Barrister	22.7%
Proctor, clerk, notary	14.0%
Other officer	10.7%
Miscellaneous	8.0%
Royal secretary	5.3%
Finance bureau officer	3.3%

Figure 6.3. Châtelet bench in 1789: professions of reference. The 54 judges, or 36% of all references, belonged to the following main courts: Châtelet (23); Chambre des Comptes (8); Parlement of Paris (7); Cour des Aides (6); Grand Conseil (1); the remainder belonged mostly to *élections* and bailliages. "Miscellaneous" (8%) included medical doctors, architects, savants of the Royal Academy, and several *chevaliers.* (A.N. Y 1867–1869).

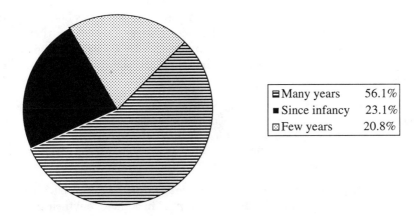

⊟ Many years	56.1%
■ Since infancy	23.1%
⊠ Few years	20.8%

Figure 6.4. References: years of acquaintance with candidates. This graph represents the 342 recommendations (both clerical and lay) for our 130 candidates, in which the duration of acquaintance was stated. This is 71% of the total of 481 recommendations; in the other 139 recommendations the duration of acquaintance was either not given or stated vaguely. "Few years" is five or less; "many" is six to fourteen. (A.N. Y 1867–1869).

or vocation.[24] There was a solitary merchant among these 287 lay references.[25] There were nine *militaires*, of whom only four were actual serving officers of the army and one of the navy.[26] One cannot conclude, from their negligable presence, that Châtelet families had no ties with military and naval officers, but one can conclude that their moral and social judgments were not prized in recommendations for the themistocracy. That was yet another powerful expression of alterity.

[24] The community that emerges from these recommendations was described poetically, in its larger parameters, by Bluche: "Monde parlementaire parisien d'une part, monde des officiers de tribunaux inférieurs d'autre part forment deux cercles et non plus deux degrés. Ne les comparons pas à des cercles de géométrie plane mais plutôt aux ondes inégales, toutes de même nature, mouvantes, interférant en grandissant. Nous pouvons imaginer, entre le grand cercle qui symbolise la société parlementaire de la capitale et les petits cercles des bailliages ou des élections, une suite d'"ondes' intermédiares, figurant la modeste cour des monnaies de Paris, puis – cercles voisins et presque égaux – la Chambre des comptes, le grand conseil et la Cour des aides. Ces liaisons mouvantes recréent l'unité de la société robine" ("Les magistrats du Grand Conseil," p. 42).

[25] He was Jean Levé, cloth merchant, who recommended Jean-François Bouquet in 1732. Bouquet's father was an *échevin* and municipal judge at the Hôtel de Ville and thus worked with leading Parisian merchants. Bouquet's other two lay references were a municipal judge and a keeper of the Paris mint. A.N. Y 1867.

[26] The other five were a lieutenant general of the Constabulary, an officer of Gendarmérie, an officer of the maréchaussée of the Ile-de-France, a retired officer who was treasurer for the Swiss Guards. In addition to the nine, there were three *chevaliers de Saint-Louis*, retired career officers ennobled by twenty years' service.

In the aggregate of lay recommendations from 1718 to 1789, the attribute most often mentioned in recommending an aspiring judge was heredity of service in magisterial or other royal civil office. This was also the attribute most stressed in many royal letters of appointment to the Châtelet. In appointing Jacques-Hypollite-Jules Michau de Montblin (age 19), for example, Louis XVI declared:

Since talent, zeal, and devotion to our Service and the public welfare are hereditary qualities in his family, We are convinced that he will follow in the footsteps of the Magistrates who compose his family and that in him the virtues, courage, industriousness, and capacity of mind that distinguished his father's performance of the important offices of magistracy in which he died will be revived.[27]

"Talent, zeal, devotion, virtues, courage, industriousness, capacity of mind": Those personal qualities were deemed essential in a judge, but their hereditary source, exemplification, and presumed guarantee were supremely desirable. "Heredity" had a particular meaning in this discourse.

Like the Maussions, this judge's family, the Michaus, were a powerful and distinguished family of the late eighteenth-century Parisian themistocracy. But their "hereditary qualities" had existed only during the four generations that preceded Jacques Michau de Montblin (b. 1770), or for some one hundred years (Chart 6.1).[28]

Four generations was a long heredity in high state office by comparison with the majority of families that gave judges to the Châtelet during the eighteenth century. Manifestly, the Michau heredity did not signify venerable lineage; it meant four generations of unbroken continuity in high and ennobling office. And that was the exact definer of the young Michau de Montblin's nobility: "fifth-degree noble." In the royal mind, the successive generations of this family were not defined at birth; they were defined by the vocations they transmitted to each other. The king employed the exalting language of heredity to characterize and pay tribute to constancy in vocation; his language was honorific metaphor. And it was as if that family did not exist, officially or pertinently, before Jacques Michau and his royal secretaryship in the late seventeenth century.

The letter appointing André-Jean Boucher d'Argis to a judgeship in the Châtelet in 1771 was graced by similar language: "We have every reason to believe that, following the path of his father who has distinguished himself at the Paris bar for more than forty years, as former judge in the Superior Court of Dombes and by his devoted service as *Echevin* of our good city of Paris, his said son will fulfill the functions of the said office with the same zeal."[29]

---

[27] A.N. V 1 537 (Apr. 22, 1789).
[28] The genealogy of the Michau family has been traced in Bluche, *L'origine des magistrates du Parlement de Paris*, pp. 313–14, and "Les magistrats du Grand Conseil," pp. 116–17. In the second, third, and fourth generations there were others of this family in the Grand Conseil and Parlement of Paris.
[29] A.N. V 1 454 (Dec. 31, 1771).

Chart 6.1. *Michau genealogy*

I	II	III	IV	V
Jacques Michau de Montaron: tax collector, Estates of Brittany; royal secretary (1671), ennobled by the secretaryship				
	Jean-Jacques Michau de Montaron (b. 1668 [Bruz], d. 1750): judge, Grand Conseil (1690–1750), died in office			
		Jacques-Marie-Jerôme Michau de Montaron (b. 1701 [Nantes], d. 1782): judge, Parlement of Paris (1722–44); intendant of commerce (1744–57); master of petitions in Grand Chancellery (1746)		
			Hyppolyte-Louis-Marie Michau de Montblin (c.1730–1777): judge, Parlement of Paris (1760–77)	
				Jacques-Hyppollyte-Jules Michau de Montblin (b. 1770 [Paris]): judge, Châtelet, 1789

Sources: Bluche, "L'origine des magistrats du Parlement de Paris," pp. 313–14, and "Les magistrats du Grand Conseil," pp. 116–17.

The selective meaning of heredity was also evident when the king was confronted with a truly venerable lineage. The Choart family had occupied significant offices of state since the fifteenth century and had been noble since the late sixteenth century. For almost 250 years, they provided treasurers, ambassadors, provosts, judges of the Chambre des Comptes, Cour des Aides, and Parlement of Paris, and councillors of state (see Chart 3.1). In appointing Louis Choart de Magny judge of the Châtelet in 1735, Louis XV invoked only briefly the "zeal and devotion that distinguished his ancestors." He identified only two of those ancestors, both quite remote in time from Louis Choart and of far less stature than his father and grandfather, Jean Choart and Gabriel Miron, who were civil lieutenants of the Châtelet in the fifteenth and early sixteenth centuries. That selection was almost dismissive of the family's subsequent distinction in lineage. The Choarts did not require exaltation. They were instead reminded of a lesser and original family office, the one to which Louis Choart was appointed.[30]

In the royal discourse of appointments, a reference to heredity signified familial vocation of important magisterial or administrative office, especially if that vocation was historically recent. The main emphasis was not on lineage but on nurturance, or the modeling of the young aspirant by the distinguished examples of his living elders, examples strengthened by the memory and reputation of their possible lineal predecessors in office. Each of these statements was a royal endorsement of the dynasticism that was inherent in venal-hereditary officialdom.

[30] A.N. V 1 301.

This royal vision was shared by the themistocracy. Socioprofessional nurturance by heredity was the essence of patrimony among themistocratic families. It was a vital element of their ethos and a dominant theme in their recommendations of candidates.

Claude-Gidéon Dumetz (judge, Chambre des Comptes), for Nicolas Besset de la Chapelle (1725): "He is of a family as distinguished by its virtues and achievements as by its fine marriage alliances."[31]

Clément-Charles-François de la Verdy (judge, Parlement of Paris), for Marc-Léonard Nau de Saint-Marc (1750): "I am convinced that the sentiments of virtue and probity that are hereditary in his family, combined with his personal capacity, will render him worthy of the office and tasks of judge of the Châtelet."[32]

Charles Quiller d'Héricourt (barrister, Parlement of Paris and royal secretary), for Pierre Nau (1780): "He belongs to one of the best-known and most honorable families of Paris."[33]

Jules-Pierre Cambault de Canthère (judge Châtelet) for François-Alexis Duval (1784): "The familial examples before his eyes and the excellent education he has received give promise that he will resemble his father."[34]

These characteristic recommendations gave greater importance to moral qualities than to purely intellectual qualities in a prospective judge. Morality and discipline were thought to be molded with greatest solidity by the extended family. That conception of moral and social pedagogy was not aristocratic. It did not refer to deep ancestry, blood lineage, or *race* in the creation of a magistrate. It lacked the historicity (whether real or mythical) and exclusiveness of a theory of character formation by lineage. It was centered on familial and clan environment, especially on the vocations of judicial and administrative service exercised within that environment. In essence, the conception was meritocratic, but with merit embodied by the living or recent family of the candidate, in both its paternal and maternal branches. The decisive figures were fathers, as well as

---

[31] A.N. Y 1867. And Jérôme Péricart, also of the Chambre des Comptes, for Besset de la Chapelle: "In the example of his father, he has a model that should render him capable of fulfilling any office in which he is placed."

[32] A.N. Y 1867.

[33] A.N. Y 1869. This was not exaggeration, if by "best-known" and "honorable" one understands several branches and generations of a family, all in prestigious and exacting royal offices. During the seventeenth and eighteenth centuries, the Naus in their various branches were treasurers, *échevins*, and bailliage magistrates at Tours; then prosecutors, recording secretaries, judges of the Parlement of Paris, Grand Conseil, and Chambre des Comptes. Pierre I Nau, chief recording secretary of the Parlement of Paris, died when his two sons were children. They were raised and educated by their uncle and guardian, Father Nau, of the Sorbonne and the Oratorian Order. Quiller d'Héricourt supervised their legal studies and recommended both to the Châtelet in 1780.

[34] A.N. Y 1869. And Jean-Nicolas Chuppin, Châtelet judge and kinsman of the Maussions, for Duval: "Because he has been raised by the care of a just and respectable magistrate father, I am convinced that he will imitate that example." Chuppin was a fourth-generation robe noble, whereas Duval was the bourgeois son of a minor judicial officer. But Chuppin was a longtime friend of that father and his son.

paternal and maternal grandfathers, uncles, and granduncles. "Fine marriage alliances" (in the characteristic phrase of Claude-Gidéon Berbier DuMetz de Rosnay) distinguished a family because they enriched its stock of notable elders, and thus power of socioprofessional nurturance for its progeny.[35] Young men were thought to be morally and socially formed, from early childhood on, by the active exemplarism of familial elders and through pervasive osmosis within an insulated environment. This concept of nurturance for the themistocracy also attentuated the fact that many Châtelet families were historically recent to officialdom. The formative power assigned to elders by the concept had politically integrative consequences for the themistocracy, for that power could be exercised by bourgeois as well as by noble patriarchs, in families that had served for only one or two generations, just as in families that had served for many. The concept of hereditary nurturance prejudiced only those families that provided no living or recent models of officialdom.

The exemplary and nurturing power of elders required submission by the child and young man. This was expressed perfectly by Robert-François Granjean de la Croix in his recommendation of Jacques Frécot (1735): "He has always been very submissive and obedient to his father, from whom he received a wise education."[36] The relation among the qualities is crystalline: Submissiveness and obedience were prerequisite to acquiring sagacity, just as in the pedagogy of the *collège*.

Here we confront more than patriarchal and corporate narcissism. We confront a hierarchy of power in which individuals occupied different positions at different stages of life and career, but always in subjection to others and to a role. Recommendations loyally expressed that vision of hierarchical order. Prescriptively and descriptively, children were formed on the model of their elders. People were supposedly inclined to emulate their superiors in status and power, even if they could never equal them. Superordination, a necessary social fact, was not only the power to command dependents and inferiors: It was, more profoundly, the power and the duty to be a model of conduct for them. The themistocracy sought to emulate the dignity and equity of the monarch. It also sought to be admired and emulated by the "people" whom it alternately protected and punished.

---

[35] Nicolas-Pierre Besset de la Chapelle-Millon, the object of Berbier Du Metz's recommendation, was at least fifth-generation noble. He entered the Châtelet in 1725, served until at least 1736, and then became principal secretary in the Bureau of Foreign Affairs. The preceding three generations of his paternity were highly versatile in royal service: regimental officer and military governor of Perpignan (François de Besset, his great-grandfather); general controller of royal buildings, inspector of *beaux-arts*, secretary of the Academy of Belles-Lettres, historian (Henri de Besset I, his grandfather); judge in the Parlement of Metz, secretary of the council of naval administration (Henri de Besset II, his father). His elder brother became intendant of Saint-Dominique. By their *belles alliances*, the Bessets were part of an equally versatile and eminent clan. It included the Gilberts de Voysin (a major dynasty of the Parlement of Paris and Council of State), the poet Boileau, the dukes of Saint-Simon, and the Chardons of the Châtelet and Parlement of Paris (De la Chesnaye-Desbois, *Dictionnaire*, vol. 3, pp. 75–7).

[36] A.N. Y 1867.

The Magistrate should be as superior to the People by his morality as he is elevated above them by the dignity of his office. How can he possibly correct others if he is susceptible to the same vices that he must punish in them, if he is not a living example of all the virtues that he must enforce? . . . Every officer of justice must render himself better than those over whom he exercises authority. Reason dictates that he who commands be more excellent than he who obeys. The higher the rank of the officer, the more he must fear God, who has given him more grace and to whom he will have a greater account to render. The higher his rank, the greater his obligation to serve the Prince who has brought him closer to the princely person and delegated to him a greater part of his power.[37]

Superordination, the essence of order, was recreated microcosmically with each son who was forged morally and socially by the authority and example of his elders. That son would continue to develop toward the perfect magistrate by emulating his seniors in the company of judges. In fact, a young judge could become accomplished in the vocation only by acquiring professional knowledge from the close example of his more senior colleagues who knew the vocation. That was so for two reasons: His legal education was doctrinal and statutory, not practical; in office, he was immediately and constantly confronted with a plethoric variety of civil and criminal cases.

When he matured as a judge and a father, the ideal themistocrat would become a source of emulation and thus perpetuate the immutable hierarchical order. The magisterial family, with its evolutive development of moral patrimony from fathers to sons, was made the model for the vocation of power, and even for the civilization.

Heredity was supremely desirable. But it was not sufficient, for references also gave strong emphasis to vital personal attributes in candidates with such pedigree:

Mathias Goudin (judge, Cour des Aides), for Augustin Testard du Lys (1746): "Born of parents distinguished by their merit and from whom he has received an excellent education, at an early age he began to perform exactly the duties required of him. Love of justice, a calm and affable temperament, studiousness, and contempt for frivolous pursuits are the essence of his character. From the study of belles lettres he passed to that of the law, in which he made rapid progress; he combines to a remarkable degree the talents of the magistrate and the virtues of the citizen."[38]

Augustin Testard du Lys (judge, Châtelet), for Pierre Lejuge (1748): "He is industrious in the study of belles lettres and the sciences vital to the public welfare; he gives every promise of being a good magistrate, a good citizen, and a good friend to the Company."[39]

Charles-Blaise-Léon Millon (judge, Châtelet), for Louis Roger Grozier de la Presle (1758): "He comes of a family that is dear to the Company. . . . He has rectitude, kindness, intelligence, and love of work."[40]

[37] Delamare, vol. 1, pp. 238–9. And by extension of this: "Le Magistrat doit être autant au-dessus du Peuple par ses bonnes moeurs qu'il y est élèvé par sa dignité: Car comment pourroit-il réformer les autres, si lui-même étoit sujet aux mêmes vices qu'il auroit à reprendre, & qu'il ne fût pas un exemple vivant de toutes les vertus qu'il en doit exiger?" (ibid., p. 238).
[38] A.N. Y 1867. [39] Ibid.
[40] Ibid. Three Roger Groziers served as Châtelet judges during the eighteenth century.

Gabriel-Nicolas Mantrol (barrister, Parlement of Paris), for Charlemagne Lalourcé (1777): "I have known him since his birth. I have observed him to be well behaved, industrious, studious, and perfectly responsive to the care that has been devoted to his education. He has continued his study of law since he was received at the Bar, and there is every reason to believe that he will acquire the reputation in the magistracy that his father acquired at the Paris Bar."[41]

Prudent de Villiers de la Noue (judge, Châtelet), for Antoine-Jean Vanin (1779): "Born of a father even more laudable for his probity than for his widely recognized learning and of a virtuous and exemplary mother, who, widowed, sacrificed everything for the education of her children, he has begun to show himself to be the worthy heir of such parents. He has distinguished himself by great devotion to his studies, and at the age of youthful frivolity and dissipation he has occupied himself with ornamenting his mind and forming his sensibility."[42]

Jean-Baptiste Bénigne Sollier de Charmon (judge, Cour des Aides), for Thomas-Antoine-Jean Maussion (1784): "I have known him for a very long time. He observes the Roman, Apostolic, and Catholic religion, is of good conduct and morals, and very devoted to the service of the King and the public. By his industriousness, carefulness, talent, and intelligence, he is capable of performing with distinction the duties of the office with which the King has honored him, and he will loyally follow in the path of his elders."[43]

The model of hereditary formation did not exclude all candidates whose families were recent, or even foreign, to officialdom. The model was strongly preferential, and it determined the selection of the majority of eighteenth-century Châtelet judges. But it was not an imperative. Other corporate values and personal accomplishments gave those without significant heredity entry to the company. But in accepting them, the corporation gave those men an opportunity to found a themistocratic family, and therefore a possibility of creating "heredity."

Pierre Pitouin's family was bourgeois and relatively obscure. He may have been its first generation in the judiciary when he was received in 1738, at the age of 25.[44] Gaspard de Ballade, judge in the Cour des Aides and second- or third-generation noble, had known Pitouin since they were in the *collège* together and wrote of him:

He distinguished himself through his diligence and brilliance in the study of belles lettres. . . . One remarks in him perspicacity and solidity of judgment, subtlety and vivacity of mind, generosity and integrity of heart. . . . He will need only to profit from the wisdom of the Châtelet in order to become an excellent judge.[45]

Gaspard de Ballade was separated by a wide social gulf from his friend, former schoolmate, and protégé Pierre Pitouin. But Ballade's great-grandfather or

[41] A.N. Y 1869.   [42] Ibid.   [43] Ibid.
[44] A certain Pierre-Paul Pitouin, barrister aged 59, recommended François-Hilaire Bouron des Clayes in 1766; he may have been the brother or cousin of Pierre Pitouin. A.N. Y 1868.
[45] A.N. Y 1867. Pitouin's two other lay references were barristers of the Parlement.

grandfather would have been a Pierre Pitouin. Ballade's act of patronage should not be regarded as a simple act of friendship or of *noblesse oblige:* It was a corporate political choice.[46]

Such recommendations and patronage of "new men" came primarily from the generational peers but socioprofessional superiors of candidates whose families were socially undistinguished and from older magistrates and officials who knew and respected the elders of such candidates. Those elders were commonly solicitors, proctors, secretaries in various lower courts and administrations, physicians, architects, or professors. Sometimes this patronage was a final act of tutelary encouragement: Jacques Sainfrais, deputy prosecutor of the Parlement of Paris and an administrator of the College of Louis-le-Grand, had known Etienne Geoffroy, the son of a physician, since childhood and had followed Geoffroy's performance at Louis-le-Grand; he certified Geoffroy's "assiduousness, predilection for work, and intellectual discernment."[47] Dagobert-Etienne Isabeau, senior recording secretary in the Grand-Chambre of the Parlement of Paris and last in a dynasty of secretaries in the Parlement, recommended the bourgeois Jean-Denis Solle, whose patrimony is unknown to us. Isabeau had personally tutored him in law for some years.[48]

The themistocracy as a corporation was revitalized in each generation through the patronage and elevation of such men. The mechanism of renewal was subtle: The new men were selected only partly because of their manifest individual qualities; they were recruited essentially because those qualities gave promise that they could be molded by their colleagues into future patriarchs and dynasts of the themistocracy. Those selections preserved the Châtelet as a prime corporate breeding ground for the sovereign courts of Paris, for a high proportion of judges in those courts were third- and fourth-generation descendants of men like Pitouin and Geoffroy. Those selections also accounted for much of the professionalism and stability of the Châtelet. Pierre Pitouin served until 1780, or a tenure of forty-two years. Many of the judges who served comparable tenures socially resemble him.

A small but constant minority of appointments in the eighteenth-century Châtelet were careful promotions of men with lesser or nonofficial patrimony. This policy, joined to the general preference for solid judicial and administra-

---

[46] So also was the decision of François Fagnier de Monslambert to sell his office to Pitouin in 1737. Fagnier had served in the Châtelet since 1706. His father had been a royal secretary and *conservateur des hypothèques* in the Treasury; his uncle was a judge in the Chambre des Comptes. François Fagnier was second-generation noble and themistocrat, and therefore resembled Gaspard de Ballade. His son, Michel Fagnier de Monslambert, became judge in the Cour des Aides and then master of petitions in the Chancellery (1775). A.N. V I 174; Roton, *Les arrêts du Grand Conseil*, p. 117; Coustant, *Chambre des Comptes*, p. 831. Louis-Quentin Maupetit gained admission to the Châtelet bench in analogous manner four decades later. He was a bourgeois of undistinguished patrimony but of distinguished performance in the *collège* and at the law faculty. In 1784, he was strongly recommended by Guillaume La Borde and Louis-Michel Damour, both noble judges of the Cour des Aides, who had been his classmates. A.N. Y 1869.

[47] A.N. Y 1869 (May 1784). Prudent-Joseph de Villiers de la Noue, a noble and very senior judge of the Châtelet bench who had served since 1743, sold his office to Geoffroy.

[48] A.N. Y 1869.

tive patrimony without regard to estate, ensured that there was no "aristocratic reaction" in the Châtelet, even after its judgeships were granted ennobling status in 1768. At least ten of the fourteen bourgeois judges who entered the court between 1777 and 1789 and who remained in office in 1789–90, entered because departing noble judges, or their families, chose them as successors and sold the office to them.[49] There were undoubtedly many qualified noble candidates for those specific positions. Sheer nobility did not constitute a valid claim to membership of the Châtelet. Between one-third and one-half of the Châtelet judges who were recommended by noble magistrates of sovereign courts across the eighteenth century were bourgeois in social condition. Those recommendations disclosed ties between families despite differences of estate, ties created by professional association and common education and then expressed through patronage and friendship. Those were the bonds of vocation.[50]

The lexicon of required attributes was narrow and concentrated, in the 306 lay recommendations. Those statements were remarkably consistent, from the 1720s to the Revolution. They converged in a language of civic and professional virtue. The qualities of mind and temperament required of a prospective judge were discipline, stamina and energy, a liking and capacity for sustained intellectual work, skill in verbal and written expression, knowledge of religious doctrine, humanistic culture, and the law, measured conviviality and urbanity, and a pronounced sense of duty to both family and the public welfare. Duty included promoting collegiality and solidarity within the corporation, which were also imperatives in juristic literature:

All magistrates must take great care to preserve among themselves peace, unity, and harmony, so as to act concertedly in the service of the Prince and the public welfare that has been entrusted to them. Envy and conflicting ambitions among them, and the divisiveness that is the inevitable result, are pernicious to the State and can cause its ruin.[51]

Intuition, imagination, and emotivity were almost completely absent from the lexicon of recommendations. Those traits were deemed incompatible with the rationalist character of the civil and criminal law, its procedures of trial and judgment, and magisterial self-discipline. Neither wealth nor noble estate figured in the lexicon. The virtues and attributes composed an austere personality, one that was analytical, introspective, ascetic yet ardent, profoundly loyal, and nomistic in thought and behavior. That corporate personality was the artifact of a professional and intellectual culture, not of a particular estate or social class.

C. Ethos

The corporate personality described in recommendations for Châtelet candidates was identical to the one delineated publicly, with careful detail and on a

[49] A.N. Y 1869, and Roton, *Les arrêts du Grand Conseil.*
[50] And they are visible in the marriage contracts and suppers for Châtelet grooms and their brides, to which colleagues of differing estate and familial distinction contributed their signatures and company (Rosset, "Les conseillers du Châtelet," pt. 1, pp. 280–8).
[51] Delamare, vol. 1, p. 239.

grand scale, in the most respected juristic writings of the late seventeenth and eighteenth centuries, the works of Jean Domat, Nicolas de La Mare, Henry-François d'Aguesseau, Daniel Jousse, and Claude Ferrière. Those writings belonged to the pedagogy of eighteenth-century magistrates.

De la Mare described the institution of magistracy as intrinsic to civilization, even as perennial:

Law without Magistrates is a soulless body of no use to government. . . . The creation and activity of Magistracy are in such conformity with right reason that the magistrates of all well-disciplined States, ancient and modern, that have existed to the present are almost all alike, although different in name.[52]

And in dramatic paraphrase of Aristotle:

What the eyes are to the hands, the head to the feet, what reason is to the senses, the soul to the body, the end to the means, repose to movement, eternity to time, such is the contemplative life to the active life. Thus the Magistrate, who must think much as well as act much, can neglect neither one nor the other. He must be constantly prepared to pass from contemplation to action.[53]

According to Jean Domat, the integrity of the judge had to be superior to that required of all other public servants (including army officers), because of the "infinite consequences" of his actions. For that reason, he exalted magistrates above all other officials.

It is not without reason that we have distinguished the probity of officers of justice from that of all other categories of officer, and by the term of "personal integrity." They have need of a rectitude so pure, so delicate, and so complete that it is far above that required for the good exercise of all other offices. This is to say that they must have the moral strength and courage necessary for their function, fear of God, knowledge and love of truth, and an aversion to greed whose intensity amounts to hatred. . . . These qualities consist principally in a spiritual disposition, and only secondarily in intellectual disposition.[54]

[52] The prestige and importance of classical studies (especially in Roman law, politics, and history) derived partly from this generic conception of themistocracy: "Les Magistrats doivent beaucoup s'appliquer à l'étude de l'Antiquité. C'est un précieux trésor où ils pourront puiser une infinité d'exemples qui serviront en semblables cas à regler leur conduite & á former leurs jugements" (ibid.).

[53] Ibid., vol. 1, p. 240.

[54] *Le droit public*, p. 125. Domat distinguished three broad categories within officialdom, or the lay political elite of France, and ranked them in importance by the ends they served: (1) "les fonctions qui regardent directement & en général le bien de l'état & le service du Prince," which applied to councillors, secretaries, and ministers of state, dukes, and peers with deliberative or executive responsibilities, provincial governors and intendants, and the officer corps of the army and navy (who protected the state from external attack and from violent internal threat); (2) "la second espèce des fonctions, qui est de celles qui se rapportent au service de la personne du Prince," mainly officers of the royal household; (3) "La troisième sorte de fonctions est de celles qui regardent *le bien commun de la société* [italics mine]; de telle sorte qu'elles ne se rapportent pas directement au bien de l'Etat comme celles de la première sorte, ni au service de la personne du Prince, comme celles de la seconde; mais qu'elle regardent le bien de la société dans les membres qui la composent, & se rapportent aux particuliers qui sont ses membres, soit pour les maintenir dans l'usage & la possession libre de leurs biens contre les entreprises de ceux qui

Henri-François d'Aguesseau, Chancellor of France (1717–51), elaborated the fullest and most intimate description of the perfect magistrate in eighteenth-century French juristic literature. His speeches, rulings, instructions, and essays were all variously didactic. They were widely read by law students and magistrates during and beyond his lifetime.[55] His account is especially rich for its negativity, its definition of social ambitions and behavior antithetical to themistocracy.

Such is the dominant character of *moeurs* in our century: a disquiet and anxiety spread throughout all professions; a ceaseless agitation, enemy of repose, rendering men incapable of work, carrying everywhere the scourge of ambitious indolence; a universal rebellion of men against their station; a kind of general conspiracy in which all are determined to be other than what they are; all professions confounded, dignities debased, propriety outraged; the majority of men . . . filled with contempt for their occupation and thereby rendering it contemptible. Constantly obsessed with what they wish to be and never with what they are, always flushed with vast projects, the only goal that eludes them is that of living happily with their profession and condition. . . . Others live only for their pleasures, for their fortune, for themselves; the perfect magistrate lives only for the republic. Free from the worries of ordinary men over their private fortune, all in him is consecrated to the public good; his days, which perfectly resemble each other, bring every year the same duties and the same virtues; and by their blissful uniformity, it seems that all of his life is but one single and same moment in which he is master of himself, and sacrifices himself entirely for his country. One searches for the man in him, and one finds only the magistrate; his dignity accompanies him everywhere, because his love for his vocation never abandons him; and, always the same in public, in private life he exercises a perpetual magistracy all the more attractive, but not less powerful, for being without the exterior apparatus that renders magistracy formidable. . . . Blessed the magistrate who, successor to the dignity of his elders, is also heir to their wisdom; who, loyal as they were to his duties, unswervingly devoted to his vocation, lives content with what he is, and desires only what he possesses. . . . Priest of justice, he

les y troubleroient, ou pour venger les crimes & les délits contre leur honneur, leur vie, leurs biens, ou pour régler les différents qui peuvant les diviser, ou pour autres usages; & les charges de cette troisième sorte, qui sont principalement exercés par les Officiers de Justice, & ceux de Police, Finances, & autres" (ibid., p. 115). This was a hierarchy of value. It placed service to both state (or public domain) and the person of the monarch before the courtier's service to the monarchy. It became an inverse hierarchy for anyone who considered that the "bien commun de la société" was a higher end than service to the state and king. The importance of purity of motive among magistrates was stressed by Ferri'ère: "Ce n'est point assez, pour être Juge, d'avoir de l'esprit & de la science. . . . Il ne suffit pas pour être bon Juge d'en faire des actions; il faut encore que l'intention soit toujours portée à faire le bien; sans quoi les meilleurs actions seroient vicieuses. En un mot, le scavoir ne renferme pas toutes les qualités d'un juge; ce n'est pas même assez, pour se bien acquitter d'un tel emploi, de réunir l'esprit, l'art & la science. . . . Il n'y a qu'une véritable et solide piété qui nous puisse porter à faire le bien, par rapport au bien même. Sans elle, les meilleurs actions que les hommes puissent faire, ont bien peu de mérite; ce ne sont pas de véritables vertus, mais des vertus en apparence" (vol. 2, pp. 71–72, 73).

55 His career: royal advocate, Châtelet (1690–1); general advocate, Parlement of Paris (1691–1700); general prosecutor, Parlement of Paris (1700–17); Chancellor (1717–51) (Antoine, *Le gouvernement*, p. 2). As Chancellor, d'Aguesseau was author of many binding rulings (*ordonnances*) in civil law. The eighteenth-century edition of his complete works filled thirteen large volumes.

honors his ministry as much as it honors him. It seems that his dignity grows with him, and that there is no office that is not rendered grand as soon as it is held by him; the offices that he transmits to his successors have been rendered more illustrious by his performance of them than they were when he received them from his predecessors.[56]

The vocation had to be its own principal reward, a reward essentially spiritual and moral. When the magistrate's primary love was of vocation, of its duties and majesty, he obtained complete satisfaction from performance of the vocation. Thus, paradoxically, what could appear as renunciation and enslavement to task was, in fact, plenitude of personal being.[57]

The modern, and basically constitutionalist, notion that public virtue among the empowered consists simply in mechanically performing the duties of an office and not transgressing the limits of its authority was alien to d'Aguesseau and other Old Regime jurists, for they understood that without personal virtue (and foremost, the love of vocation) the performance of office would degenerate eventually into laxity, error, corruption, and injustice. Material ambition and greed were anathema to the vocation: They corrupted judgment, ruined self-discipline, engendered personal discontent, squandered energy, and undermined solidarity and dignity. Ambition, greed, and luxury destroyed magisterial honor and patrimony:

One no longer recognizes one's calling; one no longer recognizes oneself; the son disdains the house of his fathers, embarrassed by its antique simplicity. Family patrimony, accumulated over so many years through moderation and frugality, is rapidly sacrificed to the entrancing spectacle of vain magnificence; or if, by an even greater misfortune, greed joins with love of luxury, one sees the rapacious magistrate ardently seeking to increase his revenue by means disgraceful to the magistracy and fatal to his family, one

[56] Henri-François D'Aguesseau, first *mercuriale:* "L'amour de son état" (1698), in D'Aguesseau, *Oeuvres choisies* (Paris, 1863), pp. 10–18. (A *mercuriale* was a hortatory address presented to the biannual plenary assembly of the Parlement by either the royal advocate or the general prosecutor.) The "dignity" of the magistrate was signified essentially by his virtue, comportment, and bearing, not by the greatness of his office or rank. According to Delamare, "Il doit aussi maintenir avec un fort grand soin l'honneur de sa Charge: premièrement par la vertu, qui en est l'unique source de sa véritable gloire; & ensuite par une gravité honorable, mais tempérée de douceur dans ses paroles & dans ses actions, & une décence proportionée à son état, dans ses habits, & dans toutes ses démarches" (vol. 1, p. 238).

[57] Domat explained why primary love of vocation was necessary for the exact and dutiful performance of vocation: "Pour se porter au travail, il faut l'aimer, parce que le coeur qui est le principe de toutes nos actions, ne peut agir que pour ce qu'il aime . . . & pour aimer le travail, il faut quelque attrait qui nous y porte & nous y engage; & parce que nous devons être toujours disposés à nous appliquer dans chaque occasion au travail & à l'application que la justice demande de nous, il faut que cet attrait qui nous y porte soit un attrait perpétuel qui dure toujours & qui nous attire dans toutes les occasions, & il ne peut y en avoir d'autres de cette nature que la justice. Elle est perpétuelle, comme dit le sage, & c'est elle qui s'offre toujours dans toutes les occasions du devoir des Juges; & c'est aussi la justice qui est la fin unique & naturelle que Dieu a prescrite au travail des Juges. Ceux qui aiment la justice, & qui ne se proposent que cette fin, sont toujours prêts à s'appliquer à rendre justice, parce que cet attrait ne manque jamais de les attirer. Mais au contraire, ceux qui agissent par d'autres fins, sont toujours dans la disposition ou dans le péril de se détourner de la justice & de négliger l'application qu'ils doivent aux fonctions de leur ministère" (p. 131).

sees him practicing the wretched art of endowing sterile metal with a fecundity contrary to its nature [i.e., engaging in usurious and illicit moneylending].[58]

The true magistrate knows that he should transmit to his children greater wisdom than he received from his fathers, but not a greater fortune; that to place in their hands a wealth limited but innocent, properties acquired slowly but justly, a fortune modest but solid, is to bequeath a sufficiently great treasure.[59]

Themistocracy could be socially and professionally conserved and developed only through duty and discipline with respect to material possessions. The force of example also made those dispositions a political necessity:

The true magistrate knows that he owes to the public not only the dispensation of justice, but also the example of virtue. The people readily imitates those whom it respects. Weaknesses in persons who are exposed to public view by their offices are more dangerous than the vices of people who are hidden by the obscurity of their condition. The greater the power enjoyed, the greater must be the care to avoid error and vice.[60]

The social cast of d'Aguesseau's portrait of themistocracy was familial and dynastic.[61] He pragmatically concentrated on the means by which patrimonial vocation could be preserved. That preservation depended far less on sheer familial retention of office than on the inner being of each magisterial scion. His spiritual description of that inner being was essentially Jansenist. According to Jansenist doctrine, divine grace was interior. It engendered virtuous behavior, but it could not be acquired from that behavior. In d'Aguesseau's conception of

---

[58] D'Aguesseau, fifth *mercuriale:* "L'amour de la simplicité" (1702), in *Oeuvres choisies*, p. 68. And: "De tous les vices contre lesquels il doit s'armer, il n'en est point de plus pernicieux que le faste et la fausse grandeur. L'esprit de simplicité prévient tous les maux que ces passions entrainent avec elles; il peut seul arréter ce poison subtil qui se communique peu à peu à toutes les parties du corps de l'Etat et qui, par un feu caché, le mine et le détruit" (ibid., p. 56).

[59] Sixth *mercuriale:* "Les moeurs du magistrat" (1702), in *Oeuvres choisies*, p. 67. This theme was developed more imperatively in the fourth *mercuriale* ("La dignité du magistrat", 1700): "C'est dans le séjour laborieux de l'austere vertu que les enfants recoivent de leurs pères bien moins les dignités que les moeurs patriciennes. Là se conservent encore, dans le déclin de notre gloire et au milieu de ce siècle de fer, les restes précieux de l'âge d'or de la magistrature. Là tous les objets qui frappent les yeux, inspirent l'amour du travail et l'horreur de l'oisiveté. La regne une vertueuse frugalité, image de celle des anciens sénateurs; une modération féconde qui s'enrichit de tout ce qu'elle ne désire point, et qui trouve dans le simple retranchement du superflu la source innocente de son abondance" (ibid., p. 48). This moral necessity was realistic. Judgeships were not economically profitable offices, unless they were used in illicit and corrupt fashion. Therefore, judges were not to be selected from families of inadequate means. For De la Mare and d'Aguesseau, the ideal fortune was a solid but only gradually increased affluence transmitted from generation to generation.

[60] "L'amour de la simplicité," in *Oeuvres choisies*, p. 56.

[61] The d'Aguesseau family was an exemplar of themistocratic dynasticism. Henri-François's grandfather had been criminal lieutenant of the Châtelet, judge and then president of the Grand Conseil, master of requests, intendant of Amiens, and a member of the Council of State. His father was judge of the Parlement of Alsace, president of the Grand Conseil, master of requests, intendant successively of Limoges, Bordeaux, and Languedoc, and councillor of state. Henri-François married a Lefèvre d'Ormesson. His sons were magistrates of the Parlement of Paris and Grand Conseil, masters of requests, and members of the Council of State (Antoine, *Le gouvernement*, pp. 1–4).

the perfect magistrate, justice and equity were conditions of mind and soul before they became consequences of action. Merit was developed from within oneself; it was not gained from birth, rank, or office. Inner being required a lifetime of cultivation, through learning, introspection, piety, and devotion to duty.[62] Honor, dignity, and power would issue from that cultivation, but they could not be its goals. The insistence on altruism, moral courage, self-discipline, and loyalty among the themistocracy may be read partly as a reformulation, for a civil elite, of the *chevaleresque* values claimed by the military elite of Old Regime France. But one must be cautious in that reading: The moral imagery was, on balance, more sacerdotal than chivalric. D'Aguesseau's explicit historical model and referent for themistocracy was the ancient magistracy and senate of republican Rome, a hereditary patriciate that legislated, judged, and administered. Although subservience to monarchy was not a theme of his *mercuriales*, subservience to God was a constant theme, because the magistrate had powers of life and death. And there was no trace of nobiliary exclusiveness in either d'Aguesseau's or Domat's description of the perfect magistrate. He could be either bourgeois or noble in social condition. Those two men incarnated that corporate unity. Henry-François d'Aguesseau was born into the high and aristocratic robe, married a Lefèvre d'Ormesson, and became Chancellor of France. Jean Domat remained a bourgeois, probably by choice. He was royal advocate in the presidial court of Clermont-Ferrand for most of his career, the most learned and influential of late seventeenth-century jurists, and a friend of both Blaise Pascal and the young Henry-François d'Aguesseau.[63] In 1681, at the age of 56, he retired from office to live, meditate, write, and then die near Port-Royal-des-Champs, the center of Jansenist piety and learning.

The themistocratic ethos, in its intellective and exalted stoicism, and whether expressed in recommendations for judgeships or in didactic and juristic literature, was neither bourgeois nor aristocratic in character. It was based on familial wealth, but was antimaterialist and antientrepreneurial. It valorized heredity, but essentially as a pedagogy, not as a pedigree. It prescribed moral

---

[62] In the "Instructions sur les études propres à former un magistrat" (1716), d'Aguesseau gave a comprehensive plan of study to be followed over many years beyond the *collège* and the faculty of law. Religion was the first of the four categories of study. Among the essential works were the Scriptures, Saint Augustine's *City of God* and *On Grace*, the treatises of Pierre Nicole, and Pascal's *Pensées*. That was a Jansenist syllabus. The value of historical study (centered on antiquity and France) was understood to be primarily spiritual: "La véritable nature de l'homme y est dévoilée bien plus clairment que dans la philosophie la plus sublime: nous y decouvrons le principe de ce mélange, et de cette contrariété étonnante de passions et de vertus, de basesse et de grandeur, de faiblesse et de force, de légerèté et de profondeur, d'irréligion et de superstition, de crimes atroçes et d'actions héroïques, qu'on trouve partout dans l'histoire, et souvant dans le même homme . . . et que rien n'est plus rare que les deux extrèmes opposés, c'est-a-dire, la vertu sans vices, et le vice sans vertus. . . . L'Etendue de l'histoire, fondée sur les principes de cette vraie philosophie, c'est-a-dire, de la réligion, nourrit la vertu, elève l'homme au-dessus des choses de la terre, au-dessus de lui-méme, lui inspire le mépris de la fortune, fortifie son courage, le rend capable des plus grandes résolutions, et le remplit enfin de cette magnanimité solide et véritable qui fait non-seulement le héros, mais le héros chrétien" (ibid., pp. 239–41).

[63] *Dictionnaire*, Prevost & d'Amat, vol. 11, pp. 466–7.

and intellectual achievement, but was hostile to individualism and originality, however creative or elegant. It required action, but action that carried little risk of death or possibility of heroism.

Themistocrats were a blend, or hybrid, of disparate, even contradictory social elements within Old Regime civilization. The majority were bourgeois in social origin. By the nature of their judicial offices, they were a technically savant, vocational, and even modernistic governing class. But since judgeships at the highest rank (the professional goal of magisterial families) were hereditarily ennobling, the social model of aristocracy – an archaic social model – exercised a certain sway over the entire themistocracy. By the eighteenth century, the model of aristocracy was indeed centered on service to king and realm. But until the Revolution, that model also retained old and tenacious values that noble themistocrats could not satisfy: respect for venerable lineage; general disdain for intellectual pursuits and vocations; a primarily agrarian lifestyle; glorification of military leadership, of physical hardship, taking risks and death on the battlefield or aboard a warship. In obedience to royal edicts that forbade magistrates to engage in trade, in partial conformity to aristocratic tradition, and from economic necessity, ennobled families of the themistocracy invested in land, became lords of the manor, gave token sons to the officer corps of the army, and occasionally married daughters into families of the military aristocracy. Yet, despite that behavior, their social identity as nobles remained vulnerable to challenge by more senior, and vocationally different, nobles.

Their ethos coherently responded to those social ambiguities and tensions, just as it coherently expressed the tasks of magistracy. It was an encompassing ideology of power, distinct from bourgeois and traditional aristocratic values and transcending both.[64] It embraced both the "perfect Catholic magistrate" of the seventeenth and early eighteenth centuries and the "enlightened" servant of the public weal during the late Old Regime. The ethos ideologically forged bourgeois and nobles into a third being, the themistocrat. That being was self-replicating, in both fact and consciousness.

Themistocrats enforced their ethos. Sons who betrayed family and professional obligations were punished, when necessary, by drastic measures: removal from office, incarceration, exile, or disinheritance.[65] Professional misconduct or scandalous behavior meant forfeiture of office, usually at the joint instigation of family, corporation, and Chancellor.[66] Confinement or exile by *lettre de ca-*

---

[64] For early constructions of the ethos by spokesmen for the Parisian themistocracy in the sixteenth century, see Colin Kaiser, "Les cours souveraines au XVIe siècle: Morale et Contre-Réforme," *Annales: Economies, Sociétés, Civilisations,* 37 (1982): 15–31.

[65] "Sous l'Ancien Régime, la notion d'enfant est extensive et se prolonge jusqu'à des âges fort avancés. Cette société partriarcale, avec une emprise familiale à la fois vaste (agnatique) et forte, engendre la notion sinon de responsabilité collective, du moins celle d'honneur familiale. D'où la répression des membres déviants" (Claude Quetel, *De Par le Roy: Essai sur les lettres de cachet* [Paris: Privat, 1981], p. 137).

[66] See Guyot, *Traité des droits,* vol. 4, pp. 18–20.

chet – the sealed royal order for which parents or guardians applied in writing – was the principal weapon and recourse of themistocratic and other propertied families against sons and daughters who rejected parental authority, disgraced the family reputation, manifested mental derangement, squandered capital, or violated professional codes. Disinheritance of disobedient and profligate sons was obtained by civil action in the courts. Rebels and miscreants from families of royal officialdom accounted for a high proportion of the 5,279 persons incarcerated at the Bastille between 1659 and 1789. Most were confined there, and in the other royal *maisons de force* at Vincennes, Charenton, and Saint-Lazare, for periods of from six months to four years. Those judged insane or incorrigible were usually confined for life.[67] Others were exiled to remote colonial islands. Such deployment of familial authority may seem brutal, but the brutality demonstrated the seriousness of themistocratic self-discipline. Incarceration or exile – on the intitiative of families, with the support of corporations, and by royal order – served as prophylaxis for family and profession, punishment and sometimes correction for their victims, and as a general warning to all children of the empowered. The commensal themistocratic household had no room for derelict progeny.

More than 900 men served as magistrates of the Parlement of Paris between 1715 and 1771. Only 10 had to be removed from office for debauchery and profligacy, mental instability, or professional misconduct. That was about 1 percent of the eighteenth-century Parlement themistocracy. Most of those removed were expelled, after a few years in office, on the initiative of their families and peers, and then ostracized with a modest pension, interned in a *maison de force*, or exiled by royal order.[68] None of the 130 Châtelet judges provoked such an action against himself.

[67] See Quetel, *De Par le Roy*, and Arlette Farge and Michel Foucault, *Le désordre des familles: Lettres de cachet des Archives de la Bastille* (Paris: Gallimard-Julliard, 1982). Charenton was the main prison asylum for those deemed insane, mentally retarded, or emotionally unstable who were from wealthy (and usually empowered) families. Inmates were committed at the request of their families and kept for many years, or for life. There were 92 inmates at Charenton in January 1789. Twenty-nine had been there since at least 1770. Most were denoted *imbécile, aliéné, fou périodique, fou furieux, maniac*, or epileptic. ("Etat des personnes detenus d'ordre du Roy dans la maison des Réligieux de la Charité de Charenton," A.N. Y 13614).

[68] Angran de Fontpertuis (cousin of the Châtelet civil lieutenant) was received in 1740 and expelled, at the request of his family, in 1741 for squandering his inheritance on drink, debauchery, gambling, and crapulous companions. They had him imprisoned at Saint-Lazare. Claude-Antoine Gobelin d'Offrement, scion of the family that made the royal tapestries, was accepted in 1720 and expelled in 1727. He had piled up 40,000 livres in personal debt in a few years. To avoid the Bastille, he escaped to Santo Domingo. His family then disinherited him. Jacques-Isidor Lottin de Charny, received in 1719, was forced from his office by his father in 1722; he had moved out of the paternal household (at age 24) without permission. Antoine-Henri Porlier de Rubelles was received in 1733 and obliged to resign by the Parlement in 1742 for professional negligence and misconduct. François Joachim de La Pierre de Talhouêt was received in 1710 and became a master of petitions in 1720. In 1727, he was tried and convicted by Parlement for forgery and betrayal of trust in office. His sentence was death. The king commuted the sentence to life imprisonment at the Bastille, and then to exile on Sante-Marguérite Islands of Canada. See Bluche, "L'origine des magistrats du Parlement de Paris," pp. 62, 197, 288, 355, 239.

The emphasis, in juristic literature, on the unity of the themistocracy had more than social resonance: It expressed a political condition. Old Regime royal courts often quarreled among themselves over jurisdiction and precedence. In spite of this, judges in royal courts, from bailliages to Parlements, and the magistracy in general lived and operated professionally in a condition of corporate democracy. Distinctions of professional rank derived principally from seniority or from differences in specialized tasks (such as the specific responsibilities of presidents, lieutenants, and royal prosecutors and advocates) or differences in the authority of courts (such as the right of judgment in first instance as opposed to final judgment on appeal). Distinctions between the chief officers (presidents and lieutenants) and the judges, within both lower and superior courts, were effaced during the trial of important civil and criminal cases. Presidencies and lieutenantcies were, at least officially, accessible to all magisterial families through purchase and appointment. Magisterial activity within any royal court was far more cooperative than competitive. Magistrates could be imperious and acerbic in dealing with nonmagistrates, but they normally were courteous and delicate in their dealings with each other. They shared the same corporate being and responsibilities.[69] The near-general solidarity that provincial Parlements and Parisian courts manifested toward the Parlement of Paris during its major eighteenth-century conflicts with the Crown, and the ease of collaboration between *parlementaires* and bailliage magistrates in the Estates-General of 1789, proceeded from that tradition of corporate democracy.

Corporate democracy was both theoretically and (for several centuries) practically compatible with a hierarchical polity (and its inequalities) whose apex was the monarchy. It became incompatible when the very articulation of the hierarchy was challenged by the Crown, in its eighteenth-century attempts at social and political reformation, and by the themistocracy, in its resistance to those attacks on its corporate rights and powers.[70]

[69] A rough modern analogy might be the social relations that obtain normatively (but not always in practice) within the officer corps of a Western army. Despite the hierarchy of rank and command authority, all officers share the amenities and fraternity of the mess and are expected to behave cordially and respectfully to each other, just as they are expected to perform their duties by established and objective rules. Both the most senior general and the youngest second lieutenant are under those obligations. The second lieutenant is a potential general, just as the general was once a second lieutenant. Both define themselves in contradistinction to enlisted men and to all civilians.

[70] Since the era of the American and French Revolutions, democracy has been cherished as a universally extensible value. Exclusionary and corporatist forms of democracy have been in disrepute since that era. But modern political experience has demonstrated that formal equality of rights cannot guarantee political democracy, no matter what the size of the group. Questions of value aside, it may be that political democracy can, in fact, endure only among those who share the same privileges (or rights), material concerns; cultural formation, and duties. Those ligatures form a community of real and conscious interests. A group without them is both unequal and uncohesive in composition. It easily dissolves into antagonistic factions, from which emerge dominating oligarchies. That became much of the political dynamic in Revolutionary France. If measured by their longevity and power of resistance to internal and external threat, the leading corporate democracies within Old Regime France were among the most successful examples of Occidental democracy.

The professional culture that we have examined largely accorded with the original royal intentions that had presided over the development of a venal-heredity judiciary and administration, and then civil ennoblement, in early modern France. During the seventeenth and eighteenth centuries, few families entered ennobling offices of state (other than the office of royal secretary) directly from commerce, private banking, or preexistent seigneurial nobility. Most rose to ennobling office after generations in lesser offices of state. Since magistracy and administration were the foremost professions in which men and their families could rise in estate, by passing from bourgeois to noble, the chief spokesmen for those professions, such as Domat and d'Aguesseau, emphasized vocation above all else. They did not emphasize nobility. Such a divisive emphasis would have falsified a dynamic social reality and violated the authority and unity of vocation. The *mercuriales* of d'Aguesseau offered clear and exacting precepts that, if followed, could lead a family over the course of generations from subaltern to superior judicial careers, that could guide it from bourgeois to noble estate, through constancy and maturity in vocation.

Jurists and moralists who argued or insinuated that true and valid nobility derived from vocations of functionally important service to state and realm, rather than from passive legal condition or sheer lineage and pedigree, were not only advancing the claims of civil officialdom: They were also reasoning in accord with royal intentions. Bernard Chérin, who succeeded the d'Hoziers as royal genealogist and thus spokesman for monarchical conceptions of nobility, evaluated the nobility of a family by five criteria, in the following order of importance: (1) venerability; (2) service to king and realm; (3) offices held; (4) quality of marriages; (5) property.[71] By at least the second through the fifth of these criteria of *noblesse*, most families of the Parisian sovereign court themistocracy far surpassed the majority of the French aristocracy during the eighteenth century. In the vision of both kings and themistocrats, the noble family that lived for generations on and from its capital but without performing civil or military service was tainted with social parasitism and moral dereliction.

An imperative of work was at the center of this ideological and political constellation.[72] A magistrate, of whatever estate or rank, deserved his office not because of inheritance or purchase but because he successfully performed the office. Patrimony, education, and privilege readied him for his duty, but the work and self-vindication were ultimately his alone. The imperative of personal work and duty grew out of the long tradition of venal-hereditary empowerment, and it survived that form of empowerment.

---

[71] Cited by Bluche, "Les magistrats des cours parisiennes au XVIIIe siècle," pp. 103–4.

[72] "Il n'y a point de condition, sans en excepter même les plus élevées, qui n'ait pour son caractère essentiel & pour son devoir capital & indispensable, l'application aux fonctions pour lesquelles elle est établie; & ceux qui prétendroient se dispenser de cet engagement, renverseroient l'ordre & violeroient la loi naturelle & la loi divine: car il est également vrai, & dans l'ordre de la rél-igion, & dans l'ordre de la nature, que l'homme est né pour le travail, & que c'est pour le travail que cette vie lui est donnée" (Domat, p. 130).

Professional culture

According to all of the leading seventeenth- and eighteenth-century jurists, service to the public was the ultimate object of the magistrate's duty and work. They also believed that service to be the duty of kings, the end for which God had ordained monarchy. The moral and political self-confidence of the themistocracy was materially based on authority, privilege, and property in office. But it was animated by the values that we have examined, and it rose to the point of revolutionary dissidence during the 1770s and 1780s.

In themistocratic ideology of the seventeenth and eighteenth centuries, we witness the germinating of some important modern conceptions of political legitimation, but through the medium of classical Greek and Roman conceptions of legitimation taught in the *collèges* and the law faculties (teaching that was subtly reinforced by Jansenist and Oratorian ethics) and through the everyday exercise of difficult, rule-bound authority. The most central conceptions were that authority can validly be exercised only by those in whom the moral vocation and intellectual competence for authority have been cultivated; that legal investiture (whether royal, corporate, or electoral in form) begins but does not complete legitimation; that authority cannot be just without adherence to principles; and that beyond the rule of law there are only arbitrary, irrational, or despotic actions by the empowered. During the crisis-ridden final decades of the Old Regime, into the Revolution, and beyond, those conceptions would prove far more powerful than their originally monarchical framework. They would both condition and survive the democracy of the Revolution.

Conclusion: Rule of law

Old Regime French criminal law required both knowledge and discipline from every magistrate: knowledge of criminal statutes and of the accurate classification of each crime; obedience to strict procedures for investigation and trial; comprehension of the fixed but subtle criteria for proof of guilt; ability to apply those criteria to the completed evidence of the case at the end of trial; and, if the defendant was found guilty, the capacity to make rule-governed selection of penalty within the range of penalties applicable to the crime. Subsequent chapters will demonstrate that those strict procedures were indeed obeyed by the judges of the eighteenth-century Châtelet and Parlement of Paris.

Judicial competence, discipline, and fidelity did not exist *sui generis* in seventeenth- and eighteenth-century France. They did not exist simply because they were mandated by the law or could be enforced by Parlements and the Chancellor.[1] They were produced through the production of that corporate being and personality that I have described.

The themistocracy was the product of a socioprofessional evolution, from *bourgeois gentilshommes* of the law during the fifteenth and sixteenth centuries to the proprietary, dynastic, and utterly professional magistrates of the eighteenth century. Their familialism was not feudal, for they defined themselves and acted in legally determined service to the state and civil society. Since they owned their offices, they cannot be considered bureaucrats in any modern sense. Their ultimate subservience was to law and vocation, not to kings. The particular social, economic, and intellectual history of the themistocracy was so interwoven with the history of criminal and civil law (from at least the Ordinance of Blois, in 1498, to the comprehensive ordinances of Louis XIV and beyond) and with the system of trial, judgment, and punishment, that the latter could not have developed without the former, and the former could not have endured without the latter.

In the most encompassing way, the themistocracy and the law were unitary. Civil and criminal law were embodied by royal edicts and codes, as well as by

---

[1] Punitive enforcement of those obligations, by Parlements over the subaltern judges in their jurisdictions, had been commanded by Article 59 of Louis XII's Ordinance of Blois, March 1498 (Isambert, vol. 11, p. 350). By Article 162, all magistrates, notaries, clerks, and summons-servers of Parlements had to swear to observe and uphold all royal ordinances (ibid., pp. 377–8).

the rulings of Parlements that Chancellors validated. These laws were enforced simultaneously on and by the themistocracy. From the Ordinance of Louis XII at Blois onward, new statues had to be read at monthly intervals in plenary sessions of Parlements; in both Parlements and royal bailliages, current royal laws had to be read in general sessions twice yearly and collections of them maintained for consultation in court libraries.[2] Chancellors and other former or serving themistocrats from sovereign courts were the chief authors of that legislation in royal councils, and thus main sources of the law, from the late Middle Ages to 1789. Those men wrote the statutes and codes that kings promulgated, an authorship that we shall examine in analyzing the Great Criminal Ordinance of 1670. The transcendence of Estate, the endogamy, and the rule-bound ethos that characterized the magistracy corresponded indispensably to the universalism and precision of the law. The two meanings of themistocracy were, in fact, one: There was a holistic legal culture in classical France, whose elements were so interdependent that significant changes (or "reforms") in any element would inevitably transform the whole. Most eighteenth-century themistocrats understood this interdependence, and therefore resisted major changes, until the very eve of the Revolution, when repeated crises of public order and social discipline made systematic change imperative. When the great transformation of law and justice occurred in 1790–1, it was equally holistic.

Modern democratic prejudice against nepotism in the judiciary and government is so firmly entrenched that it is difficult for us to believe that any venal-hereditary magistracy could have been competent, honest, and just. We associate merit and rectitude with individuals, not families, and insist that empowerment result from formal competitions among individuals. Our conviction that the only valid means for the selection of judges, and of public officials in general, is either direct election or appointment by elected executive officials has been remarkably tenacious, surviving the widely known fact that professional mediocrity or incompetence, corruption, and partisanship are recurrent, perhaps even endemic, among the judicial and other oligarchies of modern democratic states. We grudgingly recognize that fact but are unwilling to concede the validity of any other system of justice or rule. We are unwilling to believe that any nepotistic system could have been animated by principles of public duty, adherence to law, and self-discipline. Democratic political culture is in severe crisis in its historical heartland, the United States and Western Europe. Its intellectual defenders frequently reassure themselves by denigrating other political systems, past and present, and especially the "old regimes" that were supplanted by democratic political culture during the eighteenth and nineteenth centuries.

We have been accustomed by modern democratic thought, since the era of the late eighteenth-century revolutions, to believe that the rule of law cannot exist without formal constitutions. And we are encouraged to give our primary

---

[2] Articles 27–8, 78–9 (ibid., pp. 341–2, 356).

attention to constitutional mechanics – to their detail, rigor, and enforcement. We are rarely told that rule of law, and justice, also depend on the collective formation and subjectivity of those invested with the power of the law or that even the most rigorous constitutionalism cannot prevent them from committing either willful or ignorant subversion or injustice unless they inwardly prevent themselves. Constitutionalism can only purge or punish the miscreant official, usually long after the fact of costly betrayal of trust or injustice. Emphasis on the social and moral quality of the empowered would tend to personalize legal authority, and that would be dissonant with both democratic ideology and faith in constitutionalism. But that emphasis was the essence of the Old Regime themistocratic system.

"Properties acquired slowly but justly, a fortune modest but solid": The economic condition of magistrates enhanced their distinctiveness and fortified them as a transcendent elite, both materially and psychologically. The particular and confining nature of their wealth, and their strategies for consolidating and legating that wealth over generations, were also a pedagogy for judicial authority. Themistocratic capital did more than finance vocation; it also reinforced nomistic personality. Lineal property in land, long-term or lifetime *rentes*, fine artifacts, and offices, as well as dowries whose expenditure was closely restricted by marriage contracts, virtually dictated cautious, incremental, and collectivist economic behavior among the proprietors. Each generation, and individual, held that property or a portion of it in trust. Such capital powerfully dissuaded both risk taking and materialist individualism.[3] Systems of property, inheritance, education, marriage, procreation, and vocation all combined to foster discipline. Service to abstractions such as the law and the public welfare was easily comprehensible to men who lived in economic and moral obedience to familial property, kinship obligations, and profession – past, present, and future. The themistocracy was a meritocracy essentially of families, not of individuals. Individual magistrates were socioprofessional actors, and thus subjects of their own experience, but they acted as agents of family and office.

As citizens of late twentieth-century consumer democracies, we may judge themistocratic existence to have been itself carceral, stifling, and repulsive, for we measure the quality of an individual life by self-aggrandizing novelties – ever-new careers or social positions, possessions, emotional adventures, cos-

---

[3] Modern historians, both liberal and Marxian, have generally been as antipathetic to that conservative rentier economic behavior as they have been to professional nepotism and dynasticism. That is because they cherish a model of general economic development that requires entrepreneurial and speculative venturing of capital in land, banking, commerce, and manufacturing, which in turn entails a behavior of acquisitive and competitive individualism that has been made synonymous with "progress" (whether perpetually or, in the Marxian vision, as a precondition necessary for socialist revolution). The capitalist economic model is, in fact, a morality of greed. That morality was known in Old Regime France and rejected by the themistocracy. The rentier economics of the Old Regime governing elite – even of the families that grew immensely rich through systematic acquisition of real property – proceeded from its different values: duty to family, kinship group, and vocation; economic cooperation; retention and transmission of material patrimony. Those same values animated professional nepotism and dynasticism.

metic appearance, even "therapeutic" newness of personality. Such judgment is the privilege, and expression, of our relative individualism and freedom from the constraints under which Old Regime themistocrats lived. However, in making such a judgment we should reflect on the qualities of life that they enjoyed but that few of us can possibly enjoy, the qualities largely denied us by the democratic egotism and competitiveness of our era: membership in tightly woven and sustaining communities of family, kinship, and profession; clear personal and collective sense of duty; sure moral and material rewards for tasks accomplished. Themistocrats were not free, in any modern sense; but they knew and accepted who they were.

Old Regime France was governed by rule of law, but without a formal and fundamental constitution. The deep cause of that ostensibly strange effect did not lie in the codes and institutions of law – civil, criminal, and administrative. It resided in the social, political, and moral crucibles wherein each generation of the judiciary was forged. It resided in their vocation.

Youth, to which the world [of the magistracy] was opened at such an early age, entered with timidity; it could not hide its insufficiency. That world was intelligent, distinguished, solidly established in an immutable hierarchy consecrated by time: one was born to the world of the magistracy; one was expected to live that world utterly; one was expected to die in it.[4]

Themistocrats passed judgment on those from every estate, social class, and professional group. But most of all, in the criminal chambers, they confronted, tried, judged, and punished the plebeians of France, the authors and accomplices of most crimes: peasants, common and casual laborers, apprentices and journeymen, servants, soldiers, prostitutes, beggars, and vagabonds.

The relations between the Parisian themistocracy and the populace of the great city were distant and formal. The judges of the Châtelet and their colleagues in the sovereign courts of the metropolis lived in the midst of Paris (principally in the Marais, Saint-Eustache, the Cité, the Latin Quarter, and the Faubourg Saint-Germain), but maximally isolated from the popular life of the city. Their homes were thick-walled town houses from which they could gaze onto quiet and often verdant courtyards, not onto the street. When they emerged, their bodies were concealed from public view by elaborate garments. They moved about principally in carriages or on horseback. They frequented salons in private homes or patronized a few exclusive coffee shops. At the opera, and the French and Italian Comédies, they sat in well-guarded loges. They passed rapidly through the popular swarm in the streets and courtyards of the Châtelet and the Palais de Justice. Servants emancipated them from any form of manual labor. Each day they could eat to satiety, in a city and realm of periodic mass hunger. They rarely handled currency, because their capital was fixed, their incomes stable, and their credit large. They habitually spoke a cultivated, latinate French that was radically distinct from the argotic vulgate of streets,

---

[4] Pasquier, *Mémoires*, vol. 1, pp. 17–18.

shops, ateliers, barracks, and taverns. Their language was literary, especially when they spoke. They lived through intimate bonds of family and kinship. Very many metropolitan plebeians were individuals migrant over wide spaces, who were far removed or long severed from their families, who had literally to create in the city quite different and shifting bonds. Such a chasm separated themistocrats' experience of life from the plebeian experience as to render negligible, by comparison, the social differences within the themistocracy.

The memoirs of magistrates rarely mention the masses of those who lived just outside their claustral world, other than notable criminals or rioters. Despite that silence, individual judges may have been curious and reflective about the populace. But how could they have known the people of Paris?

According to eighteenth-century writers, the collective life of Paris was a broad confluence of parochial lives. The themistocracy surely lived one of the most parochial. But their parochialism meant transcendence. Their entire mode of existence sealed them off and protected them from the surrounding masses of plebeians and petty bourgeois, and thus from the criminal populace that they judged. Consequently, their knowledge of those variegated masses could not have been direct, penetrating, or empathetic. It was instead a knowledge circumscribed by jurisprudence, courtrooms and prisons, an intellective knowledge that was subsumed and defined by the categories of criminal law and justice in which judges were schooled by education and professional experience. Those thick legal categories mediated their comprehension of plebeian defendants from the beginning to the end of each trial, even during the prolonged face-to-face encounters of interrogation. Criminal law and jurisprudence, from at least 1670 onward, were voluminous and detailed; universal, they theoretically provided for virtually all human motives, actions, and material conditions. Procedures for investigation, trial, and judgment of those accused were equally meticulous. The law, not the judge, was paramount in judgment. But the legal system could not generate psychological knowledge among judges. The system-defined encounter of plebeians and magistrates forced defendants to contrivances and falsehoods, to deformations of self, while it preordained the manner in which magistrates interpreted, judged, and punished defendants. Knowledge of another is knowledge of his subjectivity, not of his social description or classification, circumstances, or even actions. Subjectivity can only be revealed by the subject in his own way, whether consciously or not, to close interlocutors and observers, over long periods. Because their social and cultural existence made it almost impossible for judges to acquire such knowledge of plebeians, they were all the more creatures of the law.

Judges were entrapped within the epistemology of the law. And that law was severely limited in its effective power over plebeians. The limitations are visible in the system of punishments, the definitions of crimes and penal liability, the procedures for trial and judgment, thus in the very substance of criminal justice.

Appendix: Letter of appointment for Augustin Testard du Lys

Conseiller au Châtelet de Paris

8e Denier	–	1559/6/8
Marc d'or	–	756
Sceau	–	90
hon	–	50

Louis par la Grace de Dieu Roy de france et de Navarre, a tous ceux qui ces présentes verront, Salut. Scavoir, faisons que pour la pleine et entière confiance que nous avons en la personne de notre Cher et bien aimé Augustin Testard du Lys, avocat en Parlement, et sur les temoignages qu'on nous a rendus de ses bonnes qualités et de ses talents et de l'attachement qu'à toujours marqué sa famille pour l'Interêt de le bien de notre Service. Nous avons au sieur Augustin Testard du Lys donné et octroyé, donnons et octroyons, par ces présentes l'office de notre Conseiller en notre Châtelet et Siège Présidial de Paris, dont il a payé en nos revenues casuels le droit de huitième denier en conséquence de la déclaration du neuf aoust 1722, et que tenoit et exercoit le sieur Claude Bruant des Carrières, qui en avoit payé le droit annuel et après le déces duquel ses enfans et heritiers nous ont nommé et presenté au dit office le d. sieur Testard du Lys par acte du onze des presans mois. Pour le d. office avoir tenir et l'exercer et jouir . . . par le d. sieur Testard du Lys aux honneurs, pouvoirs, libertez, fonctions, autoritez, privilèges, droits, exemptions, franchises, immunités, prérogatives, préeminences, entrée, rang, séance, gages, fruits, profits, revenus, emolumens, y appartenans tels et tout ainsy qu'en a joüy ou du joüir le d. feu sr. Bruant des Carrières et qu'en joüissent ou doivent joüir les autres de pareils officiers, encore bien que le d. sr. Des Carrières n'aye venu les quarante jours portez par nos Reglemens de la rigueur desquels attenda l'annuel qu'il a payé, nous avons relevé et dispensé, relevons et dispensons, le d. sr. Testard du Lys par ces présentes, a conditon toutefois que le d. sr. Testard dy Lys aye atteint l'âge de vingt et un ans cinq mois et quelques jours, suivant son extrait baptistaire du seize mars mil sept cens vingt cinq, delivré le sept novembre 1743 par le vicaire de l'Eglise parrroissiale de St. Eustache à Paris, et pourvu que le d. sr. Testard du Lys n'aye dans le nombre des officiers du d. Siège aucuns parents ni alliés aux dégrés prohibez par nos ordonnances, ainsy qu'il nous est justifié par le certificat . . . le d. extrait bapistaire, et susd. acte de nomination et autres pièces attaché sous le contrescel de notre Chancellerie, a peine de perte du d. office, nullité des presentes et de sa reception, et quant a ce qui manque au d. sr. Testard du Lys de l'âge de vingt cinq années accomplies requises par nos ordonnances nous l'en avons relevé et dispensé par nos lettres de cejourd'huy, à condition cependant que le d. sr. Testard du Lys n'aura voix deliberative que conformement aux Reglemens du d. Châtelet, S'y donnons et mandemens a notre Prévot de Paris ou son Lieutenant Civil et gens tenans le Siège Présidial au Châtelet que leurs estant apparu des bonnes vie et moeurs, âge du d. de vingt et un ans cinq mois et quelques jours, conversation et Réligion Catholique apostolique et romaine du d. sr. Testard du Lys, et ayant pris de luy le Serment requis et accoutumé, ils le reçoivent, mettent et instituent de par nous en possession du d. office et l'en fassent joüir pleinement et paissiblement aux honneurs, pouvoirs, libertez, fonctions, autoritez, privileges, droits, exemptions, franchises, immunitez, prérogatives, préeminences, entrée, rang, séance, gages, fruits, profits, revenus et emolumens susd. et y appartenans et luy fassent obéir et entendre de tous et ainsy qu'il appartiendra en choses concernans le d. office, Mandans en outre a nos amis et feaux conseillers Les Presidents Tresoriers de france et Generaux de nos finances à Paris que par les Tresoriers Receveurs payeurs et autres comptables qu'il appartiendra et des fonds à ce destinez ils fassent payer et delivrer comptan au d. sr. Testard du Lys doresnavant par chacun an aux terms en la manière accoutumez les gages et droits appartenans au d. office a commencer du jour et datte de sa reception ainsy que des presantes pour une fois seulement aux quittances de luy suffisantes, Nous voulons de d. Gages et droits etre passez et allouez en la depense des Comptes des d. Tresoriers Receveurs Payeurs et autres qui en auront fait le payemen par nos amis et feaux Conseilleurs des Gens de nos Comptes a Paris, auxquels mandons ainsy le faire sans difficulté, car tel est Notre plaisir, en temoin de quoy nous avons fait mettre notre scel a ces présentes donné a Paris, le dix neuf jour d'aoust l'an de Grace mil sept cent quarante six et de notre regne le trente unième.

Source: A.N. V 1 346.

PART II

Punishment

Introduction: Imagery

From the late eighteenth century to the present, the system of punishment has been the most widely misrepresented element of Old Regime French criminal justice. From Cesare Beccaria's *Treatise on Crimes and Punishments* (1764) and Louis-Michel Lepeletier de Saint-Fargeau's "Report on the Project of a Penal Code" (1791), to Michel Foucault's *Discipline and Punish: The Birth of the Prison* (1979), there has been a dominant imagery of that penal system.[1] It is an imagery of painful, bloody chastisements of the body, of whippings, brandings, mutilations, and executions, whereby the state publicly inscribed its sovereign power, its despotism of law, on the flesh of malefactors, and thus ruled by terror. That imagery has been convenient. It allowed Enlightenment publicists and Revolutionary legislators to discredit, in humanitarian language, a system which they were determined to replace, and with one that would be more implacably and insidiously punitive of body and personality. It has given modern historians and commentators an intellectually satisfying contrast between a tradition of corporal punishments and a modernity of imprisonment, a clear sense of rapid, dramatic change in law and power at the end of the eighteenth century, an ending and a beginning.

Those are myths. Physical chastisement (including the death penalty) was but one, and a carefully limited, sphere in the versatile Old Regime penal system. Institutions for incarceration existed on a large scale, occupied a central position in the hierarchy of penalties, and served purposes identical to those of modern penitentiaries, long before they were ever officially named "prisons." Shaming and humiliation, not physical suffering, formed the essence of Old Regime legal punishment. The overarching goal of punishment was moral correction, even salvation.

My purpose in Part II is to demonstrate these truths by reconstructing in detail the penal system as it operated in France from 1670 to 1789, from the

---

[1] Cesare Beccaria, *On Crimes and Punishments*, tr. Henry Paolucci (New York: Bobbs-Merrill, 1963); Louis-Michel Lepelétier de Saint-Fargeau, "Rapport sur le projet du Code pénal, présenté a l'Assemblée nationale au nom des Comités de Constitution et de Législation criminelle" (Paris: Imprimérie Nationale, 1791); Michel Foucault, *Discipline and Punish: The Birth of the Prison*, tr. Alan Sheridan (New York: Vintage, 1979).

most benign to the most severe of penalties. We begin with the limits on punishment, the definitions of liability and immunity. We end with annulments and mitigations of punishment, the royal pardon in law and in action.

7

Liability and immunity

Legal punishment was comprehensive in its purposes and forms, and applied to all groups in civil society – commoners, clergy, and nobility. Only the king, as sovereign, was above accusation, trial, and punishment; he could be judged and punished only by God.[1] But liability to penalty, and thus the actual reach of punishment, was restricted. The foremost restriction was established by the very definition of crime:

A crime is an act forbidden by law, through which one causes injury to another from malice or imprudence. . . . Injury inflicted without malice or imprudence can never be considered a crime, nor render its author liable to punishment.[2]

One understands by "crime" any unjust act forbidden by law which tends to harm society and disrupt public tranquillity, and which deserves a penalty. . . . It is a general principle that there is no crime without the will to commit a crime; thus illegal acts committed by the insane, or from accident, are not crimes, no matter the harm that they cause. . . . Where there is no malicious intent, there is no crime, and consequently there can be no penalty, but only damages and interests against the author of the infraction.[3]

In Old Regime jurisprudence, a crime was not simply an act that was prohibited and penalized by a law. It was also the malicious disposition – knowledge of wrong and intent to harm – that preceded and produced the act. Crime was intention and act (including an act attempted but not accomplished); both elements were required for a crime to exist and for punishment to ensue. One could be guilty of an incriminated act without being guilty of a crime. This conception of crime was implicit in royal statutes and was sometimes explicitly stated.[4] Malicious intent – *dol*, in French, from the Latin *dolus* – without any

---

[1] Jousse, *Traité*, vol. 1, p. 575.   [2] Muyart, *Institutes*, pp. 2, 9.
[3] Jousse, *Traité*, vol. 1, pp. 1, 10–11, 605. See Rousseaud, p. 1
[4] E.g., in the statutes against highway robbery and burglary (Francis I, January 1534) "Ceux qui par mauvais esprit, damnée et misérable volonté, se sont mis et mettent bien souvent par insidiations et aggressions conspirées et machinées, à piller et destrousser de nuict les allans et venans ès villes, villages et lieux" (Isambert, vol. 11, p. 400); against fraudulent and larcenous bankruptcy (Henry IV, May 1609) "les banqueroutiers faisans doleusement faillite" (ibid., vol. 15, p. 349); against dueling (Louis XIV, June 1643) "ce crime détestable, qui, en violant tout ensemble le respect qui nous est dû par nos sujets, comme à leur souverain, et l'obéissance qu'ils doivent à Dieu, comme à leur créateur et à leur juge, les pousse, par une manie prodigieuse, à sacrifier

prohibited act or attempt was sinful but not criminal. An illegal act performed ignorantly or without intent to harm was not a crime, even if it caused serious injury.[5]

Criminal intent signified malice aforethought, knowing and purposive will to commit an incrimated act. It was of two sorts: premeditated (the most serious); and impetuous or momentary, usually in the "heat of a violent passion" such as rage, sorrow, jealousy, or fear.[6] The general causes, or motives, for criminal intent were presumed to be finite and known:

All crimes have their source in concupiscence or anger. It is from anger that are born insults, assaults, homicides, betrayals, poisonings, slander, conspiracies, subornments and other crimes by which one harms his fellow man; and it is concupiscence that gives rise to drunkenness, adultery, rape, seduction, theft, simony and to all other crimes of the senses, of greed or ambition; and although some of the different crimes mentioned can have both concupiscence and anger as motives . . . all crimes in general can be attributed to one or the other of these two forces.[7]

Criminal intent, or its absence, had to be determined by judges during the course of trial; it could not be presumed, or simply deduced from commission of the prohibited action by the defendant, "since [criminal intent] cannot exist without a particular cause, such as resentment, self-interest, or contempt for the Law, for judges to be convinced of such intent it is necessary that proof of that cause be established; otherwise the crime is reputed to be purely accidental or is considered to be the result of negligence."[8] But ascertaining criminal intent was not always an elaborate process. Several common violations of the law were regarded as purposive by their nature: "There are crimes that cannot be committed without premeditation and deliberation, such as murder, dueling, poisoning, kidnapping, theft, fraud, and several others; and there are those that can be committed by premeditation, or by impetuousness, or by imprudence, such as homicide."[9] When the malicious intent was not manifest in the act, it had to be searched for in the evidence bearing upon the defendant and the act, especially that concerning his character, life history, relations with the victim,

leurs corps et leurs âmes à cete idole de vanité qu'ils-adorent au mépris de leur salut" (ibid., vol. 17, p. 13); against begging (Louis XV, July 18, 1724) "ceux qui sont en état de subsister par leur travail, mendient par pure fainéantise. . . . La dissolution et la débauche qui sont la suite de cette méme oisiveté, les portent insensiblement aux plus grands crimes" (ibid., vol. 19, p. 272).
[5] The qualities that diminished legal culpability and resulted in mitigation of punishment, as well as those that aggravated culpability and punishment, are described under the heading of "Principles" in the conclusion to Part III.
[6] Muyart, *Institutes*, p. 6. On crimes of impetuous malicious intent: "Quoique ces crimes soient moins graves que ceux commis avec un propros délibéré, néamoins, comme ils ne sont pas tout-a-fait exempts de malice, & qu'ils sont faits avec intention de nuire, ils ne peuvent aussi être exempts de peine . . . à moins que par des considérations particulières le Prince ne juge à propos d'en accorder la remission" (ibid., p. 7).
[7] Jousse, *Traité*, vol. 1, pp. 10–11. And see Domat: "l'ambition, l'avarice, la débauche, le libertinage, l'impiété, l'envie, les haines" (p. 198).
[8] Domat; p. 198. Cf. Jousse, *Traité*, vol. 2, pp. 611–13.
[9] Domat, p. 203. Cf. Muyart, *Loix criminelles*, p. 12.

and behavior before, during, and after the delictual event.[10] That was a matter for inductive reasoning by judges: "Since the external signs by which one can know the intentions of men are most often equivocal in meaning, because of the variety of circumstances and the diversity of forms within which the passions that engender malice are enveloped . . . it is difficult, even dangerous, to prescribe definite rules in this matter."[11]

Every criminal trial was an attempt to resolve two questions, through one investigation. First, did the defendant perform the incriminated act? Second, did he do so knowingly and willfully (or "wickedly," in the language of eighteenth-century guilty verdicts)? A defendant who was found innocent of malice or gross negligence but guilty of an illegal act was acquitted of the criminal charge and, at most, obliged to pay damages to his victim. He was not subjected to punishment. The need to ascertain intent had three effects on criminal trial and judgment: it individuated each defendant, beyond the issue of determining whether or not he had committed the illegal act; it determined his penal liability or immunity; and it influenced the assessment of culpability among those judged liable to punishment and affected the choice of punishment appropriate for them.[12]

The legal culture of the Old Regime incriminated evil volition – the inner disposition that caused a crime – more than prohibited behavior, or the event of a crime. Punishment was directed at putative volition, and thus at moral personality, not simply or mechanically at an incriminated act. For that reason, punishment was not conceived in terms of vengeance, despite its retributory character. It was conceived essentially in terms of correction for the criminal; instruction, by example, for others; or removal from society of the dangerous offender. These traditional, deep-rooted legal emphases on intent were a source (among others) for the psychology of suspicion that emerged widely in France, both within the state and among the populace, at times of crisis, and pervasively during the Revolution: belief in conspiracies; denunciations of guile and deceitfulness; scrutiny of statements, gestures, and actions for revelations of evil purpose.

The Old Regime conception of criminal intent derived from the medieval Christian theory of moral personality. The capacity for *dol* was an expression of rational free will. Human beings were divinely endowed with the capacity to discern and to choose between good and evil. As mature adults they were responsible for using that endowment. The 1543 Declaration of Faith and edict of Francis I gave that principle legal force: "One must believe that man has free will, by which he can do either good or evil, and also by which, even though he

---

[10] In referring to defendants and criminals in general, I use the masculine pronoun, for economy of expression and because the majority of them were of male gender.

[11] Muyart, *Loix criminelles*, p. 13.

[12] "C'est par la cause, que l'on peut reconnaître si une action est criminelle ou non. C'est par elle aussi, que l'on doit juger des différens dégrès de punition que l'action criminel peut mériter" (ibid., p. 10).

be in mortal sin, he can rise up to grace with God's help."[13] But the capacity and attendant responsibility for rational choice were not absolute, for they were vulnerable to other forces: illness; deficiencies of reason; passion; errors of judgment; accidents. Those forces belonged to the fallenness and imperfectibility of humankind.[14]

Jurists distinguished between two kinds of incriminated acts: *faute* and *dol*. *Faute* was an imprudent or mistaken act, without malicious intent, that violated law; it was "any act, or failure to act, resulting from imprudence or negligence and that causes harm to someone."[15] Such acts contained some degree of personal fault but no deleterious purpose. But the most egregious forms – gross negligence or recklessness – were criminal and liable to penalty. Acts such as leaving a fire untended in dry weather near a ripened field of grain, throwing an object from a window onto the street, or riding at a gallop through a village or town were criminal and deserving of punishment when they produced injury, for they violated moral "common sense, as when one is careless in matters that even the most stupid are expected to understand."[16] Acts of lesser imprudence or negligence – such as a midwife causing the death of a child or mother during a difficult childbirth, through haste or maladroitness, or an unskilled wagoner running someone down because he lost control of his horses, or a person who, in the company of others, testing the trigger of a musket that he believed was unloaded and accidentally wounding someone – could be exempted from punishment or punished lightly.

Penal immunity obtained when the illicit act resulted from ignorance, was purely accidental (with no imprudence or negligence), or was performed in legitimate self-defense or legitimate defense of another. Ignorance of the law did not cancel criminality and penal liability when the prohibited act was one that was also forbidden "by natural or Divine law, or by the common laws of humankind."[17] Ignorance of harm could eliminate criminality and liability, as for example, in the case of someone who found and claimed an object that he believed to be his own but that in fact belonged to another.[18] The descriptions of legitimate self-defense, in cases of assault or homicide, were highly restrictive. One had to be under attack or pursued by someone with a deadly weapon,

---

[13] In Isambert, vol. 12, pp. 821–4.

[14] Eighteenth-century jurists, like their sixteenth-century predecessors, had the canonic writings of Aquinas as their key source for the philosophy of rational will. For his formulations and their influence on French legal thought, see Michel Villey, *La formation de la pensée juridique moderne: Cours d'histoire de la philosophie du droit (1961–1966)* (Paris: Montchrestien, 1968), and *Questions de Saint Thomas sur le droit et la politique, ou le bon usage des dialogues* (Paris: Presses Universitaires de France, 1987).

[15] Jousse, *Traité*, vol. 2, p. 606.   [16] Muyart, *Institutes*, p. 8.

[17] Jousse, *Traité*, vol. 2, p. 613. The ignorance of law that did confer penal immunity was described by Muyart as "cette ignorance invincible qui est telle que celui qui a fait le crime, n'a pu avoir connoissance du mal qu'il faisoit, comme celle d'un voyageur qui fait une chose contraire à la coûtume des lieux où il passe, laquelle néamoins se pratique par-tout ailleurs" (Muyart, *Institutes*, p. 13).

[18] Muyart *Institutes*, p. 13.

not merely under threat; escape had to be impossible or self-endangering (except for noblemen and soldiers, for whom flight was dishonorable); there could be no significant interval of time between attack and defense; one must have used weapons no more deadly than that of the aggressor; the defensive violence cannot have been greater than that necessary to stop the attack; if the aggressor was killed, the defense had to be of life, not merely property. When these conditions were met, and the result was only injury of the aggressor, the defendant was usually exempted from penalty by the court.[19] However, courts could not waive penalty for those who killed by accident, out of negligence, in self-defense, or in passionate response to extreme provocation. Those cases were reserved in law for royal pardon (which was granted or refused according to the procedure described in Chapter 9).

Intent depended on the capacity to distinguish right from wrong and to act voluntarily and deliberately. Those who lacked that capacity, either permanently or at the time of their illegal act, could not be criminal and were immune from penalty. They were, foremost, children, the imbecile, and the insane.

As for the furibund and the insane, they cannot be punished for crimes if they are in that state at the time of the crime. In effect, it is only the will and knowledge of harm that one inflicts which deserves punishment. Someone enraged or insane, or a child who does not yet have ability to reason, does not know what he does.[20]

There was no stark distinction between juveniles and adults in Old Regime criminal jurisprudence and practice, although the age of majority, for most social purposes, was 25. There was, instead, a neo-Aristotelian conception of maturation by stages, stages that corresponded to the gradual development of reason, moral discernment, and self-discipline. The pace of that development differed among individuals.

Since reason has its own gradations, the Law desires that punishment be regulated according to the different grades of age, such that punishments inflicted on someone approaching the age of puberty not be as severe as those inflicted on someone at that age, and that those inflicted on the latter not be as severe as the ones against persons at the age of majority, who should be punished rigorously by the ordinary penalty for the crime. . . . In addition, experience proves that there are certain precocious minds whose age belies their capacity for malice, and others more backward, in which reason has barely developed even on the threshold of puberty; that is why the Law principally refers this matter to the wisdom of judges.[21]

The relative maturity of the youthful defendant and the nature of his crime, not biological age, were primary in trial and judgment. In most cases, judges had to estimate the age of those whom they tried. The stages of age were infancy (1–7); prepuberty (8–14 for boys, 8–12 for girls); minority (14–25 for

---

[19] Ibid., pp. 9–10.
[20] Jousse, *Traité*, vol. 1, p. 574. Cf. Muyart, *Institutes*, pp. 74–5.
[21] Muyart *Loix criminelles*, p. 27.

boys, 12–25 for girls); and majority.[22] Infants were immune from penal liability, as lacking in sufficient rationality to understand their actions. Since prepubescent children were not categorically incapable of malice aforethought, their cases required individuation. Such children were either exempted from penalty or whipped in the privacy of the court and returned to the custody of their parents. François Vincent, a 12-year-old chimney sweep, lived with his father (a knife and scissors tradesman) and mother on the rue de Berry. He was convicted by the Châtelet of stealing 9 livres from a coachman and sentenced to whipping in court; his parents were "enjoined to be more attentive to his conduct."[23]

But if the criminal act was serious, the youths showed discernment, and their parents were criminal, vagabond, absent, or of base social condition, the punishment was usually incarceration for a term in the Hôpital-Général. Jean Barbet, aged 13, a shoeblack who lived in a furnished room on the rue Saint-Antoine, was accused of stealing two silver buckles and attempting to sell them in the street. He declared in his final statement, "I do not have either father or mother. I only have a cousin in Paris, and I do not know where he lives. No one takes care of me. I did not steal the silver buckles or anything else, nor did I try to sell them. I have never committed theft, and I do not know why I was arrested."[24] He was found guilty, sentenced to whipping in custody of the court and detention for one year in the Bicêtre prison. Prepubescent children were not executed, banished, or sent to the galleys, but minors did not enjoy immunity from penal liability, for an adolescent was presumed capable of *dol*. The Châtelet and Parlement of Paris usually punished those adolescents younger than 17 minimally or moderately for their crimes, whereas those who were 18 or older were commonly invested with the same criminal responsibility as adults. Minors were sentenced to death if their crimes were notoriously immoral capital offenses and had required plotting or calculation. Nicolas Bara, aged 17, was an unemployed stonemasonry laborer who drifted around in the environs of Paris during the winter on his own, without fixed residence. Early in 1762, he was tried and found guilty of fraud, sacrilege, and burglary. In contrast to most defendants at the Châtelet, he admitted his guilt, in detail:

At the village of Villers-le-Sec I pretended to be very sick and asked to be confessed; the priest came and confessed me and then gave me the sacrament of Extreme Unction. I also faked sickness on 5 December at the village of [illegible], was confessed and took Extreme Unction. In the village of Chaumontel I pretended sickness again and was taken in by a farmer; the parish priest gave me close attention, and I stayed eight days with that farmer. When he left the house I stole 78 livres, a silver buckle, and a belt, from a chest that I opened without breaking it. I was once convicted of stealing a suit jacket at Clermont-en-Argonne [for which he had been branded and banished]. I know that I have done wrong, and I have a conscience, but it failed me in those moments. I no longer have a father or mother. My father was a builder. I have many kin who are well off. I

---

[22] Ibid., and Jousse, *Traité*, vol. 2, p. 618.   [23] August 10, 1762, A.N. Y 10518.
[24] August 6, 1762, A.N. Y 10518.

faked sickness and accepted the sacraments only because I was reduced to hunger and misery. I am sorry for what I did. That was a desperate time for me.

He was sentenced to the *amende honorable in figuris* at the portal of Notre-Dame Cathedral (wearing a placard inscribed "Thief, recidivist, impostor, and profaner of sacraments"), death by hanging on the Place de Grève, and burning of his corpse to ashes.[25]

Insanity was understood to be a malady that, in its various forms, destroyed or severely impaired reason and moral discernment.[26] Its compulsions negated freedom of will, and thus absolved the offender of criminal responsibility. Those compulsions were thought to be interior, either physiological or purely mental. Eighteenth-century jurists and magistrates regarded impulses such as "magical spells" or "demonic possession" as evidence either of extreme gullibility or insane delusion, although superstitions and vulnerabilities remained strong in popular sensibility. The mental universe of the law was "demagicalized," dominated by conceptions of rational behavior; but it was not yet refined by a psychology of abnormality.

If an incriminated act was committed by someone deemed insane at the time of the act, that defendant was beyond penal liability. "The mad do not sin, either before God or before man."[27] By a rule equally general during the eighteenth century, the insane were to be confined, either in the family household or in an institution.[28] The insane who were prosecuted for violating the criminal law were those whom the familial, administrative, and medical grid of confinement had not managed to ensnare or retain, and they were often poor, rural, or vagabond.

Lower courts were not empowered to judge defendants insane and exempt them from punishment, even if their behavior during trial was deranged. They were obliged by rulings of the Parlement of Paris, in 1702 and 1738, to try defendants for the crimes of which they were accused, according to the general

[25] Provostial judgment, February 11, 1762, A.N. Y 10517. Burglary of this sort was a statutory death offense, and his culpability was compounded by the repeated sacrilege. But there was dissension on the bench in his case, undoubtedly because of his age and circumstances; the death sentence prevailed only on the third round of voting among the seven judges.

[26] " 'Démence': C'est l'état d'une personne dont la raison est affoiblie au point d'ignorer si ce qu'elle fait est bien ou mal" (Guyot, vol. 5, p. 393). "Fury" was a violent form of dementia: "La Fureur est un emportement violent causé par un déreglement habituel de l'esprit & de la raison" (Guyot, vol. 8, p. 670). The terms *folie, demence, déreglement d'esprit*, and *délire* were often used interchangeably by jurists and magistrates.

[27] Serpillon, vol. 1, p. 396. Insanity or lucidity at the time of the criminal act, not at the time of trial and judgment, was the decisive consideration.

[28] Ibid., vol. 1, p. 398; Muyart, *Loix criminelles*, p. 28. Institutional confinement was in various royal prisons throughout France, by ministerial *lettre de cachet* when requested by the family, and in internment hospitals, when requested by directors, secretaries of state, and various magistrates, after a hearing and medical examination. Great numbers of the violently or self-destructively insane were confined in those institutions at the request of their kin, to prevent them from committing criminal acts. See P. Sérieux and M. Trénel, "L'internemant des aliénés par voie judiciaire (sentence d'interdiction) sous l'Ancien Régime," in *RHDFE*, 10 (1931): 450–86, and "L'internement par 'ordre de justice' des aliénés et des correctionnaires sous l'ancien régime," *RHDFE*, 11 (1932): 413–62.

procedure of the 1670 Criminal Ordinance. Seemingly insane behavior during interrogation by judges and confrontation with witnesses was duly recorded. Lower court judges were also to hear and record all evidence or testimony of insanity before, during, or subequent to the crime, in the course of inquiry into "justificatory facts" regarding a defendant. But they were obliged to convict those found guilty of charges and to render the appropriate penal sentence. Insanity was decided only by the Tournelle of the Parlement of the jurisdiction on appeal and in final judgment of the case.[29] It was decided from the records of the original trial, the verbal and physical behavior of the defendant in appellate trial, and the results of his examination by a physician and a surgeon of the Parlement. Physicians' and surgeons' reports were crucial. But, as Muyart de Vouglans stated, this was a "summary inquest."[30]

Jurists and magistrates were concerned with manifestations, or evidence, of insanity, not with its etiology; with the results of medical diagnosis, not with diagnostic methods. The silence of juristic literature regarding types of insanity suggests that forensic criteria were limited and crude – incoherent speech or raving, withdrawal, hysterical agitation, violent behavior during trial.[31] Many genuine paranoiacs and schizophrenics were probably found sane and sentenced to banishment, the galleys, or the scaffold. Magistrates would not have been inclined to pronounce insanity verdicts against defendants whose derangement was not obvious, for procedural time and energy had been expended to determine that the defendant had committed the crime; defendants could feign insanity; and the insanity verdict meant impunity for the crime.

The Parlement of Paris rarely found defendants insane. In 1736, from the entire jurisdiction there were only five insanity verdicts, among almost 350 persons judged on appeal; in 1762, two verdicts among more than 650 defendants; in 1787, eight verdicts among almost 750 defendants.[32] Fifteen, among some 1,750 defendants, is less than 1 percent. Nine of the 15 judged insane had been convicted of an act of murderous violence; 6 of these had been sentenced to death, 3 to incarceration for life, by a lower court. The others had been convicted of rape, arson, assault, horse theft, or theft with sacrilege and sentenced originally to banishment, the galleys, or the *hôpital-général.* All but one of the 15 were from rural jurisdictions. There was only one woman among them: Marie Pléau, convicted of arson in 1736 at Vertilly and originally sentenced to hanging.

[29] Serpillon, vol. 3, pp. 904–5; Jousse, *Traité*, vol. 2, pp. 620–4; Amiot, vol. 1, p. 33. Those rulings were enforced. In 1787, Etienne Mally, an occasional beggar, was tried for homicidal assault by the presidial court at Riom and pronounced insane. The Parlement nullified that verdict and ordered the bailliage of the Palais de Justice to re-try Mally in first instance. The bailliage court found him guilty and sentenced him to hang; the Parlement then judged the case on appeal, found Mally insane, and sentenced him to internment at Bicêtre (Inventory 450, vol. 4).
[30] Muyart *Loix criminelles*, p. 28.
[31] Other research would be required to determine the methods used by physicians and surgeons of the Parlement in diagnosing insanity among defendants.
[32] Inventory 450.

"Criminally insane" does not describe such persons and judgments. Since crime signified a discerning and deliberate action, the insane could not be criminals. But they were not innocent, for they had violated the law, and they were dangerous. They existed in a semantic limbo, whose only clarity was given by the notion of insanity. If found guilty of a criminal act, they were incarcerated indefinitely or for life, usually in an establishment of the *hôpital-général.* That was the fate of ten of the fifteen persons found insane by the Parlement in 1736, 1762, and 1787. Such persons were not segregated within those establishments from other demented inmates who had been committed by *lettre de cachet* or by the directors of the *hôpitaux.* Their incarcerations were conceived as social defense, not as punishment.

There was a gray zone, in eighteenth-century judicial doctrine and practice, between madness and coleric or irrational episodes, between the malady of insanity and isolated moments of overwhelming rage or aggressiveness among those who were usually rational and discerning. Magistrates tended to distinguish the latter cases by searching the evidence for a strong pattern of lucid behavior. If they found it, they regarded the defendant as criminally responsible for his action, especially if the rage that produced the act had a proximate and exterior cause or provocation. Rage over betrayal by a wife, husband, or friend; extreme sensitivity and aggressiveness that came from sorrow over recent loss of a loved one; violent fear provoked by threats or danger: Those passions could overwhelm moral reason, but they were not delusional. They comported with responsibility for crime but usually resulted in pardon or mitigated punishment.[33] However, if the enraged or aberrant behavior was recurrent and wanton (without reasonable cause), magistrates tended to regard the defendant as insane and immune from penalty if the crime was committed during such an episode. Jousse gave an example of how judges distinguished between insane and intentional violence:

If one man kills another with whom he had no contention, and for no apparent reason, if he does so in public, without any preceding quarrel, and if the killer stays at the site, without fleeing or hiding, then one should presume that the killer was demented at the time of the act; but the contrary should be presumed if the defendant had quarreled with the person whom he killed or wounded, and if he attempted to flee or hide after his act.[34]

The distinction was coarse and fragile, for various shadings of lucidity and will could be involved in both cases.

Dol, or evil and harmful intent, was a venerable Christian (and pagan Roman) idea that existed widely beyond the law, in common moral sensibility. It was invoked every time the sacrament of confession was administered. But law

---

[33] "La colere & l'emportement contribuent aussi à diminuer la peine du crime, sur-tout quand cette colere est occasionné par une cause légitime. . . . Mais il faut que cet emportement, ou cette colere, soit tel qu'il ne laisse pas mâitre de soi-même, & qu'on n'ait pas eu le temps de la réflexion" (Jousse, *Traité,* vol. 2, p. 615).

[34] Ibid., pp. 620–1.

and jurisprudence rigidly circumscribed its meaning. They did not differentiate between intent to commit a crime and motive, or the subjective reason for the intent and act. The "cause" according to which an act was judged criminal or not criminal, in the phrase of Muyart, was defined in terms of malice, negligence, ignorance, or accident; the specific and conscious motive for the act was not a major consideration in that judgment. Motives were classified summarily and negatively (greed, ambition, anger, hatred, lust, impiety) and then subsumed under intent. By making sheer will to criminal act decisive, jurists foreclosed possible justifications of such will among those who might have adduced morally compelling motives. Furthermore, the relations between will and action were formulated in a solipsistic manner, for some of the most important cases: To perform a criminal act such as theft or assault knowingly, deliberately, and by choice was to do so, ipso facto, with malice and intent to harm; those qualities of mind were deduced from the "nature" of such crimes, not induced from knowledge of the defendant; thus, in those cases, the act contained and manifested the intent, regardless of motive.

Others, especially defendants guilty of criminal acts, could have privately construed intent differently: "I did perform the prohibited act, but I did not do so maliciously or with evil intent, for I was personally justified in doing so." And the private justifications by motive and context could have been the following: "the tradesman, merchant or affluent bourgeois from whom I stole has a superfluity of wealth, whereas I do not have the minimum necessary for a decent existence; the person I assaulted grievously insulted me and my family, and my loyalty to self and kin obliged me to avenge and correct that insult; I indeed rioted, fought the constabulary, and broke into warehouses, because that is the only way we could stop hoarding of vital commodities or even procure them; my husband beats and degrades me and our children and, since I cannot divorce, I killed him to save myself and them." These intentions, expressed as motives, are not malicious. They were principled and even altruistic. But such self-justifications were either not admissible, or barely admissible, in legal assessment of culpability. By the definition of *dol*, those intentions and actions remained criminal in law and subject to punishment. If such motives were credited by judges, they could lead only to a lesser penalty among the range of penalties applicable to the crime. They could not annul criminality or penal liability.

Legal rigidity on the issue of intent had a major consequence. It gave defendants a moral reason, in addition to a practical reason, not to confess their crimes during trial. Defendants who did confess to the act for which they were tried virtually condemned themselves to punishment, as will be explained in Part III, Chapter 14. Beyond that notorious danger, the hypothetical defendant who believed his action to be justified, even morally imperative, would betray himself by confessing, for he would be surrendering to the legal definition of crime (malicious intent and prohibited act) that he inwardly refused. The law did not allow him a confession that distinguished between avowal of the act, implicit or explicit avowal of intent to perform the act, and denial of moral culpability. The law forced him to either accept or reject its own parochial definition of immorality. Denial was the only coherent option for such a defendant. Thus, there were two great barriers to confession by the guilty: the fact that it led most often to conviction and punishment, and the less obvious but no less genuine fact that confession was dishonest for defendants who believed themselves morally justified in performing the acts for which they were prosecuted. Complete denial – of both act and intent – was the most common choice among the defendants tried by the Châtelet and Parlement during the eighteenth century.

8

Purposes

On August 3, 1751, the Tournelle of the Parlement of Paris sentenced Jean Masson, "dit Pandour," to death by hanging on the place de Grève for robbery of his employer and murder of a tavern girl at Versailles. That was the penalty in law for intentional homicide. On the late afternoon of August 4, in the shadow of the gallows at the Grève, he confessed to both crimes before the priest–confessor and the two judges supervising the execution (Jean-Baptiste-Gaspard Bochart de Saron and Etienne-François d'Aligre). The priest intoned the final blessing for the condemned, and the ritual prayers for Masson's soul were sung by the crowd. The executioner (Charles-Jean-Baptiste Sanson) led Masson up the gallows ladder, tightened the noose, and thrust him into the air. The rope broke, and he fell to the ground. Sanson retied the rope and Masson was manhandled back up the ladder to be thrust out again. The rope parted a second time. To complete the execution of sentence, Bochart de Saron and d'Aligre ordered Sanson to strangle Masson to death on the ground with the noose. As he did so, the front ranks of the large crowd surged forward shouting, "Pardon him! Pardon him! Have mercy!" They halted when the encircling guards turned around, closed ranks, and leveled their bayonets. Sanson and his assistants retied the rope, then hoisted and held Masson's strangled corpse high up on the gallows, to demonstrate that he had indeed been hanged "until death ensues" by judgment of the Parlement.[1]

Accidents such as a defective rope were rare in Parisian executions, but they did sometimes occur. The judges had no authority to retract the sentence against Masson or to suspend his execution.[2] Their determination to carry through the sentence against him was dictated by the criminal law and the doctrine of punishment that informed the law.

It is not from cruelty that judges have the criminal who has evaded the instrument of execution brought back to that instrument; justice has no desire to sate itself on his blood; it proportions the scale of punishments to the enormity of crimes only to inspire horror of crimes, and that is why executions are performed in public and on days when

[1] A.N. AD III 8; A.N. X2b 1334.
[2] They were forbidden to do either by Article 92 of the Ordinance of Blois, May 1579 (Isambert, vol. 14, p. 404) and Article 21, Title XXV of the Criminal Ordinance, August 1670 (ibid., vol 18, p. 418).

there will be a maximum of spectators; it is necessary, for the preservation of social order, that death sentences be executed, no matter what accident occurs. If judges subscribed to the beliefs of the people, who are constantly ready to perceive the marvellous and supernatural and usually describe as miracles events that are merely extraordinary, then one would often find marvellous reasons to spare the guilty. That would give impunity to crimes. . . . Besides, judges do not have authority to pardon; their power over a defendant is consummated when they have judged him, and they cannot revoke their judgments. They are obliged to ensure that those judgments are executed.[3]

The Parlement of Paris followed the same logic in the case of Louis Martin. In December 1737, the *maréchaussée* of Orléans arrested and jailed him on charges of theft. He hanged himself in his cell while awaiting trial by the presidial court of Orléans. Suicide, a mortal sin, was also a capital offense in law. The provost of the *maréchaussée*, on his own initiative, canceled the theft charge against Martin and had him buried. The judges of the presidial vigorously protested the illegality of the provost's action. They claimed, in an appeal to the Parlement, that the jail and Martin's corpse were under the jurisdiction of the court, not the provost, and that Martin's suicide was in fact a new crime that required trial, judgment, and punishment. The cadaver should have been preserved until the conclusion of that trial. The Parlement ruled in favor of the presidial and ordered it to try the "memory" of Louis Martin on the charge of suicide, with a court-appointed trustee, or *curateur,* standing for him during the trial:

It is no longer a question of punishing the prisoner, it is the cadaver and the memory of the prisoner – over which the first judge [the provost] had no authority – that must be stigmatized; this is a fresh crime that cannot be regarded as a sequel to the first, alleged crimes, because liability for those crimes was annulled by death. . . . The principle of law is fixed in this case; conviction of the memory of the accused [on the charge of suicide] is equivalent to a death sentence.[4]

The law prescribed that if Martin was found guilty of suicide, either his cadaver or a picture of him was to be dragged on a frame through the streets of the town and then hanged from the gallows in the main public square.[5]

The execution of Masson, the trial of Martin *in memoriam* for suicide, and Serpillon's commentary proceeded from the doctrine of Old Regime legal punishment. Doctrine made such rigor necessary.

The Old Regime doctrine of legal punishment was complex, for it combined heritages of Roman law and canon law with monarchical ideology and utilitarian goals. It was at once religious and secular, as well as retributive and utilitarian.

---

[3] Serpillon, vol. 3, p. 1101.
[4] A.N. AD III 31. The procedure for trying the memory of a deceased defendant was set forth in the five articles of Title XXII of the 1670 Criminal Ordinance; such trials were restricted to deceased persons accused of capital crimes (Isambert, vol. 18, pp. 414–15).
[5] Jousse, *Traité,* vol. 1, p. 55.

Every penal sentence by the Châtelet and Parlement identified the convicted person by name and occupation or social condition; described the crime and named the victim in the case; stated the formulaic phrase "for amends of which," and then stated the punishment. Almost all of those sentences were announced publicly. Royal courts did not punish in the name of the victims of specific crimes, although they did punish on behalf of those victims. They punished in the name of law and order: "The issue is always the same: public order has been disrupted, and the general interest requires punishment [of the criminal] for that disruption and the reestablishment of order."[6] A crime was a "wound" or a "lesion" to public order (not merely to the victim) that could be remedied only by punishment of the guilty. Thus, the meaning of crime and punishment included the discrete relation between victim and aggressor but far surpassed that relation.

Retribution, understood as reparation, had distinct material forms in Old Regime penology. The first was the *réparation civile,* or award of material indemnity to plaintiff. Either the convicted person made the payment voluntarily (or arranged for it to be made) or an agent of justice distrained his money and goods to make the payment. This levy took precedence over all other fines paid from the property of the convicted; it was for "the actual harm caused the victim by the crime" and was "a legitimate debt owed by the condemned."[7] Those sums, when they could be collected by agents of the court, were in many cases reparations more symbolic than real, for they often bore little relation to the nature of the crime or the magnitude of personal loss and damage suffered by the victim. The second was the *amende,* or public monetary reparation. It was paid to the king and lawcourt, as both indemnity for the costs of trial and a form of punishment for the crime. It was classified as a defaming penalty, and it accompanied most other punishments. In the practice of the Châtelet and Parlement of Paris, such fines ranged from 3 livres, for a minor crime, to 200 livres for a serious offense. Sentences of death, incarceration for life, or banishment for life from France were also sentences of "civil death" that meant confiscation of all property. The profits of confiscation were awarded both to plaintiffs and to the state. And there was also reparation by alms, levied against those convicted of sacrilege or murder for payment to the Church. In the case of murder, the alms were to ensure that masses would be sung for the soul of the murder victim.[8]

These material retributions were subsidiary elements of punishment, in doctrine and practice. The actual punishments were themselves the essential retribution – at once act, experience, and symbol. This was expressed most clearly and dramatically in the public humiliation of the criminal, the *amende honorable in figuris* that accompanied most death sentences for violent capital offenses. It was a secular paraphrase of the sacraments of confession and pen-

---

[6] Clément L'Averdy, *Code pénal ou Recueil des principales ordonnances, édits et déclarations sur les crimes et délits, avec un Essai sur l'esprit & les motifs de la Procédure criminelle* (Paris, 1765) p. v.
[7] Muyart, *Loix criminelles,* p. 86.   [8] On reparations, see ibid., pp. 82–7.

itence. Bareheaded, barefooted, clothed only in the long woolen shirt of the condemned, wearing a placard hung from a string around his neck that proclaimed the crime, and carrying a large burning candle, the condemned person was led in broad daylight to the main door of a church. There he had to kneel, loudly proclaim his crime and the names of its victims, and then beg forgiveness of "God, the King, and Justice."[9] Retribution by those entities and the public order that they represented was generic to virtually all punishments in criminal law.

Penal doctrine was also utilitarian:

The great benefits that our subjects have received from the care that we have devoted to reforming civil procedure by our ordinances of April 1667 and August 1669 have persuaded us to give similar attention to criminal procedure, which is all the more important because not only does it preserve individuals in the peaceful enjoyment of their property, as with civil justice, but is also secures public order and restrains by the fear of punishment those who are not restrained by their sense of duty.[10]

The defense of property rights; protection of public order; restraint of the predatory and anarchic: Those were the grand purposes ascribed to criminal justice by Louis XIV. They were venerable purposes, stated habitually in the preambles to royal criminal edicts from at least the sixteenth century.[11] They

---

[9] As happened to René Plé, condemned to the *amende honorable* and to breaking on the cross and the wheel by the Parlement of Paris in December 1784, for poisoning and robbery: "condamne le dit René Plé a faire amende honorable au-devant de la principale porte de l'Eglise de Paris [Nôtre-Dame], ou il sera conduit dans un tombereau par l'Exécuteur de la Haute Justice, nuds pieds, nue tête & en chemise, tenant en ses mains un torche ardente de cire jaune du poids de deux livres, ayant écriteau devant & derrière portant ces mots: (*Empoisonneur & Voleur*); & là, étant à genoux, dire & déclarer à haute & intelligible voix, que méchamment, témérairement & comme mal avisé, il a, sous le faux nom de Dubois, de complicité avec Jacques Flatté, dit l'Oiseau, ci-devant condamné et executé à mort, & un quidam, fait entrer le nommé Paul Bourgeois, vigneron, agé de soixante-quinze ans, dans une Auberge de Châteaugaillard, sous prétexte d'une gageure qui avoit été concertée entr'eux, & dont le prix étoit une bouteille de vin, dans laquelle Auberge ils ont fait prendre audid Bourgeois, dans un vin chaud, que l'un d'eux s'étott chargé de préparer, une liqueur narcotique, assoupissante & pernicieuse, au moyen de laquelle ledit Bourgeois, après être parti de laditte Auberge, a perdu connoissance sur la route à une demi-lieue de Chateaugaillard, est tombé dans un sommeil léthargique, dont ils ont profité pour lui voler onze cens & quelques livres en or, & une tasse d'argent qu'il avoit sur lui, & par l'effet de laquelle liqueur ledit Bourgeois a été privé de l'usage de la parole pendant vingtquatre heures, & grièvement incommodé pendant cinq jours, sans pouvoir se rendre chez lui, dont il se repent & demande pardon à Dieu, au Roi & à la Justice; ce fait, ledit René Plé, mené dans le même tombereau en la Place de Grève, pour, sur un échafaud qui y sera à cet effet dressé, avoir les bras, jambes, cuisses & reins rompus vif par ledit Exécuteur de la Haute-Justice, & à l'instant jetté dans un bûcher ardent, pour ce pareillement dressé en laditte place, pour y être réduits en cendres, & les cendres jettées au vent" (A.N. AD III 15). Poisoning was made a mandatory death offense by royal edict in July 1682 (Isambert, vol. 19, pp. 396–401).

[10] Preamble to the 1670 Criminal Ordinance, in Isambert, vol. 18, pp. 371–2.

[11] As with Francis I's 1534 edict that mandated death by breaking for highway robbery and for burglary by forced entry: "Nous à ces causes, qui désirons sur toutes choses pourvoir à la tranquillité et seureté de nostredit peuple, et en tant que possible nous est, punir et corriger tels délicts, crimes et maléfices, et faire cesser lesdites entreprises, conspirations et machinations, dont sont advenus et adviennent chaque jour plusieurs maux exécrables en nostredit royaume" (Isambert, vol. 12, p. 401). Or Louis XV's 1730 edict mandating the death penalty for abduction

were elaborated by all eighteenth-century French jurists. Those ends of justice required the use of punishment, for

however intrinsically wise the Law may be, it would soon become useless to society, for whose welfare it has been established, if he who made the Law did not have the power to command respect for its authority by the punishment of those who wish to defy that authority. Therefore, the power to inflict penalties is the most essential element of Legislation, because that power alone can give strength to the Law and assure, by such means, peace and tranquillity within a State. That power, known as the Power of Life and Death, because it encompasses the lives of men, can only belong to the supreme authority that Divine Providence confers on Sovereigns. Sovereigns cannot always exercise that power themselves, because of the great extent of their States, and are obliged to confide its exercise to Judges whom they appoint, while reserving for themselves only the right of pardon, as befits Royal Majesty.[12]

Without punishment there could be no empire of the law over crimes, criminals, and the generality of civil society. Punishment was regarded as the foundation of criminal justice. Incrimination of behavior; penal liability and immunity; arrest, trial, and judgment; acquittal for the innocent; attenuation of penalty for those with mitigating circumstances; royal pardon or commutation of penalty for some of the guilty: Those acts of justice had meaning only through their relationship to punishment, without which "crimes would not be a matter of human laws, and would be ruled only by Divine Law."[13] Punishment gave force to the law and its commands and was thus the only means by which the law could exact compliance from those given or inclined to criminality. Legal punishment was all the more imperative because "victims of crime are never allowed to take justice into their own hands, except in instances of legitimate self-defense against aggression."[14] The hierarchy in punishments, from the most benign to the most devastating, established and proclaimed for the public the official moral hierarchy of crimes. It also proclaimed, by inversion of those crimes, the hierarchy of officially cherished and protected values.

and seduction (of either a male or female) for the purpose of forcing marriage: "Toutes les ordonnances qui ont été faites par les rois nos prédécesseurs, pour prévenir ou pour punir le rapt de séduction, ont eu principalement en vue d'affermir l'autorité des pères sur leurs enfants, d'assurer l'honneur et la liberté des marriages, et d'empêcher que des alliances indignes par la corruption des moeurs, encore plus que par l'inégalité des conditions, ne flétrissent l'honneur de plusieurs familles illustres, et ne deviennent souvent la cause de leur ruine: c'est par des traits si marqués que les lois ont pris soin de caractériser ce genre de crime, qu'elles ont appelé rapt de séduction. . . . Nous le devons à la sainteté de la religion, pour empêcher qu'on n'abuse d'un grand sacrement, en unissant deux coupables par un lien forcé, sans observer les solennités prescrites par les lois de l'Eglise et de l'Etat" (Isambert, vol. 21, pp. 338–9).

[12] Muyart, *Loix criminelles*, p. 38. The reasoning of Daniel Jousse was identical: "En effet la punition des crimes est la fin & le but principal de l'administration de la Justice, qui est de conserver les sujets du Roi dans une paix & une tranquillité durable, & d'entretenir entre eux le bien de la société, sans lequel auçun gouvernement ne sauriot subsister; ce qui ne peut se faire, si les excès & délits qui la troublent, ne sont réprimés par une punition prompte & exemplaire" (*Traité*, vol. 1, pp. i–ii. Cf. also Serpillon, vol. 1, p. 2).

[13] Domat, p. 196.   [14] Jousse, *Traité*, vol. 1, p. vii.

If men were not disturbed by passions and by delusions, shame alone would be a force sufficient to prevent them from unjust acts; but those passions are so strong in some persons, and dominate them so completely, that it is absolutely necessary to employ means more rigorous than shame, such as the fear of chastisement, in order to prevent them from committing crimes that are urged by their passions. All crimes that supervene in society have their source in the frivolity and inconstancy of the human mind, in lack of education, in corrupted desire, and even in contempt for Religion and the Laws, from which are born greed, idleness, debauchery, vengefulness, ambition and all the rest of life's disorders; and those passions often have a dominion so powerful over certain persons that even the fear of chastisement and torment is not sufficient to restrain them.[15]

According to this vision, all persons were subject, at least momentarily, to malicious or anarchic desires and therefore had capacity for evil and crime. That was the sense of Jousse's admonition that a judge must learn from those guilty of crimes the lesson of this own moral fragility, and of d'Aguesseau's insistence on introspection and self-discipline among magistrates. Most persons were restrained from acting on those desires by internalized disciplines other than fear of punishment, by moral sociability and fear of shame. Many others were not so restrained. Punishment was a permanent warning for the former and a permanent threat for the latter. For warning and threat to be credible and dissuasive, punishment of the guilty had to occur publicly. This was especially true in a civilization without mass communication media, one intensely local, where popular cognition was visual and aural. Whenever possible, legal punishments were inflicted publicly in the locality (village, town, or city) where the crime had been committed – for immediate deterrent example, for the shaming of the malefactor within his or her community, and also "as reparation for the scandal caused there by the crime, and to give consolation to those who have suffered from the crime."[16] The state incurred considerable expense to accomplish punishment *in situ*: For example, a person convicted of theft at Limoges by the presidial court there was transported under guard to Paris for final judgment on appeal; if the Parlement upheld the conviction and decreed even a sentence as banal as whipping, branding, and exposure in the iron collar, the person was usually transported back to Limoges for execution of that sentence.

Punishment as threat was addressed explicitly to the morally exceptional, to those who were not habitually restrained from committing crimes by religion,

---

[15] Ibid., p. ii. And Muyart: "le désir et la crainte; scavoir, le désir d'acquérir les choses qu'on n'a pas; & la crainte de perdre celles qu'on a. C'est de là en effet que l'on a vu naitre des inimités, l'envie, l'ambition & la cupidité; autant de passions funestes qui, étouffant dans les hommes des sentiments d'honneur & de justice que la Loi naturelle avoit gravés dans leurs coeurs, les ont entrainés insensiblement aux plus grands désordres. . . . Il a fallu nécessairement leur donner un frein plus puissant par la crainte des chatimens extérieurs, qui les empechent de nuire davantage à la société, en même temps qu'ils servent à la venger du scandale & du tort réel que le Crime lui a causé" (*Loix criminelles*, p. 38). Domat found the source of crimes in those same universal passions but added that their force is exacerbated by social and material conditions such as poverty, unemployment, and vagabondage (pp. 197–8).

[16] Muyart, *Loix criminelles*, p. 49.

family, profession, corporation, or general sociability; thus, to the actually criminal and to all potential criminals. As warning, its reverberations were wider and more subtle: It was suspended over every honest bourgeois momentarily tempted by fraud; over every dutiful officer or clerk tempted by peculation or forgery; over every obedient journeyman or domestic servant tempted by pilferage; over every needy plebeian tempted to riot; over every ordinary man and woman seized by lust, jealousy, or despair; over every respectable subject tempted to avenge a personal affront by violence. Its prescriptive audience was universal.

Jurists and themistocrats believed that "public order" or "social order" did not and could not exist without the criminal law. This was so despite the authority wielded by the Church, schools, and *collèges*, village and town councils, craft and commercial guilds, seigneurial landlords, and the multiplicity of other institutions in French society, and despite the fact that most of those entities had the power to punish their members with a fine, censure, suspension, ostracism, or a ritual of shaming. In the themistocratic mind, those institutions contributed to public order but remained dependents of criminal law. Law was far more than a last buttress of other agencies for social and moral discipline. It necessarily included and subsumed all of them within its protective jurisdiction. One of the most hyperbolic statements of that necessity was by Guillaume Le Trosne:

Insatiable appetite for gain, cruel vengeance, implacable hatred, murderous envy, jealous love, frantic debauchery: All passions, in a thousand different forms, combine against public security; they would burst forth and make of society a dreadful theater of treachery, horror, and carnage if justice did not present a salutary bulwark against such a torrent of crimes, if the gleaming sword in its hand was not always raised to threaten, strike, and punish the guilty. It is thus principally by the exercise of criminal justice that civil order exists and is preserved.[17]

Old Regime legal punishment was grounded in a conception of personality according to which conscience and rationality were in permanent struggle with impulses toward sin and crime, a Roman Catholic conception of humanity. Conscience and rationality were immanent capacities of humankind, but they had to be developed, educated, and continually reinforced, for they were constantly besieged by dangerous passions. Moral personality was malleable during an entire lifetime. No one was predestined to either salvation or damnation. By faith, contrition, repentance, and observing the sacraments, even the worst evildoer could win salvation, in the very last moments of life – even on the gallows or the breaking cross. Legal punishment – like the catechism, the mass, and the other sacraments – was a pedagogy in conscience. The criminal law was understood to be the ultimate and indispensable guardian of morality. Royal magistrates were, in secular life, ethical counterparts to the clergy. The punitive

---

[17] *Vues sur la justice criminelle*, 2 vols. (Paris, 1783), vol. 1, p. 245.

intervention of law occurred when virtually all other normative agencies were either absent or had failed to prevent the criminal action. Legal doctrine invested that intervention with spiritual value, in addition to other values. Judgment and punishment provided the occasion for the intercession, in extremis, of priests with malefactors. Priests were on duty inside jails and other penal institutions of Old Regime France. They had literally captive audiences for the sacrament of confession and for sermons during obligatory mass. They ministered to those who were condemned to death, from the beginning to the end of the ritual of execution. Just as lesser punishments were always penitential occasions, a death sentence was always an opportunity for salvation for the condemned. If he believed and repented, divine grace could "reach into the midst of his suffering, as happened with the thief [crucified with Jesus], who in the final moment of his life made of his torment a passage to Heaven."[18]

The first purpose of the Law in establishing penalties, a purpose that concerns all criminals except those condemned to death, is to correct by punishment, such that offenders are taught to expect new penalties if they commit new crimes. The second, which concerns only very serious crimes and those which are punished by death, is to render the guilty incapable of new crimes by inflicting the death penalty or other capital penalties. The third, which is intrinsic to all penalties and forms of punishment, is example – to restrain by the sight and fear of punishment those who are not otherwise restrained from crime, and who will abstain from evildoing only from fear of chastisement.[19]

Punishments were intended to work didactically both on the punished and on those who witnessed them. The "correction" of criminals by punishment was instruction by aversion: "This shameful, painful, or privational experience is the consequence of your evil intention and action; you will endure a more intense version of this experience if you commit another such action." The expectation was that the shame and social deprivation of whipping, public exposure, or banishment from the community for three or five years would far outweigh, in the memory of the victim, the rewards from an act of theft or casual assault, or that years of incarceration at hard labor (in *galères* and *bagnes*) or (for women) in the prisons of the *hôpital-général* would countervail any further impulses to serious theft, assault, or riot. It was also moral instruction (in a penitential sense), designed to persuade the guilty that their crimes were wrong and to induce a change in ethical attitude.

The recurrent sight of punishments was expected to produce a similar effect on the audiences, through empathetic identification with the punished: "If I commit his crime, I am likely to suffer his fate." Legal punishment was presumed to address at least a lowest common denominator of rational self-interest

---

[18] Domat, p. 197.

[19] Jousse, *Traité*, vol. 1, p. iii. Those were the main consensual aims of punishment in legal doctrine. Cf. Domat, p. 205; Ferrière, *Dictionnaire*, vol. 1, p. 345; Muyart, *Les loix criminelles*, p. 39; Guyot, vol. 13, p. 64.

among victims and audiences.[20] Public chastisements – along thoroughfares, at crossroads, on town squares – seem archaic and barbarous to modern Western sensibility (especially among intellectuals). But the purposes that underlay those chastisements – correction and deterrence – are not archaic. They remain the basic purposes of contemporary criminal justice. Only the forms, of punishment and publicity, have changed.

Exemplary punishment was expected to compensate for chronic weaknesses: in human nature; in the disciplining powers of religion, family, parish, corporation, and profession; in policing. Magistrates could always insist that such punishment had a didactic effect on the audience, precisely because the true effect could never be measured. Jurists recognized that even spectacular punishment could not dissuade the resolutely or desperately criminal. Those convicted of major crimes had obviously scorned the law's threat and had not been deterred by examples of punishment. In their persons, however, a failure of antecedent punishments was transformed into a resource for the law. They were simultaneously removed from society, by long or permanent incarceration or execution, and made to serve as examples to dissuade other, anonymous persons with a proclivity to such crimes. Thereby, social good could be produced by the law from the social evil accomplished by criminals. Since the numbers of the genuinely dissuaded could never be ascertained, jurists could assert that they were numerous. And they did so vehemently, despite the steady increase in the volume of serious crimes during the eighteenth century.

It is beyond doubt that one of the most certain means to prevent crimes and to diminish the number of criminals is to punish those who commit them in ways that make an example for others. For that reason, executions are usually performed not in prisons but in public spaces and in the most frequented sites, with a solemn display of all that can intimidate the people. And although the fear of suffering is not sufficient to prevent all crimes . . . it is nevertheless certain that punishments make crimes less frequent. If they were not punished by example, their quantity would increase daily and end by overturning the State.[21]

---

[20] The goal was expressed in more refined psychological terms by Domat: "Car comme aucun ne se porte au crime que par quelque amour illicite d'un objet qui excite la passion, on ne peut arrêter la violence de la passion qu'en substituant à l'objet qu'elle se propose un évenement contraire & assez désagréable pour suspendre sa véhémence; & c'est pour donner aux malfacteurs la vûë de cet évenement qu'on fait des punitions exemplaires, & *qu'on change en ceux qui profitent de l'exemple, le mouvement de l'amour propre & de la passion qui les porte au crime en un mouvement contraire du même amour propre qui, sans éteindre la passion, fuit ou le crime, ou au moins la peine*" (p. 205, italics mine).

[21] Jousse, *Traité*, vol. 1, pp. iii–iv. In defending the death penalty and its public execution from Beccaria's attack (*On Crimes and Punishments*, 1764), the authors of the *Répertoire universel* wrote, "Cette peine est donc utile; elle est donc nécessaire pour le maintien de l'ordre. . . . M. le marquis de Beccaria se fonde encore sur ce que, selon lui, 'l'experience de tous les siècles prouve que la Peine de mort n'a jamais empêché les scélérats déterminés de nuire à la société.' Mais ne peut on demander où sont les monumens qui établissent cette expérience? Ne seroit-il pas au contraire démontré, *si l'on avoit une confession exacte de tous scélérats* [italics mine], que la crainte du dernier supplice a seule empêché qu'ils ne commissent une infinité de crimes?" (vol. 13, p. 64).

Crimes were understood to be contagious by example. Exemplary punishment was a kind of psychological quarantine designed to create a barrier in public consciousness between crimes and their emulation. But assertions that the barrier was effective remained conjectural, for all their dogmatism. Exemplary punishment of most crimes, however uncertain its effectiveness, was deemed to be a fundamental necessity; if it were removed, the void created would be filled by thefts, violence, counterviolence, and vendettas.[22] Paradoxically, a dramatic increase in crime during the eighteenth century reinforced that fundamental conviction. Deterence by exemplary legal punishment was a tenacious concept because it was both a strategy of desperation and an incomparable display of authority.

In a sense, the ubiquitous theater, the constantly reenacted Old Regime drama of legal punishment, turned on itself. It had masses of protagonists and spectators but few determinable consequences. Its utility remained conjectural. The incidence of crimes prosecuted constantly grew between 1735 and 1789, at a rate greater than the growth of population in the jurisdiction of the Parlement of Paris. The criminal chambers of the Châtelet and Parlement were filled by recidivists. When punishment produced distinct and intended results – removal of offenders by banishment from the locality, incarceration, or death – it did so in ways that did not depend at all on spectacle. The authors of most crimes in urban areas were social analogs to the people who formed the majority in every audience of a public legal punishment. Virtually all of those convicted and punished had witnessed many legal punishments.

The dogma of deterrence by spectacle does not withstand logical and empirical scrutiny; it resembles fantasy or myth. Yet a fantasy can be internally coherent and vitally expressive of realities different from its ostensible referents (correction or deterrence of malefactors). The Old Regime dogma of exemplary legal punishment did bring into harmonious union the two supreme and interdependent moral systems of the civilization: the monarchical state and its themistocracy; and Catholic dogma and the Church. Those systems were frequently at odds, in other spheres of public life. Their harmony on the terrain of criminal justice was therefore all the more precious and dramatic.

Correction and deterrence, the proclaimed goals of punishment, may have been produced occasionally and randomly by the application of legal penalties. But in virtually every application the symbolic union of the judicious paternal state and the redeeming Church was produced. Legal punishments, when publicly enacted or proclaimed, asserted that unitary sovereignty for a world of spectators, and whether the penalty was several hours in the stocks at the

---

[22] "Car encore qu'ils soit vray que les plus grands supplices ne font cesser aucun crime, ils diminuent la fréquence, & l'impunité seroit suivie d'une multitude infinie de toute sorte de crimes. . . . Car les peines sont le seul remède qui peut retenir la license des malfacteurs; & quoique ce remede soit imparfait, & que la force des passions surmonte en plusieurs la crainte de peines, c'est l'unique voye dont on peut user pour contenir le plus grand nombre " (Domat, pp. 196, 205).

Halles, for small-time commercial fraud (a petty crime and venal sin), or breaking on the wheel at the Place de Grève for premeditated murder (a statutory
capital offense and mortal sin). They affirmed ethical rules in a way that demonstrated the capacity of state and Church to enforce those rules, for almost
every crime in law corresponded to a sin in Roman Catholicism. They celebrated the virtuous, by parading and chastising the vicious. The parading of
vices – the offenses proclaimed by court criers, described by placards hung
from the necks of criminals, advertised on posters and handbills – belonged to
the same moral pedagogy as the literature and ceremonies that exalted the lives
of saints. Legal punishments gave controlled release or purgation to public
fears and anger over criminality and were therefore a surrogate for private
vengefulness; in that meaning, they allowed king and themistocracy to display
protective benevolence, even altruism, to their subjects. And those punishments staged expiation. When the punishments were carceral labor in the galley
fleet at Marseilles or the *bagnes* at Brest, Rochefort, and Toulon, they served all
of those needs while also making the convict's expiation of crime and sin a matter of economic utility to the state.

Legal punishment was invested with Catholic spirituality, from the late Middle Ages to the Revolution. Its object was to correct evil intent, or immoral
recklessness and negligence. So long as the highest purpose of life was preparation for salvation, which required atonement for sin, the criminal law offered
a good – a spiritual resource – to the guilty who suffered appropriate punishment. That resource was the crafted opportunity for penance, purgation, and
moral change through the experience of legal punishment, even when the punishment had social or physical finalities. The offer – administered conjointly by
magistrates and priests (the ubiquitous auxiliaries of criminal justice) – mitigated, at least in principle, the severity of harsh penalties, whether or not the
criminal inwardly accepted the offer, and whether or not correction or deterrence resulted from the penal action.

9

Forms

A. Legal infamy

Of all the benefits of Society, the most precious, without question, is Honor; it is the very soul and principle of social existence.[1]

Honor (or, for commoners, good social repute), as the most valuable quality in social life, more valuable even than bodily well-being, property, or personal freedom: That assumption was the source for most of Old Regime legal punishment. Shaming and stigma, not bodily suffering or incarceration, were the core elements of punishment. They were so in two ways: through the elaborate public proclamation, enactment, or display of all but the mildest punishment, and through the stigma of legal infamy that adhered to all those who were convicted of crimes. Legal shaming and stigma were officially presumed either to diminish radically or to ruin irretrievably the honor of their victims and to damage that of their families. This was not mere judicial formalism. In the civilization of Old Regime France, honor (*honneur*) was a supreme value. *Honnêteté* (honesty and integrity) and probity were analogous values among bourgeois, artisans, and farmers.[2] All subjects of the king had rights, but there was no abstract citizenship to confer dignity. Social life-chance – expressed by the acquisition and conservation of wealth, by the possibilities one had for making a desirable marriage, gaining and keeping employment, or achieving a corporatist position – depended on reputation, even among the minimally respectable and propertied. That fact was reflected in the extreme and general sensitivity to insults that impugned honor or honesty; such insults easily unleashed the fist, any weapon to hand, or complaints in law.[3] It was also expressed by the seriousness with which the law regarded the crime of libel – insults that were written, thus both premeditated and durable in effect: "This crime is very serious:

---

[1] Muyart, *Institutes*, p. 412.
[2] As Yves Castan has demonstrated in *Honnêteté et relations sociales en Languedoc (1715–1780)*, (Paris, 1974).
[3] On that sensitivity, see Farge and Zysberg, "Les théâtres de la violence," and Brennan, *Public Drinking*.

to attack the reputation and honor of someone, which are often more precious than life itself, is to commit a kind of homicide."[4]

Infamy was both one of the three distinct categories into which penalties were classified and a quality inherent in the other two.

Legal infamy is the infamy incurred *ipso jure* from condemnation to a corporal or defaming penalty, such as the galleys, whipping, the iron collar, reprimand, etc. . . . The result of such infamy is to render the person in question ineligible for any public dignity, office, or commission. . . . Although such infamy does not deprive an official of property in his office, it does deny him exercise of that office and obliges him to resign the office. The legally infamous are not admitted to sacred Orders. A further consequence of legal infamy is that those who have incurred it cannot testify in civil and criminal cases; they are allowed to do so only if there are no other witnesses in the case; their testimony still remains suspect. . . . Once legal infamy has been incurred it lasts for the remainder of a person's life.[5]

The infamous . . . have lost all attributes that depend on a reputation for honor and probity . . . they are in a sense retrenched from civil society.[6]

Infamy ensued from conviction for a crime subject to defaming, afflictive, or capital penalties, and it began from the time of final sentencing. It was not erased, even if the convicted person received a royal letter of pardon or commutation of sentence for the crime. The stigma and its exclusions were permanent. The legally infamous retained basic property rights, but as persons stripped of "honor and probity" they were ineligible for all offices, commissions, and responsibilities that required those qualities.[7] Their word was officially without value, and they lost the privileges of taking oaths and giving witness.

Old Regime penology was divided into three general categories of punishment: capital, afflictive, and defaming. The condition of legal infamy adhered to all three.

The punishments that are inflicted on the guilty are known as "capital" when they deprive the convict of life or when they deprive him forever of his liberty or his rights. Such are death, galleys for life, banishment for life from the Realm, and incarceration for life. "Afflictive" punishments are those which are not capital but which do either afflict the body or deprive it of liberty. Such are term sentences to the galleys, whipping, branding, the iron collar, and the stocks. "Defaming" punishments are those which dishonor the

---

[4] Jousse, *Traité*, vol. 3, p. 651. Article 179 of the the 1629 Grand Ordinance made writing by hand or printing, and distributing, "écrits diffimatoires et convicieux . . . contre l'honneur et le rénommée des personnes: méme concernant notre personne [the king], nos conseillers, magistrats et officiers" crimes subject to capital penalties ("confiscation of life and property") – that is, incarceration or banishment for life, or death (Isambert, vol. 16, pp. 275–6). Article 5 of the May 10, 1728, Declaration on Printers authorized judges to punish authors and printers of libels against private persons by the iron collar, banishment for terms, or the galleys for terms (Isambert, vol. 21, p. 314).

[5] Jousse, *Traité*, vol. 1, pp. 113–14.   [6] Ferrière, vol. 2, p. 22.
[7] Serpillon, vol. 2, pp. 778–9, and Ferrière, vol. 2, pp. 22–3.

guilty person and make him infamous. Such are the public apology, term sentences to banishment, reprimand, and criminal fines. There are other punishments that are neither afflictive nor defaming. Such are admonition, alms, and warnings to be circumspect, etc.[8]

Article 13, Title 25, of the Criminal Ordinance of 1670 listed the hierarchy of capital and afflictive penalties in descending order of severity:

After the death penalty, the most rigorous is that of torture with retention of evidence, [then] the galleys for life, banishment for life, torture without retention of evidence, galleys for limited terms, whipping, public and abject apology, banishment for limited terms.[9]

Those nine broad levels of punishment included some twenty-five more specific forms of punishment, forms that were carefully defined in law and jurisprudence and used in the jurisdiction of the Parlement of Paris during the seventeenth and eighteenth centuries. This was their official hierarchy, from the most benign to the most severe:

Nondefaming

Alms
Warning or injunction
Interdiction or suspension from office or commission
Whipping in custody of the court (for minors)

Defaming

Fine
Severe reprimand
Forced witnessing of punishment (usually of capital punishment)
Promenading on a donkey

Afflictive

Banishment from the jurisdiction of the court for three, five, or nine years
Exhibition in the iron collar
Exhibition in the stocks
Public and abject apology
Suspension from the gallows by a chest strap (for minors)
Public whipping
Public branding

[8] Guyot, vol. 13, p. 62. See also Jousse, *Traité*, vol. 1, pp. 36–7.
[9] Isambert, vol. 18, p. 417.

Galleys for three, five, or nine years (men); incarceration in a *hôpital-général* for three, five, or nine years (women and men)

Interrogative torture without retention of other evidence

Amputation or splitting of the tongue

Capital

Public dragging (of the felon's corpse) on a frame and condemnation of his memory

Banishment from the realm for life

Galleys for life or incarceration in the *hôpital-général* for life

Interrogative torture with retention of other evidence

Death

Decapitation

Hanging

Dismemberment (drawing and quartering by horses)

Breaking on the Saint Andrew's Cross and exposure on the wheel

Burning at the stake

Death, by any of the above means, preceded by amputation of the hand or mutilation of the body

The Old Regime penal arsenal was abundant and carefully graded in severity. It had far more variety than modern (and French Revolutionary) penology: monetary levies, private and public shaming, exile, incarceration, forced labor, bodily pain, and execution. Two or more punishments were often combined in a sentence. Every punishment in law was a distinct act directed at the convicted person, and thus an experience. The punishments inflicted by the Châtelet and Parlement of Paris from 1736 to 1789, and their victims, are principal subjects of Volume 2. Here, our concern is with the content of the punitive acts.[10]

B. Shaming, stigma, and ostracism

Nondefaming punishments were inflicted privately, within the precincts of criminal courts, jails, or corporations (in the case of interdiction and suspension from office), not given publicity. They did not destroy the honor or reputation of the victim. Alms were a fine assessed by the court; the money went to the

---

[10] The following description of punitive actions is based principally on the sentences in A.N. AD III (Châtelet and Parlement), Y 10514–10530 (Châtelet), works of eighteenth-century criminal jurisprudence, and modern monographs, cited in this chapter. Readers of J. M. Beattie (*Crime and the Courts in England, 1660–1800* [Princeton: Princeton University Press, 1986]) will see that several of the defaming and afflictive punishments were also used in England. The distinctiveness of Old Regime French penology was in the importance of imprisonment and forced labor inside the realm, that of English penology in colonial deportation.

charitable institutions of the Church, the Hôpital-Général, or to pay for the feeding of prisoners. Fines usually accompanied sentences of "admonition" (sometimes expressed as *admonestation* or *défense de récidiver*), whereby the court warned the defendant of his harmful or delictual action and forbade him to repeat it. That sentence was defined as follows by the royal Council, in a ruling of January 11, 1741: "In our language, Admonition signifies no more than a term of charity and shame, not a penal expression; according to the Canonists, it derives from the Evangelist's exhortation for men to warn each other fraternally."[11] This sentence was commonly used for officials who had committed a minor infraction of duty. "Injunction" was similar but more forceful: It was largely reserved for a harmfully or even criminally negligent act performed without malicious intent. Sentences of interdiction or suspension from office were pronounced against public officials for more serious negligence or malfeasance: They were always for a specified period (usually less than a year), during which the official was denied the revenues of office and was replaced by a commissioner. Whipping in custody of the court – by the jailer, either in the jail or in the interrogation chamber of the court – was the customary penalty for minors convicted of noncapital crimes; it was officially a "simple correction," not a defaming punishment.

Fines, or monetary retribution to the state for crimes, were defaming penalties in themselves, although they accompanied most defaming, afflictive, and capital punishments. *Blâme*, or severe reprimand, was pronounced in the criminal chamber. But the condemned person received the sentence in abject posture, bareheaded and kneeling, and it was publicized by the court. It was always combined with alms or fines. Forced witnessing of punishment was a penalty for minors, and sometimes for adults, who were convicted of complicity in crimes that carried afflictive or capital penalties. They were obliged to watch the punishment, even the execution, of their adult accomplices, sometimes including their parents. Sometimes they were tied to the gallows post by a long rope, with a noose around their necks: a literal moral lesson. The promenade on a donkey was reserved for pimps, prostitutes, and adulterers and was combined with a sentence of whipping or banishment. The convict was seated on the donkey, facing the animal's tail. His ankles and wrists were bound with rope. He wore a high, misshapen straw hat and a placard stating his crime. The executioner slowly led the donkey through the city's main streets and squares.

Banishment for three, five, or nine years was the least severe of afflictive punishments. It was usually combined with others, and almost always with a mark that was branded onto the shoulder. It was one of the most frequent penal sentences in eighteenth-century criminal justice, applicable to a wide range of crimes. The banishment was from the jurisdiction of the sentencing court, and

[11] A.N. AD III 27b.

thus usually from the jurisdiction in which the crime had been committed. The *banni* could go wherever he or she pleased – except to Paris or the environs of the royal court. He retained full property rights during the term of sentence and could receive inheritance, annuities, and other payments from the forbidden jurisdiction (but only through intermediaries). The civil restrictions suffered were those of legal infamy. By the royal edicts of March 1682 and April 1687, any *banni* who violated sentence by returning before the expiration of the banishment term could be condemned to serve the remainder of the term, or a longer period, in the galleys or the Hôpital-Général.[12] Such violations were common in Paris during the eighteenth century, although the Châtelet and Parlement did not usually give such offenders the exacerbated punishment stipulated in 1682 and 1687. The formal punitive meaning of banishment was temporary exile from the community of family, friends, parishioners, employer, and workmates. It was also prophylaxis, to remove the offender from the environment and victims of his crime. But, as François Serpillon observed in 1767, often the criminal was only a transient in the jurisdiction where he committed the crime, and in such cases sentence of banishment was an "illusory punishment."[13] This penalty indeed reflected a vision of French plebeian life and criminality that was largely archaic by the eighteenth century. However, it served both as a warning to the *banni* and, because of the brand, a signal of his criminality for police and magistrates during the rest of his life. Yet, when banishment did cut someone off from sustaining family, community, or employment and when its brand made viable employment difficult or impossible to obtain in the region of exile, the punishment became highly criminogenic, leading to vagabondage, begging, and theft. Banishment for life from France was classified in law as a capital punishment and was reserved for crimes that were also punishable by death or by incarceration for life. This sentence could be pronounced only by a Parlement.[14]

The *carcan* was a post, set into a hole in the pavement, to which the convict was attached by a chain and a loose but locked iron collar. He wore a placard that stated his name and crime and was exhibited "to the derision of passersby"[15] for a few hours on one or more days, at different public places. This punishment was frequently ancillary to banishment and carceral penalties. The infliction of the iron collar on Emmanuel-Jean de la Coste was depicted in a contemporary engraving (Figure 9.1); Louis Vanquetin, his accomplice in fraud, was sentenced to witness the punishment and stood tied to the cart behind la Coste. The sentence (August 28, 1760) ordered

[12] That legislation is in Muyart, *Loix criminelles*, pp. 70–1.
[13] *Code criminel*, vol. 3, p. 1084.
[14] Women could not be sentenced to banishment for life from the realm; in such cases, their penalty was "la Détention perpétuelle dans une Maison de force [in a *hôpital*] ou . . . un Bannissement perpétuel hors du Ressort du Parlement. . . . Au reste, cette Peine est ordinairement accompagnée de celle du Fouet" (Muyart, *Institutes*, p. 405).
[15] Ferrière, vol. 1, p. 216.

Figure 9.1. The iron collar. (Original engraving in A.N. AD III 9. Reprinted with permission of the French National Archives.)

Emmanuel-Jean de la Coste to be attached during three consecutive days to a post set for this purpose, the first day on the place de Grève, the second in the carrefour de Bussy, & the third, in the square of the Palais-Royal, to remain there each day from noon to 2 P.M., wearing a placard with these words inscribed: "Swindler, counterfeiter of lottery tickets, author of defaming libels."[16]

The stocks, or *pilori*, of Paris was a small stone building with an open wooden platform surmounted by a roof supported with wooden beams. It could accommodate several victims, as is depicted in the contemporary engraving of three men punished for fraudulent declaration of bankruptcy (Figure 9.2). There was a revolving stock into which the heads and arms of convicts were locked. The stock was slowly turned by the executioner so that the grim countenances and dangling arms of the malefactors would be visible from all directions of the urban compass. They were exposed for two hours of each day specified in the sentence. In eighteenth-century Parisian argot, to be in the stocks was to *faire la grimace*. Until 1785, the Paris stocks were on the square of the Marché des Innocents in the Halles, one of the most densely trafficked areas in the metropolis.[17]

Sentence to abject apology, or *amende honorable*, obliged the convict to loudly confess his crime and malice and to beg forgiveness. There were two forms. *Amende honorable in figuris* (the most punitive) was enacted publicly (as described in Chapter 8). Forgiveness was begged of God, the king, and justice. *Amende honorable seche* was accomplished privately, in the criminal court, where the kneeling and bareheaded malefactor had to beg forgiveness of the offended person. Suspension from the gallows by a special leather chest strap (for no more than one hour) was a punishment reserved for minors (*impubères*) who were convicted of a crime that merited severe afflictive or capital penalties but were spared those penalties because of their immaturity. It was rarely used by the Châtelet and Parlement.

The name of the punishment known as the *fouet*, or whip, was actually a misnomer. The instrument of flagellation was not a whip but a tied bundle of branches or switches (*verges*). It did not lacerate muscle; at most, it drew blood. Few blows were struck, and only on the shoulders and upper back. The flagellation was primarily symbolic; the only trauma it could produce was emotional. It was, again according to Serpillon, a "few blows with switches, a very transitory punishment."[18] The executioner tied one end of a rope or chain around the victim's neck and the other to his wagon and then led him through the streets. At a few main squares and crossings, he gave the beating.

The brand (*la flétrissure*) was not a solitary punishment. It was joined to all sentences to *les galères* (the galleys), for whatever crime. That mark was *GAL*. It also accompanied sentences for theft in which the principal punishments were whipping and the iron collar, banishment, galleys, or Hôpital-Général; in

---

[16] A.N. AD III 9. He was also sentenced to the galleys for life.
[17] A.N. AD III 27b.
[18] *Code criminel*, vol. 3, p. 1089.

Figure 9.2. The pillory of Paris. (Original engraving in A.N. AD III, 6. Reprinted with permission of the French National Archives.)

that case, the mark was *V* (for "*voleur*," "*voleuse*"). Recidivists in theft and those convicted of theft who had a previous conviction for any afflictive or capital offense were branded with a double *V.* The mark *M* (*mendiant*) was for those found guilty of begging a second time and sentenced to a term in the Hôpital-Général. Courts could impose branding with the mark of the fleur-de-lis with a sentence of banishment for crimes other than theft. Whatever the mark, the brand was small, the diameter of a large coin. It was burned on the right or left shoulder with a hot iron after the flesh had been deadened or anesthetized. Depending on the chief punishment, branding was done in the courtyard of the tribunal, or before its main gate, or in full public view on the final day of exposure in the iron collar. (In Figure 9.1 one can see the branding iron awaiting la Coste as he stands wearing the iron collar.) The brand was simultaneously a permanent stigma and a means of identifying recidivists in crime. The stigmatic value may not have been great, for the size and placement of the brand (and techniques for effacing the imprint) meant that it could be concealed in most of daily life.

C. Incarceration

The modern French penitentiary was mandated legislatively by the Constituent Assembly in the Penal Code of 1791. But that legislation was a late stage in the long evolution of French penal incarceration. From the mid-seventeenth century onward, the Old Regime monarchy and themistocracy had created the bases for modern imprisonment by inventing and developing – on a large institutional and legal scale – the galley fleet, the *bagnes* (or penal compounds at naval bases), and the Hôpital-Général. The prison – that fortified and guarded building where inmates are surveilled, regimented, and forced to labor – was not "born," in either theory or practice, during the last quarter of the eighteenth century, contrary to Michel Foucault's assertion in *Discipline and Punish: The Birth of the Prison.* Its progenitive models were neither factory workbenches, the packing of African slaves into cargo holds and their regimen on plantations, nor the geometric alignment of soldiers on drill grounds and in military camps.

The galley fleet

The progenetive form of the modern French penitentiary, one identical to it in most respects but architecture, were the royal war galleys at Marseilles.[19] The French Mediterranean galley fleet, based at Marseilles, existed from at least

[19] The following account of the galleys is based on the excellent studies by Marc Vigié, *Les galériens du roi, 1661–1715* (Paris: Fayard, 1985), and André Zysberg, *Les galériens: Vies et destins de 60,000 forçats sur les galères de France, 1680–1748* (Paris: Seuil, 1987); "Galères et galériens à la fin du XVIIe siècle: Une image du pouvoir royal à l'âge classique," *Criminal Justice History* 1 (1980): 51–115; "Marseille, cité des galères à l'âge classique," *Marseilles: Revue Municipale Trimestrielle*, 122 (1980): 71–91.

the fifteenth century. There were six vessels in seagoing service during the reign of Francis I, twenty-four during that of Louis XIII, eighteen in 1668, twenty-eight in 1679, and then from 1694 to 1700, a maximum of forty.[20] Louis XIV and his principal naval ministers – the Colberts, father and son, and the Phélypeaux de Pontchartrain, father and son – vastly expanded the galley fleet, in ships, armaments, men, and logistics, as a major instrument for creating a French naval and political hegemony in the western Mediterranean, a "Gallic Sea," at the expense of Spain, Genoa, the Maghrebian corsair states, and, more remotely, the Ottoman Turkish navy.

A war galley had little firepower: merely five cannons, of which only one was of large caliber. They were fragile and deficient vessels on the open sea, vulnerable to swells, contrary winds, and storms, and incapable of carrying more than eight days' supply of fresh water. However, galleys could overtake most large vessels and, if those vessels were lightly armed merchantmen, they could capture them. They could successfully fight other galleys (although the French and Spanish galley fleets rarely confronted each other during the wars of Louis XIV). They could do little against multidecked gunships of the line, which, from the early seventeenth century onward, were the decisive instruments of naval warfare outside the Mediterranean. Admiral Abraham Duquesne, of the hard-fighting Atlantic and Channel ship-of-the-line fleet, contemptuously called the galleys "the demoiselles of naval war." But a galley's shallow draft, narrow beam, speed over short distances (when both sail and oars were deployed), maneuverability, and capacity to carry up to 100 soldiers made it an excellent vessel for the prowling, scouting, escorting of merchant ships, coastal raiding, and blockading that were characteristic of Mediterranean warfare during the seventeenth century. That warfare, although endemic, was of low intensity for France. The cost of constructing a galley during the late seventeenth century (approximately 30,000 livres) was a fraction of the amount required for a ship of the line that mounted only fifty guns, although the construction required the efforts of some 800 workers.

The galley at sea was labor-intensive; each had only two large sails and a normal complement of 450 officers and men, of whom some 250 to 260 were oarsmen. The cost to the royal Treasury of manning the oars of a galley with convicts was small compared to the amount required for the payment and provisioning of volunteers.[21] Manning of the galley fleet with criminals sentenced to that servitude by royal courts was sporadic and small in scale from the late fifteenth century to the 1670s. Before the advent of Louis XIV, the energy of the fleet was provided mostly by Moslem slaves (either captured directly or bought by commercial and diplomatic agents for the king in the slave markets of Malta, Majorca, Genoa, Livorno, or Crete); deserters from the royal army sentenced by court-martial; able-bodied vagabonds and gypsies arrested by

[20] Zysberg, *Les galériens*, p. 384.
[21] Vigié, *Les galériens*, pp. 26–60, 161–98; Zysberg, *Les galériens*, pp. 265–321.

municipal authorities, provosts, and criminal lieutenants; those under sentence of death who received royal commutation to galley servitude; and enlisted men.[22] Penal manning – the *peine des galères,* in the true double meaning of *peine,* both punishment and hard labor, was not institutionalized in law and practice until 1670 to 1690.[23] Article 13, Title 25, of the Criminal Ordinance of 1670 made term sentences to the galleys (three, five, or nine years, in the jurisdiction of the Parlement of Paris) the broad middle tier in the hierarchy of penalties in *grand criminel* for all bailliages, presidials, and Parlements. It also made life in the galleys a sentence alternative to death for many capital offenses. The laws of May 1680, June 1722, and August 1729 against smuggling and the illicit sale of salt, tobacco, and painted fabrics – whose transport and commerce were monopolies of the royal tax farms – made a term of servitude in the galleys the mandatory penalty for those crimes for male offenders.[24]

Between 1680 and 1748, at least 60,000 men did penal labor in the galleys. An average of 870 entered that servitude each year. In the France of the 1730s, that would have amounted to roughly 1 present or former *galérien* for every 1,000 persons in the population. Some 40 percent of the convicts were sentenced by royal courts throughout France after conviction for either *grand criminel* or vagabondage and mendicancy; 30 percent after conviction by a tax court or special commission, for smuggling salt or tobacco; 25 percent as military deserters (but only 5 percent after 1716, when the death sentence was reintroduced for desertion); and about 5 percent for practice of the Huguenot faith (but only 1 percent after 1716). Between 1716 and 1748, about 85 percent of *galériens* were men who had been tried and judged guilty of assault, theft, or smuggling by subaltern and sovereign courts throughout France.[25] The majority of *galériens* were sentenced to a term of less than ten years, but during the wars of 1680 to 1715 the intendants of the galleys contrived to keep those who

22 Article 104 of the General Ordinance of Orléans (January 1560) had commanded magistrates to order all gypsies ("ceux qui s'appellent bohémiens ou egyptiens") in their jurisdictions to leave France within two months; the males who did not leave, or who returned, were to be arrested and summarily dispatched to the galleys for three years (Isambert, vol. 14, p. 89). A royal declaration of December 1660 also threatened male gypsies with the galleys or "other corporal punishment" (ibid., vol. 17, p. 391).
23 Vigié, *Les galériens,* pp. 61–105; Zysberg, *Les galériens,* pp. 20–3, 59–64.
24 On that legislation, see Jousse, *Traité,* vol. 3, pp. 295–320.
25 Zysberg, *Les galériens,* pp. 64–115. Over the entire period 1680 to 1748, some 40% of those condemned to the galleys in *grand criminel* were sentenced by Parlements and other sovereign courts after appeals judgment, by the procedure that will be explained in Part III. Eighteen percent were sentenced by final judgment of a presidial court, and more than 30% by a provostial judgment of a *maréchaussée* tribunal (ibid., pp. 78–9). Prosecutions for smuggling salt and tobacco were effectively taken away from the jurisdiction of royal bailliages, presidial courts, and Parlements by legislation of 1667 and 1680 and placed in that of lower finance courts (primarily salt tribunals and *élection* courts). Their convictions could be appealed to Cours des Aides of Generalities only if the convict advanced the cost of transportation to the Cour des Aides, which usually amounted to at least 300 livres. This was in stark contrast to the automatic appeal to Parlements (at state expense) of lower-court sentences in *grand criminel,* guaranteed by the 1670 Criminal Ordinance. It meant that most lower finance court sentences to the galleys for smuggling were executed without appellate review (ibid., pp. 97–102).

could row for years beyond the expiration of their sentences. Intervention by the Naval Council ended that illegal practice after 1716.[26]

Convicts came to Marseilles in chains from all over France. They converged first on Paris, Rennes, and Bordeaux, where *les grandes chaines,* "the great chains," were formed, and then traversed the realm, mostly on foot, along main roads, through towns and villages, in fettered gangs of 250 to 400 under the conduct of heavily armed guards. The penal odysseys took place each spring and summer and sometimes in early winter. For Crown and themistocracy, they were an incomparable display of authority, chastisement, and warning offered to millions in every province.[27]

The Parisian chain held *galériens* from that jurisdiction and also from Normandy, Artois, and Flanders. It left from the fortress prison of the Tour Saint-Bernard on the Left Bank of the Seine. It trudged the main route to Dijon via Auxerre and Montbard, and then to Chalon. From there, the chain gang was transported on open barges down the Saône and the Rhône to Avignon. The final 70 miles to Marseilles were managed on foot, over the steep hills of Provence. The journey lasted about a month. The chain gang traveled more than 300 miles of the total distance on foot, at a forced pace of 15 miles a day, each man constantly bearing almost 40 pounds of iron around his neck and on one ankle.[28]

At its height, the *Louis-quatorzien* galley fleet of twenty-five to forty vessels – powered by 8,000 to 10,000 convict oarsmen and served by 1,000 to 2,000 more *galériens* at penal labor in the Arsenal at Marseilles – was a remarkable entity, simultaneously a naval-combat and amphibious force, an ostentatious instrument of diplomacy, an original mode of legal punishment, an ingenious political economy of labor, and a contrivance of ideal social hierarchy, both civil and military. The fleet was also an aesthetic creation of the state. The *réale,* or command galley, resembled a floating Versailles in the richness of its decorative sculptures, fittings, banners, and sails. Ordinary galleys had lavishly ornamented hulls and flags, even special coverings and sails embroidered with the fleur-de-lis for ceremonial use. Cruises and deployments *en parade,* in harbors or off coasts, were choreographed with the precision of a royal ballet or the drill of a line-infantry battalion during review.[29]

Because the fleet rather inexpensively served a plethora of valuable purposes, the monarchy preserved it until the mid-eighteenth century – long after

---

[26] Ibid., pp. 364, 371–2.

[27] "La chaîne . . . dispensait une pédagogie positive de l'Etat: la peine devenait visible par tous et partout, elle n'était plus réservée au nombre relativement petit de ceux qui pouvaient assister aux exécutions. Avec une suprenante économie de moyens, l'Etat 'médiatisait' ainsi sa puissance, la rendait familière, unifiait aussi les comportements et les pensées des populations des provinces. La chaîne symbolisait la centralisation administrative que chacun pouvait voir, donc concevoir. La régularité des convois s'intégrait dans la monotonie de la vie quotidienne ordinaire des peuples, faisant du châtiment non pas un événement extraordinaire mais l'expression familière d'une justice désormais bien réglée" (Vigié, *Les galériens,* p. 154).

[28] Vigié, *Les galériens,* pp. 135–54; Zysberg, *Les galériens,* pp. 19–39.

[29] Zysberg, "Galères et galériens de France à la fin du XVIIe siècle," pp. 51–60.

galleys had lost their naval utility to large, multigunned, sail-powered ships even in the Mediterranean, and long after the decline of the Mediterranean and the rise of the Atlantic as the vital maritime war space for France. The intricate penal system developed for the galleys at Marseilles survived the fleet. It was relocated after 1748.

"He [the convict oarsman] must first be remade in his body."[30] Jean-Baptiste Colbert described the *galérien* even more radically: His body was the "soul" of the galley fleet.[31] The principle regnant in the galleys was the exact subordination of matter, both human and inanimate, to geometric will. The principle was served through long professional training and practice for officers and petty officers, and through relentless surveillance and regimentation of the enchained *forçats* (forced laborers of the fleet). Galleys were a *système homme–machine*, in the phrase of André Zysberg.[32]

The "remaking" of the convict began immediately upon his arrival in chains at the Arsenal of Marseilles. He was entered in the registers (with a physical description) and given a number by clerks, then thoroughly inspected by physicians and officers. If deemed fit to row, he was unchained and taken aboard a training galley. His head was shaved bald (and would remain so for the rest of his sentence). He was stripped naked and issued the uniform of the *galérien:* the infamous red stocking-cap, a blue shirt and knee-length kilt, rough red stockings, and a long, heavy winter cape. He went barefoot except when detailed to work ashore. He constantly wore a leg fetter and chain aboard his training galley and, later, his war galley.[33]

The *chiourme*, or company of chained oarsmen, lived in their galleys during the entire year (except those too frail, aged, or sick to row), even in the "dead season" from November to April, when the fleet was anchored in the inner harbor of Marseilles. In winter they slept on board, under a huge canvas deck covering. During most of the "campaign" season, from April to late October, they were at sea. The interior of a French war galley was one of the most parceled and exiguous social spaces in the Occidental world during the seventeenth and eighteenth centuries. Equipment, armaments, munitions, provisions, and some 450 officers, men, and oarsmen were packed into a vessel 49 yards long, 10 yards wide, and 7.5 yards deep at its deepest (Figures 9.3, 9.4). It consisted of a cargo hold divided into twelve compartments, an elevated stern deck that contained the officers' and petty officers' quarters, a long open main deck filled with oars and rowing benches, a narrow elevated walkway that led forward to the raised prow deck, on and under which most of the sailors, soldiers, and cannons were placed, and which ended in a long ramming spur. That vessel was a platform on which an average of about 1 square yard was allocated per man.

[30] A galley chaplain, cited by Zysberg, *Les galériens*, p. 230.
[31] Quoted in ibid., p. 40.
[32] Ibid., p. 230.
[33] Vigié, *Les galériens*, pp. 156–9; Zysberg, *Les galériens*, pp. 40–58.

Figure 9.3. Convict war galley. *Recueil des planches pour la nouvelle édition du "Dictionnaire raisonné des Sciences, des Arts et des Métiers,"* vol. 2: *Marine* (Lausanne, 1781).

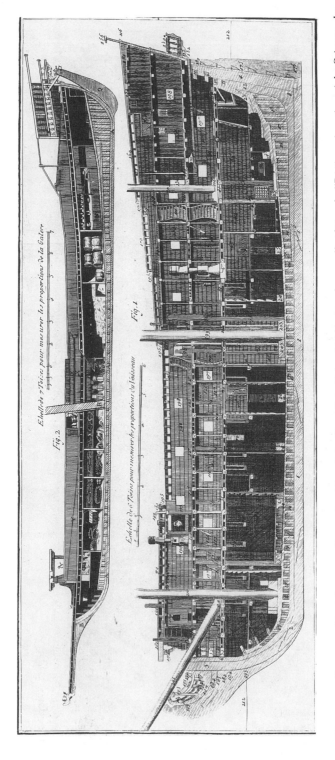

Figure 9.4. Cross-sections of a war galley and a ship-of-the-line. *Recueil des planches pour la nouvelle édition du "Dictionnaire raisonné des Sciences, des Arts et des Métiers,"* vol. 2: *Marine* (Lausanne, 1781).

The *chiourme* space was the most implacably measured. There were 5 oars-men to an oar and rowing bench, with some twenty-six benches on each side of a standard galley. Each rower was chained by one ankle. Men of varying strength were placed at different stations along the oar; the tallest and strongest at the end, the smallest and weakest at fifth position. The cushioned bench was 7 feet long and 6 inches wide, with a low, slanted back. In the rear of each there were foot planks for the rowers on the bench behind. Only 3 feet, 10 inches separated the backs of the benches; that was the space from which the galley was propelled. The standard oar was 39 feet, 4 inches long and weighed 286 pounds; 10 feet of oar were the interior pulling segment – equal in weight (143 pounds) to the outside 29 feet, 4 inches and almost three times the width. The oarsmen grasped handles fitted into the oar. The action of rowing was a mas-terpiece of disciplined kinesis. Each man occupied only 18 inches on the bench. Literally shoulder to shoulder, they moved backward and forward in unison, with their arms always extended in a straight line. André Zysberg has deter-mined that a complete oar stroke required seven distinct positions of the body (torso, legs, and feet) between the three extreme positions of torso perpendic-ular to the bench, torso jackknifed forward, torso and legs almost fully reclined in pulling. For the fifty-two oars to strike water at the same moment, all 260 oarsmen had to pull and recover in continuous, exact unison; a bench of oars-men out of rhythm, or that missed stroke, easily smashed into the oar behind. There were three regulation cadences. The normal cadence was one full stroke every 3 seconds, or twenty strokes per minute. *Galériens* were trained, and forced, to maintain such a rate for periods of more than an hour. In a calm sea and without sails, that cadence gave a speed of about 5 nautical miles per hour.

At sea *galériens* were not called on to rig sails, shift cargo, or fight in en-counters. They were exclusively propulsive energy. Rowing the galleys was a time-and-motion discipline as synchronically perfect as any devised by twentieth-century industrial engineers.[34]

Only cutting sugarcane on plantations or mining and stone quarrying were comparable in the quantity of human energy expended. Galley labor was en-forced by instruction, surveillance, and punishment. Novices were introduced

---

[34] Zysberg, *Les galériens*, pp. 194–255. Serious French involvement in the African slave trade and in plantation colonialism began during the reign and with the encouragement of Louis XIV, sec-onded by the Colberts. Those enterprises may have gotten some of their original impetus from the more precocious and constantly refined use of white slave labor (in fact, if not in legal no-menclature) in the galley fleet. To move from practicing large-scale penal enslavement and reg-imentation of French convicts, whether for a few years or life, to practicing lifelong labor enslavement (and conversion) of pagan Africans would not have been difficult, at least concep-tually and morally. The two practices briefly overlapped. During the 1670s, the Sénégal Com-pany was given a contract by Jean-Baptiste Colbert to provide Guinean slaves for the galleys. A few hundred were produced at 130 livres each (less than half the cost of an able-bodied Moslem on the Mediterranean slave markets). But most either died shortly after joining the fleet or be-came too sick to work. Such manning was discontinued, and in 1685 the 86 surviving Africans were resold by the galley intendant – for transportation to sugar plantations on Martinique (Vigié, *Les galériens*, pp. 71–2).

to rowing in training galleys, first in the harbor, then on increasingly long cruises at sea. After months of such training, they were placed in war vessels. Two petty officers on every war galley were specialist jailers and foremen. The *comite* (chief petty officer) arranged and commanded the *chiourme*. He set cadences by blowing a whistle, and those calls became bellowing shouts from the *sous-comites* on the catwalk. They used the baton or the rope to correct slow and maladroit oarsmen. The *argousin* – a blacksmith and disciplinary officer – was responsible for fettering and chaining. Those two were aided by six armed guards and, when necessary, a large contingent of mariners and soldiers. The superior officers – captain, first lieutenant, second lieutenant, and ensign – ran the ship, not its convict oarsmen. These officers were noblemen, principally from naval families of Provence. Many either belonged to or had served the Order of the Knights of Malta – that spiritual, military and mercantile community dedicated to hunting Moslems and raiding their towns and ships.[35]

Discipline, both aboard ship and in port, was based on corporal punishment. Rapid blows by petty officers – with fists, feet, batons, and lengths of rope – were frequent, for real or suspected insolence or malingering. Disobedience, insolence to officers, theft, and violence among *galériens* were punished ritualistically by tying to the mast or side of the ship or by public whipping (*la bastonnade*) with a rope. In whipping, the victim was spread-eagled on the main-deck catwalk and usually given from twenty to fifty lashes. More serious offenses (striking a guard or officer, self-mutilation to avoid the chain and oars, sacrilege, conspiracy to mutiny, or an attempt to escape) could be punished by hanging from the mainmast, in full view of the fleet.[36] Only captains and second officers could order the *bastonnade* or hanging, and only after a form of court-martial. They were under pressure from intendants and naval ministers to avoid lethal or incapacitating punishments. There were fewer than sixty hangings between 1680 and 1715.[37] The *galérien* was a commodity of value, despite the attitude expressed by Nicolas Arnoul (intendant of the galleys, 1665–73), who said, "I am in charge of four to five thousand of the most wicked scum on earth."[38]

Galleys were appendages of an industrial and command complex whose terrestrial body was the Arsenal of Marseilles. That vast and rectilinear complex of buildings occupied some 22 acres; it covered the inner basin and most of the southern bank of the harbor. The Arsenal had been designed by royal architects and constructed in two stages ("old" and "new" Arsenal) between 1665 and 1695. It recalled Versailles by its combination of baroque and classical styles, decor (façades with fleurs-de-lis), grandiosity, and purposiveness. The follow-

---

[35] Zysberg, *Les galériens*, pp. 208–20.

[36] A royal declaration of September 4, 1677, ordered that men condemned to the galleys who incapacitated themselves or had themselves incapacitated by others be punished by death (Isambert, vol. 19, p. 176). By royal edicts of December 14, 1691, and December 20, 1713, *galériens* who struck a guard with their chains or otherwise injured one were to be executed (ibid., vol. 20, pp. 614–15).

[37] Zysberg, *Les galériens*, pp. 168–71.   [38] Quoted in ibid., p. 162.

ing inscription was cut in stone over the main gate to the new Arsenal: "The Great Louis, of invincible fleets, built this citadel; from here, he dictates his laws to the subjugated ocean."[39]

The distinct buildings and areas inside the walled enclave contained the armory of the fleet, ship construction and repair yards (with pumping machines and sluice gates), foundries, forges and metal shops, rope-making shops, timber and carpentry ateliers, a canvas and textile factory, storage warehouses for the entire hardware of the galleys, a hospital, a nautical school for officers, and administrative offices and apartments for the officers and intendant. The buildings were made of stone and had mansard roofs. They were connected by paved interior courtyards, archways, and passages wide enough for heavy wagons. From 1695 to 1748, the Arsenal was possibly the largest factory in France; several thousand men – artisans, salaried or piece-rate workers, and convicts – labored in its confines. In order to demonstrate its productive capacity, on the occasion of a visit in 1679 by Jean-Baptiste Colbert de Seignelay, secretary of state for the navy, the intendant ordered the construction and launching of a complete, fifty-two–oar galley (from prefabricated parts) within twenty-four hours. That feat was accomplished by 800 paid workers and 400 convicts.[40] Industrial, the Arsenal was also bureaucratic and military. Scores of royal scribes were superimposed on masters of shops and warehouses; they kept detailed inventories of the men and materials that circulated in the Arsenal, later scrutinized by accountants and intendants. Armed guards were posted at the entries and main passages. Simultanously fortress, school, factory, and prison, the Arsenal was one of the most portentous creations of the *Louis-quatorzien* state.

A permanent complement of about 400 convicts, organized in brigades, served much of their *peine* by hard labor in the Arsenal, mainly hauling timber and iron, repairing docks, and dredging the basin. They were supplemented by others from the *chiourme* during the winter. Physicians inspected each *chain* of new *galériens* when it arrived at the port and did a triage, dividing it into three groups: the dangerously ill; those fit to row; those unfit (too young, aged, disabled, small, or generally weak). The first were sent to the hospital, the second to the training galleys, and the third to the penitentiary factory, or *bagne*, within the Arsenal. That was the main textile works, where convicts sewed and mended sails, blankets, banners, and uniforms for the fleet. One to two thousand convicts were usually occupied there, most of them for the duration of their sentences or their lives. The *bagne*, or carceral factory, was created in 1700 by the initiative of Phélypeaux de Pontchartrain, then secretary of state for the navy.[41] The factory belonged to the king and was administered by the in-

---

[39] Zysberg, "Marseille, cité des galères," p. 75.   [40] Ibid., p. 78.

[41] The word *bagne* came into French from the sixteenth- and seventeenth-century lingua franca of Mediterranean slavery, both Christian and Muslim: Its filiates were *bano* (Spanish), *banho* (Portuguese), and *bagno* (Italian). It designated either the depot where slaves were kept before sale or the building where they were lodged by their masters. Such a depot existed at Livorno, for Moslem slaves, from at least 1540; it was close to the sea and at water level. There were similar contemporary establishments at Istanbul and Algiers, but the etymology of the word was neither

tendant of the galleys. The state provided food, uniforms, guards, and medical care for the *bagnards*. Contracts for fabric and implements were let to consortia of Marseilles merchants. They provided master artisans and foremen who supervised production, sold finished goods to the state at negotiated prices, and received a subvention for each convict worker (from which they paid him a small "wage"). Although graft (primarily at the expense of the state and the convict laborers) was chronic in the *bagne,* the intendancy paid less than it would have otherwise for the great quantity of sewn goods it required, the merchants had a guaranteed and profitable market with negligible labor costs, and the *bagnards* received about 7 sous a day and an extra wine ration.

The Arsenal *bagne* crudely but unmistakably prefigured subsequent penitentiary compounds at Brest, Rochefort, and Toulon, even nineteenth-century prisons, for it was a long, stone, barracklike, two-story building with high windows and few doors. The ground floor was an immense work space, the second floor a dormitory that could accommodate perhaps 2,000 chained inmates. The regimen was severe, but less brutal than on a galley. Convicts were fettered at their worktables, dominated and punished by trustees and *argousins,* and rarely allowed into the courtyards of the Arsenal.[42]

With the constant decline in the number of serving galleys after the War of the Spanish Succession (from fifteen, in 1720, to six in 1748), labor in the Arsenal was made the principal form of punishment for most convicts. In 1737 – almost thirty years before Cesare Beccaria wrote his treatise *On Crimes and Punishments* (1764) and more than fifty years before Jeremy Bentham's *Panopticon* (1790), Bénigne du Trousset d'Héricourt, the last intendant of the galleys, wrote of the Arsenal *bagne.* "The establishment of the *bagne* factory is useful to the State and to the galleys in several ways; it provides for manufacturing, it forms workers, it occupies and instructs convicts with term sentences so that once their sentences are served they know a trade and can earn a living, it furnishes uniforms for the oarsmen at no expense to the State."[43]

The "man–machine system" was a political economy in which managers strove to balance duress, attrition, sustenance, and productivity. During most of the period 1670 to 1700, when the system was perfected, there was never a surplus of convict oarsmen for the needs of the fleet. To the state (from the kings, through the naval ministers, to the intendant of the galleys and the ship commanders) the utility of the *galérien* depended on his capacity to perform hard labor, a calculation that reflected both the modernity of the penal insti-

---

Turkish nor Arabic. It seems to have passed from Italian usage (and practice) to lingua franca, thence to French (Gabriel Audisio, "Recherches sur l'origine et la signification du mot 'bagne,' " *Revue Africaine,* 101 [1957]: 363–80, and Raymond Arveiller, " 'Barraque,' 'bagne,' guépard et la langue franque," *Etudes Linguistiques,* 9 [1970]: 81–91). From the late seventeenth century to at least the 1930s, the French word officially signified a punitive labor building or a compound for civil or military felons.

[42] On the Arsenal and its *bagne:* Vigié, *Les galériens,* pp. 239–50; Zysberg, "Marseille, cité des galères," pp. 73–9, and *Les galériens,* pp. 143–48.

[43] Cited by Vigié, *Les galériens,* p. 247.

tution and the central limit on its infliction of suffering. Preserving that capacity required preserving the health of the *galérien* with adequate food, shelter, rest and certain personal pleasures, even small profits and freedoms. These were necessary to promote docility, ward off despair, and forestall rebellion.

The daily food ration given each man consisted of about 1.5 pounds of wheat bread, a bowl of bean soup seasoned with salt and olive oil, and a liter of red wine. This diet was minimally adequate.[44] Each galley had a surgeon, a small infirmary, and medical stores. The royal hospital in the Arsenal was, by seventeenth- and eighteenth-century standards, an avant-garde facility. It was heated, well ventilated, had active resident physicians, surgeons, apothecaries, orderlies, cooks, and laundrymen, and contained 175 double beds. The diet included some meat, eggs, and fruit, and there was a large store of medicines.[45]

Galériens were given close spiritual attention. Vincent of Paul had been principal chaplain of the galley fleet during the 1620s. His legacy was an energetic religious program within the secular regime of carceral punishment, carried out principally by the Lazarist missionary fathers of his order. The *galérien* was a lost soul in a captive body; his redemption was a duty for the Church. In the hospital, mass was sung every morning and evening; there were prayers and scripture readings at mealtimes. Every war galley had a resident chaplain who led prayers in the morning and evening, celebrated mass on Sunday, read from the catechism, confessed *galériens*, and gave them communion.[46] Some chaplains protected the *chiourme* from excessive brutality by petty officers and guards.

Like regimental soldiers in most Old Regime urban garrisons, convicts of the *chiourme* were obliged to work externally, and remuneratively, during the winter months, when they were neither on campaign nor at forced labor in the Arsenal. Petty officers recruited oarsmen to work for Marseilles artisans and merchants, either aboard ship or ashore in ateliers and factories or on construction sites. Shipboard labor was mostly clothes making and leatherwork. Petty officers

[44] Zysberg, *Les galériens*, p. 118. [45] Ibid., pp. 353–58.

[46] "Il n'est guère étonnant de voir l'Eglise partager le bénéfice des valeurs d'une pénalité si étroitement intégrée au programme politique. Monarchie et religion étaient deux pouvoirs indissociables. . . . La justice du Roi rayait le galérien de la société civile, elle ne l'exculait pas de la société chrétienne. Bien que déchus, les condamnés demeuraient fils de Dieu qui en avait pitié. . . . Vincent de Paul fit surtout entrer l'espérance sur les galères en rappelant aux forcats 'que, tout criminels qu'ils étaient, Jésus-Christ les aimait encore.' A la limite, le condamné acceptant sa peine apparaissait, comme Jésus, la victime expiatoire de la communauté. Le fils de Dieu se trouvait au banc d'infamie 'souffrant pour nos crimes en la personne de ces hommes qui souffrent pour leurs propres désordres.' L'Eglise rejoignait de cette façon l'opinion populaire en développant l'idée de soumission au sort et au pouvoir ainsi que de providence justicière, tout en rappelant le caractère transitoire du pouvoir temporel face à l'Eternel" (Vigié, *Les galériens*, pp. 130–1; see also pp. 220–2). Their ministry to Catholic *galériens* was rendered more fervent by the significant numbers of determined Huguenot Calvinists among the *chiourme*, most of whom heroically resisted pressures to reconvert. They resisted in the name of the sufferings and sacrifice of Christ; for example, the baron of Salgas wrote, in a letter from his galley, "Je vis parmi les brigands, mais mon sauveur a expié entre deux voleurs" (ibid., pp. 133–4). See also Zysberg, *Les galériens*, pp. 102–11.

"contracted" with private businessmen, from whom they received fabrics, leather, and sewing implements. They paid *galériens* piece rate from the commissions they received (and shared with captains) for the finished goods. Thousands of convicts also worked ashore at low pay (10 to 20 sous a day) for entrepreneurs of all sorts, especially in soap factories and sugar refineries. They were chained in pairs, each by one ankle, and accompanied by guards. The Intendancy of the Galleys leased their labor for sums that defrayed important administrative costs. That system was triply symbiotic: It benefited the statist economy of the galleys, the merchants of Marseilles, even the felon-proletarians of the *chiourme*.[47]

Hundreds of favored, skilled, and energetic *galériens* were allowed to become petty entrepreneurs themselves, in dockside stalls adjacent to their anchored ships. There were usually at least three hundred of those primitive shops, built of old lumber and covered with rags and scraps of leather, along the entire anchorage quay of the fleet. Artisanal *galériens* engaged in hairdressing, wig making, tailoring, traded in old and new fabrics, books, leatherwork, decorative paintings, exotic birds, herbal medicine, even locks and keys, or groomed animals, pulled teeth, offered shaves and manicures – all at prices lower than in the city. The bazaar was eagerly patronized by the inhabitants of Marseilles (including thieves, for whom galley entrepreneurs fenced stolen goods) and integral to the galley system, for its large profits were shared with officers and petty officers. It included sexual traffic. Prostitutes could not board the galleys, but they did work in the jumble of the dockside *baraques*.[48]

By external labor *galériens* accumulated small coin for a carceral universe of cheap necessities. They could buy more and better food; extra wine (for the *comites* ran taverns aboard ship); fabric, leather, and wood for crafting; and sex. Because of the varied movement from ship to shore, and access to cutting and filing instruments, escape attempts were common. But between 1680 and 1748, only 800 (or 1%) of 60,000 convicts succeeded in making the break, and 140 of them did so on the march to Marseilles.[49] For all the seeming porousness, the galleys and Arsenal were a confinement system organized in some depth. Inmates were kept chained and under surveillance. As soon as one was reported missing, an alarm gun was fired, and the soldiers of the fleet began pursuit. A *galérien* was immediately recognizable in Marseilles and its hinterland by his clothing, shaved head, brand, and chain marks. The city and its environs were patrolled by police and *maréchaussée*. And the intendancy paid a handsome bounty of 60 livres to whomever captured an escapee – a brilliant means to prevent the populace of Marseilles and Provence from developing effective sympathy for *galériens*. Many of the few who made it beyond Marseilles were caught and returned by peasants of the region.

[47] Vigié, *Les galériens*, pp. 223–38; Zysberg, *Les galériens*, pp. 125–39.
[48] Zysberg, *Les galériens*, pp. 140–3, 150–62.   [49] Ibid., p. 343.

Sentence to the galleys was a mortal danger, despite administrative measures. Almost half who received that sentence between 1680 and 1748 died in consequence; the proportion was the same during the war years 1680 to 1715, when the fleet was at sea almost every year, as during the long periods of peace and of labor in the Arsenal or the city between 1716 and 1748. Few died of wounds, drowning, beatings, or undernourishment. They died mainly of dysentery, pulmonary infections, ruptured kidneys, ulcers, undefined "fevers," exposure and hypothermia, and venereal disease, or from that combination of emotional and physical degeneration expressed in the phrase *usé de galére*. The highest mortality was during the first three years of the term (one-third of those who died under sentence, including those sentenced for life), highest of all during the first year (one-fifth of total deaths). Those twelve months began with a long and enervating detention in jail, awaiting the departure of the *chain*, followed by the exhausting march to Marseilles and the first traumatic months of toil on the oars, in the *bagne*, or confined in the hospital. Many of those victims probably suffered a psychological shock and debilitation that cost them the will to survive. Beyond the threshold of three years, the hardening of the body, habituation to the environment (bacterial, viral, and social), and the regime of sustenance gave the term-sentence *galérien* a probability of survival.[50] The survivor of the galleys was a distinct physiological type: lean, with skin burnished to the color of mahogany and the toughness of hide, his hands extraordinarily powerful and calloused, his legs hard as tree trunks, and tautly muscled back and shoulders.

Galley labor left a deep imprint on French popular consciousness, one conveyed in common language for at least two hundred years:

The system survived the galleys. One reencounters it in the *bagnes* during the second half of the eighteenth century, the Restoration, and the July Monarchy, in the penal camps of Guiana during the Second Empire and the Third Republic, in those "galleys" without galleys. . . . The slang of the *bagnes* and prisons borrowed heavily from the old language of the galleys: *chiourme, taulard, argousin, forcat.* . . . It is said of someone condemned to forced labor that "he is in the galleys," as if those convicts rowed still on ghostly vessels.[51]

Before they were branded, chained, and marched to Marseilles, most *galériens* had been young or mature artisans, small tradesmen, rural or town laborers, peasants, soldiers, or vagabonds who were sentenced to three, five, or nine years for theft, fraud, assault, extortion, smuggling, desertion, or rioting. Many (except soldiers and vagabonds) had spent their lives before sentencing within one province, even within a few parishes. The galleys were a deracinating, entirely new, eclectic and complex experience for the felon who survived them, involving brutal labor, but that physically hardened and strengthened the convict; subjugation to authority, but in a constricted space that allowed close observation of those who commanded, as well as their personal obsessions, van-

[50] Ibid., pp. 347–53.   [51] Ibid., p. 389.

ities, and flaws; degradation, but also the fraternity, solidarity, and inventive lingo that prevailed on the rowing deck, and the weekly solace of mass and confession; exploitation, but accompanied by the opportunity for gain through piecework, crafting and hawking wares, performing menial services, or fencing stolen goods on the docks; erotic deprivation, but alleviated by homosexual possibilities and access to prostitutes (both of which were generally tolerated by officers); confinement, and yet expansive voyaging in the company of enchained comrades from all over the realm and much of the Mediterranean (who spoke every dialect of France and language of the Mediterranean basin, including Turkish and Arabic), comrades with a unique variety of skills and lore (including educated and upper-class Huguenot *forçats*, condemned to the galleys for violating the 1685 revocation of the Edict of Nantes); stigmatic exclusion, but from which social cunning and cosmopolitanism could be acquired, along with knowledge of criminal techniques. They were remade in more than body.

Those potencies were registered by the criminal law. Former *galériens* were forbidden to remain at Marseilles, to visit Paris, or to be within 15 leagues of Versailles or the Court. They were subject to provostial judgment (without appeal of sentence) if arrested on suspicion of a criminal act, and to the death sentence if convicted of a serious crime.[52] They were considered especially dangerous – as much for what they had become in the galleys as for what they had once been.

The bagnes

In September 1748, Louis XV ordered that the hitherto autonomous galley fleet be placed under the full control of the royal navy (which was based principally at Brest and Toulon) and that the existing *chiourme* (some 4,000 men) be transferred from galleys to naval *bagnes*.[53] In 1749, 3,000 *forçats* were sent to Toulon and 1,000 to Brest, where new *bagnes* were built for them within a few years. The galleys were rapidly decommissioned, except for one or two *réales* preserved as glorious vestiges.[54] Henceforth, all those sentenced to the galleys served their time at Brest, Toulon, or, from 1767, at Rochefort.[55] The most important of the *bagnes* – in structural innovation, size, carceral population, and naval significance – was at Brest, and felons sentenced to the galleys from the jurisdiction of the Parlement of Paris were sent there from 1749 to 1790.

The 1748 edict ended the galley fleet, but it was a refinement of the galley system, shifting convict labor from ships that had become useless to other productive forms in other strategic areas. The punishment was still called the *gal-*

<hr/>

[52] Guyot, vol. 7, pp. 716–17.
[53] The text of the edict is in Philippe Henwood, *Bagnards à Brest* (Rennes: Ouest-France, 1986), pp. 179–81.
[54] Ibid., pp. 14–17.
[55] Those three *bagnes* operated fully until, respectively, 1858, 1873, and 1852 (ibid., p. 18). After their closing, those sentenced to forced labor were deported to the Guiana penal colony, principally to Devil's Island. That institution received convicts until 1938.

ères, in both legal and popular language, until 1791, but after 1748 it was served on land. The edict marked the advent of exclusively land-based carceral labor, or the principle of the Marseilles Arsenal magnified to an Atlantic scale and purpose. During the reign of Louis XIV, the concurrent development of the galley fleet and the *peine des galères* had expressed a particular and dynamic relation between warfare and criminal justice. The relation became fully symbiotic after 1748, in the twin expansion of the French oceanic battle fleet and of the *bagnes*.[56]

Chateaubriand described Brest in his *Memoirs:*

At Brest that ocean that I would encounter on so many shores washes the extremity of the Breton peninsula; beyond that promontory, there are only limitless ocean and unknown worlds. . . . Seated on some derrick along the quai de la Recouvrance, I often watched the movements of the crowd: shipbuilders, sailors, soldiers, customs clerks, convicts passed back and forth before me. Travelers embarked and disembarked, pilots shouted maneuver orders, carpenters squared timbers, rope-makers paid out cables, ship's boys lit fires under huge pots from which poured thick smoke and the wholesome smell of tar. . . . Here, wagons backed into the water to load; there, pulley blocks and tackle lifted freight, while cranes brought down stones and dredging machines scooped out mud. Forts relayed signals, launches came and went, ships got under way or returned to harbor.

One day, I walked to the outer end of the port, to the shore. It was hot; I lay on the beach and fell asleep. Suddenly, I was awakened by a magnificent noise; I opened my eyes, like Augustus Caesar looking on the trireme galleys in the harbor of Sicily after the victory over Sextus Pompey. Salvos of artillery reverberated in succession, the roadsteads were filled with ships. The great French oceangoing high seas fleet was returning from war after the signing of the peace treaty [with England in 1783]. Vessels maneuvered under full sail, wreathed in the discharge of their saluting cannons, hoisted their flags and banners, displayed their bridge, prow, and broadsides, dropped anchor in the midst of their course, or continued to fly on the waves. Nothing has ever given me a higher idea of the human spirit; in that moment mankind seemed to appropriate something of Him who said to the sea: "You will go no further." . . . All of Brest ran to the harbor. Launches emerged from the fleet and came up to the pier. They were filled with officers, faces tanned by the sun, who had a foreign look that one always brings back from another hemisphere, but also the joy, pride, and hardiness of men who have restored the honor of the national flag.[57]

Chateaubriand experienced Brest in 1783, at the dual apogee of the port and the battle fleet. Several decades of intensive construction and expansion – much of it wrought by convict forced labor – made possible that naval achievement and its spectacle.

Jean-Baptiste Colbert and Louis XIV had chosen Brest to be the main base and construction yard for the high-seas (Atlantic and Channel) warship fleet.

[56] The eighteenth-century *bagnes*, before and during the Revolution, have not been studied archivally, as have the galleys. They require such study, for they were the long and creative intermediate stage in the history of modern French penal incarceration.

[57] François-René Chateaubriand, *Mémoires d'outre-tombe*, 2 vols. Bibliothèque de la Pléiade (Paris: Gallimard, 1966), vol. 1, pp. 72–3.

Punishment

The bay was wide and partly sheltered by islands; the harbor, formed by the Penfeld River, was narrow, deep, long, sinuous, and eminently defensible. The port was surrounded by hills on both banks. The harbor entrance was only a "half cannon shot" (or some 300 yards) wide. During the 1680s, Vauban created a continuous and thick system of fortifications that enclosed the port on both banks, and much of the town. Between 1670 and 1690, the first naval arsenal, foundries, rope and sail factories, warehouses, shipyards, barracks, and stone docks were constructed.[58] The second great period of French naval expansion began in the mid-eighteenth century, and the royal decision to move *galériens* to Brest and Toulon was a vital element in that strategy. The battleship fleet was increased from forty-eight, in 1744, to about seventy in 1773; most of the new ships were built at Brest.[59] From 1745 to 1770, the harbor was enlarged by quarrying and dredging and its installations systematically renovated or expanded – including the new Royal Naval College, the Surgeons' College, a stone naval warehouse 520 feet long, and six additional shipyards, each capable of building a three-deck ship of the line of more than ninety guns. The architect and construction engineer of the "new Brest" was Antoine Choquet de Lindu (b. 1712, d. 1790). He was, for fifty years, director of works for the port and for some thirty of those years, between 1743 and his retirement in 1784, chief engineer of the royal navy.[60] Choquet was also one of the most inventive penal architects in Old Regime Europe.

By Choquet's design and under his supervision, the *bagne* was constructed in less than three years (1750–2) of block stone (mostly granite). It was a vital element in the renovated infrastructure of Brest and, beyond, in French global navalism and colonialism. The fleet that transported Rochambeau's army to America and then defeated the English navy in Chesapeake Bay, at Yorktown, and off the coast of India, the fleet panegyrized by Chateaubriand, was in large part a product of the *bagne* and its convict laborers.

Choquet's precise and expressive "observations" on the *bagne* describe a major threshold in the history of French punishment, the creation of an establishment whose model would shape conceptions of carceral penology for the next hundred years:

The *bagne* is a prison. Its inmates are condemned to the galleys and used for the most abject and hardest work in the port, a fact that makes them little different from slaves; furthermore, it is virtually the only building that has been constructed with the exclusive purpose of confining such convicts. It was built at a cost and with a grandeur beyond any other structure of its type. Elsewhere, various buildings, originally constructed for other purposes, have been superficially altered to incarcerate convicts; thus at Marseilles, they have occupied part of the factory; at Toulon, part of the warehouse; and in the Levant, houses previously occupied by private persons.

[58] Yves Gallo, ed., *Histoire de Brest* (Toulouse: Privat, 1976), pp. 91–3.
[59] Ibid., p. 131, and G. Lacour-Gayet, *La marine militaire de la France sous le règne de Louis XV* (Paris, 1910), pp. 542–3.
[60] Gallo, *Histoire de Brest*, pp. 139–41.

Marseilles and Toulon were the only ports of France with such buildings. When His Majesty incorporated the galley fleet into the capital ship fleet, the first port was abandoned by the king [for penal purposes] and the *chiourme* was sent to the ports of Toulon and Brest, where it was lodged in the rope factory until a *bagne* was constructed. . . . Some wanted the *bagne* in the middle of the port, without examining whether the space that it would require was available there; others wanted it at the very edge of the port, at the base of the hills, without determining whether water and other indispensable necessities would be available there; some even proposed to locate it beyond the port, outside the walls of the city, which would have violated the most elementary rules of fortification; in the last case, very little support would have been available to guards in case of revolt by men who could win their freedom only by that means, and the long distance convicts would have traveled to their work would have cut in half the time they could be kept at labor. While these various proposals superseded each other, I chose the most advantageous site for the convicts – behind the [new] upper rope factory, in front of the naval-infantry barracks, and beside the hospital. That site prevents revolts, gives succor to the ill, and provides abundant water, without depriving the port of the warehouse space necessary for naval armaments. Once the site was decided, it became a matter of creating the most perfect building possible. To do so, I turned to M. Mistral, commissioner of galleys appointed by the Court for oversight of the *bagne*, and to the officers under his orders, from whom I obtained necessary insights. I shall now explain the ideas that I developed then, for achieving the ends of efficiently maintaining order among convicts, preventing their escape, and meeting the needs vital to their existence; those three purposes directed my undertaking.

The convicts were and would continue to be very numerous; the first concern had to be preventing them from conspiring to escape. Consequently, they had to be divided and subdivided in such a way that they would be unable to band together, but that subdividing could not be into an excessive number of groups; otherwise too many guards would be needed, and each division would require too much attention and provisioning. My solution was to divide the length of the *bagne* into two wings, one on each side of the centerpiece building, and to give it two levels [or storys]; by this method, the *bagne* of 130 *toises* [780 feet] was divided into four interior halls and 20,000 convicts [*sic*, error for 2,000] into four groups. The two end structures . . . were arranged to house petty officers charged with interior guard of the *bagne;* they make it impossible for convicts to carry out whatever mutinous projects they may concoct. Denied help from their comrades in other halls, constantly watched and surrounded by guards, what can they undertake?

Each hall has its own accommodations, consisting in latrines, water fountains, kitchen, and tavern; and each hall is divided lengthwise by a wall 4 feet thick.

The terrain determined the length of the building, and left me only the choice of how to provide a width that could contain 20,000 [2,000] convicts and their guards. That width had to be considerable, because the *tolas* [compartments for convicts] . . . , which are nothing other than 14-foot-square platform beds, form a kind of spine, each bed divided by a plank where the heads of convicts are placed, ten sleeping on one side of the bed, ten on the other. . . . I planned an interior wall the length of each hall [which formed two blocks per hall], with all the more satisfaction because it served other goals.

That wall . . . has along every 14 feet of its length a door or passage 5 feet high. Thus, instead of placing the camp beds up against the outer walls of the building, as had always been done, they were each placed in a space of 14 square feet, up against the central interior wall. This avoided several disadvantages: most importantly, the facility with which convicts with access to outer walls can devise often successful escape stratagems, and the inaccessibility of latrines for convicts chained to outer walls, which leads them to pollute the place with their ordures . . . and which very often causes epidemic diseases. These dangers were parried by means of [low] walls between each *tolat* . . . each wall containing a latrine niche, 2 feet deep by 2.5 feet wide, with a spigot for flushing, washing, and drinking. This arrangement gives convicts no resource for escaping; they can do nothing to the outer wall, along which there is a walkway . . . [between the outer wall and the *tolats*] constantly patrolled by guards and illuminated at night by lanterns set into the corner-pieces of the windows. . . . The entire longitudinal interior wall contains a sewage drain that flows to the vestibule, and then into the sea.

A kitchen was placed in each block; it is 17 feet long and 14 wide, enclosed by a grill of iron bars [and thus visible from outside], so as to not give convicts – who always suspect the honesty of those who serve them – any reason to grumble. On one side of each kitchen, also enclosed by a grill, is a tavern; each tavern is divided into two parts, one for distribution of the wine that the king grants to all forced-labor convicts during their eight days of hard work (after which they have eight days of rest), the other for the guards [*comites*] to sell wine to those convicts who have earned the means to buy it.

The window frames in all the halls are 6 to 7 feet above the floor, . . . which places the convicts beyond sight of and communication with the port. . . . Thus when the windows are opened, the atmosphere can be freshened in a few moments, and their elevation guarantees healthy air. Lanterns are set into the corner-pieces of each window, 7 feet high; they are beyond reach of the convicts and are kept lighted during the night for guards in their surveillance. If convicts manage to put them out, that is treated as a revolt, and those guilty are punished accordingly. The guard is composed mainly of *pertuisaniers*, each of whom is responsible for ten convicts who are chained by twos during the day when they are taken to work (and are thus known as "couples") and who are all ankle-chained at night to the base of their *tolat*. A certain number of *pertuisaniers* are detailed to watch those who might cause trouble. . . .

The spring that gives water to the naval hospital . . . was the only source that could flow to the first floor of the *bagne*, and I channeled it for that purpose, . . . but since it was not sufficiently abundant to provide for the ground floor, I built a cistern, which, by its elevation and size, amply serves the ground floor . . . and, during the day, all the latrines, kitchens, and wash stations of the entire building; this maintains cleanliness in a place filled with people who, by regulation, change their clothes only every eight days. It should be remarked that in addition to these precautions, I had an air vent installed for every latrine; the vents end above the roof and effectively remove stench; each latrine has both a lid and a small door. Furthermore, I gave the blocks high ceilings. . . .

To understand more clearly the security of the guard system, one must understand the internal layout of the structure, beginning with the building in the middle.

The centerpiece building . . . lodges officers. On the lower ground floor there is a vestibule divided into two parts. After passing the guard post, one enters a small room for the commander of the guard troop. In each part of the vestibule there is a sentry to alert the guard corps, if need arises. The remainder of the lower ground floor is cellars where the convict's provisions are kept, and they are not bulky. The commissary officer furnishes the convicts' rations each day from the royal warehouses; the other cellars are allocated to different officers for their stores. At the foot of the staircase there is an iron door 9 feet wide (the width of the entry ramp). . . . The configuration of the land led me to create this lower ground floor, which is extremely useful, for it also lodges a detachment of forty marines who reinforce the *pertuisaniers.* Off the upper ground floor, at the same level as the prisoners' blocks, two corridors lead to the halls and to the apartments of various officers. The superior officers each have two rooms with an entresol; the *comites* and *argousins* have one room each and an entresol. . . . At the end of each corridor, thus at the entry to each hall, there are two doors; the first is of strong wood, with a small iron grill in the middle for alerting the guard if necessary; the second is solid iron. The lodgings of the *comites* and *argousins* are off the corridor between the two doors. In the central vestibule . . . there is a covered altar mounted on wheels, that is pushed to the foot of the stairs and placed in view of the halls, so that mass and holy offices can be said on Sundays and saints' days without convicts leaving their places [in the *tolats*]. There is a large fire hose and pump in the same vestibule, also mounted on wheels; it gets water from the channel behind the latrine, through a leather hose. . . .

Finally, the third [upper] vestibule [on the first floor] is constructed like the second; there is an iron door at the foot of the stairs that lead to the attic. Thus, every wing and its forestructures serve to lodge commanding officers, chaplains, surgeons, *comites*, and under-*comites* who give orders to the convicts, as well as the *argousins* who control them – and who are fined if any convict escapes by their negligence. All these personnel have iron grills in their apartments to observe and forestall anything that occurs in the *bagne*, grills that can be used in last resort as firing positions for marines. That can be done with the same vigor from the building at the end of the *bagne* and revolt stifled at its first signs. From those buildings one goes by a small inner staircase to the attic, along which there is communication between all the guard posts.

The end buildings have two *cachots* [cells] on each side of a thick wall, for the punishment of *pertuisaniers;* the convicts receive no punishments other than manacles, double chains, *bastonnade,* or death, according to the case; they remain in their *tolat* until punished.

Since the attics are vast, the barracks for the *pertuisaniers* were placed there.

This sort of structure requires a very large courtyard . . . difficult to guard, despite the height of the walls . . . that also serve as an aqueduct for water to the first floor.

The courtyard is reserved for convicts' stalls and *baraques,* . . . which are small sheds without roofs, so that guards can see inside. All convicts have the privilege of working at a trade; they do so in these *baraques* and sell to the public, for whom a door was built in an angle of the wall. A guard post of *pertuisaniers* is next to the door, to inspect those who enter and leave, and prevent convicts from escaping in disguise – even though they are chained from morning until evening in their *baraques.* There is a washbasin at each end of the courtyard, 24 feet long and 8 feet wide, where convicts clean their uniforms; the water flows down through underground channels. Those channels also receive all the rainwater from the roof by a gutter pipe. Whenever I have inspected, I have found the channels as clean as on the day they were built; and the halls are without stench, contrary to the expectation of some people before the *bagne* was constructed.[61]

Two great two-story wings, with two halls on each wing, divided by interior walls into four blocks (each with about 280 inmates), each block divided into compartments for 20 men: The structure can be visualized exactly on Choquet

[61] Antoine Choquet de Lindu, *Recueil de planches pour la nouvelle édition du Dictionnaire raisonné des Sciences, des Arts et des Métiers,* vol. 3 (*Architecture*) (Lausanne, 1781), pp. 37–45.

de Lindu's construction blueprints (Figures 9.5 through 9.8). The galleys and the Marseilles *bagne* had depended essentially on guards and individual chaining to control convicts. The Brest establishment went beyond those rudimentary devices to a new architecture whose sole purpose was incarceration. The structure enclosed convicts in self-contained, semicellular spaces (blocks and *tolats*). It reduced their movements to a minimum, a reduction whose ultimate refinements were the latrines, within reach of the enchained *tolards*, and the portable altar that, theoretically, could be seen from the *tolats*. It kept them under multivantaged interior surveillance and denied them physical and visual access to the exterior world, other than marching to and from work sites. It was the prototype for the *maisons de force* that were mandated in the Revolutionary Penal Code of 1791 and for nineteenth-century *maison centrale* prisons. The Brest *bagne* remained traditional in the practice of constant chaining, the high proportion of guards to inmates (perhaps 1 to 8), the convict uniform, administrative hierarchy and language (of the galleys), and the commerce in the courtyard *baraques* (which replicated the dockside bazaar at Marseilles). Its limitations were not in penal or architectural imagination but were physical: The scale was immense, but the structure could reasonably accommodate only 2,240 inmates, and then only by dense crowding. It filled rapidly. Between May 1750 and July 1755, 2,917 convicts arrived on the *chaines* (1,539 from Paris).[62] During most of its one-hundred-year existence, the Brest *bagne* usually housed from 2,500 to 3,500 prisoners.[63]

Security and sanitation were the driving obsessions of the *bagne* regime. Both obsessions were starkly utilitarian. *Bagnards* were forced laborers of great value to the navy, proletarians with little or no wage who, en masse, could not be replaced. They performed both skilled labor and heavy gang labor indispensable to the base and its shipyards. Architecture, chaining, and surveillance were contrived to subdue convicts psychologically, to countervail inevitable conspiracies to escape or revolt, and to allow rapid suppression of such acts before they became contagious. These measures were contrived to produce the effect described by Vidocq, a former *bagnard:*

Even the most fearless convicts have admitted it; however hardened one is, the first sight of this place of misery gives a profound shock. Each hall contains twenty-eight platforms, called benches, on which 600 convicts are chained; those long lines of red uniforms, those shaved heads, those sunken eyes, those forlorn countenances, the constant rattle of chains, all combine to fill the soul with a secret terror.[64]

The sanitary system, constructed to protect the laboring capacity of the *bagnard,* was quite advanced. The building was constructed on a shelf excavated from the slope of Kéravel Hill; its concealed sewage pipes, located below the spring

---

[62] Henwood, *Bagnards à Brest,* p. 32.   [63] Ibid., p. 69.
[64] Quoted from ibid., p. 91.

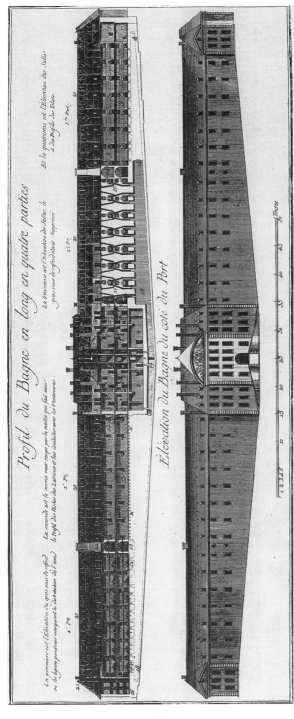

Figure 9.5. Frontal view of the Brest bagne. *Recueil des planches pour la nouvelle édition du "Dictionnaire raisonné des Sciences, des Arts et des Métiers,"* vol. 3: *Architecture* (Lausanne, 1781).

337

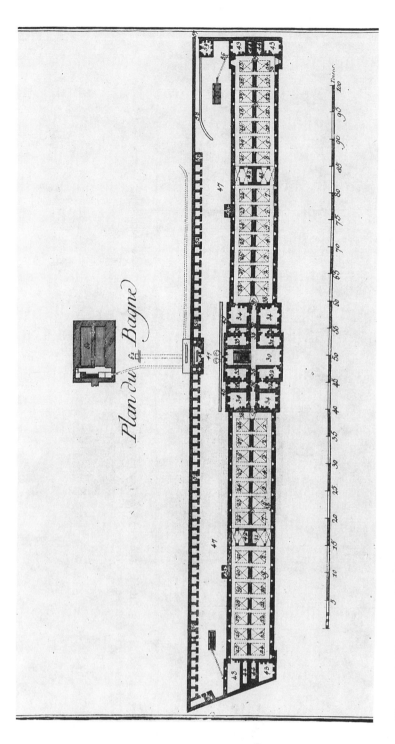

Plan du Bagne

Figure 9.6. Floor plan of the Brest *bagne*. 1–28. compartments (*tolats*) for convicts, twenty men per compartment; 29. staircase; 30. main vestibule; 31. administrative office; 32. officers' lodgings; 33. chaplain's and surgeon's lodgings; 34. petty officers' and *argousins'* lodgings; 35. corridors; 36. heavy wooden doors; 37. iron doors (leading to prison blocks); 38. four prison blocks (*salles*), each with fourteen compartments (see items 1–28); 39. latrines; 40. latrine pipe; 41. kitchens for prisoners; 42. tavern for prisoners; 43. guards' lodgings; 44. punishment cells for guards; 45. ramps leading to courtyard; 46. latrines leading to courtyard; 47. courtyard; 48. prisoners' latrines 49. latrines; 50. fountains; 51. rubbish area; 52. prisoners' shops (*baraques*); 53. guard posts; 54. water pumps; 55. wash-houses; 56. rain trap leading to main sewage channel; 57. external gate; 58. gate ramp; 59. gatekeepers' and guards' lodgings; 60. cistern; 61. canal for rainwater and cistern overflow. *Recueil des planches pour la nouvelle édition du "Dictionnaire raisonné des Sciences, des Arts et des Métiers," vol. 3: Architecture* (Lausanne, 1781).

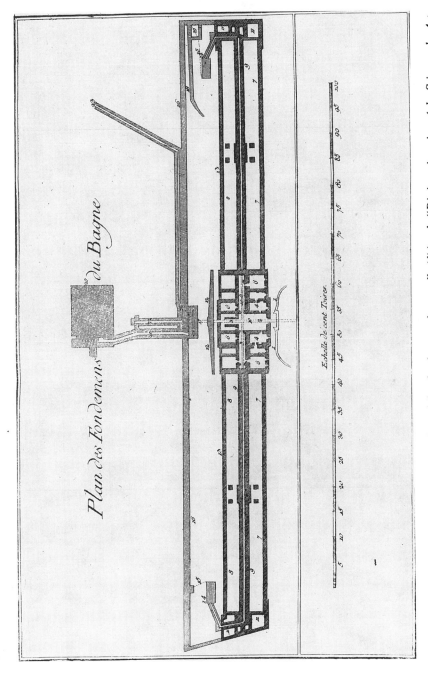

Plan des Fondemens du Bagne

Echelle de cent Toises

Figure 9.7. Foundations of the Brest *bagne. Recueil des planches pour la nouvelle édition du "Dictionnaire raisonné des Sciences, des Arts et des Métiers,"* vol. 3: *Architecture* (Lausanne 1781).

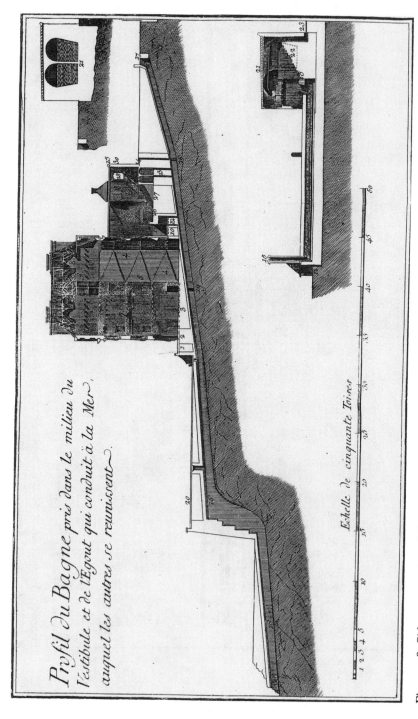

Profil du Bagne pris dans le milieu du Vestibule et de l'Egout qui conduit à la Mer, auquel les autres se reünissent

Echelle de cinquante Toises

Figure 9.8. Side cross-section of the Brest *bagne*. (Antoine Choquet de Lindu, *Recueil des planches pour la nouvelle édition du "Dictionnaire raisonné des Sciences, des Arts et des Métiers,"* vol. 3: *Architecture* [Lausanne, 1781].)

and cistern, were continually flushed by gravity into the harbor tidewater. Its three floors were well ventilated. The adjacent hospital, like its predecessor at Marseilles, was large, aerated, well furnished, and well staffed.[65]

Yet the *bagne* was chronically humid and ineluctably debilitating. Because of fog and rain, Brest and its hinterland were known colloquially as the "piss-pot of France." The only heat in the cavernous blocks was given by kitchen cook-fires and bodies packed together in *tolats*. The regulation space for each prone *bagnard* was 18 inches wide – exactly that of an oarsman on a rowing bench of the old galleys.[66] His basic ration was also that of the former *galérien:* about 1.5 pounds of bread, a bowl of bean soup, a liter of wine. That quantity of wine, most of it consumed every evening between 6:00 and 8:00 P.M., was a soporific drug.

> The *comites* are forbidden to tolerate laziness among the convicts, and if any convicts who do not know a useful skill refuse to learn one, the *comites* are ordered to inform the ledger-keeper, who will give the list of their names to the commissioner of the *chiourme*, so that he will put their names more frequently than those of others on the roster for hard toil in the arsenal.[67]

Time and energy, like space, were carefully organized in the *bagne*. Reveille was just before dawn. The convicts were formed into work brigades of ten, led past the guard, who inspected their chains individually, then escorted by armed guards to their work sites. They remained guarded and ankle-chained in pairs at work; the length of the chain was adjusted to the task they performed. They were usually fed a small amount of bread and wine on site at midday and worked until late afternoon, when they were marched back to the *bagne*. Their principal meal was in the early evening; it could be supplemented with meat, cheese, butter, extra wine, and other provisions that were sold by privileged convicts in the kitchens, under the supervision of *comites*. There followed about two hours of enchained leisure in the *tolats*, when drinking, smoking, singing, accordion playing, storytelling, dominos or cards, and crafting wares were permitted. That ended abruptly at 8:00 P.M., when the *comites* blew their whistles. Silence, if not sleep, was obligatory from that hour until reveille.[68]

The *bagnards* were divided roughly into two groups or shifts. Each one worked at *fatigue*, or hard toil, within the port for eight days and was then relieved by the other. The division of labor among *bagnards* on *fatigue* duty has not been studied closely for the period 1750 to 1789, although it seems to have duplicated the general division of labor within the port. All of them worked

[65] Ibid., pp. 143–4.
[66] André Zysberg, "Politiques du bagne, 1820–1850," *L'impossible prison: Recherches sur le système pénitentiaire au XIXe siècle*, ed. Michelle Perrot (Paris: Seuil, 1980), p. 188.
[67] A mid-eighteenth-century naval regulation for *bagnes*, cited by Henwood, *Bagnards à Brest*, p. 105.
[68] Henwood, *Bagnards à Brest*, pp. 123–40.

either with or close to the free laborers and artisans of Brest employed by the navy, and its technical personnel. Prisoners were assigned to the least skilled and most tiring tasks (*"la grande fatigue,"* in administrative language): draining of drydocks and yards; dredging and cleaning of the harbor (often in diving suits); quarrying and hauling stone; carrying, stacking, or loading and unloading ships' stores, cannons, shot, anchors, sails; masting and demasting vessels; cleaning and scraping holds and hulls; building and repairing docks and piers; shoring up banks; excavating foundations; sawing heavy timber and cutting stone blocks; hauling materials within, to, and from warehouses and magazines; pulling barges; winding and slipping anchor ropes. This was the heavy manual labor by which a fleet lived, and most of it was accomplished at Brest by the corps of *bagnards*. Many had been artisans and had manual skills. Those men were integrated into the ateliers of the port (*la petite fatigue*) – the foundries and forges, shipwright and carpentry shops, rope, sail, and uniform factories – and some of them were paid at piece rate by the navy, as incentive to do high-quality work. They were the aristocracy of *forcats*, men who accumulated a *pécule* to spend in the *bagne* and for the day of their release. Others, who were literate, served *la petite fatigue* as clerks at the port or in the *bagne* or hospital. The society of *bagnards* thus approximately replicated the hierarchy of external society: a mass of mostly rustic and unskilled men, destined for the hardest and most dangerous tasks, and an elite with artisanal and cultural skills whose work was privileged and individuated.[69]

During the eight days of reprieve from port labor, they did maintenance tasks in the *bagne* and hospital, or crafted and sold wares in their courtyard *baraques*. They did not work for private businesses, although they were occasionally loaned to the Municipality of Brest for landscaping and construction (and were paid a small sum). *Baraques* were a general privilege accorded *bagnards* by the 1748 edict, for reasons of both morale (thus discipline) and economy. In the galleys, this privilege had been limited by the favor of petty officers. During a few of each eight days' respite from port labor, convicts – who were allowed to appropriate small amounts of leather, wood, and metal from naval work sites and to possess engraving and hammering tools (but not files) – sold their artisanry in the courtyard. The privilege of artisanry was one of the most fragile elements in the security system but also probably the strongest force in relieving tension among *bagnards* and, one suspects, in maintaining acquiescence.[70] As with the galleys, their commercial profits were spent in the *bagne*. They bought meat and cheese – and thus strength for labor – for which the king did not have to pay. In contrast to the world of the galleys, and like that of

[69] Ibid., pp. 105–23; Zysberg, "Politiques du bagne," pp. 178–83.
[70] Some of their woodcrafting was superb, wrought in exotic hardwoods (see the illustrations in Henwood, *Bagnards à Brest*, p. 136). Few seem to have escaped from within the *bagne*. Successful escapes were mostly from the port, accomplished with the aid of *pertuisaniers*, sailors, and free workers, paid with money earned at skilled work or in the *baraques* (ibid., pp. 155–68).

nineteenth- and twentieth-century prisons, they had no easy sexual access to women.[71]

Thirty-two to forty thousand men served sentences in the three *bagnes* between 1749 and 1790, at a rate of 750 to 950 sentences per year for all of France. That low rate meant that the ordinary courts, especially the Parlements, pronounced the penalty of *galères* restrictively (for reasons that will be explained in the next section of this chapter and in Chapter 10). Those sentenced by the courts and Parlements of Paris, Artois, and Flanders were taken to the Tour Saint-Bernard in Paris and formed into the Paris chain; the great majority of them then went to Brest, as did the chains from Normandy and Brittany. *Galériens* sentenced by courts and Parlements in Guyenne, Burgundy, Franche-Comté, and Alsace went to Rochefort, those from Languedoc, Roussilon, Provence, and Dauphiné to Toulon. Among the 8,000 men in the Parisian chains (1749–90), 44 percent were sentenced for theft, 30 percent for smuggling salt and tobacco, 7 percent for desertion from the army or some other military offense, 6 percent for violent crimes, and 6 percent for mendicancy and vagabondage. These were essentially the same proportions as in the galleys between 1716 and 1748. Their terms were as follows: three years, 32 percent; five years, 24 percent; six years (mostly soldiers), 4 percent; nine years, 16 percent; life, 22 percent.[72]

The march from Paris to Brest (usually via Dreux, Alençon, Laval, Rennes, and Saint-Brieuc) was even more harrowing than the old route to Marseilles. The distance was more than 400 miles, and it was crossed in twenty-four days of trudging over hilly terrain, often through chilling rain or drizzle and mud. The mortality rate among eighteenth-century *bagnards* has not been researched, but studies of mortality in the *bagnes* during the first quarter of the nineteenth century (within a penal and medical regime almost identical to that of 1752 to 1790) suggest that it was much lower than in the galleys from 1680 to 1748.[73] It seems that Choquet de Lindu and his successors at Brest did, in fact, go far toward realizing the venerable seventeenth-century goal of a carceral proletariat that was simultaneously inexpensive, securely entrapped, and punished by degradation and deprivation, but still able to do hard, productive labor and to survive the sentence.

The Hôpital-Général

The Hôpital-Général of Paris became the model for one of the most polyvalent institutions of Old Regime civilization. It was created in 1656 by Cardinal

---

[71] Unless by the clandestine goodwill of their guards, which could be bought. The Kéravel quarter was densely inhabited, and its winding, alley-like streets were filled with taverns and bordellos frequented by *bagne* guards, sailors, and marines (ibid., pp. 155–8).

[72] Marc Vigié, "Justice et criminalité au XVIIIe siècle: Le cas de la peine des galères," *Histoire, Economie et Société*, 3 (1985): 352–63.

[73] Annual deaths in the Brest *bagne* averaged 37 per 1,000 prisoners between 1816 and 1827; that 1 in 27 was about four times the annual mortality rate of the adult French population but far below the death rate in the galleys (Zysberg, "Politiques du bagne," pp. 190–3).

Mazarin, acting in the name of the young Louis XIV, and under the insistent influence of Saint Vincent of Paul, the Sisters of Charity, and the Company of the Holy Sacrament. To form the Hôpital-Général, the cardinal combined four existing Parisian charity institutions (Scipion, la Pitié, la Salpêtrière, and Bicêtre) into one large administration, to which six other institutions were later annexed. In the name of charity and redemption, destitute or invalid paupers, mendicants, and vagrants were to be interned in those hospices. The purpose was to extract "masterless" men, women, and children from their anarchic freedom and vulnerability and to place them, at least temporarily, under the mastery of the state – behind walls, subjected to religious discipline, constrained to work – and thereby to rid the streets of their parasitic and delictual presence. The state, through the agency of the Hôpital-Général, became a surrogate and stern parent for paupers, beggars, vagrants, and orphaned, abandoned, or fugitive children who lacked the sustenance of work and the discipline of family. The Hôpital-Général of Paris was replicated in several provinces in the ensuing decades.[74]

The monarchy endowed the Hôpital-Général with corporate political and economic autonomy. Its permanent titular directors were the first president and general prosecutor of the Parlement of Paris, the presidents of the Chambre des Comptes and Cour des Aides, the provost of merchants, the lieutenant-general of police, and the archbishop of Paris. There were also twenty-six administrators, each appointed for life; when one died, the directors and administrators co-opted a successor. None of those supreme offices in the Hôpital-Général were venal, hereditary, or remunerated; they were philanthropic responsibilities ancillary to professional careers. In theory, this large body formed a *bureau central* that set policy, ordered internments, and commanded the resident administrations of the ten separate institutions of the Hôpital, in practice, the latter enjoyed wide latitude within their domains. The Hôpital had its own police force, the *archers*, who were empowered to arrest beggars and other delinquents, and the governors had extensive punitive authority over internees. Revenue came from fixed *rentes* on various royal and municipal domains, urban properties, and excise taxes, percentages of the money earned by the Comédie-Française, the Comédie-Italienne, and various fairs in Paris, judicial confiscations and percentages of alms collected by courts, and from private benefactions. The funds were apportioned among the ten institutions, with little budgetary variance from year to year.[75] The Hôpital-Général

---

[74] On the ideas and politics that led to its creation, see Jean-Pierre Gutton, *La société et les pauvres: L'exemple de la généralité de Lyon, 1534–1789* (Paris: Les Belles Lettres, 1971), pp. 303–50; Olwen Hufton, *The Poor of Eighteenth-Century France, 1750–1789;* and Michel Foucault, *Madness and Civilization: A History of Insanity in the Age of Reason* (New York: Doubleday [Vintage], 1973). For a comprehensive study of the uses of the *hôpitaux* in Normandy, see Robert M. Schwartz, *Policing the Poor in Eighteenth-Century France* (Chapel Hill: University of North Carolina Press, 1988).

[75] Emile Richard, *Histoire de l'hôpital de Bicêtre: (1250–1791)* (Paris, 1889), pp. 21–4.

was a peculiar entity: The aegis was royal, the ideology was ecclesiastical, but the political being was secular, autonomous, and essentially repressive.

The founding purposes of the institution – charity and salvation for the destitute, joined with social prophylaxis against their "excesses" – were stated in the preamble to the April 1656 edict:

The wantonness of beggars has become excessive, by an unfortunate self-abandonment to all manner of crimes, crimes that call down God's curse on states when they go unpunished; those who have been occupied in charitable activity have learned that many beggars of both sexes live together without matrimony, their children unbaptized, and that nearly all live in ignorance of religion, disdain for the sacraments, and habituation to all manner of vices. . . . Considering these poor mendicants to be living members of Jesus Christ, and not useless members of the state, and carrying out this great work [internment and redemption], not by imperatives of police, but by the sole motive of charity . . . [76]

"Imperatives of police" were soon made paramount. Royal legislation against begging and vagabondage was increasingly punitive from 1660 onward. Its enforcement – primarily by the lieutenant general of police and the *archers* – furnished the Salpêtrière and Bicêtre with a continuously swollen and revolving carceral population of mendicants and vagrants until the Revolution.[77]

In 1786, the total population of the ten units that formed the Hôpital-Général of Paris was about 12,000, counting both inmates and staff. That was approximately 1 person in 50 of the city's population. More than 9,800 of the 12,000 were in either the Salpêtrière (reserved for women) or Bicêtre (reserved for men).[78]

The Salpêtrière. The Salpêtrière was a walled town on the periphery of the metropolis. It can be seen at the top center of the "Plan de Turgot" (see Map 1). In 1789–90, its population was officially 6,796, of whom 5,699 were in various situations of confinement. The remaining 1,097 were guardians, maintenance personnel, and administrators, most of whom also lived within the walls.[79] It was a carceral universe of women, their children, and their guards.[80]

[76] Isambert, vol. 18, pp. 326–7.
[77] The most informed and sensitive works on the social world of beggers and vagabonds are Bronislaw Geremek, *Truands et misérables dans l'Europe moderne (1350–1600)* (Paris: Gallimard/ Julliard. 1980); Gutton, *La société et les pauvres;* Hufton, *The Poor.*
[78] Armand Husson, *Etude sur les hôpitaux* (Paris, 1862), p. 280.
[79] Louis Boucher, *La Salpêtrière: Son histoire de 1656 à 1790* (Paris, 1883), p. 137. During the eighteenth century, there was 1 employee for every 5 or 6 inmates, and they absorbed most of the Salpêtrière's budget. The institution was managed by lay women, with conventual titles and costume: a "superior" (recruited from the Parisian nobility); a hierarchy of some 1,092 "sisters," matrons, governesses, cooks, and maintenance personnel (most of them women); 86 resident artisans and journeymen; 42 armed male guards (*archers*) and officers (ibid.). There was also a resident rector, assisted by twenty-two priests.
[80] But its history from 1656 to the Revolution has not been written systematically, from serial archives. Our knowledge of the Salpêtrière is limited and based on the following works: Boucher, *La Salpêtrière;* Husson, *Les Hôpitaux;* Jacques Hillairet, *Gibets, piloris et cachots du vieux Paris* (Paris: Editions de Minuit, 1956); Benabou, *La prostitution et la police des moeurs au XVIIIe siècle;*

The architecture of the Salpêtrière embodied the combination of monumentalism and obsession with sociospatial detail that was characteristic of the *Louis-quatorzien* state. The site had previously been occupied by a royal saltpeter refinery and gunpowder works, under the administration of the Arsenal. In implementing the 1656 edict, Louis XIV donated the site and some thirty surrounding acres to the Hôpital-Général. Most of the new charitable and carceral *cité* in the Faubourg Saint-Victor was designed by leading royal architects – notably Louis Levau and Libéral Bruant – and built between 1660 and 1700, although there were important additions during the eighteenth century. The entire area was walled. It was constructed to be ecologically self-sufficient, with vegetable gardens, stockyards and slaughter pens, a flour mill, reservoirs, water pumps, lumberyards, ateliers and clothing factories, infirmaries, wards for the insane and epileptic, laundries, schools, apartments for guards and administrators, dormitories and prisons, a cemetery. The Saint-Louis Church (designed by Bruant on commission from Louis XIV) loomed over the complex and visually dominated the entire Faubourg Saint-Victor, thereby asserting the redemptive vocation of the Salpêtrière. With its high, octagonal dome, two great arcades, four naves (each with a chapel), and an altar in the center of the dome that was visible from each nave, the church was constructed to accommodate, and to segregate, thousands of worshipers.[81]

When the Salpêtrière was constructed in the seventeenth century, the region of the Faubourg Saint-Victor was rural and thinly populated. It filled, during the eighteenth century, with populations and activities that created a pestilential environment for the Hôpital: the log pile and lumberyards of the Porte Saint-Bernard, infested with rats; stone quarries and their pools of stagnant water; the horse market and its excrement; the Bièvre Creek – lined with tanneries and laundries and filled with their waste – that flowed past the Salpêtrière into the Seine; quantities of fetid shacks, apartment buildings, and ateliers.

The Salpêtrière is the largest hospital of Paris, and perhaps of Europe: this hospital is both a hospice for women and a prison for convicts; it receives pregnant women and girls, nursing women with their babies, male children from the ages of 7 or 8 months to 4 or 5 years, every sort and age of young girl, old married couples, women who are violently insane, imbecile, epileptic, paralyzed, blind, crippled, afflicted with infectious diseases, incurably ill, scrofulous children, etc., etc.[82]

The eclecticism of the Salpêtrière, as witnessed by Tenon in 1788, resulted from a series of different functions that were grafted by the state onto the original poorhouse over a long period after the 1656 foundation. The grafting pro-

Bloch and Tuetey, *Comité de Mendicité* (notably the duke of LaRochefoucauld-Liancourt's "Rapport fait au nom du Comité de Mendicité des visites faites dans divers hôpitaux, hospices et maisons de charité de Paris," 1790); Alexandre Tuetey, ed., *L'assistance publique à Paris pendant la Révolution, vol. 1: Les hôpitaux et hospices, 1789–90* (Paris, 1895); Jacques-René Tenon, *Mémoires sur les hôpitaux* (Paris, 1788).

[81] Boucher, *La Salpêtrière*, pp. 27–33; Husson, *Les hôpitaux*, pp. 280–4.
[82] Tenon, *Mémoire*, p. 85.

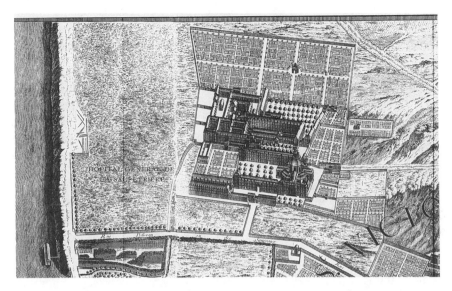

MAP 9. The Salpêtrière of Paris (detail from Map 1).

duced a transformed and highly original institution. The charitable and prophylactic enterprise of 1656 had grown, by the 1720s, into a grandiose penal establishment. Between at least 1730 and 1789, approximately 1 inmate in 4 of the Salpêtrière was a convict – prostitute, delinquent, or criminal. During the late eighteenth century, the Salpêtrière was made into a major laboratory for medical experimentation on the venereal and the insane, in the name of science.[83]

The Salpêtrière remained, foremost, a poorhouse for women and girls. The largest group of inmates (almost 4,000 in 1679, and 4,657 in 1789) were mendicant, vagrant, and destitute females, most of them arrested by the police, *constabulary,* or *archers* of the Hôpital for those reasons, some of them admitted at their own request. Those aged 60 or over, domiciled in Paris for at least two years, whose poverty was certified by their parish priest and who presented themselves voluntarily, were known as *bonnes pauvres;* the term was also used to describe other paupers who were life residents of the Hôpital. During the eighteenth century, most of the younger or able-bodied women interned for begging were interned for less than six months.[84] Some thirty large dormitories lodged

---

[83] See Foucault, *Madness and Civilization.* In 1786–9 there were more than 500 deranged inmates, some 150 feebleminded, and about 300 epileptics; in addition to those 1,000 who were congenitally afflicted, there were about 350 seriously ill, most from veneral or skin diseases (Tenon, *Mémoire,* pp. 1, 218; Tuetey, *L'assistance publique,* pp. 269, 274). The Salpêtrière had, after the Hôtel-Dieu, the largest concentration of maladies in eighteenth-century Paris.

[84] Between August 1764 and December 1773, 18,523 persons were interned (in a *hôpital* or *dépôt de mendicité*) for begging or vagabondage in the Generality of Paris; 11,895 were released; 3,158 died inside; 1,963 escaped (Hufton, *The Poor,* p. 389).

paupers, usually four to a bed. The residents were distributed among dormitories (named after women saints) in groups: the invalid; children without mothers; nursing mothers; the contagiously diseased; the venereal; epileptics; the sick and convalescent; the insane; the deformed and imbecile; the violent and "vicious"; able-bodied women and girls without children. There were also elderly mendicant or destitute married couples. These latter numbered some 200, occupied small apartments in the buildings of the front facade, and were given piecework.

Their poverty was regimented, but it was not hidden. The able-bodied and well behaved were allowed out on certain days (but not at night); they had to wear Hôpital uniforms and were forbidden to beg, although a cohort was formed to collect alms for the Salpêtrière. The administration rented certain of them out to important familes for their funeral corteges, "following the hearse, chanting prayers and incantations to make easier the path of the deceased to heaven where the poor were apparently more esteemed than the rich."[85]

The Salpêtrière's population was not only continually replenished by new internees; it was also self-replicating. A great many inmate girls were children of beggars, vagabonds, prostitutes, and criminals. They were put into a huge common nursery until the age of 7. Then they were moved into school and factory dormitories. Most were taught to read and do sums, but few to write. All worked at sewing, knitting, and spinning. This was to prepare the "daughters of the Salpêtrière" for supervised release, between the ages of 20 and 25, into a respectable and laborious life. The administration attempted to place them in Parisian ateliers and households, even to marry them to artisans and workers. It awarded a trousseau and 300 livres of dowry to each young woman who did contract an honest marriage. But the attempts rarely succeeded, and most of the minority who were placed returned, or were forcibly returned, within a few years, often with their babies, after falling prey to sexual abuse, unemployment, desertion, and then debauchery, begging, or prostitution.

The habits of irresponsibility and indolence that they have acquired in the Hôpital, their ignorance of social conventions, the pronounced besottedness in which they have been raised, and often their infirmities render them incapable of housekeeping or domestic service, the only occupations to which they can aspire. Most of those who leave turn out very badly, and even when they do not sink into debauchery they are fired and reenter the Hôpital. Finally, it is almost incredible that although the directors of the establishment give a trousseau and 300 livres to the girls who marry, there are no more than two (in an average year) who manage to do so. Thus, the Salpêtrière devours entire generations that it rears at great expense, or that it recruits from the most degraded classes of society.[86]

---

[85] Ibid., pp. 146–7.
[86] LaRochefoucauld-Liancourt, in Bloch and Tuetey, *Comité de Mendicité*, p. 621.

The majority of the Salpêtrière's daughters never left. They remained as *bonnes pauvres* or were recruited to be cooks, nurses, or low-level guards. When the Salpêtrière morally reformed derelict girls, it usually did so by fabricating dependencies that riveted them to the institution for life.

It was also a prison depot for street prostitutes, publicly libertine women, and for debauched or rebellious girls interned at the request of their parents or guardians. A royal edict of April 20, 1684, laid the legal foundations for the public "moral policing" of Paris until the Revolution and for the first thoroughly punitive purpose of the Salpêtrière.[87]

Its preamble targeted and amalgamated "the wretches who prostitute themselves with scandal and disturbance," "women of public and scandalous debauchery," and "those who corrupt others in order to prostitute them." Prostitutes who solicited publicly, in streets, marketplaces, taverns, boardinghouses, and apartment buildings and women who were notoriously promiscuous in public were to be penally interned in special buildings of the Salpêtrière, separate from pauper women. In those buildings, they and their children were to be "instructed in their religious duties and forced to work in a manner capable of changing their immoral dispositions." The 1684 edict was directed textually at public prostitution and debauchery, not at the private and concealed world of bordellos, concubines, and *femmes galantes* for the affluent. It also established a dual criminal jurisdiction. The lieutenant general of police of Paris was empowered to judge summarily those arrested on such charges, in his audiences at the Châtelet, without appeals decision by the Parlement of Paris. He could also decide the terms of their sentences to the Salpêtrière. However, the Châtelet and other courts retained the authority to try and judge prostitutes and publicly libertine women, but their judgments were henceforth excepted from appeal to the Parlement.

A royal declaration of July 1713 further refined the policing of female public morals. It distinguished between "public debauchery and scandalous living" by women and girls and "public prostitution or pimping." The distinction was, implicitly, between those who gave sex gratuitously and promiscuously and those who did so for money. The former offenders were subject primarily to lesser defaming and afflictive penalties (fines, alms, banishment, or confiscation of property for the profit of the Hôpital-Général); they were to be judged by the lieutenant general, but with appeal to the Parlement. The latter were subject to both the aforementioned penalties and imprisonment at the Salpêtrière; they were to be judged preferentially by royal courts (not the lieutenant general), according to the procedure of the Criminal Ordinance of 1670 and with appeal to the Parlement. Both categories of offenders, however, could be "provisionally" imprisoned at the Salpêtrière until appeals decision.[88] But Erica-Marie Benabou has determined that in Parisian practice, from 1684 to the Revolution,

---

[87] In Isambert, vol. 19, pp. 441–5.　　[88] In Isambert, vol. 20, pp. 603–5.

the judgment and punishment of prostitutes and libertine women per se was done almost wholly by the lieutenant generalcy, despite the jurisdictional distinctions and accommodations of 1713.[89] The Châtelet and Parlement acquiesced to his authority over those sordid prosecutions. A key reason for the acquiescence was the sheer volume of such cases, five hundred to eight hundred a year during the eighteenth century. By Benabou's estimate, there were about 15,000 full-time or frequent prostitutes in Paris at any time during the century (or about 1 in 38 of the population, a ratio similar to that in Bangkok or Calcutta today).[90] Most of them were the girls and women of the streets, for whom Mercier invented the term *vulgivagues*.[91] The Châtelet and Parlement frequently tried and judged prostitutes and "debauched" women, but rarely for those crimes alone. Women convicted of prostitution and debauchery by provincial courts and given afflictive or capital penalties were judged on appeal, usually with moderation or leniency, by the Parlement of Paris.[92] Parisian common prostitutes (especially those who had not secured the favor of police inspectors) were permanently threatened by expeditive judgment followed by incarceration at the Salpêtrière, outside the trial procedure and protections of the Criminal Ordinance of 1670. In consequence, the great majority of women imprisoned for prostitution and debauchery at the Salpêtrière were there by sentences of the Lieutenant Generalcy of Police, not by those of a royal court or the Parlement. The same was true of the women (and men at Bicêtre) imprisoned for the offenses of begging and vagabondage.

---

[89] "Il faut aussi souligner combien, dans son application, certains points de la Déclaration de 1713 furent négligés ou ignorés. C'est en masse que les débauchées sont jugées sommairement en audience par le Lieutenant Général de police. Dans la seconde moitié du XVIIIe siècle, elles défilent à la moyenne de 600 à 800 par an. Le tribunal criminel du Châtelet, lui, n'est saisi, au plus, que d'une ou deux affaires de prostitution ou libertinage par an; quelquefois d'aucune. Quant à l'appel d'un jugement de police au Parlement de Paris, de longues recherches ne nous ont pas permis d'en trouver un seul exemple" (*La prostitution*, p. 25).

[90] Ibid., p. 328.

[91] *Tableau de Paris*, vol. 3, p. 68. *Vulgivagues*, with its mixture of irony and sympathy, expresses an attitude different from the official one of Ruhlière, inspector for the Constabulary of the Ile-de-France, who referred to his clients as "whores of the lowest sort" (quoted by Benabou, *La prostitution*, p. 61).

[92] Even those cases were rare in the Tournelle. For example, in 1736 the Parlement judged 344 defendants on appeal in *grand criminel*, almost one-third of them women. Only four had been convicted exclusively of pimping or prostitution. Jean Denis was convicted of pimping in public by the Tours presidial court and sentenced to promenade on a donkey, branding with the fleur-de-lis, the iron collar, and banishment from the jurisdiction for nine years; the Parlement confirmed the sentence. Cathérine Gendre was convicted of public prostitution by the same court; her sentence to promenade on a donkey and banishment for nine years was confirmed. Cathérine Masson and Marie-Anne Pineau were both sentenced by the La Rochelle presidial to the Hôpital-Général for three years for prostitution; the Parlement reduced their sentences to three months in jail, under decree of *plus amplement informé*, and then dismissal of charges (Inventory 450, vol. 2). No more than a few hundred such cases figured among the 40,000 to 50,000 judged by the Tournelle from 1700 to 1789, by the computation of Benabou, *La prostitution*, p. 59. Only research into the records of local courts will disclose how the judicial policing of prostitution and debauchery was accomplished in the provincial jurisdiction of the Parlement during the eighteenth century.

During the eighteenth century, arrested prostitutes were detained in the Saint-Martin jail on the street of that name. Once a month, they were convoyed to the Châtelet for the lieutenant general's audience of *Grande Police:*

Contemporaries have given us more than one scandalous description of those audiences: After being penned in a waiting room of the tribunal . . . , up to a hundred at a time were led into the audience hall. Immediately, there ensued a vicious exchange of crude insults, even blows and projectiles, with their lovers, the "accomplices of their debauchery," who filled the hall, or with spectators who provoked them from the galleries. "It is incredible that the preparations for a public and stigmatic correction in justice should be a type of crapulous, orgiastic festival," as [police commissioner] Des Essarts wrote indignantly. . . . Silence fell as soon as the magistrate entered; kneeling, the accused heard their sentences read by the lieutenant general and then left the hall one by one, on their way to the Hôpital.[93]

The monthly convoys of open wagons, filled with prostitutes and public *debauchées*, that wound from the rue Saint-Martin in northern Paris to the Châtelet and from there across the Latin Quarter and southern faubourgs to the Salpêtrière, were integral to the human landscape of Paris. They were described by Mercier:

They stand all pressed together in the wagons. One is weeping, another is trembling, another hides her face. The most brazen return the stares of the ridiculing populace; they shout back curses and defy the hooting that reverberates along their route. This scandalous cortege traverses a large part of the city in full daylight; the language that it provokes is an insult to public decency.[94]

This penology was tautological. Most were sentenced to the Hôpital for a term of less than nine months.[95] They were released – unreformed, embittered, and even more destitute than before – to make room for others, and very many became recurrent inmates of the Salpêtriére. The cycle was usually broken only by incapacitation or death.

Children, whether boys aged under 25 or girls, of artisans and poor inhabitants of the city and faubourgs of Paris, inhabitants exercising a trade or with some employment, who mistreat their fathers or mothers, who refuse to work out of debauchery or laziness, and girls who have debauched themselves or *who are in evident danger of doing so,* will be locked up in places designated for that purpose, that is to say: boys in Bicêtre and girls in the Salpêtrière. . . . The boys and girls will hear mass every Sunday and Holy Day, pray to God for a quarter hour every morning and evening, be carefully instructed in the catechism, and listen to readings from books of piety during their work. *They will be made to work, as long as possible and at the hardest labors that their strength and conditions of detention can permit;* should their behavior suggest that they wish to reform, they will be taught trades suitable to their sex and their aptitudes, trades by which they can earn a

---

[93] Translated from Benabou, *La prostitution,* p. 62. At midcentury, 59% of these defendants were banished from Paris; 26.5% were sentenced to the Salpêtrière; 6.8% were warned to desist. The percentage of those imprisoned steadily increased from 1750 to 1789 (ibid., pp. 63–4).
[94] *Tableau de Paris,* vol. 3, p. 106.   [95] Benabou, *La prostitution,* pp. 64, 80.

living, and they will be treated with degrees of gentleness commensurate with the proof of their reformation. . . . Laziness and other faults will be punished by reducing their soup ration, increasing their work, confinement [in cells], and other penalties used in the Hôpital, as the directors deem appropriate [italics mine].[96]

These passages of the 1684 edict, which prescribed the Salpêtrière and Bicêtre as prison reformatories for wayward and rebellious youths from poor or socially modest families, were suffused with the ethical imperatives of the French Counter-Reformation: piety; sexual ascesis or restraint; hard, sustained labor (as a device to promote contrition, atonement, and subjugation of the passions); parental authoritarianism; economic and social productivity. The imperatives formed the ideology, both statist and ecclesiastical, that reigned officially, with varying degrees of intensity and application, over the entire Hôpital-Général, even over the galleys and then the *bagnes*. The ideology was both penal and salvational. It was a semisecularized monasticism. It preceded the Enlightenment by more than one hundred years.

Fathers, mothers, or, if the parents were dead or incapable, uncles, aunts, tutors, guardians, even parish priests could apply to the office of the Hôpital-Général for the correctional internment of such youths in their charge. The presiding director of the office was to select one or two other directors to hear the applicants and their witnesses (and the young person, if possible). On their recommendation, and with the signed assent of two other directors, the youths were to be interned "for as long as the directors in charge of the case deem necessary" and could not legally be released without their order. They could order the provost or the lieutenants at the Châtelet to have the delinquent arrested and placed in the Hôpital.

Judgmental and internment authority over the debauched or rebellious offspring of laboring and shopkeeping families was subsequently assumed also by the lieutenant general of police, the Chancellor, and royal ministers (via *lettres de cachet*). And it also came to include preventive or correctional imprisonment of miscreant and dangerous adults, on petition of their families.[97]

The second significant change in the Salpêtrière, and the one of greatest import to this study, was accomplished by the Parlement of Paris and its subaltern courts. After the promulgation of the Criminal Ordinance of 1670, they began to use the Salpêtrière as a carceral penalty in cases of *grand criminel*, though the frequency of that use is not known before the middle of the eighteenth century. One of the earliest royal laws to order that practice was the declaration of April 1687. It stated that women who were sentenced to banishment by provostial or presidial judgments and who violated those sentences were to be "condemned to confinement in the nearest *Hôpital-général;* which we desire to be especially practiced as regards the *maison de force* of the Hôpital-Général of our good city

---

[96] 1684 edict, Isambert, vol. 20, pp. 442–4.
[97] Benabou, *La prostitution*, pp. 74–7; Quetel, *De Par le Roy*, pp. 183–4.

of Paris, where such women and girls will be imprisoned . . . without judges being at liberty to mitigate this penalty, but at liberty only to determine whether it will be for a term or for life, according to the case."[98]

A March 1724 royal declaration on theft stipulated that women convicted of theft from a church, those convicted of recidivism in theft, and those convicted of theft who had been branded for any previous offense were to be sentenced to a term or to life in a *maison de force*, that is, in the prison section of a *hôpital*.[99] The August 1729 declaration on smuggling ordered that women convicted of that offense a second time be sentenced either to banishment for life or life imprisonment in a *hôpital*.[100] By the 1730s, the Parlement and its subaltern courts were using the Salpêtrière as a penalty analogous to the galleys – for women convicted of crimes that, in the case of men, were punishable by term or life sentences in the galleys at Marseilles, or later in the *bagnes*. Kings and Chancellors permitted the analogy, and by midcentury this type of sentencing had become a frequent practice.[101] The Salpêtrière therefore contained women convicted by royal courts and sentenced to incarceration for one, three, five, or nine years or life and women under death sentence who received royal commutation to life imprisonment. And because the Salpêtrière had extensive buildings for the mentally deranged, the Parlement also used them for the detention (usually for life) of many of the women convicted of a serious crime who were judged insane by its physicians. The Tournelle, unlike the Lieutenant Generalcy, made restrained use of the Salpêtrière. Of the approximately 130 women judged on appeal in 1736, only six were sentenced to the Hôpital: two minors, one for six months and the other for one year; two thieves for five years; two women found guilty of murderous violence and committed for life as insane.[102] Provostial and presidial courts, that principally judged mendicant or vagrant criminals without appeal, made greater use of the Salpêtrière.

During the years 1684–1700, a *maison de force* was built in the Salpêtrière, on royal order and in consequence of the 1684 edict. It was the large yet compact rectangle of buildings shown in the center of Map 9. The *maison de force* consisted of two long, parallel buildings, each with a ground floor, three stories, an attic, and a peaked roof, that were joined at right angles by four buildings of the same dimensions but shorter. The southernmost segment was further divided by a seventh building parallel to the two large ones. The entire structure enclosed three small and dank stone courtyards. There were few windows and only the most elementary plumbing. The guards' barracks were adjacent to the main entrance of the *maison de force*. The *maison* was divided into three carceral sections during the eighteenth century: The northernmost, *le commun*, was reserved for prostitutes. The central section was the *prison*, for women convicted

---

[98] Isambert, vol. 20, pp. 47–9.   [99] Ibid., vol. 21, p. 260.
[100] Jousse, *Traité*, vol. 3, pp. 295–320.
[101] See Yvonne Bongert, "Quelques aspects de la prison au XVIIIe siècle," in *Etudes dédiés à la mémoire du Professeur Gérard Dehove* (Paris: Presses Universitaires de France, 1983), pp. 79–80.
[102] Inventory 450, vol. 2.

of crimes. The southernmost, *la grande force*, was designed principally for women criminals sentenced to life imprisonment by the courts or to long-term detention by royal order. The middle building, which divided *la grande force* into two subsections, contained forty cells for solitary confinement of the most dangerous or intractable. Each cell was 6½ by 5 feet. It had a small barred and shutterless aperture that faced on a courtyard, a heavy door with a judas hole for guards, a wooden bed and straw mattress with a blanket, and sheets that were changed every six weeks. The other parts of the *maison de force* were common halls (*dortoirs*). Wooden platform beds with straw mattresses lined the walls of each, with four or six women allotted to each bed. Worktables and benches filled the middle portion of each hall.[103] Prisoners were not chained.

The house of correction (*maison de correction*) was just below but adjacent to the *maison de force*, within the northern garden. It was the prison for the delinquent and libertine girls defined in the 1684 edict, most of whom were incarcerated for a few years. Confinement there was in 150 individual cells, most of which had only one inmate. Because their families or guardians were obliged to pay annual *pensions* of 100 to 300 livres for the *correctionnaires*, they were fed better than criminals and the poor. They also had use of the courtyard and, occasionally, the garden. They were put to work at sewing and mending.[104]

The penitential regime of the entire Salpêtrière resembled that of a convent. At the time of internment, inmates' hair was cropped short to a burr and kept that way. They wore a uniform consisting of a coarse linen blouse, a skirt, a grey gown of rough serge, grey woolen stockings, wooden clogs, and a round bonnet.[105] This was to de-eroticize them, in the manner of nuns. The standard fare in the *maison de force* during most of the eighteenth century was a bowl of soup with some beans, peas, or lentils, and almost 2 pounds of black bread each day. By the 1780s, the ration had been increased by a few ounces of boiled meat, butter, and cheese. No wine was provided.[106] There was a quarter hour of obligatory common prayer each morning and evening and mass every Sunday and holy day; the catechism was read aloud at intervals during every twenty-four hours. Convict inmates were remunerated at piece rate for their labor inside the *maison de force*, as in the galleys and *bagne*. But that was pittance income. The spinning, sewing, crocheting, and embroidery work to which prisoners and *correctionaires* were constrained (at least officially), and that was "purchased" by the

---

[103] Hillairet, *Gibets*, pp. 269–72.   [104] Ibid., pp. 269–70.
[105] Ibid., p. 272.
[106] Tuetey, *L'assistance publique*, p. 278. But there was a tavern within the walls. During at least the 1780s, it made more than 15,500 livres a year from selling wine and strong drink to guards, artisans, administrators, and inmates who could pay; that was 18% of the entire annual revenue generated by the Salpêtrière (Bloch and Tuetey, *Comité de Mendicité*, p. 627; Tuetey, *L'assistance publique*, p. 280). It was off-limits to convicts, but they could obtain wine – and sex – illicitly from *archers* and the various artisans, gardeners, and stockmen of the Salpêtrière. The total revenue from all of the commodities fashioned in the establishment was only 16,998 livres in 1789 – as against the 15,500 livres of the tavern (Tuetey, *L'assistance publique*, p. 279).

administration, seems to have been more spiritual and disciplinary than economic in purpose. During an average year of the period 1750 to 1789, it amounted to only a few thousand livres in commercial value, although it was done ostensibly by several hundred women.[107]

Penury, not physical duress, was the essence of the eighteenth-century Salpêtrière. The total expenses for the establishment in 1789 were 109,813 livres, equivalent to the annual income of one comparatively wealthy *parlementaire* family. About 73,750 livres of that budget were paid to administrators, guards, maintenance personnel, artisans, and clerics for their services.[108] The average sum expended on maintaining an inmate (whether pauper or prisoner) was 75 to 79 livres annually, or about 4 sous, 2 deniers per day.[109] The principle of obligatory labor – as simultaneous discipline, penance, and sustenance – was intrinsic to the Salpêtrière (and to most of the Hôpital-Général) from its creation, but the practice in the Salpêtrière seems to have been desultory.

Inmates of the Salpêtrière were not endowed with economic value, in contrast to *galériens* and *bagnards*. They seem to have worked only sporadically, whereas prayers and mass apparently were enforced rigorously. The autarchy intended by the founders of the Salpêtrière became a system of material dearth for all but high-ranking personnel.

The explicitly penal buildings usually contained about 1,000 inmates during the eighteenth century: 400 to 600 prostitutes; 250 to 350 criminals; 150 to 200 *correctionaires*. The worst was the *maison de force* – a "dreadful abode," in the judgment of the duke of LaRochefoucauld-Liancourt, dark, cramped, humid, poorly ventilated, and stench-ridden. It faced onto the river, and the main sewage ditch of the Salpêtrière flowed past its northern façade. There, the qualities that LaRochefoucauld noticed generally within the Salpêtrière of 1790 – administrative and medical negligence or indifference, disorder, filth, structural and human decay – were most acute.[110]

---

[107] Ibid., p. 277, Cf. Benabou, *La prostitution*, p. 82. The administrators stated in 1790 that only 1,800 of the some 4,500 pauper inmates were physically or mentally capable of work (Tuetey, *L'assistance publique*, p. 275).

[108] Ibid., pp. 279–84.   [109] Bloch and Tuetey, *Comité de Mendicité*, p. 82.

[110] François Doublet, member of the Royal Society of Medicine and former deputy-inspector of civil hospitals and *maisons de force* of Paris, was more knowledgeable and expressive than La Rochefoucauld: "La maison de la Salpêtrière a trois parties très distinctes; dans la première sont renfermées les femmes condamnés à une prison perpétuelle. Tout est triste et morne dans ce département, et y offre l'image d'une vie si languissante et si misérable, qu'elle rassemble à une mort lente ou prolongée. D'une côté, une petite cour sombre et infecte, le long de laquelle sont rangées des cellules étroites, et qui sont froides et humides dans toutes les saisons; d'un autre côté, des dortoirs où des femmes sont rassemblées dans un très-petit espace, et condamnées à vivre sans cesse les unes auprès des autres: par-tout de l'entassement et un air étoufée; par-tout l'empreinte sévère et rigoureuse d'une détresse et d'un chagrin qui n'ont jamais allégé par l'espérance. La seconde partie de la prison de la Salpêtrière, destinées aux femmes dont la détention est limitée, présente bien l'idée de la gêne, mais la contrainte y paroît moins profonde, et le licence méme n'y est qu'à demi-étouffée. Ce qui l'excite assez souvent à paroître, c'est que les renfermées sont extrêmement pressés dans des salles basses et étroites, et que, malgré des travaux particuliers aux-quels on les assujettit, elles sont on ne peut plus mal nourries. La troisième division, dite de *la correction, est une espèce de cloître* [italics mine] com-

Many of the poor and mendicant were already aged or sick when first interned at the Salpêtrière. Even so, the general mortality among them and prisoners was high. Before the construction of a hospital building in the early 1780s, the annual mortality rate among inmates of the institution was about one-sixth; afterward it fell to one-tenth.[111]

In February 1790, there were 176 women incarcerated in the *maison de force* by appeals sentences of the Parlement of Paris.[112] The most senior inmate (Anne Lebrun of Reims, aged 75) had been sentenced for life in 1744, the most junior (Marie Foucaud of Bourg-en-Saintonge) for three years in December 1789. The 176 form a profile of the Salpêtrière's criminal population during the second half of the century, by term of sentence, age, marital condition, and geographical origin. Through their diversity in those respects, the convicts of the Salpêtrière resembled *galériens* and *bagnards*.

Sixty-seven (39% of those whose sentences are given) were imprisoned for life; 50 (29%) for nine years; 31 (18%) for five years; 17 (10%) for three years; 7 (4%) without stated term. Most of the 7 were either girls below the age of seventeen, whose cases were subject to review at maturity, or women found to be insane at the time of conviction. Most of those sentenced for life had been convicted of a criminal act or complicity subject to the death penalty, and their high proportion expressed a form of judicial clemency. A further 6 had been sentenced to death and then granted royal commutation of penalty to life imprisonment. One hundred eighteen were branded with a single *V*, which meant conviction for at least theft or complicity in theft; 5 with a double *V*, which meant recidivism in theft; and 11 with the fleur-de-lis, for other capital or afflictive offenses (principally violence or complicity in violence).

Their ages at the time of conviction and incarceration were as follows: 16 (2); 16 to 20 (10); 21 to 30 (71); 31 to 40 (60); 41 to 50 (21); 51 to 60 (5); 61 to 70 (3); 70 or older (1). The Parlement rarely used the rigors of the Salpêtrière for

posée de cellules particulières et isolées, ouvrant sur des galères assez aérées; c'est la seule partie de la prison de la Salpêtrière qui paroisse disposée d'une manière salubre, et c'est cependant la seule dont on ne fasse aujourd'hui aucun usage" (*Rapport sur l'état actuel des Prisons de Paris, lu à la Séance publique de la Société Royale de Médecine, le 28 août 1791* [Paris, 1791], pp. 6–7).

[111] Report of LaRochefoucauld-Liancourt, 1790, in Bloch and Tuetey, *Comité de Mendicité*, p. 625. *La gale*, a virulently contagious skin disease that could lead to fatal blood poisoning, was the principal scourge of the Salpêtrière, according to Tenon and LaRochefoucauld. Because neither halls nor bedding were disinfected, inmates continually spread contagion to each other. The infirmaries and hospital merely segregated the most diseased, gave them some treatment, and then returned them to the halls, where they were usually reinfected. On May 19, 1790, in their response to the inquiry of the Mendicancy Committee, the administrators of the Salpêtrière acknowledged the mephitic condition of the establishment, the prevalence of *gale* and various deadly "fevers," but they blamed the pestilential site, not their primitive regime (Tuetey, *L'assistance publique*, p. 270).

[112] "Etat des personnes détenues par arrêts de la Cour du Parlement en cette maison [Salpêtrière] à compter du 7 juillet 1744 jusqu'a et compris le 8 fevrier 1790," ms. A.N. BB 30 19. In 1789, at least, there were an additional 125 prisoners by order or sentence of the following authorities: provostial and presidial judgments without appeal (36); audience of lieutenant general of police (34); general prosecutor, Parlement of Paris (55) (Boucher, *La Salpêtrière*, p. 137).

the correction of delinquent girls; it reserved them for women. Three-fourths of the inmates were aged between 21 and 40 when locked into the *maison de force*. Marital condition is known for 165 of the 176: 81 (49%) were single; 54 (33%) were married; 30 (18%) were widows. The number of single and widowed women was twice that of those with husbands. The *maison de force* was essentially a world of those who had formerly lived outside matrimony – either single; in periodic liaisons, concubinage, and criminal complicities with men; or in the quasi solitude and, one suspects, poverty of widowhood. Those qualities were striking among the 152 who were in full maturity:

Age	Single	Married	Widowed
21–30	49 (69.0%)	16 (22.5%)	3 (4.0%)
31–40	17 (28.0%)	26 (43.0%)	15 (25.0%)
41–50	3 (4.0%)	7 (33.3%)	10 (48.0%)

The crimes of the women who were crowded into the *maison de force* ranged from stealing old clothes from a traveling tradesman or chickens from a farmer, assault and battery or rioting, domestic theft, burglary or participation in armed robbery, to calculatedly lethal actions. Jeanne Bateau was sentenced in 1768 by the presidial court of Montargis (in provostial judgment, without appeal) for concubinage, errancy and vagabondage for three years with Antoine Alphond, and for having been in his company when he was arrested in possession of stolen goods. Louise d'Auvergne of Sentenay-en-Brie used arsenic to poison some two hundred sheep that belonged to the farmer for whom she worked in revenge for his beating of her husband. (Such slaughter of livestock was a hanging offense, but she was sentenced instead to life imprisonment by the Châtelet and Parlement.) There were also women convicted of active complicity in murder. There was little segregation of inmates inside the *maison de force*, despite the administrative rule. Those sentenced to three or five years for nonviolent offenses, those sentenced to nine years or life for violent crimes, those guilty of a single offense, recidivists guilty of multiple crimes and complicities, the young, the old, and the hardened were mixed together in the same halls and platform beds. Only those deemed most violent and "vicious" were placed in the cells and halls of *la grande force*. The community of the *maison* was corruptive, abrasive, tension-ridden, and criminogenic.[113]

[113] In April 1791, a commissioner for the keeper of the seals reviewed the cases of the women who had been imprisoned for more than twenty years and interviewed several of the *maison de force*. He recommended only three for release on pardon: They had behaved well in prison and seemed genuinely repentant. One, Charlotte LaGrogne from Champagne, had been incarcerated since 1762, on life sentence as a recidivist felon, able-bodied beggar, and vagabond who was convicted anew of multiple thefts. She had no one on the outside and asked to remain in the Salpêtrière as a *bonne pauvre*, with attendant privileges. Jeanne Bateau (previously cited) also stated that she no longer knew anyone outside but wished to go to Auxerre (where she had once been) to practice the trade of seamstress she had learned in prison (A.N. BB 30, 19).

The *maison de force* was Parisian only in location, for it was peopled by inmates who came from virtually all of France north of the Loire. Less than one-fourth of the 176 sentenced to the Salpêtrière on appeal by the Parlement had been tried and judged by the Châtelet. More than three-fourths had been tried in first instance by seneschalcy, bailliage, or presidial courts throughout the jurisdiction of the Parlement. Only 37 were from cities or large towns: 12 from Paris, and 1 to 3 each from Reims, Cambrai, Liège, Troyes, Sens, Laôn, Moulins, Nevers, Lyons, Aurillac, Riom, Bourges, Orléans, Blois, Chateaugontier, Le Mans, Angers, Nantes, and Bordeaux. The provenance (place either of birth or of residence at the time of trial) of the remaining 129 was rural: villages and small *bourgs* dispersed throughout northern, northeastern, central, and western France. Many of the convicts had been peasants rather than urban immigrants or long-term vagabonds. For them, the Salpêtrière would have been a strange and searing experience.

Bicêtre. Bicêtre was the institution for males that formed a counterpart to the Salpêtrière within the structure of the Hôpital-Général of Paris. Between 1656 and 1789, it was subjected to the same permutations in use as the Salpêtrière. By the late Old Regime it had acquired an even more notorious reputation among the official, the cultivated, and the propertied:

Sloth, vice, and villainy have their refuge at Bicêtre; bitterness, jealousy, and putridity are ceaselessly at work in the Salpêtrière. Idleness enervates the men of Bicêtre; forced labor kills the children of the Salpêtrière. The slovenliness is the same in both, but it is more dangerous for the health of the women; the impression given by Bicêtre is more frightening, that by the Salpêtrière more disgusting.[114]

Bicêtre: A terrible ulcer on the body politic, a large, deep, and suppurating ulcer that one can stand to face only by looking aside. The very air of the place, that one smells a half-mile away, tells you that you are approaching a site of incarceration, of misery, of degradation, of misfortune. . . . Because it has become the receptacle for all that is most impure and vile in society, and is populated mostly by all manner of libertines, crooks, police spies, thieves, counterfeiters, pederasts, etc., the imagination is injured as soon as the word is uttered, a word that calls to mind every turpitude.[115]

Putrescence; savagery; evil: These dominant images of Bicêtre register the fact that its prison subsumed its poorhouse, insane asylum, and hospital, in at least official and educated consciousness. The Salpêtrière signified physical malady and misery, whereas Bicêtre signified criminality and moral rot. It was an axial site within "the geography of haunted places as in the landscape of the moral universe."[116] The latter meaning was powerfully reinforced by the fact that, from the early eighteenth century, Bicêtre was the major institution within the Hôpital-Général for the treatment of lower-class or delinquent men and women

---

[114] LaRochefoucauld-Liancourt, in Bloch and Tuetey, *Comité de Mendicité*, p. 629.
[115] Mercier, *Tableau de Paris*, vol. 8, pp. 1–2.   [116] Foucault, *Madness and Civilization*, p. 57.

with venereal disease, the malady of vice.[117] In consonance with that general reputation, the first tests of the prototype guillotine, early in 1792, were conducted on the corpses of inmates in a yard of Bicêtre prison.[118] And in fact, Bicêtre had consistently, from at least 1701 to 1789, a higher proportion of prisoners (including able-bodied vagabonds) to paupers, invalids, and *bons pauvres* than the Salpêtrière: at least 1 in 3 inmates.[119] Although the history of Bicêtre remains to be written, two contemporary sources provide compelling and concordant descriptions, from 1772–73 and 1789–90.[120] Both addressed long-term conditions within the penal establishment, yet both followed on large-scale convict riots. They reveal striking disjunctions between institutional architecture and purpose and the true carceral situation.

Bicêtre was located on a ridge a few miles south of Paris, between the villages of Gentilly and Villejuif, near the Fontainebleau road (see Map 2). In 1633, Louis XIII designated the site for the construction of a royal military hospital, and the main buildings were completed within a few years. In 1656, Louis XIV ordered the removal of the invalid soldiers from the hospital to Paris, the donation of the site to the Hôpital-Général, and construction on a grand scale, most of which was completed by 1690. The walls of Bicêtre enclosed several acres of buildings for all purposes, as well as yards, vegetable gardens, a sheepfold, windmills, a tannery, and a cemetery. Like the Salpêtrière, it was designed

---

[117] Venereal women were brought from the Salpêtrière for treatment at Bicêtre and then returned. During 1755, 423 males (ranging in age from 4 to 80) and 450 females (babies, children, pregnant girls, the elderly) were given the *grand cure* at Bicêtre – emetics, bleeding, steam baths, and repeated rubbing with a mercury pomade (Richard, *Bicêtre*, p. 79). According to the chief administrator, Bicêtre had given the cure to 6,400 during the years 1780–90 (Tuetey, *L'assistance publique*, p. 234). Mercier's representation of Bicêtre as a "suppurating ulcer" was an adumbrated image of the syphilitic body.

[118] Daniel Arasse, *La guillotine et l'imaginaire de la Terreur* (Paris: Flammarion, 1987), p. 34.

[119] Specifically, 520 prisoners to 946 paupers and invalids in 1701; 697 prisoners to 1,427 paupers and invalids in 1726; and 800 or more prisoners to 2,305 paupers and invalids in 1789. Richard, *Bicêtre*, pp. 143, 146; Bloch and Tuetey, *Comité de Mendicité*, p. 599; Tuetey, *L'assistance publique*, pp. 222 ff. At any given time, at least one-third of inmates were ill from congenital or contagious diseases, crippled, or senile; many were in this condition when first interned at Bicêtre and simply worsened there. The annual mortality rate during the 1780s was close to that of the Salpêtrière, about 1 in 7 inmates. During the eighteenth century the permanent staff consisted of a governor, or *économe*, in reality a general accountant; 24 under governors and masters of ateliers; 33 workers and apprentices; 33 female officers; some 235 *gens de service;* 5 priests; some 80 guards. The *maison* was divided into seven sections, or *emplois;* each was a nearly autonomous satrapy, with its own governor and personnel. The entire staff was lodged, fed, and paid within the establishment (Richard, *Bicêtre*, pp. 40–43). They seem to have been even more parasitic on the budget of the Hôpital-Général than their colleagues in the Salpêtrière.

[120] We have two sets of descriptions. The first is in A.N. Y 13614. In 1772, Michel-Pierre Guyot, a Parisian police commissioner, was assigned by Lieutenant General Sartine to investigate the causes of rioting in Bicêtre and the general penal regime there. He devoted six months to the task and submitted a comprehensive report with an "Etat général des prisonniers," based on registers and his questioning of several hundred convicts. These were accompanied by a *mémoire* on the guard force of Bicêtre, written by an anonymous administrator. The second set are LaRochefoucauld-Liancourt's inspection report (in Bloch and Tuetey, *Comité de Mendicité*) to the Mendicancy Committee and the abundant correspondence on Bicêtre between its administrators, the committee, and municipal officers of Paris in 1789–90 (Tuetey, *L'assistance publique*).

to be a self-contained community. In 1734, a spectacular well, 168 feet deep and 15 feet in diameter, was dug through bedrock; it was served by a pumping machine that brought water to the central reservoir, (see Figure 9.9).[121] Yet Bicêtre was a mephitic place, despite its hydraulic marvel and a rural location with fresh winds. Underground tunnels drained a daily average of 12,600 gallons of polluted water and sewage into central, open aqueducts that flowed downhill to an open basin (the *puisard*). The latter was full by 1775 and overflowed during rains into the surrounding fields, creating the marshes of sewage and the stench that so appalled Mercier. The solution aggravated the problem; between 1781 and 1789, sewage was diverted from the *puisard* to six old stone quarries nearby.

Bicêtre was, architecturally, a trompe l'oeil. The long and high frontal edifice (where administrators lived) and its spacious courtyards disguised an interior of squalid, forbidding stone penal buildings, pauper dormitories, infirmaries, and ateliers. The penal section was at the core of the complex. It was formed by the *salles de force*, the *cabanons*, the *correction*, Saint-Léger infirmary, the *cachots* or cells (inside the walled quadrangular zone in the corner of the main courtyard), and, from at least 1770, the *batiment neuf* (Figure 9.9). The *salles de force* normally held between 400 and 500 prisoners – by order or sentence of the lieutenant general of police, royal *lettre de cachet*, or by a court sentence – in common halls, several to a straw bed. These were two-story buildings, with low ceilings and barred windows. Only an iron grill with a single large door separated the halls from the entry vestibules. As in the Salpêtrière, those with money from their families received better rations.

Saint-Léger, constructed during the 1760s, was the central infirmary for sick and convalescent prisoners (see Figure 9.10).[122] Like the *salles de force*, Saint-Léger consisted of large, grilled halls. It was adjacent to collective latrines and to an open sewage aqueduct.

The *cabanons* were individual cells. There were 296 of them, in two blocks, each consisting of five low-ceilinged stories. Each cell was 8 feet square, with a bed, table, and chair. Like modern prison cells, they had iron grills instead of doors. They held police spies and agents convicted of crimes (who would have been killed in the convict halls), prisoners with money or protectors, and notably dangerous convicts.

The *correction* lodged delinquent juveniles. Simultaneously prison, school, and workshop, it also provided choirboys for the Bicêtre church. The *correction* was divided into two sections: the *petite correction*, for boys under 15 interned for begging, vagabondage, or crimes, who were placed, at age 17, in the *grande correction* with those imprisoned for delinquency, debauchery, or rebellion against parental authority. The first, and presumably more innocent category, thereby "graduated" into the company of the stronger, more maturely and resolutely

---

[121] The late eighteenth-century *plan général* for Bicêtre is in A.N. F 14 10253.
[122] The plans for the infirmaries are also in A.N. F 14 10253.

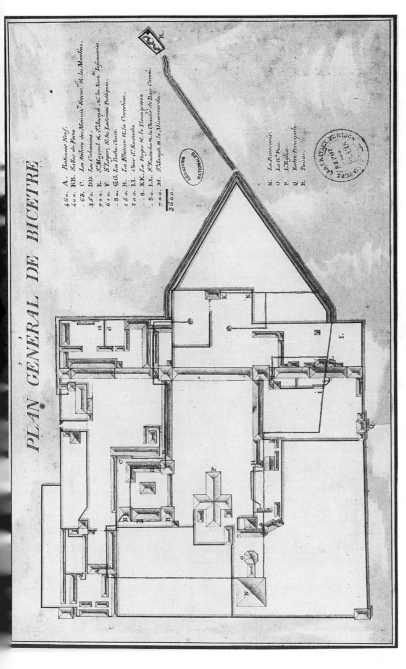

PLAN GÉNÉRAL DE BICÊTRE

460. A. Bâtiment Neuf.
400. BB. Salles de Force.
63. C. Les Cabanons.
350. DD. Les Ateliers des Menuis. Serur. & les Moulins.
700. E. S.ᵗ Mayeul & S.ᵗ Joseph & la Non. Infirmerie.
640. F. S.ᵗ Leger & les Latrines Publiques.
50. GG. La Basse Cour.
160. H. Les Hôtics. & la Correction.
200. II. Cour S.ᵗ Antoine.
8. KK. Le Foyer & la Mantquerie.
50. LL. S.ᵗ Prudence & la Chapelle & le Bois Carré.
700. M. S.ᵗ Joseph & la Miséricorde.

N. Le Réservoir.
O. Le Gᵈ Puits.
P. L'Église.
Q. Entrée Principale.
R. Puisar.

Figure 9.9. General plan of Bicêtre. The penal zone was formed by the *batiment neuf* (*A*), the *salles de force* (*BB*), the *cabanons* (*DD*), the Saint-Léger infirmaries (*F*), the *correction* hall (*H*), and the *cachots*, which were inside the walled quadrangular zone in the corner of the main courtyard. *N* is the reservoir; *O* is the pumping machine; *R* is the sewage basin. (A.N. F 14 10253). Reprinted with permission of the French National Archives.

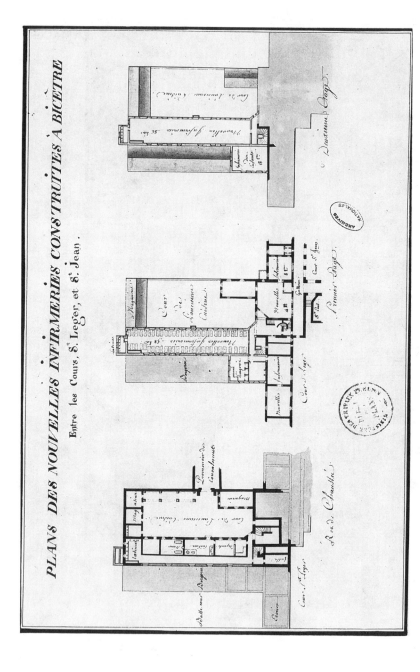

Figure 9.10. Floor plan of the Bicêtre infirmaries. This plate shows the ground floor, first floor, and second floor of the infirmaries. (A.N. F 14 10253. Reprinted with permission of the French National Archives.)

delictual. The regime in the *grand correction* was similar to that of the *maison de correction* in the Salpêtrière.

The eight *cachots* were small, holelike cells some 15 feet underground, each ventilated and illuminated by a single shaft and secured by a double door. Their inmates were men whose death sentences had been commuted to life imprisonment and prisoners guilty of serious violence inside Bicêtre. Those prisoners were chained; the others were not.

That was the regulation geography of penal Bicêtre, its official segmentations and segregations. The interior reality was far more promiscuous. New convict inmates were often placed wherever there was room for them at the moment of their entry – *salles de force, correction,* the infirmary – regardless of their ages, histories, or crimes. Very many juveniles incarcerated for begging, petty theft, or libertinage were put in the *salles de force* with recidivist and violent convicts. Robust multiple offenders who were sick on arrival were placed in the infirmaries and remained there for months or years after recovery. In 1773, Guyot wrote of the *salles de force* and Saint-Léger: "It is with consternation that I see pederasts confined in these halls; I believe that they must be locked up separately."[123]

Penury of service, if not of means, was even more drastic in Bicêtre than in the Salpêtrière. Bicêtre had a staff of 800 employees, on the payroll of the Hôpital-Général, of which 435 were pauper inmates paid with extra food and a salary of 4 livres a month (expended in the tavern).[124] There was a significant complement of physicians, surgeons, apothecaries, and their students, but when LaRochefoucauld inspected the *maison* he discovered that in most of the infirmaries, including Saint-Léger, there were hundreds of inmate patients but only 2 guards and virtually no nurses or orderlies: "The sick care for each other as best they can."[125] Even the 270 highly active inmates of the insane and epileptic asylum were attended by only 13 employees.[126] In 1790, the administration admitted that the insane, epileptic, feebleminded, paralyzed, incontinent, and asthmatic, both paupers and prisoners, were given no medical treatment.[127] The Saint-Léger infirmary had been allowed to become a center for malingering, drinking, fighting, and rioting soon after its construction. That chronic situation was described by an overseer of the Hôpital-Général early in 1790:

It is in the infirmary that plots are hatched among prisoners. They invent every pretext to get put there; they threaten officers and surgeons with riot or suicide if they refuse to oblige. They want the infirmary because there they do not work, they have wine and better food, they live in common and hold a school for crime. Among the 197 now in the

---

[123] A.N. Y 13614.
[124] There was prodigious consumption of alcohol in Bicêtre. The tavern earned an average of 46,000 livres a year; that was three times the amount earned (and consumed) within the Salpêtrière, and by a population half the size. Most able-bodied prisoners were not given a wine ration, although inmates of the infirmaries were. The principal customers of the tavern were undoubtedly administrators and employees.
[125] In Bloch and Tuetey, *Comité de Mendicité,* p. 603.   [126] Ibid., p. 604.
[127] Tuetey, *L'assistance publique,* p. 234.

infirmary, not 40 are bedridden, and those unfortunates are cruelly tormented by the clamor and drunkeness of those who are well. Superior officers are no longer able to get the healthy out of the infirmary and back to any work.[128]

The force of armed guards for Bicêtre was small: 66 men and officers in 1772, 85 in 1790. In the aftermath of a bloody convict riot in 1772, an administrator described the inadequacy of this force:

Of all the *maisons de force* in the Realm, that of Bicêtre is the largest and the least secure, as much by the construction of its buildings as by the number of prisoners confined, which is always about 900. Two great halls, each containing 200 and often more prisoners – of which the majority are branded, thieves, or other scoundrels of the same type – closed by simple grills of iron bars, 248 *cabanons* or small rooms 8 feet square, grilled in the same manner and separated by weak walls, that is the prison. In addition, there are the buildings of the *correction* . . . and those for the insane, which are hardly any more secure. The great number of prisoners assembled in the two *salles de force*, sleeping on straw, filled with misery, vermin, and badly nourished, leads them periodically to revolt, to vandalize, finally to do anything to escape. To guard this quantity of prisoners, there is only a company composed of 60 riflemen, 5 sergeants, and a captain. . . . When there are riots, which are frequent, this force is not sufficient to control the prisoners, and in those moments we have to depend on the Paris Guard, of which strong detachments of cavalry and infantry march [7 miles] to Bicêtre on order of the lieutenant general of police.[129]

Commissioner Guyot was more scathingly explicit in his report to Lieutenant General Sartine:

The soldiers of the guard are easy and familiar with the prisoners. . . . I regard the poor recruitment and indiscipline of the soldiers of this troop as one of the worst abuses in the establishment, and the chief cause of its disorders; I can truthfully say that these soldiers are military only in name and uniform. . . . the recruitment and punishment of the soldiers depends on the administration, not on their captain.[130]

[128] Ibid., p. 222. And Doublet, in 1791: "Dans les infirmaries des prisons de Bicêtre, nous avons trouvé les lits, les vases et tous les ustensiles détruits ou mutilés par les malades eux-mémes" (Rapport, p. 15). This entire situation contravened the *reglement* issued in 1774 by Lenoir, lieutenant general of police, for security in Saint-Léger infirmary and the *salles de force:* Prisoners were to enter or leave, one by one, through a special wicket-gate (to be built into the grill), where they were to be held and searched; surgeons were to visit the halls every day, accompanied by four armed guards; the *économe*, a locksmith, and a stonemason escorted by guards were to inspect the halls every eight days to look for damage to walls, barred windows, and doors, then to punish those responsible and make prompt repairs (A.N. Y 13614). And LaRochefoucauld on the infirmaries: "tous les âges sont réunis, le criminel et le malheureux, l'homme sans raison et l'homme sain d'esprit, enfin celui qui la pitié a sauvé de la corde, qui a vieilli dans le crime, et le malheureux enfant, coupable à peine d'une légère faute. C'est là que ces misérables tiennent école de vices et de crimes, et corrompent de toutes les manières ces infortunés enfants" (Bloch and Tuetey, *Comité de Mendicité*, p. 606).

[129] A.N. Y 13614. The prison guard force was divided into three squads: One did picket duty; one patrolled; one rested or enjoyed time off-duty in the tavern. The dispersion of the force was thus extreme. The author urged that the guard force (which cost the Hôpital 22,470 livres a year) be pensioned off and replaced with a company of 102 riflemen from the royal military hospital at the Invalides. That was not done.

[130] A.N. Y 13614.

The guards were responsible for ruling over more than 1,500 paupers and mendicants, in addition to almost 1,000 convicts and delinquents. The guards were not young men. Most were retired, long-service veterans of the royal army. They lived inside Bicêtre, and many continued to live there as pensioners after they retired from the guard corps. They lived cautiously, if not fearfully. Guards did not usually brutalize prisoners; rather, they avoided confrontation with them.[131] Prisoners brutalized each other, and occasionally guards.

In 1790, the administration claimed that "at least half" of all inmates (some 1,500) were capable of some work.[132] But there was virtually no forced labor in any area of late eighteenth-century Bicêtre, except for juveniles in the *correction*, who made bootlaces. The fact was surely, if unavowedly, derived from the tenuous security within Bicêtre; the administration lacked the means and the will to force labor.[133] Paupers who were more or less fit, reliable, and willing were recruited for menial tasks, but prisoners were given little opportunity to work voluntarily for pay.[134] From at least the early 1770s to 1790, 60 to 80 prisoners (most of them inmates of the *cabanons*) polished mirror glass that was provided by the royal glass works in the Faubourg Saint-Antoine.[135] During the same period, a permanent detail of only 72 prisoners worked the water-pumping machine, in shifts of 24, replacing the team of oxen that had previously turned the wheel of the machine. Each shift of 24 worked for one hour at a time – against a wheel pressure of only 9 pounds. Smaller groups were detailed to turn the blades of the flour mill.[136] They were paid derisory sums, for derisory work. The great majority of convicts ate, occasionally drank, languished, amused, or defended themselves in the halls and cells for the duration of their confinement. That ambiance was evoked in a regulation of the 1770s that strictly (and uselessly) forbade prisoners to chant, shout, howl, curse, or sing blasphemous or obscene songs.[137]

When the Mendicancy Committee asked the chief officer of Bicêtre to state the governing principles of the administration, he replied: "Vigilance, force, and prudence."[138] Only the last principle seems to have been genuine.

---

[131] But they did not avoid contact. One Commissioner Guyot's recommendation, Lenoir's December 1774 "Reglement concernant la discipline des prisonniers détenus à Bicêtre" contained the following articles: "12. Les Soldats ne pourront, sous quelque prétexte que ce soit, se charger de lettre, soit de la part des Prisonniers, soit pour eux, sous peine de cachot & d'être ensuite chassés. 13. Il leur sera défendu, sous pareilles peines, d'entretenir conversation avec eux, de se charger de leurs commissions en tout temps, & singuliérement lorsqu'ils seront en faction dans les Guérites de fer devant les grilles des Prisonniers & dans les Cours le long Cabanons" (A.N. Y 13614).

[132] Tuetey, *L'assistance publique*, p. 240.   [133] Ibid., pp. 247–8.

[134] "Le plus grand mal de cette maison, le vice qui nous a le plus frappé, parce qu'il porte sur une plus grande masse d'hommes, et qu'il pourroit être facilement réparé, c'est le défaut de travail dans toutes les classes de la maison" (LaRochefoucauld, in Bloch and Tuetey, *Comité de Mendicité*, p. 612).

[135] Tuetey, *L'assistance publique*, p. 247.   [136] Richard, *Bicêtre*, p. 92.

[137] Ibid., p. 138.   [138] Quoted in ibid., p. 251.

Escapes, violence, and rioting were common in Bicêtre during the eighteenth century.[139] In 1740, the inmates of the *correction* rioted and set fire to the building. There were general riots in the *salles de force* and Saint-Léger in February 1752 and May 1772, during which guards and prisoners were killed, and again in December 1789. The 1772 riot provoked Guyot's thorough investigation of Bicêtre's convict population, its carceral regime and society, and his detailed record of the penal use of the institution by ministers of state, the lieutenant general of police, and the Parlement of Paris.

According to Guyot, the most dangerous sections were the most crowded, the *salles de force* and Saint-Léger:

Prisoners are assembled there in great numbers and with no distinction between them. . . . Without any work to do, they spend all their time inventing ways to avoid surveillance and prepare escapes. . . . They are not in fact adequately watched, because they easily obtain knives and other tools which they use to get out, either by digging or by striking personnel who approach them. . . . Those in the *salles de force* always damage and vandalize the building, and never use violence on staff; those in Saint-Léger always use force and threats, and never vandalism. . . . Both groups are equally malign and determined; their different locations explain their different actions. The prisoners in *la force* are on the ground floor, and seek to escape by digging; that is not practicable for those in Saint-Léger, who are on upper floors, and they use violence.

Guyot's recommendations for a new carceral regime in Bicêtre show the influence of the *bagnes*. Prisoners must be divided up into *chambrées* of 25 to 30 each. They must be made to work. They must be classified and segregated by the gravity of their crimes, the violent separated from the nonviolent, the libertine from the criminal, pederasts and sodomists from all others. A special building must be constructed to punish the refractory and thereby intimidate the others, a building where up to 30 can be kept in chains and fetters ("like *galériens* in the Tour Saint-Bernard"). Large iron sentry boxes must be placed near the grills of Saint-Léger and the *salles de force* and manned day and night; each would be "a kind of small fort from which one can dominate and beat to ruin all the prisoners in those halls, from which one can observe all that they may do." The guard force must be replaced with a much larger one of militarily disciplined men, themselves under threat of serious punishment for negligence, cowardice, or complicity with prisoners. The sentry boxes were the only proposal that seems to have been implemented, and they apparently only served to give the guards more protection from the prisoners.

---

[139] The frequency of escapes was known to the Chancellor and recognized in the April 1778 edict of Louis XVI: "Sa Majesté aurait reconnu la nécessité de prendre de nouvelles précautions pour empêcher ces évasions et prévenir les désordres qui pourraient en résulter." The "new precautions" ordered were a mandatory black and grey uniform and regular haircuts for all prisoners – so they could be recognized and caught once they escaped Bicêtre (quoted in Richard, *Bicêtre*, pp. 137–8).

In 1772–3, Guyot inventoried a total of 690 prisoners in the *cabanons* (258), Saint-Léger (223), and *salles de force* (209).[140] He specified the authorities responsible for the incarceration of 467 of them; for 258 in the *cabanons*, 154 in Saint-Léger, 55 in *la force*. His inventory validates Lieutenant General Sartine's terse yet comprehensive description (1770) of penal Bicêtre.[141] This was principally the realm of royal ministers with the authority of *lettre de cachet* and of the lieutenant general of police: They accounted for 89 percent of specified incarceration orders. (See Table 9.1.)

Twenty-nine percent of the inmates in the *salles de force* and Saint-Léger (and 32% in the *cabanons*) were imprisoned, by ministerial *lettre de cachet* or police order, on formal request of their parents or families, for such misbehavior as

[140] "Etat général des prisonniers," A.N. Y 13614. He chose to examine only the prisoners incarcerated in 1769 or earlier. He did not inventory the *correction*. His method was to transcribe the information entered on the prison register for each inmate (name, birthplace, occupation, judicial history, reason for incarceration, incarcerating authority, date of incarceration, age in 1772 or 1773) and then to interview each on the reasons for his incarceration. The great majority either declared innocence of the charges against them, or claimed ignorance of why they were imprisoned, or claimed they had been persecuted by malicious enemies. Guyot commented as follows on the denials and self-exonerations: "Ces nottes contiennent pour la plupart des histoires que ces prisonniers on fabriquées pour prouver qu'ils sont les victimes sacrifiées: les uns a la cupidité de leurs parens qui les ont fait arretter pour s'emparer de leurs biens, les autres de l'intrigue et de la mauvaise conduite de leurs femmes, d'autres enfin du crédit et de la puissance de leurs ennemis, de leurs maîtres ou de personnes constituées en dignités. Ceux qui ont été repris de justice et portent sur leur personne l'empreinte de leur infamie prétendent qu'ils ont été jugés injustement ou soutiennent qu'ayant subi leur peine il est contre toute équité de les retenir en captivité. . . . Je croyais en trouver quelqu'un qui fût oublié je me flattais au moins d'y déterrer quelque innocent opprimé, je l'ai cherché et je ne l'ai pas trouvé. . . . Ils m'ont parus tous plus ou moins coupables, du moins ceux dont les charges sont connues."

[141] "Ces maisons [Bicêtre and the Salpêtrière] . . . servent en partie de prisons pour renfermer les mauvais sujets de toute espèce et entre autres ceux qui ont été repris de justice, tels que ceux qui ont été condamnés au fouet et au bannissement, lorsque l'on juge qu'il y aurait du danger de leur rendre leur liberté après leur jugement. On y retient également ceux qui ont essayé des procès pour crimes, mais contre lesquels il ne s'est point trouvé de preuves suffisantes pour les condamner, lorsque d'ailleurs il existe des présomptions assez considérables contre eux pour les regarder comme coupables. Elles servent encore de maisons de correction pour les femmes de débauche qui ont été arrêtées pour désordres, pour les libertins qui se sont livrés à certains excès, les perturbateurs du repos public, les escrocs, les gens du bas peuple qui remplissent partie du service public, et qui ont manqué essentiellement à la discipline à laquelle ils sont assujettis, ou qui ont commis des violences contre ceux qui les ont employés, pour les forcer à leur payer un salaire excessif; les ouvriers et les domestiques qui ont agi de la même manière à l'égard de leurs maîtres ou de ceux dont ils dépendent, etc. Enfin on renferme encore dans ces maisons, pareillement à titre de correction, à la sollicitation des familles, les gens mariés parmi le peuple qui ruinent leur ménage par leur débauche ou leur mauvaise conduite, les jeunes gens de la même classe dont les actions, le libertinage, l'oisiveté et les liaisons suspectes qu'ils contractent donnent lieu de craindre à leurs parents qu'ils ne s'abandonnent à des excès ou à des crimes capable de causer leur déshonneur. Ainsi ces maisons remplissent deux objets essentiels: 1. elles servent à séparer de la société tous ceux qui ont donné lieu de les regarder comme ne pouvant y rester sans danger pour la sûreté et le repos de autres; 2. à la correction de ceux dont les désordres, n'étant pas encore que la suite des passions, laissent quelque espérance qu'une punition momentanée pourra produire en eux avec le temps et la réflexion un heureux changement" ("Mémoire sur l'administration de la police en France," 1770, in *Mémoires de la Société de l'Histoire de Paris et de l'Ile-de-France*, 5 (1879): 83–4).

Punishment

Table 9.1. *Incarcerating authorities for Bicêtre prison*

	Cabanons	Saint-Léger	La force	Totals
Ministerial "lettre de cachet"	155 (60%)	76 (49%)	40 (73%)	271 (58%)
Order, lieutenant-general of Police	92 (36%)	49 (32%)	3 (5%)	144 (31%)
Judgment, Parlement of Paris	0	17 (11%)	8 (13%)	25 (5%)
Order, general prosecutor, Parlement of Paris	0	4 (3%)	2 (4%)	6 (1%)
Judgment, Prévôté de l'Hôtel du Roi	0	6 (4%)	2 (3%)	8 (2%)
Royal commutation	11 (4%)	2 (1%)	1 (2%)	14 (3%)

The actual percentage of incarcerations in *la force* by order of the lieutenant general was undoubtedly far higher than is shown in this table, since many of Guyot's notations for that section of Bicêtre do not specify the imprisoning authority or do not distinguish between ministerial orders and those of the lieutenant general. I have counted only those in which the distinction is clear. For the same reason, numerous inmates of *la force* may have been there by judicial sentence of the Châtelet.

Source: A.N.Y. 1361 ("Etat général les prisonniers," 1772).

assault, theft, insubordination, debauchery, profligacy, public indecency, or chronic drunkenness. Louis Mirot, for example, was placed in Bicêtre at age 17 for debauchery and stealing. François LeMercier, of Dieppe, was imprisoned at 18 for having stolen money from his widowed mother. Henri Tranchant, aged 23, whose father was a sutler of the royal *gendarmes* at Versailles, was imprisoned for inveterate drunkenness. Ambroise Hoüy, from a village near Chartres, was incarcerated at age 24 for having attempted to shoot his uncle with a pistol. Several such prisoners were mature men: François Bardel, a farmer, was imprisoned at age 51 for debauchery, on petition of his brother, a priest in the diocese of Lisieux. Claude Fessier, a Parisian wigmaker, was imprisoned at the age of 32 by petition of his brother-in-law, as dangerously violent, for having assaulted a family member. An additional 5 percent were servants or employees imprisoned at the formal request of their masters for similar reasons. Vincent Dubois, 40, had been household manager for the princess of Talmont; on her petition, he was incarcerated for fraudulent appropriations. Yves Ledeusc, a Breton manservant, was imprisoned for libertinage and insulting his master, a shipping merchant at Saint-Mâlo. Those were ostensibly preventive detentions, intended to forestall acts that would lead to prosecution by royal courts; to preserve, in extremis, the authority, property, and reputation of economically modest families and the social image of important *maisons*, to protect communities from the violent or licentious and from the contagiousness of their behavior.

A further 17 percent in the *salles de force* and Saint-Léger were *repris de justice*, who wore the brand (M, V, or GAL); most were imprisoned by order of the lieutenant general, Chancellor, or a minister for having violated sentences of banishment or permanent exile from Paris (acts for which many could have been sent to the *bagnes*). Dominique Avaux, former Parisian domestic servant, had been convicted of theft, then whipped, branded, and banished for three years; he returned after two years at Lyons, was caught and sent to Bicêtre in 1764. Jean-Baptiste d'Allegre was arrested in a boardinghouse and incarcerated in 1768; he had done three years in the *bagne* for theft of silver. Pierre Deniset, from Dôle in the Franche-Comté, had been convicted of theft by the Châtelet, branded, and banished; he seems never to have left Paris. Most of the remaining extrajudicial imprisonments, by order of the lieutenant general or ministers of state, in the *salles de force* and Saint-Léger were of persons without apparent conviction records, who were imprisoned for military desertion, gambling, sexual deviance, public disturbance, criminal associations, or strong suspicion of criminal activity. Laurent Delaitre, an 18-year-old drapery worker, was arrested by the police and imprisoned by the lieutenant general for "frequenting suspect persons." Jean-Pierre Lot, a tailor's apprentice aged 15, was imprisoned on suspicion of thefts at fairs. Nicolas Jambon, aged 19, was arrested as a transvestite for "accosting men on the boulevards while disguised as a woman." François Du Terrat, public letter writer on the rue Dauphine, was imprisoned in 1769 for repeated indecent exposure in the streets. Jean-Phélippe Gueret, a stonemason and soldier of militia, was imprisoned for prowling the streets at night and insulting a watch patrol. François Troquon was a fisherman of the Gros Caillou Quarter on the Seine; he was incarcerated for fighting with the River Guards who had confiscated his nets. In ordering the incarceration of such persons at Bicêtre, the lieutenant general used his royally conferred authority to "purge the city of those who can cause disorder."[142] And there were those who had been tried and judged by a royal court and given sentences other than confinement in a *maison de force* – usually *plus amplement informé* " (an interlocutory judgment short of conviction and formal penalty), whipping, the iron collar, or banishment – and who were then subjected by the lieutenant general or a minister of state to detention at Bicêtre, as social defense or aggravated punishment. There were 22 of them in the *salles de force* and Saint-Léger, or 10.5 percent of the 209 for whom incarcerating authorities were noted. (The details on this group are presented in Table 9.2.) Half of them had been given the sentence of *plus amplement informé* by their judges, because of insufficient proof for conviction and legal penalty, which police or ministerial authorities transformed into longer-term detention at Bicêtre.

[142] As stated in the March 1667 edict that created the lieutenant generalcy, Isambert, vol. 18, p. 100.

Table 9.2. *Postjudicial detentions at Bicêtre, by police or ministerial order*

Accusation	Sentence	Year	Reason for detention	Detention year
Theft	P.a.i. at liberty	1760		1761
Theft	Whipping in custody; Bicêtre 1 year	1764	Dangerous thief	1764
Theft	P.a.i. 6 months prison	1760		1767
Theft	P.a.i.	1763		1765
Theft from church	P.a.i.	1755		1756
Theft				1755
Theft	Released	1768	Public security	1769
Theft	Whipping in custody		Dangerous thief	1766
Theft	P.a.i. 6 months			1768
Complicity in murder	Released		Insane	1761
Attempted murder	P.a.i. 1 year prison			1766
Theft	P.a.i.			1764
Theft	P.a.i. prison "Bagne"		Dangerous thief	1766
				1765
Theft	P.a.i. 6 months			1769
Theft	P.a.i.			1766
Theft	P.a.i. 3 months prison			1768
Theft	Released	1769		1769
Theft				1769
Theft			Request of family	1766
Burglary	Banishment			1768
Theft	P.a.i. 3 months			1768

Abbreviation: p.a.i.–plus amplement informé.
Blank spaces signify no information given.
Source: A.N.Y. 13614.

The Parlement of Paris made quite limited use of Bicêtre. (The details about 23 of the 25 whom it sentenced to confinement there are given in Table 9.3.) Only 2 of them were 25 years old or older; 17 were juveniles under 20. The most frequent sentence was three years, and the administration of Bicêtre does not seem to have respected the terms. The Parlement virtually reserved the Hôpital-Général as a severe penalty for male juveniles found guilty of authorship or complicity in crimes that, in the case of adults, were punished by long-term banishment, the *bagnes*, or death; men too old for the *bagnes;* convicted offenders who were judged insane; and, rarely, to imprison violent criminals for life under a sentence of *plus amplement informé* (a practice described in Part 3).

Detention for an indeterminant period was the rule in Bicêtre. Many imprisonments by order or sentence of the lieutenant general did not state a term;

Table 9.3. *Detentions at Bicêtre by judgment of Parlement of Paris*

Crime	Judgment	Occupation	Birthplace	Age	Years
Theft	Bicêtre for life	Laborer	Picardy	23	21
	Bicêtre 2 years	Farrier		25	5
Theft	Whipping in custody; Bicêtre	Shoeblack	Brittany	12	3
Domestic theft	Bicêtre	Servant	Lyonnais	23	5
Theft	Bicêtre for life			21	4
Theft	Whipping in custody; Bicêtre to age 25	Laborer	Ile-de-France	12	7
Theft	Whipping in custody; Bicêtre 2 years	Cabinetmaker's boy	Paris	11	5
Theft	Bicêtre 3 years		Paris	12	3
Theft	Bicêtre 5 years		Ile-de-France	10	5
Theft	Bicêtre for life	Soldier	Paris	21	4
Theft	Bicêtre 3 years		Paris	11	5
Theft	Whipping in custody; Bicêtre	Servant	Ile-de-France	13	5
Theft	Bicêtre 3 years	Pedlar of rabbit skins	Ile-de-France	13	3
Domestic theft	Bicêtre 3 years	Farm laborer	Normandy	12	5
Theft	Whipping in custody; Bicêtre 3 years	Tailor's apprentice	Normandy	12	3
Theft	Bicêtre 3 years	Weaver	Lorraine	12	5
Theft	Bicêtre 3 years	Basketweaver	Flanders	12	4
Theft	Bicêtre 3 years	Servant	Burgundy	11	5
Theft	Bicêtre 3 years		Paris	10	4
Theft	Bicêtre 3 years			10	4
Theft	Bicêtre 3 years		Picardy	11	4
	Criminal insanity; Bicêtre for life	Locksmith	Paris	17	7
Theft	Bicêtre for life	Laborer	Picardy	38	3

Blank spaces signify no information given. *Years*–years in Bicêtre at the time the record was made.
Source: A.N.Y. 13614.

all ministerial *lettres de cachet* for imprisonment were issued with the ominous clause "until further order to the contrary." The prisoners of Bicêtre had reason to despair; more than four-fifths of them could not know when they would be released. That indeterminacy belonged to the ideology of correctional policing but not to that of royal criminal jurisprudence. Ideally, such prisoners were to earn their release by giving sign of reformation. In fact, the sheer pressure of familial, ministerial, and police demand for incarcerations in the limited space of Bicêtre led to relatively short terms and high turnover. During the approximately six months of Guyot's inquiry, a total of 73 prisoners, 10.5 percent of the 690, were released (without any recommendation on his part): 12 percent of those in the *cabanons*, 9 percent of those in Saint-Léger, and 11 percent of those in La Force. Doubled, that would represent a release rate of 1 in 5 prisoners per annum. Eleven men, or 1.5 percent of 690, died. High turnover is also suggested by the actual time served by 363 prisoners in La Force and Saint-Léger:

Years in prison	La Force (N)	Saint-Léger (N)	(%N = 363)
4	74	94	46.0
5	41	40	22.0
6	23	9	9.0
7	12	8	5.5
8	8	11	5.0
9	10	3	3.5
10	5	3	2.0
11–15	10	5	4.0
16–20	2	4	2.0
21 +	1	0	2.0

Sixty-eight percent had been imprisoned for four or five years, only 8 percent for ten to twenty. Since Guyot chose to inventory only those interned in 1769 or earlier, not those interned from 1770 to 1773, the actual number of short-term inmates (who served only one to five years) must have been much higher than figures in the table suggest.

The convict world of Bicêtre was extremely youthful, both at the time of incarceration and in the period of Guyot's inquiry. In 1772–3, the following age groups are found among the 353 inmates of the *salles de force* and Saint-Léger: age 15 to 20 (22%); age 21 to 30 (35%); age 31 to 40 (23%); age 41 to 50 (15%); age 51 to 60 (4%); over 61 (1%). One in five of these prisoners was an adolescent, many of them delinquents incarcerated by *lettre de cachet* or police order who should, officially, have been in the *correction*. More than 50 percent of the total were between the ages of 15 and 30. Guyot noted only about 7 inmates of Saint-Léger as "sick." Their youthfulness at the time of their incarceration is striking:

Age at incarceration (years)	Salles de force	Saint-Léger	(%N = 354)
11–14:	17	49	19
15–17	13	30	12
18–20	21	14	10
21–25	30	34	18
26–35	60	19	22
36–45	32	14	13
46–55	9	10	5.5
56–65	2	0	0.5
66 +	0	0	0

Almost one-third were between the ages of 11 and 17 when first imprisoned; more than one-half were young men below the age of legal majority (25). They seem to have been put into the *salles de force* or Saint-Léger directly on their admission to Bicêtre, which suggests that the *maison de correction* was reserved for juveniles whose families paid for their maintenance.

Late eighteenth-century accounts of the *maisons de force* in the Salpêtrière and Bicêtre do not describe prisons or labor compounds. They essentially describe pariah warehouses built of stone and iron, human *foutoirs*. Eighteenth-century observers insisted that most prisoners in the Salpêtrière and Bicêtre were undisciplined and idle, in contrast to *galériens* and *bagnards*. Their "license" resulted from administrative negligence or fear and from the live-and-let-live arrangements between guards and convicts. Surveillance and labor – hallmarks of modern prisons and organized facts in the galleys and *bagnes* –were haphazard and feeble in the carceral halls of the Hôpital-Général. License allegedly produced filth, viciousness, violence, and physical and moral depredations.[143]

What elite observers characterized as de facto anarchy inside Bicêtre (and to a lesser extent in the Salpêtrière) was in fact an order fashioned by inmates, an order based on complicities with employees and guards, conventions of behavior in the halls, loyalties within gangs and factions. We should therefore ask, What was the punitive value of Bicêtre or the Salpêtrière? Prisoners had col-

---

[143] The morbid and sensational language of such late eighteenth-century descriptions does suggest the fascination alleged by Foucault: "What the classical period had confined was not only an abstract unreason which mingled madmen and libertines, invalids, and criminals, but also an enormous reservoir of the fantastic, a dormant world of monsters supposedly engulfed in the darkness of Hieronymus Bosch which had once spewed them forth. One might say that the fortresses of confinement added to their social role of segregation and purification a quite opposite cultural function. Even as they separated reason from unreason on society's surface, they preserved in depth the images where they mingled and exchanged properties. The fortresses of confinement functioned as a great, long silent memory; they maintained in the shadows an iconographic power that men might have thought was exorcised; created by the new classical order, they preserved, against it and against time, forbidden figures that could thus be transmitted intact from the sixteenth to the nineteenth century" (*Madness and Civilization*, p. 209).

lective freedom to control much of their daily and nocturnal lives behind the walls. They were not *esclaves de la peine*, as were *galériens* and *bagnards*. Their existence inside differed from that of their plebeian counterparts outside only by aggravation of rigors common to both: crowding, violence, coarse food, exposure to disease. They suffered limited opportunities for sex and wine, and they were incarcerated – but in a malleable environment that was not alien for most, that could not durably terrify or transform the criminal or dissuade them from future crimes.

And yet, despite the degenerated administrative regimes, those *maisons de force* were prototype prisons in the modern sense. They were given the basic characteristics of prisons at their legal creation and physical construction in the late seventeenth century.[144] Guyot, a senior policeman of the Old Regime, Doublet, an administrator and medical savant, and LaRochefoucauld-Liancourt, a leading Revolutionary legislator, all wanted to fulfill that purpose by imposing a *bagne*-style regime within Bicêtre.

Jails

Eighteenth-century jurists fastidiously insisted that in France prison was not a penalty in law. They did not define the galleys, *bagnes*, and *hôpitaux* as prisons; judicial incarceration in the *hôpital-général*, for example, was defined as "réclusion dans une maison de force," not as imprisonment. To them, *les prisons* had two meanings: It signified either the royal chateaus and fortresses (such as the Bastille and Vincennes in Paris) reserved for those interned by *lettre de cachet*, not by the courts; or it meant the jails, adjacent to courts and under their supervision, in which defendants were confined for trial and judgment until they were either acquitted and released or sentenced to various punishments. But courts did in fact use those jails as punishment, by the formal legal device of *plus amplement informé*. That was an interlocutory judgment (one that in most cases was appealed for decision by the Parlement of the jurisdiction), rendered at the conclusion of trial investigation, by which a court detained a defendant against whom there was strong evidence of guilt, for a period of one month, three months, six months, or one year (in the jurisdiction of the Parlement of Paris), for the official purpose of awaiting further evidence in the case before final judgment. It was, simultaneously, a trial procedure and a punishment. (Its uses will be explained in Chapter 10, and its incidence described in Volume 2.) Since *plus amplement informé* was widely employed by the Châtelet and Parlement of Paris during the eighteenth century, it made of their jails penal institutions.

Kings, chancellors, and magistrates conceived jails as places for temporary detention of those suspected but not convicted of crimes; thus, as holding places for both the genuinely innocent and the possibly guilty. Their carceral condition was meant to be a sphere intermediate between civil society, with its

---

[144] This point was made lucidly and forcefully by Benabou, *La prostitution*, pp. 84–5.

privileges and freedoms, and the defamed community of the criminal, and far closer to the former than to the latter. The official purpose of jails was simply to secure defendants until judgment, not to correct or punish them. Successive royal edicts and rulings by Parlements expressed and amplified that conception and prescribed a regime that accorded the prisoners of tribunals many of the hierarchies, rights, and amenities that obtained in civil society.

Title XIII of the Criminal Ordinance of 1670, which concerns prisons, jailors, and the supervisory responsibilities of magistrates, was one of the longest titles of that ordinance. Jailers, their secretaries, and turnkeys were agents of courts and answerable to magistrates. They were to keep precise registers of all those jailed. They were forbidden to extort money from prisoners or to physically abuse them. Prisoners could purchase food from jailers to supplement their rations, and the latter were obliged to give receipts for the amount paid. All decrees, sentences, and judgments regarding a prisoner had to be announced to him by the court recorder within 24 hours of their issuance. If the court ordered the liberation of a prisoner, he could not be retained because of any money he owed the jailer. Prisoners who were not in special cells were allowed to have food, wood, and bedding brought in to them at their expense. They could not be chained unless they were violent or accused of a serious crime and unless the chaining was ordered by the instructing judge of the case. All those accused of a serious crime were to be confined in cells (separately, if suspected of complicity in the same crime). Jailers were liable to a heavy fine and even corporal punishment if they violated these and other rules. Prosecutors were obliged to visit prisons each week to receive any complaints from prisoners.[145]

In 1717, the Parlement of Paris issued a general ruling for all courts and jails in its jurisdiction that was yet more comprehensive and fastidious. Mass was to be sung every morning and prayers said every evening in prison chapels, with sermons every Sunday and holy day; attendance by prisoners was obligatory. Prisoners were to be allowed daily exercise in a courtyard, where they could also receive visits from family members. Wives could visit husbands in their cells (but not in the common rooms and halls). Turnkeys and inmates were forbidden to require or accept any payment or gift from new prisoners. Fixed, exclusive prices for lodgings and services were mandated: 1 sou per day for a sleeping place on the straw in the common hall and 1.5 pounds of bread; 5 sous for a single bed, 3 sous each for a double bed; for those paying board, a maximum of 3 livres a day, with 1 livre additional for a shared room with a fireplace or 1 livre, 15 sous, for a single room with a fireplace. Boarders had the right to regular service from turnkeys, including fresh linen and clean tableware. Judges of the Parlement, in the company of deputy prosecutors, were to inspect the Parisian prisons five times each year. Finally, this ruling and preceding royal edicts on prisons were to be read aloud in prison chapels on the first Sunday of

---

[145] Ibid., vol. 18, pp. 393–8.

each month and permanently placarded on main gates and in courtyards to inform prisoners of their rights.[146]

The central flaw in all this humane legislation was that it presumed adequate facilities, funds, and administrative will in court prisons. The first two necessities were lacking throughout France, and the third was consequently deficient.

The Grand Châtelet. The Grand Châtelet, headquarters of the lawcourt and its principal jail, was a high-walled fortress built in 1130 by order of Louis VI. When Phillip Augustus constructed the northern ramparts of the capital in the 1190s, the Châtelet became militarily redundant and was given to the provost of Paris as the seat of his court. There were only partial renovations during the late fifteenth century and in the 1680s. It was one of the oldest, most decayed and congested official structures in eighteenth-century Paris. The complex of buildings formed a rough square at the base of the rue Saint-Denis; it was divided into two parts by a covered passageway that narrowly funneled the rue Saint-Denis into the quay on the rue Trop-va-qui-dure and the entry to the Pont-au-Change. The Châtelet abutted the banks of the Seine, its humidity and seepages.[147] Until its demolition in 1802, it remained closely surrounded by the Halles, especially the meat market, with its refuse and stench. The main courtyard and the judicial chambers (in towers or on upper stories) were in the western portion of the Châtelet; the prison area was in the eastern, least renovated, portion. The prison of the Grand Châtelet was composed of fifteen different jail areas; most were in multistoried, low-ceilinged buildings around small, obscure courtyards. Inmates were segregated by sex and by class. The most comfortable and salubrious areas were in the northeastern towers. Below, there were common halls and rooms of various sizes, with one to three inmates per bed, others where inmates slept on piles of straw (*les pauvres de la paillasse,* who could not afford better), and cells with fetters and chains for the dangerous, violent, and escape-prone.[148] There were also subterranean cells and common rooms that had once been storage cellars of the fortress. Pierre Giraud, the municipal architect who supervised the demolition of the Châtelet, described those dungeons in 1805,

which received light only through high apertures that were half obstructed by fine-meshed grills that gave onto courtyards or onto the neighboring butcher stalls and fish market, and even onto the main sewer, which constantly disgorged monstrous rats that

---

[146] A.N. AD III 27b.

[147] So also did the smaller auxiliary prison of the court, the Petit Châtelet, on the Left Bank at the foot of the Petit Pont (see the Turgot map of the Ile de la Cité, frontispiece). It was closed in 1782.

[148] When John Howard inspected the Grand Châtelet in 1783, he found 305 prisoners, 209 of whom were *pauvres de la pailliase* (*Etat des prisons, des hôpitaux et des maisons de force,* vol. 1 [Paris, 1791], p. 371).

cats were afraid to attack. . . . Rainwater and even the urine of other prisoners constantly filtered, through cracks in pavement and ceilings, into the cells beneath the courtyards.[149]

As in all Old Regime prisons, the chief jailor, or *greffier-concièrge*, was both a venal-hereditary officer of state (whose office at the Châtelet cost some 30,000 livres in the 1780s) and a hostelry entrepreneur. New inmates negotiated their lodging with him, immediately after being registered in the jail book. Unless police or magistrates ordered otherwise, those who could pay were placed in the towers or in the rooms and halls with beds, and fed according to their means; those who paid full board could dine at the jailer's table on his ample fare.[150] Those who could not pay, the majority of inmates at the Grand Châtelet, were put on straw in common rooms (which was changed once a month) and given the daily ration of water and 1.5 pounds of bread.[151] During the late Old Regime, certain of those rooms contained up to 120 inmates, who slept in shifts on pallets that measured 22 by 19 feet and whose straw was "filled with vermin and devoured by a prodigious quantity of mice."[152]

Detention at the Grand Châtelet was harsh and corrosive for all but a minority of inmates. That condition was not produced by cruelty of intent or behavior among jailers or by indifference among magistrates. It was produced by chronic overcrowding in ancient, deteriorated, poorly ventilated and heated structures, a minimal budget, and the unwillingness of the monarchy to incur the great cost of demolishing and replacing the building and the many others equally dilapidated. The unwillingness was reinforced by the fact that most inmates were jailed for less than two months, the normal duration of investigation, trial, and judgment. Those sentenced to *plus amplement informé* with detention for six months or a year were often transferred from the Châtelet to the Conciergerie of the Parlement, Bicêtre, or the Salpêtrière.

During the period 1779 to 1789 inclusive, an average of 750 persons were jailed each year at the Grand Châtelet as suspects or defendants in *grand*

---

[149] "Plans et descriptions historiques de prisons et maisons d'arrêt du département de la Seine. . ." (Paris, 1805), pp. 6–7. See also Doublet, *Rapport,* pp. 2–3.

[150] As expressed by the *greffier-concièrge* of the Châtelet in 1789; "Les gages des concièrges consistent en une somme fixe, & au produit des chambres particulières qu'ils louent pour leur compte" ("Adresse à la municipalité de Paris par le Greffier-Concièrge du Châtelet," ms., Paris, 1789, p. 18, Bibliothèque Nationale Rp. 3557). The 1717 ruling established a list of the payments they could require from prisoners or their families; the highest was 1 livre, for registering an inmate in the book or providing a copy of the order for discharge from prison. Turnkeys were not to collect any money from prisoners; they were hired and paid by the *greffier-concièrge,* but at a minimum legal wage of 100 livres a year. They lived in the jails.

[151] The Parlement acknowledged, in a ruling of November 1760, that the bread given prisoners in Paris jails was "always made poorly from inferior ingredients, and occasions rumors and revolts in prisons." That was not surprising, for the Parlement let six-month provisioning contracts to the bakers who bid lowest. The "solution" adopted in 1760 was to award a nine-year contract to one large-scale baker, while stipulating that each of his 22-ounce prison loaves was to contain one part rye, one part wheat flour, and one part mixed wheat and meal (A.N. AD III 27b).

[152] Giraud, *Plans,* p. 4.

criminel, or an approximate total of 8,250.[153] Between October 1785 and October 1786, 807 were jailed there, and for the following lengths of time before sentencing: less than one month (40.0%); one to two months (29.0%); two to four months (25%); four to six months (4%); six to eight months (1.5%); more than eight months (0.2%).[154] Fifty were sentenced by the criminal chamber to *plus amplement informé* in prison: for three months (26), six months (14), or one year (10). Most served that time in the Grand Châtelet or the Conciergerie. Thus, approximately three-fourths of those jailed in 1785–6 had to endure the Châtelet jail for less than three months before they were either freed without trial, tried and acquitted of charges, or convicted and given exterior punishment.

That was long enough for men and women – most of whom were in their prime, between the ages of 18 and 40, to become dangerously ill within the cells and halls of the Grand Châtelet and for a few to die. Twenty-one inmates died between January 1779 and December 1789; the causes of their deaths are given in Table 9.4.[155] Most of the 21 died from contagious respiratory diseases and various "fevers," or from intestinal and blood diseases of the sort caused by malnutrition or contaminated food or water. They represent a minuscule fraction (0.25%) of the some 8,250 inmates during those eleven years. In some years there were no deaths. But more than 200 others who contracted the same maladies or suffered various injuries were transferred to the Hôtel-Dieu, where many undoubtedly died.[156] The sum of about 250 represents a biological attrition rate, of 3 percent among 8,250 inmates, or about 1 in 30 during relatively short periods of detention. Fifteen of the 21 dead had been inside for more than two months, whereas only about 30 percent of all inmates were detained that long. Those 15 were probably killed by the environment of the Châtelet.

The Conciergerie. The Conciergerie was the jail for the Parlement of Paris and for the bailliage court of the Palais de Justice. It was located virtually at the topographical core of the grounds of the Palais, surrounded on the east and west by the main buildings of the Parlement and on the south by the Chambre des Comptes and the court of the *élection* of Paris. The Conciergerie occupied almost one-third of the entire area of the Palais de Justice. Criminal defendants judged in first instance by the Parlement of Paris, as well as the hundreds judged by the Parlement each year on appeal from subaltern courts,

---

[153] Estimated from the registers of jailings in A.N. Y 10648–10650.

[154] A.N. Y 10648. The majority of those released after less than one month of detention were discharged by the criminal lieutenant or provost because there was insufficient evidence of guilt to warrant their prosecution and trial; the majority of those detained for more than two months were tried and sentenced.

[155] Data were constructed from "Ordonnances d'inhumation des Prisonniers décédés en Prison," A.N. Y 10551. The cause of death was stated by physicians of the Châtelet after examination of the corpse.

[156] A.N. Y 10551.

Table 9.4. *Causes of death in Châtelet prison, 1779–1789*

Date of jailing	Date of death	Duration of detention	Gender	Cause of death
June 20, 1780	December 24, 1780	6 months	m	Consumption
July 12, 1780	September 22, 1780	2 months	m	Generalized dropsy
September 4, 1780	September 22, 1780	2–3 weeks	m	Malignant fever
January 1, 1781	March 18, 1781	2–3 months	m	
January 2, 1781	January 10, 1781	1 week	f	Asthma
August 18, 1781	December 14, 1781	4 months	m	Lung disease
October, 1781	February 8, 1782	4 months/p.a.i. 3 months, January 19, 1782	m	Dropsical swelling, chest
July 5, 1782	August 28, 1782	7 weeks	m	Malignant fever
January 21, 1784	May 20, 1784	4 months/p.a.i. 3 months, March 3, 1784	m	Indigestion
March 2, 1784	March 1, 1785	1 year/p.a.i. 1 year, May 26, 1785	m	Diarrhoea
November 15, 1784	February 22, 1785	2–3 months	m	Putrid and malignant fever
February 10, 1785	November 12, 1785	9 months	m	Fever and diarrhoea
July 23, 1785	February 17, 1786	6 months	m	Diarrhoea
November 21, 1785	June 2, 1786	6–7 months	m	Mange
March 29, 1788	September 13, 1788	5–6 months	m	Inflammation of lungs
October 13, 1788	October 28, 1788	2 weeks	f	Pneumonia
November 18, 1788	December 25, 1788	5 weeks	m	Gangrenous infection of lungs
January 19, 1789	February 25, 1789	5 weeks	m	Inflammatory fever
January 26, 1789	May 14, 1789	3–4 months	m	Emaciation/atrophy
April 19, 1789	September 27, 1789	6 months	m	Diarrhoea/atrophy
April 30, 1789	November 21, 1789	6–7 months	m	

Abbreviations: **m**–male; *f*–female; *p.a.i.*–*plus amplement informé.*
Source: Data constructed from "Ordonnances d'inhumation des Prisonniers décédés en Prison," A.N.Y. 10551.

were confined there. Between 1735 and 1789, its annual inmate population ranged from 500 to almost 1,000. The Conciergerie was a thick-walled, fortresslike artifact of the fourteenth and fifteenth centuries, but it was far better maintained than the Grand Châtelet. There was the same sociospatial hierarchy among inmates, ranging from individual apartments to common halls with beds of straw, as in the Châtelet, but the Conciergerie was far more capacious, labyrinthine, and logistically self-contained.[157]

The mid-eighteenth-century diagrams of the Conciergerie depict the ground and first floors on a north–south axis.[158] The three round towers to the north faced onto the Quai de l'Horloge; they were, from west to east, the Tour Bon-Bec, which housed the *chambre de la question,* or torture chamber; the Tour d'Argent, which housed the criminal appeals chamber or Tournelle, and its twin, the Tour César, where civil appeals were judged. Just below and behind the twin towers, on the ground floor, was the *salle des gardes,* divided into jail cells and guards' apartments. The large, ornate, high-ceilinged hall of the Grand-Chambre of the Parlement was on the first floor, above the *salle des gardes.* Here, as in the Châtelet, themistocrats worked in very close proximity to the living quarters of those whom they judged. The *chambre des criminels,* for those awaiting final hearing and judgment in the Tournelle, was just below and to the east of the Grand-Chambre. The Conciergerie was bisected on the east–west axis by long corridors that wound from the great staircase and the boutiques off the Cour du Mai (on the east) through the *promenoir des hommes* to a square tower (on the west). The men's carceral section was to the north of those corridors. It was spatially dominated by the rectangular main courtyard, or *préau de la Conciergerie pour les hommes.* On the inner, or eastern, side of the yard were the common halls for inmates without money, those who slept on straw (the *pailleux*). On the western and northern sides were the much smaller *chambres des pistoliers* (named after a coin, the *pistole*), for prisoners who could pay for a bed. The men could dine in one of two large refectories. The women's section was to the south of the east–west corridors, centered on the *cour des femmes.* The same social distinctions obtained there. There were many rooms with only one or a few beds, and common halls of *paillasses.* Finally, there were various keeps reserved for inmates held under maximum security, such as the brigand leader "Cartouche" in the 1720s, or for high-born, wealthy, and distinguished prisoners – from Philippe de Commynes in the fifteenth century, to the marquise of Brinvilliers in the late seventeenth, to the count of Favras in 1790.

There was a large chapel, but only two small infirmaries, for this population of men and women. The women's infirmary had no more than twenty beds and

---

[157] On its history, see Jacques Hillairet, *L'Ile de la Cité* (Paris: Editions de Minuit, 1969), and Henri Stein, *Le Palais de Justice et La Sainte-Chapelle de Paris* (Paris, 1912).

[158] When referring to floors in a building, the European system is used here (i.e., "ground floor" corresponds to the American "first floor"; "first floor" corresponds to the American "second floor," etc.). The original drawings are in A.N. F 14 10253.

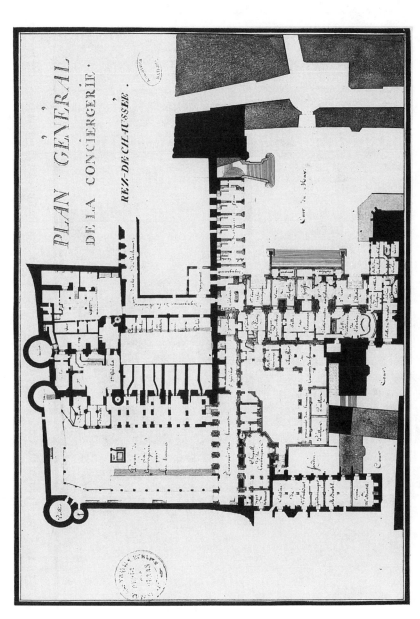

Figure 9.11. General plan of the Conciergerie: ground floor. (A.N. F 14 10253. Reprinted with permission of the French National Archives.)

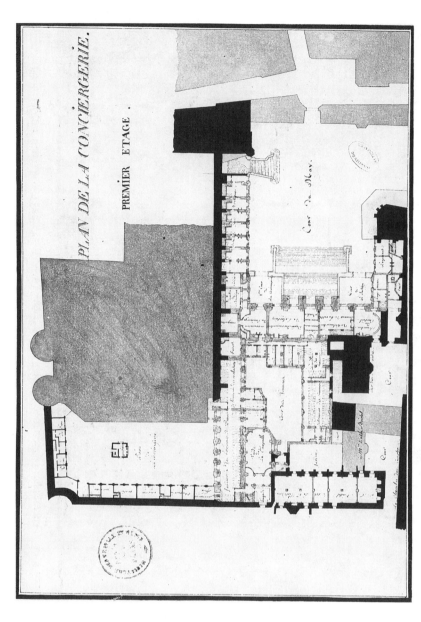

Figure 9.12. General plan of the Conciergerie: first floor. (A.N. F 14 10253. Reprinted with permission of the French National Archives.)

was on the floor above two halls for *pauvres de la paillasse;* the men's had about fifty beds in a space measuring 36 yards by 9 yards. However, the Conciergerie was more salubrious than the Châtelet: It was high above the Seine and had solid foundations. There was abundant water from fountains and wells. Most of the carceral buildings received light and air from courtyards, the passageways were high and vaulted, and many blocks and cells were separated by iron grills rather than stone walls.

D. Torture, mutilation, and death

The Criminal Ordinance of 1670 classified torture, or the *question*, as a penalty in *grand criminel.* In fact, however, torture was a trial procedure, given the status of penalty in 1670, but not that of autonomous penalty. The *question préparatoire* could be decreed, under precise and severe restrictions, as an interlocutory judgment for defendants accused of a capital offense and against whom there was strong but not conclusive evidence of guilt. Its outcome had a decisive effect on final judgment of the defendant. The *question préalable* could be decreed against those convicted of a capital offense and sentenced to death when there was strong evidence of complicity in the case and to obtain further evidence against accomplices either at large or under accusation. It was administered immediately before the ritual of execution. Both forms of the *question* will be closely examined in Part III.

Mutilation of the body had almost disappeared from French criminal justice by the late seventeenth century, although it survived in military punishments and could be inflicted on fugitive colonial slaves.[159] Extreme and recidivist blasphemy – "to blaspheme, curse, and execrate the Holy Name of God, to utter words against the honor of the Very Holy Virgin . . . and the Saints" – could be punished by mutilation. But the royal declaration of July 1666 provided a generous scale in the punishment of such blasphemy: fine for a first conviction; progressive doubling of the fine upon each conviction up to the fourth; at fifth conviction, fine and the iron collar; at sixth, piercing of the upper lip with a hot iron, at the pillory; at seventh, amputation of the lower lip; at eighth, cutting out of the tongue.[160] Attempted or accomplished murder of a spouse, sibling, or parent was an offense calling for a mandatory death sentence. In such cases, hanging, breaking, or burning was sometimes immediately preceded by severing of the offending hand at the site of execution. When that was ordered in the judgment, the executioner placed the arm on a block, chopped off the hand with a hatchet, thrust the stump into a small sack filled

[159] The edict of March 1685 on fugitive slaves in the American colonies mandated " 'que l'esclave fugitif qui aura éte en fuite pendant un mois, à computer du jour que son maître l'aura dénoncé en Justice, aur des oreilles coupées, & sera marqué d'une fleur de lis sur l'épaule; que s'il récidive un autre mois, à compter pareillement du jour de la dénonciation, il aura le jarret coupé, & sera marqué d'une fleur de lis sur l'autre épaule; & que la troisième fois il sera puni de mort' " (quoted by Jousse, *Traité,* vol. 4, p. 105).

[160] Isambert, vol. 18, pp. 86–7.

with bran to stanch the blood, tied the sack around the victim's arm, and proceeded with the execution.

Between 1735 and 1789, the death sentence was statistically rare within the jurisdiction of the Parlement of Paris, comprising only from 4 to 8 percent of all final penal sentences in *grand criminel.* But it did not appear so to contemporaries, for its execution was public, spectacular, and enveloped in a long ritual (described in Volume 2). Between 1670 and 1789, judicial death was inflicted by five methods: decapitation; hanging; breaking on the Saint Andrew's Cross, followed by exposure on the wheel; burning at the stake or drawing and quartering (dismemberment) by horses. Judges did not arbitrarily choose the form of execution: Each was reserved for distinct categories of capital offenses and capital offenders.

Decapitation by the executioner's sword was reserved for nobles, but only if their crimes were not derogating of nobility by their baseness or viciousness:

This punishment, which is quite venerable, is rarely inflicted among us except on noble persons and is normally utilized for offenses which mean the gallows for commoners, such as unpremeditated murder, abduction, sedition and revolt, etc., but with the following distinction: In cases of crimes that, by their nature, dishonor and render infamous the culprit, such as effractive burglary, highway robbery, premeditated murder, etc., nobles are condemned to the same punishments as commoners.[161]

Hanging was the most common executionary method in eighteenth-century France. The technique of hanging was primitive; it involved a rough physical encounter between the executioner, his assistants, and the victim. It required great dexterity and strength on the part of the executioner. There was no raised scaffold with a trapdoor and no deadfall to ensure a broken neck. There was only a wooden gallows post, 12 to 15 feet long, with a single beam at the top. A gallows was constructed for each execution and set into a hole in the pavement. Muyart de Vouglans accurately described the typical Parisian hanging:

This penalty is executed as follows: Three ropes are fixed around the Criminal's neck, to wit, two *tortouses* [hanging ropes], which are of the thickness of a finger and with a slipknot noose, and the *jet,* so called because it serves only to aid the Executioner in thrusting the Criminal off the gallows ladder; the Criminal is then made to climb onto the Executioner's wagon, where he is seated on a cross-bench, his back turned to the horse, the Confessor at this side and the Executioner behind him. At the Gallows, a ladder is propped and tied, and the Executioner climbs the ladder backward, guiding the Criminal up, also backward, by using the ropes around the neck. The Confessor then climbs, facing forward; and while he exhorts the *Patient* [the official term for the condemned person], the Executioner ties the *tortouses* around the Gallows beam; when the Confessor climbs down, the Executioner knocks the *Patient* off the ladder by thrusting with his knee and pulling on the *jet;* the *Patient* dangles in the air with the nooses press

[161] Jousse, *Traité,* vol. 1, p. 46.

ing into his neck. The Executioner then holds onto the beam, presses with his feet on the bound hands of the *Patient*, knees him in the stomach, shakes him about, and thus ends his agony by causing his death.[162]

That death was by strangulation, and it was not always so rapid as Muyart suggested.

Execution on the wheel, *la roue*, was the most prolonged and agonizing of Old Regime capital punishments, when it was not abbreviated by secret instructions from the sentencing court. It was reserved for men and inflicted in two stages: breaking and exposure. A high platform was erected, on which a large wooden Saint Andrew's Cross (shaped like an X) was placed. The victim was tied horizontally to the cross. The executioner struck two blows to each limb and two or three to the kidneys or stomach with a long, heavy iron rod. That was "breaking." The shattered body was then removed from the cross and tied horizontally, arms and legs bent back, to a carriage wheel fixed on top of a 10-foot pole. The pole was raised and set into a pavement hole. He remained on the wheel until he died or, in the unvarying formula of the sentence, "his face turned to the Heavens, to remain there so long as it shall please God to conserve his life." In practice, executions by the full duration of breaking and exposure were rare within the jurisdiction of the Parlement of Paris during the eighteenth century. The Parlement, and the Châtelet (when it pronounced that sentence without appeal), usually issued secret instructions, or *retenta*, for the executioner to strangle the victim rapidly with a leather garrote (*le moulinet*), after striking a few blows with the rod or after a specified time on the wheel. *Retenta* were issued primarily for a spiritual reason: Because the pain of breaking and the wheel was so intense, it easily provoked blasphemous curses that sabotaged the ministrations of the priest.[163] Every execution, no matter the method, was considered both an extinction of a physical life and a salvational opportunity for a soul. The man who died uttering blasphemy was damned.

Burning "alive" was done at an 8-foot stake, around which kindling and wood were piled in a pyramid (whose base was about 6 feet in diameter), with a hollow space near the stake and a passage for the executioner. Only the victim's head protruded from the pile. Burnings were only exceptionally in vivo. *Retenta* were customary; the executioner garroted the victim at the stake, inside the pile of wood and beyond sight of the crowd, before the fire was started. Those hanged or broken for particularly "atrocious" crimes were sometimes burned to ashes immediately after being executed on the gallows or wheel.

Drawing and quartering by a team of horses, which was preceded by various mutilations, was the rarest of capital punishments. It was reserved in law for

---

[162] *Loix criminelles*, p. 58.

[163] "Afin d'empecher que la rigueur extrême de ce Supplice, ainsi que celui du Feu vif, n'expose le Salut du Condamné par le desespoir où elle pourroit se jetter, les Juges des Cours supérieures ont attention le plus souvent d'ordonner par un 'Retentum,' qu'ils mettent au bas de l'Arrêt, que le Condamné sera étranglé dans le tems de l'Exécution" (Muyart, *Institutes*, p. 401).

regicides and those who attempted violence against members of the royal family or princes of the blood. There was only one such execution in Paris during the eighteenth century: of Damiens, in 1757, for attempting to kill Louis XV.

Finally, there was occasional public figurative execution of people who were already dead: persons convicted of suicide or defendants convicted of "atrocious" capital offenses who had died in custody of the court. Jousse described executions of the dead:

The condemnations [to death] pronounced against the corpse of the deceased culprit order that he will be dragged on a hurdle frame, his face turned toward the ground, through the streets and crossroads of the place where the judgment has been pronounced, then hanged from the gallows and thrown on the refuse dump; and that his property will be confiscated. When the corpse has not been preserved, an effigy is drawn of that man or woman, and the judgment is executed against the effigy, as if it were the corpse.[164]

Sentences to death, banishment for life from the realm, or life in the *hôpitaux*, galleys, or *bagnes* were not directed only at the person of the convicted; they also comported "civil death," and thus financially damaged the convict's family. Civil death meant that all property of the condemned was subject to confiscation by the state, a provision that sometimes resulted in complex civil litigation to protect conjugal and lineal property from confiscation. Civil death, an official annihilation of economic being, was the ultimate expression of the concept of infamy that permeated Old Regime punishment.

E. Spectacles

Parades of the infamous, theaters of defamation: These were not metaphoric, symbolic events or accessories to physical chastisement. Such spectacles belonged to the essence of Old Regime punishment, and they punctuated the daily life of every eighteenth-century French city. It is impossible to comprehend eighteenth-century French urban attitudes regarding justice, state, and church, or shame and the body, without examining those spectacles.

Dozens of punishments each month, amounting to hundreds each year, were publicly enacted in Paris. The inner city, on both banks of the river, was traversed by processions of the chastised, most of whom wore placards with their names and crimes in bold letters. The processions wound, in fixed trajectories, from the Châtelet, Parlement, and other courts through densely populated and commercial quarters to the sites of punishment. Publicity was aural and literary, as well as visual. Penal judgments were proclaimed at the sound of a trumpet

[164] Jousse, *Traité*, vol. 1, p. 55. Those sentences were accompanied by formal condemnation of the deceased person's memory: "Afin de laisser à la posterité une note genérale et éternelle du crime, contre celui qui l'a commis; par exemple, à l'égard des nobles, en les déclarant roturiers & leurs descendants; & en ordonnant que leurs armoires seront brisés; leurs châteaux, ou maisons, abattues; leurs bois coupés, & leurs noms supprimés" (ibid.).

and then posted in the streets by court criers. They were grandiloquent texts, such as the typical appellate judgment by the Parlement reproduced as appendix to Part II.

The common geography of Parisian punishment remained constant across the century: the Place de Grève, in front of the Hôtel de Ville; the Portes Saint-Martin and Saint-Denis; the Croix du Trahoir and the pillory, in the Halles; the square of the Palais-Royal; the main portal of Nôtre-Dame Cathedral (where the *amende honorable in figuris* was usually performed); the squares of Saint-Michel, Maubert, the Montagne Sainte-Geneviève, and the carrefour de Buci on the Left Bank. There were no executions on Sundays, but the other punishments were enacted seven days a week. Ritualistic spectacles of punishment were equally intrinsic to criminal justice and to the public life of the metropolis. Brandings, whippings, *amendes honorable,* the iron collar and pillory, convoys to the Salpêtrière and Bicêtre, chain gangs leaving for the galleys or *bagne,* and the corteges of executions alternated, competed for attention and space, and often intermingled with a multiplicity of other ceremonial events in eighteenth-century Paris. Every year there were thirty-two religious processional festivals that traversed much of the city, and some forty parishes had annual processions to honor their patron saints. Corteges marched for the feast day of Saint-Louis, the reliquary of Sainte-Geneviève, the *rentrée* of the Parlement, royal visits to the City, major guild celebrations, and the funerals of municipal notables, high officers of state, and aristocrats. Images of the Virgin in three Parisian churches were sites of pilgrimage and annual marches. Between 1600 and 1789, 248 royal Te Deums were celebrated in Paris, two hundred of them during the reign of Louis XIV, twenty-four between 1750 and 1789.[165] That compressive promiscuity of sacred or profane celebratory rituals and punitive spectacles underlay François Vermeil's despairing statement, "We celebrate our public festivals on sites of carnage, all sprinkled with blood."[166]

The year 1762 was an ordinary year in the criminal justice of the Châtelet and Parlement. There were no serious riots or unusual collective prosecutions during that or the preceding year. The cases tried, judgments rendered, and punishments enacted in 1762 were typical of midcentury Paris. During those twelve months, the Parlement rendered 235 appellate penal judgments against defendants first judged in *grand criminel* by the Châtelet, 60 women and 175 men.[167] Most of those judgments were publicized by court criers. One hundred and forty-six of the punishments were enacted or displayed publicly: banishment and branding, usually combined with whipping (82); the preceding combined with the iron collar (9); branding and the *bagne* (19); the Hôpital-

---

[165] Annik Pardailhe-Galabrun, "Les déplacements des parisiens dans la ville aux XVIIème et XVIIIème siècles," *Histoire, Economie et Société* (1983): 205–53. See also René Héron de Villefosse, *Nouvelle histoire de Paris: Solemnité, fêtes et rejouissances parisiennes* (Paris: Hachette, 1980).
[166] *Essai sur les réformes à faire dans notre législation criminelle* (Paris, 1781), p. 136.
[167] Inventory 450, vols. 5–8.

Général, usually after branding and/or the iron collar (20); hanging (12); breaking (3); burning (1). In addition, the criminal chamber of the Châtelet rendered 42 penal sentences in final provostial or presidial judgment, of which 14 were executed publicly: branding and banishment (3); the Hôpital-Général (4); the *bagne*, usually preceded by the iron collar (5); hanging (2).[168] The actual number of public judicial chastisements in Paris and its *banlieue* during 1762 was three to four times greater than the sum of 160 ordered by the Châtelet and Parlement. Sixteen other royal courts or tribunals had some independent criminal jurisdiction over the metropolis and its region. Five to six hundred public chastisements a year, of which at least eighteen were capital executions, formed a massive presence within Paris and its environs. The metropolis was a *cité des supplices*.

Those spectacles were enacted by the public executioner and his assistants. The executioner's official title was "Executioner of criminal sentences and judgments" and, sometimes, "Executioner of High Justice." He enjoyed the royally conferred, and quite rare, privilege of carrying offensive and defensive weapons "for the security of his person, because of his office." But he was known colloquially, and with sinister mockery, as *le bourreau* – the tormenter, the butcher.[169] The antagonism of nomenclatures expressed the unique and perennial tension of his position: He was utterly indispensable to state and themistocracy, and correspondingly privileged and protected; he was also a social pariah, defiled by his work and ostracized from the normal life of his community. "He is the most vile citizen of the city."[170] Yet the opprobrium was mixed with other attitudes. The enactor of punitive spectacles was a fascinating personage, highly visible and widely known. He even wore formal attire for capital executions: powdered wig, high collar, black frockcoat and breeches, white stockings and buckled shoes.

The lowest class of the people is perfectly familiar with his countenance; he is the great tragic actor for the vulgar populace that flocks to these dreadful spectacles. . . . The common people talk frequently about the executioner. . . . There are cobblers who know the history of the hanged and their executioners as thoroughly as men of cultivated society know the history of the kings of Europe and their ministers.[171]

Executioners were reputed to have great and arcane knowledge of the body. Some capitalized on the repute by concocting potions (that occasionally included blood, urine, ejacula, or flesh from the executed) and giving various medical treatments, clandestinely and illegally.[172]

---

[168] A.N. Y 10517–10518.

[169] Addressing or publicly referring to the executioner by that insulting term was outlawed, under penalty of fine, by the royal Council of State in January 1787 (A.N. AD III 31).

[170] Mercier, *Tableau de Paris*, vol. 3, p. 161. See also Ferrière, vol. 1, p. 572.

[171] Mercier, *Tableau de Paris*, pp. 161–2.

[172] Michel Bée, "Le boureau et la société d'ancien régime," in *Actes du 107e Congrès national des Sociétés Savantes: Histoire moderne et contemporaine* (Paris, 1984), vol. 1, pp. 61–73.

The office both sustained and entrapped its incumbents, and their progeny, during the Old Regime and subsequent regimes. As François Desmarest, assistant to the Paris executioner, wrote to the minister of justice in 1796: "Our occupation is incompatible with all others."[173] The dynasticism and marital endogamy of Old Regime executioners surpassed even those of *parlementaires*. There were more than one hundred executionary offices throughout France from the late seventeenth century to 1791. They were held by about twenty intermarried families.[174] Their scions addressed each other formally, as "Monsieur de Paris," "Monsieur de Tours," and so forth. They were a caste.

Executioners, like magistrates, were venal-hereditary officers of state and complete professionals in their task.[175] The office was made lucrative, in contrast to magisterial offices. From at least 1485 to the Revolution, kings granted considerable title, remuneration, and protection to the executioners of France. They did so because of the singular importance of the office, the general opprobrium that made recruitment difficult, and the consequent need to sustain dynasticism. In the provinces north of the Loire, remuneration was by a combination of *gages;* set fees for execution of judgments; reimbursement of travel costs; exemption from most indirect taxes; free lodging (the "executioner's house"); and right to a quota, paid in money or in kind, of most foodstuffs brought to market. This last, the *droit de havage*, was highly profitable.[176]

The executioner of Paris served all courts in the jurisdiction of the provostry, including the Parlement and other sovereign courts of the city. His *havage* privileges on the city's markets were correspondingly extensive, until 1775:

One egg from each merchant carrying eggs in a sack or basket, two eggs from each with a pack saddle, one dozen from each with a wagon; 1 sou for each basket of apples, pears, grapes, and other produce arriving by land or by river, 2 sous for each horse or wagon thus loaded; a full ladle of all green peas, medlars, hemp seed, mustard seed, millet, walnuts, chestnuts, hazelnuts, green walnuts transported by land or river; 6 deniers from each merchant carrying butter, cheese, poultry and fowl, or freshwater fish in a sack or basket, 1 sou from each carrying the same in a pack saddle, 2 sous from each with a

---

[173] A.N. BB 3 209. Another executioner's assistant, at Dijon, wrote, in requesting appointment to the recently vacated office there: "Le Préjugé public ne permet plus de retour vers une autre profession, après les essais dans celle-ci; ne permettez donc pas qu'un citoyen, après s'être dévoué à l'exécution de la vindicte publique se voit repoussée pendant le reste de sa vie des autres professions de la vie civile" (April 1801, A.N. BB 3 209).

[174] "Tableau des Exécuteurs existants dans le Royaume," ms. late 1791, A.N. BB 3 206. See also the documents in BB 3 207–209. Other than the Sansons of Paris, the most prominent long-term executionary dynasties were the Fereys (who held the office at Rouen and other Norman cities for more than three generations before 1789) and the Jouënnes of Normandy and Touraine. In 1791–2, the Revolutionary government abolished several executionary offices and appointed one salaried executioner for each of the eighty-three *départements;* it selected them from among the large *corps* of Old Regime executioners. Most of the dynasties lasted well into the nineteenth century.

[175] On their duties and their formal relations with prosecutors and judges, see Jousse, *Traité*, vol. 1, pp. 404–7.

[176] In most provincial towns, it gave executioners an annual revenue of from 2,000 to 6,000 livres. "Tableau des exécuteurs," A.N. BB 3 206.

wagon, 1 livre and a carp from each boatload; 1 sou for each sack of shelled peas, 6 deniers for each basket; 1 sou from each merchant carrying cases of oranges and lemons; one dozen oysters from each wagon of oysters, a proportionate number from each boatload; one broom from each person bringing brooms, two from each packload, six from each wagon; a bucketful of coal from each coal merchant; rope from the rope-makers, for executions.[177]

Each week the executioner's assistants, or *valets,* exacted these payments at the various ports and markets of Paris. They, or tradesmen commissioned by the executioner, sold the produce in stalls adjacent to the executioner's official lodgings at the *maison du pilory* in the Halle Centrale, often at prices below those of other tradesmen. Thus the craftsman of chastisements and death was also a prosperous food merchant. Turgot suppressed these *droits d'havage* throughout France in 1775. Henceforth, the executioner of Paris was paid 16,000 livres a year. He earned an additional 1,500 to 2,500 livres annually in set fees for executing criminal sentences.[178] He, and his colleagues in the provinces, could also traffic licitly in the clothes worn by the executed. There was a brisk market for those ghoulish souvenirs, especially when the criminal was notorious, or socially distinguished, or had died splendidly.[179]

The Sansons were the most renowned dynasty of *bourreaux* (see Chart 9.1). That family held the office of executioner for the "city, provostry, and viscountry of Paris," and then for the Department of Paris and of the Seine, from 1688 to 1847 – during 159 years, three reigns, and five subsequent regimes. Members of the family also held the office for long tenures at Reims, Tours, and Provins during the eighteenth century.[180] Their most epic tenure at Paris was that of Charles-Jean-Baptiste. He was appointed (in succession to his deceased

---

[177] From the letter of appointment of Charles-Jean-Baptiste Sanson to the office of executioner for the city, provostry, and viscounty of Paris, September 9, 1726, A.N. V 1 540. Executioners were also exempted from all payments of or for the Watch or Guard or for bridges, tolls, or customs duties on wine and spirits.

[178] "Tableau des exécuteurs," A.N. BB 3 206.

[179] The office was, in fact, a business that required considerable expenditure by the executioner. Charles-Henri Sanson, executioner of Paris from 1778 to 1795, itemized his average annual outlay, for that business and his household, in a "mémoire justificatif" to the Constituent Assembly in 1790 or 1791; 600 livres each to his two brothers, whom he deputed to execute judgments in his place (usually outside Paris); 1,200 livres in salary to four servants who assisted him; 300 livres each to three wagoners for conveying the convicted to punishment; 200 livres for a cook; 2,000 livres for purchase or renting of four horses; 350 livres for their harnesses, feed, and shoeing; 300 livres for the building of four wagons and a cart; 1,200 livres in pension to his mother; 9,600 livres in food for a household of sixteen persons, including eight servants or employees (after the abolition of *havage*); 4,000 livres for general maintenance of himself, his wife, and children; 4,800 livres in rent on his main residence, storehouse, and stables (in the Faubourg Poissonnière); 2,048 livres in *capitation* tax; 5,000 livres for tips, gratuities and gifts to various personnel, medical treatment for servants and employees, and for repair or replacement of the instruments of the trade. Sanson alleged a total average annual outlay of more than 32,000 livres. One is struck by the number of persons materially implicated in one executioner's office; they also included carpenters from whom he purchased gallows, iron-collar posts, and scaffolds (A.N. BB 3 206).

[180] Roger Gaulard, *Une lignée d'exécuteurs des jugements criminels: Les Sanson, 1688–1847* (Melun: Librairie Archambault, 1968). The genealogy of the Sansons is from this work.

Chart 9.1. The Sanson family

I	II	III	IV	V	VI

Charles I Sanson (1635–1707): soldier, infantry regiment; executioner at Paris (1688–1707) oo Marguérite Jouënne (1675), daughter, executioner at Caudebec-en-Caux

Charles II (1681–1726): executioner at Paris (1707–26) oo Jeanne-Renée Debut (1707)

Anne Renée (1710–?) oo Nicolas-Charles-Gabriel (1721–95): executioner at Reims (1745–77)

Jean-Louis (c.1750–?): executioner at Reims (1777–c.1795) oo Marie-Josèphe Sanson (1794), his first cousin, daughter of the following:

Charles-Jean-Baptiste (1719–78): executioner at Paris (1740–78) oo 1. Madeleine Tronson (1737), daughter of his tutor; oo 2. Jeanne-Gabrielle Berger (c.1742), daughter of executioner in Touraine

Madeleine-Claude Gabrielle (c.1738–c.1779) oo Pierre Hérisson, executioner at Melun

Louis-Charles Martin (1744–c.1812): executioner at Tours (1768–96), at Dijon (1801–7), at Auxerre (1807–12) oo Marie-Victoire Collet de Charmoy (1776)

Chart 9.1. *(cont.)*

I	II	III	IV	V	VI
					Louis-Victor (c.1776–c.1824): executioner's assistant at Tours (father), Blois (uncle), La Rochelle and Saintes (uncle), executioner at Montpellier (1800–2)
				Nicolas-Charles-Gabriel II (1745–c.1800): assistant to Charles-Henri below; torturer at Paris (1779–91); executioner at Blois (1795–99)	
				Louis-Cyr Charlemagne (1748–94); executioner at Provins (1768–88), at Versailles (1788–94) oo Marie-Madeleine Hérisson (1779), daughter, executioner at Melun; oo Marie-Fare Gendron (1792), daughter of miller	
				Charles-Henri (1739–1806): assistant to father (1750–78); executioner at Paris (1778–95) oo Marie-Anne Jugier (1776), daughter of market-gardener	
				Henry (1767–1840): assistant to father; executioner at Paris (1795–1840) oo Marie-Louise Damidot (1792)	
					Henri-Clément (1799–1889): assistant to father; executioner at Paris (1840–47)

Sources: A.N. BB 3 206 ("Tableau des Exécuteurs existants dans le Royaume," 1791); A.N. V 1 540; Roger Gaulard, *Une lignée d'exécuteurs des jugements criminels: les Sansom, 1688–1847* (Melun: Archambault, 1968).

father) in 1726, at the age of 7. Georges Hérisson, torturer at the Châtelet, and François Prudhomme (both relatives of the Sansons) filled the office by interim appointment, and trained the boy, until he reached the age of 21 and fully assumed the office in 1740. With the aid of his sons, he exercised the office until his death in 1778. He and his assistants would have inflicted close to fifteen thousand public chastisements during those 38 years, chastisements that ranged from branding and whipping petty thieves to decapitating the count of Lally-Tolendal, French commandant in India during the Seven Years' War. The performances of Charles-Jean-Baptiste Sanson and his successor Charles-Henri at the gallows, wheel, and stake from 1740 to 1789 are recounted in Volume 2.

10

Royal mercy

Remission of penalty, and related acts of mercy or clemency by the authority and in the name of the monarch, were derived from fundamental principles of French political culture. Kings ruled in the name and for the purposes of God, who was the source of their sovereignty. God and his Christianity were legalistic. They commanded justice among humankind. Divine laws were revealed in the commandments of Scripture and in the canons and sacraments of the church. Those were prescriptive models for secular law. Every French king from Louis XI to Louis XVI swore to these principles in the two coronation oaths.[1] They were expressed forcefully by Jean Domat, one of the most royal of seventeenth-century jurists:

The first and most essential of all duties of those whom God raises up to Sovereign governance is to recognize this truth, that it is from God that they hold all their power, that it is His place that they occupy [among men], that it is through Him that they must reign, and that it is from Him that they must derive the intelligence and wisdom which should be in them, the art of governing. . . . A sovereign should consider himself as father of the people who compose the body of which he is the leader; otherwise he will have to answer to the severe judgment that God passes on those who have badly used the power he has conferred on them. . . . Thus, the power of sovereigns being a participation in that of God is like the arm and force of justice, which should be the soul of government.[2]

Mercy, or forgiveness, was an attribute of the divinity. The monarch, God's temporal justiciar, shared in the power of mercy, "by virtue of his sovereign power, and by the authority that he holds from God alone."[3] He did so exclu-

---

[1] The first of the two oaths sworn was to the Church, in the persons of the bishops of France: "I promise to all of you and grant that to each of you and to the churches entrusted to you I shall protect the canonical privilege, due law, and justice, and I shall exercise defense of each bishop and of each church committed to him, as much as I am able – with God's help – just as a king ought properly to do in his kingdom" (quoted in Richard A. Jackson, *Vive le Roi! A History of the French Coronation from Charles V to Charles X* [Chapel Hill: University of North Carolina Press, 1984], p. 57). In the second oath, sworn to the people of France, the king promised "to forbid all conditions and ranks of persons to commit any and all crimes and iniquities" and "to instruct all judges to use equity and mercy, to the end that a clement and merciful God will grant me and you His Mercy" (Isambert, vol. 9, p. 458).

[2] Domat, pp. 7, 15.   [3] Jousse, *Traité*, vol. 2, p. 405.

sively, from the reign of Louis XII to the Revolution.[4] The monarch was the "fount," or source, of secular law and justice. Criminal law consisted principally of royal statutes. He had, therefore, the authority, even the duty, to intervene in the course of justice on behalf of the guilty who merited mercy or clemency when the law forbade judges to spare them punishment for their acts.[5] He thus preserved the law and its universalist incriminations, while tempering its application in morally exceptional cases. That relation between law and mercy may be illustrated by the following proposition: Homicide is a crime and requires punishment, but not everyone who kills deserves punishment. This was to conciliate positive law with equity. Every petitioner for royal *grace* had to admit his guilt of the incriminated act, thus validating the law. Each act of sovereign grace announced royal ideology: the attributes of supremacy, vigilance, equity, and benevolence. Each was widely publicized and served to eclipse momentarily the great distance that separated the monarch from his subjects, especially from the delinquent among them.

Certain crimes were unpardonable, because of the evil intent deemed inherent in them. According to the Criminal Ordinance of 1670, there could be no royal grace for those accused or convicted of dueling, premeditated murder (including accomplices), rescue of prisoners of justice, abduction with violence, or violence against magistrates and agents of justice during the exercise of their duties. Courts and chancelleries customarily assimilated rape, poisoning, arson, heresy, and treason to unpardonable crimes.[6] If letters of grace were issued for such crimes, courts were forbidden to ratify them; they had to refer them back to the Chancellery.[7] Assessments of intent and moral personality were crucial in decisions on royal mercy and clemency in all other cases.

By a very old principle of jurisprudence, all who killed, even accidentally, were liable to the death penalty and obliged to seek royal pardon. That principle created the main, active sphere of royal mercy. But such pardons could not have effect unless they were ratified by magistrates, after full trial and judgment of the offender.

---

[4] During the Middle Ages, grace or pardon was also a prerogative of dukes, peers, and various *seigneurs.* It was taken from them by the ordinances of 1498 and 1507, which made grace or pardon in justice a royal monopoly (Jacques Foviaux, *La rémission des peines et des condamnations: Droit monarchique et droit moderne* [Paris: Presses Universitaires de France, 1970], pp. 50–1). The only exceptions were the cathedral chapter of Rouen and the bishop of Orléans; they were authorized by royal legislation to give pardons, in a highly limited and vestigial manner, and did so until the Revolution. Each year on Ascension Day, the chapter of Rouen could pardon one prisoner under death sentence, who then marched in the front of the procession to the cathedral, garlanded with flowers. Each new bishop of Orléans, upon his entry to the diocese, could pardon and liberate prisoners in the town who were not accused or convicted of murderous crimes or a number of other unpardonable capital offenses (Muyart, *Loix criminelles,* pp. 600–2).

[5] "Le pouvoir qu'à le Souverain d'établir les peines & de les rendre plus sévères ou les modérer, renferme celui d'accorder en particulier des grâces à ceux qui sont accusez de crimes, si quelques justes considérations peuvent l'y porter" (Domat, p. 12). Those interventions should be only in cases "ou la sagesse & la clémence peuvent s'accorder" (ibid., p. 17).

[6] Serpillon, vol. 2, p. 768.

[7] 1670 ordinance, Title XVI, Article 4, Isambert, vol. 18, p. 403.

There were several distinct types of royal lettres de grace (letters of grace) all issued in the king's name and with his signature.[8] They either saved the recipient from punishment for his incriminated act or reduced that punishment.

Letters of "remission" of penalty were reserved for homicides. Article 2, Title XVI of the Criminal Ordinance ordered that remissions be issued only for involuntary and accidental homicide and for homicide in self-defense, without antecedent quarrel.[9] Those letters were to be issued in the petty chancelleries attached to Parlements. Decrees of November 20, 1683, and May 22, 1723, extended eligibility for remission to violent but accidental homicide, as described by Serpillon: "When one man kills another in a brawl, the penalty is reduced if he who is killed was the aggressor; the same is done if it appears that the killer did not intend to kill, if he did not use a deadly instrument, and if there are other circumstances suggesting that the homicide was accidental."[10] That definition could be stretched to include homicides or injuries committed in spontaneous rage and as a result of extreme provocation. Remission of penalty for accidental but quarrelsome and violent homicide could be issued only by the Grand Chancellery attached to the Parlement of Paris, under the great seal of the king.[11] During the eighteenth century, those who had killed in duels strove to place themselves in this legal category.

Letters of pardon were issued in petty chancelleries for crimes that did not carry the death penalty. In principle, thefts were not pardonable: "Theft is a vile and shameful action, which does not deserve grace; it is usually committed by premeditation and with calculated intent."[12]

Letters of "abolition," or annulment, of penalty, were for serious criminal acts, other than those subject to remission or pardon, but that were not among those legally unforgivable.

"Amnesties" were collective; they were reserved for military desertion or rebellions and for sedition by villages or communities. They were awarded directly by royal edict, not by letters of chancellery. General amnesties and pardons were issued on the occasion of coronations, to those detained or condemned for pardonable crimes in jails at Reims (the coronation site) and in jurisdictions along the route from Paris or Versailles to Reims. Those were celebratory and propitiatory acts of grace, performed to announce both a new, benevolent reign and the continuity of royal authority. From 1610 to 1775, they were accompanied symbolically by the freeing of caged birds inside Reims Cathedral.[13]

---

[8] They are described thoroughly by Foviaux, *La rémission*, pp. 69–91, and Muyart, *Loix criminelles*, pp. 598–603.
[9] *Isambert*, vol. 18, p. 403.   [10] Serpillon, vol. 2, p. 757.
[11] Ibid., pp. 749, 751, 757.   [12] Ibid., p. 759.
[13] Jackson, *French Coronation*, pp. 94–103. Those pardons were large-scale: more than 3,500 by Louis XIV in 1654; 511 by Louis XV in 1722; 112 by Louis XVI in 1775. But they were not indiscriminate. Royal commissioners sifted through trial records and interrogated prisoners to

Letters of "commutation" of penalty were issued by the Grand Chancellery to condemned persons who appeared to merit reduction of penalty (for example, from death to galley servitude, from the galleys to banishment, or from banishment to defaming punishments) because of services they had rendered to the realm, or the destitution of their families, or for considerations that mitigated their culpability.

Letters of "recall" from banishment or the galleys effectively liberated their recipients from the remaining term of those sentences, but they did not remove legal infamy.

Letters of "rehabilitation," also issued by the Grand Chancellery, were for those who had been judged and punished and who petitioned for removal of the infamy and civil death they had incurred.

Letters of "right to plead" (*ester à droit*) were for those who had been judged and condemned when contumacious and who had remained contumacious for more than the five years that the Criminal Ordinance allowed for appearance and retrial. Such letters waived the five-year limitation and authorized them to be retried in person.

Remissions, annulments, pardons, and amnesties were acts of mercy; commutations, recalls, rehabilitations, and letters of right to plead were acts of clemency. They could be requested and obtained only for crimes that carried capital or afflictive penalties.

Letters of grace were "sovereign" acts only in nomenclature. The twenty-eight articles in Title XVI of the Criminal Ordinance, supplemented by later decrees, established the mechanics of royal grace until the Revolution. They made those acts rule-bound and harmonious with trial procedure in *grand criminel*. From 1670 onward, they were not arbitrary interventions in the course of justice but, in effect, selective extensions of criminal trial. Remissions, annulments, or pardons for unintended or even passionate homicide or serious injury were applications of the doctrine of penal immunity (described in Chapter 6) but accomplished through the king's grace and by the final agency of magistrates.

The accused person, or his family, friends and patrons, initiated the process that led to a letter of grace. He could do so while at large or in trial detention. He prepared (or had someone else prepare) a petition to the king for grace. Frequently those petitions were actually written and dispatched by a local priest, domainal *seigneur*, municipal officer, or even a magistrate who had jurisdiction over the case. The accused person informed his judges that he was petitioning for grace, and they registered that fact. The court of first instance carried on with trial and judgment while the petition made its way. Execution

select those suitable for mercy (ibid., pp. 94–7). Pardons were also issued to selected prisoners on the occasion of a royal marriage, birth, or baptism, the marriage of a dauphin, a royal entry into a town, and in celebration of a military victory (Foviaux, *La rémission*, p. 57).

of sentence, in first instance or on appeal to a Parlement, was suspended until the petition was decided.

The petitioner had to state his social condition.[14] He had to give a detailed factual account of the criminal event, explicitly admit guilt of the incriminated act, and then state the circumstances or considerations that should absolve him of punishment or justify clemency. Confession was a necessity both spiritual and judicial: "It is for the accused, who cannot be ignorant of his crime, to set it forth completely and to hide nothing, because the Justice and mercy of the King imitate that of God, who absolves the sins of people only when they have sincerely confessed."[15] Petitions were often accompanied by letters of recommendation from influential persons, sometimes from entire parishes. Petitions for grace were literally personal supplications to the king: "His heart filled with pain, with tears in his eyes and sobs in his soul, he begs pardon of His Majesty."[16] The suppliant took a great risk in satisfying the imperative of confessing that he was guilty of the act; if the petition was refused by the royal Council or if the letter of grace was rejected by the court, he would most probably be convicted and punished with the full rigor of the law. The imperative of confession made the supplicatory act all the more genuine, and psychologically intense.

Petitions were to be addressed either to the king or to the keeper of the seals in the Grand Chancellery. They were then distributed among the approximately eighty-five masters of requests in either the Grand Chancellery or the petty chancelleries attached to provincial Parlements, depending on the type of grace involved. Masters of requests acted as deputies of the Chancellor in regard to petitions for royal grace. Each was a former sovereign court magistrate and thus experienced in criminal justice. The master of requests asked the local magistrates or the general prosecutor of the Parlement (whether Parisian or provincial) for the trial records and usually solicited their opinion on the case. He then reported favorably or unfavorably on the petition to the royal Council, with the Chancellor present. The decision on most petitions was taken in Council. This procedure in chancellery and Council was virtually a simulacrum of criminal trial. If the decision was positive, the letter was prepared by a royal secretary in the Grand Chancellery or a petty chancellery, presented for the king's signature and the countersignature of a secretary of state, and then sealed. The letter textually incorporated the narration given in the petition for grace. A set fee for services was levied on the recipient.

The letter of grace was sent to the beneficiary and to the court with jurisdiction over his case. There was a presentation audience, on request of the de-

---

[14] "Il est juste que le Roi soit informé de la qualité de celui qui lui demande une grace; la qualité de Gentilhomme le rend moins favorable; il est censé par sa naissance avoir des sentiments qui aggravent le crime: ainsi ce seroit une obreption dans l'exposé des lettres, si l'impétrant Gentilhomme y avoit célé sa qualité. . . ." (Serpillon, vol. 2, p. 778).

[15] Omer Talon, during the discussion of Title XVI of the Criminal Ordinance (*Conférences*, p. 187).

[16] From a typical petition cited by Foviaux, *La rémission*, p. 61, note 3.

fendant. Nobles who obtained letters had to present them to the Parlement of the jurisdiction for ratification, not to the local court that had tried them in first instance, even if their case was still before that court. This was to insulate the ratification hearing from nobiliary pressure; *parlementaires* were presumed to have greater immunity from such pressure than many local magistrates.[17] Commoners presented letters to the judges of their local court if it belonged to a presidial jurisdiction; if it did not, to the Parlement of the region. If they received letters when in appellate custody of a Parlement (the most frequent occurrence), they presented them to that Parlement. All had to present their letters within three months of obtention, and all had to be judicial prisoners at the time of presentation (especially those who were contumacious when they petitioned). Judges had to keep them in detention until the court either ratified or rejected their letters. Virtually all crimes subject to royal mercy were also crimes judged definitively on automatic appeal by Parlements or in last resort by a presidial court. This fact, coupled with the time required for a letter of grace to be granted and dispatched, meant that ratification or rejection of most letters occurred in Parlements (and in the Grand'Chambre, not the Tournelle), or on presidial benches (for those judged provostially without right of appeal). Decision on royal letters was vested essentially with those high ranking magistrates.

Judicial ratification or rejection of letters of grace was a strict procedure, carefully defined by Title XVI of the Criminal Ordinance.[18] Court clerks transmitted the full trial records to the judges and prosecutor of the case. The intention of the ordinance was that the ratification hearing should take place only after definitive instruction of the case and when sentencing was either imminent or had occurred, in either original trial or on appeal. The prosecutor was authorized to require further inquiry by judges, even further hearing of witnesses and confrontation of them with the defendant, before he gave his written opinion on ratification to the bench. A copy of the letter was also given to the plaintiff, to permit him to state written objections. The reporting judge interrogated the defendant in jail on the charges against him, and his responses were compared with the account of the crime given in his letter. He was interrogated a last time by the bench at the commencement of the hearing on ratification. The two interrogations were vital for determining the veracity of the account in the letter, and thus for the decision on ratification. At the ratification hearing recipients of letters of remission, annulment, and pardon had to present themselves bareheaded and on their knees, "in order to show, by that humiliating posture, the submission to Justice due from defendants who have avoided the penalties they merit only by the mercy of the Prince."[19] That posture was also to remind them that they were not yet absolved of penalty, even though they had been granted royal mercy, that they still remained suppliants of

---

[17] Ibid.

[18] Isambert, vol. 16, pp. 403–7, and Serpillon's commentary, vol. 2, pp. 745–805.

[19] Serpillon, vol. 2, p. 794.

magisterial justice. They had to swear that the letter was truthful, that they had authorized the petition, and that they would respect the letter if it were ratified. The bench then compared the details of the letter with the full trial documentation, especially with the charges, interrogations of the defendant, depositions by witnesses, and the confrontation between the defendant and the witnesses against him.[20] If there were no significant contradictions between the letter and the trial records and if the crime was pardonable, the letter was ratified and proclaimed to both the defendant and the public. Two sorts of contradiction suspended or prevented ratification of a letter: if it contained mendacious statements about the crime and the participation of the defendant; if it erred by omission of significant facts against him, as they had emerged during trial. In those cases, and if the letter had been issued by the Grand Chancellery, judges suspended ratification and referred the case to the Chancellor for reconsideration. If the letter had been issued by a petty chancellery (pardons, commutations, recall from the galleys or banishment, and certain types of remission), judges of the Parlement were authorized to reject the letter entirely and pass immediately to definitive judgment and execution of sentence. When a letter was ratified before judgment had occurred, no infamy attached to the defendant; if ratified after condemnation, infamy remained and could be removed only by a further letter of "rehabilitation." Remissions, annulments, and pardons waived penalty, but the beneficiary remained responsible for trial costs, damages to the plaintiff, and alms (in cases of homicide).

By the provisions of the Criminal Ordinance, the monarchy affirmed that, in each case, a royal act of grace was subordinate to judicial truth as determined from trial evidence by judges and prosecutors. In that sense, remission, annulment, pardon, and commutation were sovereign acts only in appearance. The court that had jurisdiction over the case announced ratification to the defendant and publicized the letter, just as it did with final judgment. The king's personal role in the granting of individual letters was minimal. Decisions by masters of requests, royal councillors, the Chancellor, and judges were paramount. The elaborate procedures for obtention and ratification of letters ensured that those officers all shared in the moral prestige of royal grace. Through each letter of grace, the monarch did reintegrate himself into the system of justice that was officially his creation but from whose everyday operations he was normally distant. He thereby reminded the magistracy of his sovereign authority and vigilance.

Letters were formulaic. They recounted the crime as it had been described in the petition, stated the grounds for mercy or clemency, and concluded with the award of grace. The conclusion to a letter of remission for Nicolas Le Roux (guilty of involuntary homicide) was typical:

[20] "Que pour scavoir si les Lettres sont conformes aux charges, il faut voir toutes les charges & le procès entier. Que ce n'est pas la seule information qui fait la charge, mais que c'est la confrontation qui lui donne la forme & la perfection"(Lamoignon, in discussion of Title XVI of the ordinance, *Conférences*, p. 198).

For these reasons [the particulars of the case described in the body of the letter] and desiring to prefer mercy over the rigor of the laws, from our special grace, full power and royal authority we have remitted, discharged, and pardoned, do now remit, discharge, and pardon for the said Nicolas Le Roux, through this document signed by our hand, the action and the case described herein, along with all penalties and corporal, civil, and criminal amends which he may have incurred; we annul all decrees, defaults, contumacies, sentences, and judgments that may have been pronounced against him; we restore him to his good name and to all his property not confiscated by justice, on condition that he make reparation to the plaintiff, if he has not done so and if such is due, and with the instruction that he remain in prison for two months from this date.[21]

But that mercy (literally *miséricorde*, a religious term) was in fact a finely tuned equilibrium of royal and magisterial powers. It was produced by a circuitous procedure that began with judicial inquiry and ended with judicial decision.

During the years 1735 through 1749, a total of 420 death sentences were either pronounced by the Parlement of Paris on appeal and executed (319), or pronounced by a lower court, confirmed or suspended by the Parlement, and then annulled by ratification of a letter of remission, annulment, or commutation (101).[22] In the last category, the Parlement ratified 39 remissions or annulments and 62 commutations of the death sentence.[23] Thus, 1 in 4 of the 420 convicted of a capital offense, in original trial or on appeal, had his life spared by royal grace; 319 were executed, or an average of 21 each year throughout the jurisdiction of the Parlement of Paris. That grace was qualified: Most of the 55 men who received commutations were sent to galley servitude for life or for long terms. Those commutations served both ideological and material interests of the monarchy, for they provided labor for a completely royal penal establishment.

The beneficiaries of royal mercy or clemency during the period 1735 to 1749 are represented in Tables 10.1 and 10.2. These were successful outcomes of petitions for grace; the sources do not disclose those specific qualities of the criminal acts or of their authors that either caused or contributed to outcomes of mercy. That could be determined only by research into the judicial and chancellery records for each case.

The ratio of remissions, annulments, or commutations to executions of the death penalty was high, but it was limited essentially to crimes of homicidal or injurious violence. All of the 39 remissions and annulments were of that nature, as were 38 of the 62 commutations. There was a total of 257 individual convictions and death sentences for authorship or complicity in such crimes in the

[21] May 1752, in Foviaux, *La rémission*, p. 152. The requirement of two months in jail was to allow judges time for the ratification proceedings and to assess reparations against the defendant. For model letters of grace of various types, see Jousse, *Traité*, vol. 4, pp. 569–80.

[22] Inventory 450, vol. 2. This figure does not include those sentenced to death by provostial or presidial judgments, whose cases were not eligible for appellate judgment by the Parlement. An unknown number of them would have received royal clemency, ratified by a presidial court.

[23] They have been identified by cross-referencing Inventory 450 with Inventory 449, no. 401, "Table chronologique des lettres de rémission et de commutation de peines, enregistrées au Parlement de 1704 à 1767," ms. A.N. U 995.

period 1735 to 1749; 77 (30%) of the persons convicted were pardoned or received commutation. Of the 319 persons actually executed for all capital offenses, 180 (56%) went to the gallows, wheel, block, or stake for murderous violence (which was often accompanied by other crimes). Old Regime justice executed primarily for violence, just as it reserved mercy primarily for those guilty of violence when they could establish that they had acted without premeditation – accidentally, in self-defense, or under extreme provocation. None of the remissions and annulments, and only 22 of the commutations, were for theft. Eighteen commutations were for burglary with exterior or interior breaking and entering, a statutory death offense (edict of Francis 1, January 1534).[24]

Gender inequality is evident in the dispensation of mercy and clemency. Death sentences were pronounced or confirmed on appeal against 72 women, more than half for abortions, infanticide, or exposure of infants. None of them received a remission or annulment; only 7 received a commutation. Six male servants received commutation of the death penalty for burglaries and thefts, which were probably from the households in which they worked. Only 2 female servants, among 16 sentenced to death for domestic theft, received such clemency. One of them, Elisabeth Toillier, was spared the gallows only because she was pregnant – with the child of her master, according to her declaration.[25]

Most of those who received grace had been severely chastised by being forced to endure months of anguish and uncertainty in jail, under sentence of death, before their letters of grace were finally ratified. (That fact emerges from comparison of columns *G* and *I* in Table 10.1 and columns *G* and *H* in Table 10.2. For those who received a remission or annulment, the average lapse of time between the death sentence in first instance and ratification of the letter was almost five months; only 9 of 33 waited two months or less, whereas 6 waited at least eight months. The lapse of time was dramatically longer with commutation of penalty. All but 3 of the 62 commutations issued were ratified only after final judgments – and death sentences – by the Parlement. Those beneficiaries of grace had been condemned to death by the Tournelle. Their letters were ratified at least four months, on average, after condemnation. To those periods (between the dates in columns *G* and *H* on Table 10.2) must be added the weeks or months since the trial and conviction in first instance.

There may well have been an element of calculation, inside chancelleries and Parlements, behind the long delays in granting, dispatching, and ratifying letters, in addition to the obstacles of crowded agendas, slow transport, and fastidious procedure. Each of those defendants was obliged to live on borrowed time, in imminent threat of public execution. Inner supplication for mercy, and gratitude when it arrived, were undoubtedly all the more intense for that reason.

[24] Isambert, vol. 12, pp. 400–2.
[25] Thomas Gueulette, "Arrêts de Mort," ms, A.N. AD III 19.

Table 10.1. *Royal remissions and annulments of death penalty: Parlement of Paris, 1735–1749*

A	B	C	D	E	F	G	H	I
Ancelu, Jean	31	Shoemaker	Homicide	Coudry	Hanging	Aug. 22, 1741	Suspension	Oct. 24, 1741
Basque, Bernard	41	Schoolmaster	Homicide	Lusson	Hanging	Feb. 16, 1748	Suspension	Mar. 30, 1748
Bertrand, Etienne	30	Woodcutter	Homicide	Chateauroux	Hanging	Oct. 8, 1745	Suspension	June 15, 1746
Blanchard, Pierre	55	Painter	Brawl	Tours	Hanging	Oct. 18, 1743	Suspension	Apr. 21, 1744
Bourgeois, Jean	55		Murder	Savigny	Hanging	Jan. 23, 1746	Suspension	Oct. 14, 1746
Breton, Nicolas	27	Wagoner	Homicide	St. Germain-en-Laye	Hanging	July 11, 1742	Suspension	Oct. 18, 1742
Briard, Jean			Murder	Langres	Hanging	July 22, 1738	Suspension	Jan. 29, 1739
Coupdelance, Blaise	33	Guard	Duel	Chateauthierry	Hanging	Jan. 9, 1747	Suspension	July 4, 1748
Caudon, Charles	28		Brawl and murder	La Roche Guyon	Hanging		Hanging	Jan. 9, 1739
Chama, Louis	37	Farmer	Homicide	Berisson	Hanging		Hanging	Aug. 3, 1745
Chériau, Urbain	27	Summons clerk	Rape and violence	Angers	Hanging	Apr. 16, 1742	Suspension	Jan. 14, 1743
Cheval, Etienne	30	Officer	Homicide	Châtelet	Hanging	May 20, 1746	Suspension	Aug. 20, 1746
Coutelot, Paul	22	Servant	Homicide	Châtelet	Hanging	Mar. 19, 1742	Suspension	July 28, 1742
De la Chesnaye, Pierre	38	Gendarme	Homicide	Châtelet	Hanging	Oct. 21, 1737	Suspension	Dec. 13, 1737
De Vismes, Nicolas	25		Brawl and murder	Provins	Hanging		Suspension	June 21, 1737
Deleix, Antoine		Count of Marsin	Brawl	Parlement	Decapitation		Suspension	Dec. 17, 1738
Dudefoy, Charles	24	Schoolmaster	Murder	Pontoise	Hanging	July 5, 1742	Suspension	July 24, 1742
Durand, Antoine	24		Homicide	Abbeville	Hanging		Suspension	May 15, 1739
Fontenay, Pierre	30	Stonemason	Murder	Châtelet	Hanging	Sept. 19, 1737	Suspension	Dec. 3, 1737
Gauline, Antoine	50		Homicide	Montlucon	Hanging	Dec. 30, 1734	Suspension	May 26, 1735
Gauline, Etienne	24		Homicide	Montlucon	Hanging	Dec. 30, 1734	Suspension	May 26, 1735
Gerard, Claude	28		Homicide	Bar	Hanging	Sept. 5, 1740	Suspension	Sept. 28, 1740
Grisdelair, Antoine	25		Brawl	Châtelet	Hanging	Oct. 13, 1739	Suspension	Mar. 4, 1740
Guillebaud, François	26		Murder	Rochefort	Hanging		Suspension	Aug. 21, 1738
Hameau, Charles			Brawl	Angers	Hanging	July 21, 1738	Suspension	Oct. 24, 1738

Table 10.1 (*cont.*)

A	B	C	D	E	F	G	H	I
Havard, Pierre	31	Sawyer	Murder	Noyon	Hanging	Dec. 12, 1741	Suspension	June 22, 1742
Laplace, Claude	22	Cavalry soldier	Brawl	La Rochelle	Hanging	Mar. 5, 1748	Suspension	July 9, 1748
Lemaindre, Etienne		Wheelwright	Brawl		Hanging	Apr. 27, 1741	Suspension	June 9, 1741
Manchon, Mathias			Duel	Parlement	Hanging	Jan. 9, 1740	Suspension	Mar. 30, 1740
Maurice, Pierre	36		Homicide	Thizy	Hanging	Jan. 9, 1736	Suspension	Apr. 28, 1736
Pavaillon, François	21	Farmer	Assault	Poitiers	Hanging	June 18, 1742	Suspension	Aug. 9, 1742
Pouilly, Pierre	42	Laborer	Murder	Ardres	Hanging	July 18, 1737	Suspension	Dec. 16, 1737
Prevost, Pierre	23	Laborer	Brawl	Peronne	Hanging	Dec. 2, 1740	Suspension	Dec. 31, 1740
Questier, Pierre	26	Farmer	Homicide	Angers	Hanging	July 12, 1740	Suspension	Jan. 7, 1741
Regnault, Jean	34		Brawl	Rochefort	Hanging	Aug. 21, 1738	Suspension	Oct. 24, 1738
Rodde, Gilbert	41	Summons clerk	Brawl	Thiers	Hanging	Dec. 1, 1742	Suspension	May 6, 1743
Roy, Edmé	32		Homicide	Auxerre	Hanging	Apr. 16, 1739	Suspension	June 3, 1740
Ruteau, Jean	18		Murder	St. Cyran	Hanging	July 22, 1738	Suspension	Mar. 4, 1739
Triozot, Pierre	21	Soldier	Homicide	Issoire	Hanging	Sept. 16, 1740	Suspension	Oct. 20, 1740

Explanation of column headings: A, name; *B*, age; *C*, occupation; *D*, accusation; *E*, court in first instance; *F*, verdict; *G*, date of verdict; *H*, sentence of Parlement on appeal; *I*, date Parlement ratified remission or annulment.

Data constructed by cros-referencing Inventory 450 with Inventory 449, no. 401: "Table chronologique des lettres de rémission et de commutation de peines, enregistrées au Parlement de 1704 à 1767," ms. A.N. U 995.

Table 10.2. Royal commutations of death penalty: Parlement of Paris, 1735–1749

A	B	C	D	E	F	G	H
Barthelemy, Nicolas	20		Murder	Bar-le-Duc	Hanging	June 9, 1739	Aug. 29, 1740
Blot, Martin			Homicide	Angers	Hanging	June 6, 1741	Aug. 3, 1741
Bouvard, Marguerite	28		Infanticide	Sethiviers	Hanging	May 11, 1746	Mar. 28, 1747
Bretonneau, François	32	Farmer	Murder	Restigny	Hanging	Mar. 5, 1748	July 26, 1748
Bridault, Jacques			Murder	Châtelet	Hanging	Jan. 26, 1745	Apr. 30, 1745
Bruneau, Laurent	25	Soldier	Homicide	Châtelet / hanging	Suspension	Apr.1, 1743	
Brunet, René			Murder	Argenton / hanging	Suspension	Mar. 19, 1744	May 11, 1744
Champagne, Charles	35	Vintner	Burglary	Meaux	Hanging	Dec. 11, 1747	Feb. 9, 1748
Chauvin, Jean	23	Servant	Burglary	Châtelet	Hanging	May 11, 1745	Jan 12, 1746
Couturier, Jean			Burglary	Châtelet	Hanging	Mar. 5, 1739	Apr. 22, 1739
Delacroix, Jean	39	Law clerk	Homicide	Poitiers	Hanging	Aug. 14, 1745	Aug. 13, 1746
Delahaye, Nicolas	26		Brawl	Joigny	Hanging	Oct. 2, 1740	
Desjardins, Firmin	25		Murder		Hanging	June 17, 1738	Oct. 28, 1738
Duchesne, Martin	65	Weaver	Rape and violence	Chinon	Hanging	Feb. 10, 1745	
Dufour, Pierre	35		Murder		Hanging	Oct. 6, 1738	Jan. 16, 1739
Duprez, Nicolas			Burglary	Châtelet	Hanging	Apr. 10, 1745	June 8, 1745
Fort, Jacques	20	Servant	Theft	Poitiers	Hanging	Apr. 29, 1746	Apr. 15, 1747
Fournier, Antoine	44	Surgeon	Murder	Montaigne	Hanging	July 15, 1745	
Fournier, Louis	48	Farmer	Murder	Boulogne-sur-Mer	Hanging	Mar. 19, 1744	June 6, 1744
François, Etienne		Miller	Murder	Sens	Hanging	Mar. 12, 1744	Aug. 19, 1744
Gilterre, Pierre	18	Servant	Burglary	Châtelet	Hanging	Mar. 8, 1745	Jan. 18, 1746
Gobert, Jean	32	Servant	Burglary	Châtelet	Hanging	Oct. 21, 1747	Dec. 30, 1747
Gombert, Pierre	44	Vintner	Murder	Cognac	Hanging	Apr. 8, 1743	Dec. 31, 1743
Handet, Louis	25	Carter	Burglary	Orléans	Hanging	June 19, 1744	July 19, 1744
Jacquot, Pierre	25	Soldier	Brawl	Auxerre	Hanging	May 5, 1749	Aug. 3, 1749

Table 10.2 (cont.)

A	B	C	D	E	F	G	H
Joffroy, Louis	21	Soldier	Murder	Reims	Hanging	July 5, 1748	Oct. 22, 1748
Jolivet, Michel	23	Stonemason	Burglary	Châtelet	Hanging	Jan. 26, 1747	Jan. 30, 1747
Joubert, Jean	21		Burglary	Lyons	Hanging	Jan. 17, 1749	June 4, 1749
Jourdain, François	25	Goldsmith	Assault	Châtelet	Hanging	June 23, 1745	Sept. 27, 1747
Lafosse, Suzanne	25		Infanticide	Dreux	Hanging	July 6, 1747	Aug. 7, 1748
Lange, Marie		Vintner	Infanticide	Vitry-le-François	Hanging	May 13, 1748	June, 1745
LeBeyre, Pierre	20		Poaching	Rambouillet	Hanging	Feb. 1, 1745	July 1, 1744
Lebrun, Anne	37	Spinner	Infanticide	Reims	Hanging	June 12, 1744	
Lecompte, Jean	32		Murder	Reims	Hanging	May 22, 1738	
Lelièvre, Michel		Soldier	Murder	Le Mans	Hanging	Dec. 4, 1748	May 9, 1749
Lelièvre, Jacques		Haberdasher	Murder	Le Mans	Hanging	Dec. 4, 1748	May 9, 1749
Lemounier, Pierre			Burglary	Angers	Hanging	Sept. 28, 1740	Oct. 29, 1740
Masson, Antoine	20	Vintner	Murder	Bourges	Hanging	Aug. 13, 1739	
Merimé, Antoine	36		Murder	Chinon	Hanging	May 5, 1738	Aug. 28, 1738
Montreuil, Michel	35		Homicide	Baugé	Hanging	Aug. 30, 1746	Jan. 11, 1747
Morel, Jean	17	Apprentice tailor	Burglary	Meaux	Hanging	Apr. 27, 1744	May 7, 1745
Palette, Denis	58	Shoemaker	Theft	Argenteuil/hanging	Suspension	Apr. 25, 1741	
Pelletier, Charles	39	Guard	Homicide	Corneille	Hanging	Dec. 2, 1743	
Picard, Jean	28		Burglary	Baugé	Hanging	May 16, 1741	Aug. 8, 1741
Percheron, Urbain	25		Burglary	Saumur	Hanging	Mar. 11, 1740	May 23, 1740
Pichon, Edmé	22	Carter	Murder	Vielmanay	Hanging	Jan. 25, 1742	June 1, 1742
Quasy, Joseph	21	Surgeon	Homicide	Châtelet	Hanging	Aug. 1, 1749	Dec.10, 1749
Regnier, Jean	17	Servant	Burglary	Châtelet	Hanging	Dec. 3, 1744	Jan. 4, 1745
Regnier, Jacques	22	Servant	Burglary	Châtelet	Hanging	Dec. 3, 1744	Jan. 4, 1745
Remy de Layens, Pierre		Military officer	Murder	Châtelet	Breaking	June 13, 1747	
Renoux, Patrocle			Murder	Montaigne	Hanging	Sept. 17, 1737	Mar. 28, 1748

A	B	C	D	E	F		
Rousseau, André	35	Soldier	Homicide	Blois	Hanging	Aug. 29, 1747	May 27, 1748
Roy, Cathérine	25	Servant	Infanticide	Sens	Hanging	Feb. 14, 1749	May 3, 1749
Sauvageot, Francois	60	Farmer	Murder		Hanging	Jul. 29, 1745	Dec. 31, 1745
Senau, Léonard	18	Soldier	Burglary	Villeneuve-le-Roy	Hanging	Jan. 17, 1744	May 16, 1744
Soullier, Étienne	31	Coppersmith	Counterfeiting	St.-Quentin	Hanging	May 9, 1749	
Tavernier, Jean		Locksmith	Burglary	Châtelet	Hanging	Oct. 6, 1735	
Thibault, Louis	23	Soldier	Murder	Châtelet	Hanging	Aug. 19, 1737	
Thomas, Pierre			Murder	Châtelet	Hanging	Jul. 10, 1739	
Toillier, Elisabeth	20	Servant	Household theft	Châtelet	Hanging	Jan. 19, 1740	May ?, 1740
Tuffière, Pierre	25	Servant	Household theft	Le Mans	Hanging	Jan. 11, 1746	Mar. 9, 1746
Vielle, Marie	20	Servant	Burglary	Senlis	Hanging	May 24, 1746	

Explanation of column headings: A, name; B, age; C, occupation; D, accusation; E, court in first instance, and sentence (if only sentence in case); F, sentence of Parlement; G, date Parlement ratified letter of commutation.
Source: See the source note to Table 10.1.

Only 2 among the 101 beneficiaries of royal grace were socially distinguished: Antoine Deleix, count of Marsin, and Pierre Remy de Layens, army lieutenant. The others were plebeians, artisans, scribes, and small property owners, all of them typical figures of popular France and socially identical to the mass of those judged and punished in *grand criminel.* They were from highly varied rural and urban jurisdictions. In selecting them, royal benevolence reached deep into the lower strata of French society and far into its provinces.

Grace had wider prehension in the form of pardons for offenses not subject to the death penalty, commutation of penalties other than death, and recall, or liberation, from banishment and the galleys. At least 172 such letters were ratified by the Parlement of Paris in the period 1735 to 1749: 83 pardons or "discharges" from penalty (mostly from sentences to the galleys); 74 commutations; 8 liberations from the galleys; 6 recalls from banishment; one liberation from the Hôpital-Général.[26] But those 172 dispensations were granted to less than 5 percent of all those convicted and sentenced to defaming, afflictive, and nonlethal capital penalties during the fifteen years. That minuscule percentage must be set against the 30 percent of death sentences remitted, annulled, or commuted. Priority in royal mercy and clemency was reserved for those whose lives were at stake, thus for the most spectacular cases in *grand criminel.*

In Old Regime France, as in Hanoverian England, royal and magisterial mercy could, and probably did, serve as political theater.[27] Suppliants were cast in extremely deferential roles, which they had to perform over long periods. Authority – incarnated by *seigneurs,* local notables, priests, notaries, barristers, or magistrates who encouraged defendants to petition or drafted petitions for them, masters of requests, royal councillors, and chancellors who received and approved petitions, judges who ratified them – acted out both power and benevolence. Each time mercy or clemency was granted by will of the king and addressed directly to the suppliant in the king's language and name, the monarch ceased to be remote and abstract. Royal mythology suddenly became real, exerting an indelible effect on the beneficiary and all his dependents. But political theater does not adequately describe those events in Old Regime France. Beyond their propagandistic value, royal mercy and clemency formed the ultimate safeguard within a system of justice that was based on binding statutory laws but that also individuated defendants and apportioned punishment to their moral responsibility and character; that defined crime in terms of volition, not merely action; and that gave both obedience and enforcement to Catholic doctrine.

[26] Inventory 449, no. 401.
[27] See Douglas Hay, "Property, Authority and the Criminal Law," in *Albion's Fatal Tree: Crime and Society in Eighteenth-Century England* (New York: Pantheon, 1975), pp. 17–63.

Conclusion: Tradition and modernity

French penology of the period 1670 to 1789 was a remarkable combination of tradition and modernity. It utilized venerable devices such as fines, public shaming, banishment, violence to the body (more often symbolic than real), stigmatizing, and spectacular ritualized executions, as well as new and proto-modern carceral punishments: the galleys, the *bagnes*, the *hôpitaux*, and imprisonment by sentence of *plus amplement informé*. From the mid-seventeenth century to the Revolution, monarchy and themistocracy either preserved from the past or created the leading purposes and methods that modern penologists would deploy from the 1790s onward, including the remaking of the felon into a regimented proletarian who produced capital for the state and for private enterprises (a process that was most advanced in the Brest *bagne*), and the priestly cure of criminal souls (especially in places of detention, at the gallows, and on the breaking cross), which, in the twentieth century, has become secular enterprises for reformation of felons during and after imprisonment. In contrast to the penology of the Revolution, punishment was not implacable: Responsibility for crime and liability to punishment were measured; defendants were individuated in sentencing; royal pardon and clemency were accessible when life was at stake.

During the Old Regime, the most prevalent "confiscation of criminal bodies" (to use Foucault's phrase) was not on executionary scaffolds. It was by galleys, *bagnes*, and *hôpitaux* for periods of three to nine years. Chains, fetters, and ropes were used commonly across the array of punishments, from the lesser forms (iron collar, whipping, promenade on a donkey) to the galleys, the *bagnes*, and execution. They were both more than pragmatic restraints and, despite their abrasiveness, less than corporal punishments. They were meant to symbolize, even to induce, a condition of humiliating servility, for they converted the malefactor into a penitential slave, if only for a few hours.

If one excepts forced labor and execution, there were only four forms of corporal punishment in Old Regime penology: whipping; branding; amputation of the lips, the tongue, or the hand; and investigative torture. Whipping and branding were frequent; they inflicted only momentary pain and no bodily disablement. Amputation was extremely rare. Mutilation was inflicted only as an element in a small number of death sentences. Investigative torture was closely restricted by law after 1670, and it was not disabling. Penology consisted over-whelmingly in shaming, banishment, incarceration, or death. Shaming and ban-ishment were the most common and (archaic forms) of eighteenth-century punishment. They postulated a local community (real or imaginary) to which the offender belonged, from which he was severed, or within which he was stripped of honor.

The French prison was not conjured philosophically in the Enlightenment and created legally and practically by the Revolution. Under other names, it was instrumentally fashioned, in law, architecture, and regimen, by the highest pow-ers of state – kings, chancellors, *parlementaires*, ministers, lieutenant generals of police, and prominent ecclesiastics – from the mid-seventeenth century to the mid-eighteenth century. Between 1660 and 1750, the French monarchy de-veloped carceral institutions that were as original, systematic, and grand in scale as was the English system of penal deportation to overseas colonies.[1] Nor was the Old Regime discourse of incarceration – the system of thought, expression, and social purpose behind the galleys, *bagnes*, and Hôpital-Général – conceived *sui generis*. It proceeded from the confluence, during the late seventeenth cen-tury, of two other systems: the ethics of the Counter-Reformation, and the con-temporary sciences of fortification and naval architecture. "Nothing can be more effective than to confine them [able-bodied vagabonds and beggars] in

---

[1] Those royal decisions had consequences beyond criminal justice. The English state heavily pop-ulated its empire in the Americas and Australia by deporting convicts during the seventeenth and eighteenth centuries, and thereby made those colonies productive and durable. The first such law was promulgated in 1597, 39 Elizabeth c.4, the "Acte for Punyshment of Rogues, Vagabonds and Sturdy Beggars" (see Beattie, *Crime and the Courts in England, 1660–1800*, pp. 450–519; Robert Hughes, *The Fatal Shore: The Epic of Australia's Founding* [New York: Knopf, 1987]). The French monarchy instead practiced penal servitude within France. The long-term result was underpop-ulation and vulnerability in Canada and Louisiana. There was, however, a brief experiment with the alternative. During the years 1718–22, four royal laws ordered that various categories of con-victed beggars, vagabonds, and violators of judicial banishment be sentenced to colonial depor-tation. Those were acts of the duke of Orléans, regent of France, and they were issued to further John Law's schemes for populating Louisiana. Only a few hundred such persons were in fact deported to America. Most of them soon died, and the practice was abandoned; its only legacy was a sentimental classic, the Abbé Prévost's *Manon Lescaut*. That legislation was rescinded by laws of July 5, 1722, and July 18, 1724, which reverted to territorial incarceration of such of-fenders (Isambert, vol. 19, pp. 168–71, 179–80, 271–3; Jacques Depauw, "Pauvres, pauvres mendiants, mendiants valides ou vagabonds? Les hésitations de la législation royale,"*Revue d'His-toire Moderne et Contemporaine*, 21 [1974]: 412–13). During the seventeenth and eighteenth cen-turies, the French monarchy did selectively and sporadically practice colonial deportation against persons at the opposite social extreme from convicts and vagabonds: rebellious and delinquent young men from affluent and distinguished families. Those were transatlantic exiles by royal *let-tres de cachet*, not by judicial sentences. Families had to formally request and pay for the depor-tation. The number of exiles, and their fates in Canada and the Caribbean, have not been established. English and French differences in penology reflected differences in grand political strategy. The English state was globally expansionist after the late sixteenth century and excar-cerated convicts and pariahs within the matrices of its incessant maritime colonialism. The French state was, for at least eight hundred years, principally a territorial polity that expanded by conquering and annexing contiguous regions: the Midi, Brittany, Flanders, the Rhineland, the Alps, and the Pyrenees. The French state grew through absorbing populations into its realm and its laws, the English state through exporting populations to its colonies.

places destined for that purpose, and there to punish them by the loss of their freedom, the food they are given, and the work they are forced to accomplish": This crystalline passage in the royal declaration of March 23, 1720, came out of that confluence, and it anticipated by seventy years the punitive language of the Constitutent Assembly and its Penal Code of 1791.[2]

The legislators of the Revolution inherited those carceral institutions, then renamed, modified and greatly expanded them. Their only genuine inventions in penal law were death by guillotining and deportation. The latter was reserved for recidivists in crime and political offenders; it was an emulation of English practice and a grim extension of an already abundant forced-labor legacy within France. The architects of the new constitutional, formally democratic and liberal polity selected the *bagne* – that creation of the old monarchical and themistocratic polity – as their model for carceral punishment when they drafted the Penal Code of 1791. This fact tells us much about the inner authoritarianism of the Revolution, the plasticity of its ideology, and the historical weight of the Old Regime.

[2] Isambert, vol. 21, p. 180.

Appendix: *Arrest de la cour du Parlement*

QUI condamne LOUIS-LEOPOLD-CASIMIR-CÉSAR DE BARBINS, ci-devant Décroteur, Marmiton, Laveur de vaisselle, garçon de cuisine, Soldat & actuellement sans état, au Carcan, à la Marque & aux Galeres, pour avoir été Escroc & Imposteur insigne.

Extrait des Registres du Parlement, du 5 Décembre 1761.

VU par la Cour le Procès criminel fait par le Prevôt de Paris, ou son Lieutentant Criminel au Châtelet, à la requête du Substitut du Procereur Général du Roi, Demandeur & Accusateur, contre Louis-Léopold-Casimir-César de Barbins, ci-devant Décroteur, puis Marmiton, ensuite Laveur de vaisselle, Garçon de Cuisine, Soldat, & actuellement sans état, Défendeur & Accusé, Prisonnier ès Prisons de la Conciergerie du Palais, Appellant de la Sentence contre lui rendue sur ledit Procès, le 28 novembre 1761, par laquelle il est déclaré dûement atteint & convaincu des différentes escroqueries, manoeuvres, fourberies & suppositions par lui faites & pratiquées, en se présentant sous le nom d'une personne de la première qualité, prenant des titres de Marquis, Comte & Duc, & se décorant des marques des Ordres de Sa Majesté, ainsi qu'il est mentionné au Procès; pour réparation, il est condamné à être attaché au Carcan pendant trois jours consécutifs; scavoir, le premier aux Halles; le second au Carrefour de Bussy, & le troisième en la Place de Grève, & y demeurer depuis midi jusqu'a deux heures, ayant écriteaux devant et derriere, portant ces mots: (ESCROC ET IMPOSTEUR INSIGNE), & ledit troisième & dernier jour flétri par l'Exécuteur de la Haute-Justice, d'un fer chaud en forme des lettres GAL. sur l'épaule droite; ce fait, conduit à la chaîne, pour y etre attaché & servir le Roi comme Forçat sur ses Galères, pendant le tems & espace de neuf ans: il est dit en outre que ladite Sentence sera à la diligence du Substitut du Procureur Général du Roi, imprimée, lue, publiée & affichée dans tous les lieux & carrefours accoutumés de la Ville, Fauxbourgs & Banlieue de Paris, & par-tout où besoin sera. Ouï & interrogé en la Cour ledit Louis-Léopold-Casimir-César de Barbins sur ladite cause d'appel & cas à lui imposés; tout considéré:

LA COUR met l'appellation au néant, ordonne que ladite Sentence sortira son plein & entier effet, condamne ledit Louis-Léopold-Casimir-César de Barbins en l'amende; ordonne que le présent Arrét sera imprimé & affiché dans tous les Carrefours & lieux accoutumés de la Ville, Fauxbourgs, Banlieue de Paris, & par-tout où besoin sera. Et pour faire mettre le présent Arrét à exécution, renvoie ledit de Barbins Prisonnier devant le Lieutenant Criminel du Châtelet. Fait en Parlement le cinq Décembre mil sept cent soixante-un, Collationné, Laudumiey,

Signé, RICHARD

A PARIS, chez P. G. SIMON, Imprimeur du Parlement, rue de la Harpe, 1761.
Source: A. N. AD III, 9.

PART III

Trial and judgment: the procedure of the 1670 Criminal Ordinance

Introduction: Origins and legend

The *Grand Ordonnance Criminelle* of 1670 governed the procedure of the judiciary in criminal cases throughout France until 1789–90. It was a complete system for judicial investigation and decision. To its procedural rules were attached explicit penalties for violations by magistrates and other personnel. The ordinance also defined jurisdictional competencies and powers among the various types of courts, both seigneurial and royal. It was essentially a constitution for criminal justice. It encompassed all tribunals: small rural bailliages or seigneurial courts, great urban presidials like the Châtelet, and the sovereign courts of France.

The ordinance, promulgated by Louis XIV at Saint-Germain-en Laye, was the last of the great royal procedural codes: Louis XII at Blois (1498) and Lyons (1510); Francis I at Villers-Cotterêts (1539); Charles IX at Moulins (1566); Henri III at Blois (1579); Louis XIII at Paris (1629). It was more comprehensive, precise, and imperative than earlier codes. It consisted of 28 titles, with 407 specific articles or provisions. They prescribed virtually all elements of criminal inquiry, trial, and judgment. Prescription was fastidious, including even procedures for prosecuting or receiving testimony from deaf-mutes (Title XVIII), trying rebellious guilds, villages, or towns (Title XXI), prosecuting in memoriam an accused person who had died subsequent to the crime (Title XXII), verifying signatures and other writings (Title VIII), converting civil cases into criminal cases and vice versa (Title XX).[1]

In 1670, a significant number of venerable current practices were annulled, and several major innovations of procedure were introduced. The ordinance completed the triumph of royal and *parlementaire* criminal procedure over va-

---

[1] The following analysis of criminal procedure is based on the text of the Criminal Ordinance of 1670 in Isambert, vol. 18, pp. 371–423; the minutes of the final drafting conferences (*Procès-verbaux des conférences tenues par ordre du roi entre Messieurs les Commissaires du Conseil et Messieurs les Députés du Parlement de Paris pour l'examen des Articles de l'Ordonnance civile du mois d'avril 1667 et de l'Ordonnance criminelle du mois d'août 1670* [Louvain, 1700]); commentaries by Amiot, Denisart, Desmarquets, Ferrière, Guyot, Jousse, Muyart, Rousseaud de la Combe, Serpillon, and Soulatges; and records of trials and judgments by the Châtelet and Parlement. Adhémar Esmein, *Histoire de la procédure criminelle en France* (Paris, 1882), and André Laingui and Arlette Lebigre, *Histoire du droit pénal:* vol. 2, *La procédure criminelle* (Paris: Cujas, 1979) have also been consulted.

rieties of local customary law and seigneurial justice. For that reason, its advent was epochal in the histories of French criminal law, themistocracy, and the state. It compares in importance with the judicial revolution of 1789 to 1791 and the consummation of that revolution in the Napoleonic criminal codes of 1808 and 1810. From a perspective of long historical time (and in echo of Alexis de Tocqueville), the successful imposition of the 1670 ordinance on the magistracy of France laid the foundation for the national codifications of procedure and penology during the years 1789 to 1810. There was epistemological affinity between the two systems, despite substantive differences between them. In 1670 and its long aftermath, as in the period 1789 to 1810, the legislating state was the source of all judicial authority, and the validity of judicial acts derived from their conformity to rules mandated by the state. Both regimes were integrative and absolutist. The latter built on the legacy of the former.

The ordinance was produced through intensive conciliar work by members of the royal Council and serving magistrates of the Parlement of Paris. The initiative for a new codification of civil and criminal procedure came from Jean-Baptiste Colbert, minister of state, and his uncle Henri Pussort, of the royal Council. In 1665, they persuaded Louis XIV to appoint a Council of Justice to solicit recommendations for procedural reforms from Parlements and other superior courts throughout France and then to draft codes. That council was composed of ten members of the royal Council and presided over by Chancellor Pierre Séguier. At least eight of the eleven were former judges of the Parlement of Paris and members of illustrious themistocratic families. At the close of 1665, Guillaume de Lamoignon, first president of the Parlement of Paris, created an independent commission of *parlementaire* magistrates to deliberate on reform of civil and criminal procedures. For a year, its activities paralleled those of the royal Council of Justice. In January 1667, Lamoignon persuaded Louis XIV to invite his group of *parlementaires* to join with Séguier and the Council of Justice in completing the civil and criminal codes. The result was a working assembly of thirty-nine, with little subsequent change in membership. The Civil Ordinance was promulgated by the king in April 1667. The Criminal Ordinance required another three years of drafting and was completed in final discussions that took place from June 6, 1670, to late July. Twenty-eight of the thirty-nine commissioners who did the final work of debating and emending the draft of the Criminal Ordinance, article by article, were *parlementaires*.[2] The conciliar product was promulgated by Louis XIV at Saint-Germain-en-Laye in August 1670. The text blended royal authority with the criminal jurisprudence of the Parlement of Paris.

[2] *Conférences.* The *parlementaires* included all thirteen presidents of the Parlement of Paris; six judges from the Grand'Chambre; one from each of the four Enquêtes; the general prosecutor; and the general advocate. Several of the great themistocratic dynasties described in Part I were represented among them: Lamoignon, Novion, Molé de Champlatreux, Bragelonge, LePelletier, Bignon, Talon, and Maupeou. Lamoignon (first president of the Parlement), Omer Talon (general advocate), and Henri Pussort (councillor of state) were the three most active discussants in the conferences on the Criminal Ordinance.

The ordinance terminated the independent criminal authority of seigneurial courts. Manorial lords and their bailiffs henceforth retained only a narrow prerogative. They could try a case only if they commenced a formal inquest and issued a summons to the accused persons or witnesses within twenty-four hours of the commission of a crime in their jurisdiction. Beyond twenty-four hours, the case passed automatically to the competence of the local royal court.[3] The seigneurial courts were bound to follow the procedure of the ordinance when they retained competence. All of their interlocutory judgments and sentences in *grand criminel* went to appellate review and final decision by Parlements. They were forbidden to prosecute the following crimes, which were "royal cases," reserved for royal courts (either bailliages or presidials): treason and sedition; sacrilege and profanation; rebellion against orders or agents of justice; illicit bearing of weapons; riot, illegal assembly, and public violence; counterfeiting of money; crimes by officers of state; heresy; disruption of religious services; kidnapping; effractive burglary; robberies on highways and thoroughfares; premeditated murder; crimes by soldiers, vagabonds, and recidivists.[4]

Those provisions meant a deep change in authority within provincial France. Magistrates of royal bailliage, seneschalcy, and presidial courts, most of whom were commoners in estate, were given concrete preeminence over manorial lords, most of whom were nobles. Those magistrats were invested with unchallengeable judgmental and punitive authority over the populace, including peasants on manorial domains.[5] The provisions applied equally to the courts of ecclesiastical *seigniories*.

The ordinance incorporated the main provisions of the 1580 Edict of Melun regarding criminal liability of clerics. They were to be tried for secular crimes exclusively by royal courts, but clerical judges (from diocesan religious tribunals) had to participate in judgment of their cases. They were judged on appeal by the Grand'Chambres of Parlements (which always had ecclesiastical judges), not by Tournelles. When convicted in *grand criminel*, clerics were subject to the same penalties in law as lay persons, including death.

---

[3] Ordinance, Title I, Article 9, p. 373. Lamoignon accurately observed that this provision would rardically diminish seigneurial authority and prestige: "Étant certain que les Gentilshommes, n'ont rien plus à coeur, que la conservation de leurs Justices; parce qu'il n'y a rien qui les distingue plus d'avec des autres Sujets du Roi que l'avantage de faire rendre la Justice en leur nom" (*Conferences*, p. 15). The seigneurial courts within the jurisdiction of the Châtelet were divested of criminal jurisdiction by the same article.

[4] Ordinance, Title I, Articles 11–12, pp. 373–4.

[5] Chancellor Séguier eloquently defended the preeminence of royal magistrates. He argued that criminal justice consists in the authority to punish all subjects of the king. It can be conceded, under restrictions, to lords of manor, but they can never correctly lay claim to an independent right of its use. "La véritable propriété de cette justice, qui s'appelle *jus gladii*, est un droit de Sang sur les sujets du Roi, residant à proprement parler, en la main de sa Majesté; qui le communique à ses Officiers . . . que les Officiers du Roi aîent du moins la Prévention dans les affaires criminelles dont la vengeance apartient particulièrement au Souverain, comme étant un droit Régalien de sa Couronne, qu'il n'est jamais présumé abandonner entièrement" (*Conferences*, p. 17).

Trial and judgment

The procedure mandated by the ordinance was directed to three ends, each of which corresponded to successive phases of inquiry and decision: (1) investigation of the material detail of a crime ("preparatory instruction"); (2) determination of the guilt or innocence, or the degree of either, of those suspected and then accused of that crime ("definitive instruction", trial review, interlocutory judgment); (3) verdict and decision on penalty for those found guilty (sentence in first instance and final judgment on appeal). Judges were supreme in this procedure, but their exercise of authority at each stage was defined and governed by the provisions of the ordinance. The procedure was nonpredilective in regard to the innocence or guilt of defendants; it expressed neither will to condemn nor will to acquit. It was inquiry into a crime and its possible authors and their accomplices, inquiry by methods that resembled those of modern science. The inquiry was closed to the public (and its pressures), formally logical, and fully objectified in documentation of all proceedings.

That such a procedure could have been mechanistically neutral in regard to defendants, and that its treatment of them could have been equitable, may seem difficult to grasp or credit. Modern sensibility is intuitively hostile to judge-dominated "inquisitorial" procedure.

That hostility has produced a tenacious "black legend"of Old Regime criminal procedure, one transmitted from Enlightenment polemicists in the 1760s to modern historians and commentators. Articulators of the black legend have shared belief in a certain judicial ideology, of which the following are the major tenets: presumption of the innocence of defendants until their guilt is proven in court; active legal counsel for defendants before and during trial; trial and verdict by jury; the "visible" and "oral" trial, open to public attendance and scrutiny, as against secret investigation based on documentation; binary verdicts of either guilt or innocence; a statutory fixed penalty, or narrow range of penalties, for each crime, as against widely discretionary penalties and penal individuation of defendants by judges. Those are the passionately held tenets of modern liberal jurisprudence. They form the dogmatic perspective from which the criminal procedure of the 1670 ordinance has been described by most authors for the past two hundred years.[6]

---

[6] The black legend originated with Beccaria, Voltaire, Diderot, and lesser Enlightenment publicists; it was amplified by the legislators of the period 1789 to 1791 when they repudiated the Old Regime procedural system. For modern statements of the black legend, see Peter Gay, *The Enlightenment: An Interpretation* (New York: Knopf, 1969), vol. 2: *The Science of Freedom*, pp. 295, 303; Gordon Wright, *Between the Guillotine and Liberty: Two Centuries of the Crime Problem in France* (New York: Oxford University Press, 1983), pp. 4–5; Michel Foucault, *Discipline and Punish* (New York: Vintage, 1979), pp. 3–47. Adhémar Esmein's *Histoire de la procédure criminelle en France* has remained the seminal work on the Old Regime procedural system for modern French legal historians and a major statement of the black legend. Esmein was professor of criminal law at the University of Paris during the early years of the Third Republic and a self-conscious heir to the liberal and ostensibly democratic jurisprudence of the French Enlightenment and Revolution. His representations of traditional inquisitorial procedure were frequently tendentious. They are echoed by Jean Imbert, "Principes généraux de la procédure pénale (XVIIe–XVIIIe siècles)," in *Quelques procès criminels des XVIIe et XVIIIe siècles* (Paris: Presses Universitaires de France, 1964). None of the preceding authors did significant research into actual seventeenth-

It may be instructive to examine the first tenet of modern liberal jurisprudence – that all defendants are to be presumed innocent of charges until they are proven guilty in court – and thereby to illuminate the quite different cast of mind that was embodied by the 1670 ordinance. Since not all defendants are in fact innocent, the presumption of innocence is false in regard to many of them. But when it is true of the others, it is true accidentally, not because of any inherent accuracy. One encounters two recurring arguments for the presumption; both are arguments from projected consequences. If the innocence of the defendant is presumed, then the requirements for proof of his guilt, in the minds of those judging him, will be greater than they would be otherwise, and the margin for an erroneous guilty verdict will be narrower. The presumption leads to a greater likelihood that those who are indeed innocent will be found innocent and that those convicted will in fact be guilty. These two likelihoods are given greater moral importance than the accompanying likelihood that considerable numbers of those who are indeed guilty will be found innocent, precisely because of the presumption of innocence and heightened reluctance to convict. In other terms, it is more desirable to protect the innocent from conviction, and to have indubitable proof of guilt before convicting the guilty, than to convict most of those who are actually guilty. The second argument is an extension of the first. If courts do not presume the innocence of defendants, they will tend to presume their guilt. If they presume guilt, the psychological requirements for proof of guilt will be weaker than otherwise, and courts will convict on dubious evidence of guilt. In doing so, they will indeed convict the majority of those actually guilty but also numbers of those actually innocent. The injustice of the latter outcome cancels the justice of the former.

The flaw in these arguments is their exclusiveness. They postulate that those who judge, especially jurors, will necessarily presume either the guilt or the innocence of defendants from the outset of trials. They discount the possibility that those empowered to judge, in any system, can be nonprejudicial regarding defendants or devoted only to ascertaining the truth of the crime and the defendant's relation to that truth. They also discount the possibility that the rules for proof of guilt could be strict and rational in systems where the innocence of defendants is not presumed. Those possibilities were realized by the procedural system of the 1670 ordinance. So too was the individuation of each case in justice. The system contained interlocking safeguards against errors in judgment. It required and was served by a learned professional magistracy.

and eighteenth-century trials and judgments. Historians who have done so present a quite different evaluation of the 1670 ordinance: cf. Louis-Bernard Mer, "Réflexions sur la jurisprudence criminelle du Parlement de Bretagne pour la seconde moitié du XVIIIe siècle," in *Droit privé et institutions régionales: Etudes historiques offerts à Jean Yver* (Paris: Presses Universitaires de France, 1976), pp. 505–30, and "La procédure criminelle au XVIIIe siècle: L'enseignement des archives bretonnes." *Revue Historique*, 555 (1985): 9–42; Ian Cameron, *Crime and Repression in the Auvergne and the Guyenne, 1720–1790* (Cambridge: Cambridge University Press, 1981).

11

Initiating judicial action

Court jurisdictions and their police forces were highly varied in Old Regime France, as were the means for judicial arbitration, rather than prosecution, of offenses between persons. Those means were often used in petty crimes, subject to only monetary penalties, and they have been described by Nicole Castan.[1] The concern here is with investigation in cases of *grand criminel* (subject to defaming, afflictive, or capital penalties), cases for which arbitration was not legally permissible. They included virtually all forms of theft, most instances of physical aggression, and all the royal cases previously mentioned. Their judicial priority was established by Title XXV, Article 1 of the ordinance: "We order all judges, even of Parlements, to expedite criminal cases in preference to all others."[2]

The several ways in which judicial action on serious crimes could be initiated were set forth in Titles I, III, and XXV. They were summarized by Desmarquets:

The criminal investigation begins with a complaint made by a victim to a Judge, in Paris to the Criminal Lieutenant or more frequently to a police commissioner; in the provinces, it is made to the local Judge or by denunciation to the Provost of Constabulary. The trial can also begin with a denunciation of the guilty person to the royal prosecutor, or to the prosecutors of seigneurial courts. They then request the Criminal Lieutenant or another Judge to order inquiry, and the Judge authorizes inquiry; on his decree the suspect is arrested. Alternatively, the investigation begins when the malefactor is taken in flagrant delict, either by the Watch, the Provost's men, or other officers of Justice; those officers submit their written report of the crime and arrest; on the basis of that report, which is equivalent to a denunciation, the prosecutor requests investigation, and the Judge orders the opening of inquiry.[3]

Complaints by injured parties were reserved for judges or police commissioners. They had to be written, either by the plaintiff, or for him and in his presence by a court clerk; he, the clerk, and a judge had to sign each page. The plaintiff could elect to name himself "civil party" to the case, although he was

---

[1] *Justice et Répression en Languedoc à l'époque des Lumières* (Paris: Flammarion, 1980). For such arbitrations in Paris, see Farge, *La vie fragile.*
[2] Ordinance, p. 415   [3] Desmarquets, p. 65.

not obliged to do so. He remained eligible for monetary reparations if the accused was convicted, even though he had not elected to be civil party. But if he did choose to be civil party, he was liable for trial costs should the case be dismissed or the accused be found innocent of charges.[4]

Denunciations of crimes and their authors were made to prosecutors, not judges. They were transcribed into a special register and signed by the denouncer. The prosecutor addressed the written denunciation to the presiding judge and requested inquiry. From that moment, all of the prosecutor's actions in the case were governed by the ordinance and subordinate to the authority of judges. Magistrates had to keep the identities of denouncers secret, and the latter could not serve as witnesses against the accused. If the accused was acquitted of charges and the denunciation judged baseless or malicious, the denouncer was liable for fines and trial costs. He could also be prosecuted for slander. The same liability attached to plaintiffs whose accusations were judged to be willfully false.[5] Judicial investigation was to be a solemn public action, not one that subjects could instigate with impunity in order to satisfy hatred or greed.

Arrest in flagrant delict, whether by police or ordinary persons, was a common source of judicial action. Its frequency largely accounts for the high proportion of convictions. Persons captured in the act of crime or its immediate aftermath could be jailed and questioned by seigneurial judges, but those judges had to notify immediately the principal judge of the local royal court and transfer the prisoner to the custody of that court, if the crime was a royal case. In cases of flagrant delict, police commissioners of the Lieutenant Generalcy and the Châtelet of Paris were authorized to interrogate the culprit, order his jailing, take depositions from witnesses and complaints from victims. They had to send copies of those written actions to the registry of the Châtelet within twenty-four hours.[6] All captures and jailings in consequence of flagrant delict had to be communicated to judges, and by them to royal prosecutors. Except in cases of flagrant delict and specific provostial cases, suspects could not be jailed without warrant from a judge, nor could their domiciles be searched.

Judges could initiate judicial action themselves, without a complaint, denunciation, or arrest in flagrant delict, in instances of notorious crimes, public clamor, or duels. They had to communicate such initiatives and their documentation to prosecutors.

Judges and prosecutors of royal or seigneurial courts were obliged to translate denunciations and complaints into accusatorial inquiry when they estab-

---

[4] Ordinance, Title III, Articles 1–5, pp. 379–80. Most plaintiffs at the Châtelet did not choose to be civil parties to their cases; they deferred to the prosecutor as "public party" and thus avoided liability for trial costs. Letter from the Châtelet judges to the keeper of the seals, October 1789 (A. N. BB 30 158).

[5] Ordinance, Title III, articles 5–8, p. 380.

[6] Ibid., Article 3, pp. 379–80, Rousseaud, p. 224.

lished that a serious crime had been committed.[7] Those crimes, all of which carried afflictive or capital penalties, were public matters; no transactions or deals between victim and aggressor could cause judicial action to cease once it had commenced. Judges and prosecutors had to follow that action through to sentence.[8] All trials were to be by the court of the jurisdiction in which the crime was committed.[9]

[7] Guyot, vol. 1, p. 117. Guyot gave a thorough inventory of the crimes: "Les délits qu'ils [judges and prosecutors] dovient poursuivre sont (1), tous ceux qui offensent la majesté divine, tels que l'hérésie, le blasphème, le parjure, le sacrilège, l'abus des sacramens, le trouble fait au service divin, etc. (2), Les délits qui offensent le souverain, tels que les crimes de lèse-majesté, la fabrication & exposition de fausse monnaie, les leveés de troupes sans commission du roi, les assemblées illicites, les séditions & émotions populaires, les malversations & prévarications d'officiers dans leur fonctions, le péculat, le crime de concussion, la rébellion aux ordres & mandemens du roi & et de la justice, le recèlement des voleurs & gens condamnés & décretés par la justice, les entreprises de ceux qui par violence empechent l'établissement des gardiens & commissaires, ou l'éxécution des jugemens, etc. (3), Tous les crimes qui troublent l'ordre et la tranquillité publique, tels que le vol avec violence, le délit de ceux qui, par force ou à main armée, chassent les particuliers des biens qui leur appartiennent ou dont ils sont en possession; qui emprisonnent ces particuliers, les frappent, les maltraitent, les engagent par force & violence au service du roi, enlevent les femmes ou filles, etc. L'usurpation des dixmes & des biens des bénéfices, les monopoles, le duel, l'usure, la polygamie, l'inceste, les crimes contre nature, le macquérelage, la prostitution publique, l'exposition d'enfans, le recèlement de grossesse, l'enlèvement de bornes, la séquestration des titres des biens de villes & communautés, fait par des seigneurs dans la vue de s'emparer de ces biens, etc. (4), Différens délits privés tels que l'homicide, le larcin, le recèlement des choses volées, l'abigiat, les banqueroutes fraudulentes, le faux, le stellionat, l'incendie, le viol, les blessures notables, l'impérité grossière, les libelles diffamatoires, l'accusation calomnieuse, etc." (ibid.).

[8] "Enjoignons à nos procureurs et à ceux des seigneurs, de poursuivre incessament ceux qui seront prevenus de crimes capitaux ou auxquels il echerra peine afflictive, non obstant toutes transactions et cessions de droits faites par les parties: et à l'égard de tous les autres, seront les transactions exécutées, sans que nos procureurs ou ceux des seigneurs puissent en faire aucune poursuite" (Ordinance, Title XXV, Article 19, p. 418).

[9] Ordinance, Title 1, Article 1, p. 372.

12

Preparatory instruction

Preparatory instruction was the formal commencement of trial, and its opening phase was the *information*. The instructing judge, who usually supervised the investigation and trial to judgment, visited the site of the crime and its victims, ascertained the nature of the crime, inspected and collected evidence. At the Châtelet, this duty was usually accomplished by the criminal lieutenant. If a police official had already collected evidence and heard witnesses, he had to deposit such material and documentation with the court within twenty-four hours. The judge ordered a medical report on any injured persons or corpses. From this point onward, secrecy was obligatory for judicial personnel, an obligation enforced by severe penalties.[1]

Witnesses were designated to the judge by either the prosecutor or the plaintiff, and the judge could also designate them himself. The witnesses were issued imperative summonses to appear in the criminal chamber within a specified period; if they failed to answer a first summons without valid reason, they were fined; if they failed to answer a second, they could be arrested and jailed. There were no social exceptions. They were paid set amounts for travel and testimony. The hearing of witnesses was closely regulated by Title VI. Each had to swear an oath to speak the truth and give the following information: name; age; occupation; place of residence; whether or not a servant, employee, or relative of the plaintiff or the accused (if there was yet an accused person). Each was heard separately by the judge, accompanied by his recording secretary. Neither the prosecutor nor the plaintiff could be present. Witnesses were insulated from them and, by the secrecy of the hearing, from outside pressures. Judges were authorized to read the text of the complaint or denunciation to wit-

---

[1] Ordinance, Title VI, Article 15, pp. 382–3. In October 1789, the magistrates of the Châtelet argued the traditional case for secrecy: "Une grande partie des procès criminels qui s'instruisent à Paris commence par la détention des délinquents, mais souvent tous les complices ne sont point arrêtés. Ne sera-t-il point à craindre si dès le lendemain de l'imprisonnement on donne un conseil à l'accusé, si le premier intérrogatoire se fait publiquement, si l'information qui se fera ensuite est également publique, que les complices soient toujours avertis, et qu'il ne soit presque jamais possible de pouvoir les arrêter? Ne pourroient-on point encore appréhender que des témoins ne voulussent pas déposer publiquement, dire tout ce qu'ils pourroient scavoir du délit, dans la crainte de se faire des ennemis et que par la l'impunité ne devint très fréquent?" (A.N. BB 30 158).

nesses; they always urged witnesses to disclose all their knowledge of the crime and its authors. Judges were forbidden to interrogate witnesses, and the Parlement of Paris issued punitive decrees against subaltern court judges who did so.[2] Each witness could testify only once during preparatory instruction. Depositions were transcribed literally by the clerks; they were read to the witness and then signed by him, the judge, and the clerk. Depositions were classified either as *a charge* (incriminating the defendant) or as *à décharge* (either nonincriminatory or evidence for the defendant's innocence). The prosecutor and plaintiff could read copies of the depositions. If the rules for hearing and transcribing depositions were violated, the depositions were nullified and the judges or clerks penalized.[3] The strictness of procedure for the hearing of witnesses reflected the fact that testimonial evidence was the primary source for most prosecutions and judgments.

Judges could summon ecclesiastical cooperation, in the form of *monitoires,* during preparatory instruction of cases subject to capital and afflictive penalties. They could do so, however, only if the number and quality of witnesses heard were inadequate to advance the case, if their depositions were vague or contradictory, or if no plausible or identifiable suspects had emerged from the depositions. In those circumstances, the instructing judge could ask the bishop of the diocese to order parish priests to exhort their parishioners, from the pulpit, to reveal any knowledge they had of the crime, under threat of excommunication for withholding such knowledge. That exhortation was a *monitoire.* The priest could mention only the date, place, and nature of the crime, never the names of suspects. The *monitoire* was repeated on three consecutive Sundays. If parishioners gave information directly to the priest, he had to receive it outside the confessional, transcribe the information, and send it under seal to the court with jurisdiction.[4] The practice involved not only parish priests and vicars in criminal justice; it involved entire communities.

Nothing is more glorious than the concourse of the two powers in the punishment of crimes; the Church lends its censure to the Magistrate for the discovery of truth, while the Magistrate continues inquiry. He both punishes crimes and enforces the execution of sentences rendered by ecclesiastical tribunals, when they call upon the secular power. The temporal power has always needed the authority of religion for the preservation of order, and the Church has always had recourse to secular authority to preserve its laws and discipline. The two powers, although distinct, unite to lead men to truth and to justice.[5]

---

[2] Serpillon, vol. 1, pp. 479–80.
[3] Ordinance, Title VI, Articles 1–19, pp. 381–4.
[4] According to Talon and Pussort, the most common practice was for a parishioner with information to give only his name and address to the priest, which he transmitted to magistrates (*Conférences*, p. 93–4).
[5] Serpillon, vol. 1, p. 501.

But *monitoires* were more an expression of the state's supremacy over the Church than of equal collaboration between the two. Bishops and priests could not refuse requests for *monitoires* without risking prosecution for obstruction of justice and penalties, which could include confiscation of revenues from their benefice.[6]

The *information* was not a relentless statist inquisition. Its outcome was determined essentially by the local community. If no witnesses came forward, or if those who did gave only vague or implausible testimony, no suspects could be arrested for trial. Inquiry was either canceled or suspended indefinitely. The frequently lengthy proceedings of *information* had a dual purpose: to permit the judges to develop extensive knowledge of the crime before ordering arrests and making formal accusations; to protect innocent persons from being arrested and accused. This scrupulosity gave a certain protection to the guilty – time to escape the jurisdiction. During the eighteenth century, a high proportion of those indicted after the *information* were, and remained, contumacious especially in criminal cases with coauthors and accomplices.

Judges could order the jailing of suspects without conducting an *information* only in the following cases: captures in flagrant delict or as a result of public outcry; duels; complaints by prosecutors against vagabonds suspected of crimes; complaints by masters against servants for crimes in households or service.[7] In all other cases, they could issue writs that ordered suspects to appear, or to be arrested, for questioning only after hearing of witnesses and presentation of written requests from the prosecutor.

There were three forms of writ. Summons to appear for questioning (*l'assignation pour être ouîe*) was the most benign. Summons to personal adjournment meant interdiction from exercise of any public office or charge during the period of custody and was thus punitive. *Prise de corps* was an arrest and jailing warrant, and it was the most common writ against suspects when strong indications of their guilt had emerged from the *information*. Failures to comply with writs to appear, within a specified period, led to arrest warrants.[8] Social distinctions affected the choice of writ: "The suspect will be either summoned to appear, personally adjourned, or arrested according to the nature of the crime, the evidence, and the person."[9] Vagabonds and those of low condition were usually arrested and jailed; the socially respectable and resident were often merely summoned, unless the evidence against them was strong.[10] Execution of arrest warrants could not legally be delayed or obstructed by anyone, through protests, appeals, or alleged immunities. Agents of justice were empowered to enter any property (except royal palaces) and to summon any armed force – civil or military – they might require for the execution of those warrants.[11] Ecclesiastical

---

[6] Ordinance, Title VII, Articles 1–11, pp. 384–5.
[7] Ordinance, Title X, Articles 8–9. p. 389.   [8] Ibid., Articles 3–7, pp. 388–9.
[9] Ibid., Article 1, p. 388.   [10] Serpillon, vol. 1, p. 536.
[11] Ordinance, Title X, Articles 12, 14–15, pp. 389–90.

sanctuary or asylum for those against whom summonses or warrants were issued (even clerics) had been forbidden in 1579, by Article 193 of the Ordinance of Blois.[12]

Suspects jailed in flagrant delict or by warrant were to be questioned within twenty-four hours by the instructing judge or, if he was physically unable to do so, by another judge, either in the jail or the council chamber of the court. The purpose of interrogation was to determine if the suspect should be formally accused of the crime. Neither torture nor any form of duress could be used. He was not presumed innocent, for he was jailed only because some significant evidence of his involvement in the crime had emerged from the *information*. Nor was his guilt established. The magisterial goal was to learn as much as possible about the crime and the possible involvement of the suspect, directly from the suspect. The quality, or pertinacy, of the interrogation largely depended on the detail and coherence of the antecedent *information*.

No matter the number of suspects, each had to be questioned separately. They were sworn on Scripture to speak the truth. They were given an interpreter if they did not know French. They were not to be informed of the specific charges against them but rather questioned on the crime. But they were to be shown, and asked to explain, any material evidence against them. The judge's clerk had to transcribe the entire interrogation; if there were gaps or crossouts the interrogation was nullified. At the end, the transcript was read to the suspect; he, the judge, and the clerk signed. Two or even three interrogations were customary during preparatory instruction. The prosecutor and plaintiff were forbidden any contact with the jailed suspect. They could give the judge written suggestions of facts, allegations, or questions for him to use, at his discretion. The prosecutor received transcripts of interrogations. He then recommended either sentence or further instruction of the case to the presiding judge.[13]

Those suspected of capital crimes were forbidden aid of defense counsel. Judges could authorize counsel or advice for suspects in noncapital cases and those that required technical and documentary defense: embezzlement, forgery, fraudulent bankruptcy, extortion, and bribery, but they could do so only after interrogating suspects.[14]

Pre-Revolutionary and subsequent critics have stigmatized interdiction of defense counsel as oppressive. The interdiction was, however, cogent within the jurisprudence of the ordinance. The goal of its procedure was to disclose the truth of a crime and, in doing so, the guilt or innocence of those accused. The premise of the entire system was that the culpability or nonculpability of the

[12] Isambert, vol. 14, p. 426.
[13] Ordinance, Title XIV, Articles 1–7, 10–21, pp. 398–400.
[14] Ibid., Articles 8–9, p. 399. A counsellor, when authorized, could meet with the suspect only in prison; he could not be present during interrogations and subsequent confrontations with witnesses, nor could he speak for the suspect. In cases not subject to capital penalties, judges could allow suspects to confer with specific friends, relatives, associates, or advisers.

suspect was known most completely to himself alone; the purpose of inquiry was to elicit and then corroborate that knowledge. Permitting defense counsel would have introduced obscurantism, prevarication, and mendacity into the proceedings.[15] Procedure was so constructed that if the suspect or defendant was innocent, or guilty only in a limited degree, judges would be capable of determining that from evidence, depositions, interrogations, and confrontations of accused with accusers during the last stage of trial. They, not prosecutors, conducted the instruction and trial.

One must visualize the mise-en-scène of an interrogation, in the jail cell or council room of the court, to understand its psychology. The judge was be-wigged, draped in the dramatic black gown of justice, and usually seated in a raised, high-backed chair. The suspect was dressed in rough clothing and seated on a low wooden stool, the *sellette*. At the judge's side, a silent clerk wrote mechanically and incessantly at his table. The suspect was faced with an imposing authority. This mise-en-scène simulated the confessional, without the curtain of separation, just as the black gown resembled the priest's robe. This setting was meant to work on at least the traces of Catholic moral sensibility in the suspect. The proceedings commenced when he was summoned to swear on Holy Scripture to answer the judge's questions truthfully. Although the oath was without penal consequences, it was intensely suggestive. As Pussort re-marked, "There are timorous souls that the fear of perjury can lead to admit the truth."[16] He was not informed of the specific charges against him, their sources, or the extent of the judge's knowledge of the crime and of him. The entire situation was contrived to deprive him of guile, to incline him toward responsiveness and candor from the onset of questioning.

Eighteenth-century jurists, most of whom were former or serving judges, de-scribed the proper techniques for interrogating suspects during preparatory in-struction and defendants at later stages of trial. They urged judges to begin the questioning with known circumstances of the crime and then move closer to the suspect's possible involvement.[17] Questions needed always to be as precise and

---

[15] As expressed by Pussort, "Que l'experience faisoit connaître, que le conseil que étoit donné se faisoit honneur & se croïroit permis en toute sûreté de conscience, de procurer, par toutes voïes, l'impunité à l'accusé" and to "immortaliser son procès" (*Conférences*, pp. 164–5). See Guyot on this issue, vol. 1. p. 121.

[16] *Conférences*, p. 160. The interrogation oath was a new requirement, and it was energetically de-bated in the conferences. Lamoignon argued that it would force guilty suspects to perjure them-selves and to show contempt for God, as well as debase the authority of all judicial oaths. Talon retorted that the utility of the oath was precisely in religious intimidation: "Les Chrétiens doivent dire la vérité par tout, & ne la peuvent dissimuler sans manquer à leur devoir; & si quelque chose pouvoit dispenser de prêter le serment, c'est qu'en tout tems, en toutes recontres, on doit expliquer les choses conformément à la vérité, & qu'il n'est jamais permis de la déguiser" (ibid., p. 161).

[17] "La première [rule] est de ne jamais interroger l'Accusé sur la substance même du délit, si ce n'est que cet Accusé avouât toute de lui-même aussitôt après les serment par lui prêté. Mais hors ce cas, & lorsque l'Accusé paroit disposer à nier, (ce qui arrive le plus communément) le Juge l'interrogera seulement sur les circonstances du délit, & sur les différens indices qui sont prouvés au procès, & qui resultent des charges & informations, en commençant d'abord par les

material as possible, without lies, threats, or promises.[18] The judge had to watch closely the facial expressions, gestures, and general demeanor of the suspect. Beyond a certain point in questioning, especially if the suspect was evasive or obstinate in denials, the tone could become accusatory. Such a tactic was not simply entrapment; it could serve to test the innocence of the suspect, to lead him into disclosing what he did not know of the crime.[19]

False confession of guilt was as undesirable in law as mendacious denial. Judges became most patient and meticulous in questioning when the suspect began to confess, in order to learn as much as possible about the crime and accomplices, to gain from him as much detail as possible for testing the confession against depositions by witnesses. Such detail was necessary for gauging the veracity of a confession. It was required by the ordinance, for sheer confession of guilt did not form legal proof of guilt; confession had to be convincing and concordant with material, circumstantial, or testimonial evidence of guilt.[20] But confessions of any sort were rarely obtained in the interrogation rooms of the eighteenth-century Châtelet and Parlement.

plus généraux, & par ceux qui ont un rapport plus éloigné du fait principal, & venant ensuite aux particuliers. Par exemple, il lui demandera ou il étoit tel jour & avec qui; s'il n'a pas connoissance qu'il ait été commis un tel crime, & par qui; de qui il l'appris; qui sont ceux qui y étoient présents; & s'il s'en est entretenu avec eux; s'il ne s'est pas trouvé dans l'endroit ou le crime a été commis le jour même du crime. . . . Car il arrive par ce moyen que l Accusé à coutume de convenir de plusieurs faits qu'il avoit dessein de nier, & que souvent on peut tirer de ses propres réponses des arguments détachés dont l'aveu sembloit ne pouvoir lui causer aucun préjudice, mais qui etant ensuite réunis ensemble, l'obligent nécessairement à avouer son crime ou du moins à dire des choses entièrement contraire à ce qu'il avoit dit précédement, & à le convaincre du mensonge, ce qui formera alors un présomption contre lui." (Jousse, *Nouveau commentaire*, vol. 1, pp. 263–4).

[18] "Il [the judge] doit aussi interroger avec assurance & d'un ton ferme, & il seroit peu convnenable qu'il se laissât émouvoir par une foiblesse & une compassion déplacée: car il doit toujours avoir en vue qu'il est préposé également pour la conviction comme pour la défense de l'Accusé. En un mot, il doit se comporter dans toute la suite de l'interrogatoire avec dignité, intérroger d'un même ton de voix, & garder toujours la modération & la prudence. . . . S'il doit user de beaucoup d'art pour découvrir la vérité, ce doit être aussi sans aucune tromperie, & sans alarmer le criminel par de fausses craintes, ou sans le gagner par de fausses espérances." (ibid., pp. 262, 265–6).

[19] "La première chose a considérer, c'est la qualité de l'accusé; un homme du common doit être interrogé autrement que celui qui est d'une condition plus distingué, on doit avoir pour lui plus d'égards. Celui qui paroit résolu & ferme, doit l'être différemment du timide; l'intrépidité est souvent la marque d'un mauvais sujet. Un accusé qui a l'air fourbe et rusé, exige plus de précaution & d'activité en l'interrogeant qu'un homme simple & sans déguisement. La fourbe doit être fatiguée, aussi bien que l'intrépide, par plusieurs interrogatoires. . . . Le Juge doit dicter son interrogatoire, à haute voix, afin que l'accusé ait le temps de faire réflexion à sa réponse. . . . Les plus habiles ont toujours les yeux sur l'accusé. Ils observent avec attention tous ces mouvements. S'il pleure, s'il soupire, s'il tremble & pâlit, ils lui en demandent la raison" (Serpillon, vol. 2, p. 649).

[20] "Lorsque le Juge aura une fois la confession de l'Accusé, il ne manquera pas de l'interroger sur toutes les circonstances du crime qui concernent le lieu, le temps, l'occasion, les armes, la manière dont il a été commis, & autres semblables. . . . Le Juge persévera ainsi à interroger l'Accusé jusqu'à ce qu'il ait tiré de lui toute la confession; & cela afin d'avoir par ce moyen une information ample & exacte, & de pouvoir conclure par le moyen de toutes ces circonstances, si effectivement le crime a été commis conformément à la déclaration de l' Accusé" (Jousse, *Nouveau commentaire*, vol. 1, pp. 268–9).

After one or more interrogations, the instructing judge, in consultation with two other judges, could decide for the suspension or dismissal of charges against the suspect. If he had been arrested and jailed, the prosecutor had to concur in writing for him to be released. Judges liberated suspects, on decrees of *sorti sur requête* (release on request), when their responses, juxtaposed with the depositions of witnesses, did not justify further prosecution. *Sorti sur requête*, with or without surety from another person, was a common result of preparatory instruction by the Châtelet.[21] It meant freedom, but the former suspect usually had to choose residence in the jurisdiction and swear to reappear if summoned.[22]

The suspect became the "accused" in formal terminology, or a "defendant" in our usage, if substantial evidence of his guilt emerged from interrogations and depositions by witnesses. But he could not be judged and sentenced at the conclusion of preparatory instruction unless the following three conditions were met: The crime had to be one subject only to defaming penalties; he had to request judgment; the prosecutor had to concur with that request. Otherwise, and in the vast majority of cases, definitive instruction was required before he could be judged and sentenced.[23] These provisions gave defendants substantial protection. The principal beneficiaries were those accused of crimes subject to afflictive and capital penalties.

[21] During the judicial year October 1785 through October 1786, 808 persons were jailed in the prison of the Grand Châtelet by arrest warrants or captures in flagrant delict. Fully 285 (35%) of them were liberated (255 by decreees of *sorti sur requête*) after the interrogation in preparatory instruction (A. N. Y 10648).
[22] On liberations and discharges, see Jousse, *Traité*, vol. 2, pp. 560–71; vol. 4, pp. 540–5.
[23] Ordinance, Title XIV, Articles 19–20, p. 400.

13

Definitive instruction

Definitive instruction was the most expansive and dramatic stage of criminal inquiry. It bore close resemblance to a modern criminal trial. Both in the ordinance and in practice, definitive instruction was known as the *réglement à l'extraordinaire*. It comprised four phases, performed in fixed sequence: the verification (*récolement*) of witnesses and their testimony; the confrontation of the witnesses for the prosecution with the defendant; the final written conclusions or recommendations of the prosecutor; the written conclusions of the plaintiff.[1] When these phases of definitive instruction were completed, the bench passed to trial review and judgment.

Testimony by witnesses was the most important source of evidence in Old Regime procedure. To commit witnesses to their testimony, to fix that testimony as evidence and thereby to begin "verification" of the depositions, were the purposes of the *récolement*. During that proceeding, conducted by a judge, the witnesses against the defendant were themselves on trial. They were summoned and had to appear, under threat of arrest and fines for noncompliance. All who had given testimony classified as against the defendant during preparatory instruction, or who had emerged since then, were heard separately and secretly after taking an oath to speak the truth. Each was read his original deposition and was then asked if he wished to add or subtract in any way. If he did so, those changes were transcribed by the clerk. The new and final deposition was read to him, and he was asked to sign on each page. If he refused to sign or make a mark, that fact was noted and could invalidate all or parts of his testimony at the time of judgment. Testimony of witnesses *à charge* was now frozen. The threat of prosecution hovered over them, for if they changed their testimony when confronted by the defendant, or during questioning by judges after his challenges, they could be indicted for perjury.[2] Perjury had been a crime subject to the death penalty (depending on the particulars of the case) since a 1532 edict of Francis I.[3] The severity derived from the fact that verbal

---

[1] Ordinance, Title XV, Articles 1–24, pp. 400–3, set forth the rules for definitive instruction.
[2] "Les témoins qui depuis le récolement rétracteront leurs dépositions ou les changeront dans les circonstances essentielles, seront poursuivis et punis comme faux témoins" (ibid., Article 11, p. 401).
[3] Isambert, vol. 12, pp. 357–8.

testimony was often the core of proof in criminal law, and its content could therefore mean life or death for a defendant. The ordinance did not require judges to inform witnesses *à charge* of that liability, although it allowed them to do so.

All witnesses against the defendant had to undergo *récolement* and then confrontation with the accused. Witnesses whose testimony was classified as either neutral regarding the defendant or indicative of his innocence (*à décharge*) were subjected only to *récolement*. They were, in a sense, allowed to stretch the truth or modify their testimony with relative impunity, for they were not subjected to the threatening rules of the confrontation. Their testimony was presented to the bench after the confrontation, in its review of the trial. Thus, the last testimony heard before judgment was favorable to the defendant.

The defendant confronted the witnesses individually and successively in the criminal chamber. He was on the *sellette*, but he was also the dominant protagonist of the confrontation. The presiding judge swore both to speak the truth, then asked them if they knew each other and in what capacity. Each witness's declared name, age, occupation, place of residence, and relations with the plaintiff and defendant were read aloud. The judge invited the defendant to challenge the personal creditability of the witnesses, to offer any challenges (*reproches*) concerning his identity, reputation, or past relations with him and the plaintiff. The defendant stated his challenges to the judge, who was obliged to question the witness on them. The secretary then read aloud both the witness's original deposition and his deposition in *récolement*. The judge invited the defendant to challenge that testimony, thus to point out any contradictions within or between the two depositions, and any omissions. If he did so, the judge questioned the witness on the challenges. The witness was now, figuratively, on the *sellette*, for he was obliged to answer those questions. If he persistently refused to do so, the challenged elements of his testimony were nullified, and he could be indicted for obstruction of justice. If there were blatant contradictions between his answers and his deposition in *récolement*, he could be indicted for perjury.[4] The defendant was also shown, and invited to comment on, any material evidence against him. The ordinance neither required nor forbade confrontation of the defendant with the plaintiff(s); that was a matter for judicial discretion. If there was more than one defendant in the case, and any had inculpated others during interrogations, these defendants had to be confronted with each other, by the same procedure for confronting defendants with witnesses. Defendants were allowed to submit written challenges after the confrontation and before judgment. Days could become weeks of confrontation, in trials with several defendants and many witnesses for conviction, but the procedure had to be followed methodically to its conclusion. Clerks had to transcribe every statement in these proceedings, and judges had to ensure that they did so accurately: "If it is necessary for the witnesses to be heard a second time

---

[4] Jousse, *Nouveau commentaire*, vol. i, p. 318.

in confrontation or for there to be re-trial because of any invalid procedure [*nullité*], the Judge responsible will be assessed the costs of second hearing or re-trial, the fees for the judge who presides, and damages and reparations for the parties involved."[5]

The confrontation brought voices, accounts, and allegations that were originally solitary and isolated into dialectical contact with each other. From the dialectic, judges could acquire revelations and even syntheses that were not obtainable otherwise. Judicial confrontation resembled philosophical inquiry by disputation, by the scholastic method. Transcripts of confrontations were regarded as the most important single category of documentation in an Old Regime criminal trial, more important even than interrogations.

Prosecutors were barred from confrontations. When that proceeding was completed, they received copies of the confrontation, just as they had received all other documentation in the case, from which to prepare their final summary and recommendation of sentence to the bench. They were forbidden to attend the judges' review of trial and decision on the case. Their conclusions were presented in writing and read to the bench, except at the Châtelet, where the prosecutor read his conclusions himself. Prosecutors had to conclude for one of the following actions: conviction and specific penalty; acquittal; continuation of inquiry (*plus amplement informé*); proof of justificative allegations; the *question préparatoire*, or torture of the defendant to obtain confession (but only in cases subject to the death penalty). Those were also the sentencing alternatives for judges. The plaintiff could submit his written recommendations. The defendant was given a copy of this document and an opportunity to reply in writing to the bench, by the hand of a court clerk if he required such assistance.

There now occurred review of the trial.[6] The bench had to be composed of at least three judges in a subaltern court, and at least seven in a presidial or Parlement. Ten judges were customary in the Tournelle of the Parlement of Paris. The defendant was always given a final hearing in person, on the *sellette*. This was a last opportunity for him to defend himself in his own words, by denying guilt or admitting to the action and offering self-justification. The judges then heard the prosecutor's conclusions, the plaintiff's recommendation, the defendant's written statement (if there was one), the written depositions of wit

---

[5] Ordinance, Title XV, Article 24, p. 403.

[6] During the review the minutes of confrontation were to be examined closely: "Tous les reproches, tant proposés verbalement que par écrit, se jugent en voyant le Procès au fond; & avant de juger, les Juges opinent préalablement sur la validité de ces reproches. Si le reproche est déclaré valable, & qu'il soit justifié, on ordonne que le Témoin sera rejetté, & on ne lit point sa déposition. S'il est jugé non valable, on ordonne que, sans y avoir égard, il sera passé outre à la lecture de ce Témoin. Enfin il arrive quelquefois que la reproche, quoique valable, n'est pas suffisamment justifié: alors les Juges ordonnent qu'il en fera fait preuve, tant par titres que par témoins; mais cette preuve ne doit pas s'ordonner lorsqu'il y a d'ailleurs une preuve suffisante par la déposition des autres Témoins; c'est pourquoi il fait surséoir jusqu'après la visite du Procès avant de l'ordonner" (Jousse, *Nouveau commentaire*, vol. 1, pp. 316–17).

nesses *à décharge*, and, finally, the reporting judge of the case, who recommended sentence. The bench then passed immediately to judgment of the defendant, according to the set method of "opining," or voting, that will be described shortly.

14

Interlocutory judgment

The Criminal Ordinance did not require interlocutory, or provisional, judgments, although it carefully defined their use. They were pronounced when the bench decided, after definitive instruction and review of the trial, that there was not yet sufficient evidence for either a verdict of acquittal or conviction and penalty. They then postponed definitive judgment of the defendant. There were three forms of interlocutory sentence: proof of justificative circumstances (*la preuve des faits justificatifs*); suspension of judgment for a specified period, to allow for the possibility of uncovering additional evidence (*plus amplement informé*); investigative torture, or the *question préparatoire.*

A. Proof of justificative circumstances

"Justificative circumstances" were those that supported a case for innocence, diminished culpability, or penal immunity. They were either alleged by defendants or emerged from review of the trial. The most convincing were alibi, doubtful or mistaken identity, evidence that the crime was an accident or response to aggression and provocation (in homicide and injury cases), proof that the crime in question was beyond the capacities of the defendant, proof that he was not in possession of the implements of the crime when it was committed or that another person had been convicted of the crime (presumably by a different court), insanity, or mental debility.[1]

The investigation of justificative circumstances was closely regulated by Title XXVIII of the ordinance. Judges selected the precise circumstances or allegations to be verified and notified the defendant of their selection. He was invited to name witnesses who could testify on his behalf, and they were summoned for depositions. Medical or other experts could be appointed to give opinions. The prosecutor was given this documentation and submitted his recommendations. The bench then passed to definitive judgment and sentence.

[1] They are discussed by Jousse (*Traité*, vol. 2, pp. 574–5), and Muyart (*Institutes*, pp. 392–4).

B. *Plus amplement informé*

The sentence of *plus amplement informé* signified that definitive judgment of a defendant would be postponed, for a specified period, to allow time for the emergence of further evidence in his case. It prolonged instruction of the case, if only in a technical sense. *Plus amplement informé* was the most common of interlocutory judgments pronounced by the Châtelet and Parlement of Paris during the eighteenth century. Although this judgment was not mentioned in the ordinance, it was used by subaltern and superior criminal courts well before and long after 1670.[2] The silence of the ordinance was a confirmation of custom. Use of *plus amplement informé* was determined by jurisprudence and surveilled, in practice, by the Tournelle of the Parlement and the Chancellor. Judicial custom grows where statute is silent, and over time its growth can subtly alter the spirit of statutory law. The spirit of the ordinance was to delineate a clear progress to definitive judgment: either acquittal, or conviction and assignment of specific penalty. During the eighteenth century, *plus amplement informé* was made into an alternative to both full acquittal and formal conviction, becoming a disguised penalty, intermediate between banishment and long incarcerations in the galleys or *hôpitaux*.

Within the jurisdiction of the Parlement of Paris, it was pronounced against defendants for periods of one month, three months, six months, or one year. They were either held in prison during the period or released under oath and surety to reappear if summoned by the court during their term. Parlements could pronounce the sentence for an indefinite period (*plus amplement informé indéfini*), without detention of the defendant. But they customarily did so only at the expiration of a term of imprisonment under the sentence (usually one year), and customarily only in cases subject to the death penalty.[3] Even *plus amplement informé à temps* (at liberty) was a defaming sentence, for the defendant remained under suspicion and barred from holding public office while it was in force. During the period of sentence – whether in prison or at liberty, for one month or for a lifetime – the prosecutor was empowered to conduct further inquiry into the case, to search for or receive further evidence that could be con-

---

[2] According to Amoit (vol. 1, p. 218), it began to be used by the Parlement of Paris during the 1640s. Similar postponements of definitive judgment, with continued imprisonment of the defendant, were practiced by the Parlement in the mid-sixteenth century (Bernard Schnapper, "La justice criminelle rendue par le Parlement de Paris sous le regne de Francois Ier," *RHDFE*, 52 (1974): 252–84).

[3] "Le plus amplement informé indéfini ou *usquequio* ne se prononce presque jamais que quand il y a déjà eu contre l'accusé un plus amplement informé avec prison, & lorsque après ce temps fini, il demande son élargissement. Ce plus amplement informé *usquequio* n'a lieu que dans les grands crimes & ne se prononce toujours avec l'élargissement de la personne de l'accusé. Quelque-fois néamoins, avant de l'élargier, on ordonne encore un second plus amplement informé à temps avec prison . . . ce qui arrive sur-tout dans les crimes atroces, ou il y a contre l'accusé une preuve assez considérable, mais non suffisante pour le condamner à la question préparatoire" (Jousse, *Traité*, vol. 1, pp. 834–5).

clusive against the defendant.[4] If or when new evidence emerged, the case was reopened and final judgment occurred. *Plus amplement informé avec prison* (in prison) was virtually reserved for cases subject to capital or afflictive penalties. For that reason, the possibility of new and conclusive evidence of guilt was threatening and punitive for those defendants. But prosecutors and judges had already conducted a full trial of the defendant. Further evidence for guilt or innocence rarely appeared, and further judgment of defendants who were under the sentence rarely occurred at the Châtelet and Parlement during the eighteenth century.

The sentence of *plus amplement informé* was supple. Its various forms were applicable to the full range of crimes judged in *grand criminel*, from simple thefts to homicides. It included several options for judges. If no new evidence for conviction emerged, they could decree one of the following at the expiration of the term: renewal of the sentence for an indefinite period and assignment of the defendant to residence in the jurisdiction; judgment of *mis hors de cour* (dismissal of the case), which was a de facto acquittal and liberation, but without full and formal absolution of charges; one further sentence of *plus amplement informé* for a specified term, in prison or at liberty, that would be followed by either the indefinite form of the sentence (at liberty), a decree of *mis hors de cour,* or by definitive judgment with absolution or conviction and penalty. Exceptionally, and only with cases subject to the death penalty, the Tournelle would decree that at the expiration of a one-year term of *plus amplement informé* in prison the defendant be incarcerated for life in the Hôpital-Général.[5] A defendant at liberty under sentence of *plus amplement informé* was summoned for judgment if new evidence emerged; if he failed to appear, the court decreed him contumacious and judged him in absentia.

[4] "Les plus amplement informé est ordonné lorsque les faits ne sont pas assez éclaircis, ni les preuves assez fortes pour absoudre ou pour condamner" (Serpillon, vol. 3, p. 1090). "L'effet du plus amplement informé pour un temps limité, ou indéfini, est que le Procureur du Roi est toujours en droit d'agir & de suivre le procès, si l'occasion de prouver la vérité se présente" (Jousse, *Traité*, vol. 2, p. 559).

[5] This rarely used device was explained by Joly de Fleury, general prosecutor of the Parlement of Paris, in a memorandum to the keeper of the seals on April 11, 1790: "Si lors du rapport d'aucuns des dits procès, la Chambre [the Tournelle] ne trouve pas la preuve conforme à la loy, pour raison des crimes dont sont prévenus ou même convaincus par la sentence des premiers Juges, l'accusé ou aucuns des accusés, les Magistrats qui alors ne voient pas la preuve comme Juges, mais qui comme hommes sont convaincus que l'accusé ou les accusés en soit véritablement les auteurs, infirment la Sentence des premiers Juges et prononcent contre l'accusé ou les accusés un plus amplement informé d'un an de prison; quelquefois même un second plus amplement informé, *mais avec une notte sur le registre de la Chambre* portant qu'à l'expiration du plus amplement informé l'accusé ou les accusés (accusés de crimes horribles) et que la Justice regarde comme ne devront plus rentrer dans la société, seront effectivement privés de leur liberté. Laquelle notte à son effet à l'expiration du plus amplement informé prononcé contre eux. Le Greffier me remet alors un extrait de l'arrêt et *de la Notte portés sur le registre;* et à l'expiration je donne un ordre à mon huissier pour transferer l'accusé ou les accusés au Château de Bicêtre pour y être detenus au désir de l'arrêt. Ces nottes sont très rares à la Tournelle; il faut que les délits soit attroces pour la Justice se détermine, malgré la conviction intime que les Magistrats en ont comme hommes et comme Juges, aux termes de la Loy, pour qu'ils se déterminent dis-je, Monseigneur, à mettre cette Notte, pour la sûreté et la tranquillité publiqué" (A.N. BB 30 19).

This interlocutory judgment was both an investigative device and a punishment. As investigation, it was an alternative to torture (the *question préparatoire*) in cases subject to the death penalty. As punishment, it was an alternative to formal capital or afflictive penalties. Because it contained these two qualities, *plus amplement informé* in whatever form appears to be a contradiction in the logic of the law and one oppressive of defendants: Why was the defendant not fully acquitted if there was not sufficient proof of his guilt? How could he be punished if he had not been convicted of the crime? These appearances are deceptive.

Court records and jurists reveal that this judgment was frequently rendered exclusive of the *question* in cases subject to the death penalty: "It is a wise compromise that has been devised for cases in which there is not sufficient proof, either to convict or to entirely absolve the defendant, and principally to spare him the *question préparatoire*."[6] But as a mode of investigation, it was mostly a subterfuge. It was not, in practice, an extension of inquiry, for instruction, trial review, and possible investigation of justificative circumstances were all dynamic procedures in which judges actively sought evidence for or against the defendant. That activity practically ceased when he was sentenced to *plus amplement informé*. If decisive evidence was not sought and discovered by a zealous prosecutor or his deputies (who were engaged in other, active cases), it had to emerge accidentally and then be credited as authentically new and conclusive by judges. The meticulous character of the entire procedure that preceded the sentence made such an outcome highly improbable and in fact rare.

By the rules of proof that governed Old Regime criminal law, judges could not convict on the basis of presumption or innermost persuasion of guilt. For conviction and formal penalty in crimes subject to capital and afflictive penalties, they required at least two of the following: indubitable material evidence; incontrovertible testimony by at least two eyewitnesses; coherent and sustained confession of guilt. Strong persuasion of guilt could be established far short of those criteria for proof of guilt, especially when the evidence for innocence was comparatively weak. *Plus amplement informé* was a recourse that filled the gap between considerable evidence of guilt and formal proof of guilt, in a manner that was prudent and scrupulous. And it did so with special benefit to the defendant, when his case was subject to the death penalty, the evidence against him was very strong but not conclusive, and the alternative was the *question*. Despite the appearance of oppressiveness, it was in most cases a lenient judgment.

Plus amplement informé also expressed judicial determination that those probably guilty receive some punishment.[7] As punishment, it was ingenious and cre-

---

[6] Muyart, *Loix criminelles*, p. 79.

[7] That was affirmed in a ruling by Chancellor d'Aguesseau (January 1734): "Ou la preuve du crime est complètte, ou elle n'est l'est pas; au premier cas il n'est pas douteux que l'on doit prononcer la peine portée par les Ordonnances, mais dans le dernier cas il est aussi certain que l'on ne doit prononcer aucune peine & que l'on ne peut ordonner que la question, ou un plus amplement informé, suivant la nature des crimes ou le genre des preuves" (quoted by Serpillon, vol. 3, p. 1542).

ative; technically, it was not penal incarceration but rather prolongation of trial detention. But it meant the reality of imprisonment and its stigmas.[8] The genesis and early development of short-term penal incarceration by judicial sentence (other than the formal penalties of the galleys and *hôpitaux*) was through this device.

Eighteenth-century jurists agreed that *plus amplement informé* in all forms, but especially with detention, was a serious punishment even though it was not a penalty in law, and that it was most commonly used in that manner by the courts.[9] Those under any form of this sentence were, for its duration, interdicted from holding offices or commissions, making wills, receiving inheritances, or testifying in law. They were defamed. Because of their penal character, after 1670 all such interlocutory judgments by subaltern courts were appealed for decision to sovereign courts. Most sentences to *plus amplement informé à temps* by eighteenth-century courts resulted, at the expiration of the term, in definitive judgments of *mis hors de cour,* or dismissal of charge, but without exoneration of the defendant. He was rarely "absolved," or fully acquitted of the charge, and therefore could not claim damages. He continued to suffer a condition of social infamy for not having been found innocent.[10] *Plus amplement informé indéfini* (indefinite) at liberty was, at least technically, a stigmatic and menacing punishment. When pronounced in cases subject to the death penalty, and when there was strong evidence of the defendant's guilt but evidence deemed insufficient for either the *question* or final judgment and the death penalty, the defendant under that sentence remained under threat of the death penalty should new evidence against him emerge, evidence that could "complete" formal proof of his guilt. "For that reason, *plus amplement informé* [indefinite] is considered a more severe penalty than the galleys; it places the defendant in danger of being condemned to death, whereas the penalty of the galleys preserves life."[11] However, there was not one case of conversion of *plus amplement informé indéfini* into a death sentence by the Parlement of Paris during either of the periods 1735 to 1749 or 1775 to 1789. For lesser crimes, *plus amplement informé à temps* – even without prison – was, according to the jurisprudence of the Parlement of Paris, a sentence less severe than terms in the galleys or *hôpitaux* but more severe than term banishment, by the reasoning that new evidence could mean conviction and incarceration in the galleys or

---

[8] The royal declaration of February 1723 stated that those indicted for notorious duels could not be absolved by courts until they had served sentence of *plus amplement informé* with prison for one year. Quoted in Muyart, *Institutes,* p. 362.

[9] "Ce plus amplement informé [with term] est plutôt prononcé comme une peine, que comme un moyen pour acquérir la preuve nécessaire du procès" (Jousse, *Traité,* vol. 2, p. 558).

[10] Muyart, *Loix criminelles,* pp. 78–9; Serpillon, vol. 3, 1090.

[11] Serpillon, vol. 3, p. 1090; Muyart, *Loix criminelles,* p. 78. This was also the opinion of Omer Talon in the discussions on the ordinance: "Tout ce qui avoit trait à la mort étoit une grande peine, qu'aucuns ont estimé que 'le plus amplement informé' étoit un avis plus rigoureux que celui des Galères" (*Conférences,* p. 248).

hôpitaux.[12] Here again, jurisprudence was more intimidating than practice: In the great majority of cases judged by the Châtelet and Parlement during the eighteenth century, the outcome of *plus amplement informé à temps* with prison was permanent liberation of the accused at the expiration of his prison term (usually less than a year), whereas the outcome of *plus amplement informé à temps* without prison was simple cessation of judicial pursuit at expiration, if not long before.

Plus amplement informé was an ambiguous judgment because it embraced two quite dissonant meanings: (1) punishment of a defendant against whom legal proof of guilt was not established during trial but against whom there was sufficient evidence for judges to conclude that guilt was likely; (2) punishment of a defendant against whom proof of guilt was sufficient for either the *question* or for conviction and a formal penalty other than death but to whom judges decided not to apply torture or hard penalties (terms or life in the galleys or *hôpitaux*). During the eighteenth century, the incidence of *plus amplement informé* with prison reflected two developments: magisterial repudiation of torture as an investigative device; desire for a form of short-term penal incarceration alternative to formal capital and afflictive penalties.

The increasing frequency of the sentences across the century (which will be recounted in Volume 2) brought de facto changes in the criminal law and in the politics of punishment. It brought a movement from public, theatrical, and physically hard sanctions to more psychological and privatized sanctions, a movement away from the scaffold, the chain gang, the brutalities of the *bagne* and the Hôpital-Général to the concealed but anxiety-ridden domination of jailing, deprivation of civil rights, *résidence surveillée,* and threat of further punishment. Those magisterial decisions prefigured major uses of imprisonment in Revolutionary criminal justice.

C. The *question*

Judicial torture existed in two distinct forms in Old Regime criminal law. The *question préparatoire* was used to extract confession of guilt after trial review and before definitive judgment. It was pronounced as an interlocutory judgment, "preparatory" to final judgment. The *question préalable* accompanied certain death sentences; its purpose was to force the disclosure of accomplices, and it was inflicted immediately before execution of the condemned person.

Preparatory to judgment

The *question préparatoire* was regulated by the twelve articles in Title XX of the ordinance. It was, however, an element anomalous and disjunctive within the

---

[12] "Pour le plus amplement informé, on ne doute point qu'il ne soit plus rude que le bannissement à temps" (Amiot, vol. 1, 102).

general procedure of the 1670 ordinance, and the authors of the Code seriously considered abolishing the practice.[13] It was preserved in 1670, a remnant of much older jurisprudence and one whose use was carefully restricted. Contrary to the black legend, the ordinance did not culminate the development of investigative torture; it forced the decline of torture by radically diminishing its scope, harshness, and probative value. Eighteenth-century magistrates, acting in consonance with the ce ordinance, had largely discontinued the *question préparatoire* long before its abolition by royal edict in 1780.

Judicial torture had developed in France out of the Roman–canonical law of proof, which became orthodoxy in criminal practice between the thirteenth and fifteenth centuries. That law of proof was designed to protect defendants from conviction by presumptions or "intimate convictions" of their guilt on the part of judges. It applied especially in cases subject to capital penalties, by the maxim that for the death sanction to be applied proof of guilt must be "more clear than daylight." In such cases, a combination of the following categories of evidence of guilt was required for conviction: (1) strong material, character, or circumstantial evidence (or *indicia*); (2) incriminating writing in the hand of the defendant; (3) concordant testimony by two irreproachable eyewitnesses to the crime; (4) confession by the defendant, made directly to his judges. Any two of these four categories of proof were theoretically sufficient for conviction and the death penalty. But the premise of Roman–canonical jurisprudence was that confession established guilt as no testimonial or material evidence could. Confession was regarded as the "queen of proof."[14]

The premise expressed a certain idea of truth, which one might call the "epistemology of first-person authority." Who can know with absolute certainty whether this defendant committed that criminal act? Only the defendant, if he is sane and does not suffer amnesia, can know with absolute certainty. A dozen witnesses to the crime can give mutually corroborative testimony to the guilt of the defendant. But, theoretically, they could all be either mistaken or mendacious, and mutually reinforcing in their error or falsity. Notoriety is often subject to contingencies that can undermine its truth value: confusion; rumors; gullibility; forgetfulness over time.[15] Even with extensive testimony as to the defendant's guilt, judges can only calculate the probability of his guilt. Only the defendant has certain and subjective knowledge of his action or nonaction. And

---

[13] *Conférences*, p. 224.

[14] On Roman–canonical jurisprudence in the development of early modern European criminal procedure, see especially Jean Gilissen, "La preuve en Europe du XVIe au debut du XIX siècle," and Jean-Philippe Lévy, "Le problème de la preuve dans les droits savants du Moyen Age," in Recueils de la Société Jean Bodin pour l'Histoire Comparative des Institutions, no. 17, *La Preuve* (Brussels: 1965), pp. 137–67; John Langbein, *Torture and the Law of Proof: Europe and England in the Ancien Régime* (Chicago: University of Chicago Press, 1976); Edward Peters, *Torture* (New York: Blackwell, 1986), and *Inquisition* (New York: Free Press / Macmillan, 1988).

[15] As with the example given by Lévy: "L'exemple type est celui du flagrant délit. Sa superiorité sur toute preuve vient . . . de ce qu'ici la réalité est percue directement par les sens, par la vue, et que la connaissance immédiate par les sens est, selon l'enseignement d'Aristote et d'Averroes, supérieure à celle même qui resulte de la raison. . . . La difficulté est plus grande pour un éven-

only he can communicate that knowledge. Truth, as against probability, can come only from him, for he alone possesses that truth. This persuasion made confession the queen of proof.

Even in late medieval and early modern jurisprudence, for the confession to be conclusive it needed to accord with at least one other category of evidence, whether some powerful *indicia*, the testimony of one irreproachable eyewitness, or incriminating writing. Conviction and the death penalty could be pronounced without confession, but only if there were two irreproachable eyewitnesses and either strong material and circumstantial evidence or indubitable written evidence of guilt. Such an array of objective evidence for conviction was rare. Witnesses for the prosecution were vulnerable to challenge, according to the high standards of late medieval and early modern jurisprudence. Numerous qualities of such witnesses could invalidate testimony *à charge:* immaturity (those aged under 20); feeblemindedness; marriage, parency, or close blood relationship to the defendant; legal infamy (those who had received defaming penalties in law); mendicancy and vagabondage.[16] Since the Ordinance of Villers-Cotterets in 1539, all witnesses for the prosecution had to undergo verbal confrontation with the defendant. As for incriminating writing, most early modern and Old Regime defendants in *grand criminel* could not write a text. Serious crimes usually left material traces of their authors, but *indicia* were often fragmentary and difficult to interpret. They could establish presumptions of guilt, but rarely proof of guilt. The strictness of traditional rules of evidence, a strictness that protected defendants, also made confession the queen of proof. The *question préparatoire*, or extortion of confession by physical duress, developed within that exigent tradition. Roman–canonical jurisprudence assumed that the guilty would be induced to confess by torture and thereby condemn themselves to the scaffold. This meant, in long practice, that for judges to conclude the innocence of a defendant against whom there was strong evidence, the innocent defendant had to be tortured and refuse to confess. However circumscribed in the 1670 ordinance, this primitive implacability remained intrinsic to the *question préparatoire* from its medieval origins to its abolition.

The 1670 ordinance and its subsequent jurisprudence revised the probative status of confession, both voluntary and coerced. Article 5 of Title XXV stipulated that if there were no witnesses against the defendant, he could be convicted on the basis of confession made voluntarily during the instruction, but only if that confession was corroborated by either incriminating writing in his hand or by strong material and circumstantial evidence of guilt. Article 17 of Title XIV was even more restrictive: In cases subject to capital or afflictive

ement isolé. Qu'un meurtre soit commis sur la place publique et devant une foule nombreuse, sur le moment le crime n'est pas niable. Mais si l'on doit juger longtemps après ou en un autre lieu, le fait est-il encore notoire?" ("La preuve dans les droits savants du Moyen Age," in *La Preuve*, p. 163).

[16] The most thorough presentation of rules on the admissibility and credibility of witnesses in traditional French criminal law is by Bernard Schnapper, " 'Testes inhabiles': Les témoins réprochables dans l'ancien droit pénal," *Legal History Review*, 38 (1965): 575–615.

penalties, if the defendant confessed during the preparatory instruction or even later, he could not receive immediate judgment; the trial had to follow the full course of definitive instruction, despite his confession. Evidence gathered during full instruction was required for judges to gauge the veracity of his confession. These provisions expressed a Cartesian attitude of doubt applied to confession.

The defendant's confession . . . cannot alone form proof sufficient for conviction.[17]

In criminal cases, a defendant's confession can be divided into its elements; but whatever its content, it never serves as perfect proof against him, because it may be the result of confusion or despair.[18]

Ferrière stated the main criteria by which the validity of a voluntary confession was judged:

The confession must be clear and determined, it must concern a known consequence, one susceptible to legal judgment, and which is not manifestly false. . . . The confession must be made without errors.[19]

Such evaluation of confession required exterior and independent evidence. It also required the following analytic cast of mind:

Study of man's heart should be the unique purpose of the judge. He should discern the motive that causes someone to speak, to distinguish the various elements of the confession, and his goal, in civil as in criminal cases, should always be to discover the truth.[20]

Even voluntary and passionate confession was therefore not, ipso facto, revelation of truth. This skeptical approach to criminal confession resembled the orthodox attitude to ecclesiastical confession in eighteenth-century France:

The Confession should be complete, which means admission and detailed account of all mortal sins that the confessant can recall after serious and mature examination of himself. It should be sincere, which is to say, made without any equivocation and with true contrition. It should be made to a Priest who has the juridical power to absolve sins.[21]

Judges carefully analyzed the statements by defendants during interrogations: Non sequiturs, contradictions, manifest confusion, recurrent evasiveness, and distress, could legitimately be interpreted as evidence of guilt.[22] But inferences of guilt from statements of denial never equaled, in law, the potency of confession. However, from 1670 onward "confession" meant sustained, coherent, and repeated admission of guilt, an admission that had to be persuasive empirically. Even voluntary confession had to be convincing in both its subjectivity and objectivity.

[17] Muyart, *Instruction criminelle*, p. 696.
[18] Denisart, vol. 1, p. 603. See also Ferrière, vol. 1, p. 335, and Serpillon, vol. 2, p. 675.
[19] Ferrière, vol. 1, p. 335.   [20] Ibid., vol. 1, p. 336.
[21] J.-F. Brézillac, *Dictionnaire ecclésiastique et canonique portatif ou abregé méthodique de toutes les connoissances necéssaires au Ministres de l'Eglise*, 2 vols. (Paris, 1755), vol. 1, p. 425.
[22] Ferrière, vol. 1, p. 362.

Nothing could be more obstructive of justice, according to the investigative system and logic of the ordinance, than false confession of guilt. It was even more obstructive than perjury by witnesses against the defendant, because of the residual moral authority of the confessional act. If the danger of entire or partial falsity lurked behind every voluntary confession, even in capital cases, that danger was magnified when confession was forced by pain. If confession was no longer the queen of proof, what logic could there be in attempting to force confession?

These problems were confronted, but not resolved, by Article 1 of Title XIX. The *question préparatoire* could be decreed only under all of the following conditions: if the crime was subject to the death penalty; if the commission or event of the crime had been proven; if there were strong evidence (*preuve considérable*) against the defendant, but evidence insufficient for conviction and capital punishment.[23] The purpose of judicial torture was to obtain confession and thereby to complete proof of guilt. Eighteenth-century jurists were in accord on the nature of the strong evidence required for judges to decree the *question:*

To sentence someone to torture there must be . . . evidence of guilt that is almost complete proof and generative of strong presumption of his guilt, at least the testimony of one witness above reproach, from which one concludes that had there been one other such witness the defendant would have been convicted, and in addition strong material or circumstantial evidence [*indicia*] is required.[24]

Neither the testimony of one witness, unsupported by other evidence, nor public clamor of the defendant's guilt was sufficient for the *question.*[25] Blatant contradictions among the depositions of witnesses against the defendant, if those contradictions bore on principal elements of the crime, invalidated their depositions as bases for torture. Even if the dying victim of a homicide had denounced the defendant as his murderer, directly to judges, that was not sufficient for torture.[26]

For torture to be decreed, testimony by witnesses had to be reinforced by material and circumstantial evidence of the defendant's guilt.

As for denunciation of the defendant by one of his accomplices in crime, even one condemned to death, it is not sufficient reason for the defendant to be put to the *question,* if that denunciation is not supported by other evidence. Sometimes material and circumstantial evidence alone suffices for the *question,* especially in major crimes and in those committed secretly: but that evidence must be multiple and strong, its elements closely related to the criminal event. . . . For example, in a case of theft, if the defendant

---

[23] Ordinance, p. 412.
[24] Serpillon, vol. 3, p. 911. See also Soulatges, vol. 3, pp. 34–6.
[25] "Le bruit public est encore fort sujet à tromper; il ne faut pas le prendre pour une forte présomption [of guilt] . . . Le bruit public ne se forme que sur des ouï dire, souvent l'accusateur en est l'Auteur" (Serpillon, vol. 3, p. 914).
[26] "La Déclaration faite par un blessé en mourant que c'est un tel qui l'a assassiné, est une forte présomption; mais elle ne suffiroit pas pour le faire condamner à la question; parce qu'il a pu se tromper, & dans les frayeurs de la mort qui lui ont troublé les sens ne pas dire la vérité" (ibid.).

is found in possession of the stolen goods, or if he has been seen carrying the stolen goods near the site of theft, without being able to give a good account of those circumstances, and especially if he has a bad reputation.[27]

Character evidence and social condition – a reputation for immorality, or furtiveness and evasiveness during trial, attempted escape from the jurisdiction, vagabondage, lack of employment or respectable livelihood – could supplement but not replace material and circumstantial evidence of guilt in decisions on the *question préparatoire*.[28] In sum, for the *question* to be decreed, the instruction had to have generated a combination of testimonial, material, circumstantial, and character evidence against the defendant – a combination that made his guilt highly probable but that fell short of proof.

Judges could decree the *question* either "without reserve of evidence" or "with reserve of evidence."[29] The first meant that if the defendant either refused to confess under torture or retracted his confession immediately after torture he thereby nullified all evidence against him and could not be convicted of the crime.[30] This decree was extremely rare after 1670, if not long before. From 1670 to 1780, when the *question* was decreed it was commonly with reserve of evidence. This meant that if the defendant did not confess or retracted confession, the evidence against him was still retained by the court in final judgment; on the basis of that evidence, he could be sentenced to *plus amplement informé* with prison or convicted and sentenced to afflictive penalties, even to the galleys for life, but not to death. The ordinance intended that judges be virtually convinced of the defendant's guilt before they ordered the *question* with reserve of evidence.[31] Denial of guilt under torture or retraction of confession immediately after torture made the death penalty inapplicable, whether the *question* was administered with or without reserve of evidence.

Immediately it was rendered, the judgment ordering the *question* had to be read to the defendant in the torture chamber of the court, where he was brought for that audience.[32] But it could not be executed until and unless it was confirmed by decision of the Parlement, or another sovereign court, of the jurisdiction; all sentences to the *question préparatoire* by subaltern courts were suspended and appealed automatically.[33] This was a highly significant innovation by the ordinance, and one that radically diminished the use of investigative torture. The defendant and the full documentation of his trial were transported, at the lower court's expense, for hearing and review by the Parlement. The authority of the Parlement was wide in this matter. They could uphold the

[27] Jousse, *Nouveau commentaire*, vol. 2, pp. 390–1.
[28] Muyart, *Institution criminelle*, vol. 1, p. 698.
[29] Ordinance, Title XIX, Article 2, p. 412.
[30] Muyart, *Institution criminelle*, vol. 1, p. 699.
[31] Jousse, *Nouveau commentaire*, vol. 2, pp. 393–4.
[32] Ordinance, Title XIX, Article 6, p. 412.
[33] Ibid., Article 7, p. 412.

sentence and return the defendant to the lower court. They could uphold the sentence and execute it themselves. They could, and very frequently did, annul the sentence and order the subaltern court to proceed to another interlocutory judgment or to definitive judgment. They could even confiscate the case and judge it definitively. Any subaltern court that ordered the *question préparatoire* risked losing control of its trial and defendant. The defendant had been placed in terror of the *question* by lower-court judges, but that mental terror could become physical reality only after the long delay of review by the Parlement. He was given time to prepare his psychosomatic defenses against the ordeal.

The ordinance mandated extensive precautions in the execution of the *question*. They were strengthened by a 1697 ruling of the Parlement of Paris, binding on all courts within the jurisdiction. The interrogations that comprised the *question* had to be conducted by two judges, assisted by a secretary who had to record everything, and under the supervision of the court surgeon or medical doctor. The surgeon was empowered to order diminution or cessation of the torture, for it was not intended to maim or endanger life. The torturer was a professional officer of justice responsible to the court. The prosecutor was barred from attendance. By custom, invalids, pregnant women, minors under the age of 16, those aged 70 or over, the seriously ill, and the mentally deranged could not be put to the *question*.

The *question* was administered in a sequence of three interrogations during one session.[34] Only one interrogation was by duress, or with torture. The three interrogations had to be transcribed verbatim, including gasps, screams, or curses by the defendant. Each page of the minutes had to be signed by the two judges and secretary, who also had to sign the completed transcript. The defendant had to be invited to sign the first and third interrogations at their conclusion; if he refused or was unable, that fact had to be noted. Signatures authenticated the transcription of the interrogations. Those transcriptions formed the evidence, for guilt or innocence, obtained from the *question*. They were studied by judges in definitive judgment, and by *parlementaires* on appeal. They were the means by which Parlements policed the administration of the *question* by subaltern courts.

The *question* was usually administered early in the morning, before the defendant had eaten. After he was sworn to speak the truth, he was given the first or preliminary interrogation on the stool; this was frequently the most lengthy and detailed of the three. When they finished, the judges and secretary signed the text of questions and answers. It was read to the defendant, and he was invited to sign. Then the court physician examined the defendant and recommended which of the two forms of torture be used.

In 1697, the Parlement of Paris ordered all subaltern courts within its jurisdiction to use only torture by leg braces (*brodequins*) or by stretching and

---

[34] Ibid., Articles 8–11, pp. 412–13.

forced ingurgitation of water (*la question de l'eau avec extension*).[35] That ruling was enforced until the abolition of the *question* in 1780 (*préparatoire*) and 1788 (*préalable*). Physicians had to oversee the proceedings, and they were empowered to intervene if there was danger of maiming or death.

Leg braces were the customary form of torture in the jurisdiction during the eighteenth century. The defendant was seated on the stool. Two oaken planks were placed on the inside of each leg, extending from the feet to above the knees; a plank of the same length was placed on the outside of each leg. The six planks were secured by ropes passed through holes at their ends, and the ropes were then wound tightly around the planks to form a casing for both legs. Pain was inflicted, and controlled, by means of wooden wedges. The torturer hammered them between the two planks inside each leg, from the vicinity of the knees down to the ankles. Each wedge increased the pressure. The ordinary *question* by leg braces was four wedges; the "extraordinary" was eight. After each wedge was driven in, the judges asked one or two specific questions concerning the crime and the culpability of the defendant.

In torture by stretching and forced ingurgitation of water, the defendant was tied by the wrists to two rings in the wall of the torture chamber and by the ankles to two rings in the floor, so that he was stretched face upward in a diagonal position. A wooden trestle was placed under the ropes binding his ankles to the floor, which increased the stretching. The torturer pinched his nostrils shut and slowly poured water into his mouth from a two-pint container. From time to time, he was allowed to breathe. The maximum quantity of water allowed by the Parlement's ruling was eight containers-full, or about 2 gallons – a very large quantity. After each container was poured, the judges questioned the defendant. This was the most dangerous method of torture. It was rarely used during the eighteenth century.

The leg braces applied duress to the most resistant part of the human anatomy. The muscles and bones of the ankles, calves, knees, and thighs are the largest and strongest in the body, and the legs have few nerve ganglia. Since the planks extended up the thighs, they bent with the wedges and distributed some of the pressure along their entire length. The quantity of pressure could be controlled exactly by the torturer. But the defendant watched the entire process. Beyond the mounting pain, especially at the knees and ankles, the increasing constriction probably caused him to fear that his legs were being crushed, when in fact they were not. Inducing that pain and fear, without inflicting crippling pressure, was the purpose of torture by leg braces. Eighteenth-century jurists affirmed that the maximum duration of torture was from an hour to an hour and fifteen minutes.[36] The ordinance urged judges to moderate the *question* if the defendant began to confess.[37] At the end of interrogation under torture, the

---

[35] In Isambert, vol. 20, pp. 281–4.
[36] Jousse, *Nouveau commentaire*, vol. 2, p. 401; Serpillon, vol. 3, p. 933; Muyart, *Instruction criminelle*, p. 717.
[37] Title XIX, Article 10, p. 413.

defendant was untied, placed on a mattress (near a fire, in cold weather), allowed to rest, and attended by the doctor. He could not be tortured again.[38]

The third and last interrogation "on the mattress" was decisive in regard to final judgment and penalty. If the defendant denied guilt in preliminary interrogation, confessed under torture, and then retracted his confession during interrogation on the mattress, he thereby nullified his confession as proof sufficient for the death penalty, whether or not evidence against him had been reserved. He could be condemned to afflictive penalties but not to death. For the death penalty to ensue, a confession extorted by torture had to be repeated voluntarily on the mattress. That necessity largely undermined the legal efficacy of the *question préparatoire.*[39]

After 1670 the *question préparatoire* remained a duel between magistrates and defendants, but the physical and legal conditions under which the duel had to be fought distinctly favored defendants who had some presence of mind and power of will. It also remained an ordeal, an avatar of early medieval trials by fire and water. But unlike those ordeals, defendants did not have to resist the pain, or fear of the pain, to save themselves from the scaffold; they had only to recover their resistance on the mattress, when they were free from duress. These facts were probably widely known within plebeian culture during the eighteenth century.

The three interrogations that formed the *question préparatoire* were conducted on the assumption that the defendant was guilty. But in their questioning, judges had to lead him to reveal specifics of his guilt. Their goal was not a simple plea of guilty. Just as with interrogations during instruction of the trial, the quality of the confession obtained depended largely on the precision and coherence of the questions asked. If the defendant indeed confessed under torture and did not retract on the mattress, judges had to evaluate his confession by comparing its details with the evidence against him. If it accorded with that evidence, it was accepted as completion of proof. Errors or non sequiturs regarding known elements of the crime either invalidated or weakened the confession, certainly as proof sufficient for the death penalty.

Confessions made under torture have always been regarded as uncertain. . . . Since strong evidence of guilt is required to condemn someone to the *question,* according to the Ordinance, one must conclude that when the evidence is reserved and the defendant admits the crime under torture, it is not his admission of guilt alone that causes

---

[38] "S'il a été délié et entièrement ôté de la question, il ne pourra plus y être remis" (Title XIX, Article 10, p. 413).

[39] "L'ordonnance exige un troisième interrogatoire, après la question préparatoire, afin de voir si l'accusé qui auroit avoué son crime, ou quelques circonstances essentielles, y persiste; mais si dans ce dernier interrogatoire, il déclaroit expressément qu'il n'a rien dit, ni avoué, que par la rigueur des tourmens, & qu'il révoque ses aveux, ne les ayant fait que pour faire cesser ses peines; ce désaveu fait sur le champ affoibliroit & anéantiroit presque entièrement les avantages que l'on auroit pu tirer contre lui, de ses réponses" (Serpillon, vol. 3, p. 934). Cf. Muyart, *Instruction criminelle,* p. 718.

him to be convicted; his confession is only a supplement that gives perfection to the evidence reserved.[40]

The ordinance did not oblige judges to decree the *question préparatoire*, under any circumstances. The same weight of evidence against a defendant that was required for the *question* could be used for sentence of *plus amplement informé*. Judges could alternatively pass directly to definitive judgment and, on the basis of the evidence, to conviction and penalties other than death. And they could condemn defendants to death without recourse to the *question* if the evidence of guilt accorded with canons of proof.

After 1670, the *question préparatoire* was riddled with systemic contradictions. The most obvious was the forcing of confession, as against the generally diminished probative status of confession. The *question* could force someone who was innocent or only marginally guilty to confess authorship of a crime; the same person could then further confound the inquiry by retracting his confession on the mattress. If he did not retract, judges could establish the validity of the confession only by its concordance with preexistent evidence against him. Through strict adherence to the ordinance, they had to make that evidence – and not his confession – the basis for conviction. If they used his confession to "override" ambiguities in preexistent evidence, to convict and sentence him to death, they risked judicial murder of an innocent and an unsolved crime. The great majority of those probably guilty refused to confess under torture during the eighteenth century. Judges were obliged to convict them on the basis of reserved evidence – in a sense, as if they had never been put to the *question* – or to acquit them despite that evidence (when it had not been reserved), simply because they had resisted torture. In such cases, the *question* either vitiated the death penalty or produced freedom for the guilty and an unsolved crime. Torture with reservation of evidence was a redundancy in the trial. Without reservation of evidence, it was a blind throw of the dice by judges.[41]

All was contrived to impress on the defendant sentenced to the *question préparatoire* the gravity of the event. But he had already been interrogated in depth several times by the same judges, from preparatory instruction to trial review. He knew their tactics in questioning and the extent of their knowledge of him and the crime. Automatic appeal of those sentences meant that he was thor-

---

[40] Serpillon, vol. 3, p. 923.
[41] "La question est un dangereux moyen pour parvenir à la connoissance de la vérité; c'est pourquoi les Juges ne doivent pas y avoir recours sans y faire réflexion. Rien n'est plus incertain, ni plus équivoque. Il y a des coupables qui ont assez de fermeté pour cacher un crime véritable au fort de la question; d'autres, innocens, à que la force des tourmens a fait avouer des crimes dont ils n'étoient pas coupables. La véhémence de la douleur, ou l'infirmité de la personne, fait confesser à l'innocent ce qu'il n'a pas commis, & l'obstination des autres, qui se trouvent robustes & *plus assurés dans leurs crimes* leur fait tout dénier. Ainsi, la question est une invention qui peur faire perdre un innocent qui à la complexion faible & qui peur sauver un coupable qui est robuste" (Ferrière, vol. 2, p. 433, italics mine). And Pussort in the *Conférences:* "Qu'au surplus la question préparatoire lui avoit toujours semblé inutile, & que si l'on vouloit ôter la prévention d'un usage ancien, l'on trouveroit qu'il est rare qu'elle ait tiré la vérité de la bouche d'un condamné" (p. 224).

oughly forearmed for the encounter in the torture chamber. All of this undoubtedly served to fortify self-defensive resolve. Pain alone could not break down that resolve, unless it was either unbearable or life-threatening. Leg braces were neither.

Both the guilty and the innocent knew that their lives were at stake in the torture chamber – not by the duress, but by their behavior under and after the duress. The *question* presupposed that the innocent would act rationally under torture; they would not falsely confess, because they imperiled their lives by doing so. They would resist the pain because resistance was necessary, and they would also do so in the strength conferred by innocence. But the guilty were subjected to the same pain and threatened with the same consequences. The *question* somehow presupposed that they would act irrationally: that they would confess and thereby condemn themselves to the scaffold. By secular logic, such a presupposition was incoherent. But according to Catholic morality and a venerable pentitential spirituality, the presuppositions had coherence. The authors of the ordinance probably retained the *question préparatoire* as a legal vestige of that venerable spirituality.

In the eighteenth century, the *question préparatoire* was still occasionally referred to as the *question purgative*.[42] This was semantic residue of canon law, of a jurisprudence according to which pain could "purge" guilt and therefore act as a catalyst of moral truth. Since at least the High Middle Ages, penitential doctrine had assumed that those objectively guilty of mortal sins – and most capital offenses were mortal sins – experienced remorse and guilt. That was "raw" contrition, yearning to be alleviated in penitence. Such a person would act out in the torture chamber, under the insistent suasion of his judges and torturer, a simulacrum of ecclesiastical confession. In confessing guilt, he purged remorse. Priests waited in the antechambers of every Old Regime prison to receive confessions and to administer the sacraments on the eve of execution. According to both theologians and jurists, the guilty defendant who sacrificed his life to the law by confession could win salvation of his soul. By the same reasoning, the innocent – without burden of remorse over mortal sin and capital crime – would not confess. But what of defendants who, in Ferrière's phrase, were "confident in their crimes" or devoid of remorse, who did not believe in the efficacy of confession, who valued their lives more than their possible salvation on the scaffold? What of those who were only marginally guilty but who were suicidally despondent, or those who no longer valued life but did value the partners in crime whom they could save by false confession, or those who preferred death to a long term or life sentence in the galleys or Hôpital-Général?

The *question préparatoire* was also in contradiction with Title XVII of the ordinance, on the prosecution and judgment of the contumacious. If a defendant refused a summons to appear for questioning or escaped arrest and became

---

[42] Denisart, vol. 4, p. 453.

fugitive, the court was to commence instruction of his trial in absentia eighteen days from the date of the summons or arrest order.[43] If found guilty on the basis of testimonial, material, circumstantial, and character evidence, he was to be convicted and sentenced according to the gravity of the crime. "Only condemnations to death will be executed by effigy; those to the galleys, *amende honorable*, life banishment, branding, and whipping will be written on a placard without any effigy; effigies and placards will be displayed in public squares."[44] If the sentence was death or life in the galleys or Hôpital-Général, the contumacious defendant was pronounced legally and civilly dead five years from the date of judgment, but any contumacious defendant who turned himself in or was arrested within five years of judgment was re-tried in vivo. Flight was not proof of guilty, and contumacious defendants were tried, and acquitted or convicted, on the basis of objective evidence, including the same categories of evidence used to decide on the *question préparatoire*.[45] Such trials and judgments, in which guilt or innocence was decided without any interrogation of defendants, were common at the Châtelet and Parlement of Paris during the eighteenth century.

The *question préparatoire* was dissonant with penology. By Article 13 of Title XXV, it was defined as a formal penalty. But it differed fundamentally from all other penalties in law: It was executed before the defendant had been found guilty; it was executed secretly, not publicly and didactically. In the ordinance, the *question* with reserve of evidence was placed after the death penalty, thus indicating that it was second in gravity only to the supreme punishment.[46] There were two reasons for this: the *question* inflicted pain and was therefore corporal punishment; when inflicted with reserve of evidence, it meant probable death if the defendant confessed and was therefore potentially more severe than incarceration or banishment for life.[47] But the very intimacy between the *question* and the death penalty served to weaken the death penalty, to undermine the most powerful instrument of penology. If a defendant did not confess under the *question*, he could not be sentenced to death, no matter the atrociousness of the crime or the weight of evidence against him. In a sense, the state negated itself in Article 13 of Title XXV: Royal statutes mandated death for many offenses, but defendants accused of such crimes who resisted the *question* had to be spared the death penalty, even if they were subsequently convicted. By enduring sixty to seventy-five minutes of the leg braces or ingurgitation of water, assassins, poisoners, rapists, or homicidal thieves and arsonists could mock royal punitive will. As constructed in the ordinance, the *question préparatoire* protected all but the weak and the innocent from the death penalty. Its legal and

---

[43] Ordinance, Title XVII, Articles 13–14, p. 408.
[44] Ibid., Article 16, p. 408. [45] Ferrière, vol. 1, p. 381.
[46] "Après le peine de mort naturelle, la plus rigoureuse est celle de la question avec réserve des preuves en leur entier, des galères perpétuelles, du banissement perpétuel, de la question sans réserve des preuves, des galères à temps, du fouet, de l'amende honorable, et du banissement à temps" (Ordinance, Title XXV, Article 13, p. 417).
[47] *Conférences*, p. 248.

practical meanings were the opposite of those assigned to it by Michel Foucault and an entire modern historiographical tradition.[48]

Judicial torture was far more destructive of the authority and perspicacity of judges than of the lives and limbs of defendants. At the moment of the *question*, the magistrates' genuine authority over the defendant ended: They could neither force him to confess nor make him tell the truth. Paradoxically, at this moment of physical power over the defendant, they were at the nadir of their intellectual and legal power over him. Liberal commentators, from the Enlightenment to the present, have been blind to the fact that after 1670 power in the torture chambers of France resided with defendants, not with their judges. By lying or retracting confession, a guilty defendant could defeat the death penalty and compromise the investigation of criminal truth. This potential for subversion was the greatest contradiction between the *question préparatoire* and the jurisprudence of the ordinance. The power relations between judges and defendants were the opposite with the other interlocutory judgment available in capital cases: *plus amplement informé* with prison. That is why it was preferred to the *question* by the Châtelet and Parlement of Paris.

After 1670, the *question préparatoire* did not stand in central relation to proof. It stood in central relation to the death penalty – as a barrier to the death penalty. The defendant who resisted the *question* could still be found guilty and sentenced to a penalty other than death. A defendant sentenced to the *question* had to confess both under and after duress, and his confession had to be confirmed by evidence, for him to receive the death penalty.

The ordinance and subsequent jurisprudence did not require confession, and therefore judicial torture, for the death penalty. Severe penalists, especially those obedient to royal statutes that mandated the death penalty, could not intelligently decree the *question* unless they expected that the defendant would confess. But that expectation was rarely practical. Eighteenth-century court records reveal that only a small fraction of defendants confessed or revealed accomplices under torture.[49] Severe penalists, acting logically, would opine for conviction on the basis of evidence and penalty of death or incarceration for life. We shall see that the probability of their obtaining the death penalty was low; via the *question*, it was yet lower. Moderate and lenient penalists could not intelligently decree the *question* unless the evidence against the defendant was very strong, he was charged with a statutory death offense, and his only chance of escaping death was by defying torture.[50] Under those conditions logic required

---

[48] *Discipline and Punish* and the other authors cited in note 6 to "Origins and Legend," the introduction to Part III of this volume.

[49] For the Châtelet: A.N.Y 10018–10417 (cases in *grand criminel*, Châtelet, 1702–80) and A.N.Y 10514–10526 (registers of judgments in *grand criminel*, 1747–76). For the Parlement: A.N. Inventory 450, 1736–80.

[50] In condemning such a tactic, Serpillon implied that it was occasionally used: "Il seroit très irrégulier de condamner à une question préparatoire un accusé suffisamment convaincu de son crime; ce seroit un expédient inventé pour lui sauver la vie; parce que s'il n'avouoit pas à la question, on ne le pourroit plus condamner à la mort, quoique les preuves eussent été réservées en entier" (vol. 3, p. 919).

them to vote for either *plus amplement informé* or conviction and long-term in-carceration, because of the risk that the defendant might confess under torture and thereby doom himself to the scaffold. Such judges enjoyed a high proba-bility of obtaining penalties other than death, without recourse to the *question*.

Prolonged and repeated torture would undoubtedly have generated far more confessions than were produced in the torture chambers of the eighteenth cen-tury. Such extreme duress was interdicted in 1670 and 1697.[51] The interdiction was both rational and humane: Sustained or repeated torture could maim or kill; it could also produce false confessions, and thereby unsolved crimes and judicial murders.

The ordinance was not the apogee of judicial torture. It annunciated and im-pelled an obsolescence. Subaltern and sovereign courts were subtly discour-aged from imposing the *question préparatoire;* the execution of every such sentence was suspended until reviewed and confirmed by a sovereign court; the sovereign court was allowed to interrogate defendants in the torture chamber without using torture; the same type of evidence required for the *question* could be used to decree *plus amplement informé* or even penalties other than death. In sum, the ordinance attenuated the *question préparatoire* to such an extent that its utility was undermined, thereby impelling long-term desuetude of the proce-dure and, ultimately, a movement for abolition.

Inventory 450 of all judgments by the Tournelle of the Parlement of Paris allows close examination of the incidence and results of the *question préparatoire* in that jurisdiction from 1700 to 1780. The fifteen years 1735 to 1749 have been chosen for study, because that was a period before the development of literary and philosophical attacks on judicial torture.[52]

We may begin with a single year, 1736. During those twelve months, a total of 294 interlocutory and definitive judgments from provincial courts (183) and the Châtelet (111) were decided on appeal by the Tournelle. Provincial courts decreed the *question préparatoire* lavishly, against 20 (11%) of 183 defendants. This meant that a near-majority of those accused of capital offenses in the pro-vincial courts were sentenced to the *question*. The Châtelet was circumspect: It sentenced only 3 of its 111 defendants to the *question*. The Tournelle invali-dated, and thus prevented, 19 of those 23 sentences. It confirmed 4: the 3 by the Châtelet but only 1 by a provincial court. Two of those defendants did not confess; the behavior and fate of the other 2 cannot be determined. One of the

---

[51] Alfred Soman, "La justice criminelle aux XVIe–XVIIe siècles: Le Parlement de Paris et les sièges subalternes," in *La faute, la répression et le pardon: 107e Congrès national des Sociétés Savantes* (Brest, 1982), pp. 16–52, examined all sentences to the *question préparatoire* that were upheld or decreed by the Parlement of Paris during the years 1539 to 1542 and 1604 to 1611. Of the 71 persons tortured during the period 1539 to 1542 whose behavior is known, only 6 (8.5%) con-fessed. In the period 1604 to 1611, the confession rate was 2.3%. During those periods, the Parlement used only leg braces or water and only one application of torture. Those were the methods legislated in 1670 and 1697. Soman argues that the late seventeenth-century restric-tions on the *question préparatoire* were the culmination of a long development within the Parle-ment of Paris.

[52] Data constructed from Inventory 450, vols. III–IV.

2 who did not confess was sentenced by the Tournelle to the galleys for nine years, the other to *plus amplement informé* for one year with prison and then indefinite *plus amplement informé* at liberty. All but 1 of the sentences to the *question* by provincial courts were invalidated and transformed into other sentences by the Parlement (see Table 14.1). In a indictment for a capital crime where the evidence of guilt was strong but did not meet the canons of proof, *plus amplement informé*, not the *question*, was a correct alternative to torture. In only one of the cases reviewed in 1736 did the Tournelle deem the evidence sufficient for proof, thus conviction and the death penalty. Adequacy of proof made the *question* unjustifiable.

During the fifteen years 1735 to 1749, the Tournelle judged approximately 6,500 defendants on appeal of interlocutory or definitive judgments by subaltern courts. Some 1,110 defendants were prosecuted for or convicted of capital offenses by those courts. The Tournelle pronounced 417 death sentences. Sixty-nine of the condemned received royal pardons or commutations. The others – 348 – were executed. Only 2 of them were executed in consequence of the *question préparatoire.*

In those same years subaltern courts pronounced some 350 interlocutory judgments to the *question*, or against about one-third of all those tried for capital offenses. With emphatic repudiation, the Tournelle upheld or ordered the *question* against only 41 defendants: 21 confirmations of original sentences; 13 ameliorations (of original convictions and sentences to death or to life in the galleys); 2 aggravations (of original sentences to *plus amplement informé*). Thus, only about 3.5 percent of those judged for capital offenses were actually put to torture. Had final decision remained with subaltern courts, some 35 percent of them would have been tortured.

Table 14.2 discloses the incidence and results of the *question préparatoire* in the Tournelle during the period 1735 to 1749. Behavior in the torture chamber is known for 28 defendants. Only 2 confessed. Twenty-six who were tied into the leg braces or stretched and then bloated with water either resisted duress or retracted on the mattress. The post-1670 *question préparatoire* was clearly futile as coercion against the majority of defendants. Those 26, like the majority of their analogs in *grand criminel,* were either young or in the prime of maturity; they were also inured to hard, abrasive labor. They won in the torture chamber by stamina of body and presence of mind. The majority of them were probably guilty. Legal proof of guilt in these 41 cases may or may not have been adequate for the death penalty without confessions. But there was only the slightest chance that confessions would be obtained from the *question.* Thus, when the Tournelle sentenced these men and women to torture, it was giving them an opportunity to save themselves from the scaffold. It was applying the following maxim: "One makes the defendant, so to speak, the judge of his own case as regards the death penalty."[53] That was subtle clemency.

---

[53] Rousseaud, p. 424.

Table 14.1. *Invalidations of lower-court sentences to the question préparatoire by Parlement of Paris, 1736*

Court	Accusation	Final judgment, Parlement
Compiègne	Murder	Hanging
Etampes	Murder	P.a.i. 1 year prison
Fontenay-le-Comte	Murder	P.a.i. 1 year prison
Montbrison	Murder	P.a.i. 1 year prison; indefinite at liberty
Pontoise	Murder	P.a.i. 6 months prison; indefinite at liberty
Clermont-Ferrand	Complicity in murder	P.a.i. 1 year prison; indefinite at liberty
Saumur	Fratricide	P.a.i. 1 year prison; indefinite at liberty
Saumur	Fratricide	P.a.i. 1 year prison; indefinite at liberty
Crépy-en-Valois	Murder	P.a.i. 1 year prison; indefinite at liberty
Senlis	Complicity in murder	P.a.i. 1 year prison; indefinite at liberty
Coucy	Poisoning	P.a.i. 1 year prison; indefinite at liberty
Coucy	Poisoning	P.a.i. 1 year prison; indefinite at liberty
Coucy	Effractive burglary	P.a.i. 1 year prison; indefinite at liberty
Auxerre	Arson	P.a.i. 1 year prison; indefinite at liberty
Villeblevin	Arson	P.a.i. 6 months prison; indefinite at liberty
Provins	Threatening and seditious letters	P.a.i. 1 year prison; indefinite at liberty
Montfort l'Amaury	Thefts	P.a.i. 1 year prison; indefinite at liberty
Lyon	Thefts	P.a.i. 6 months prison; indefinite at liberty

Abbreviation: p.a.i. – plus amplement informé
Source: A.N. Inventory 450, vols. III–IV.

Moderation by the Tournelle in punishment of those who did not confess during the *question* was not subtle; it was transparent. Technically, the Parlement could have sentenced these triumphant veterans of the *question* to life or several years in the galleys. Only 5 of the 26 were sent to the galleys: 1 for life; 2 for nine years; 2 for three years. Nine of the total of 41 received sentences to the galleys, including the instructions *ex nihil*. Twenty of the 26 who resisted the *question* were sentenced to *plus amplement informé* with prison. Those judgments conformed to the spirit of the ordinance, which placed the *question* with reserve of evidence (always the form used by the Parlement of Paris) immediately after death in the hierarchy of punishments. To pronounce life or several years in the galleys against those who had already endured the *question* would be to punish them twice, with near-maximal severity each time, for the same crime. The Tournelle chose to do so in only 7 of 41 cases. Here again, the subversive potency of the *question* is manifest: It not only negated the death penalty; it also compromised the alternative of long-term carceral penalties.

By sentencing veterans of the *question* to *plus amplement informé* with prison, usually followed with indefinite *plus amplement informé* at liberty, the Parlement both adhered to the spirit of the ordinance and accomplished a penal casuistry. In jurisprudence, indefinite *plus amplement informé* at liberty was more severe than even incarceration for life, because the defendant could be convicted and given the death penalty should new and conclusive evidence supervene.[54] *Plus amplement informé* with prison for six months or a year was considered less severe than the galleys or *hôpital* for several years but more severe than banishment. By combining *plus amplement informé* with one- or two-year prison terms and the indefinite form of the sentence at liberty, the Parlement combined real clemency with a symbolic, or fictive, severity. It conveyed the legal semblance of serious punishment for veterans of the *question*. But that was little more than semblance: None of the 20 was later convicted and sent to the scaffold or the galleys. Only 1 of them – Martial Tabourin, accused of having poisoned his wife – was kept in Bicêtre for life, by a *note* issued at the expiration of his second term of *plus amplement informé* with prison. After a year or two behind walls, usually at Bicêtre, 19 of the 26 victors in the torture chamber walked out of prison, through doors and gates opened for them by the law. Their freedom was a consequence of their having been put to the *question*. I have found no evidence that the consequences of the *question préparatoire* were different between 1670 and 1735.

The rarity and investigative futility of the *question préparatoire* were not unique to the Parlement of Paris. The Tournelle of the Parlement of Burgundy judged 998 persons during the period comprised by 1715 to 1717, 1728 to

---

[54] Article 2 of Title XIX provided that defendants who had denied guilt in the *question* could be sentenced to death if new and conclusive evidence emerged after the *question*. That technically was a further reason for sentences to *plus amplement informé* with prison, after torture. But I have not found one case in which the Parlement decided that sufficient evidence had arisen to warrant death for someone who had resisted the *question* and been given *plus amplement informé*.

Table 14.2. *Incidence and results of the* question préparatoire *in jurisdiction of Parlement of*

Year	Name	Age	Occupation	Court	Crime
1747	Jean Chertier	63	Farrier	Chateauroux	Poisoning
1749	Barthélemy Charton	40	Farmer	Moulins	Murder
1735	Jean Dumesnil	24	Unknown	Châtelet	Murder and theft
1735	Etienne Frémont	40	Unknown	Crépy-en-Valois	Complicity in murder
1735	Ebon Darde	33	Unknown	Sens	Fratricide
1735	Pierre Prudhomme	50	Unknown	Unknown	Complicity in murder
1735	Pierre Thierry	39	Unknown	Senlis	Complicity in murder
1736	Joseph Monnet	42	Soldier	Châtelet	Effractive burglaries
1736	Pierre Tessier	20	Unknown	Cognac	Murder
1737	Alexandre Bouret	22	Unknown	Châtelet	Murder
1737	Michel Rigault	19	Unknown	Châtelet	Murder
1737	Martial Tabourin	?	Roofer	Issodun	Poisoning his wife
1739	Pierre Lamorail	?	Soldier	Châtelet	Theft
1740	Georges Garret	22	Farmer	Riom	Murder and theft
1740	Jean Vié	30	Farmer	Riom	Complicity in murder and theft
1740	Michel Vié	47	Weaver	Riom	Murder and theft
1740	Philippe Treillard	28	Unknown	Lyon	Murder of his wife
1741	André Jacquin	31	Winemaker	Soulières	Effractive burglary
1741	Antoine Boivin	22	Old clothes dealer	Châtelet	Domestic theft
1742	Jean Pelletier	32	Hempcomber	Semur-en-Auxerrois	Theft from church
1742	Antoine Fauché	25	Unknown	Châtelet	Effractive burglary
1742	Anne Gaultier	33	Unknown	Auxerre	Unknown
1746	Thomas Quéneur	38	Farmer	Romorantin	Murder of his wife
1746	Louis Bertrand	27	Soldier	Châtelet	Effractive burglary
1747	Jean Jeannot	44	Day laborer	Châtelet	Murder
1747	Jean Mansuet	34	Wagoner	Châtelet	Murder
1748	Joseph Helvin	26	Servant	Châtelet	Domestic theft
1749	Jacques Charton	32	Farmer	Moulins	Complicity in murder
1735	Gaspard Paris	50	Unknown	Unknown	Unknown
1735	François Hémon	?	Unknown	Montdidier	Unknown
1735	Florent Lefebvre	35	Unknown	Montdidier	Burglary
1736	Pierre Noël	18	Apprentice painter	Châtelet	Complicity in armed robberies
1736	Guillaume Laidier	36	Unknown	Châtelet	Effractive burglary
1738	Silvain Bonneau	28	Unknown	St. Pierre-le-Moutier	Murder
1739	François Tiron	30	Unknown	Langres	Arson
1741	Marie Tartereau	?	Unknown	Sens	Poisoning
1742	Denis Lebigre	20	Leather merchant	Châtelet	Effractive burglary
1747	Michel Bouret	25	Floor polisher	Châtelet	Effractive burglary
1748	Pierre Bouret	25	Woodturner	Châtelet	Multiple thefts
1748	Pierre Robelot	34	Farmer	Troyes	Arson
1749	Alexandre Courtois	24	Journeyman painter	Châtelet	Murder

Notes: The column "Parlement judgments and dates" gives the sequence of decisions on each case by the Tournelle and the date of each decision, where given in Inventory 450. The abbreviations are as follows: *p.a.i.–plus amplement informé; ques.–question; indef. lib–*indefinite at liberty. The last 13 entries in the column "Behavior under the *question*," are cases in which it is impossible to know with certainty from the inventory whether or not the defendant confessed. In most of these cases, the defendants were put to the *question* by the original courts after

Paris, 1735–1749

Original sentence	Parlement judgments and dates	Behavior
Hanging	Ques. Feb. 16; hanging Feb. 17	Confessed
Breaking	Ques. Mar. 27; breaking Mar. 28	Confessed
Question	Ques. Sept. 1; p.a.i. indef. lib.	Did not confess
Unknown	Ques. Mar. 7; p.a.i. 1 yr. prison Mar. 8; p.a.i. indef. lib June 25, 1736	Did not confess
Question	Ques. May 5; p.a.i. 1 yr. prison July 6	Did not confess
Unknown	Ques. Mar. 7; p.a.i. 1 yr. prison Mar. 8; p.a.i. indef. lib. Apr. 25 1736	Did not confess
Unknown	Ques. Mar. 7; p.a.i. 1 yr. prison Mar. 8; p.a.i. indef. lib. June 25 1736	Did not confess
Question	Ques. May 29; galleys 9 yrs. June	Did not confess
Question	Ques. July 17; p.a.i. 1 yr. prison July 18; p.a.i. indef. lib.	Did not confess
Question	Ques. Mar. 14; p.a.i. 1 yr. prison Mar.; p.a.i. indef. lib. Aug. 8 1738	Did not confess
Question	Ques. Mar. 12; p.a.i. 1 yr. prison Apr. 2	Did not confess
Breaking	Ques. July 19; p.a.i. 1 yr. prison July; p.a.i. 1 yr. prison Aug. 1738; prison for life Aug. 1739	Did not confess
P.a.i. 1 yr. prison	Ques. Mar. 18; p.a.i. 1 yr. prison Mar. 19; p.a.i. indef. lib. May 12, 1740	Did not confess
Breaking	Ques. Oct 21; galleys 3 yrs. Oct. 22	Did not confess
Breaking	Ques. Oct. 21; galleys 3 yrs. Oct. 22	Did not confess
Breaking	Ques. Oct. 21; galleys 9 yrs. Oct. 22	Did not confess
Question	Ques. Jan. 26; p.a.i. 1 yr. prison Jan. 27	Did not confess
Hanging	Ques. May 4; p.a.i. 1 yr. prison May 5	Did not confess
Hanging	Ques. Jan. 2; galleys for life Jan. 4	Did not confess
Question	Ques. Mar. 5; p.a.i. 1 yr. prison Mar. 6; p.a.i. indef. lib.	Did not confess
Unknown	Ques. Mar. 12; p.a.i. 1 yr. prison Mar. 15; p.a.i. indef. lib. Mar. 1743	Did not confess
Question	Ques. Mar. 5; p.a.i. 1 yr. prison Mar. 6	Did not confess
Breaking	Ques. May 17; p.a.i. 1 yr. prison May 18; p.a.i. indef. lib. June 1747	Did not confess
Question	Ques. Jan. 14; banished 9 yrs. Mar. 4	Did not confess
Question	Ques. July 27; p.a.i. 1 yr. lib. Aug. 27	Did not confess
Question	Ques. July 27; p.a.i. 1 yr. prison Aug. 29; p.a.i. indef. lib. Sept. 18, 1748	Did not confess
Question	Ques. June 18; p.a.i. 1 yr. prison July 9	Did not confess
Breaking	Ques. Mar. 27; p.a.i. 1 yr. prison June 11	Did not confess
Question	Ques. Sept. 1	Unknown
P.a.i. 3 mos. prison	Ques. Aug. 22	Unknown
Question	Ques. "si nihil galères à perpétuité" Aug. 22	Unknown
Unknown	Ques. "si nihil ad omnia citra mortem" Jan. 30	Unknown
Question	Ques. Mar. 15	Unknown
Question	Ques. "si nihil ad omnia citra mortem" Feb. 6	Unknown
Galleys for life	Ques. "si nihil galères à perpétuité" Feb. 25	Unknown
Hanging	Ques. Mar. 8	Unknown
Hanging	Ques. "si nihil galères" July 16	Unknown
Question	Ques. "ad omnia citra mortem" Oct. 25	Unknown
Question	Ques. "Si nihil galères à perpétuité" July 30	Unknown
Question	Ques. Oct. 25	Unknown
Question	Ques. "si nihil ad omnia citra mortem" Jan. 22	Unknown

authorization by the Parlement. In 8 of these cases of unknown behavior, the Tournelle gave instructions as to penalty in the event of no confession: *si nihil galères à perpétuité* or *galères* (if no confession, then galleys for life or galleys); *si nihil ad omnia citra mortem* or *ad omnia citra mortem* (if no confession, then any penalty other than death). It is probable that few of the 13 confessed.
Source: A.N. Inventory 450, vols. III–IV.

459

1730, 1748 to 1750, and 1758 to 1760. It sentenced 129 (12.9%) of them to death. Only 17 (1.7%) of the 998 were sentenced to the *question*. After 1766, the Parlement of Burgundy dispensed entirely with the *question* and invalidated all those interlocutory judgments by its subaltern courts.[55] From 1750 to 1780, the Parlement of Brittany passed final judgment on almost 6,000 defendants, several hundred of whom were accused of capital offenses. The Tournelle authorized or pronounced 11 sentences to the *question préparatoire* during those three decades. Only 1 defendant confessed and was sentenced to death.[56]

Lower courts, like Parlements, had at their disposition the penalties of galleys, Hôpital-Général, and *plus amplement informé*, but they commonly preferred the *question*. With the exception of the Châtelet, the subaltern courts in the jurisdiction of the Parlement of Paris tried to use the *question* lavishly until at least the mid-eighteenth century. They were prevented from doing so by the Tournelle. There was considerable fluctuation in the frequency of the death sentence at the Parlement of Paris during the century: The frequency was low and relatively stable until the mid-1740s; it rose almost steadily from then until about 1770; from the early 1770s to 1785 there were short-term oscillations but a cumulative decline; in 1786, the decline became precipitate. None of those fluctuations had any discernible relation with the incidence of the *question préparatoire*, which was both numerically rare and declining over the entire period. The only relation possible between the incidence of the *question* and that of the death penalty was negative: More sentences to torture would have resulted in fewer sentences to death. From the early 1770s onward, there was general increase in sentences to the *bagne*, Hôpital-Général, and *plus amplement informé* in capital cases. But that increase did not express any relation to the *question préparatoire*, which had long since passed into desuetude in the Tournelle. It did express the rising political and moral crisis of the death sanction and its execution.

After 1670, the *question préparatoire* could produce only four possible results: (1) a guilty defendant confessed guilt; (2) a guilty defendant denied guilt; (3) an innocent defendant denied guilt; (4) an innocent defendant confessed guilt. The optimal theoretical efficacy of the *question* in eliciting truth was only 50 percent in any individual case. But the practical efficacy within the jurisdiction of the Parlement of Paris during the years 1735 to 1749 was between 5 and 10 percent, for that was the percentage of confessions obtained from defendants against whom there was strong objective evidence of guilt. When the *question* did produce subjective truth, the value of the product was primarily aesthetic: harmony between objective evidence of guilt and subjective avowal of guilt, or between lacunae in objective evidence of guilt and subjective denial of guilt. In those rare cases, it closed an epistemological circle and produced "beautiful proof." But when the *question* produced falsity – in 50 percent of all possible

[55] D. Ulrich, "La repression en Bourgogne au XVIIIe siècle," *RHDFE* (1972), 50:398–437.
[56] Mer, "La procédure criminelle au XVIIIe siècle," pp. 28–9.

cases and perhaps 90 to 95 percent of actual cases – it produced far more than falsity. Since denials of guilt by the guilty had to be credited as possibly true, the guilty could not be punished as their crimes merited in law but only by the *question* itself and subsequent lesser penalties. This meant that, after the *question*, arsonists, highway robbers, and murderers received the same punishments as ordinary thieves: *plus amplement informé* with prison or a term in the galleys.

The decline of judicial torture during the eighteenth century was a repudiation of torture by magistrates of sovereign courts who were loyal to the 1670 ordinance, to its procedural strictures and its penology. Their repudiation was nourished by obdurate and successful plebeian resistance to the *question*. The power to judge and punish rationally required that judges renounce the power to torture, which was the result subtly intended by the authors of the ordinance.[57]

In many capital cases – burglaries, armed robberies, assaults, and murders – eighteenth-century judges in towns and cities confronted new types of defendants: ever-greater numbers of deracinated and migratory plebeians for whom these and lesser crimes were a form of survival, an aggrandizement, an affirmation of virility; who lived amid violence; who experienced little or no remorse or repentance; who regarded their indictments as bad luck; who had no inner deference to the black-gowned figure of the judge; who were obstinate and cunning in defying interrogative skills; who were not terrified by judicial torture. Most of them owned, in durable property, only the strength and prowess of their own bodies. For them, to refuse confession under torture was also to affirm self. Rousseaud de la Combe wrote of such defendants, speaking from long experience in the Parlement of Paris, "These defendants admit to virtually nothing, such that most often the *question préparatoire* has no effect; they suffer the torment of the *question* without confessing anything and if they speak at all, it is to deny everything."[58]

---

[57] The inefficacy of the *question préparatoire* and its subversion of due punishment, not the inhumanity of the practice, were the reasons given for its abolition in the royal declaration of August 24, 1780: "Nous avons été informés que lors des conférences tenues préalablement à la rédaction de l'Ordonnance du mois d'Aôut 1670, des Magistrats recommandables par une grande capacité & par une expérience consommée, s'étant expliqués sur ce genre de Question, auroient déclaré qu'elle leur avoit toujours semblé inutile; qu'il étoit rare que la Question préparatoire eût tiré la vérité de la bouche d'un accusé, & qu'il avoit de fortes raisons pour en supprimer l'usage; & il nous paroit qu'on n' a cédé pour lors qu'à une sorte de respect pour son anciennêté. Nous sommes bien éloignés de Nous déterminer trop facilement à abolir les Loix qui sont anciennes & autorisées par un long usage. Il est de notre sagesse de ne point ouvrir des facilités pour introduire en toutes choses un droit nouveau qui ébranleroit les principes & pourroit conduire par degrés à des innovations dangereuses; *mais, après avoir donné toute notre attention à l'usage dont il s'agit, avoir examiné tous ses rapports & tous ses inconveniens, & les avoir balancés avec les avantages que la Justice en a pu rétirer, & qui pourroient en résulter par la suite pour la conviction & pour la punition des coupables, Nous ne pouvons Nous réfuser aux réflexions & a l'experience des premiers Magistrats, qui nous laissent entrevoir plus de rigueur contre l'accusé dans ce genre de condamnation, que d'espérance pour la Justice de parvenir, par l'aveu de l'accusé, à completter la preuve du crime dont il est prévenu* [italics mine]. Nous ne pensons donc par devoir différer de faire cesser un pareil usage" (Isambert, vol. 26, p. 374).

[58] P. 422.

Eighteenth-century defendants generally refused to confess guilt, no matter the crimes of which they were accused. The scale of refusal is disclosed by their final hearings, immediately before judgment. One year at the Châtelet has been selected to illustrate this phenomenon. During 1748, that court heard and judged 251 defendants (159 men, 92 women) in *grand criminel*.[59] Final statements are legible for 153 of them; the crimes for which they were tried were mostly minor and subject to defaming and afflictive penalties. Only 4 (or 2.6%) of the 153 confessed. Nine others admitted to some involvement (with others) in the crimes with which they were charged, but several of those admissions were vague as to personal guilt. Two of the 4 who confessed had been caught in violation of banishment from Paris and Versailles. Françoise Bonnet, a seamstress aged 56, had been branded, whipped, and sentenced to the Hôpital in 1723. When her term was completed, she was released and forbidden to ever return to Paris. She claimed that she had respected the proscription for many years and had returned only recently to seek work. She was sentenced to the Salpêtrière for life. Jean Goynet, a weaver aged 68, was a branded former *galérien* who had been caught near Versailles. Because of his age, he was released under sentence of banishment. The other 2 confessed to the charges against them – and attempted to exonerate themselves. Philippe de Canville, aged 61 and a retired officer of the royal household, was accused of stealing silver tableware from a home where he dined regularly. He had been found in possession. But he claimed that the *maître d'hôtel* of the household owed him 6 livres, he intended to return the silver as soon as he was paid. He was sentenced to whipping, branding, and banishment for nine years. Marie-Philippe Bouillerat, soldier in a dragoon regiment, admitted to having killed someone during a sword fight in a cabaret. He claimed that he did not know his adversary, insults were exchanged, both drew swords and fought. He asserted involuntary homicide in self-defense. He was authorized to petition for royal pardon.

Fully 142 (93%) of the 153 vehemently denied the charges against them. Most did so in the face of extensive testimonial and material evidence of their guilt. Martin Laugé, a gardener at Bonneuil near Paris, was accused of stealing a silver fork from one of the homes where he worked. He was there on the day of the theft, and he was arrested soon after in possession of the fork. But he insisted that he had not stolen it: He went to the local tavern, where he drank with a soldier he had never seen before and whose name he could not remember; the soldier slipped the fork into his pocket. The sentence was unanimous: branding, whipping, and banishment for three years. Marie Girard, a pedlar in the Halles, was accused of stealing a gilded snuffbox from a tailor in a wineshop: there were eyewitnesses to the theft; she was arrested in flagrant delict; she had the snuffbox on her person; the police commissioner had testified that she admitted to taking the box when she was arrested. She denied everything

[59] A.N. Y 10514.

and received the same sentence as Marie Laugé. Louise-Elisabeth Courtois, embroideress, was accused of active complicity in a gang of street and highway robbers, a gang that had murdered. At least two convicted members of the gang had given evidence against her in confrontations and death testaments. She denied all charges, insisted that she had not known any members of the gang except in prison, that their allegations were vindictive lies, that the stolen goods found in her possession had been given to her by various other persons. By a vote of five to three, the judges of the Châtelet sentenced her to the *question* with reserve of evidence. The Parlement overturned their sentence and pronounced death by hanging.

Denial of guilt had no relation to the gravity of the charges among the 142; only 10 to 15 percent were tried for capital offenses. It had little relation to judgments. The Châtelet pronounced sentences of acquittal or *plus amplement informé* for brief terms at liberty for some one-third of the 153. It convicted two-thirds of them. The Tournelle pronounced the death sentence against 6 of the 153; none of them had confessed.

Denials of guilt were general at the Châtelet and Parlement during the eighteenth century, and they were actions of great judicial import. Denial should not be understood only as self-protection, even though most defendants convicted in original trial would receive final judgment on appeal and had an incentive to assert innocence from the beginning of inquiry. But these defendants also rejected the very evidence of their guilt when it was set before them; in doing so, they rejected the linear and empirical reasoning by which judges ascertained guilt. Some undoubtedly refused any intimate culpability of the crimes for which they were tried, either because they were morally confident in their officially criminal behavior or considered the meaning of their actions to be private and not legal. When such persons asserted innocence in the face of evidence of their guilt, they were not simply lying. They were also repudiating the rigid, legalist description of their actions as crimes, as evil actions that required inquiry and formal punishment.

The subjectivities of most eighteenth-century defendants remain opaque to us. They were made opaque to the scrutiny of judges. But through systematic denial, those defendants indubitably defied, and incrementally altered, the canons of jurisprudence. They rejected the contritional or purgative value of confession, and by withholding avowal of guilt they made first-person truth virtually unattainable in law. They forced judges into the realm of probabilities and, in doing so, they forced significant changes in methods of judgment. Eighteenth-century courts would have lost all capacity to convict and punish guilty defendants had legal proof of guilt depended on confessions. They retained such capacity by extensive and predominant reliance on other forms of proof, a reliance that was encouraged by the 1670 ordinance.

The decline of the *question préparatoire* after 1670 belonged to the general decline, in practice, of first-person authority in judgment. Both movements registered the ascendancy of testimonial, material, circumstantial, and character evidence in judgment, the ascendancy of the objective evidence on which eighteenth-century jurists insisted so emphatically. That meant skepticism and methodical induction by judges of guilt or innocence from evidence that existed independently of denials or avowals by defendants. The seventeenth-century intellectual revolution expressed by Descartes's *Discourse on Method* was present in the 1670 ordinance. It clearly penetrated jurists and superior magistrates during the first half of the eighteenth century. That is not surprising; from the late seventeenth century onward, the *Discourse* shaped the logic segment of the obligatory philosophy course in most *collèges* where royal magistrates were educated.[60] The consequence of this epistemological shift was the practical development of modern rules of evidence in French criminal law.

Testimony had always been second only to confession in the traditional canons of proof. But early modern jurisprudence had severely restricted the deployment of witnesses. The ordinance removed most of the restrictions.

In Roman–canonical jurisprudence, the following had been *testes inhabiles*, or persons barred from testifying for prosecution in criminal cases: those aged under 20; parents against children; children against parents; brothers against brothers; domestic servants or bondsmen against their masters; those of defaming social condition. Only in crimes of *lèse-majesté*, and in the absence of other witnesses, could their testimony be heard.[61] These disbarments protected social hierarchies and corporatist bonds. But for judges to determine the guilt or innocence of a defendant, they required the fullest possible spectrum of testimony, especially when two eyewitnesses were necessary for conviction. Exclusion of potential witnesses because of youth, gender, familial relations with the defendant, or social condition obstructed rational inquiry and royal justice. And it led to torture of defendants in capital cases.

Title VI of the ordinance removed the most important restrictions on eligibility of witnesses:

Children of both sexes, below the age of puberty, can be admitted to testify; judges are to be attentive to the necessity for and credibility of their testimony.[62]

Witnesses will be sworn to tell the truth and will be asked to give their name, forename, occupation, residence, and to state whether or not they are servants, parents, relatives or spouses of the parties to the case, and in what degree.[63]

The same criteria for evaluation of testimony were to be applied to their depositions as to all others, and they were subjected to the same procedures of *récolement* and confrontation. Wives, husbands, siblings, parents, and children could be summoned to testify against each other in cases of the most serious crimes (those subject to penalties of death or long-term incarceration). In other

---

[60] Brockliss, *French Higher Education*, pp. 200–9.   [61] Schnapper, "Testes inhabiles."
[62] Ordinance, Title 6, Article 2, p. 381.   [63] Ibid., Article 5, p. 382.

cases, their testimony for the prosecution had to be voluntary.[64] Domestic servants could be summoned to testify against their masters in all cases of *grand criminel.*[65] Even beggars, vagabonds, prostitutes, and others of defaming occupation could be summoned, although jurists insisted that judges had to scrutinize their testimony with particular care.[66] Social distinctions no longer determined the eligibility of witnesses. Such distinctions remained important in the evaluation of testimony: The testimony of the respectable was to be accorded greater credit than that of the socially base or defamed, when the two were in contradiction.[67]

The new and democratic eligibility of witnesses in criminal justice altered the character of the confrontation, to the general disadvantage of defendants. They could no longer invalidate the testimony of adverse witnesses simply by pointing out their youth, occupations, or kinship. The authority of judges over defendants, and over the gathering of evidence, was increased correspondingly.

Increase in the number of witnesses meant increase in the volume and importance of the fourth category of evidence in the Roman–canonical system: *indicia,* or material, circumstantial, and character evidence. In eighteenth-century practice, there were twenty-six chief "indications" of guilt for most crimes: (1) bad reputation; (2) past criminal behavior; (3) presence in suspect places; (4) presence at the site and time of the crime; (5) leaving that site at the approximate time of the crime; (6) affiliations with those who commit similar crimes; (7) threatening words or gestures against the victim before the crime; (8) enmity with the victim; (9) flight from the locale or jurisdiction; (10) personal or material benefit from the crime; (11) personal belongings or traces found at the site of the crime; (12) public clamor; (13) manifest lying during trial; (14) contradictory statements during trial; (15) distress and trembling; (16) silence or refusal to answer under questioning; (17) accusation by the victim, especially if the victim persists while dying (in homicides); (18) accusation by an accomplice to the crime; (19) attempt to compensate or come to terms with the victim of the crime; (20) foreknowledge of the crime, without divulging that knowledge to magistrates; (21) hiding or aiding any known authors of the crime; (22) insistence on informing against alleged authors of the crime, without having been summoned to do so; (23) preparing all things necessary for the crime to be committed; (24) being able to prevent the crime and not doing so;

---

[64] Serpillon, vol. 1, p. 468. "Du moment que le témoin est déclaré bon témoin, malgré sa parenté, sa déposition marche d'un pas égal à celle de tous les autres témoins, pour servir tant pour la conviction que pour l'absolution. . . . Le parant qui a été déclaré bon témoin est censé ne parler que le langage de la vérité, il ne peut être bon pour une partie de sa déposition, sans l'être pour le tout" (ibid., vol. 1, pp. 466–7).

[65] Ibid., p. 469.

[66] Ibid., pp. 461–2, and Rousseaud, p. 374.

[67] "Il arrive quelquefois dans une information respective que les preuves paroissent égales de part & d'autre; dans ce cas, l'usage est de peser les dépositions, c'est-à-dire, d'examiner la qualité & suffisance des témoins. Un homme en dignité, un Gentilhomme, un bon Bourgeois, & autres d'une fortune, d'un état distingué & d'une réputation connue fait plus de foi qu'un Laboureur, un artisan, ou un journalier" (Serpillon, vol. 1, p. 461).

(25) possession of goods from the crime; (26) facility to commit the crime, by reason of proximity to or cohabitation with the victim.[68] The absence of these indicators suggested innocence.

Testimony remained the primary source for such evidence.[69] Eighteenth-century jurists concurred that such evidence required careful evaluation and, at best, could establish only "conjectural," not indubitable, proof of guilt. *Indicia* that were numerous, concordant, and directly related both to the crime and the person of the defendant could establish proof sufficient for conviction and formal penalty. But such evidence alone, without testimony by one eyewitness or accomplice to the crime, was not deemed sufficient for the death penalty by most eighteenth-century jurists and many magistrates. Their conservatism will be illustrated by a murder case in Part IV. Conjectural proof would not wholly replace first-person authority and direct eyewitness testimony until the Revolution and the advent of decision by jury.

The ordinance expanded the range of evidence that could provide legal proof of guilt. As royal courts admitted the testimony of those previously excluded, they effected a silent political transformation, one that prefigured the democracy of voice in Revolutionary criminal law. For the purposes of justice and the rational ascertainment of guilt or innocence, sexual, familial and social hierarchies were temporarily leveled in courtrooms: Women were made the near-equals of men; children the near-equals of their parents; domestic servants the near-equals of their masters; apprentices and journeymen the near-equals of their employers. Even social pariahs were integrated to the royal community of testimony in criminal justice. This development contributed powerfully to rendering the *question préparatoire* obsolete. Liberal commentators and historians have been so fascinated by the barbarity and irrationality of judicial torture that they have not perceived the repressiveness inherent to the expansion of testimonial evidence and to the magnified role of *indicia.*

The repudiation of the *question préparatoire* by superior magistrates during the eighteenth-century signified an epistemological shift in judgment. It may be expressed as follows: In deciding the guilt or innocence of defendants we shall renounce the possibility of obtaining truth, first-person avowal of guilt, because the quest for that truth entails the far greater likelihood of obtaining falsity, first-person lying; for truth we shall substitute probability, the probability of

---

[68] Jousse, *Traité,* vol. 1, pp. 752–3. This work gives the most thorough exposition of evidence and rules of proof in post-1670 criminal jurisprudence; it agrees with the positions of Muyart, Serpillon, and most other eighteenth-century jurists, except on some points of detail.

[69] Thus the insistence on critical evaluation of testimony: "En effet, la déposition d'une témoin doit être claire, juste, précise, sans équivoque ni variation. Car si elle est concue en terms obsurs, & à double sens, ou si cette déposition est chancelante, & que le témoin soit lui-même en doute de ce qu'il déclare, cette incertitude & ces variations rendent sa déposition incertaine, & elle ne doit faire aucune impression dans l'espirit du Juge; toute la force d'une déposition consistante dans cette justesse & dans cette conformité qu'elle doit avoir avec la vraisemblance du fait; en telle sorte qu'en lui donnant un sens raisonable, elle ne puisse prouver aucun fait que celui dont il s'agit, ni avoir un double sens qui renferme quelque contrariété" (Jousse, *Traité,* vol. 1, p. 720).

guilt or of innocence that can be inferred from evidence. This epistemological shift made defendants objects of judgment. They ceased to be subjects of their own judicial truth and fate in capital cases. This was a greater victory for the state than for humanity.

Preliminary to execution

The *question préalable* against those condemned to death was used as a source of evidence against their accomplices, who were either in custody and on trial or at large; so also were the "death testaments," or final statements of the condemned at the site of execution. Those devices belonged both to criminal procedure and to the ritual of execution. (Their significance for the latter will be described in Volume 2.) Our concern here is with the *question préalable* and death testaments as elements of procedure, essentially as testimonial evidence.

When decreed, the *question préalable* followed immediately upon notification of the death sentence to the condemned person and immediately before the execution ritual. It was identical to the *question préparatoire* in form: water or leg braces; a long preliminary interrogation followed by a shorter interrogation under duress; a third and final interrogation on the mattress; attendance by a court physician; verbatim transcription of the entire proceeding; signing of the transcript by the condemned person, his judges, and the clerk. Judges could do this only once, as with the *question préparatoire*.[70]

According to the ordinance and subsequent jurisprudence, the *question préalable* was to be decreed only under the following conditions: The defendant had been convicted of a capital offense and sentenced to death in final judgment, either by a provostial court judging in last resort or by a Parlement on appeal; the crime probably involved accomplices; the condemned person had denied having accomplices, refused to identify them, or withheld information on their complicity during his trial.[71]

The last two of these conditions were frequently satisfied in the capital cases judged by the Châtelet and Parlement of Paris during the eighteenth century: Many capital offenses involved accomplices; most defendants systematically denied both personal guilt and accomplices. A defendant against whom there was compelling testimonial, material, circumstantial and/or character evidence of primary guilt in a capital offense was sentenced to death. The court of final judgment usually added the *question préalable* to its death sentence when strong but unavowed evidence of complicity had emerged during trial. If the condemned person denounced accomplices during the *question* or in his death testament at the site of execution, he thereby became a witness against those persons, and his denunciation could be used as evidence against them. That

---

[70] Ordinance, Title XIX, pp. 412–13.
[71] Ibid., Article 3, p. 412. And Jousse: "Elle ne doit jamais s'ordonner contre l'accusé lorsqu'il avoue & nomme ses complices, à moins qu'il ne paroisse par les preuves et circonstances du procès qu'il déguise la vérité, & qu'il a d'autres complices que ceux qu'il nomme" (*Traité*, vol. 2, p. 486).

testimony could be used to complete proof against those under accusation or to initiate prosecution of those at large. But without strong and independent supporting evidence, it could not result in conviction of those denounced. The *question préalable*, like the *question préparatoire*, accorded its subject the power to lie and conceal, and thus to confound judicial inquiry. However, eighteenth-century jurists and magistrates concurred on the utility, in principle, of the *question préalable*, as an important source of evidence in intricate cases with several defendants.[72] According to traditional doctrine, revelations by the condemned person during the *question préalable* or a death testament were to be given probative importance: The speaker was at the threshold of death, of damnation or salvation, and therefore at a moment of truth; to die in speaking lies was to expire in sin, not in penitence, and therefore to risk damnation. That doctrine was echoed in eighteenth-century jurisprudence.[73]

But there were important strictures on the conversion of such denunciations into evidence against alleged accomplices. To protect those denounced, the ordinance enjoined that they be brought for direct confrontation with the condemned person, just as in the confrontation period of a trial.[74] The Châtelet and Parlement of Paris did so scrupulously, if accomplices denounced under the *question* or in death testaments were in custody or could be arrested within the jurisdiction. The confrontations were held in rooms adjacent to the site of execution. The transcript of the denunciation by the condemned person served as *récolement* of his testimony. It was read aloud to those denounced, and each was invited to challenge or refute the allegations of complicity. The entire event was transcribed as if in a courtroom. The semipublic proceedings of death testaments and confrontations at the site of execution sometimes lasted for many hours and often meant that sentence of death was executed late in the night. Those who could not be arrested for confrontation within a reasonable time were given opportunity to challenge the deposition of the condemned person after his execution.[75]

Accounts of confrontations at eighteenth-century executions in Paris reveal that the majority of those denounced and arrested were released by officiating judges of the Châtelet or Parlement soon after confrontation; the majority of those against whom the incriminating testimony was retained were already on

---

[72] "Cette question est bien importante, car elle découvre souvent des complices & des associés pour voler, tuer ou assassiner; les condamnés au dernier supplice, qui voient qu'il n'y a plus d'espérance de sauver leur vie, & qu'il faut mourir, se laissent plus facilement convaincre par cette question, à parler & découvrir leurs complices & associés, que les accusés qui souffrent la question préparatoire" (Rousseaud, p. 422). Cf. Jousse, *Traité*, vol. 2, p. 476, and Serpillon, vol. 3, p. 924.

[73] "La raison est, qu'on ne peut pas présumer qu'un homme voulut mentir lorsqu'il ressent sur sa personne les effets de la colère de Dieu & des hommes, lorsqu'il voit audessus de sa tête la glaive foudroyante de la Justice, & qu'il se trouve prêt de comparoitre devant le Tribunal de celui qui est la Vérité & la Justice même" (Ferrière, vol. 2, p. 694). Cf. Jousse, *Traité*, vol. 1, p. 774.

[74] Ordinance, Title XIX, Article 4, p. 412.

[75] On the formalities of these confrontations, see Serpillon, vol. 3, pp. 924–6, and Jousse, *Traité*, vol. 2, pp. 494, 546, 554.

trial. Eighteenth-century jurists and magistrates regarded such denunciations with rational skepticism.

The statement made by a condemned person under torture against someone he accuses of complicity is not of itself strong evidence against that person, because the speaker has been declared infamous by the Judgment that condemned him to death; the statement can properly serve to cause the arrest of the alleged accomplice, especially if he is already suspect and of base condition. There are criminals who remain vengeful unto death. Thus, in cases where a condemned person accuses someone of respectable social condition and good reputation of complicity, one may arrest and confront that person, but the ordinance does not state that he must be arrested and jailed. That action depends on the charges emerging from the denunciation and confrontation, the verisimilitude of the allegations and responses, the condition, occupation and reputation of the alleged accomplice. Thus, according to the specific circumstances and the plausibility of the charges, the Judge can order arrest, summons to personal adjournment, or simple summons to appear; he can even refuse to order any decree against the denounced person.[76]

In fact, it often happens that the condemned denounce persons virtually unknown to them, with whom they have had no affiliations, from motives of despair, hatred, hope of postponing execution, or fear.[77]

Incriminating testimony by those condemned to death had to be coherent – precise, detailed, and without contradictions – and in accord with other evidence to complete proof of guilt against suspected or alleged accomplices or to warrant judgments of the *question préparatoire* against them.[78] In collective prosecutions, only when Châtelet and Parlement judges had already accumulated considerable evidence against a defendant did his sustained denunciation by one or more persons convicted of the crime lead to interlocutory or final penal judgments.

Very often we see that the condemned admit nothing under the *question préalable*, and that they speak and make revelations only when they are on the scaffold or at the gallows, at the very moment when they are to be executed. Is this from spite? Is it to prolong their lives for a little while, for a few hours at most? One can only imagine or conjecture the reasons.[79]

This was so in eighteenth-century Paris. The most common result obtained by the Tournelle of the Parlement from the *question préalable* was not revelation

---

[76] Serpillon, vol. 3, p. 925.   [77] Jousse, *Traité,* vol. 1, p. 775.

[78] Il [denunciation by a condemned person] ne sert à l'égard des complices que d'indice contr'eux, à l'efffet de les faire emprisonner. Cependant deux testamens de mort conformes contre une même personne forment un soupcon violent & peuvent, suivant les circonstances, suffire pour faire appliquer à la question, sur-tout quand il y a eu confrontation. . . . Quoi qu'il en soit, les testamens de mort ne font jamais une preuve complètte. . . . Ceux au contraire que leur mauvaise manoeuvre à réduits à finir leur vie en public par un supplice qu'ils ont mérité, ne respirent souvent que rage, que déséspoir, que fureur, & qu'un désir funeste d'en voir tomber d'autres en de semblables malheurs" (Ferrière, vol. 2, p. 695).

[79] Rousseaud, p. 422.

of accomplices. It was obstinate denial of both personal guilt and accomplices. The same general behavior among defendants that vitiated the *question préparatoire* was present in the *question préalable*. To illustrate this pattern, ten cases of the *question préalable* have been selected randomly from among the hundreds administered or authorized by the Parlement of Paris during the period 1750 to 1770.[80] The following were the names, ages, occupations, principal crimes, and dates of torture and execution for the ten: Pierre Bouvet, 31, journeyman wood-turner, burglaries with effraction, July 11, 1750; Didier Merelle, 27, former soldier, robbery and murder, August 31, 1750; Michel Houdé, 35, public letter writer, burglaries with effraction, February 19, 1751; Nicolas Porcher, 24, weaver, burglaries, October 4, 1754; Pierre Merienne, 32, tavern-keeper, burglary and armed robbery, February 29, 1762; Gilbert Laville, 34, farmer, arson, July 22, 1763; Jean Bouvier, 36, day laborer, burglaries with effraction, August 4, 1763; André Labbé, 19, apprentice rope-maker, burglaries with effraction, March 27, 1765; Pierre Normand, 36, edge-tool maker, burglaries with effraction, September 24, 1765. Like the majority of those convicted of capital crimes by the Parlement of Paris, they were young male plebeians. The exceptions were the letter writer and the tavern-keeper.

Each had been convicted of at least one capital offense; several were vehemently suspected of other crimes. The interrogations reveal that all but one had been convicted on the basis of testimonial, material, and circumstantial evidence; only Pierre Bouvet had been sentenced to the *question préparatoire*, and he had confessed. In each case, the interrogating judges knew the names of suspected accomplices and elements of their relations with the defendant. Several of those suspected were on trial. The judge's questions concerning accomplices were nominative, detailed, and reiterative. The preliminary or first interrogation of the *question* was the most lengthy in each case; judges inquired about the culpability of the condemned person, the material execution of the crime(s), then the identities and actions of accomplices. The convicted person was then put in leg braces, and eight wedges were used. One, at the most two, short and precise questions were asked after each wedge was placed; most had been asked at least once and in greater detail during the first interrogation. Actual duress was brief in the ten cases, from thirty minutes to one hour. Only when there had been avowals or denunciations was there a third interrogation on the mattress.

Five of the ten denied all personal guilt and refused to incriminate anyone. Two admitted to the crimes and denounced accomplices during the first interrogation and then simply repeated under torture; one of them, Pierre Bouvet, had confessed much earlier in the *question préparatoire*. One admitted to partial guilt and denounced an accomplice who was already on trial; he did so from the beginning of the first interrogation. Only two of the ten admitted personal guilt under duress, after having denied during first interrogation, but only one de-

---

[80] The transcripts are in A.N.X2b 1334.

nounced an accomplice. Both began confession at the third wedge. In four of the ten cases the *question préalable* resulted in denunciation of at least one accomplice, but in only one of the ten cases did torture produce a denunciation. Even when magistrates succeeded in extracting personal confessions during the *question préalable*, that success did not necessarily lead to any information on accomplices.

The magistrates of the Châtelet and Parlement had almost discontinued the *question préparatoire* by 1750. They continued to utilize the *question préalable* until its abolition by royal decree in May 1788. At least one-half of capital crimes prosecuted during the years 1775 to 1789 involved more than one malefactor, and there was always the possibility of obtaining information on accomplices from the *question préalable*, information that could be of probative value when compared with other evidence. But this does not seem to have been the exclusive reason for the longevity of the practice.

There was a standard strategy or technique of interrogation in the *question préalable* inflicted by the Châtelet and Parlement of Paris during the eighteenth century. During the first interrogation, the subject was repeatedly asked about his personal culpability, a questioning seemingly intended to reconstruct his guilt for him and thereby to elicit confession. Only after such questioning at length did magistrates interrogate on accomplices, while frequently shifting back to elements of personal guilt. Questions on material details of the crime were woven into these two phases of questioning. Judges strove to present such a persuasive case for the existence, often the identities and explicit actions, of accomplices that the subject would be led to reveal and confirm their roles. In five of the ten cases analyzed, the strategy produced only systematic denial – of guilt and accomplices.

By this strategy, magistrates made the *question préalable* into a partial avatar of the archaic *question préparatoire*. That fact probably contributed to the relative futility of the *question préalable* as a source of information on accomplices. By concentrating on the primary guilt of the subject, by urging him to confess that guilt during most of the proceeding, magistrates provoked him to continue his stubborn denials of guilt during trial and judgment. By reactivating that resistance, they disposed him to deny any and all accomplices. Such insistence on obtaining confession of personal guilt was all the more peculiar since he was already convicted on the basis of compelling evidence. His confession or denial of guilt in the *question préalable* could have no legal import for his case, for neither action could alter the judgment against him and his imminent fate. But the issue was probably of moral import to magistrates. When judges pressured condemned persons to confess guilt in the *question préalable*, they were urging them to validate the magistrates' own judgments, to validate the death sentences they had pronounced. Their need for such avowals was also an avatar to the old idea of confession as the queen of proof. Those condemned to death, most of whom had been self-defensively defiant from the outset of trial, could have perceived that magisterial need in the long preliminary interrogation of the *question préa-*

lable. Most commonly, they refused to give their judges any such reassurance and, by extension of that attitude, to reveal accomplices.

As will be demonstrated in Volume 2, persons condemned to death by the Châtelet and Parlement of Paris frequently reversed themselves in the presence of the gallows or the scaffold. Many who had denied guilt and accomplices during the *question préalable* admitted and named both in death testaments at the site of execution. At that moment and place, the strongest pressure on them was spiritual, not magisterial. They were under the ministrations of the priest and confronted with Pascal's Wager. When they did speak, they gave judges raw testimony that had to be refined by comparison with other evidence against suspected accomplices.

15

Definitive judgment

Interlocutory judgments of *plus amplement informé* or the *question préparatoire* were decreed in a minority of trials by most subaltern courts within the jurisdiction of the Parlement of Paris, although the Châtelet used the former judgment extensively. Subaltern court judges usually proceeded directly to definitive judgment after trial review.

Definitive judgment was the most important judicial act in Old Regime criminal justice. It is also an act whose mechanics have received little study from modern historians. It occurred in two stages for defendants accused of crimes subject to defaming, afflictive, or capital penalties, unless they were judged by provostial or presidial courts in last resort: judgment by the subaltern court that tried the case; final judgment, on appeal, by the Parlement of the jurisdiction. The ordinance required that judges give priority to definitive judgment of criminal cases over all other matters pending and that their deliberations begin in the morning and continue until they reached a verdict.[1] The process was identical, in both instances: final statement by the defendant; prosecutor's conclusions and recommendation of sentence; summary of the case and recommendation of sentence by the reporting judge (often the criminal lieutenant, who had also instructed the case in part or in full); opining, or voting, on sentence by each of the other judges.

Definitive judgment in a subaltern court had to be by a minimum of three judges. Appellate judgments by a Parlement had to be by a minimum of seven. That was also the number of judges required in provostial and presidial cases that were not subject to appeal.[2] During the eighteenth century, each case judged on appeal in the Tournelle of the Parlement of Paris was decided by a panel of at least ten judges. That number is only two less than a modern American criminal jury.

There were various forms of acquittal. *Absolution* nullified all charges against the defendant and thus declared his complete innocence. That verdict was announced publicly by court criers, and a line was drawn through the defendant's

---

[1] Ordinance, Title XXV, Articles 1 and 9, pp. 416–17.
[2] Ibid., Articles 10–11, p. 417.

name on the jail register, as if he had never been there. He could sue for damages against the plaintiff. Absolution was rare. *Renvoi hors de cour* or *mis hors de cour* (dismissal of the case) was more common. It meant that there was not sufficient evidence to form a conviction, or to decree either *plus amplement informé* or the *question* (in capital cases), but there remained some specific evidence of criminal involvement. Because of that evidence, the defendant could not cogently be absolved of charges. Prosecution ceased and he was freed, but under the stigma of lingering suspicion. He could not sue for damages.

Conviction required sentence to a specific penalty in law. Conviction by a Parlement on appeal of original sentence required sentence to a specific penalty and execution of that penalty within the shortest possible time, unless royal pardon or commutation was granted. There were no "suspended sentences" in Old Regime criminal law, except for pregnant women sentenced to death. In apportioning penalties to crimes and criminals, judges were to observe the letter or spirit of royal criminal statutes, most of which allowed some choice in penalty. That statutory law was very ample by the early eighteenth century. When statutes were silent, judges were to respect the penology customary within the jurisdiction. In judgment of a case, there was no separate decision on guilt or innocence. Judges who concluded either for innocence or against conviction opined for some form of acquittal or for *plus amplement informé*. Those who concluded for guilt opined for a specific penalty.

The ordinance required that all sentences by subaltern courts (except in provostial cases) to afflictive, corporal, or capital penalties or to the *question préparatoire* be judged on appeal and with finality by Parlements. This *appel de droit* required no action by those who had been convicted; it was mandatory and automatic. Defendants sentenced to lesser penalties could appeal either to Parlements or to their local royal bailliage court if they had been tried by a seigneurial court.[3] Provostial judgments were subject to final appellate judgment, if the provostial court was in a city that was the seat of a Parlement. Prosecutors and civil parties in subaltern courts could appeal *a minima* against acquittals and penalties they considered too mild; in those cases, final judgment was also by Parlements.[4] Sentences rendered by subaltern courts in all of the cases just described could not be executed unless they were confirmed by Parlements.[5]

The 1670 ordinance, code of the classical monarchy, made judgment of criminal defendants funnel upward to final decision by the Tournelles of Parlements, by magistrates at the summit of the themistocratic hierarchy. Neither Revolutionary justice nor Napoleonic and post-Napoleonic justice would guarantee the convicted such systemic protection against punishment by those who had tried and judged them in the locality of the crime.

[3] Ordinance, Title XXVI, Articles 1 and 6, pp. 419–20.
[4] Ibid., Articles 11 and 13, pp. 420–1.
[5] The most detailed description of appeals procedure after 1670 is by Serpillon, vol. 3, pp. 1138–1201.

At state expense, a complete transcript of the original trial and judgment, along with all defendants in the case, were transported to the Parlement of the jurisdiction for review, hearing, and final judgment.[6] This was the principal activity of the judges who served by rotation in the Tournelles of France. *Parlementaires* were in no way bound to the original judgments or to the recommendations *a minima* of prosecutors. They had complete independence of review and decision: They could acquit those found guilty, convict those acquitted, and ameliorate or aggravate original penalties. They had the authority to censure subaltern courts and to order re-trials, along with the responsibility to recommend to the Chancellor that lower-court magistrates be fined or suspended if they violated procedural rules. Criminal jurisprudence and the politics of penology were thus centered on Parlements and other sovereign courts. Their appellate decisions were overseen by the Chancellor and the royal Council. By endowing Parlements with supreme responsibility for most judgments and punishments, the ordinance also endowed them with potential for creativity in criminal justice.

The ordinance stated the boundaries within which penal judgment had to be exercised. The official hierarchy in severity of the major penalties was set forth in Article 13 of Title XXV:

After the death penalty, the most severe is that of the *question* with retention of evidence, followed by galleys for life, banishment for life, the *question* without retention of evidence, galleys for terms, whipping, *amende honorable*, banishment for terms.[7]

Article 12 of Title XXV stated the rule for decision in criminal judgment:

Judgments, whether definitive or interlocutory, will be according to the most benign opinion stated, if the most severe opinion stated does not prevail by a majority of one voice in cases subject to appeal, or if it does not prevail by a majority of two voices with cases judged in last resort or on appeal.[8]

This meant that when a defendant was judged by a subaltern court, whose verdict was subject to appeal, for the most severe sentence opined to prevail (e.g., conviction and penalty instead of acquittal, the *question* as against *plus amplement informé*, death as against galleys for life) that opinion had to be voted by a majority of one in the panel of judges. Otherwise, the most benign verdict or penalty opined among them would prevail automatically. When judgment was final, by a Parlement on appeal or a provostial court without appeal, for the most severe sentence opined to prevail that sentence had to be voted by a majority of two: five of seven, six of eight, six of nine, or seven of ten judges. Otherwise, the most benign sentence opined among them would automatically become the judgment. This rule was an innovation. Coupled with *appel de droit*, it was one of the most consequential provisions of the ordinance.

---

[6] Ordinance, Title XXVI, Articles 6–14, pp. 420–1.
[7] Ibid., p. 417.   [8] Ibid.

Article 12 meant, in practice, that if there was not strong consensus on guilt among judges in a case or on penalty in that case, within the discretionary range of penalties applicable to the crime, the defendant would be acquitted, or he would receive a benign penalty. It made convictions difficult when significant doubt remained in the mind of a few judges. It made the death penalty rare among the aggregate of offenders convicted of capital crimes, for most of those crimes could also be punished by life or long terms in the galleys or *hôpitaux* or by *plus amplement informé* with prison. The authors of the ordinance presumed dissention on penalty among judges and subtly encouraged dissention by Article 12. The presumption accorded with fundamental jurisprudence: All cases were potentially individual, not generic, and required individuation of penalty, for they had varieties of defendants and of aggravating or ameliorating characteristics. Article 12 determined simultaneously how dissention would be expressed and how it would be resolved in criminal chambers.

If there were three or more opinions on sentence voiced on the bench of judges, they were reduced to two "categorical" opinions. In the second round of voting, all judges were obliged to choose one of those two. If the most severe of the two opinions was embraced by a majority of one (in a subaltern court subject to appellate decision) or by a majority of two (in a sovereign court or a provostial case), it automatically became the judgment in the case. Otherwise, the least severe of the two categorical opinions automatically became the judgment.

The reduction or narrowing of several opinions to two was accomplished by a strict procedure. Those opinions that received the least votes in the first round of judgment were discarded as options, and the judges who held them were obliged to "default" to one of the two opinions that received the most votes. The order of opining among judges remained the same in the second or third round as in the first; the practice in the Tournelle of the Parlement of Paris was for judges to opine in fixed order of seniority, after the reporting judge: the most junior *parlementaire* first; the most senior last. In a second round, the reporting judge, as the first to opine, had to default first if his opinion was either the most minoritarian of three or more opinions voiced or if his default was required to break deadlock. In their turn, each of the other judges whose opinions were most minoritarian were also obliged to default to one of the two most majoritarian opinions. As the records of judgment by the criminal chamber of the Châtelet reveal, when judges defaulted they did so usually to the possible opinion that was closest to their original opinion in the hierarchy of severity. The result was always the same, no matter how many opinions were voiced initially or how many rounds occurred: two opinions on sentence. The least severe automatically became the final, executed judgment in the case, if the most severe had not received a majority of two votes.[9] "The reason [for this rule] is humaneness, which is natural to humankind."[10]

[9] On the procedure, see Rousseaud, p. 456; Serpillon, vol. 3, pp. 1067–8; Amiot, vol. 1, pp. 87–8.
[10] Ferrière, vol. 2, p. 296.

Definitive judgment

To illustrate the mechanics of final judgment by seven judges in the Tournelle of a Parlement or in a provostial court, one may project a hypothetical offender whom all seven judges considered either certainly or probably guilty and whose crime was subject to one of the following penalties: (1) death; (2) galleys for life; (3) galleys for nine years; (4) *plus amplement informé* with one year imprisonment. The reporting judge always opined first.

Scenario 1: (three penalties are opined)

First vote

Judges   Penalties opined

1	Galleys, life
2	Death
3	Death
4	Galleys, life
5	Galleys, nine years
6	Galleys, nine years
7	Death

The reporting judge must default. His opinion is minoritarian, and its number of voices is equaled by the number of voices for galleys, nine years. In consequence, the fourth judge must also default.

Second vote

1	Death
2	Death
3	Death
4	Galleys, nine years
5	Galleys, nine years
6	Galleys, nine years
7	Death

The judgment is galleys for nine years.

Scenario 2: (four penalties are opined)

First vote

1	Death
2	Death
3	Galleys, life
4	Galleys, life
5	Galleys, nine years
6	Galleys, nine years
7	P. a. i.

The dissention is extreme. The reporting judge is obliged to default. His opinion is not in smallest majority, but it is equaled by two other opinions, and there is deadlock. The second and seventh judges must also default.

Trial and judgment

Second vote

1	Galleys, life
2	Galleys, life
3	Galleys, life
4	Galleys, life
5	Galleys, nine years
6	Galleys, nine years
7	Galleys, nine years

The judgment is galleys for nine years.

Scenario 3: (four penalties are opined)

First vote

1	Death
2	Death
3	Death
4	P. a. i.
5	Galleys, life
6	Galleys, nine years
7	P. a. i.

The fifth and sixth judges must default.

Second vote

1	Death
2	Death
3	Death
4	P. a. i.
5	Galleys, life
6	P. a. i.
7	P. a. i.

The judgment is *plus amplement informé*.

Scenario 4: (three penalties are opined)

First vote

1	Galleys, life
2	Death
3	Galleys, life
4	Death
5	Death
6	Galleys, nine years
7	Galleys, nine years

The reporting judge and the third judge must default.

Second vote

1	Death
2	Death

3	Galleys, nine
4	Death
5	Death
6	Galleys, nine
7	Galleys, nine

The judgment is galleys for nine years.

Such a hypothetical case was common in the Tournelle of the Parlement of Paris: burglaries without violence; thefts of sacred objects from churches; assaults in the course of riots; complicities in deadly violence. Simple logic leads to the conclusion that the combination of at least seven judges, four possible penalties, the default rules, and the requirement that the most severe opinion receive five votes to become the judgment would dictate a very low incidence of death sentences, a low incidence of galleys for life, and high incidence of galleys for nine years and *plus amplement informé* with prison. It also leads to the conclusion that when three judges (in original judgment) decided among the same four penalties, with two votes required for the most severe penalty to prevail, there would be higher incidence of death and galleys for life and lower incidence of galleys for nine years and *plus amplement informé* than in Tournelle. But how high and how low at both levels of judgment?

To answer that question with mathematical accuracy, Roger Blumberg of the Columbia University Heyman Center for the Humanities has constructed a model for predicting the outcomes of judgment on our hypothetical case. The model incorporates the rules for penal decision in the 1670 ordinance and its jurisprudence. It reveals the fundamental tendencies of decision in all cases that were subject to penal discretion after 1670. (See the appendix to Part III.)

The model demonstrates that when our hypothetical case was decided by seven judges either provostially or on appeal, the probability for severe outcome (death) was 4 to 11 percent, for moderate outcomes (galleys for life or for nine years) respectively 23 to 24 percent and 33 to 37 percent, for most benign outcome (*plus amplement informé*) 33 to 35 percent. It demonstrates that the rules for penal decision promoted highest incidence of sentences that were lenient and a close secondary incidence of sentences that were moderate within the hierarchy of sentencing options available. Those rules systematically limited, and almost precluded, outcomes of maximum severity. The model also reveals that even when division on penal options among seven judges was minimal (only two sentences opined) the great probability was that the most benign of the two would prevail. When division was more extensive, the probability of moderate and lenient outcomes increased dramatically. But in lower courts, with a minimum of three judges and a one-vote majority for the most severe sentence, the rules for decision had different consequences. They were not biased to moderation or leniency. They created a near equality of chance between severe, median, and lenient sentences.

From 1670 to 1790, decisive judgment of most cases in *grand criminel* was by Tournelle. Their judgments formed the punitive reality of Old Regime criminal justice. It is impossible to describe this system of judgment as repressive of defendants, if by repressive one means a bias to punish and, within that bias, to punish severely.

Article 12 of Title XXV rarefied the death penalty in final judgment. The authors of the ordinance were experienced magistrates, and they surely intended that result. For there to have been high incidence of the death penalty in Parlements after 1670, there would have had to be both high incidence of capital offenses and a durable consensus on severity among five of seven, six of eight, or seven of ten judges. Dissention among judges over discretionary capital offenses made statistically low incidence of the death penalty inevitable. Article 12 was dynamic. It subtly promoted evolution from severe to median punishments within the hierarchy of penalties. The rules for decision were elastic, in the sense that they accommodated long-term changes in penal behavior among judges. They did not absolutely ensure benign outcomes irrespective of magisterial opinions, but they did predispose judges in Parlements to moderation and thereby rendered them susceptible to public or intellectual pressures in that direction. The changes in capital punishment that began during the final decade of the Old Regime occurred within the matrix of this system and, in a sense, as a subtle product of the system. Finally, the effects of Article 12 were global. They favored the interests of defendants in final judgment and deescalated all punishments in the hierarchy of penalties. Article 12 governed decision by a Tournelle on a simple case of public theft – a crime that could be punished by a short term in the galleys or *hôpital*, by a term of banishment, or by whipping and the iron collar – just as on a capital offense.

The galleys (until 1748), the *bagnes* (after 1748), and the *hôpital-général* were the main carceral penalties. Those royal institutions were the penalties applicable to the largest range of crimes during the eighteenth century. Most cases of theft, fraud, sedition, and violence could be sanctioned by them as well as by other penalties either more or less severe. Only banishment rivaled, but did not equal, those carceral penalties in its range of applicability. By the statutory and customary apportionment of penalties to crimes, carceral penalties were either maximal, median, or least severe for approximately 70 percent of all *grand criminel* offenses tried by subaltern and sovereign courts. Close to one-fifth of those judged on appeal by Parlements during the eighteenth century had been found guilty of capital offenses by subaltern courts, and for most of those offenses the galleys or *hôpital* were discretionary penalties. The hierarchy of penalties set forth in Article 13, Title XXV was minimalist. The actual hierarchy of penalties used was as follows, from most benign to most severe: alms; warning; interdiction or suspension from office or commission; whipping in custody of the court (for minors); fines; severe reprimand; forced witnessing of punishment (usually the death sentence); promenading on a donkey; banishment from the jurisdiction for three, five, or nine years; *plus amplement informé* for terms at liberty; exhibition in the iron collar or in the stocks; public and abject apology; suspension from the gallows by chest strap (for minors); public whipping; public branding; *plus amplement informé* for terms in prison; galleys for three, five, or nine years, and the *hôpital* for three, five, or nine years; interrogative torture without reserve of evidence; public dragging of the felon's corpse on a frame and condemnation of his memory; banishment for life; galleys or *hôpital* for life; interrogative torture with reserve of evidence; death, by decapitation, hanging, breaking, burning. Most crimes prosecuted in *grand criminel* were punishable by one or more of at least two of these penalties, according to the particulars of the case. Incarcerations for three, five, or nine years were the median penalties in both the official and actual scales of punishment.

Let us compare predicted outcomes of judgment with actual outcomes in eighteenth-century subaltern and sovereign courts, bearing in mind that only those sentences of acquittal against which subaltern court prosecutors appealed *a minima* were heard and decided by Parlements and that, in consequence, the number of acquittals reviewed by Parlements was inferior to their actual number in subaltern courts. For the Parlement of Paris and its subaltern courts, two calendar years separated by five decades have been selected: 1736 and 1787. Those years differed in only two significant legal respects: the *question préparatoire* was no longer a sentencing option after 1780; 1787 belonged to the period in which the Parlement of Paris both diminished the death penalty and redirected its application. In comparing those two years, our concern is with the specific relations between sentencing by subaltern courts, with few judges and a majority of one required for most severe sentence, and by the Parlement, with ten judges and a majority of two required for most severe sentence – despite the distance of more than fifty years. Tables 15.1 and 15.2 have been constructed from Inventory 450. The numerical surplus of the total of persons judged by the Tournelle over the total judged by subaltern courts – thirty-six in 1736 and fifty-four in 1787 – expresses cases that had been judged by subaltern courts during the preceding year or that were judged in first and final instance by the Parlement.

The judgments by the Tournelle were generally harmonious with those by the Châtelet in 1736 and 1787. The majority of Châtelet sentences were to median penalties – banishment or incarcerations for three and five years and *plus amplement informé* with prison terms. Those were 50.4 percent of the total judgments appealed in 1736 and 68.4 percent in 1787. In the Tournelle, they were respectively 50 percent in 1736 and 59.9 percent in 1787. The incidence of severe penalties in the Châtelet – galleys or the *hôpital* for life, death – was low in 1736 and 1787, and comparable to that in the Tournelle during both years. In 1736, the Parlement confirmed 51 percent of judgments by the Châtelet, ameliorated 41.7 percent, and aggravated only 7.7 percent. In 1787, the percentages were respectively 48.6, 30.2, and 21. During both years, the majority of ameliorations were either within the same category of penalty or to the nearest category below the original: reduction of banishment from nine or five years to five or three years; of galleys from five years to three or to banishment for

Table 15.1. Sentences by Parlement of Paris and its subaltern courts, 1736

Sentences	Provincial courts (183)		Châtelet (111)		Parlement (330)	
	Number	%	Number	%	Number	%
Final judgment						
Nullity of procedure	0	0	0	0	11	3.3
Hors cour or dismissal of charges	12	6.5	0	0	70	21.2
Injunction, admonition	5	2.7	0	0	14	4.2
Blâme	7	3.8	1	0.9	7	2.1
Fine or alms (only)	0	0	0	0	1	0.3
Whipping (principal)	4	2.1	0	0	1	0.3
Carcan (principal)	0	0	0	0	1	0.3
Pillory (principal)	0	0	0	0	1	0.3
Banishment, 3 years	13	7.1 ⎫	17	15.3 ⎫	38	11.5 ⎫
Banishment, 5 years	13	7.1 ⎬ 35.7	14	12.6 ⎬ 32.4	29	8.7 ⎬ 25.6
Banishment, 9 years	23	12.5 ⎥	4	3.6 ⎥	17	5.1 ⎥
Banishment, life	18	9.8 ⎭	1	0.9 ⎭	1	0.3 ⎭
Galères, 3 years	7	3.8 ⎫	7	6.3 ⎫	15	4.5 ⎫
Galères, 5 years	4	2.1 ⎬ 16.6	6	5.4 ⎬ 18.9	7	2.1 ⎬ 10.5
Galères, 9 years	10	5.4 ⎥	2	1.8 ⎥	8	2.4 ⎥
Galères, life	7	3.8 ⎭	1	0.9 ⎭	1	0.3 ⎭
Hôp. gen., 3 years	2	1	3	2.7	1	0.3
Hôp. gen., 5 years	0	0	0	0	3	0.9
Hôp. gen., 9 years	0	0	2	1.8	0	0
Hôp. gen., life	1	0.5	0	0	0	0
Insane, hôp. gen. or prison	0	0	0	0	4	1.2
Detention, juveniles	0	0	1	0.9	4	1.2

	Provincial No.	Provincial %	Châtelet No.	Châtelet %	Parlement No.	Parlement %
Hanging	23	12.5	3	2.7	14	4.2
Wheel	4	2.1	3	2.7	4	1.2
Burning	0	0	0	0	0	0
Decapitation	0	0	0	0	0	0
Witness (*assisté*) execution	1	0.5	0	0	0	0
Interlocutory judgment						
Question préparatoire	20	10.9	3	2.7	4	1.2
P.a.i. without prison						
No period specified	0	0	5	4.5	1	0.3
1 month	1	0.5	0	0	0	0
3 months	0	0	3	2.7	5	1.5
6 months	2	1.0	20	18.8	11	3.3
1 year	0	0	0	0	5	1.5
P.a.i. with prison						
3 months	2	1.0	3	2.7	13	3.9
6 months	2	1.0	3	2.7	12	3.6
1 year	1	0.5	4	3.6	23	6.9
P.a.i. indefinite (at liberty)	0	0	0	0	5	1.5
Indeterminant sentences	0		5		0	0

Grouped percentage totals (indicated by braces):
- Hanging–Decapitation: Provincial 14.6; Châtelet 5.4; Parlement 5.4
- P.a.i. without prison (1 month–1 year for Provincial; No period–1 year for Châtelet; 1 month–1 year for Parlement): Provincial 1.5; Châtelet 26; Parlement 6.3
- P.a.i. with prison (3 months–1 year): Provincial 2.5; Châtelet 9; Parlement 14.4

Abbreviation: p.a.i. – plus amplement informé

On Tables 15.1 and 15.2, columns 2 and 3 show the number of sentences in the provincial courts to specific penalties, in ascending order of severity, with the percentage that each number represented of the total of persons judged by those courts during the year (excepting provostial cases). Columns 4 and 5 give the same information for the Châtelet. Under the heading "Parlement," columns 6 and 7 give the number of sentences to those penalties and their percentage among the total judgments rendered by the Parlement on appeal of lower court sentences. This last was the final outcome or penalties executed. Interlocutory judgments of the *question préparatoire* and *plus amplement informé* have been listed at the end of the tables.

Source: A.N. Inventory 450, vols. III–IV.

Table 15.2. *Sentences by Parlement of Paris and its subaltern courts, 1787*

Sentences	Provincial courts (538)		Châtelet (152)		Parlement (744)	
	N	%	N	%	N	%
Final judgment						
Nullity of procedure	0	0	0	0	6	0.8
Hors cour or dismissal of charges	34	6.3	2	1.3	72	9.6
Injunction, admonition	6	1.1	5	3.2	30	4.0
blâme	8	1.4	0	0	3	0.4
Fine or alms (only)	0	0	0	0	0	0
Whipping (principal)	9	1.6	13	8.5	16	2.1
Carcan (principal)	9	1.6	1	0.6	2	0.2
Pillory (principal)	0	0	0	0	0	0
Banishment, 3 years	67	12.4	14	9.2	63	8.4
Banishment, 5 years	25	4.6	19	12.5	34	4.5
Banishment, 9 years	23	4.2	10	6.5	22	2.9
Banishment, life	4	0.7	0	0	0	0
		} 21.9		} 28.2		} 15.8
Bagnes, 3 years	65	12.0	15	9.8	86	11.5
Bagnes, 5 years	43	7.9	8	5.2	28	3.7
Bagnes, 9 years	48	8.9	11	7.2	49	6.5
Bagnes, life	48	8.9	4	2.6	37	4.9
		} 44.4		} 27.9		} 31.1
Hôp. gen., 3 years	10	1.8	1	0.6	11	1.4
Hôp. gen., 5 years	10	1.8	1	0.6	7	0.9
Hôp. gen., 9 years	7	1.3	3	1.9	13	1.7
Hôp. gen., life	10	1.8	0	0	4	0.5
Insane, hôp. gen. or prison	0	0	0	0	10	1.3
Detention, juveniles	1	0.1	4	2.6	18	2.4

Hanging	32	5.9	⎫ 8	4	2.6 ⎫	3	0.4 ⎫ 1
Wheel	11	2.	⎬	2	1.3ª ⎬ 3.9	5ᵇ	0.6 ⎬
Burning	1	0.1	⎬	0	0	0	0
Decapitation	0	0	⎭	0	0	0	0
Witness (*assisté*) execution	5	0.9		0	0	2	0.2
Interlocutory judgment							
P.a.i. without prison							
No period specified	0	0	⎫	0	0	0	0 ⎫
1 month	1	0.1	⎬ 2.2	0	0	0	0 ⎬
3 months	1	0.1	⎬	3	1.9 ⎫ 6.4	16	2.1 ⎬ 11.2
6 months	4	0.7	⎬	4	2.6 ⎬	59	7.9 ⎬
1 year	7	1.3	⎭	3	1.9 ⎭	9	1.2 ⎭
P.a.i. with prison							
1 month	0	0	⎫	0	0	0	0 ⎫
3 months	2	0.3	⎬ 8.9	3	1.9	8	1.0 ⎬ 16.9
6 months	17	3.1	⎬	15	9.8 ⎫ 14.9	69	9.2 ⎬
1 year	30	5.5	⎭	5	3.2 ⎭	47	6.3 ⎬
notte	0	0		0	0	3	0.4 ⎬
Indefinite at liberty (as initial sentence)	0	0		0	0	1	0.1 ⎭

ª In addition to these six death sentences that were judged on appeal by the Parlement, the Châtelet rendered two provostial death sentences that were not subject to appeal; both were breakings of armed highway robbers.

ᵇ An additional 8 persons were given the death sentence by the Parlement but received royal pardon or commutation of sentence.

A.N. Inventory 450, vols, III–IV.

terms; conversions of *plus amplement informé* with prison terms to the same at liberty. The aggravations were similar: extending terms of *plus amplement informé*, converting terms of banishment to terms in the galleys or *hôpital*, increasing the terms of incarcerations. In 1736, the Tournelle confirmed five of the six death sentences rendered by the Châtelet; in 1787, it confirmed three of six. This relative harmony in judgment between the Châtelet and Parlement constrasted dramatically with the dissonance between the Tournelle and provincial subaltern courts.

Theoretically, penal judgments by the Châtelet should have resembled those by other subaltern courts, not the penology of the Parlement. On the Châtelet bench, only a one-vote majority was required for the most severe sentence opined to prevail. But the Châtelet had a large bench in the criminal chamber. During regular sessions, most cases were judged by eight to twelve judges; during judicial vacations they were judged by five to eight. The registers of judgment reveal that in cases subject to afflictive or capital penalties there were frequently at least three opinions stated among more than eight judges in the initial voting; often, one of those opinions was *plus amplement informé*. The likelihood of the most severe among three or four opinions surviving the reduction to two, and then obtaining even a one-vote majority, was low. In practice, more judges meant greater dissention in judgment; dissention meant high probability of moderate and benign outcomes. Its size, combined with the rules for judgment, caused the Châtelet to resemble the Tournelle, causes that existed independently of the socioprofessional affinities between the two companies of magistrates.

Decisions by the Tournelle almost systematically deescalated decisions by provincial courts in 1736 and 1787. In the column for provincial courts (Tables 15.1, 15.2), if one reads up the hierarchy of penalties from most benign to most severe, and up the hierarchy in interlocutory judgments, the numbers rise cumulatively in a progression of harshness. Most of those courts had three to six judges, and their tendency was to near-maximal severity with most cases. The great exception was the distribution of sentences to banishment in 1787. Yet in that year, provincial courts sentenced almost as many persons to the *bagnes* and *hôpitaux* for nine years or life as they did for three or five years. Many of those persons were not convicted of offenses subject to the death penalty. The reverse obtained in the Tournelle. The numbers decline as one reads up the hierarchy of penalties. In 1787, the large number of sentences to nine years or life in the *bagnes* and to *plus amplement informé* with one year of imprisonment was meliorative, for those sentences were the main reason for the 1 percent of death sentences pronounced by the Parlement.

In 1736, the Tournelle confirmed 27.3 percent of judgments by provincial courts, ameliorated 61.2 percent, and aggravated 11.4 percent. The proportions were similar in 1787: 27.1 percent confirmed; 52.6 percent ameliorated; 20.2 percent aggravated. In 1736 and 1787, the majority of judgments confirmed were acquittals; banishments for three, five, or nine years; sentences to *plus am-*

plement informé; and galleys or *hôpital* for three or five years. Ameliorations were across the entire hierarchy of penalties, but most numerous at its upper tiers: reductions of death to incarceration or *plus amplement informé* (usually with prison); of incarceration for life or nine years to five or three years or to banishment for terms. In 1787, aggravations of original sentences were overwhelmingly within the lower ranges in the hierarchy of penalties: iron collar and reprimand to banishment for terms; banishment to *plus amplement informé* (often with prison for three or six months) or to the galleys or *hôpital* for three or five years. Only 8 of 109 aggravations in 1787 were to severe afflictive or capital penalties.

The systemic differences between judgment by provincial courts and judgment by the Tournelle were most dramatic with offenders subject to the death sanction. They are expressed by Tables 15.3 and 15.4.

Ten of the eleven death sentences confirmed by the Tournelle in 1736 were for premeditated or intentional murder, a crime for which the death sentence was mandatory by royal statute. The other, domestic theft, was a mandatory death offense by the royal Declaration on Theft of March 1724. Eleven of these 27 cases concerned offenses for which the death penalty was discretionary. These offenses were of the type that were decided by the rules of penal judgment that have been described and modeled mathematically. If one excepts the cases pardoned or given verdict of insanity, the outcomes on the other 9 were as follows: (1) death: 2, or 22 percent; (2) the *question:* 1, or 11 percent; (3) galleys: 3, or 33 percent; (4) *plus amplement informé:* 3, or 33 percent.

In 1787, provincial courts (including the bailliage of the Parlement) rendered forty-three death sentences (see Table 15.4). The Tournelle confirmed only five, ameliorated thirty-eight (including five insanity verdicts and five endorsements of royal pardons). All of those confirmed were for murder or infanticide, statutory death offenses. Twenty-two of the forty-three cases were discretionary capital offenses. Domestic theft is included in that number, for by 1787 the Parlement was treating that crime as a discretionary, not mandatory, death offense. Penal outcomes in the Tournelle on the twenty-two cases were as follows: (1) death, 0; (2) *bagne* or *hôpital* for life, 4, or 18.2 percent; (3) *bagne* or *hôpital* for terms, 13, or 59 percent; (4) *plus amplement informé*, 5, or 22.7 percent.

Provincial courts sentenced 14.6 percent of those whom they found guilty to death in 1736; the Tournelle passed the death sentence against 6 percent of that total. In 1787, the percentages were respectively 8 percent and 1 percent. In 1787, some 60 percent of death sentences by provincial courts were still for nonviolent crimes, mostly thefts. In 1736 and 1787, the Parlement ordered the death sanction almost exclusively for blood crimes, most of which were statutory death offenses, and only when the guilt and sanity of the defendant were indubitable. The reason was not essentially humanitarian: The rules for penal decision made the death penalty extremely difficult to obtain in appellate judgment of all cases subject to penal discretion. It was not difficult to obtain by a majority vote of one on a bench of three to five judges.

Table 15.3. *Appellate decisions by Parlement of Paris on death sentences pronounced by lower courts, 1736*

Lower Court	Death sentence / crime	Parlement of Paris
Soissons	Domestic theft	Confirmed
Bougé	Murder	Confirmed
Fontenay-le-Comte	Murder	Confirmed
Bellesme	Murder	Confirmed
Compiègne	Murder	Confirmed
Provins	*Burglary	Confirmed
Angers	*Burglary	Confirmed
Villeneuve-le-Roy	Murder and burglary	Confirmed
Bellesme	Murder	Confirmed
Bellesme	Murder	Confirmed
Bellesme	Murder	Confirmed
Fontainebleau	Murder	Nullification of procedure
Clermont-Ferrand	Murder	P.a.i. 1 year prison
Angoulême	Murder	P.a.i. 1 year prison
Loudon	*Burglary	Galleys, 9 years
Amboise	*Multiple thefts	Galleys, 5 years
Sénonches	Theft of horses	Galleys, 5 years
Crépy-en-Valois	Murder	P.a.i. 1 year prison
Tours	*Homicide	P.a.i. 1 year prison
Provins	*Arson	P.a.i. 1 year prison
Soissons	*Arson	P.a.i. 1 year prison
Thizy	*Homicide	Royal pardon
Vertilly	*Arson	Insanity, detention for life
Montéreau	*Theft of silverware	Galleys, 9 years
Riom	Murder	Insanity, detention for life
Riom	Infanticide	P.a.i. 1 year prison
Melun	*Homicide	Question, *ad omnia citra mortem*

Abbreviation: p.a.i. – plus amplement informé.

The asterisks denote offenses for which the death penalty was discretionary according to the case, not mandatory by statute.

Source: A.N. Inventory 450, vols. III–IV.

The same rules impelled the Parlement of Paris to carceral penology in cases of *grand criminel.* In 1736, sentences to the galleys, *hôpitaux,* and *plus amplement informé* with prison totaled 36 percent of all penal judgments by the Tournelle. In 1787, they totaled 57.7 percent, of which 77.4 percent were to incarcerations for five years or less.

Definitive judgment

Table 15.4. *Appellate decisions by Parlement of Paris on death sentences pronounced by lower courts, 1787*

Lower Court	Death sentence / crime	Parlement of Paris
Soissons	Murder	Confirmed
Angoulême	Parricide	Confirmed
Auxerre	Murder	Confirmed
Moulins	Infanticide	Confirmed
Beauvais	Murder and theft	Confirmed
Bourges	*Complicity in burglary	*Bagne*, 9 years
Le Mans	*Complicity in burglary	*Hôpital*, 9 years
Le Mans	*Bigamy and fraud	*Bagne*, 9 years
Sténay	*Recidivism in theft	*Bagne*, 9 years
Sens	Domestic theft	*Bagne*, 9 years
Montlucon	*Violent assault	*Bagne*, 5 years
Chartres	Domestic theft	*Bagne*, life
Melun	*Burglary	*Bagne*, life
Bourges	*Complicity in burglary	*Bagne*, 3 years
Pontoise	*Theft	*Bagne*, 9 years
Abbeville	*Burglary	*Bagne*, 9 years
Le Mans	*Theft	*Bagne*, 9 years
Bourges	*Thefts	*Bagne*, 9 years
Meaux	*Recidivism in theft	*Bagne*, life
Le Mans	*Complicity in burglary	*Hôpital*, 9 years
Guise	*Thefts	*Bagne*, 9 years
Vaucouleurs	*Thefts	*Hôpital*, life
Montbrison	*Complicity in poisoning	P.a.i., 1 year prison
Troyes	*Theft of sacred objects	P.a.i. , 1 year prison
Abbeville	*Complicity in theft	P.a.i., 6 mos. at liberty
Chaumont-en-Bassigny	Murder	P.a.i., 1 year prison
Lyon	Domestic theft	P.a.i., 1 year prison
Lyon	*Complicity in theft	P.a.i., 6 mos. prison
Montargis	Infanticide	P.a.i., 1 year prison
Civray	Murder	P.a.i., 1 year prison
Aurillac	Infanticide	P.a.i., 1 year prison
Calais	Murder	P.a.i., 1 year prison
Etampes	Murder	Insanity, Bicêtre
Versailles	*Theft and profanation	Insanity, Bicêtre
Château-Thierry	Murder	Insanity, Bicêtre

Table 15.4.(*cont.*)

Lower Court	Death sentence / crime	Parlement of Paris
Bailliage, Parlement	*Assaultive violence	Insanity, Bicêtre
Angers	Murder	Insanity, Bicêtre
Montlucon	*Homicide	Royal pardon
Riom	*Homicide	Royal pardon
St. Pierre-le-Moutier	*Homicide	Royal pardon
Hérisson	*Homicide	Royal pardon
Angers	*Homicide	Royal pardon
Mamers	Domestic theft	Acquittal

Abbreviation: p.a.i. – plus amplement informé.

The asterisks denote offenses for which the death penalty was discretionary according to the case, not mandatory by statute.

Source: A.N. Inventory 450, vols. III–IV.

During the period 1775 to 1785, the Tournelle judged on appeal some 8,700 persons, an average of 790 a year. The following were the percentile averages, with extremes of high and low, for each main type of sentence pronounced during those eleven years.[11]

Sentence	Extremes (%)		Average (%)
Absolution,	9.3	6.1	7.7
Hors cour and warning	14.6	8.0	11.3
Alms, fines, reprimand	1.2	0.1	0.6
Whipping, iron collar	9.2	5.8	7.5
Banishment for terms	20.4	9.4	14.9
P. a. i. with and without prison	38.7	18.7	28.7
Bagne and *hôpital,* for 3, 5, or 9 years	24.9	14.8	19.8
Banishment for life			0.8
Bagne and *hôpital* for life	8.0	4.6	6.3
Death	9.7	3.7	6.7

Approximately one-half of all sentences to *plus amplement informé* were without prison, which means that almost 30 percent of those judged were either acquitted or released de facto, almost the percentage of the same actions in 1736. More than 40% of the total found guilty by the Tournelle during the period 1775 to 1785 were given various carceral penalties.

The Brittany courts have been studied by Louis-Bernard Mer and his students, especially for the decade 1750 to 1760. Local courts judged 550 persons

[11] From Jean Lecuir, "Criminalité et moralité: Montyon, statisticien du Parlement de Paris," *Revue d'Histoire Moderne et Contemporaine.* 21 (1974): 445–93, especially 485.

in *grand criminel* during that decade. The following were their sentences and the judgments of the Parlement at Rennes on those cases:[12]

Sentence	Local courts (%)	Parlement (%)
Acquittal or release	12.4	30.7
Fines	0.7	2.0
Banishments	16.5	21.0
Galleys and *hôpital*	14.6	24.9
Jail	0.7	1.7
Death	48.2	11.3

The hinterland of Brittany was the domain of judicial thanatos; local courts sentenced almost half of all those they judged to death. The Parlement confirmed only 18 percent of judgments by local courts, ameliorated 73.5 percent, and aggravated 8.5 percent. It overturned convictions by almost 60 percent and death sentences by 75 percent. As in Paris, the penology of the Brittany Tournelle centered on incarcerations: They were the penalties accorded some 40 percent of all those found guilty on appeal.[13]

For the decades 1750 to 1790, Nicole Castan tabulated all sentences by the subaltern courts of Languedoc that were judged on appeal by the Parlement at Toulouse and divided them into categories of rural and urban defendants. "Rural" signified those accused of crimes in communities of less than 2,000 inhabitants. Some three-fourths of the population of eighteenth-century Languedoc lived in such communities. "Urban" signified communities of 2,000 or more. Rural offenders comprised 55 to 65 percent of the cases judged in *grand criminel*.[14]

| Sentence | Local courts (%) | | Parlement (%) |
	Rural	Urban	
Acquittal or release	13.0	15.0	29.0
Fines, whipping, iron collar	4.0	8.0	4.0
Banishment	18.0	28.0	19.0
Bagnes or *hôpital* for terms	30.0	24.0	26.5
Bagnes or *hôpital* for life	12.0	10.0	8.0
Death	17.0	13.0	9.5

The three Parlements resembled each other in their appellate judgments, which may be summarized as follows: high rates of acquittal or release under *plus amplement informé* without prison (25% to 35%); low incidence of defaming

[12] "Criminalité et répression en Bretagne: Appréciation statistique, 1750–1760," in *Mélanges en l'honneur du doyen Pierre Bouzat* (Paris, 1980), pp. 10–41.
[13] The pattern continued to the end of the Old Regime: See Mer, "Réflexions sur la jurisprudence criminelle du Parlement de Bretagne pour la séconde moitié du XVIIIe siècle."
[14] *Justice et répression en Languedoc*, p. 275.

and corporal punishments as main penalty (5% to 10%); moderate and stable incidence of banishment for terms (15% to 20%); highest incidence of carceral penalties (25% to 40%); low incidence of the death penalty (6% to 11%). Those were the sentences executed. Their simple reality contradicts most representations of Old Regime penology.

Most subaltern courts in these three jurisdictions judged with maximal severity. If their sentences had been executed, villages and towns would have been studded with the gallows and the breaking cross, while the galleys and *hôpitaux* would have been packed with offenders condemned for nine years or life. Provincial courts within the jurisdiction of the Parlement of Paris generally obeyed the procedural rules of the ordinance: The Tournelle ordered only 3.3 percent of trials nullified in 1736 and 1 percent in 1787. But the frequency with which the Tournelle overturned convictions and acquitted or released defendants – 31 percent in 1736 and 10 percent in 1787 – suggests that provincial courts did not conscientiously observe the canons of proof.

The severity of lower courts in the jurisdiction of the Parlement of Paris was most blatant in judgment of minors, aged 16 or under. Provincial courts usually sentenced them as adults, and the Parlement invalidated most of those sentences. The following are representative cases from 1787. Marie Cameroy, age 14, was convicted at Tours of stealing livestock and sentenced to whipping, branding, and banishment for three years. The Tournelle reduced this to whipping in custody of the court and in presence of her parents. Cathérine Gontier, age 16, was convicted at Sézanne for stealing bedding and sentenced to whipping, the iron collar, branding, and the *hôpital* for three years. The sentence was reduced to *plus amplement informé* for three months, at liberty. Pierre Montel, age 15, was convicted of theft at Montreuil-sur-Mer and sentenced to the iron collar, branding, and the *bagne* for three years. The Parlement decreed *plus amplement informé* for six months, with detention in Bicêtre. Guillaume Pezé was convicted at Mondidier of complicity with his father in theft and violence; he was sentenced to nine years in the *bagne*. The Parlement gave him *plus amplement informé* with six months of detention.

Throughout France, local seigneurial and bailliage courts were usually in small towns or large villages that were inhabited or surrounded by impecunious laborers, cottage pieceworkers, and indebted tenant peasants. Most such courts had sparse police forces, unlike the magistrates of the Châtelet and Parlement, who were both served and protected by the largest and most effective force in France, the Lieutenant Generalcy. Provincial judges were probably inclined to compensate for their weakness in policing by severity in punishment. But it was mathematically facile for a few judges to conclude, by a majority of one, for severity. That facility could easily have become habitual behavior. It was mathematically difficult for such a result to ensue from ten judges in a Tournelle. Those judges were thereby conditioned to moderation. This system of appellate judgment did cast *parlementaires* in a highly benevolent judicial, and thus political, role with the mass of defendants, even if they were not individually benevolent. That consequence was not accidental: The authors of the system in 1670 were all dynasts of sovereign courts.

Since the actual sentences by many judges, over long periods and in various subaltern courts and their Parlements, on cases subject to discretionary penalties statistically resembled the frequencies predicted by the mathematical model of judgment, we are obliged to conclude that the rules for judgment set forth in the ordinance produced those sentences. Eighteenth-century judges probably believed that their votes in judgment were matters of rational choice. Whatever their beliefs, the results of voting were largely determined by the system of decision. That was the intention of those who drafted the 1670 ordinance.

Penal discretion – which has been decried as arbitrary and oppressive by Enlightenment, Revolutionary, and modern critics of Old Regime criminal law – benefited defendants, especially those convicted of offenses subject to the death penalty. The benefit was systemic in nature. It resulted from two factors: (1) appellate decision by several judges and the necessity of a two-vote majority for the most severe sentence opined to prevail; (2) the necessity that the most benign sentence opined prevail, when that majority did not occur. That system accommodated, even subtly promoted, changes in magisterial attitudes toward punishment, such as the pronounced shift away from corporal penalties toward carceral penalties that occurred during the final decades of the Old Regime.

Conclusion: Principles

Old Regime trial procedure was inquisitorial, not prosecutorial. Prosecutors could not interrogate defendants. They could not be present when judges heard testimony. They were barred from the confrontation, trial review, and (except at the Châtelet) judgment. They translated complaints and denunciations into accusations, recommended witnesses for summonses, presented evidence and arguments for conviction, recommended sentences, and appealed against acquittals or inadequate penalties if they so decided. Virtually all of their trial actions were written, not verbal. They worked in concert with judges and under their authority.[1] The most important responsibility of prosecutors commenced after judgment; it was to ensure that all decrees, sentences, and judgments were executed with exactitude by subaltern personnel.

The role of judges was not to prosecute defendants. It was to seek the truth of a crime. They were endowed with supreme authority in criminal inquiry and judgment, but their exercise of authority was methodically rule-bound. The 1670 ordinance was also a penal code for the criminal judiciary. Forty-seven of its 407 articles stated mandatory penalties against judges and recording clerks who violated those articles, and most of them were provisions that directly concerned the interests of defendants. Penalties consisted in payment of trial costs and damages to plaintiffs and/or defendants, fines of from 100 to 500 livres, suspension from office and its revenues, even dismissal from office. Article 24 of Title XV referred to all main elements of trial from the information through the confrontation; it stated that if witnesses had to be heard anew or the trial re-done because of errors or omissions in form by judges, those guilty of such deficiencies were to pay all costs and damages accrued and all expenses of re-trial. Parlements and the Chancellor enforced these rules.

The ordinance was grounded in certain basic principles of jurisprudence. They were expressed by Daniel Jousse.[2]

---

[1] "En effet, il est constant & c'est une maxime qui ne souffre aucune difficulté, que les fonctions du ministère public, quant à la poursuite des crimes, résident éminemment dans les Juges; & que par une conséquence nécessaire, les Juges peuvent poursuivre le punition d'un crime, & en informer independamment des Procureurs du Roi ou Fiscaux" (Jousse, *Traité*, vol. 3, p. 66).

[2] In the *Traité*, vol. 1, p. 658, and vol. 2, pp. 574–77.

494

1.   It is an unvarying maxim . . . that facts cannot be presumed, and must be proven; which is especially true in criminal matters. It is not sufficient that a crime be notorious and known to everyone for it to be punished by the Judge, even when everyone is persuaded of the actuality of that crime and the identity of its author. For example, a murder committed in public, in front of a crowd and even under the eyes of the Judge, is a notorious event, one which cannot be doubted; however, the Judge who has witnessed that murder cannot condemn the guilty person on the basis of notoriety and his own certainty. He must hear witnesses and observe the same formalities of trial as if the event were not notorious.

2.   Judges must search for all evidence that can establish the innocence of the defendant. In effect, the rigor of the law is directed against the defendant during instruction of the trial; but when conviction is at issue, it is their duty to search for innocence.

3.   In their review and judgment of criminal trials, judges must adhere exactly to the Laws of the Realm.

4.   They must conduct and examine with integrity and all possible care the criminal trials entrusted to them; the life, liberty, honor, or reputation of the accused, and sometimes of his entire family, often depends on their judgments. They must especially avoid precipitancy and not hasten to judge. They must be constantly aware of the maxim that precipitancy is the companion of injustice. Divine justice orders them to scrutinize repeatedly the cases submitted to their decision. If they wish to avoid the damnation of their souls, they should not fear being slow in deciding cases.[3]

5.   In their judgments, judges should consider justice itself; when in doubt, they should not act against their conscience, but with reference to God to whom they must all one day render account of their actions.

---

[3] Haste in judging usually came from *prévention*, or prejudice and presumption against the defendant. Such presumption was, according to d'Aguesseau, an emotional, unstable, and irrational attitude, one founded on appearances: "il est, si nous n'y prenons garde, des jours de grace et de miséricorde, où notre coeur n'aime qu' à pardonner; il est des jours de colère et d'indignation, où il semble ne se plaire qu' à punir; et l'inégale révolution des mouvements de notre humeur est si impénétrable que le magistrat, étonné de la diversité de ses jugments, se cherche quelquefois, et ne se trouve pas lui-memê. . . . [the dutiful judge] sait que le vrai, qui se dérobe presque toujours à l'impetuosité de nos jugements, ne se refuse jamais *à l'utile pesanteur d'une raison modeste qui avance lentement* [italics mine], et qui passe successivement par tous les dégrés de lumière dont le progrès insensible nous conduit enfin jusqu'à l'évidence de la vérité" (*Oeuvres choisies*, pp. 151, 153). Cleverness or quickness of mind easily led to precipitant and erroneous judgment, when it was not controlled by legal reasoning and observance of procedural rules (ibid., p. 71).

6.   In the exercise of their authority to punish crimes, judges should be entirely devoid of the passions ordinarily found in those who are high in rank and dignity. Thus, instead of deriving from their power reasons for conceit and vanity, they must derive from the failings of others reasons to fear their own human frailty. In effect, a judgment or opinion can be objectively just, without proceeding from merit in the judge. A judge can opine for the conviction of a criminal only to present an advantageous image of his virtue and his zeal for justice and the public welfare; sometimes he declaims with force and energy all the circumstances of a crime, but in order to display his eloquence, and not from sincere love of justice. Holy Scripture doubtless refers to such men when it says that God will judge even the judges. . . . On that day, He will tear off the masks and appearances that conceal vanity from others and even from ourselves.

7.   Judges should be entirely free in their judicial opinions, free from any constraints or other pressures that could prevent them from acting according to their knowledge, wisdom, and convictions.

Realization and enforcement of these principles virtually required written trial procedure. Written procedure – which has been derided by Esmein and other exponents of the black legend as studded with formalities, as needlessly arcane, fastidious, and time-consuming – in fact habituated magistrates to intellectual discipline, distanced them from emotional involvement with defendants, and allowed Parlements and Chancellors to police trials in subaltern and superior instances. Written procedure made judicial actions objective and discernable. Trial reviews always preceded judgment, and the first obligation of the reporting judge – whether in a lower court or on appeal in a Tournelle – was to determine from transcripts "if the necessary formalities, which are the substance of trial, have been observed" and then to evaluate the quality of proof revealed by the record.[4]

The ordinance was constructed to guide judges toward accurate determination of the guilt or innocence of defendants. It was constructed to achieve two goals: The innocent were not to be convicted; the guilty were not to escape some punishment. The process was meticulous and frequently slow. It could be onerous for the innocent or marginally guilty, but its outcome was generally equitable. It acted to prevent judges from deciding the fates of defendants by presumption or intuition.

To describe the 1670 ordinance as repressive is fallacious. It was foremost an investigative system that contained rules for the determination of penalty should proof of guilt emerge from the investigation. The modern dichotomy (at

[4] Jousse, *Traité*, vol. 2, pp. 578–9.

least in political theory) of rule by scientific or technical expertise as against rule by force did not exist in the criminal justice of Old Regime France. Both modes of rule were unified in the judiciary, with the second rigorously subordinated to the first. A crime and a defendant were made objects of quasi-scientific inquiry for a long period before judgment occurred. Convictions were then reviewed by Parlements. Punishment, when it occurred, was at the end of a long intellective process, at considerable temporal remove from the crime – even if the crime had been notorious – and generally moderate.

The procedural system did act to isolate popular defendants from the social and cultural *milieux* familiar to them and from their suspected codefendants. It placed them in dependence on their judges.[5] The system also made defendants active protagonists in their trials. The ordinance gave them successive opportunities to state their case: in interrogations; in confrontation with witnesses; in allegation of justificative facts; before original judgment; before final judgment on appeal. Criminal trials partially simulated a religious encounter in their staging, with black-robed judges cast as confessors and defendants as penitents, in rough clothing, seated on the wooden stool.[6] The simulation was intended to elicit humility and candor from defendants. But the force of simulation was blunted by Catholic doctrine. Guilty defendants could make the distinction between judicial authority and ecclesiastical authority; they could and did refuse to confess their crimes to judges, while confessing them to priests who attended them in the jails. By canon law and criminal jurisprudence, priests were forbidden to disclose such information to judges: The secret of ecclesiastical confession was inviolable, in jails, prison chapels, even at the site of execution. Priests could urge the guilty to confess to magistrates; they could not compel them. Judges could not request such information from priests.[7] The law al-

---

[5] See the remarks of Arlette Farge in *Délinquance et criminalitè: Les vol d'aliments à Paris au XVIIIe siècle* (Paris: 1974) pp. 233–5.

[6] "L'accusé devoit être in *vestitu sordido*. En effet il seroit indécent qu'un accusé prisonnier, prévenu d' un crime considérable, paroit devant ses Juges avec un habillement trop recherché. Cette situation n'est pas convenable à l'humiliation qui doit être inséparable de son état" (Jousse, *Traité*, vol. 3, p. 61).

[7] "Qui dit Secret, dit un dépôt sacré qu'il faut garder saintement & réligieusement, tout ainsi qu'une confession ouie auriculairement, dont le sceau est inviolable. . . . Il ne resulteroit donc qu'un très-grand inconvenient de cette révélation; c'est que de quelque nature que fût le délit commis ou projetté, cette infidelité forcée ou voluntaire de la part du Confesseur seroit pernicieuse, par les suites & les conséquences qu'elle produiroit. On ne regarderoit pas le Tribunal de la Pénitence [the confessional] que comme un piège; & un seul exemple de Confession révélée seroit un motif assez puissant pour détourner une multitude de Pecheurs de se confesser" ("Consultation de MM. les Avocats du Parlement [of Paris] avec celle de MM. les Curés de Paris, touchant l'obligation de garder le sécret promis," January 27–9, 1746, A.N. AD III 31). This was also the position of the Diocesan Council of Paris, which stated that any revelation made by a defendant to a priest, even outside the confessional, had to be kept secret by the priest: "quoique ce ne soit pas dans la Confession que ce secret lui ait été confié. . . . Cependant le sceau sous lequel l'accusé le lui a confié ce secret, n'en est ni moins sacré, ni moins inviolable. . . . Le Confesseur doit plutôt mourir que de révéler les pechés qu'on lui dépose" (ibid.). See also Ferrière, vol. 1, p. 336, and Jousse, *Traité*, vol. 2, pp. 100–1. The only cases in which priests could be requested to disclose what had been revealed to them were those of heresy and regicide.

lowed the guilty to purge their conscience by confessing to priests, while denying guilt to judges.

Sin was integral to human life; so too was crime to society. This meant that neither sin nor crime could be entirely removed from collective experience by any human codification or authority, and that was not the ambition of either church or state. It was accepted that ultimate judgment of all criminals, and ultimate retribution for their crimes, would be divine, not human. The judiciary and its system sought to preserve an equilibrium between the inevitability of crimes, equity in treatment of defendants, and the necessity to punish the guilty. Crime required punishment, just as sin required expiation. But punishment, like expiation, was apportioned to both the malefactor and the offense. Even in cases involving capital offenses (many of which were mortal sins), penal retribution was not usually implacable or extreme, for the character, motives, the moral and social being of the offender, as well as the circumstances of the crime counted in judgment and in the assessment of penalty. Except for the most serious offenses, the emphasis in trial and judgment was on both the offender and the crime. Equity in judging persons, not merely crimes, required consideration of aggravating and mitigating circumstances and also discretionary penalties.

In jurisprudence, there were seven circumstances of the person or the offense that aggravated culpability and penal severity: (1) motives of personal betrayal, greed, hatred, or knowing and manifest contempt for the law; (2) rank or social condition, if the offender was infamous, a recidivist, a vagabond, a noble or a soldier who committed a base action, or a public official who abused his authority for criminal purposes; (3) if the victim was an illustrious personage, a magistrate, a parent, master, or superior of the offender, or someone weak, invalid, or incapable of self-defense; (4) if the crime was committed in a church, a royal or princely palace, a judicial building, a public square, on a street or highway, in a cabaret or wine shop, or in a private home; (5) if the crime was committed by assault or surprise, or with a weapon, or by breaking and entering, or with blatant scandal; (6) if it was committed at night, during a judicial audience or the celebration of divine services; (7) if the crime was widespread and recurrent.

There were twenty-seven qualities of the person or the offense that mitigated culpability and diminished penalty. In addition to those discussed in Chapters 7 and 10, they were: (1) long trial detention; (2) motives such as realistic fear, love, commiseration or pity, consanguinal affection, obedience to the orders of a master or superior, reaction to personal injury or offense, extreme poverty (but only in the case of theft of necessities of life) (3); drunkenness, if it was neither habitual or planned; (3) ignorance, dullness or simplicity of mind (*la rusticité*); (4) female gender; (5) high social status or nobility; (6) past or present services to the realm; (7) eminent and socially important talents; (8) good reputation; (9); voluntary confession of guilt; (10); nonconsummation of the crime; (11) beneficial consequences of the criminal act, particularly if they were part of the motive.[8] Personal wealth, social distinction, nobiliary estate, and ecclesiastical office were aggravating considerations in judgment and punishment when the crime was base or brutal in nature. Such crimes by such persons were regarded in law as betrayals of honor, status, estate, or vocation, as particularly evil. They were often punished with dramatic public severity.

Individuation of defendants was most evident in the treatment of complicity and accomplices. Complicity and its punishment were carefully defined in jurisprudence but only occasionally by royal statutes.[9] The definitions were observed by the Châtelet and Parlement. In all cases, courts had to establish that accomplices had acted knowingly and voluntarily for them to be punished.

There were three categories of complicity: (1) participating in a crime before, during, or after the action; (2) advising, persuading, ordering, or hiring someone to commit the crime; (3) "adhering" to the crime by sharing in its profits or giving approbation, reward, refuge, or aid ex post facto to its authors. Complicity by participation included virtually every form of material assistance, but penal liability was measured in gradations. The participating accomplice could receive the same penalties as the author of the crime only in the following cases: (1) if he were involved in the planning of the crime; (2) if he facilitated the crime by his presence or direct actions; (3) if he served as lookout or decoy while the crime was being committed. Jousse enumerated some seventeen other forms of complicity by participation, including providing lodging and tools for the criminal and hiding evidence of the crime, for which accomplices customarily received lesser penalties than authors. Advising or inciting someone to commit a crime was a lesser form of complicity than hiring or ordering him to do so, as a husband to a wife, a parent to a child, a master to a servant. Those who hired or ordered were liable to the same penalties as their agents. But in such cases, ocular and aural witnesses or written evidence of command or payment was essential for equal penalty.[10] Those who advised or incited the criminal could be punished by equal penalty only if it was established that the crime probably would not have been committed otherwise or that the incitor gave instruction in how to commit the crime. There were exceptions even to this general rule: If the advice was given in jest or without manifest intent that it be acted on; if it was followed by a criminal act different from the one spoken of; if the incitation was general, not specific. Otherwise, those who advised or incited were either not liable to punishment or were liable to lesser penalties. Complicity ex post facto was also divided into categories. Even loud approbation of a crime or criminal was not punishable unless it was established that the

[8] Muyart, *Institutes*, pp. 392–4.
[9] There is a comprehensive and succinct presentation of complicity in Jousse, *Traité*, vol. 1, pp. 20–35. See also André Laingui, "La théorie de la complicité dans l'ancien droit pénal," *Legal History Review 45* (1977): 27–65.
[10] "Mais dans le doute, le mandat ne se présume point; & si le crime qui est commis procure un avantage à celui qui a engagé de le commettre, & à celui l'a commis, on présume plutôt que c'est un conseil qu'un mandat" (Jousse, *Traité*, vol. 1, p. 26).

crime had been committed for the person giving approbation. A large body of royal statutes penalized seditious and heretical incitements, especially when the incitements were written, but rarely treated them with the same severity as actions, such as actual profanation, treason, or regicide. Those who gave refuge to criminals, shared in the profits of a crime, or fenced stolen goods were subject to lesser penalties than authors.

One could not be prosecuted for neglecting to inform authorities of an imminent crime, except in cases of treason, poisoning, and murder plots. Those who were forced into complicity by actual or threatened violence were not liable to penalty. Wives of criminals could not be punished, even if they had foreknowledge of crimes and hid stolen goods or other evidence, unless it were proven that they had aided in crimes or shared directly in profits. Mistresses and concubines were not so exempted, but they could not be punished equally with authors unless their complicity was participatory. Aiding a criminal to escape arrest was prima facie evidence of participation in crime, except when it came from a relative or servant. Such aid was presumed to be natural, and not evidence of criminal involvement.

Complicity had to be proven, and such proof was often difficult. Possession of implements and goods from the crime, witnesses to involvement, and denunciation by authors of crimes were accepted as conclusive when they combined. Sustained and close association with convicted authors of a crime was evidence for complicity, but only in supplement to other evidence. Denunciation by authors of a crime was powerful evidence, but it was not sufficient for conviction, for it had to be supported by other indices of complicity. This disposed judges to pronounce the death sentence against those convicted of a serious crime for which others were on trial as accomplices, for only the death sentence could produce the *question préalable* and the death testament.

Complicities in crime expressed the ramified sociability of eighteenth-century French plebeians. They lived, worked, drank, and traveled in groups. When they lodged, it was several to a room and often to a bed. The life of an individual was frequently migratory and transient, but at each halting place it was enveloped by relations with others. Conviviality and sharing were normal, just as friendships, both pragmatic and affective, were formed easily. Crimes were often a form of pragmatic friendship, of association in need.

Close to one-third of all death sentences pronounced by the Parlement of Paris during the periods 1735 to 1749 and 1775 to 1789 were against two or more persons convicted of the same crime or crimes. But close to two-thirds of those cases involved others who were convicted of complicities and given lesser penalties.

During the judicial year October 4, 1785, through October 7, 1786, a total of 808 persons were jailed at the Châtelet on suspicion of crimes that carried defaming, afflictive, or capital penalties.[11] Fully 640 (79.2%) of them were

---

[11] A.N. 10648.

charged with theft. Of these 640, 196 (30.6%) were charged as accomplices or partners in theft. The rate of complicity in theft was therefore almost one-third, in the Paris of 1785 to 1786. The complicities most common involved three to five persons, especially in burglaries: one or two principles, one or two lookouts or carriers; one or two who hid or fenced stolen goods. By the end of the judicial year, the Châtelet had judged 137 of the 196. Sixty-one were released by decrees of provisional liberation or withdrawal of charges, because of insufficient evidence (27 within ten days of first interrogation; 23 after subsequent interrogations). Six were acquitted and 3 given sentences of warning or reprimand, after full trial. Thirty-six (25%) were convicted and penalized as follows: branding and banishment (18); *bagnes* (9); Hôpital-Géneral (2); whipping in custody (5); death (2). Thirty-one (22.6%) were sentenced to *plus amplement informé*, 15 of them with prison for terms of three months to one year.

This qualified conception and treatment of complicity, with its gradations of moral responsibility and penal liability, was grounded in Catholic humanism. Full moral responsibility, and thus liability to full penalty, resided only with the person who knowingly and voluntarily committed the violent or larcenous act; only those whose authority or aid were either integral or indispensable to the act were full accomplices. All others involved were in some degree accessory, and at some degree of lesser moral responsibility. Magistrates were obliged by the law to select carefully from the sea of accomplices and associates whom they encountered in criminal chambers. This weakened Old Regime criminal justice as a system of power, a weakness that gave heightened importance to the public punishment of those who were convicted. Those spectacles masked the numbers of accomplices who were either not convicted and punished or who received benign sanctions.

The majority of those tried, convicted, and punished in *grand criminel* were plebeians, especially in the towns and cities. That fact did not register class prejudice by magistrates; it registered a social actuality of crimes. For every plebeian sent to the galleys or scaffold, there were numerous others guilty of complicity in the same offense or of similar offenses who received lesser penalties, and many of them remained invisible to the public. However, certain groups were categorically suspect of criminality and liable to severity in penalty if found guilty of crimes. Their social and presumed moral beings were aggravating considerations in judgment and could also form evidence against them.

It is the duty of Judges to weigh the nature of crimes, the quality of proof, the conditions or ranks of defendants and plaintiffs, and other considerations that can serve to aggravate or mitigate penalties, before they pronounce judgment.[12]

With very serious crimes, if the defendant is of evil repute one does not refuse to condemn him to banishment or even to the galleys, even though proof of guilt is not complete.[13]

[12] Soulatges, vol. 1, p. 185.   [13] Serpillon, vol. 3, p. 1072.

Mal-famé, or evil repute, signified foremost those with previous criminal convictions. That infamy lasted for life, unless it was removed by special royal pardon. Such persons became *répris de justice* if they were arrested and tried for a crime; if convicted, they were liable to the penalty of maximal severity for that crime. The brand was the literal mark of infamy, and it identified the bearer as socially dangerous. Infamy was a powerful form of character evidence against a defendant. The royal declaration of March 4, 1724, mandated severe penalties against recidivists.[14]

Vagabonds, beggars, and others without respectable means of support were a major population of the *mal-famé*. During the seventeenth and eighteenth centuries, a voluminous succession of royal edicts defined and redefined them as pariahs.[15] The fundamental legal definition was set forth in the royal declaration of August 17, 1701:

We declare to be vagabonds and people without good repute all those who have no profession, no trade, no fixed domicile, no property from which to live, and who are not vouched for, and cannot be certified to be of good life and morals, by persons worthy of belief.[16]

Vagabonds, beggars, *gens sans aveu*, and *répris de justice*, as well as soldiers and deserters, came under the jurisdiction of provostial and presidial courts that judged without appeal, when such persons were accused of crimes that carried defaming, afflictive, or capital penalties. Titles I and II of the ordinance set the limits of such jurisdiction, limits that were refined by the royal declaration of February 5, 1731.[17] Cases were subject to judgment without appeal either by the nature of the suspect or the nature of the crime. If the suspect belonged to the aforementioned categories he was to be tried by the provost of constabulary (or his deputy) as instructing judge, when the crimes had been committed outside the town or city, and its faubourgs, that was the seat of the court; if committed within, the case was tried and judged presidially, under the authority of the criminal lieutenant.

In addition, the following crimes were subject to judgment without appeal: highway robbery; burglary by breaking and entering or with weapons; sacrilege

---

[14] "Ceux et celles qui, après avoir été condamnés pour vol, ou flétris pour quelque crime que ce soit, seront convaincus de recidive en crime de vol, ne pourront être condamnés à moindre peine que, savoir: les hommes aux galères à temps ou à perpétuité, et les femmes a être de nouveau flétries d'un double V, si c'est pour recidive de vol, ou d'un simple V, si la première flétrisseur a été encourue pour autre crime, et enfermées à temps ou pour leur vie dans des maisons de force; le tout sans préjudice de la peine de mort, s'il y échoit, suivant l'exigence des cas. Ceux qui seront condamnés aux galères à temps ou à perpétuité pour quelque crime que ce puisse être, seront flétris avant d'y être conduits, des trois lettres GAL, pour en cas de récidive en crime qui mérite *peine afflictive* [italics mine], être punis de mort" (Isambert, vol. 21, p. 260).

[15] For that legislation, see Jacques Depauw, "Pauvres, pauvres mendiants, mendiants valides ou vagabonds? Les hésitations de la Législation royale," *Revue d'Histoire Moderne et Contemporaine*, (1974): 401–18, and Mohamed Grissa, *Pouvoirs et marginaux à Paris sous le regne de Louis XIV (1661–1715)*, (Tunis: Université de Tunis, 1980).

[16] From Rousseaud, pp. 597–8.

[17] The declaration is in Desmarquets, pp. 287–96.

committed during burglary; seditious assembly and riot; recruitment of soldiers without royal commission; counterfeiting of money. When such crimes were committed outside the town or city of the court, they were judged provostially; when inside, presidially. In cases of concurrent inquiries and multiple crimes, presidial jurisdiction had precedence over provostial.

These last-resort competencies were qualified. Clerics, nobles, and officers of the law were not liable to provostial or presidial trial. Crimes provostial or presidial by their nature could not be judged in last resort when they had been committed within a town and its faubourgs that was the seat of a Parlement, unless they were committed by those whose social condition was of provostial and presidial nature. Otherwise, the case was decided on appeal by the Parlement. Thus, in Paris only those aforementioned persons could be tried and judged in last resort by the Châtelet, under the supervision of the provost if the crime had been committed outside the city and its faubourgs, under that of the criminal lieutenant if inside. If a suspect in a provostial crime was captured in flagrant delict or arrested by order of a local bailliage judge before the provost had ordered his arrest, the local royal court tried and judged the case, with decision on appeal of its judgment. If a suspect was simultaneously accused of crimes provostial by their nature and crimes that were not provostial, he was to be tried for all offenses by ordinary justice, with appellate decision. In a trial with several suspects, if any were charged with nonprovostial crimes or were nonprovostial in social condition, all had to be tried and judged by ordinary judges subject to appellate decision.[18] A panel of seven judges in the local royal court, not the provost of constabulary or the criminal lieutenant alone, determined whether a case was provostial, presidial, or ordinary, after reviewing the information and questioning the suspect. They had to establish that a suspect was indeed vagabond, *sans aveu*, a previous offender, or a soldier; they could not merely ascribe that condition to someone.[19] They had to inform suspects that they were to be judged in last resort and were required to send copies of all

---

[18] Article XX, 1731 declaration, ibid. Serpillon described the consequences of this: "Cet article prouve encore bien clairement la faveur accordée aux Lieutenants Criminels; le renvoi dans tous les cas leur est fait, quoique ce soit d'autres Juges qui aient informé & décreté, aussi-tôt que l'on depouillât les Juges en dernier ressort. . . . Il suffit suivant cet article que dans un procès prévôtal il y ai un accusé prévenue d'un crime ordinaire, c'est-à-dire, qui seroit de la connoissance du Juge des lieux, notre nouvelle Ordonnance [1731] renvoie le tout dans les Bailliages et Sénéchaussées, & si tous les accusés étoient gens de guerre, vagabonds, ou répris de Justice, la plus petite accusation qui surviendroit dans le même procès contre un domicilié, seroit encore une imcompétence totale contre le dernier ressort des Prévôts; le procès seroit de même renvoyé au Lieutenant Criminel" (vol. 1, pp. 336–7).

[19] In October 1768 the Chancellor reprimanded the officers of the Châtelet for declaring the provost competent to judge someone arrested at Melun, on the grounds that the latter was "suspected of being a beggar and vagabond." He reminded them that suspicion is not grounds for provostial or presidial trial and recited the formula for determining jurisdiction in such cases: "Copie de la formule de Sentence de compétence tant pour les jugements prévôtaux que présidiaux en matière de vagabondage: Nous. . . attendu que le dit. . . n'a pu justifier d'un domicile ni de l'exercice d'une profession depuis six mois, ni se faire avouer depuis sa détention, jusqu'à présent par gens dignes de foi, avons déclarer le Prévôt compétent pour luy faire son procès comme à un vagabond" (A.N. Y 10510, fol. 23).

such decrees to the general prosecutor of the Parlement every six months. All provostial and presidial cases had to be judged by at least seven judges, of which the provost or criminal lieutenant was only one. As in a Tournelle, a majority of two was required for the most severe sentence opined to prevail; without that majority, the most benign sentence opined prevailed. It will be shown in Volume 2 that penal outcomes in provostial and presidial cases judged by the Châtelet did not differ significantly from penal outcomes in cases judged on appeal by the Parlement of Paris. These qualifications on trial and judgment without appeal, even of the socially dangerous, came from a scrupulosity embedded within the ordinance and its jurisprudence: "Jurisdiction in last resort is not favorably regarded; it is curtailed on all possible occasions, because it is an extraordinary means which should always be abandoned in favor of defendants' interests, whenever there is doubt of its appropriateness."[20]

Contrary to a tenacious legend, those subjected to provostial or presidial trial and judgment were not subjected to a distinctive or summary procedure. They were tried by the exact procedure described in these chapters and accorded the same rights as all other defendants, except for appellate judgment. Provostial and presidial justice was no cynosure of repression. The ordinance and the 1731 declaration subordinated the need to isolate, judge, and punish those regarded as most dangerous to social order – actual or former anarchs who were inclined to criminal acts by their very character and existence – to an abiding, overarching moral concern with judging accurately and punishing equitably in individual cases.

[20] Serpillon, vol. 1, p. 336.

Appendix: Penal decision, a mathematical model

Given the rules of deliberation and the procedure by which judges opined and arrived at a sentence, we can model the structural features of this system in an effort to examine its structural bias. In doing so, we will use a combinatorial model, treating judges as objects being stochastically assigned different sentences. We will then look at the penal outcomes of the different patterns of sentencing and calculate the frequency with which each sentence might be expected in such a system. We will limit ourselves to seven judges and four possible sentences. Though the identities of the sentences are not so important, so long as they are all different in severity, our four sentences will be death *(Death)*, *bagnes* for life *(BL)*, *bagnes* for nine years *(B9)*, and *plus amplement informé (p.a.i.)*.

We begin by noting that with seven judges, each of whom may cast his initial vote for any one of the four sentences, the number of possible permutations is equal to 4^7, or 16,384. We may divide this outcome space into four partitions: (1) initial judgment in which only one sentence is present, in which case the initial vote is unanimous; (2) initial judgment in which two and only two sentences are present, in which case a penal outcome may be seen, as the "narrowing to two" step is unnecessary; (3) initial judgment in which three and only three sentences are represented, in which case a narrowing step is necessary in order to arrive at a penal outcome; and (4) initial judgment in which all four sentences are represented, in which case the narrowing step is again necessary. We may list the possible outcomes in each of the four partitions and then examine the sentences associated with each combination.

Using the lists of possible combinations and penal outcomes, we may calculate the frequency with which each sentence occurs within a given partition and then calculate the systemwide frequency associated with each sentence.

The first partition is mathematically the most elementary. If the decision of the judges is unanimous during their initial opining, the sentence is decided. Therefore, we can say that in the first partition there are only four possible combinations and each can only occur in one way. Assuming (as we are) that the judges are objects, equally likely to "vote" for one sentence as for another (that is, ignoring them as choice-makers), we may say that within this partition the

Roger Blumberg is the author of this appendix.

Appendix

Table A.1. *Initial judgment: unanimous decision*

Death	BL	B9	P.a.i.
7	0	0	0
0	7	0	0
0	0	7	0
0	0	0	7

Four possible outcomes, the probability of each being .25 within this category.

Table A.2. *Initial judgment: two sentences*

A	B	#	Outcome
6	1	42	A
1	6	42	B
5	2	126	A
2	5	126	B
4	3	210	B
3	4	210	B

Here $p(A) = 168 \div 756 = .22$
$p(B) = 588 \div 756 = .77$

likelihood of each of the sentences is the same: .25. A list of the possible outcomes may be found in Table A.1.

Table A.2 shows the outcome list for partition 2. Here, with two and only two sentences represented, one may deduce the outcome by applying the plus-two majority rule. The identities of sentences A and B are not given; we know only that sentence A is the more severe, and we note that in this partition there is a bias toward the most benign sentence (a bias due entirely to the plus-two requirement). We have calculated the number of ways each combination is possible (#), using the multinomial coefficient. In order to see how Table A.2 reflects specific sentences, we look at the possible correlations between A, B, and the four sentences with which we are dealing. There are six such correlations:

	Death	BL	B9	P.a.i.
1	A	B		
2	A		B	
3	A			B
4		A	B	
5		A		B
6			A	B

Thus, of the 756 possible outcomes, or combinations of judges' opinions, 378 (half) have death as the more severe sentence. In calculating the frequency

Table A.3. *Initial judgment: three sentences*

A	B	C	#	Outcome
5	1	1	168	A
1	5	1	168	B
1	1	5	168	C
4	2	1	420	B
4	1	2	420	A,C
2	1	4	420	C
2	4	1	420	B
1	2	4	420	C
1	4	2	420	B
3	2	2	840	A,B,C
2	3	2	840	B
2	2	3	840	C
3	3	1	560	B
3	1	3	560	C
1	3	3	560	C
		Total	7,224	

Here $p(A) = 658 \div 7{,}224 = .09$
$p(B) = 3{,}108 \div 7{,}224 = .43$
$p(C) = 3{,}458 \div 7{,}224 = .48$

of the death sentence, we simply note that half of the outcomes contain A in the Death column, and so, multiplying the expected frequency of A (which we will refer to as "$p(A)$") by .5, we find the frequency of death to be .11 in this partition. (Henceforth, and in the concluding tables, "p of x" means the expected frequency of X.) Similarly, the frequency of the BL sentence is $\frac{1}{6}$ the frequency of B $+ \frac{2}{6}$ the frequency of A, or .20. The frequency of B9 in this partition is .29 and that of p.a.i. is .39. These positional fractions indicate expected frequencies within this partition, given that all 756 combinations are equally likely. This given is necessary in order that we preserve the idea of judges as nonagents, equally likely to "vote" for one sentence as for another.

From these frequencies, and the numbers in Table A.2, which show the expected frequencies of each unspecified sentence, $p(A)$ and $p(B)$, we can see that in this partition the system is biased in favor of the most benign of two sentences. Because all voting in the system except for unanimous decision is, in theory, eventually reduced to two sentences, we would expect this bias to be reflected in all sentencing of the seven-judge court.

Table A.3 shows the contents of partition 3. We begin by listing the correlations between the unspecified sentences A, B, and C and the four particular sentences we are considering:

Death	BL	B9	P.a.i.
A	B	C	
A	B		C
A		B	C
	A	B	C

Thus, in .75 of the cases in this partition, A will represent the death sentence.

There is a complication in this partition, because we cannot deduce a penalty from the three-sentence configuration, as we did in Table A.2. According to the rules of deliberation, a first-round opinion that contained three sentences had to be reduced to two sentences, and this reduction was to occur through the movement of judges, in a second round, in the order in which they first opined. Because we wish to avoid mention of judges as choice-makers, we will project the penal outcome from a given three-sentence combination by making three modest assumptions: (1) that judges followed the rules of deliberation closely, particularly those that governed when a particular judge had to default on his position; (2) that when such a default or movement occurred, the judge in question always moved to a position as close to his original position as possible; and (3) that a judge holding either the majority or clear first minority opinion will not default in the second round.

Given these assumptions, assumptions that historical evidence supports, it is possible to project the specific outcomes of each combination (see Table A.3), except for two combinations (and the 1,260 ways these combinations might occur with seven judges opining) in which movement could end in one of two or three sentences. We have factored these cases into the frequency calculations by saying, for example, that in the case of 4A, 1B, and 2C half of the 420 cases will conclude A and the other half C. In doing so we are saying that in half of the cases the lone judge for sentence B will default to A, and in the other half he will default to C. What is clear is that he is the one who must default, and the position in which he opined initially does not in this case matter.

In fact, the order of opinion, important as it is to the appearance of the court, matters only for one combination in partition three: 3A, 2B, 2C. In this case, different outcomes might come from different default orders, though even this is not certain. We factored the 840 cases of this combination into the frequency figures by saying that 280 cases would result in A, 280 in B, and 280 in C; this assumption is generous to the A sentence, since it is clear that more movements result in B or in C than in A.

We may now calculate the frequencies with which specific sentences may be expected in the third partition, and we do so by combining the correlation table given earlier with the frequencies for unspecified sentences presented in Table A.3. Thus, for example, since A represents the death sentence .75 of the time, the expected frequency of the death sentence is .75 multiplied by the expected frequency of the A sentence, $p(A) = .09$, which gives us the expected fre-

Table A.4. *Initial judgment: four sentences*

Death	BL	B9	P.a.i.	#	Outcome
4	1	1	1	210	A,B,C,D
1	4	1	1	210	B
1	1	4	1	210	C
1	1	1	4	210	D
3	2	1	1	420	B,C,D
3	1	2	1	420	C
3	1	1	2	420	C,D
2	3	1	1	420	B
2	1	3	1	420	C
2	1	1	3	420	D
1	3	2	1	420	C
1	3	1	2	420	B,D
1	2	3	1	420	C
1	2	1	3	420	D
1	1	2	3	420	D
1	1	3	2	420	C
2	2	2	1	630	B,C
2	2	1	2	630	B,D
2	1	2	2	630	B,C,D
1	2	2	2	630	B,C,D

Total   8,400

Here $p(\text{Death}) = 52.5 \div 8400 = .006$
$p(\text{BL}) = 2{,}082.5 \div 8400 = .25$
$p(\text{B9}) = 3{,}447.5 \div 8{,}400 = .41$
$p(\text{p.a.i.}) = 2{,}817.5 \div 8{,}400 = .34$

quency of death in this partition $p(\text{Death})$ as .07. The expected frequencies for all sentences are

$p(\text{Death}) = .07$	$p(\text{B9}) = .33$	
$p(\text{BL}) = .24$	$p(\text{p.a.i.}) = .36$	

We note the bias toward leniency here is very similar to that of the second partition, and here there is even a greater bias against the extremes of death and p.a.i.

Table A.4 shows the contents of the fourth partition. Here, as in the third partition, one cannot deduce penal outcome from the initial opinion; rather, we must project what outcomes could occur given different opining orders and judicial movements. In making these projections we will hold to the three assumptions we made for movement in partition 3 and project the possible outcomes by looking at what could happen when minority-opinion judges move in different orders.

Appendix

Table A.5. *Outcome space*

7 judges, unanimous =	4
7 judges, 2 sentences =	756
7 judges, 3 sentences =	7,224
7 judges, 4 sentences =	8,400
4^7 =	16,384

Table A.6. *Systemwide expected frequencies*

$p(A) = p(A_{11})p(1) + p(A_{12})p\,(2) + p(A_{13})p(3) + p(A_{14})p(4)$

(a) If $p(1) = \quad 4 \div 16,384 \qquad p(3) = 7,224 \div 16,384$
$\qquad\ p(2) = 756 \div 16,384 \qquad p(4) = 8,400 \div 16,384$

then $\quad p(\text{Death}) = .04 \qquad p(\text{B9}) \quad = .37$
$\qquad\quad p(\text{BL}) \qquad = .24 \qquad p(\text{p.a.i.}) = .35$

(b) If $\quad p(1) = p(2) = p(3) = p(4) = .25$

then $\quad p(\text{Death} = .11 \qquad p(\text{B9}) \quad = .33$
$\qquad\quad p(\text{BL}) \qquad = .23 \qquad p(\text{p.a.i.}) = .33$

While order is indeed important in this partition, it in no way overrides the power of the system's structure, and we note that only in this partition is the order in which the judges opined important. Since there is but one correlation between unspecified sentences and the sentences we are considering, we may use the calculated frequencies in Table A.4 and find the following expected frequencies in this partition:

$p(\text{Death}) = .006$		$p(\text{B9}) \quad = .41$	
$p(\text{BL}) \qquad = .25$		$p(\text{p.a.i.}) = .34$	

Here again we note the structural slant of the system, away from death; the system seems to weight both moderation and leniency, and in practice one would expect the former to come from the "narrowing to two" step and the latter to come from the "plus two majority" rule governing outcome.

Table A.5 shows that the outcome spaces for each of the four partitions add to the number of permutations that we noted were possible at the start: 4^7, or 16,384.

Table A.6 shows the expected frequency of each sentence in the system as a whole. This calculation was made using an adaptation of Bayes' Theorem, which (applied to our problem) says, for example, that the frequency of a given sentence is the sum of the frequencies of that sentence in each partition multiplied by the frequency with which that partition can be expected. In other words: $p(\text{Death}) = p(\text{death in partition 1}) \cdot p(\text{partition 1}) + p(\text{Death in par-}$

tition 2) · p(partition 2) + p(Death in partition 3) · p(3) + p(Death in partition 4) · p(4). We have done the calculation two ways. In the first (a) we said that the frequency of each partition is the number of cases in that partition divided by 4^7. Thus: $p(1) = 4 ÷ 16,384 = .0002$; $p(2) = 756 ÷ 16,384 = .046$; $p(3) = 7,224 ÷ 16,384 = .44$; and, $p(4) = 8,400 ÷ 16,384 = .51$. In the second case (b) we calculated the frequencies using the rather ridiculous assumption that the probability of each partition is the same, namely .25. This is ridiculous if only because in making the assumption we are saying that the frequency of unanimous decision is equal to the frequency of initial judgments in which three sentences are represented (something we know is not the case). Still, case b can be seen as an upper limit to the frequency with which the structure of the system will produce the death sentence, since it gives unfair weight to the first partition, where the frequency of death is .25.

In the situation of maximal dissention among judges (see Table A.4), the "strongest" opinion is *bagnes* for nine years. And systemwide (see Table A.6), when all combinations of opinions are accounted for – unanimous opinion, two opinions, three opinions, and four opinions – *bagnes* for nine years is also the "strongest" opinion, followed closely by *plus amplement informé*.

The expected frequencies with which the sentences Death, BL, B9, and p.a.i. occur in the systemwide expected frequencies allow us to make certain observations about the system as a whole. First, it is clear that, independent of judicial behavior, the structure of the decision rules and procedures strongly determines penal outcome. Second, this determination weights both moderation and leniency. Third, once initial opining takes place, we see that in a large majority of cases a precise penal outcome may be either deduced or projected; thus, in these cases it seems that the only judicial behavior that counts is initial input, after which the structure of the system takes over.

Finally, the order in which judges opine and must default does not seem to matter, except when the initial opinion shows a spread over four sentences. However, if the initial opinion so determines the final outcome, we would conclude that the judges with the most influence would be those who opine last, because they are the ones who can mold the initial opining and thus would be the ones to "give" the initial opinion to the system. It seems clear that, for example, the seventh judge would, in most cases, know what penal outcome would follow upon his voting for a particular sentence, even when that outcome is not the one for which he voted. This foresight would probably influence voting behavior, especially in senior judges who are familiar with the system, and especially in those senior judges who wish to dictate the court's decision.

Another question we might ask is "What does it mean if the historical data were to match our expected frequencies?" If that were so, we would say that the penal outcomes of the system were almost entirely rule-bound, a product more of the structure of the judicial system than of the judges. We would say that the personalities and legal philosophies of the individual judges did not exert much influence on the system of decision. Because our model treats judges as objects, not as "rational" decision-makers, we would say that whatever the judges thought they were doing, they behaved *as if* they were objects being stochastically assigned sentences in various combinations.

In our model, we might think of the seven judges seated in a row, each choosing to put on one of four penal hats during the initial opining. We find that once the hats are in place, in a large majority of cases the structure of the system dictated fashion. That is, the structure of the system dictates a very low incidence of death sentences, gives great weight to moderate sentences, and adds to that a weighting of lenient sentences.

In order to evaluate the bias of the seven-judge system and recognize its moderation and leniency, let us consider a system in which three judges vote for one of four sentences. Here, as earlier, the identities of the sentences are not very important, so long as they vary in their severity, but for the sake of convenience and comparison we shall again use "Death," "*bagnes* for life," "*bagnes* for nine years," and "p.a.i." as our four specific sentences. This system corresponds more to the structure of the provincial courts, but we will model the system in a manner similar to the seven-judge example. We will treat the decision process as the stochastic distribution of three objects into one of four partitions, and we will abide by the rules of procedure followed earlier. Of course, the influence of such rules will be lessened here, because the second round of opining, or the "narrowing to two" step, will be necessary only in cases where three opinions are represented.

Given the rules, three judges, and four sentences, Table A.7 lists all possible combinations, the number of ways each combination is possible, and the penal outcome associated with each combination. We construct Table A.7 using the same combinatorial techniques that were used in constructing the preceding tables and displays. We begin by noting that in this system, each of the three judges may "vote" for any one of four sentences. Thus, the number of possible outcomes is 3^7, or 64.

Unlike the seven-judge example, few of the combinations will require a second round. Thus, for all but the last four combinations we may deduce the penalty that results from the three judges' initial opining. For the final four combinations, we follow the rules of procedure and find that in each case the order in which the judges opined (and thus the order in which they must default in the attempt to reduce the number of opinions to two) will determine the penal outcome. Following the assumptions made to determine judicial movement in the seven-judge example, holding to the principle that all combinations are really likely, and considering that all orders are equally likely (e.g., the judge who voted for death is as likely to have opined first, as second or third), we may calculate the expected frequencies of each specific sentence in the three-judge, four-sentence model:

$$p(D) = 15 \div 64 = .23 \qquad P(B9) = 17 \div 64 = .27$$
$$p(BL) = 17 \div 64 = .27 \qquad p(p.a.i.) = 15 \div 64 = .23$$

Table A.7. *Initial opinion: possible outcomes*

Death	BL	B9	P.a.i.	#	Outcome
3	0	0	0	1	Death
0	3	0	0	1	BL
0	0	3	0	1	B9
0	0	0	3	1	P.a.i.
2	1	0	0	3	Death
2	0	1	0	3	Death
2	0	0	1	3	Death
0	2	1	0	3	BL
0	2	0	1	3	BL
0	0	2	1	3	B9
1	2	0	0	3	BL
1	0	2	0	3	B9
1	0	0	2	3	P.a.i.
0	1	2	0	3	B9
0	1	0	2	3	P.a.i.
0	0	1	2	3	P.a.i.
1	1	1	0	6	Death, BL, B9
1	0	1	1	6	B9, p.a.i.
0	1	1	1	6	BL, B9, p.a.i.
1	1	0	1	6	Death, BL
			Total	64	

In comparing these figures with those in Table A.6, several things are apparent:

1. The expected frequency of the most severe sentence is greatly increased as one moves from seven to three judges. The frequency of the death sentence is more than five times that in the seven-judge model.

2. Because there are only three judges, the moderating influence of the "plus two" majority rule is not relevant. The symmetry between severity and leniency, revealed in the pattern $p(\text{Death}) + p(\text{BL}) = p(\text{B9}) + p(\text{p.a.i.})$, is one associated with a "plus one" majority rule.

3. The frequency of the most benign sentence decreases as one moves to the three-judge model, as does the frequency of the B9 sentence. The decrease is a good representation of the percentage of sentences converted and/or ameliorated by the rules and structure of the seven-judge court.

4. The differences in sentence distribution between the three- and seven-judge court is great enough that it should be visible even with a relatively small data sample. One should pay

particular attention to the frequency with which the death
sentence is passed.

Despite the possible reduction of four penalties to two, and despite the certain requirement of a one-vote majority for most severe sentence, the penal outcomes in the three-judge court are almost evenly distributed among the four penalties, as shown in the preceding table in text; death had as solid a chance of being the sentence as any of the other three penalties. In only one, and the rarest, of the four combinations or partitions of opinion in a Tournelle was this the case: unanimity of opinion among the seven judges (Table A.1).

PART IV

Trials and judgments: illustrative cases

Introduction: The case record

The cases that are reconstructed in Part IV exemplify the judicial procedure described in Part III. I have examined 100 from among the some 1,200 judged by the Châtelet and the Parlement during the years 1748–9, 1761–2, 1780–1, and 1785–1787. The following 3 cases – one of assault on police agents, one involving theft from a tavern, and one of murder and robbery – have been selected from that 100. These cases were chosen for their relative banality: the banality of the crimes, defendants, trials, and outcomes. Our concern here is with common social protagonists, environments, and forms of *grand criminal*. The changing incidence of such cases and their penal outcomes will be disclosed in Volume 2, which concerns crimes and judgments from 1736 to 1789.

Documentation is complete for each case. We possess the record of all evidence that prosecutors and judges possessed; we lack only the physical presence of defendants and witnesses, therefore the facial expressions, gestures, and inflections of voice that magistrates also studied. But occasionally we can even infer that behavior from documentation. Most depositions by witnesses are translated in full, as are dialogues between magistrates and defendants during interrogations.[1] Detail was almost sovereign in Old Regime criminal justice, for it was from detail that patterns of intelligibility emerged for magistrates. This often meant redundancies that we, like eighteenth-century magistrates, must endure for the sake of comprehension. Written procedure formed a narrative. Like most narratives, it was often sinuous, with themes that persuaded by their recurrence in different voices, and with subtle changes in emphasis and direction.[2]

[1] Recording clerks rendered depositions by witnesses and interrogations of defendants in the third person: "Il a dit qu'il a été présent au moment du crime"; or "a lui demandé s'il a frappé le plaignant" and "a repondu que non." In actual practice, judges asked their questions in the second person ("Did you hit the plaintiff?") and defendants answered in the first person ("No, I did not"), just as witnesses made their statements in the first person ("I was present at the moment of the crime"). In translating, I have respected the natural form of deposition and interrogation.

[2] The case method used here gives "transparency" to criminal procedure, a procedure whose records were filled with voices. It transmits an integral dossier to the reader. Selective and summary presentation of trials and judgments is the opposing method of modern French legal historians. By compressing large documentation into brief juristic narration and analysis, such historians both superimpose themselves, as judges, on past magistrates, defendants, and witnesses, and prevent the reader from questioning their judgments. That method also obscures the

Illustrative cases

In exploring these cases, we explore an intensely dynamic yet frequently opaque world of lies and half-truths, concealed intentions, fragmentary actions, contrived or ambiguous social identities, stubborn resistances to judicial authority and legal reasoning, complicities and loyalties that were often dissimulated or tormented. Magistrates of the Châtelet and the Parlement were obliged to enter that world every day of their service in the criminal chambers, armed only with the rationalist procedure and jurisprudence of the 1670 ordinance.

human richness of the judicial archive and its power of social disclosure. For examples of French method, see Jean Imbert, ed., *Quelques procès criminels des XVIIe et XVIIIe siècles* (Paris: Presses Universitaires de France, 1964).

16

Assault

The Watch (*Guet*) and the Guard were the two most important police forces in Old Regime Paris. Eighteenth-century Parisians frequently conflated these two forces in nomenclature, although they were organizationally different. When Parisians did distinguish between them, they reserved most intense opprobrium and derision for the Watch.

The Old Regime Watch descended from the medieval archers of the Châtelet, and popular language retained that term for the foot soldiers of the Watch, along with a full lexicon of insults. In the eighteenth century, they were armed with muskets and bayonets. The force was small, from 125 to 150 (of which one-third were mounted), until 1770, when it was reduced and amalgamated with the Guard. During the same period, the Guard numbered from 600 to 900 foot and horse police. The men of the Watch, unlike those of the Guard, were not salaried. They purchased their rank and resembled a militia. Remunerations were a 5-percent annual interest return on the purchase price, small fees for jailings and giving testimony, and exemption from most royal taxes. The force was composed primarily of artisans and small tradesmen, many of whom were over the age of 40. They were liable for station and patrol duty two of every three nights. Although the Watch had its own titular commander until 1770 (the *chevalier du Guet*), it was under the superior authority of the lieutenant general of police, and thus of the Châtelet. It was stationed in squads of 7 to 10 men at guardposts in most of the twenty administrative Quarters of Paris; the squads were at the immediate disposition of local police commissioners. But the Watch was most present in the outer areas of the Inner City and in the faubourgs, whereas the Guard was responsible for patrolling the river, the Halles, and the ramparts. The Watch, like the Guard, normally patrolled in squads of 5 or 6 men, commanded by a corporal or sergeant. This was a significant unit of force, in appearance if not always in fact.

The Watch, and all other police and judicial agents, were forbidden by law to use injurious force in making arrests unless they were resisted violently or with weapons. Otherwise they were liable to sanctions and even criminal prosecution. By Articles 6 and 14 of Title X of the ordinance, the charge of resisting arrest had to be established by judicial investigation.[1] Police commissioners of the Châtelet were authorized to record such charges and, on order of the criminal lieutenant, to conduct a formal investigation. Judges, not police officials, decided the validity of the charges and of the use of force by arresting agents.

The duties of the Watch were multitudinous and primarily nocturnal: shutting down and clearing out drinking and dancing establishments at legal closing hour; arresting beggars, vagabonds, street prostitutes, and pimps, hustlers, charlatans, brawlers, disturbers of the peace, drunks who were violent, threatening, or stupefied, variously delinquent soldiers and recruits. Many of these "offenses" were not crimes in law but rather violations of police and military ordinances. The Watch was also the first-line, confrontational force of order against rioters. Units of the Guard and detachments of the regular army (the French and Swiss Guards regiments) were normally held back in reserve and to cordon off the area of riot. During riots of even small dimensions, men of the Watch were frequently overwhelmed and injured, and occasionally they were killed. They regularly guarded the courtyards and environs of the large Parisian jails and prisons, and they served as police at executions. When the plebeians of Paris attended the execution of a social analog, the usual force whose bayonets separated them from the victim was the Watch.

For most of the eighteenth century, the Watch also served as a general-purpose arresting force for various authorities, both judicial and nonjudicial. These included military officers. Until the last decades of the Old Regime, there were no military police for the many thousands of soldiers garrisoned or billeted in Paris. Officers frequently summoned the Watch to arrest and jail absconded recruits, soldiers absent without leave, and soldiers guilty of various insubordinations. The Watch complied, without need of judicial warrant. Such operations stretched the legal authority of the Watch to the extreme limit: The above were violations of military disciplinary codes, not crimes; the Watch was technically a judicial police force subject to the rules that limited the arresting powers of the Lieutenant Generalcy and the Châtelet. The tension was not only within law. As Jean Chagniot has demonstrated, the soldiery had multiple insertions within the collective life and values of plebeian Paris, insertions where solidarities coexisted with frictions. That soldiery, in its aggregate, came from the same social and provincial origins as the plebeian city. Most soldiers had volunteered to escape the rural penury and confinements that also impelled plebeian immigration to Paris. Many soldiers exercised trades in their off-duty time, married or found mistresses in the city, and settled in Paris after their

---

[1] Isambert, vol. 17, pp. 389–90. And Jousse: "Pour constater cette résistance de la part de l'accusé, ou même de la part d'autre personnes, & en général pour constater la rébellion, les Archers, Huissiers, ou Sergens doivent dresser leur procès-verbal. Ce procès-verbal doit être recordé de témoins, & rémis sur-le-champ entre les mains du Juge. Sur ce simple procès-verbal, le Juge peut décréter les coupables d'ajournement personnel; mais ils ne peuvent être décrétés de prise-de-corps, qu'après ces Archers ou Sergents & leurs records auront été répétés" (*Traité*, vol. 4, p. 79).

term of enlistment expired. They shared regularly in the popular conviviality and violence of bordellos, estaminets, dance halls, and street fairs.

Its duties and tasks placed the Watch in almost constant abrasive contact with popular and laboring Paris. By the canons and the procedures of criminal jurisprudence, certain of those tasks and the means by which the Watch fulfilled them were of doubtful legality. The men of the Watch were generally loathed and derided: In popular lingo, they were the *savetiers* (bunglers), *tristes-à-pattes* (flatfeet), and *happe-chairs* (flesh-snatchers) of public authority. They were often spontaneously attacked, especially at night and when they were making unpopular arrests.[2]

Several chronic urban tensions were most extreme during the night. The respectable and the harmless were inside, not moving through the city. The human diversity of circulation in the daylight metropolis narrowed at night, mostly to three groups: plebeians inflamed by drink, the delinquent and the desperate; a fearful and vigilant police. On penumbral and semideserted streets, chance encounters easily became confrontations.

The four defendants in our case of assault were young menservants of the count of Lussan who resided in his household (*l'hôtel des Charolais*) on the rue des Francs-Bourgeois in the Marais: Jean Moussard, "dit Comtois," coachman and postillion, age 26, native of Neuville-là-Charité near Besançon (Franche-Comté); Lorient Caignote (or Gaignote), aged 27, native of Vatan (Berry); Laurent Riqueville (or Biqueville), aged 32, native of Stil near Molzheim (Alsace); Jean Baptiste Loyer, "dit Hilaire," age 28, native of Marolles-sur-Seine (Ile-de-France). They were comrades in work and play. Like the majority of eighteenth-century Parisian domestic servants, they were born in villages and into settings of poverty and demographic surfeit. Beneath their aristocratic livery, they were uprooted young peasants.[3] Their household was in the aristocratic *quartier* of the Marais, but they took their pleasures in the plebeian *guingettes* of the Porcherons.

The Porcherons was an area of cabarets, open-air taverns, and restaurants with orchestras and dancing (*guingettes*), inns, and bordellos in the western portion of the Faubourg Montmartre. It lay just beyond the boulevard of the Ramparts that separated Inner Paris from the northern faubourgs, and was bisected by the course of the northern sewer. The main (and few) streets were the rues

[2] On the eighteenth-century Watch and its antagonists, see the following: Chagniot, *Paris et l'Armée*, pt. I, chaps. 2–3; Williams, *Police of Paris*, pp. 67–70; Arlette Farge, *Vivre dans la rue à Paris au XVIIIe siècle* (Paris: Gallimard/Juilliard 1979), pp. 173, 187, 206–7; Christian Romon, "Mendiants et policiers à Paris au XVIIIe siècle," *Histoire, Economie et Société* (1982): 259–95.

[3] Jean-Pierre Gutton, *Domestiques et serviteurs dans la France de l'Ancien Régime* (Paris: Aubier, 1981), has emphasized the rural origins of most domestics in eighteenth-century Paris, their relative youthfulness, the economic precariousness of their situations in the city and the frequency of unemployment among them, their clannishness, and the general propensity of male domestics to use insults and violence against police authorities and even to riot. And he suggests that they were torn between two identities: one plebeian, by origins, economic insecurity, and associations outside the household; the other aristocratic, by service and the livery. See also Roche, *Le peuple de Paris*, pp. 27–9.

Saint-Lazare, de la Croix-Blanche, des Martyrs, and especially the rue du Faubourg-Montmartre (known colloquially during the eighteenth century as the *chemin des Porcherons*). Before the last two decades of the century, the region was desolate, semirural, and meagerly populated – except at night. The Porcherons, like the Nouvelle France in the Faubourg Saint-Denis and the Courtille in the Faubourg du Temple, was one of the great nocturnal pleasure areas of the plebeian city: Drink was plentiful and cheaper than in the inner metropolis; police authority was more sparse and generally more permissive. The region magnetized plebeians from Paris *intra muros*. Freedoms, anonymities, and fugitive identities were all accessible there, both in the drunken and congested promiscuities of the *guingettes* and outside, in the darkness of a Quarter with few street lamps.

The complaint against the four servants was made near midnight on February 26, 1749, by Jacques-Phillippe Bollard, corporal commanding a Watch patrol from the guard post at Saint-Joseph (Montmartre Quarter), to Pierre Regnard, police commissioner of the Quarter, at Regnard's *hôtel* near Saint-Eustache:

About two hours ago, I was at the squad guard post near the Saint-Joseph Chapel [at the corner of the rue Saint-Joseph and the rue Montmartre] when a naval officer ("le Sieur Renard") summoned me to take a squad to the Porcherons to arrest three soldiers of naval infantry who are "suspect" because they habitually return to their billet at midnight or even later, and to take them to the military prison at Fort-l'Evêque [on the rue Saint-Germain l'Auxerrois and close to the Châtelet and the river]. I complied. We found and arrested the three, in the cabaret "at the sign of the Rat." While descending the rue du Faubourg-Montmartre, six or seven domestic servants in livery approached and began insulting us, calling us *bougres* [bastards] and *jean-foutres* and shouting that if they were in charge they would not arrest those three, that it gave them heartache to see three good fellows hauled away like that. [The soldiers' wrists had been tied when they were arrested.] As we crossed the boulevard of the Ramparts, the domestics conferred loudly among themselves about rescuing the soldiers, and then continued bellowing more insults and threats at us. When we arrived near the Saint-Joseph guard post, four of the domestics approached us and demanded to know why we had arrested the three soldiers. Suddenly, one of them jumped me, grabbed my halberd and bit my right hand [the bite marks were confirmed by the commissioner] to make me release it. The other domestics attacked the squad with fists and feet and rescued two of our prisoners, both of whom fled into the night. One of the domestics, named Moussard, is known to have been involved in a riot at the home of M. Desmoulins, where he was a servant, during which riot he smashed all the furniture. When I tried to arrest Moussard, he resisted like a wild man. In the struggle his head was bruised against the cornerstone of a wall.[4]

The squad had arrested the four servants in flagrant delict of *rébellion à la justice*, and the commissioner questioned them. He asserted in his report that they admitted in his presence to plotting and attempting the rescue of the three prisoners. But he did not formally interrogate them, and therefore his assertion

---

[4] Translations and citations of documents in this case are from the records in A.N. Y 10123.

had little probative value.[5] He attested to the physical damage suffered by Bollard and to the bruises and torn uniforms of the other Watchmen and then ordered the four servants to be taken to the prison of the Châtelet.

On the following day, February 27, they were interrogated by the criminal lieutenant at the Châtelet.

Jean Moussard, "dit Comtois"

Ques: Did you and three of your comrades not make a pact to rescue three persons that were under arrest by the Watch?

Ans: No. We had left the cabaret, and someone exclaimed that the Watch was hauling off three persons; I merely stated that the Watch are only bunglers and not worth attention.

Ques: Did you not grab the corporal's halberd and then bite his hand to make him release it?

Ans: No. When we and the patrol neared the Saint-Joseph guard post, I politely asked the sergeant [Bollard, corporal in command] what the three under arrest had done. In answer, the sergeant accused me of having been in the Desmoulins riot, and then hit me on the head with the halberd. The other Watchmen held me, tied my hands, and dragged me off to the commissioner. I did not resist.

Ques: Why did you and your comrades presume to interfere with the Watch and resist its authority?

Ans: My motive was only curiosity. I had no intention of rescuing the prisoners.

Ques: Did you not resist violently when the Watch tried to arrest you?

Ans: No. The sergeant told me that the action of the patrol was none of my business and to be off, and then struck me with the halberd as I was turning away. Then, one of the other Watchmen shouted that I had been part of the Desmoulins affair, strode toward me, struck me on the head with his musket butt, and shouted to the other Watchmen, "Arrest this joker" [Arrêtez-moi ce drôle-la!]. When they grabbed me, I did not resist.

Ques: Have you ever been in prison?

Ans: Yes, once for fifteen days when I was in the service of M. Desmoulins, about six months previous.

Ques: Are you willing to believe the testimony of witnesses?

Ans: If they speak the truth.[6]

Lorient Caignote

Ques: Did you and three of your comrades attempt to rescue three prisoners that a squad of the Watch was taking to jail?

Ans: No.

---

[5] Regnard was not obliged by law to do a formal swearing and interrogation of the four suspects at that late hour. He deferred the task to the criminal lieutenant.

[6] Magistrates of the Châtelet ended virtually every interrogation of defendants in *grand criminel* with this formulaic question. Defendants consistently replied in some variation of "Yes, if they speak the truth." In this and subsequent cases, I have omitted that formulaic question and its answer.

Ques: Did you not verbally abuse the squad and then attack it to rescue the prisoners?

Ans: No. My comrades and I asked the patrol why they were taking away the prisoners. Several Watchmen then ran toward us, and we ran away. When we saw that Comtois [Moussard] was not with us, we went back to the squad, which had arrested Comtois. We urged the squad to let him go, and when they refused, we insisted on accompanying the squad to the commissioner's office. The commissioner had us all taken to prison.

Ques: Why did you presume to attempt rescue of the squad's prisoners?

Ans: Neither myself nor my comrades had any hand in saving any prisoners.

Ques: Have you ever been in prison?

Ans: No.

Ques: Did you not aid in the escape of two prisoners that were in custody of the Watch last night?

Ans: I had nothing to do with that. One of my comrades named Comtois saw a patrol of the Watch leading away two persons and said, "Let's find out why they are being arrested." The squad handled Comtois very roughly.

Ques: Did you not help Comtois in rescuing the prisoners?

Ans: No. I only went to see what was happening to Comtois, saw him being beaten, and then I insisted that Comtois be taken to the commissioner.

Ques: Did you not continue to insult the patrol and prevent it from accomplishing its task?

Ans: No. I am calm by nature and incapable of such rowdy behavior.

Ques: You are not telling the truth. You tried to rescue Comtois from the squad and gave it strong resistance.

Ans: I am telling the truth. I only pleaded with the squad to stop beating Comtois.

Ques: Have you ever been in prison?

Ans: No.

Jean-Baptiste Loyer, "dit Hilaire"

Ques: On February 26, did you not participate in an attempt to rescue three prisoners from a Watch squad, and why did you do so?

Ans: I was not involved in any such act. The Watch has alleged that.

Ques: Did you not insult the squad, throw stones, and use your fists to make it let go of the prisoners?

Ans: No.

Ques: When you saw that the squad had Comtois, did you and your comrades not fight to rescue him?

Ans: No. The squad was repeatedly hitting Comtois with musket butts on the head, the sides, and the back. I pleaded with them to stop and to take Comtois to the commissioner.

Ques: Why did you participate in rescuing two prisoners from the squad?

Ans: I did not. Comtois, and only Comtois, asked the squad why they were arresting the three soldiers and what they had done. In response, the squad turned on him. My comrades and I went back to get the squad to stop beating Comtois.

Ques: Have you ever been in prison?

Ans: No.

Moussard and Riqueville declared that they could not sign their names. Loyer and Caignote signed in fluent script.

On request by the prosecutor and order of the criminal lieutenant, commissioner Regnard began the *information* by issuing summonses to Bollard and seven members of his Watch squad (March 4). He heard their depositions on March 6. Each of them was read the text of the February 26 complaint before he testified. Bollard's testimony repeated the substance of the complaint and added detail:

We were ordered to arrest the three soldiers and take them to the Fort-l'Evêque prison. We found one in an inn at the Porcherons and asked him where the other two were; he told us. We arrested him and then went to the cabaret "at the sign of the Rat." We found the two drinking with several other customers and arrested them in the cabaret. Soon after and at a short distance from the cabaret, we saw that we were being followed by a group of six or seven domestic servants, who began to insult us; neither I nor any member of my squad said anything back. When we turned in the direction of the Saint-Denis Gate, I overheard the domestics say, "We've got to jump those bastards; we can't let them haul off those three good boys" [Qu'il falloit tomber sur ces gueuz-la et ne point laisser emmener ces trois bons garçons]. We continued along without answering back. Near Saint-Joseph Chapel, four of them came up to us, and the one in grey and white livery asked why we were arresting the three soldiers. I told him that this was none of his business and to be on his way. Then I was attacked by that domestic, he tried to grab away my halberd and bit flesh from my hand. The three other domestics attacked the squad and pulled away two of the soldiers, who escaped. While we were struggling to arrest the servants, a carriage appeared. Someone dressed in black, wearing a wig and a sword, and who looked to be a bourgeois, got out. The bourgeois asked me why we were arresting the servants. I told him what had happened and that the servants had rescued two prisoners from my squad. He replied that we were right to do our duty. His coachman was about to take sides with the servants, since Moussard had shouted "A moi la livrée!" But the bourgeois prevented him and made him get back on his carriage seat, and they drove away. We managed to tie Moussard, the most violent and vicious of the four, and led them all to the commissioner's office. Once there, one of the domestics in red livery, who speaks German [probably Riqueville, who was Alsatian], said that if they had known that the squad would not fire on them, they would have sliced the whole squad to pieces. On the way to the Châtelet, Moussard tried to escape and became violent again. As we handed him over to the jailor, he shouted at me, "Sooner or later you will pay for this; I'll kill you even if you have ten thousand lives."

The five Watchmen who had been with Bollard during the entire incident gave testimony. Their statements echoed the substance and much of the detail of Bollard's. They claimed that Moussard was the primary aggressor but also incriminated the other three for insults and violence. They particularly emphasized the insults: "bougres"; "jean-foutres"; "bougres de savetiers"; "gueux"; "misérables"; "foutus happe-chairs" (fucking flesh-snatchers). Three claimed that they had suffered minor injuries. Antoine Morand stated that he was holding two prisoners; one of Moussard's comrades shouted, "Let go of those men!", kicked him in the thigh, and hit him in the stomach; as a result, he lost hold of a prisoner. Hilaire Abraham stated that while he was fighting off one of the servants, another one cut the rope binding the wrists of his prisoner, and that prisoner fled into the night. All six alleged that the battle occurred quite near Saint-Joseph Chapel and guard post.

The other two witnesses had not participated in the alleged battle between the squad and the servants. Michel Delisle had been ordered to remain on guard near Saint-Joseph when the squad went to the Porcherons. At about 11:00 P.M., he heard loud noises and went to investigate. He saw the squad struggling with a domestic dressed in grey and white livery, whose hands were tied and whom he recognized as having been in the Desmoulins affair some months earlier. He also saw three other domestics in red livery; his squad mates told him that the three had helped the one in grey and white to rescue two of the soldiers and had also insulted the squad. He accompanied the squad to the commissioner's office. Jacques Autant had also remained on guard duty. He was relieved at 11:00 P.M., and soon after he encountered the squad. It was holding a domestic in grey and white livery, who struggled and cursed the squad. He saw three other domestics who followed along with the squad. He also accompanied the squad to the commissioner's office and then to the Châtelet. At the threshold of the commissioner's office, the one in grey and white said that if he had been able to grab a musket he would have killed them all, and that if they (the four) had been more numerous they would have "exterminated" the squad. On the way to the Châtelet, the one in grey and white tried to escape and resisted the squad. But Delisle and Autant were not witnesses to any battle between the four domestics and the squad or to the escape of two prisoners. Neither claimed to have directly seen or heard any insulting, threatening, violent or resistant behavior by the three in red livery (Caignote, Riqueville, and Loyer). That battle and behavior may have occurred as the other six witness–participants alleged, but these two were not present.

Also on March 6, and independently of the *information*, the four defendants petitioned the criminal lieutenant for liberation from jail, or for decrees of *sorti sur requête*. Moussard claimed that he had established his innocence of the charges in his interrogation by the criminal lieutenant and that he was also innocent of "any evil purpose or any intention to insult or incite revolt against the Watch." Each of the others, in petitions that were almost identically worded, asserted his own innocence but incriminated "one of his comrades" and by the following phrase: "having taken no part in the disturbance caused by one of his comrades or in the violence and resistance against the Watch by that comrade." By implication, the "comrade" in question was Moussard. The petitions were denied.

The criminal lieutenant interrogated the defendants for a second and final time on March 10. His questioning incorporated the testimony obtained from the *information*.

Assault

Jean Moussard

Ques: During the night of February 26, when you were returning from the Porcherons and when you encountered a Watch squad, why did you call the squad "foutus gueux," and "bougres de jean-foutres," and exclaim loudly that it gave you heart-ache to see good fellows hauled away like that?

Ans: One of my comrades made sign to me that the Watch was holding three prisoners. I replied that the Watch are only "savetiers" and that they probably would not be able to hold on to those three. But I did not insult the squad.

Ques: Did you not approach the squad and ask why they were arresting the three, and when the sergeant told you that such was none of your business, did you not assail the sergeant and bite his hand to make him release the halberd?

Ans: All of that is false. I only asked the sergeant why they had arrested the three. The sergeant told me to be off. As I was leaving, one of the Watchmen gave me a blow with his musket butt that caused me great pain.

Ques: Did not all four of you attack the men of the Watch with fists and feet, and by this violence cause the squad to lose two prisoners?

Ans: There was no violence on our part. I do not know how those prisoners escaped; but I was arrested at once.

Ques: Once arrested, did you not continue to threaten the Watch, and exclaim that if you had known that they would not shoot, you would have slashed them up, and that you would kill them?

Ans: All of that is false. We committed no violence against the squad, but the sergeant insulted and physically abused me even after I was arrested.

Ques: Have you ever been in prison?

Ans: Yes, I was once in jail for fighting.

Lorient Caignote

Ques: Were you not with a group of five or six other domestic servants on the Porcherons road at about 10:00 P.M. on February 26?

Ans: There were four of us, and we were returning from the Porcherons.

Ques: Why did you and your comrades insult a Watch squad when it passed by?

Ans: We were returning from the Porcherons, just as I said, but one of my comrades, named Moussard, coachman in the service of the count of Lussan, called the men of the Watch "jean-foutres de savetiers" and told them that if they [the servants] were in the situation of the three soldiers, the squad would not be able to haul them off. The sergeant arrested Moussard; we simply followed along to the commissioner's office. We did not insult the squad.

Ques: Were you and your comrades not in concert to harass the squad, and did you not attack it in order to cause the escape of the squad's prisoners?

Ans: We had no plan or intention of causing the prisoners to escape. We only entreated the Watch not to mistreat our comrade who had been arrested for insulting the squad.

Ques: Is it not true that all four of you rushed the squad, hit out with fists and feet, and by that means caused the escape of two prisoners?

Ans: We struck no blows. I do not know how the prisoners escaped – unless it was when one of my comrades first attacked the squad, but I was not in on that.

Ques: Did you or the others not shout, "A moi la livrée!", to summon all domestics
 within earshot and call them down on the squad?
Ans: No.
Ques: When you were at the commissioner's office, did not one of you say that if he had
 known that the squad would not shoot, he would have slashed up all of them, and
 then tell the sergeant that he would get him sooner or later, even if he had ten thou-
 sand lives?
Ans: I heard no such thing. We were guilty of no violence.
Ques: Have you ever been in prison?
Ans: No.

Laurent Riqueville

Ques: On February 26, when you and your comrades encountered a squad of the Watch
 while returning from the Porcherons, did you not insult the squad and attack it?
Ans: We did not insult the squad. The coachman of the count of Lussan simply said
 to him and the others that the Watch are "savetiers," and that it pained him to see
 them hauling off three good fellows. I myself did not insult the squad.
Ques: Did you and your comrades not attack the squad with fists and feet and force it
 to release two prisoners?
Ans: My comrades and I neither insulted nor attacked the squad. The coachman had
 disappeared from our group, and we went to find him. We found him in the hands
 of the squad, being abused, and we entreated the Watchmen to stop the abuse.
Ques: Did not one of you bite the sergeant's hand to make him release his halberd?
Ans: I did not see that, but I certainly did not do it.
Ques: Did you or the others not shout, "A moi la livrée!"
Ans: No.
Ques: Did you not threaten to kill the sergeant, even if he had a thousand lives?
Ans: We made no threats.
Ques: Have you ever been in prison?
Ans: No.

Jean-Baptiste Loyer

Ques: When you and four or five others were returning from the Porcherons, did you
 not plot to attack a squad of the Watch that was passing by?
Ans: We did not plot against anyone.
Ques: When you and the others saw that the squad had three prisoners, did you not call
 the Watchmen "jean-foutres de bougres" and declare that it gave you heartache to
 see those good fellows arrested?
Ans: That is not true.
Ques: When one of the Watchmen told you that the arrest was none of your business,
 did you not then attack the squad and cause the escape of two prisoners?
Ans: None of that is true. When we saw that one of our comrades had been arrested
 by the squad, we followed along to see what would happen to him; but we were not
 insulting or violent.
Ques: Did you or the others not shout, "A moi la livrée!", to bring down other domestics on the squad?

Ans: We did not call out for anyone, and we had no bad intentions.

Ques: Is it not true that one of you declared that if he had known that the squad would not fire on them, he would have slashed them to pieces?

Ans: No. We made no threats.

Ques: Have you ever been in prison?

Ans: No.

Caignote incriminated Moussard for insulting and attacking the squad. The prosecutor requested *récolement* and confrontation of Caignote with Moussard. This was done on March 12. Caignote's statements were read to him in the presence of Moussard; he swore to their authenticity, affirmed that he had indeed referred to Moussard, and "that he upholds those statements as true in their entirety." Moussard denied Caignote's allegations of insults and assault, but he did admit to having called the Watch "savetiers" in speaking to his comrades. Caignote's statements were read to him a last time, and he signed.

On March 28, Jean Moussard was transferred from the Châtelet prison to the hospital of the Hôtel-Dieu. He died there three days later. The death certificate did not state the cause, but it was probably the head injuries he had suffered in the altercation with the squad.

Récolement of the eight witnesses for prosecution and their confrontation with Caignote, Riqueville, and Loyer were accomplished on April 17 and 18. In *récolement*, none of the eight changed their depositions of March 6. During the confrontations, there was no mention, by any party, of Moussard's death. It is probable that the witnesses and defendants did not yet know that he had died.

Each confrontation of accusing witness with a defendant was in the fixed sequence mandated by the ordinance: (1) Witness and defendant were sworn to speak the truth; (2) each was asked if he knew or recognized the other; (3) the name, age, occupation, and place of domicile of the witness were read to the defendant, and he was asked if he wished to challenge that information or the personal credibility of the witness (none of the three defendants did so); (4) the depositions of the witness in *information* and *récolement* were read aloud, and the witness was asked if he persisted in the testimony as read and if he wished to make additional statements; (5) the defendant was invited to challenge the depositions and any additional statements; (6) the witness was given opportunity to respond to the challenges or simply to reiterate his statements as truth; (7) a transcript of the confrontation was read to the witness and the defendant, and both were summoned to sign in authentification of their respective statements.

The eight witnesses persisted in the depositions made during the *information* and *récolement;* these alleged insults, assault, and attempt to rescue prisoners by the three defendants. When Bollard and the five members of his squad who had been in the altercation were confronted successively with each of the three defendants, they identified each as one of the three in red livery who had insulted and attacked them along with Moussard. The only variation in the incriminations was by Emmanuel Giraud: When Caignote denied his testimony, Giraud answered that Caignote was "one of the least troublesome" of the four.

The defendants denied the accusations. But two of them equivocated. Nicolas Fontaine, who had been with Bollard, accused the three of attacking the squad soon after Moussard's attack on Bollard, and of attacking him when he aided Bollard. He identified Caignote as one of the attackers. Caignote replied in challenge, "I accept the deposition as true except as regards me; I was neither violent nor insulting." This was to imply, under oath, that some or all of the others had been insulting and violent. Riqueville's "challenge" to Fontaine's identical testimony against him was similar: He denied personal guilt but credited the testimony against the others. All three of them realized that the testimony of Delisle and Autant did not directly incriminate them and was dubious as testimony for prosecution. They accepted Delisle's general statement, while explicitly denying its hearsay element. They accepted Autant's testimony, each adding that "it does not incriminate me." Both Riqueville and Loyer asserted that they were arrested by the squad only because they had insisted on accompanying the squad and Moussard to the commissioner's office.

The opposition between the two versions of the incident remained almost as complete at the end of the confrontation as it had been before. The testimony of Delisle and Autant was, in a sense, neutral. It did not incriminate the three, but it did not disculpate them of charges of insult, assault, and rescuing prisoners; it only signified that the defendants were not doing such things when the two arrived on the scene. The defendants did not challenge the eyewitness status of the five members of Bollard's squad, nor did they allege justifacatory facts or suggest possible witnesses in their defense after the confrontation. The third soldier, whom the squad had managed to place in Fort-l'Evêque, was never mentioned or summoned as a witness by the prosecutor or the defendants. Finally, there is no documentary trace of any intervention on their behalf by the count of Lussan or his family.

This case, like so many judged by the Châtelet and the Parlement during the eighteenth century, formed a Rashomon-like enigma. Discrepancies between testimony, responses in interrogation and confrontation, and material evidence made it impossible for judges to know what precisely had occurred before, during, and immediately after the confrontation between the squad and the defendants. Like us, they could only use this documentation as the basis for deducing plausibilities and probabilities within the event and for rendering a judgment.

The four defendants had been arrested in flagrant delict of *rébellion à la justice*, or resisting and obstructing legal authorities. They were charged with four offenses in law: (1) insulting the Watch; (2) assaulting the Watch; (3) rescuing prisoners; (4) violently resisting arrest (Moussard only). These charges were retained by the prosecutor and the instructing judge from the *information* through the confrontation. The second and third of the charges were the most serious in penal liability.

The prosecutor made his written recommendation of sentence on May 10. He found the three guilty of "insults and violence against a squad of the

Watch." He did not find them guilty of plotting or attempting to rescue prisoners or of resisting their own arrest. He recommended that the three be banished from Paris for three years (the minimal term of banishment) and fined 3 livres each (a minimal fine). They were judged by the bench of the Châtelet on May 20. They were heard separately in their final statements before judgment, but they virtually echoed each other. Each admitted that he had been drinking at the Porcherons and on the way home had passed a squad of the Watch with three prisoners. Each denied that he had insulted or assaulted the squad or conspired or acted to rescue the prisoners. The denials of culpability were complete, and probably collusive. But each of them, in almost identical language, incriminated the deceased Moussard: "Comtois who is dead had an altercation with the Watch, but I do not know what happened" (Riqueville); "The one who is dead said something to the Watch" (Caignote); "Comtois said something to the Watch about releasing their prisoners" (Loyer).[7] The reporting judge concurred with the prosecutor's recommended verdict and sentence. But Judge Pierre Pitoin objected that their violence against the squad was an aggravated offense, for it had produced the escape of two prisoners. He opined for nine years of banishment, the maximum term of that sentence that a subaltern court could pronounce. His opinion prevailed, but only after two rounds of opining and by a majority of one among nine judges. On May 24, the three defendants and the documentation of their case were transferred to the Parlement for final judgment. They were judged by the Tournelle on June 6, found guilty only of assault and violence against the Watch, and given definitive sentence of banishment for three years and fine of 3 livres each.[8]

Magistrates of the Châtelet and the Parlement were not required by the ordinance or custom to give the reasons for their judgments, and they did not usually do so in trial records. Therefore, we do not know the reasoning that led the prosecutor, presiding judge, three other judges of the Châtelet, and the bench of the Tournelle to refuse Pitoin's opinion, to find the defendants guilty of insulting and assaulting the Watch but not of rescuing the prisoners, and to punish them rather leniently. But we may conjecture the following reasoning, from details of the case and principles of jurisprudence.

By their own admission, the four domestic servants had followed the squad and its prisoners for a long distance, from the close environs of the cabaret "at the sign of the Rat" to near the Saint-Joseph guard post on the rue Montmartre, and along dark and semideserted streets. If their immediate destination had been the household on the rue des Francs-Bourgeois, they would not have taken such a route. This stalking of the squad did not suggest innocent curiosity, and one may surmise that the stalk was accompanied by derision and insults. Witnesses asserted that Moussard was the initial and most vehement aggressor among the four, both verbally and physically. He was accorded a

---

[7] From the minutes of judgment of their case in A.N. Y 10514.
[8] A.N inventory 450, vol. 3.

similar role by the defendants, in muted terms by Riqueville and Loyer, explicitly by Caignote. These three, while denying all charges of insulting and assaulting the squad, did avow that they approached the squad and stayed with it only to protect their friend Moussard. Five of the witnesses alleged that the three became violent soon after the battle was joined between Moussard and Bollard. Quite probably, Caignote, Loyer, and Riqueville physically intervened against the Watchmen to aid their workmate and comrade Moussard, who was being beaten by at least Bollard. They probably did so with the spontaneous and immediate intention of siding with Moussard against his antagonists (whom they also despised) but not with the purpose of rescuing the soldiers. Their intervention probably facilitated the escape of two prisoners. But that intervention was not deemed by the Parlement to have been rescue of the prisoners.

Criminal responsibility required criminal intent. The consequences of a distinct act did not establish the motives for that act. Motives or intent had to be induced by judges from details of the act, the character of the defendant, and statements by the defendant. During the two interrogations, the criminal lieutenant repeatedly asked the question "Why?": Why had they attacked the squad? Why had they presumed to rescue the prisoners? His locution should not be read only as a tactic for entrapping the defendants into admitting that they did attack the squad and attempt to rescue its prisoners. It also had literal meaning. The criminal lieutenant inquired insistently as to the defendants' motives. He was urging them to state their subjective conceptions of their personal behavior, even to justify their alleged act. They denied both culpable intent and culpable acts, and yet the judge persisted in this questioning of personal motive. The criminal lieutenant and his colleagues were probing for intent before deciding on the charge of rescuing prisoners. Rescue signified an intentional act. This was the charge that the defendants denied most consistently and vehemently. Ultimately, their denial of intent to rescue was given credence. They were not found to be criminally responsible for the escapes. The judges would also have known that Bollard and his squad members needed to insist that the four had attacked them to rescue the prisoners, for they needed to avoid responsibility for the escape of the prisoners. In its decision on this case, the Parlement sacrificed the interests, and even the authority, of the police to rules of jurisprudence.

Behind the case, there was a concordance between popular and jurisprudential conceptions of just and unjust police actions. According to the popular conception, the arrest and jailing of the three soldiers was a typically unjustified and oppressive police action: The soldiers had not been disorderly in the cabaret; they were not charged with any crime; they had not resisted arrest; they had simply violated a military curfew. One may surmise that the servants were actuated by that notion of injustice: they followed the squad, insulted it, and repeatedly demanded to know why the soldiers were being arrested. When Moussard became most threatening, the corporal reacted with violence, and the three others joined the altercation. But in arresting the three soldiers, the Watch had acted at the extreme limits of its legal authority, as those limits were defined in criminal jurisprudence.

By a principle of jurisprudence that dated from at least the sixteenth century and that had been upheld in specific decisions by the Parlement of Paris during the seventeenth and eighteenth centuries, there were situations in which rescue of arrested persons or resistance by third parties to their arrest were meliorative acts, not subject to normal penalties for *rébellion à justice:* when it was manifest that the arrest was made by unauthorized persons, and without flagrant delict; when it was equally evident that the arrest was without cause, valid order, or warrant. The exceptions to the latter principle, or persons whom judicial and police agents could arrest without warrant and flagrant delict, were also eloquent and relevant to this case: vagabonds; those illegally carrying weapons; those suspected of violating sentences of banishment.[9] The three soldiers were not such persons. By the same principle, there were cases in which resistance to arrest was not a crime but a legitimate exercise of self-defense against an unlawful act.[10]

The trial had not established intent to rescue prisoners as the three defendants' motive for insulting and then probably attacking the Watch squad. Therefore, the Parlement found them guilty only of violence. But by its refusal to find them guilty of rescuing prisoners, one may speculate that the Parlement was also implicitly questioning the validity of the arrest and jailing of those prisoners by the Watch.

Rébellion à justice, the principal crime in this case, was a very common offense in the jurisdictions of the Châtelet and the Parlement during the eighteenth century. Definitions were comprehensive: "those who directly or indirectly prevent, by violence or assault, the execution of judicial orders or sentences";[11] "whenever someone insults or mistreats Magistrates, Officials, Summons-servers, or Sergeants who are carrying out and executing judicial actions."[12] The definition encompassed all police authorities. These were royal cases, and they could not be tried by seigneurial courts. Incrimination and penaliza-

---

[9] "Au reste, cette distinction n'a pas lieu [between permissible and impermissible arrest] dans le cas où les Archers peuvent arrêter sans ordonnance de Justice; comme quand on est trouvé portant les armes defendues; ou à l'égard de celui qui enfreint son ban; ou quand il s'agit de vagabonds; car alors comme les Archers peuvent arrêter d'eux-mêmes & sans decret du Juge, il n'est pas permis de leur résister" (Jousse, *Traité,* vol. 4, p. 74).

[10] "Cela a lieu principalement lorsque celui qui veut arrêter est sans caractère [without authority to arrest]; ou lorsq'ayant caractère, il n'a point les marques de son ministère; ou bien lorsqu'il porteur d'un mandaement, ou décrêt d'un Juge sans caractère; ou lorsqu'il a excédé son pouvoir; ou qu'il n'a point observé les formes de Justice. En effet, cette résistance est plutôt une défense légitime qu'une rébellion. . . . Ainsi, il est permis alors à celui qu'on veut arrêter importunement, non seulement de résister, mais encore d'appeller ses amis & ses voisins à son secours, pour l'aider à se défendre" (ibid., pp. 79–80).

[11] Ibid., p. 68.

[12] Muyart, *Institutes,* p. 461.

tion were by royal edict.[13] The statutes embodied the determination of the monarchy to protect its developing judicial and police authority. But the determination was subtly countervailed by jurisprudence. The forms, circumstances, and motives that attended most cases of *rébellion à la justice* made penalties discretionary in practice. Judgment was subject to mitigating considerations, and penal outcome was frequently anodyne. Both in fact and in penal law, police authority remained fragile in eighteenth-century France. The case illustrates that fragility.

Customary penalties for *rébellion à la justice* ranged from payment of damages and fines (of up to 200 livres), whipping, the *carcan*, branding, to banishment for from three to nine years. Insults to officials of the law were comprised within the general definition of the offense.[14] The most violent and aggravated forms of the offense (armed assault or resistance against judicial agents in their duty or armed rescue of prisoners) were subject to capital penalties: *galères*, *hôpital-général*, or death. To resist arrest was a crime, but one subject to discretionary penalty according to the circumstances and the nature of resistance.[15] Rescue of prisoners or arrested persons from police and judicial agents was an offense customarily subject to afflictive or carceral penalties. But if the rescue was of a *galérien* from the chain or of a person who had been condemned to death, the penalty could be death. This fact of law partially explains the rarity of attempts by sympathetic crowds to rescue condemned persons during eighteenth-century Parisian executions. However, "if the apprehended person has not yet been convicted, or if the crime for which he was arrested is minor, the punishment should be of lesser severity and at the discretion of the judge."[16] That was exactly the situation in the case of the soldiers and the four servants.

---

[13] And in the most general terms by Article 190 of the Edict of Blois, May 1579: "Defendons sur peine de la vie à nos sujets de quelque qualité qu'ils soient, excéder et outrager aucuns de nos magistrats, officiers, huissiers ou sergents faisans, exercans et exécutans acte de justice. Voulons que les coupables de tels crimes soient rigoureusement châtiez, sans espoir de miséricorde, comme ayant directement attenté contre notre autorité et puissance" (Isambert, vol. 14, p. 426). Cf. Articles 29, 31, and 33 of the Ordinance of Moulins, February 1566 (ibid., pp. 197–8).

[14] "C'est encore une rébellion à la Justice que d'outrager ou insulter les Juges, & autres Officiers de Justices dans leurs fonctions ou à l'occasion de leurs fonctions" (Jousse, *Traité*, vol. 4, p. 68).

[15] "La peine qui se prononce, dans ce cas, est ordinairement une peine arbitraire, suivant les circonstances & la qualité du fait. Ainsi lorsque celui qu'on veut arrêter, excite & appelle à son secours, ou lorsqu'il oppose la violence avec des armes, & qu'il blesse & maltraite les Archers, ou Sergents qui l'arrêtent; dans ce cas, il peut être puni de peine capitale, surtout s'il étoit prévenu d'un crime qui emportât cette peine. . . . Mais si l'accusé n'opposoit qu'une violence privée sans aucunes armes, ou moyens de laquelle il se sauvât des mains de la Justice, il doit étre condamné à une peine plus légère, suivant les circonstances du fait. De même, si celui qu'on veut arrêter, appelle & excite le peuple à son secours, sans opposer aucune violence publique, il doit aussi être condamné à une peine arbitraire" (ibid., pp. 76–7). Thus, the characteristics that especially aggravated the resistance and made it subject to capital penalties were the gravity of the crime for which the subject was being arrested, resistance with weapons, and injuring the arresting authority. For a full discussion of *rébellion à la justice* in law and jurisprudence, see ibid., pp. 67–95.

[16] Ibid., p. 72.

This case also illustrates the volatility of relations between the populace of Paris and its uniformed police. That volatility was enduring. But the case was also a harbinger, among many in 1749, of the great antipolice riots of May 1750. Those were among the most severe riots in the history of eighteenth-century Paris, by their scale and their violence. They were provoked essentially by the mounting arbitrariness and brutality of Watch, Guard, police commissioners, and inspectors in their arrests and jailings, notably of beggars, vagabonds, and other "delinquents" (including children suspected of vagabondage, begging, and street crime). The riots were triggered by the rumor that there were off-spring of Parisian artisans and tradesmen among the hundreds of children who had been swept from the streets and into the Hôpital-Général during these po-lice operations of 1749–50 (which was true), and that all of them were destined by secret royal order for deportation to French Canada along with cargoes of adult beggars and vagabonds (which was false). But the rumor circulated at the end of a long period of sporadic local resistance to Watch arrests of locally known and "protected" beggars, and a long period of general abrasiveness between police and plebeians. The judgmental response of the Parlement of Paris to the great "sedition" of 1750 was fundamentally comprehending and clement.[17] And it included sanctions and penalties against police officials and agents.

In cases of *"rébellion à la justice,"* the magistracy of the Châtelet and the Par-lement acted generally with caution, discrimination, penal moderation, and even leniency. The primary loyalty of that magistracy was to principles and procedures of the criminal law, not to the discourse and interests of police authority.

---

[17] For excellent accounts of the 1750 riots, see Farge, *La vie fragile*, pt. III, chap. 3, and Christian Romon, "L'affaire des 'enlèvements d'enfants' dans les archives du Châtelet (1749–1750)," *Revue Historique*, 270 (1983): 55–95.

17

Theft

Thefts accounted for approximately three-fourths of the crimes prosecuted in *grand criminel* by the Châtelet and the Parlement from 1735 through 1789. They formed a considerably higher percentage of crimes prosecuted in the urban jurisdiction of the Châtelet than in the jurisdictions of provincial courts. The frequency and complexity of theft in Old Regime France was addressed by fastidious classification and penal gradation of thefts in the criminal law. Opportunistic and furtive thefts of small or easily portable objects from public or semipublic places – such as work sites, stalls and markets, shops, taverns and inns, washing lines, fields, pastures, and orchards – were the most common form of the crime during the eighteenth century. The great majority of such thefts were classified in law as *vols simples*.[1] Subsequent to the royal declaration of March 1724, the minimal and mandatory penalty for first offenders in theft was whipping and branding with the mark of *V* (*voleur/voleuse.*)

Women were a salient proportion of the thieves prosecuted, particularly by the Châtelet.[2] Most of them were tried for simple theft. When they were accused of aggravated thefts, it was usually as domestic servants or as accomplices of men. A high proportion of those women were unmarried or widows. Their economic condition was generally more base and precarious than that of men,

---

[1] *Vols qualifiés* (or aggravated thefts, which were punished more severely) were of the following types: theft at night; theft from domiciles, churches, royal edifices or properties; theft by breaking and entering, with weapons or violence; by apprentices or journeymen from their masters, by domestic servants from their households; by previous offenders or vagabonds; multiple thefts. The circumstances of a theft and the character of its author were accorded greater importance in law and penalty than the monetary value of the objects stolen, in stark contrast to the criminal justice of eighteenth-century England. On contemporary English justice in regard to theft, see especially Douglas Hay and E. P. Thompson, *Albion's Fatal Tree: Crime and Society in Eighteenth Century England* (New York: Pantheon, 1975), and Peter Linebaugh's superb *The London Hanged: Crime and Civil Society in the Eighteenth Century* (Cambridge: Cambridge University Press, 1992).

[2] During 1762 (the year of the case), approximately 575 men were judged on appeal by the Parlement of Paris. One hundred seventy-six of them (or 30%) had been judged by the Châtelet. Of that total, 148 (or 84%) were judged for thefts. Close to one-sixth of the 148 were accused of nocturnal burglaries or thefts with violence. One hundred thirty-eight women were judged on appeal from the entire jurisdiction; 97 (or 70%) were accused of theft. Sixty-one of these women had been judged by the Châtelet, and a total of 58 (or 95%) of them were accused of theft (inventory 450, vols. 5–8).

and their material need more chronic and intense. Single women attracted by the labor markets of the metropolis and severed from their provincial families, and widows in the metropolis, were prey to multiple exploitations and expropriations. Their larcenies were often acts of survival and defiance. And their common dress facilitated opportunistic theft. It was ideal for concealment: wide, billowing skirts with folds, layers, and deep pockets; loose blouses; long and thick shawls in winter. But they were frequently caught, whether during the act, in its proximate aftermath, or when they attempted to sell stolen goods, for many of them lacked artifice in theft.

At noon on Monday, October 26, 1761, Police Inspector Philippe-Edouard Roulier came into the office of François-Simon Chastelus, police commissioner of the Saint-Jacques de la Boucherie Quarter, with a woman whom he had just arrested on suspicion of theft.[3] She had attempted to sell two engraved silver forks to street pedlars on the rue des Arcis. Chastelus first heard one of the pedlars: Marie-Elizabeth Bonneval, *revendeuse*, domiciled rue des Nonaindiers.[4]

As I was walking on the rue des Arcis this morning with two associates, the woman who has been arrested came up and offered to sell two silver forks for 6 francs [the equivalent of 6 livres]. I bargained with her, first offering 4 livres, then 5, then 5½). While we were bargaining, inspector Roulier had been informed. He arrived and arrested her. When arrested, she admitted that the forks belonged to a tavern owner on the rue de la Harpe, that she had dined there yesterday with another woman, and said that she did not know how the forks came to be in her pocket.

Each of the forks was engraved clearly with the initials "E. J." Chastelus then sent for the presumed owner – Elie Jouan, tavern-keeper (*marchand de vin*) on the rue de la Harpe, at the corner of the rue Poupée. He arrived and made the following statement:

Yesterday [Sunday, October 25] two engraved silver forks were taken from my tavern. I suspected two women who left at 10:00 P.M., one of whom is the woman under arrest. [Chatelus showed him the two forks; he identified them as those missing from his stock.] I served those women with these forks when they dined. When I counted the silver at closing time, I saw that they were missing. I asked my serving boy if he had served the two women with forks. He answered yes. I described the missing forks to him. Then I asked the two women, who were drinking in the saloon, if they had returned the forks. They answered yes. We then searched all over the tavern, and the two women saw the trouble we were taking to find the forks. I should have searched them, but I did not go that far. I let them leave with the other customers.

Chastelus interrogated the woman.

[3] The records of the case are in A.N. Y 10237.
[4] *Revendeuses* were pedlar women who bought used goods (mostly clothing, accessories, linens, and household articles) for resale in public; they either sold from stalls or laid out their goods on walkways. Women formed the majority of such ambulant street pedlars in eighteenth-century Paris.

Ques: What are your name, surname, age, occupation, birthplace, and residence?

Ans: I will not tell you my name. I would rather die than tell. I live wherever I can, and sometimes I beg. I am from Paris, from the parish of St. Nicolas du Chardonnet, where I live.

Ques: Are you married?

Ans: I am a widow, with no children. [She began to weep.]

Ques: What is your name?

Ans: I would rather die than tell you my name, because of my family.

Ques: I summon you to state your name.

Ans: I will not.

Ques: Where were you baptized?

[She did not respond]

Ques: Yesterday evening, did you drink in Jouan's tavern on the rue de la Harpe with another woman, and then leave at about 10:00 P.M.?

Ans: We also dined [lunched] there. It was then that I took the two forks. I returned to the tavern with my friend after supper. That was my misfortune. Jesus Mary, am I to be ruined, and my family dishonored, because of a miserable moment?

[She was shown the forks, and asked if they were ones she had taken from Jouan.]

Ans: Yes, and the same that I tried to sell this morning.

Ques: When you and your friend left the tavern at 10:00 P.M. did the owner ask you to hand over the forks?

Ans: No, he did not. I took them earlier.

Ques: What is the name of the woman who was with you in the tavern?

Ans: I will not tell you. She is not guilty of this theft. I took the forks.

Ques: Was the woman with whom you dined yesterday the same woman with whom you supped?

Ans: Yes, it is the same woman. But she had nothing to do with the theft. I took the forks carelessly, without thinking ["par mégarde"]. They were in my hand when I walked out of the tavern. Then I put them in my pocket outside, without thinking. If the owner had asked me for them then, I surely would have given them to him.

Ques: What is your occupation?

Ans: I have been a bonnet stitcher for the twenty years that I have lived in Paris.

Ques: What is your name, and where do you live?

Ans: I will never tell you.

Her clothing was searched, and nothing was found in her pockets. The secretary read aloud the transcript, asked if she accepted it as authentic and her answers as true, and invited her to sign. She declared that she could neither read nor write, began weeping again, and exclaimed that the commissioner could learn about her from Father Bachelet at the Celestins Convent.

Ques: What should I ask him, and about whom?

Ans: You only have to ask him about Marie-Cécile Gosset.

Ques: Is that your name?

Ans: Yes.

Ques: What was your husband's name?

Ans: You can ask Father Bachelet, and he will tell you.

Ques: How old are you?

Ans: I am forty-five.

Ques: Where are you from?

Ans: Amiens. I ask to be locked up. I deserve that. But God forbid that my family suffer this blemish!

Chastelus ended the interrogation. Marie-Cécile Gosset was read the transcript and accepted it as authentic. The forks were kept as evidence, and she was jailed at the Grand Châtelet.

At 10:30 P.M. inspector Roulier returned with another woman whom he had just arrested on the rue de la Harpe, as the companion of Marie-Cécile Gosset. She was interrogated by Chastelus. She identified herself as Françoise Legrand, unmarried, age 26 or thereabouts, housemaid and occasional beggar, native of Apremont (Franche-Comté), domiciled in the lodging house of Madame Goulart on the rue Percée near the rue de la Harpe, where she paid 4 sous a night for her room.[5]

Ques: With whom did you spend last evening?

Ans: With Dame Bonneuil [Marie-Cécile Gosset].

Ques: Where did you go to meet her?

Ans: At Mme. Haribate's on the rue Percée, which is where Dame Bonneuil works and is next to Goulart's lodging house. Dame Bonneuil suggested that we go drink two *sétiers* of wine [16 pints] at a tavern on the rue de la Harpe. On the way, Dame Bonneuil bought 4 sous' worth of salt pork for our dinner. At the tavern, we were given two silver forks for our pork. At the end of the meal, at about 3:00 or 4:00 in the afternoon, Dame Bonneuil took the forks with her when she went to pay at the counter. I had given her 9 sous for my bill. We left together. I thought she had deposited the forks at the counter when she paid. She did not tell me that she had taken them. We parted outside the tavern. We live in the same lodging house, run by Mme. Goulart. I have a small room to myself. Dame Boneuil lives in the common room with several other women. I went back to my room to sleep. At about 9:00 P.M., Dame Bonneuil came in and urged me to drink with her at the tavern. She was drunk. I declined to go, giving the excuse that I did not have money for more drinking. She told me not to worry, that she had money. She said that she had been to the Courtille [a large and famous *guingette* in the Faubourg du Temple] and that friends there had given her drink money. We returned to the same tavern on the rue de la Harpe. She knew people there and talked with several of them. After a while, she took up with a man and left with him. I was afraid that she had left me to pay the bill. But she returned at 10:00 P.M., just before closing time. The owner was loudly searching for two forks and complaining that they had been taken. He asked Dame Bonneuil if she had them. She denied having them and said she had given them back after dinner. We had not eaten in the evening, only drank. We left the tavern and went to a café. The man Dame Bonneuil was with earlier was in the

---

[5] This was a furnished room (or *garnie*) in a lodging house. These were the cheapest rental units in eighteenth-century Paris. By the calculations of Petrovitch ("Recherches sur la criminalité à Paris dans la seconde moitié du XVIIIe siècle"), some two-thirds of defendants in *grand criminel* at the Châtelet during the years 1755, 1765, 1775, and 1785 lived in furnished rooms, and most in lodging houses (pp. 241–3).

café. They left together, and I stayed in the café until midnight. This evening I returned to the tavern looking for Dame Bonneuil. That is when I was arrested by the inspector.

Ques: How long has Dame Bonneuil lived at Mme. Goulart's?

Ans: For about a month.

Ques: Does she also use the maiden name of Marie-Cécile Gosset?

Ans: I have heard her use that name.

Ques: Do you know her particularly well?

Ans: I have heard that she recently lived with a printer named Garnet in a furnished room in the Faubourg Saint-Denis, but I do not know the street.

Ques: Are you certain that Dame Bonneuil and Marie-Cécile Gosset are the same person?

Ans: I believe so.

Ques: Have you ever been in jail?

Ans: I have only been locked up in the Hôpital-Général by the Archers of the Poor.[6]

Nothing suspect was found in her pockets. She declared that she could not sign her name. Chastelus ordered her jailed at the Petit Châtelet.

The criminal lieutenant, Jean-Charles-Pierre Lenoir, interrogated Marie-Cécile Gosset at the Châtelet on October 29.[7] She readily identified herself as follows: Marie-Cécile Gosset, widow of Nicolas Bonneuil (carter); bonnet seamstress; aged 45; native of Amiens: domiciled on the rue Percée Saint-Andre-des-Arts at Goulart's, lodger.

Ques: On the twenty-sixth last, did you attempt to sell two silver forks to ambulant tradeswomen on the rue des Arcis?

Ans: That is true.

Ques: How much did you ask for the forks?

Ans: I asked 6 francs.

Ques: Where did you get the forks?

Ans: I took them carelessly from Jouan's tavern on the rue de la Harpe, where I had dined and supped the day before.

Ques: Did you take them at dinner or at supper?

Ans: I took them at dinner when I paid my bill and absentmindedly put them in my pocket. When I returned to the tavern in the evening, I had forgotten that I had them. I did not hear anyone in the tavern say that they were missing. Only when I returned home late at night did I realize that they were in my pocket.

Ques: If you had indeed taken the forks thoughtlessly, you would have returned them to the tavern instead of attempting to sell them.

---

[6] These were police employed by the Hôpital-Général, under the supervision of the lieutenant general, to arrest beggars in the streets of Paris (Williams, *Police of Paris*, p. 91).

[7] J.-C.-P. Lenoir was the son of Jean-Charles-Joseph Lenoir, who served as particular lieutenant of the Châtelet from 1718 to 1754 (the longest tenure in that office during the eighteenth century). Jean-Charles-Pierre became judge–councillor in April 1752 and succeeded his father as particular lieutenant in 1754. He rose to the office of criminal lieutenant in 1759 (at the age of 27), where he remained until August 1774. In 1774–5 and from 1776 to 1785, he was lieutenant general of police. He acquired a reputation as one of the most proficient, sophisticated, and reformist magistrates and administrators of eighteenth-century Paris (A.N. V 1 370; Y 1867; Williams, *Police of Paris*).

Ans: I was confused. I should have done that, but unfortunately I did not.

Ques: Why did you not leave the forks on the table when you went to pay your bill?

Ans: I ate in the lower room of the tavern, and when I took the forks with me to the pay counter I had no intention of wrongdoing.

Ques: Were the forks served to you when you came in? And who was with you?

Ans: The forks were served. I ate with a girl called Franchon who lives in the same lodging house. But she is not guilty in any way. I took the forks. She had no knowledge of what I did.

Ques: Why did you refuse to tell the commissioner your name, and is your name indeed Marie-Cécile Gosset?

Ans: That is my true name. I refused because I wanted to save my family's reputation. [She was shown the two forks and asked if she recognized them.]

Ans: I am not sure. I did not examine the forks when I took them or when I tried to sell them. If I had examined them, I would surely not have tried to sell them.

Ques: Have you ever been in jail?

Ans: No.

On request of the prosecutor and order of the criminal lieutenant, Commissioner Chastelus summoned witnesses for the *information*. Their depositions were heard on October 31.

Marie-Elizabeth Bonneval

Age 50; wife of Sébastien Bachoux (master founder); street pedlar; domiciled rue des Nonaindiers, near the Place aux Veaux. On the twenty-sixth, at about 10:30 A.M., I was walking with two friends on the rue des Arcis when a woman unknown to me came up and offered to sell two silver forks for 6 livres. I examined the forks. I saw that they were both engraved with the letters "E. J." and were of different shapes. I doubted that they were solid silver because of the price the woman was asking. I showed them to one of my friends and said, "These forks look to be silver, but maybe they are only silver-plated." She whispered that they are definitely silver. Then in a low voice I told her, "Fetch the police, while I distract this woman." I kept her attention by bargaining for the forks. When we arrived at a price of 110 sous, I pretended that I did not have the full sum on me and invited her for wine in a nearby tavern. We drank some *chopines*. I sent my other friend after the inspector and told the woman that I was sending her to fetch money for the forks. When the inspector arrived, I told him the story. He arrested her, and we all went to the commissioner's office. She admitted that she had stolen the forks from a tavern owner on the rue de la Harpe where she had eaten the previous day. But she refused to tell her name, until she learned that she would be jailed at the Châtelet.

Eloy Jouan

Age 34; tavern owner; domiciled rue de la Harpe, at the Golden Sun tavern, near the rue Poupée. On the twenty-fifth, at about 1:00 P.M., two women came into my tavern. I knew one of them by sight, since she came in almost every day to drink wine by the bottle. They had brought a portion of salt pork and went to the dining room. They were served with two forks and wine. I went out on errands. When I returned at about

7:00 P.M., I saw the two women return with a morsel of meat. I asked if they had returned their forks. They said yes. At about 10:00 P.M., the serving boy collected the last forks at tables. He urged me to count the silverware. I was surprised at this. The boy had counted up the forks and come up short. I did the count and discovered that two forks were missing. I asked the boy why this was so. He said that he had served two women with forks at midday, women who were in the saloon, and did not know if they had returned them. I went to the saloon and yelled out that forks were missing. I described them. The drinkers said that they had not seen the forks. We searched in the saloon. I made the two women get up from table and asked them if they had taken the forks. They said no. I was angry and said to everyone how strange it is that among regular drinkers I could have lost two forks. But I went no further with it and let everyone leave. The next day I was summoned to the commissioner's office. He showed me two forks, and I immediately recognized them as the two stolen. I also recognized the woman who had been arrested for trying to sell the forks as one of the two who had been in the tavern the day before. She admitted that she had taken them but insisted that the other woman was not guilty. I had never seen the arrested woman before the previous day. The other woman, who regularly came to drink, was the one whom the arrested woman said was not guilty of the theft. The arrested woman refused to tell her name. At about 9:30 that evening, the other woman, whom I knew by sight, came in looking for her friend. I told her that her friend had been arrested for stealing my forks. She said that she had no involvement in that, and that after they had dined the other woman had taken the forks to the counter when she went to pay. She left. Then, agents of Inspector Roulier came in. I told them about her visit and our conversation. They immediately ran after her and caught her near the rue Percée. That is all I know. [He signed.]

Simone Chévigny

Wife of Jean Dubuisson (tanner); street pedlar; age 44; domiciled near the Saint-Jean Cemetery. On Monday the twenty-sixth, at about 11:00 A.M., I was walking on the rue des Arcis with two associates when an unknown woman came up to us and offered to sell two forks for 6 francs. When we saw that the forks were silver, we decided to distract the woman until we could notify someone in authority. We enticed her into a tavern on the rue des Lombards, where we all drank a pint of wine. I left the tavern on the excuse that I had to get money for the bill and managed to take the two forks with me. Our other associate went to find M. Desfosses, who is an agent of Inspector Roulier. I had the forks examined, and they were silver. I returned to the tavern with them. Soon after, our associate came with Desfosses. He arrested the woman on suspicion of theft. We all went to the commissioner's office. She admitted that she had taken the forks from a tavern on the rue de la Harpe [She could not sign.]

François Desfosses

Age 52; police agent; domiciled rue des Lionnais, parish Saint-Médard. At about noon on the twenty-sixth, I was at the security office of the quarter when Mme. Talière, a pedlar and a relative of mine, came in and told me that a woman in a tavern on the rue des Lombards had tried to sell her two silver forks for 6 livres and that the forks were suspect. She showed them to me. They were silver, and I told her that there is no doubt that they have been stolen. I instructed her to return to the tavern with the forks and to tell the woman that she has just had the forks weighed by a goldsmith who said they were worth 8 livres and wants to buy them but who insists on meeting the seller. This ruse worked. I waited a short while and then went to the tavern on the rue des Lombards. The three pedlars were just leaving the woman. I followed them down the rue de la Vielle Monnaie until they passed all by the guard post. Then I came forward, brought them all into the guard post, and sent for Roulier, my inspector. The woman admitted to the commissioner that she had stolen the forks from a tavern on the rue de la Harpe, and that she had been with another woman who was innocent of the theft. [He signed.]

Marie-Anne Dubuisson

Age 40: wife of Jean Taliére (laborer); street pedlar; domiciled rue Jean Pain-Mollet. On Monday the twenty-sixth at 11:00 A.M. a woman on the rue des Arcis tried to sell two silver forks for 6 livres. My friends and I asked where she lived. She said she lived in the building of a hatter in the Faubourg Saint-Denis, and that he had given her the forks to sell. We pretended not to have enough money on us for the purchase, and lured her into a tavern on the rue des Lombards. My sister [Simone Chévigny] told the woman that we were going to get money and we left Mme. Bachoux [Marie Bonneval] there with her. I took the forks with me to the security office and showed them to M. Desfosses. He said they were certainly stolen and that we should not buy them but return to the tavern and tell the woman that a goldsmith wants to buy them but insists on seeing the seller. I did as he said. I told the woman this tale to get her to leave the tavern with us. We led her along the rue de la Vieille Monnaie while Desfosses followed us. When we neared the guard post, he arrested her and we accompanied him to the commissioner. She admitted that she had taken the forks from a tavern on the rue de la Harpe. When the tavern owner arrived, he recognized the forks as his. [She signed.]

Noel-Edmé Duché

Age 15; tavern boy; domiciled with a tavern owner on the rue Mouffetard. On Sunday, the twenty-fifth, at about 1:00 P.M., two women came to Jouan's tavern, the Golden Sun, where I lived and worked then. They ordered a *chopine* of wine each. One of them went out to buy a piece of salt pork. She returned, and I served them with two forks. They stayed in the tavern until about 3:00 P.M. But they did not pay me when they left, for I had gone to deliver wine. They must have paid M. Jouan himself. They came back at about 8:00 that evening, with a morsel of boiled beef wrapped in paper. I gave them a plate and asked if they needed forks. They said no. After I had cleared the tables before closing, I asked Jouan to count the silver. It seemed that four forks were missing. We found two of them, but two were still missing. He knew their engravings and marks. We searched a long time. He even asked the two women if they had returned their forks after dinner. They answered that they had. We let them leave with everyone else. The next morning Jouan was informed that one of the two women who had stolen his forks was arrested. That same evening, the other woman came to the tavern looking for her comrade. He told her that she had been arrested. She said that she was surprised, that she had never believed her friend to be a thief, and that she herself was completely innocent of any theft. She said that after they had dined, the other woman took the forks to the counter when she went to pay. [He signed.]

Prosecutor Moreau requested a second interrogation of Marie-Cécile Gosset and Françoise Legrand, and definitive instruction of the case (*récolement* and confrontation). Lenoir complied and delegated the definitive instruction to André-Louis Huerne.[8] On November 4, Huerne interrogated Françoise Legrand.

Ques: Do you know the widow Bonneuil?
Ans: Yes.
Ques: Were you with her in the tavern "at the sign of the Golden Sun" on the rue de la Harpe?
Ans: Yes.
Ques: When you were together there, did you see her take two silver forks?
Ans: Yes.
Ques: Were you with her when she tried to sell the forks?
Ans: No. I thought that she had given the forks to the tavern owner.
Ques: For how long have you known widow Bonneuil?
Ans: For about a month, since she has lived in the same boardinghouse as me.
Ques: Have you ever been in prison?
Ans: No.

On the following day, Françoise Legrand petitioned for dismissal of charges and release from prison. The prosecutor approved her release, and on November 19 the criminal lieutenant granted decree of liberation with assigned residence (*sorti sur requête*).

Marie-Cécile Gosset was interrogated for the last time on November 12.

Ques: Did you offer two silver forks for sale to street pedlars on the rue des Arcis at about 10:00 A.M. on October 26?
Ans: Yes.
Ques: Where did you obtain the forks?
Ans: From the Golden Sun tavern on the rue de la Harpe, where I had dined the day before. I put them in my pocket. I only realized that I had them at about midnight. On the morrow, I gave in to temptation and tried to sell them.

The witnesses (Bonneval, Jouan, Chévigny, Desfosses, Dubuisson, Duché) were subjected to *récolement* on November 24. They all swore to the testimony that they had given during the *information;* none altered or added to his deposition. The confrontation followed immediately. Marie-Cécile Gosset did not challenge the credibility or the depositions of the witnesses; she only remarked that Jouan had not asked her for the forks when she paid for dinner. She acknowledged that the forks shown to her during the confrontation were the ones she had taken from the tavern and attempted to sell. Six days later, she was examined by the doctors of the Châtelet. They found no trace of branding.

---

[8] Huerne was 28 in November 1761. He had been a judge since September 1759 (A.N. V 1 400; Y 1867).

There was an unusually long delay between the close of definitive instruction and judgment of her case. On January 18, 1762, the prosecutor summarized the case documentation and recommended sentence. He found her guilty of stealing two silver forks and requested that she be sentenced to whipping, branding with the V, and banishment from the jurisdiction of the Châtelet for a term of five years. But she was not judged by the bench until March 26. In her final hearing, she said only the following: "I drank with Legrand in a tavern. I carelessly put two forks in my pocket and left the tavern with them. I tried to sell the forks because I was afraid to return them." Huerne was reporting judge. He opined for whipping, the brand, and three years of banishment. The six other judges (including Lenoir) concurred with that sentence.[9] On April 5, that sentence was confirmed by the Tournelle. Françoise Legrand was acquitted.[10]

Marie-Cécile Gosset confessed her crime during the first interrogation, before Chastelus asked if she had stolen the forks. She may even have confessed to Inspector Roulier immediately upon her arrest. She effused shame and moral regret, and her demeanor was consistently repentant from arrest to judgment. She denied premeditation in taking the forks from the tavern, but she did not attempt to deny the immorality or criminality of her actions. She did not plead drunkenness or destitution as mitigation of responsibility. In explanation for her actions, she claimed carelessness, confusion, temptation, and weakness. Self-condemnation was accompanied by altruism: She was primarily concerned to protect the reputation of her family (presumably at Amiens), to disculpate Françoise Legrand of complicity, and perhaps to conceal the identity and role of the man who was her companion on the night of October 25. The anguish over reputation was not implausible, for condemnations by the Châtelet and Parlement were widely publicized. Her comportment before the magistrates was almost a simulacrum of comportment before the tribunal of penitence. It had those qualities of simplicity, humility, pertinence, sincerity, and emotional pain that signified contrite and genuine religious confession in Church doctrine of the seventeenth and eighteenth centuries.[11]

Marie-Cécile Gosset was probably devout. But judges were not father-confessors. They were not endowed with the power to absolve the guilty. The judicial meaning of confession was not purgation of sin. It was elucidation of criminal truth. When confession was substantiated by evidence, it confirmed guilt and resulted in punishment. The consequence of punishment ensued necessarily, unless it was established that the defendant could not be held morally responsible for the criminal act. And that consequence was the principal reason for the extreme rarity of confessions among eighteenth-century Parisian defendants.

[9] Minutes of judgment, March 26, 1762 (A.N. Y 10517).
[10] Inventory 450, vols. 6–7.
[11] On the post–Council of Trent doctrine of confession, see A. Vacant and E. Mangeot, *Dictionnaire de Théologie catholique* (Paris: Letouzy, 1911), vol. 3, pp. 953–60.

But her confession did not constitute proof of her guilt. To guarantee against conviction on the basis of false confession, the ordinance (Titles XIV and XV) required definitive instruction (*récolement* of witnesses and their confrontation by defendants) before judgment of all defendants accused of crimes that carried afflictive or capital penalties. This included all such defendants who had confessed during preparatory instruction.[12] For the authors of the ordinance, and for eighteenth-century jurists and magistrates, plenitude and exactitude of proof derived from plenitude and exactitude of evidence, despite the major probative importance of confession. Marie-Cécile Gosset would undoubtedly have been convicted of theft had she not confessed; the combination of material, circumstantial, and testimonial evidence against her was indubitable. Her trial beyond confession both exemplified and vindicated the exigencies of the ordinance, for it produced a perfection in proof of guilt.

The minimal penalty in law for her crime of "simple theft" was whipping and branding; the customary supplement to that punishment in the jurisdiction of the Châtelet was public exposure in the *carcan*, with a placard describing the crime. She was spared the defamation of the *carcan*. By tradition of the Châtelet and the Parlement, the maximal penalty applied to her crime was three or five years in the Hôpital-Général. Banishment for three years was only one gradation above minimal penalty for such theft. That leniency in punishment may well have been in recompense for her confession and manifest repentance.

Marie-Cécile Gosset lived her quotidian existence in direct subordination to female, not male, power: to Mme. Haribate, the bonnet-maker who employed her (probably at piece rate); to Mme. Goulart, the lodging-house owner whom she paid for a bed in a common room. Her arrest and ultimate conviction resulted from cunning ensnarement by the three pedlar women. Their act was also an expression of power. It was cruel, but it was not gratuitous. They were themselves ensnared within a larger matrix of power – masculine power.

Revendeuses sold secondhand goods that they acquired by purchase or barter from homes, shops, ateliers, individuals, and other pedlars. They sold publicly

---

[12] Jousse gave the two principal reasons for the requirement: "Il faut que la confession de l'accusé soit vérifiée par une information exacte des circonstances & des qualités [of the crime], surtout de celles qui sont substantielles, & que l'accuse aura spécifiées dans sa confession, pour scavoir si ces circonstances & qualités se trouvent conformes à son aveu; de *maniér qu'il n'y ait plus lieu de douter de la vérité du fait* [italics mine]. . . . Car on ne peut douter que celui qui peut déclarer exactement les circonstances du délit, qui se trouvent ensuite bien vérifiées, ne soit auteur au complice de ce délit; surtout lorsqu'il déclare des circonstances de l'action, qui soient telles qu'elles ne puissent être connues de ceux qui n'auroient pas été présents" (*Traité*, vol. 1, pp. 677–8). "D'ailleurs, en matière criminelle, il faut tout mettre en usage: & la preuve qui résulte de la déposition des témoins sert à justifier celle qui résulte de la confession de l'accusé" (ibid. vol. 2, p. 333). The Parlement of Paris went farther than the requirement of the ordinance: By an *arrêt* of May 1717, it forbade subaltern courts within the jurisdiction to judge any defendant accused even of a crime subject to defaming penalties without definitive instruction. Quoted in Jousse, ibid., p. 332. By Title XXV, Article 5, of the ordinance, only if there were no witnesses (and thus no *information* or possibility of definitive instruction) could defendants who confessed be judged solely on the bases of their confession and whatever material or character evidence were available.

and rapidly at haggled prices, in streets, squares and marketplaces. Habitually, they trafficked in stolen goods, whether knowingly or unknowingly. Their trade was closely and penally regulated by a June 1698 ordinance of the Lieutenant Generalcy of Police: they were required to have permits from the Lieutenant Generalcy; they were forbidden to buy from anyone whose identity and address were unknown to them or whose goods appeared suspect; they were forbidden to buy plates, dishes, utensils, jewelry, or objects in gold and silver from any but artisans and tradesmen licensed to sell them; they were required to keep a record (for police inspection) of all goods sold and the buyers (although many, if not most, of them were illiterate). Violations of these and other provisions were punishable by fines to the sum of 400 livres.[13] That law permanently confronted street pedlars with a choice between extinction and illegality, and thereby guaranteed both illegality and wide discretionary police authority. Pedlars could survive in business only by violating the regulations most of the time, while complying with them some of the time. But the police could enforce the regulations at will. The 1698 ordinance led to collective blackmail, to an extortion of services from pedlars.

Street pedlars (like tavern-keepers) were valuable to the police of eighteenth-century Paris as informers, as agents of pervasive surveillance. They were basic conduits between criminals, popular consumers, and the police. There were legions of them throughout the city. Most had a fixed, small, and jealously guarded commercial territory of one or a few streets. They purchased their illegality, and their gain from the sale of stolen and smuggled goods, by periodically denouncing genuine and suspected criminals to the local police.[14] To the three *revendeuses* in our case, Marie-Cécile Gosset was an ideal victim for such a transaction: Her forks were obviously stolen; she was alien to the rue des Arcis; she had encroached on their territory; she was solitary and guileless. On October 26, 1761, the three pedlars complied with the law, calculatedly and cynically. Marie-Cécile Gosset violated the law with confusion and remorse.

---

[13] The text of the 1698 Police Ordinance is cited in Jousse, *Traité*, vol. 4, pp. 246–8.

[14] On street pedlars in their relations with the populace and the police, see especially Williams, *Police of Paris*, pp. 95, 195; Roche, *Le peuple de Paris*, pp. 187–9; Reinhard, *Nouvelle histoire de Paris: La Révolution*, pp. 86–8; David Garrioch, *Neighbourhood and Community in Paris, 1740–1790* (Cambridge: Cambridge University Press, 1986), pp. 22, 122.

18

Murder

Homicide was carefully defined in Old Regime criminal law, through a hierarchy of five specific types: involuntary and accidental (by an action that was neither negligent nor blameworthy and whose homicidal result could not be foreseen); accidental, but as a result of negligent or imprudent action; necessary or legitimate (in self-defense from unprovoked murderous attack or in defense of another from such attack); voluntary or wilfull, but without premeditation or deliberation (such as in spontaneous rage or during a fight); premeditated and deliberate.[1] The fourth and fifth were subject to the death penalty. All but the fifth offense were subject to royal remission or commutation of penalty, and such homicides accounted for the great majority of royal pardons issued during the eighteenth century within the jurisdiction of the Parlement of Paris.

Premeditated murder was expressed in law by the terms *le meutre de guet-à-pens* (by surprise or stealth) and *l'assassinat*. Those terms were used synonymously, although *l'assassinat* also designated the hiring of someone to commit murder.[2] Intention, design, and readiness to kill distinguished this crime from other forms of homicide.[3]

This was a supreme crime, for it was one of the few placed, by royal legislation, beyond the authority of royal pardon or commutation of penalty. That exceptionality was formally stated in article 4, Title XVI, of the 1670 ordinance: Letters of pardon and commutation could not be issued to persons convicted of premeditated murder, no matter what motive or justification they gave for the murder; should such letters be issued by error, the courts were forbidden to ratify them. By the same article, attempt to commit premeditated murder, "even if there has been only plotting or attempt, without consequence of

---

[1] Jousse, *Traité*, vol. 3, pp. 480–1; Muyart, *Institutes*, pp. 511–21.

[2] Jousse, *Traité*, vol. 1, p. 194; Rousseaud, p. 86.

[3] "'C'est donc la 'Trahison' qui forme le principal caractère de ce crime, & cette Trahison se manifeste ordinairement par les circonstances qui l'accompagnent ou le précedent . . . . Comme cette espèce d'Homicide est le pur effet du Dol & et de la Malice, & qu'il ne peut être excusé en aucune manière, c'est contre lui que se sont élevées principalement toutes les Loix, & qu'elles prononcent irrémissiblement la Peine de mort." Muyart, *Institutes*, pp. 516–17.

effect," was beyond pardon or commutation.[4] By these provisions, the otherwise sovereign monarchy declared itself juridically incompetent to forgive and spare those convicted of murder by design. The only forgiveness possible was divine. The categorical penalty, whether the murder was accomplished or simply attempted, was death. Accomplices to such murder were also subject to the death penalty. The juristic notion of complicity in murder was broad. It specified

those who give assistance to the murderer, whether before the act, by giving him money, weapons, horses or men to aid him, whether during the act, by accompanying him or joining with him to facilitate execution of the act, whether after the act itself, in hiding the murderer in their homes and in giving him means to avoid capture by Justice.[5]

Premeditated murder was also a sovereign crime because its commission nullified a crucial social distinction in fact and in law. Nobles convicted of other capital offenses and sentenced to death were executed by decapitation with the sword. This was the least painful, most rapid, and most "honorable" of penal deaths. But after the July 1547 edict of Henry II, conviction for premeditated murder annulled that privilege.

Henceforth all persons without distinction, gentlemen as well as commoners, of whatever estate or condition they may be, who have committed murders and homicides by stealth and assassination, will be punished by the penalty of death on the wheel, without possibility of commutation to any other penalty whatsoever.[6]

Death by breaking on the Saint Andrew's Cross and exposure on the wheel was the most spectacular, prolonged, excruciating, and debasing of executionary forms.[7] No crime of theft – even theft of sacred objects from churches accompanied by profanation, or theft from royal palaces and treasuries – was defined and punished so implacably in early modern and Old Regime France.

Murder by design was more than the most aggravated form of homicide. It was also a supreme sin in Catholic doctrine, one for which the penalty in canon law was excommunication.[8] Its essence was evilness of purpose and willful treachery, not the sheer action of killing. By that essence, it was a paradigmatic *crime atroce* in Old Regime law. Here, there was perfect conceptual symmetry

---

[4] This article reaffirmed the impossibility of royal pardon for premeditated murder – plotted, attempted, or accomplished – that had been stated in Article 195, Ordinance of Blois, May 1579: "Nous voulons la seule machination et attentat estre puni de peine de mort, encore que l'effet ne s'en soit ensuivi, dont aussi n'entendons donner aucune grace ou rémission" (Isambert, vol. 14, p. 427).

[5] Jousse, *Traité*, vol. 3, p. 249.

[6] Isambert, vol. 13, p. 27.

[7] Women were never broken. When convicted of premeditated murder, they were either hanged or hanged and then burned. Men and women sentenced to death for nonpremeditated voluntary murder, and who did not receive pardon, were hanged, not broken.

[8] Eighteenth-century jurists asserted that according to medieval canon law, premeditated murder was the only crime that deserved the death penalty. See Muyart, *Institutes*, pp. 517–18, and Guyot, vol. 1, pp. 663–5.

between criminal law and Catholic morality. Yet even premeditated murder was also given, in jurisprudence and practice, an internal hierarchy of gravity: It was more atrocious to murder a blood relation, family member, dwelling mate, or friend than to murder a stranger; it was more atrocious to murder for larcenous purposes than in response to insult or abuse; it was more atrocious to murder those aged, weak, or defenseless than those robust; it was more atrocious to murder through concealment or at a distance, by poison, arson, or firearms, than to murder face-to-face, with knife, sword, or bludgeon; it was more atrocious to murder and mutilate or dismember than simply to murder.[9] Murder committed in the course of a robbery, and of the victim of that robbery, was treated in law as premeditated murder, especially if the robber was armed with a lethal weapon; the juridical assumption was that the robber was volitionally prepared to kill in order to accomplish the theft. Such qualities of the specific murder and of the author's relation to his victim had penal consequences: They determined whether death on the cross and wheel or at the stake would be abbreviated by *retenta* of the court (secret instructions to the executioner to strangle the victim before burning, to strangle after a specified number of blows on the cross or after a specified time of exposure on the wheel) or would be inflicted by full duration of the execution.

Eighteenth-century Paris engendered all forms of murder, but not murder with impunity. The metropolis was characterized by intense human compression and abrasiveness, quantities of migratory transients, ex-convicts, and persons variously desperate and parasitic, by abundance of commodities and larcenous opportunities, and fierce competition among most social groups for survival or aggrandizement. These qualities of metropolitan life incited duplicities, greed, hatred, and violence. But compression and abrasiveness were accompanied by general vigilance and suspiciousness, by a collective gaze whose beneficiaries were police commissioners and the criminal judiciary. Parisian murderers were surrounded by eyes, ears, and memories. They were especially vulnerable because the majority of murders in the eighteenth-century city were among people acquainted with each other; a high proportion of them were among neighbors, family members, drinking companions, or associates in work and business. Rarely was the murderer a complete stranger either to his victim or to that victim's social environment. The metropolis entrapped: It propelled to violence; it exposed the violent to detection. The case of Nicolas Gérard illustrates that entrapment and its consequences.

The rue de Cléry was the chief locale of this case; it was the site of the crime and the residence of both victim and primary suspect. That long street extended from the Porte Saint-Denis to the rue Montmartre; it contained more than one hundred densely inhabited buildings, most of them tenements with shops on the street floor and ateliers in the rear. There were few residential

---

[9] Premeditated murder of blood relations and spouses could be punished by burning at the stake, and that punishment was inflicted during the eighteenth century.

hôtels of bourgeois or nobles. The parish was Notre-Dame de Bonne-Nouvelle. The Quarter was the Porte Saint-Denis.

The Quarters of the Portes Saint-Denis and Saint-Martin demarcated inner Paris from the semirural expanses of the northern faubourgs. Along much of the rue du faubourg Saint-Denis, visual perspectives were radial and horizontal over pastures, stables, quarries, and vegetable gardens. Suddenly, at the approaches to the Porte and through its arch, perspectives became vertical: a ravine of continuous walls, formed by the scabrous, bulging façades of the five-and six-story buildings along the entire length of the rue Saint-Denis, and all of its vertebral streets, as far as the river. The Quarter was defined by that artery and permanently congested with human and commercial traffic, for it was a zone of passage for transport, travel, and migrations to and from northern and northeastern France. Those trajectories encompassed absolute social extremes: the kings of France making their solemn entries into Paris through the Ludovician Arch of the Porte; daily arrivals of desperate provincial immigrants to Paris.

The Quarter of the Porte Saint-Denis was one of the most architecturally tangled and densely populated on the Right Bank. Most of the buildings on the streets, alleys, and *culs-de-sac* near the Porte (including the rues de Cléry, de la Lune, des Filles-Dieu, de Bonne-Nouvelle, and Basse-Porte Saint-Denis) had been constructed during the seventeenth century, out of debris collected from the demolition of the ramparts of Charles V, Charles IX, and Louis XIII. The *voies* of many streets followed the traces of old moats and ditches; they were narrow, sunken, humid, and dark. The most notorious *cour des miracles* (repair of beggars and thieves) in medieval and early modern Paris had been at the heart of the Quarter, near the Convent of the Filles-Dieu.[10] The Quarter figured saliently in eighteenth-century Parisian criminality, prostitution, and casual violence.[11] And yet, during the same period, the larger region of the two Portes (bounded on the west by the rues de Cléry and Montmartre, on the south by the rues Saint-Sauveur and Grénéta, and on the east by the rue Saint-Martin) was the most concentrated manufacturing region of the city in fabric, textiles, clothing, accessories, and cheap luxury articles, one of the most concentrated for the building and decorative trades, and the most important for haulage enterprises.[12] All gradations of bourgeois capital and enterprise coexisted there with all forms of plebeian survival.

At 11:00 A.M. Sunday morning, January 7, 1781, Hubert Mutel, police commissioner of the Saint-Denis Quarter, his recording secretary, and Elie San-

---

[10] On the topography of the Quarter, see the following: J. Hillairet, *Dictionnaire historique des rues de Paris* (Paris: Editions du Minuit, 1963), vol. 2; *Dictionnaire de Paris* (Paris: Larousse, 1964); Bernard Rouleau, *Le tracé des rues de Paris: Formation, typologie, fonctions* (Paris: CNRS, 1967); Reinhard, *Nouvelle histoire de Paris: La Révolution*.

[11] See especially the following: Farge and Zysberg, "Les théâtres de la violence"; Abbiateci and Petrovitch, "Criminalité à Paris," pp. 248, 254; Benabou, *La prostitution*, pp. 195–210.

[12] Author's computations from the records of Parisian artisan, merchant, and manufacturing enterprises, 1790 to 1792 (A.N. F 30 115–160).

terre, inspector of the Quarter, arrived at a characteristic tenement building of the rue de Cléry (between the rue Sainte-Clothilde and the rue des Filles-Dieu) – a ground floor of shops and back rooms, a single building entrance that gave directly onto the street, a single staircase, four low-ceilinged landings divided into individual rooms, an attic garret, a shallow and dank rear courtyard. They had been notified of a corpse found in a third-floor room.[13] Jacques Pain, who was "principal occupant" (or building superintendent and rent collector) and a master locksmith with a small shop on the ground floor, gave them an initial account in a second-floor room facing the courtyard:

Nicolas Kerse, German by nation and master tailor, has lived for about a year in the room above [on the third floor]. His rent is 100 livres a year.[14] Two weeks ago I gave him notice to move out on the eighth of this month, and he gave me a key to the room so I could show it to prospective tenants when he was not there. During the past three days, he has not been seen in the building. Last evening [January 6] between 7:00 and 8:00 P.M., Françoise Forgère, a cook and maid who works in the room where we are now, heard noise from Kerse's room above, and then noise on the staircase. She went to investigate and found two individuals carrying out a chest of drawers. She lit a candle to see and noticed that one of them was wearing a gray frock coat. When she asked what they were doing with the chest, one of them answered that they were taking it to be repaired. She saw another individual – also with a gray frock coat but black-haired and thin-faced – who was carrying a faience shaving bowl, a sack, a worn brown woolen jacket, two lengths of blue and white cotton cloth that looked to be from bedding belonging to Kerse's room, and two books. She asked them why they were taking these things from the room, and since she knew that Dorville [a second-floor tenant] had given Kerse a jacket for repair she asked if they were not also taking the jacket. He answered that the jacket was in the room and shouldered his way down the stairs. Then Mlle. Orry came out of her room and rushed down to the building entrance; there, she stopped one of the individuals and demanded to know if he was taking Dorville's jacket. He hit her in the chest with his fist, dropping the belongings as he did so, and began running up the street. Mlle. Orry gathered them up and gave them to my keeping

[13] When referring to floors in a building, the European system is used here (i.e., "ground floor" corresponds to the American "first floor," "first floor" corresponds to the American "second floor," etc.). The records of this case are in A.N. Y 10418.

[14] This was an unfurnished room. One hundred livres a year was very low on the scale of late eighteenth-century Parisian rentals. It amounted to 5 sous, 6 deniers a night, or about 8 livres, 6 sous a month. In the socially mixed Quarters of central Paris, the average monthly bourgeois rental for an apartment of some three or four rooms on the *rez-de-chaussée* or the first floor was 30 to 40 livres; the shabbiest of furnished rooms in the tenements of "sleep merchants" (a level of habitation not far below that of Pain's building) went for 2 sous a night or about 3 livres a month. Some 60% of all Parisian rentals in the decade 1780 to 1790 were in the range of 40 to 200 livres a year; in 1780, 48% of the total were 40 to 100 livres. And 63% of total rented habitations were single rooms. In that total, there was an average of almost three persons residing per room (Roche, *Le peuple de Paris*, pp. 112, 120; Reinhard, *Nouvelle Histoire de Paris: La Révolution*, pp. 42–3). Annual rentals were due in quarters: at Easter, St. Jean Day (end of June); St. Rémy Day (October), and Christmas Day. In 1790, the average daily pay of a journeyman carpenter or stonemason (when he had work) was from 2 to 3 livres. That sum should be matched against the rentals just noted and the drinking bills of protagonists of the case in the taverns around the Porte Saint-Denis. To pay rent, the plebeian had either to save income or acquire a large sum of money at the end of the quarter.

when I returned to the building later that evening. [He showed the belongings to Mutel; in addition to those mentioned earlier, there were a small razor strop, a wooden razor sheath, and two Catholic devotional books written in German. And then Pain spoke for himself.] I returned to the building at about 11:00 P.M. that night, and Mlle. Forgère told me all of the above. I was worried that Kerse had moved out without paying the rent he owed. I went to the room and knocked. There was no answer. So in the company of Dorville [Jean-Baptiste Riau, "dit Dorville," second-floor tenant] and his mistress Mlle. Orry [also referred to by Pain and others as "la Dorville"], I unlocked the door and went inside. We saw that most of the furniture had been removed. We left, and I locked the door. This morning I was advised to ascertain what might have become of Kerse, so with Dorville and his woman I went back to the room and unlocked it. Dorville found Kerse's dead body hidden underneath his tailor's bench, and I notified the commissioner.

Mutel and the other officials then went to Kerse's room. Underneath the tailor's bench, hidden by a rug hanging that was nailed to the top edge of the bench, they found the body of a man aged about 40. His throat was cut widely and deeply. The left side of the face was badly disfigured. He was wearing a shirt, a worn frock coat, old breeches and stockings (but not shoes); most of the clothing was bloodstained. In his pockets, Mutel found a rent bill from Pain that was dated October 21, a folding knife, a rosary with a small copper cross, and a Saint Francis of Xavier medallion. His inventory of the room's contents described a penurious existence, with little ornamentation: a small earthen cookstove; an old leather bellows; an iron candlestick and candle extinguisher; a tinderbox; two large pots; a pine workbench mounted on trestles, with a hanging piece of rug; a small pine table; four old wooden chairs stuffed with straw and a straw-stuffed armchair; a wooden sleeve-board and a wooden box; a wig on its stand; two iron needles; a bed 3 feet wide and 6 feet long with a straw mattress; a blanket that was rolled into a bundle and that contained two short sheets, a worn mattress cover, a blue-and-white–striped cotton curtain, a large rag, and several pieces of fabric; and on the wall, a painting of the Virgin and Christ Child, four small prints, a small canvas painting, and a seemingly un-completed painting of a woman's head. He also found a plank that had been torn from the closet chest next to the chimney and several blood-soaked rags on the hearthstone and in the ashes of the fireplace. Mutel consigned the objects found on Kerse's person to Inspector Santerre as evidence and placed the room and its contents under the guard and responsibility of Pain.

The next person heard by Mutel was Jacques-Louis Legoy, general laborer and messenger at the Porte Saint-Denis who lived in a room off the passage Saint-Laurent near the Porte. He had been arrested in the company of the three men who were suspected of Kerse's murder and who were now in Santerre's custody.

Yesterday between 5:00 and 6:00 P.M. I was at my usual place near the Porte where I wait for work and commissions. Someone who later identified himself as Gérard called me to come with him to the rue de Cléry for a moving job. We came to this building and this room. There were two other individuals, who were named Thibault and Méclet. They met us at the corner of the rue Saint-Denis and the rue de Cléry and came here with us. The one named Gérard said to me, "The bourgeois who owns this building owes me 60 livres but refuses to acknowledge the debt; I am going to get back at him by moving out without paying the rent, and that is why I have brought my two friends here and hired you." The other two agreed that this was true. I set to work carrying down the big chest with Thibault. We carried it to the rue Guérin-Boisseau, to the workshop of a founder–smelter. After we deposited the chest there, we went to the tavern "à l'enseigne de l'Esprit-Saint" on the same street. We drank there until about 7:00 P.M., waiting for the man who was to come and pay for the chest; I was assured that I would be paid from that money. But he did not come. Instead, Gerard arrived and asked me to come with him back to the rue de Cléry for the rest of the things in the room. He had me wait outside the building for the things to be brought down. But a short while later, he came downstairs and said that nothing more could be moved that evening. I then insisted on being paid for my labor. Gérard told me not to worry and took me to another tavern on the rue de la Lune. He left me alone there for about a half hour and then returned with a woman who carried a pair of black velvet breeches and a black velvet jacket. She spoke briefly with Gérard and then left. Gérard stayed and ordered wine. The woman came back at about 11:00 P.M. and told Gérard that she had not been able to find anyone to buy those clothes. It was past closing time and the tavern-keeper insisted on being paid for the wine we had drunk. Gérard offered me the breeches and jacket as security if I would pay the bill and promised that he would get my money the next morning. I agreed and gave the tavern-keeper an *écu* of 6 livres, which he changed; I gave Gérard 3 livres, which he used to pay the bill. He assured me that he would get a good sum for the chest from the founder–smelter on the rue Guérin-Boisseau. He did not keep his promise to me.

Legoy handed over the breeches and jacket to Mutel; they were consigned as evidence.

Inspector Santerre then brought the three suspects to the second floor for a formal *interrogation d'office* by Mutel. Each was searched, sworn, and then asked his name, age, birthplace, occupation, and domicile.

The first was François-Louis Thibault: age 45; native of Paris, parish Saint-Gervais; public letter writer; lodged at the home of Méclet, cabinet-maker, on the rue des Filles-Dieu.

Ques: How long have you known Méclet?
Ans: I have known him for two years, as a cabinet-maker. I have never known him to do anything wrong.
Ques: How long have you known Gérard?
Ans: For about fifteen days, during which time he visited Méclet.
Ques: How long have you known Kerse, master tailor, who lives in the room above?
Ans: I never saw or knew him. But yesterday at about 3:00 or 4:00 P.M. Gérard visited Méclet and me. He told us that he was living with a tailor on the third floor of this building, that the tailor had gone to Versailles, and that before leaving he had instructed Gérard to move out his furniture and sell some of it because he could not pay the rent. Gérard asked us to help him do this. We agreed. Gérard hired a porter at the Porte Saint-Denis. He opened the door to the room with a key. I helped carry a walnut chest to the shop of a founder–smelter on the rue Guérin-Boisseau.

Ques: Is it not true that you, Gérard, and Méclet also carried off numerous personal belongings from Kerse's room?

Ans: I only learned this morning that Gérard had taken a mirror from the room and sold it to the founder–smelter.

Ques: Did you not take other belongings from the room?

Ans: During the past five or six days, Gérard brought various things to Méclet's room, such as a mattress, clothes, a cotton velvet jacket, and said that these things belonged to the tailor where he lived and whom he was moving out.

Ques: Is it not true that you, Méclet, and Gérard jointly murdered Kerse in his room by cutting his throat and then hid his body under the workbench?

Ans: I did not murder or help in murdering that man. I knew nothing of his murder until I was arrested and brought here.

[Mutel then had Thibault taken upstairs and shown the corpse.]

Ques: Did you not kill this man or help in his murder?

Ans: I never knew and do not know this man. I did not kill him or help in killing him. I was only in this room yesterday to move furniture, and I did not see a corpse.

Ques: Have you ever been in prison or arrested?

Ans: No.

Thibault signed.

Next was François Méclet: age 46; native of Paris, parish Sainte-Marguérite (Faubourg Saint-Antoine); journeyman cabinet-maker in a shop on the rue Neuve Saint-Denis; domiciled in a furnished room on the fifth floor, rue des Filles-Dieu. In his pockets, Mutel found a package of blue-and-white–striped cloth, several pieces of braid, two kerchiefs, and a receipt for the sum of 30 sous made to Nicolas Kerse for payment of dues in the Parisian guild of tailors and old-clothes dealers, dated November 3, 1780.

Ques: How long and by what relations have you known Gérard?

Ans: I have known him for about two months, because of work that he gave the woman I live with, Mlle. Colin, a clothes-mender.

Ques: Did you know Nicolas Kerse, who lived in the room above?

Ans: I never knew him.

[Méclet was taken upstairs and shown the corpse.]

Ques: Do you recognize this man?

Ans: No, I have never seen him before.

Ques: Did you not murder or aid in the murder of this man?

Ans: No.

Ques: What, then, were you doing in this room yesterday?

Ans: Last Friday [January 5] Gérard came to my room with a mirror that had a gilded top and frame and left it with me. Yesterday in the morning he came and asked me to find a buyer for the mirror. I spoke to Bazin, founder–smelter. He agreed to buy it for 10 livres; I arranged a meeting, and he paid Gérard. Gérard said that he also had a chest to sell. Bazin replied that he was interested but wanted to see it first. He told Gérard to have it brought to his shop so he could inspect it. That afternoon, Gérard returned to my room and asked me and Thibault to help him move the chest and other furniture. He hired a porter, and we all came to this building. The porter and I carried the chest to Bazin's shop. Gérard told us that the furniture and other things in the room belonged to Kerse and that Kerse had asked him to sell them.

[Mutel then showed him the objects found on his person and asked him how he got them.]

Ans: The two kerchiefs are mine. The other things fell out of a drawer in the chest as we were carrying it; I picked them up and put them in my pockets.

Ques: Is it not true that Gérard brought several articles of clothing and other things to your room over several days?

Ans: Yesterday afternoon Gérard and I brought from Kerse's room to my room a mattress, several old clothes, two tailor's cutting squares, a large pair of scissors, and other things that I do not recall. I only kept these things in my room because Gérard told me that his friend and the tailor had asked him to sell them.

Ques: Have you ever been in prison or arrested?

Ans: No.

Méclet signed.

Nicolas Gérard was interrogated last: age 35; native of Burgundy, but claimed not to know the name of the village where he was born, only that it was 8 or 9 leagues from Dôle; stonemason's laborer; domiciled in the room occupied by Kerse. In his pockets they found a bone-handled spring knife, a long straight razor wrapped in a dirty and stained piece of stiff paper, a pair of long scissors in a cardboard sheath, four combs, a small copper compass, and an S-shaped key about 6 inches long.

Ques: How long did you know Kerse?

Ans: I have known him for about four months. He did some tailoring work for me.

Ques: Is it not true that during the past several days, with the help of Thibault and Méclet, you removed most of the furniture and belongings from Kerse's room?

Ans: I did so because Kerse asked me to.

Ques: On what day did you see Kerse for the last time?

Ans: I saw him last on Sainte-Geneviève Day [Wednesday, January 3]. He told me then that he was going to Versailles to collect some money owed him. He gave me the key to the room and told me I could stay there while he was gone, and asked me to sell the mirror and chest for him because he needed the funds.

Ques: Did you not indeed sell the mirror for 10 livres to Bazin, master founder–smelter on the rue Guérin-Boisseau, and also have the chest transported there?

Ans: Yes.

Ques: What did you do with the money you got for the mirror and chest?

Ans: I have not yet sold the chest. I got 10 livres for the mirror. I kept 6 in repayment for the 6 livres I advanced to Kerse for his trip to Versailles. The remaining 4 paid for the drink I stood the men who helped me move furniture and other things from Kerse's room.

Ques: What else did you take from Kerse's room?

Ans: Clothes, a mattress, tailor's implements, pieces of fabric, all of which I brought to Méclet's room. I was storing those things there for Kerse until his new room on the rue des Petites-Ecuries in the Faubourg Saint-Denis was ready for his occupancy.

Ques: And what did Kerse intend to do with the money from the sale of the furniture?

Ans: He intended to pay the back rent he owed Pain.

Ques: You are lying. In all of this, your only intention was to rob Kerse, as you indeed did. In order to conceal that robbery, you told others that the furniture and objects in the room belonged to you, and with equal falsity that the superintendent of the building owed you 60 livres and denied owing it, that to get back at him you were moving out without paying the rent.

Ans: I have told the truth. What you claim is false.

Ques: You are lying. You planned to rob Kerse. To accomplish that robbery you killed him by cutting his throat.

Ans: What you are saying is completely false.

[Mutel then showed Gérard the spring knife and razor, and asked if these were the instruments he used to murder Kerse.]

Ans: I did not murder Kerse. The knife and razor are mine, for my personal use.

Ques: Were you not sentenced to the galleys?[15]

Ans: Yes, I was sentenced to the galleys for stealing game.

[He was shown the corpse and asked if he recognized it.]

Ans: Since the face is so badly disfigured, I am not sure I recognize it. The clothes look like those worn by Kerse.

Ques: On what day and at what hour did Kerse leave for Versailles?

Ans: On January 3 at 7:00 A.M.

Gérard declared that he did not know how to sign his name.

The prosecutor and criminal lieutenant of the Châtelet were notified of these actions early in the afternoon, and copies of the minutes were prepared for them by Mutel's recording secretary. Mutel ordered that the three suspects be held under arrest at the rue de Cléry, pending the arrival of the criminal lieutenant, and went with Santerre to search Méclet's room on the rue des Filles-Dieu. What they found resembled the interior of an old-clothes dealer's shop, not the furnished room of a journeyman cabinet-maker: a mattress and long pillow, a blue-and-white–striped cotton curtain (this was a basic fabric from Kerse's room) with copper rings; two old frock coats; sleeves of embroidered mousseline; a mousseline collar; a length of white satin; seven pieces of green taffeta; two striped kerchiefs; a suit cut from coarse brown cloth; two old woolen jackets, tailor's cutting squares and scissors, many pieces of fabric and linings. Seals were placed on the room, and they went to the home of Antoine-Claude Bazin, master founder–smelter on the rue Guérin-Boisseau. The building was of a certain status, for it had a carriage entrance and a large courtyard; Bazin's apartment was on the ground floor, facing the street; his atelier was in the rear, off the courtyard.[16] He was present. Mutel and Santerre found

[15] When Gérard was searched just before interrogation, Mutel and Santerre probably noticed the scar on his shoulder.

[16] The building was owned by one of the Mermillod brothers. That family was among the wealthiest and most prominent dynasties of merchant–manufacturers in the region of the rues Saint-Denis and Saint-Martin from the last quarter of the eighteenth century into the early nineteenth. They were decorative wood-turners and enamelers, originally from a small village (Villars) in the Jura, about 50 miles from the town of Dôle. The patriarch during the late Old Regime and Revolution, Claude-François, had immigrated from Villars to Paris in 1757; two

a large polished walnut chest with several drawers and a mirror whose top and frame were in gilded hardwood. Bazin made the following statement:

Yesterday morning Méclet sold me the mirror for 10 livres. He was with someone named Gérard, who said he owned the mirror and wanted to sell it to pay his rent; they also proposed to sell me a chest of drawers that Gérard said he owned. This Gérard claimed that he was a hairdresser who had been unemployed for a long time. I have known Méclet since we were children, and since Gérard was with Méclet, I thought I could buy these things without risk of fraud or incrimination. But I said that I wanted to see the chest before buying. At about 9:00 P.M. I returned home and found the chest in its present place; I was told that it had been brought by a porter and someone else. At about 10:00 P.M. I went to the tavern "at the sign of the Holy Spirit" for supper. Méclet was there with someone else, whom he introduced as Thibault, a locksmith by trade. We ate and drank together. Our bill was over 2 livres; Méclet and Thibault said that they did not have enough to pay their portion. I paid their bill.

Mutel had the mirror and chest brought back to the rue de Cléry.

Soon after their return, Joseph Chatillon, tavern boy, arrived on his own initiative to make a statement. He was employed by Chéron, owner of a tavern on the rue Notre-Dame de Bonne-Nouvelle.

About six weeks ago, a stranger who called himself François, "dit Bourguignon," who I learned is also called Gérard, journeyman stonemason, owed me 4 livres for drink consumed in the tavern. In pledge of payment he gave me a gold box watch. He had also given a silver watch in pledge to Chéron, the owner, for another wine bill. He paid Chéron the money and took back the silver watch. Since the gold watch was worth much more than his bill, I allowed him another 12 livres of credit in drink. He sent me a letter in which he offered to sell me the watch for 7 gold louis; the letter is signed "François" and dated December 20 at Saint-Denis.

Mutel confiscated the watch and letter as evidence.

That afternoon, two medical doctors of the Châtelet examined Kerse's body at the rue de Cléry on order of the criminal lieutenant. They certified a long slash wound of the throat, almost from ear to ear. The wound was regular and deep, for it had severed the esophagus, all major arteries and muscles. The left side of the face and both hands were badly burned. They estimated that death had occurred between thirty-six and forty-eight hours previous to the exami-

younger brothers followed him in 1778 and 1782. By 1790, the elder Mermillod owned the largest manufacture of fancy-turnery, parquetry, and wood engraving in Paris and many rental buildings in the Saint-Denis and Saint-Martin Quarters. During the Revolution, Claude-François Mermillod was the largest purchaser of auctioned ecclesiastical property in the region. He and his younger brother Pierre were also Jacobin executives of the Gravilliers section in 1792 to 1794 (A.N. F 30 135, doss, Mermillod; D 111 253, liasse 12; Fib 11 Seine, 18; F7 4795, register of "cartes de sûreté," "Gravilliers" section; *Sommier des biens nationaux: Département de Paris*, Section des "Gravilliers"; *Almanach national*, an II, p. 461). The Mermillods were at an extreme socioeconomic distance from the defendants in this case, yet they lived and worked in permanently close proximity to men like Thibault, Méclet, and Gérard. This intensity of social contrast is heightened by the fact that the Mermillods were emigrants from the same mountainous region of eastern France as Nicolas Gérard.

nation (or between the late afternoon of Friday, January 5, and the early morning of Saturday, January 6).

At about the same time, Charles-Simon Bachois de Villefort, the criminal lieutenant of the Châtelet, arrived at the rue de Cléry with his recording secretary to inspect the site and interrogate the three suspects.[17] Bachois had read Mutel's reports and minutes of interrogation. After viewing the body, he interrogated the three separately in the second-floor room of Riau, "dit Dorville." Thibault gave biographical information slightly different from that which he had given Mutel: He told Bachois that he was formerly a journeyman locksmith, had been a soldier in various regiments, and was presently enrolled in the Mantes battalion of the royal militia but made his living as a letter writer for illiterate workers in Paris.

Thibault

Ques: How did you come to know Méclet and Gérard?

Ans: I have know Méclet for two years, and lived with him for three months. I have known Gérard for the past fifteen days, during which he visited Méclet three or four times.

Ques: Did you know the Kerse with whom Gérard lived?

Ans: I never saw him.

Ques: Why did you join with Méclet and Gérard in carrying off Kerse's furniture and belongings?

[Thibault repeated almost verbatim his response to the same question from Mutel, and added, "I have just been shown a corpse that I am told is that of the tailor with whom Gérard lodged in the room above. But when I was in that room yesterday, I saw no corpse. I am innocent of the murder. I can give you no information about the murder."]

Ques: It is very difficult to believe that you knew nothing of Kerse's murder and that you were not involved.

Ans: I am innocent, and incapable of such an atrocity. I have always behaved honorably wherever I have been.

[He was shown the body once again, as asked if he recognized it.]

Ans: I do not recognize that corpse. I never saw Kerse. I know nothing of his murder. I hardly know Gérard – whom I heard Méclet address as "Lionnais."

[He was shown the mirror, chest, and most of the objects inventoried in Méclet's room and then told, "Since you live with Méclet, and you have been found in possession of the near-totality of Kerse's belongings, it is very difficult not to regard you as an accomplice to Kerse's murder."]

[17] Bachois de Villefort was an astute and energetic criminal lieutenant. He was of a magisterial family; one of his elders, Charles-Simon Bachois, was judge of the Cour des Monnaies at mid-century. Bachois de Villefort was received into the office of judge of the Châtelet in March 1762, at the age of 25. He replaced Augustin Testard du Lys as criminal lieutenant, or chief criminal judge, of the court in March 1774, at the age of 37. He presided over the trials and judgments of most of those prosecuted by the Châtelet for the massive bread riots in the spring of 1775 and did so with skill and discernment. He remained in office until the suppression of the court in 1790 and was thus the Châtelet's last criminal lieutenant (A.N. V 1 411; Y 10510, fol. 28).

Ans: Those objects were placed in Méclet's room by Gérard and Méclet. I only helped carry the chest. I am innocent. I never saw Kerse. I had no part in his murder. I saw no dead body when I was in his room.

Ques: Have you ever been in prison?

Ans: The only times I was ever in jail were by action of military discipline.

Méclet

Ques: Did you know Kerse?

Ans: No, I never saw him.

Ques: How long have you known Gérard?

Ans: For about two months, since Gérard brought my wife some stockings and breeches to be mended. Since then he visited me three or four times. He works as a mason's laborer, but I think that he was once a hairdresser. I do not know him well. Last Friday he brought a mirror to my room. I do not know if my wife let him in or if he opened the door himself. All I know is that when I came home that night the mirror was there. Next morning, Saturday, at about 9:00 A.M., Thibault and I went to his room in this building. Gérard was in bed. He told me to sell the mirror, that Kerse, his roommate, was in Versailles and had asked him to sell the mirror and the chest to pay the rent and to move out his other belongings. I believed him and did not think that I would compromise myself in selling the mirror or helping in the move. I sold the mirror that day to Bazin. Gérard came for Thibault and me to complete the move that evening. We took the chest, a mattress, and other things. I saw no corpse or anything suspicious in the room. I am innocent, and I believe that Thibault is also innocent. No one but Gérard could have done this vile thing. I am very afraid that I am doomed if Gérard does not confess, just like my unfortunate friend Thibault. But the truth is that we are both innocent. We only wanted to aid Gérard. If I knew anything about the murder, I would tell you.

Ques: Almost all of the belongings of the unfortunate Kerse were found in your home. His body was found hidden under the workbench in the very room from which you removed those belongings. How can I believe you when you say that you perceived nothing suspicious?

Ans: I insist that I am innocent.

[He was taken upstairs, shown the body, and asked if he recognized it.]

Ans: I have never seen this man before today.

[He was shown the mirror, chest, mattress, and other things found in his room. He identified them and repeated his previous explanation of how they came to be there.]

Ques: Have you ever been in prison?

Ans: No.

Gérard

Ques: Were you not once sentenced to the *bagne?* Tell me by which court you were sentenced, when you were released, and why and for how long you have returned to Paris.

Ans: It is true that I was sentenced to the *bagne* for stealing game [*braconnage*]. I do not recall by which court. I left on the chain from Dôle about four years ago. We were taken to Dijon and joined with the chain that went from Dijon to the Rochefort *bagne.* I was three years in Rochefort. Then I escaped. I moved about from town to town, such as Orléans, Tours, and smaller places, working in masonry. I came to Paris about four months ago. I lived for two months in lodgings on the rue du Faubourg Saint-Denis, near the Porte. For the last two months I have shared Kerse's room. He did some tailoring for me and invited me to share the room and split the costs of rent and food. I accepted.

Ques: And why did you remove furniture from that room yesterday?

Ans: Last Wednesday, Sainte-Geneviève Day [January 3], Kerse told me that he was very worried about the rent, that he did not have the money to pay the period coming due. He said that he was going to Versailles to collect from someone who owed him money. He left me the key and told me that if he was not back by Friday or Saturday, I should sell the mirror and chest for rent money. Therefore on Friday I took the mirror to Méclet and asked him to sell it. He did so for 10 livres, which he gave me. I only know Méclet from the taverns in the *quartier.* I do not know the other man who was arrested with us, except that he is one of Méclet's friends. I do not know his name. Yesterday I asked Méclet to help remove the remainder of Kerse's belongings. He agreed. That evening the chest was taken to Bazin's shop. He had already bought the mirror and said that he would buy the chest. The other things were in Méclet's room. I intended to leave them there until the eighth, when Kerse's new room in the Faubourg Saint-Denis would be vacant and ready for him.

Ques: You are giving the most incredible account of your behavior. You admit to having been in the *bagne,* because you cannot conceal that fact. But you refuse to disclose which court convicted you. If in fact Kerse had told you to sell his belongings to pay rent, you would have waited until the rent was due [according to Pain, the rent was due by January 8], before which date Kerse was expected to return from Versailles. It is not possible to doubt that you and Méclet planned to rob Kerse. And since Kerse's body was in the room, it is not possible to doubt that you are the author or accomplice of that murder. Moreover, the doctors report that Kerse had been dead for some two days before today; the body was jammed under his workbench and hidden by a rug hanging; the rags used to stanch his blood were half buried in the chimney ashes. You have admitted to sleeping in the room on Friday night, to having removed the mirror during the day on Friday, the chest and other things during the day on Saturday. It is not possible to doubt that you are the murderer and that Méclet and Thibault are your accomplices.

Ans: I insist that I am innocent. I thought that Kerse was at Versailles. I never had any reason to harm that dear man.

Ques: Your manner of denying that you committed this atrocity only confirms your guilt. And it seems that you have committed other thefts. You gave a tavern boy a gold watch and a silver watch. Where did you get them?

Ans: I am innocent of murder and of any thefts. I gave the tavern boy the gold watch in pledge for 120 livres that I owed for drink and food. It belonged to me. I bought it five months ago for 8 gold louis from a traveler near Tours.

Ques: Is your true name Villemain? Is not your real trade that of hairdresser? Were you not tried and convicted in Paris under the name of Villemain? I seem to remember once having interrogated you at the Châtelet under that name. We have been assured that you were once known as Villemain.

Ans: I have told you my true name. I am innocent.

[He was shown the body, and asked to recognize it.]

Ans: I recognize the clothing as Kerse's, but I cannot recognize the face because of disfigurement.

Ques: The neighbors have all recognized this corpse as that of Kerse, despite the disfigurement. He is disfigured because his vicious murderers tried to prevent identification. All of the evidence taken together establishes an overwhelming case against you and your accomplices; there are even fresh bloodstains on the pillow that you took from here to Méclet's room. I summon you to admit the truth.

Ans: I am innocent. The bloodstains on the pillow are from a scratch on my nose.

[He was shown the various goods removed from Kerse's room and asked to recognize them.]

Ans: I recognize those things. I removed them on instructions from Kerse.

[He was shown the knife, razor, compass, scissors, three combs, and key found on his person.]

Ans: The key is to Kerse's room. The other things are mine.

Ques: The three combs and razor do not suggest that you are a masonry laborer but rather a hairdresser. The razor is worn from use; the upper part of the blade has pieces missing, as if it had been drawn across a hard surface. The paper sheath has red stains that look like blood. Is this not the razor that you used to kill Kerse?

Ans: I am innocent. Those are tobacco stains, not bloodstains. There is nothing unusual about the razor. I have used it for a long time to trim my beard and cut my hair. I use the combs on the wig that I own and wear. I am a masonry laborer, not a hairdresser.

Ques: Your wig is black, matted, and looks like it has not been combed for months. Your beard is quite long.

Ans: I trimmed my beard a few days ago. I regularly comb the wig.

Ques: Have you ever been in prison in Paris?

Ans: I was in prison at Dôle, and never in Paris.

Bachois ordered that Gérard be imprisoned at the Grand Châtelet, Méclet and Thibault at the Petit Châtelet.

During the late afternoon of January 7, immediately after the interrogations, Bachois ordered an inquiry into the criminal archives of the Châtelet and the Tournelle of the Parlement of Burgundy at Dijon. The first inquiry yielded results within a few days: A certain Villemain had been convicted by the Châtelet, under the assumed name of François Castel, on June 30, 1777, for theft of a horse. He was whipped, branded with a *V*, and banished from the jurisdiction for three years. He was rearrested on suspicion of violating banishment in July 1778 and gave his name as Villemain. The presidial chamber of the Châtelet then ascertained, by visual and voice recognition, that Villemain and Castel were the same. The sentence was benign: His term of banishment was renewed for three years, and he was released.

By January 23, 1781, the criminal lieutenant had received information from the Tournelle of the Parlement of Burgundy that a certain Villemain, also known as Nicolas Gérard, branded with a *V*, had been convicted on appeal by the Tournelle, in April 1779, for theft from a home in Burgundy where his wife was employed; he was branded *GAL* and sentenced to the *bagne* for three years. The Nicolas Gérard of the present case closely fit the physical description of Villemain / Castel / Gérard. Bachois de Villefort had been criminal lieutenant since 1774; in that office, he would have presided over the judgment of Villemain / Castel / Gérard in 1777. Magisterial memory and judicial archive converged on Nicholas Gérard.

As a previous offender, Gérard would have been subject to presidial trial without appeal of judgment. But Méclet and Thibault, his codefendants, were not so liable. All three had therefore to be tried and judged by the Châtelet, with appellate decision by the Tournelle of the Parlement of Paris.

On request of the prosecutor and order of the criminal lieutenant, Commissioner Mutel began the formal *information* on the evening of January 7. By then, Prosecutor Moreau had formulated the charge: "Nicolas Gérard, François Méclet, and François-Louis Thibault, suspected of premeditated murder committed against the person of Nicolas Kerse, master tailor, and of theft of various articles of furniture and personal effects from the room of said Kerse." Mutel heard Jacques Pain and Louise Orry.

Jacques Pain

About fifteen days ago, Kerse gave me a key to his room. He was due to move out on the eighth of the month. He had another key. I did not see Kerse for three or four days before his body was found. Yesterday afternoon my servant woman heard noise in Kerse's room. In the evening, at about 6:00 or 7:00, she heard noise on the staircase. She went to investigate and saw three men carrying out Kerse's furniture. This morning I went to the room with other persons. We found his body with the throat cut, stuffed under the workbench. We sent for the commissioner. Gérard shared that room with Kerse. He calls himself a masonry journeyman or laborer.

Louise Orry

"Ditte Dorville": unmarried; age 21; hairdresser; domiciled with Riau, "dit Dorville." Yesterday at about 7:00 P.M. I returned to the building and saw three strangers leaving. They are the same as the ones who have been arrested. The one who is named Gérard was carrying a bundle; he said to me that Kerse is moving out. I answered that only crooks move out at night. I was afraid that he was taking away the jacket that Dorville, with whom I live, had given Kerse for repair. I tried to stop Gérard. He dropped the bundle and ran. I gave the bundle to Pain. This morning we went into Kerse's room and found his dead body.

The next action in the case was January 15. The three defendants were examined in prison by doctors of the Châtelet. They found no trace of branding on Méclet and Thibault. On Gérard's shoulder they found a scar with the diameter of a large coin, which appeared to have been made by a hot iron; there was distinct trace of the letter *L*.

On January 16, by request of the prosecutor and order of the criminal lieutenant, Commissioner Mutel conducted the final *information* at his office. The witnesses had been carefully and intelligently selected by the prosecutor and criminal lieutenant. All of those summoned gave depositions. Their hearing closed preparatory instruction of the case.

Pierre Poirier

Age 26; keeper of the tavern "Louis the Great" on the rue de la Lune; lodged on the rue des Tournelles by Vé, owner of the tavern. In mid-December I noticed a man who had been coming frequently to the tavern. He was big in size and height, wore a frock coat and a mason's apron, was aged about 38 or 40, had dark-brown hair, wore a wig and a dirty hat. He was often with a woman scarred by smallpox, who also had a scar near her mouth and another under her chin. She looked to be about 34. This man always sought out conversation with the other drinkers and seemed to be a skillful talker. One day, I overheard him tell a customer who was a domestic servant that he had deposited a gold watch with the tavern-keeper "at the sign of the Drum" on the rue Bonne-Nouvelle in pledge for 5 or 6 louis that he owed there. He offered to sell the watch to the servant. I suspected that he had come to my tavern to drink because he owed too much "à l'enseigne du Tambour." Around December 31, a small man wearing a wig and dressed simply, and who spoke French poorly, came looking for the garrulous stranger. They left together. The next day the small man returned and approached me. He said he was a tailor. He showed me a pair of black velvet breeches and a black velvet jacket and asked if I wanted to buy them. I told him no, they were too fancy for my work. A few days before that, the large man was in the tavern, drinking from morning to evening. He was joined by another man, whom I did not know. At closing time, the large man said that he did not have money to pay his bill. I was angry, and asked him why he had drunk all day, and ordered drinks for others, knowing that he could not pay. He asked for credit. I refused. In pledge of payment, he offered a snuffbox, a razor, a pair of scissors of the sort used by wigmakers. He said that he was a wigmaker and always carried these with him. I accepted those things in partial pledge of payment. A few days later he came back, paid his bill, and I returned his things. On about the third, he returned. I served him wine. Soon after, the same tailor as before joined him. They drank together for a half hour, and the tailor left. I have not seen him since. At about 5:00 or 6:00 P.M. on the sixth, the big man came into the tavern with two women and bought wine for them all. One of them was the scar-faced woman; the other is a washerwoman in the *quartier*. The big man left and came back at about 7:00 P.M. with a porter. They drank. The porter gave me an *écu* of 6 livres in exchange for 2 *écus* of 3 livres. He gave one of them to the big man to pay for their drink, and they left together. The next morning I heard in the *quartier* that a tailor had been murdered on the rue de Cléry, by men who drank in my tavern. People told me that the murdered tailor was the one who had been in my tavern with the stonemason.

Antoine-Claude Bazin

Age 49; master founder–smelter; domiciled rue Guérin-Boisseau. Saturday morning between 10:00 and 11:00 on the sixth, I encounted Méclet as I was passing in the courtyard of Saint-Nicolas-des-Champs. I have known him since childhood. He asked me if I wanted to buy a mirror. I asked him if it was of value. He said that it is going for 12 livres, and belongs to a friend who needs to sell it to pay rent. I said that I would buy it for 10 livres. Méclet left to speak to the owner. About fifteen minutes later I was back at home. Méclet came with a stranger who said that he owned the mirror. He introduced himself as Gérard. He said that he was a hairdresser, out of work for a long time, and needed to sell the mirror to pay rent. I bought it for 10 livres. Gérard exclaimed, "Let's drink to this!" Since Méclet is an old friend, I agreed. We went to Breton's tavern "at the sign of the Holy Spirit" on the rue Guérin-Boisseau. We stayed there until about 2:00 P.M. Gérard told me that he also had a chest to sell. I said that I wanted to see it. He and Méclet replied that they would bring it to my home right away, and they left. I went home. I waited until 5:00 P.M. and then went out. When I returned at about 9:00 P.M., I was told that my companions were waiting for me in Breton's tavern. I went there. Méclet and another man he introduced as Thibault told me that while I was gone they had placed the chest in my atelier and asked if I wanted to settle on the price. I replied that it was too late in the evening, that I would look the chest over and decide on the morrow. Then they told me that while they were waiting for me they had run up a wine bill of 2 livres, 7 sous, and did not have the money. Would I pay for them? They said I should not worry, because the chest was in my atelier. I paid. The next morning [Sunday] at about 9:00 Méclet came to my home. I was still in bed and told him to return in an hour. He did, and we went to the atelier. I looked the chest over and then asked the opinion of one of my neighbors, who is a cabinet-maker. I offered 15 livres. Méclet said he would convey the offer. Just as he was leaving the atelier, we saw several men escorting Gérard and Thibault, whose hands were tied. Méclet ran back inside, up the stairs, and into a water closet. When these men told me they were looking for Méclet, I told them where he was. They arrested him. As they took him away, I told Méclet that he had tricked and compromised me. He shouted that he was innocent. Soon after, the commissioner and inspector arrived. I showed them the chest and mirror. They took my statement.

Honoré Breton

Age 65; tavern owner, rue Guérin-Boisseau. Saturday the sixth at about 11:00 A.M. Bazin came into my tavern with two men unknown to me. He introduced me to one of them, as a cabinet-maker with whom he was raised in the Faubourg Saint-Antoine and with whom he had served in a regiment. The three drank together until about 2:00 P.M. At about 6:00 in the evening, the same two who were with Bazin in the morning came in. They were with a porter from the Porte Saint-Denis and a man unknown to me. After a while one of them left with the porter. The other two stayed and drank. Sometime after 9:00, Bazin arrived and sat with them. They drank together. When it was time to pay, I heard one of them tell Bazin that they could not pay their bill, and would he pay for them. Bazin paid.

Jacques-Louis Legoy

Age 24; general laborer and porter; domiciled rue Basse Porte Saint-Denis, passage St. Laurent. Saturday the sixth, at about 5:00 or 6:00 P.M., I was hired by a man who called himself Gérard to help carry a heavy chest. We went to a building on the rue de Cléry and were met there by two other men. We went to a room on the third floor that Gérard opened with a key. I saw a large chest, a bundle on the bed, and a workbench with a tapestry hanging nailed to the top edge. Gérard told me that I only had to move the chest. It was in the middle of the room. He said the two others would move the other things. He also told me that he owned the furniture and other things in the room, that the landlord owed him 60 livres but refused to acknowledge the debt, that he is getting revenge for this bad faith by moving out without paying rent. The other two introduced themselves as Méclet and Thibault and said they were there to help Gérard move. Those two helped me move the chest down the stairs and onto the street. They accompanied me with the chest to the founder–smelter's atelier on the rue Guérin-Boisseau and then back to the rue de Cléry, in case Gérard needed help with the other things. Méclet and Thibault went up the stairs, and I followed behind. I heard a woman on the staircase shout at them, "You have carried off the chest, but you will not take anything else! It is shameful for a master tailor to move out without paying rent!" Méclet answered that they were not moving, but only taking the chest to be repaired. Another woman said, "You have taken my husband's jacket, you must bring it back!" Gérard replied, "We have not taken the jacket, it is in the room." Then Gérard, Méclet, and Thibault came down and told me to come with them to the tavern on the rue Guérin-Boisseau where we would have a bottle and wait for the founder–smelter to come with money for the chest. We waited and drank for a long time. I asked Gérard for the money he owed me. He replied that he did not yet have it, but would soon, and invited me to go with him to another tavern, "at the sign of Louis the Great" on the rue de Bonne-Nouvelle. We went. He ordered wine and left, telling me he would return. About forty-five minutes later he came back with a woman who was carrying a pair of black velvet breeches and a black velvet jacket. She told me that she was going to get money with those clothes so that I could be paid. She left and returned a half hour later. She spoke privately with Gérard, gave him the clothes, and left. Gérard then told me that it was too late at night for him to get the money he owed me, and that he did not even have enough to pay the wine bill. It was 11:00 P.M., closing time, and the tavern-keeper insisted on payment. I gave him a 6-livre *écu* to change; from that I gave Gérard an *écu* of 3 livres to pay the bill. He gave me the velvet clothes as security and promised to pay me at my workplace near the Porte the next morning. He did come there, early in the morning. He took me to another tavern on the rue des Filles-Dieu. Then he went to fetch Méclet and Thibault. After we had all drunk a *chopine*, Méclet said he was going to get the money for the chest from the founder–smelter. Not long after he left, the police arrived. They arrested Gérard, Thibault, and me.

Jean-Baptiste Riau

"Dit Dorville": age 22; clerk–agent of Police Inspector Lescaze; domiciled rue de Cléry.[18] I live in the same building as did Kerse, on the second floor, just below his

---

[18] Riau "dit Dorville" was a police agent employed and supervised by Lescaze, inspector in the Quarter of Saint-Germain-des-Prés. Such agents were known officially as clerks or subinspectors; they were known colloquially and vituperatively as *mouches* or *mouchards*. There were a few hundred of them during the 1780s. They worked semiclandestinely in searching for persons

room. Around last December 15, I noticed that Kerse was sharing his room with someone who called himself a journeyman mason and who was known in the building by the name of "Bourguignon." During the night of Thursday/Friday, the fifth of this month, at about 2:00 A.M., I heard footsteps in Kerse's room and a noise like that of chairs being overturned. At about 5:00 A.M., I heard the door being shut. When I returned home at about 10:30 at night on the sixth, I was told that Kerse had moved out without paying his rent. The woman who lives with me told me that some men had also tried to take away the jacket I had left with Kerse but that she prevented them. They dropped a bundle of clothes, which she gave to Pain, the superintendent. Pain came home at about 11:00 P.M. He was also told that Kerse had moved out. He went up to see if there was still anything in the room that could be used to pay the rent. I and some others went with him. On the bed we saw a large bundle wrapped in a blanket. Pain exclaimed, "Ha! They have not taken everything!" I looked around the tailor's bench for my jacket. When I looked under the rug hanging, I saw a leg with a black stocking and no shoe, and then a dead man. We all immediately left the room, and Pain locked the door. When the commissioner arrived the next morning, I recognized the body as that of Kerse. I also learned that the furniture and other things had been taken by "Bourguignon," who also calls himself Gérard, and by two other men named Méclet and Thibault.

Jean Marie

Age 29; haberdasher; domiciled rue de Cléry [but not in the building of the murder]. At about 7:30 in the evening on Saturday the sixth I was walking down the rue de Cléry, in front of the building where Pain is superintendent. People were saying that Pain is being moved out on. I answered: "Ho! If Pain is being moved out on, the furniture won't be heavy!" Then I saw someone come out of the building, carrying a mattress; he headed for the rue des Filles-Dieu. I asked him what he was doing. He told me to mind my own business. The next morning, the seventh, I heard that a man had been murdered in Pain's building and that furniture and personal belongings had been stolen. I went there immediately and told Inspector Santerre that I had seen someone carrying a mattress out of the building and down the rue des Filles-Dieu. He asked me to go with Latelle, one of his agents, and try to find out where the mattress had been taken. We learned that it was taken to the room of a certain Méclet, on the 5th floor of a building on the rue des Filles-Dieu. We reported this immediately to Santerre. Meanwhile he had learned that the men who had carried off the furniture were in a tavern on the rue des Filles-Dieu and had them arrested.

Antoinette Liébaut

Age 32; laundress; domiciled rue de Cléry. Since I live in the same building as Kerse, I noticed that for about three weeks before he was murdered he shared his room with a

against whom there were warrants, violators of sentences of banishment, escapees from the *bagnes* and prisons, and in reporting criminal plots and activities. Many of these "clerks" were recruited from among former criminals, for reasons of efficiency. They ranged throughout the city and were often most active in areas where they did not reside. See Williams, *Police of Paris*, pp. 104–11.

man who said he was a stonemason but that others said was a hairdresser. I saw him come and go frequently. The last time I remember seeing Kerse was around December 31. On Saturday, the sixth of this month, at about 7:00 P.M., as I was going downstairs I saw this mason or hairdresser carrying a heavy chest along with a porter whom I had never seen before. When I came back about a half hour later I saw another stranger [whom I later learned is named Méclet] carrying a mattress down the staircase. I knew that Kerse was the only tenant due to move out at the end of the rent period. I thought that the chest and mattress were from Kerse's room and that he was moving out without paying, all the more so because it was dark and these men tried to hide their faces, and Pain was not in the building at the time. The next morning at about 11:00 I learned that Kerse was found murdered in his room. I recognized his corpse.

Joseph Chatillon

Age 24; tavern-keeper for Chéron, rue Nôtre-Dame de Bonne Nouvelle; domiciled same street. During the past three months a man who called himself sometimes François, sometimes Bourguignon, and said he was a stonemason, came now and then to my tavern. By early December he owed me a bill of 5 livres. I pressed him to pay his bill. He offered me a gold watch in pledge of payment but told me that it was already in pledge with Decoffe, grocer on the rue des Petits Carreaux, for food. He suggested that I pay Decoffe the 4 livres that he owed, thereby get the watch and keep it as security until he paid his wine bill. I did this. Since I had the watch, I let Gérard have further credit. This François or Bourguignon or Gérard now owes me 149 livres, 13 sous. He sent me a letter stating that he wanted to sell me the watch for 7 *louis d'or* to cancel that bill. Sunday morning on the seventh I heard that a man had been found with his throat cut in a room on the rue de Cléry and that Gérard had been arrested as a suspect. I went there immediately, made my statement to the commissioner, and gave him the watch and letter. Gérard often came into my tavern with two women, one of whom was large-necked and shabbily dressed, and with an older man about 5 feet, 3 inches tall.

Pierre David

"Dit Latelle"; age 38; clerk–agent of Inspector Santerre (Saint-Denis Quarter); domiciled rue de la Vannerie: I know only the following of this case. Sunday morning I went with Inspector Santerre to the building on the rue de Cléry where Kerse the tailor had been found murdered. Santerre had discovered that an individual known as Villemain, who was an escapee of the *bagne* and who used different names such as Bourguignon, François, and Gérard, was suspected of the murder and of having stolen furniture and belongings from Kerse's room. Santerre had also learned that this individual was then in a tavern on the rue des Filles-Dieu. I was sent to arrest him, and I did.

The criminal lieutenant conducted final interrogation of the three defendants on January 23. He was armed with the depositions by witnesses on January 7 and 16 and the results of a search of the criminal records of the Châtelet and the Parlement of Burgundy.

Murder

Thibault

Ques: How long and how have you known Gérard and Méclet?

Ans: I have known Méclet for about six months. We have lived together for about three months. I knew Gérard under the name of Lionnais for about fifteen days before I was arrested. I knew him through Méclet. I heard him say that he was formerly a women's hairdresser and now a stonemason.

Ques: Did you not aid Gérard and Méclet in taking various things from the room that Gérard shared with Kerse? Are you aware that Kerse was found dead in that room, with his throat cut, and dead for almost forty-eight hours before you were in the room, and consequently that it is impossible not to suspect you and your friends of having killed Kerse with the purpose of robbing him?

Ans: I am innocent of the murder. I am in the pitiful situation of being under accusation with my friend Méclet. It is true that on January 6, after urging by Gérard, we helped him move objects from that room. Gérard told us that his roommate was at Versailles, and instructed him to sell the chest and mirror to pay the rent, and to take out the other things. We believed him. We saw no corpse, and we had no reason to suspect Gérard of any such crime. We never knew or saw Kerse.

Ques: When you were in the building with the porter, you heard Gérard tell the porter that he owned the furniture and that the landlord had refused to pay 60 livres that he owed Gérard. From this it follows that you knew you were participating in an illegal act.

Ans: I never heard Gérard say any such thing. I believed that the money from the mirror and the chest would go to pay the rent. Lionnais tricked me into this miserable business, but I am innocent.

[He was shown all the confiscated objects and asked to identify them. He did so.]

Méclet

Ques: How did you come to know Gérard? What are his true names and occupation?

Ans: I met Gérard about two months ago, to my great misfortune. I thought he was honest. But he is a crook who has caused me to rot in this prison. Before being a stonemason he was a hairdresser. I knew him only by the name of Lionnais. Because of him my friend Thibault and I are suffering in prison innocently. We had no knowledge of Kerse's murder. I never saw or met Kerse. I only reproach myself for having in good faith helped Lionnais move Kerse's belongings, sell the chest and mirror, and store things in my room.

Ques: Since you furtively carried away the belongings of the unfortunate Kerse, you are strongly suspected of his murder. Your excuse, that you only sold the chest and mirror to facilitate the rent payment, is false. It is clear from the depositions that Gérard said in your presence, when he was trying to sell the chest, that the things were his, and that he was moving out to get back at the landlord who owed him money.

Ans: I did not hear him say such a thing. I had no intention of being part of a furtive move. I sincerely believed that with the money from the mirror and chest Lionnais would pay the rent owed. I also believed him incapable of crime and especially of a murder so atrocious. Thibault and I are absolutely innocent. It is horrible that the two of us, who are known to be honest and for whom forty people can attest, are compromised like this, locked up in cells with our reputations ruined.

[He was shown all the goods taken in evidence and asked to identify them. He did so, and gave the same explanation as before.]

Gérard

Ques: I call upon you to state your real name. It is not Nicolas Gérard. We believe that your real name is Charles-François Villemain and that you were once a hairdresser. We believe that you have been tried on criminal charges under various names. The first trial was in 1763, on a charge of burglary. You were released for lack of proof. The second was in 1777 for stealing a horse. You were convicted, branded with a *V*, and banished from Paris under the name of François Castel, by judgment of June 30, 1777. In July 1778 you were arrested in Paris for violating that sentence. You gave your name as Villemain. The Châtelet ascertained that Villemain was the same convict who had been banished under the name of Castel. By presidial judgment your sentence of banishment was renewed from July 1778, and you were released. In April 1779 you were convicted on appeal by the Parlement of Burgundy for theft from the home of a gentleman who employed your wife and who had given you hospitality. You were sentenced to the *bagne*.

Ans: That is all false. I have never been a hairdresser. I have worked in stonemasonry for twenty years. I have never been tried in Paris. Nicolas Gérard is my only name. I was tried and convicted for stealing game and sentenced to the *bagne* for three years. I escaped last June.

Ques: How long did you live with Kerse and by what arrangement?

Ans: I shared the room with him for two months. We agreed that I would pay half the rent and food.

Ques: On the fourth or fifth of this month, did you not murder Kerse and then, with the help of Méclet and Thibault, move out most of his furniture and belongings, taking some of them to their room and others to Bazin's shop for sale?

Ans: I did not murder Kerse. [He repeated exactly the version of his actions that he had given in previous interrogations.]

Ques: You have admitted to seeing Kerse in the morning of January 3. No one else has seen him since then, except dead. During your previous interrogation, you stated that you slept in the room during the night of the fifth/sixth, that the removal took place during the day and evening of the sixth, and that you slept elsewhere during the night of the sixth/seventh. You were arrested on the morning of the seventh, after the body was found. It is impossible to doubt that you are the murderer, given these circumstances, your admissions, and your obviously furtive behavior. I exhort you to admit the truth. And I emphasize that you are morally obliged to do so, for by your denials of guilt you seriously endanger Méclet and Thibault, who may be innocent.

Ans: I am innocent. Pain had a key to the room. He could have murdered Kerse.

Ques: On the sixth, when you brought a porter to Kerse's room, did you not tell the porter that the furniture and other goods were yours, that you were moving out on the landlord because he owed you 60 livres and refused the debt?

Ans: That is false. I never said that.

Ques: Where did you get the gold watch that you gave in pledge of payment to the tavern-keeper Chatillon? Do you recognize this letter sent in the name of François to Chatillon, in which you proposed to sell the watch to Chatillon? [The letter was shown and read to him.]

Ans: I had that letter written and sent to Chatillon. I bought the watch from a pedlar near Tours, for 8 gold louis.

[He was shown the things found on his person when arrested and asked to identify them. He claimed them as his.]

Preparatory instruction of the case was completed by these interrogations.

Definitive instruction was begun immediately, by the *récolement* of the three defendants. They were separately read the transcripts of their interrogations on January 7 and on this date, asked if they wished to alter any of their statements (which they did not), and then asked if they swore to the veracity of those statements (which they did). Immediately after this *récolement*, Méclet and Thibault were confronted with Gérard, for both had variously incriminated him. This confrontation between the defendants and the subsequent *récolement* and confrontation of witnesses with the defendants were conducted by judge Claude-Thomas Nau de Champlouis.[19]

When he was read the full texts of Méclet's and Thibault's interrogations and *récolements*, Gérard only denied that he had ever said he was a hairdresser or used the name Lionnais; he challenged no other element of their statements. In conclusion, both of them reiterated the veracity of their statements.

Récolement of all witnesses and their confrontation with the three defendants were conducted on January 25. In the *récolement*, Poirier, David "dit Latelle," Marie, Chatillon, Bazin, Breton, Legoy, and Orry adhered to their previous depositions, without alteration. Antoinette Liébaut added that she did not see Thibault in the building when Kerse's belongings were removed. Riau "dit Dorville" and Jacques Pain offered new disclosures:

Riau

At about 11:00 P.M. on the sixth [and presumably immediately after he had discovered the dead body], Pain and I went to Commissioner Mutel's *hôtel*. He was not there. We then went to the *hôtel* of Commissioner Leblond.[20] His clerk told us that the commissioner was in bed and that it would be wrong to disturb him. He asked us if the death was natural. We answered that we did not know, since we were seized with dread and afraid to examine the body.

[19] The Naus were a leading dynastic family of the Châtelet and the Parlement of Paris since at least the late seventeenth century. Nau de Champlouis and his brother Pierre were both received as judges in 1780, at the respective ages of 21 and 24. It was customary at the Châtelet for novice judges to be assigned the supervision of *récolements* and confrontations, two of the most formulaic procedural actions (A.N. V 1 499; Y 1869).

[20] Leblond was police commissioner of the Grève Quarter and lived near the rue des Arcis. It is strange that they went to his office; the Saint-Denis Quarter had two resident commissioners in addition to Mutel (Williams, *Police of Paris*, pp. 146–7).

Pain

Between 10:00 and 11:00 P.M., soon after I returned and learned of the move, I entered the room with Dorville and my two small children. I wanted to see if everything had been moved from Kerse's room or if enough remained for payment of the rent due. As Dorville was searching for a jacket he had given Kerse for repair, he saw a leg under the workbench; he looked more closely and exclaimed, "There is a dead man here!" I too saw the leg. We were all terrified and did not touch or examine the body. We left the room immediately, and I locked the door. Dorville and I went to fetch Commissioner Mutel. He was not in. We went to Commissioner Leblond's *hôtel.* His clerk told us that Leblond was not commissioner for the Saint-Denis Quarter and that we should go elsewhere. We then returned home. Commissioner Mutel arrived the following morning.

Thibault did not challenge or attempt to refute either the credibility of the witnesses or any of their depositions in his regard. He merely asserted his innocence of any criminal act and referred to his answers in interrogation. Only Louise Orry and Legoy recognized Thibault as having been one of the three who removed Kerse's belongings. Méclet's behavior in confrontation was similar. His only challenges were to parts of the depositions by Bazin and Legoy: He asserted that he ran into the water closet *chez Bazin* to relieve himself, not to escape arrest; he denied that he had ever said that the chest was being taken out of Kerse's room for repair, and that he had ever heard Gérard say that he owned the furniture and other goods in the room. For the rest, he adhered to his previous statements.

Gérard was alert and aggressive in confrontation. He energetically challenged most of the depositions that incriminated him, in the following terms:

To Poirier: I have never said that I was a hairdresser. The velvet jacket and breeches belonged to me. I bought the fabric from a secondhand dealer, and Kerse made it into breeches and a jacket. But they were too tight in fit, and I returned them to Kerse so he could sell them.

To Legoy: I never said that I owned the furniture in Kerse's room or that the landlord owed me money.

To Riau, "dit Dorville": This witness is a police spy, and he cannot be believed. It is strange that this witness and Pain went into the room and supposedly found a corpse that I, who slept in the room the preceding night, did not see.

To David "dit Latelle": I never took the name Villemain. My real name is Gérard. Sometimes I did use the names François and Bourguignon; that depended on the ateliers where I worked and if there were other workers with those names. I was in the *bagne,* but only for poaching.

To Orry, "la Dorville": This witness is a prostitute and cannot be believed. She is lying when she says that she forced me to drop a bundle of clothes. I set the bundle on the staircase, and she took it away.

To Pain: The witness says in his deposition that he entered Kerse's room at 7:00 A.M. on the seventh. But in *récolement* he says that he entered the night before and saw the dead body. He surely knew where the body was, because he found it immediately. He had a key to the room all the time. Besides, the building is inhabited by whores and *mouchards* [public spies]. I am not responsible for what goes on there. [In response to this, Pain reaffirmed his deposition in *récolement*.]

All of the witnesses persisted in their depositions after Gérard's challenges. Definitive instruction of the case was now concluded.

None of the defendants petitioned the criminal lieutenant for inquiry into "justificative facts" in their defense. Méclet had claimed that forty persons could vouch for his honesty, but he did not name one as a character witness. The Châtelet passed to judgment of the case.

On January 26, the prosecutor summarized the entire police and judicial actions of the case (including the convictions record of Villemain / Gérard from the registers of the Châtelet and Parlement of Burgundy) and recommended sentence:

Requests for the King that the said Nicolas Gérard be declared duly convicted of the premeditated murder committed against the person of Kerse, master tailor, who had offered and given him hospitality and shelter in his home, after which murder he appropriated and stole the furniture and belongings of the said Kerse, which he had removed by men acting as his agents. . . . In reparation, and since he has previously been branded and sentenced to the *bagne*, from which he escaped before the expiration of his sentence, that he be broken alive on a scaffold to be erected at the Saint-Denis Square and Gate; that, once broken, his body be placed on a wheel with his face turned to the heavens, to remain there so long as it shall please the Lord to conserve his life; that his properties be confiscated in the name of the King, from which properties the sum of 200 livres be paid in damages and costs to the King's justice and the sum of 200 livres be donated for masses and prayers that will be said for the repose of the soul of Kerse, his victim; that before execution the said Gérard be subjected to torture both ordinary and extraordinary so as to learn from his mouth the truth concerning all facts of his crime and the names of his accomplices in crime; that judgment of François Méclet and François-Louis Thibault be suspended until after execution of sentence against Gérard, which sentence shall be printed, read publicly, and placarded in all the customary places and crossroads of the city, faubourgs, and outskirts of Paris.

On January 27, the three defendants were heard by the bench of the criminal chamber and then judged.[21] These were their final statements.

Gérard

I was sentenced at Dôle to the *bagne* for poaching. I have never changed my name or been a hairdresser. I have never used the names Villemain or Castel. I was never tried or judged at Dijon, and only passed through the town. I lived with Kerse for two months. I had the key to his room because he had to go to Versailles for a few days and gave me authority to sell the furniture and other articles in his room, which I was doing when I was arrested. I am not the murderer of Kerse or the accomplice of his murderer. I do not

[21] Register of the Criminal Chamber, January 27, 1781, A.N. Y 10528.

know who is guilty. I did not know that he was dead and hidden under the table, although I did continue to sleep in the room, except for one night when I ate and drank with a soldier. I never said that I was the owner of the furniture and other articles, or that the landlord had cheated me. I am innocent of all the accusations. I neither murdered nor robbed Kerse.

Méclet

I knew Gérard for a few months. He told me that he was a hairdresser. I knew nothing of Kerse's murder and did not see his body under the table. I am innocent of his murder. I have explained during the trial what took place between me and Gérard.

Thibault

I did not see the murder of Kerse. I was not involved in it and do not know who did it. Everything I said during the trial and am saying now is the truth. I am innocent of the charges.

The bench consisted of thirteen: Bachois de Villefort, criminal lieutenant and reporting judge, and twelve other judges. Its composition was balanced in generations and experience: Three judges had been received during the 1730s and 1740s and were in their sixties; three had been received during the 1750s and 1760s and were middle-aged; seven had been received between 1771 and 1780 and were in their twenties and early thirties. Their verdict was a perfect example of the workings and bias of the rule of *l'avis le plus doux* in a situation of dissenting opinions among several judges.

Bachois de Villefort, as reporting judge, opined first. He declared,

Gérard convicted of the theft of furniture and belongings from the person who lodged him, and *strongly suspected* [italics mine] of the murder of that person, for reparation of which, and in view of the fact that he has two previous convictions, he be sentenced to hanging, 200 livres of *amende,* and the *question préalable,* with suspension of judgment of the other two defendants until execution of that sentence.

The vote then proceeded as follows:

Judge	*Opinion*
Avril	Same as reporter
Bellanger	Same as reporter
Boucher d'Argis	*Plus amplement informé* [hereafter *p.a.i.*] during one year in prison for Gérard; same at liberty for Méclet and Thibault
Garnier	Same as reporter
Devin de Fontenay	Same as reporter
Baron	Same as reporter
Cambault de Canthère	Same as Boucher d'Argis

Murder

Phéllipe de la Marnière	*Bagne* for life for Gérard; p.a.i. for one year at liberty for Méclet and Thibault
Nau de Champlouis	Same as la Marnière
Baron	Same as la Marnière
Pelletier	Same as reporter
Fosseyeux	Same as Boucher d'Argis

The first round produced three opinions: death by hanging for Gérard and suspension of sentencing for the other two (7 votes); p.a.i. during one year in prison for Gérard, and at liberty for the other two (3 votes); life sentence to the *bagne* for Gérard and p.a.i. during one year at liberty for the other two (3 votes). The rules for decision required that the three opinions be reduced to two. Those who opined for the second minority sentence *(bagne)* were obliged to default; those who opined for the first minority sentence (p.a.i.) were not. Reduction was accomplished by a second, and possibly a third, round of opining:

Judge	Opinion
Bachois de Villefort	Death for Gérard, suspension of sentence for the others
Avril	Same as Bachois de Villefort
Bellanger	Changed from death to p.a.i.
Boucher d'Argis	P.a.i. with prison for Gérard, at liberty for the others
Garnier	Changed from death to p.a.i.
Devin de Fontenay	Death for Gérard, suspension of sentence for the others
Baron	Same as above
Cambault de Canthère	P.a.i. with prison for Gérard, at liberty for the others
Phéllipe de la Marnière	Changed from *bagne* to p.a.i. with prison for Gérard, at liberty for the others
Nau de Champlouis	Same as above
Baron	Same as above
Pelletier	Death for Gérard, suspension of sentence for the others
Fosseyeux	P.a.i. with prison for Gérard, at liberty for the others

Two of the seven judges who had originally opined for the death sentence against Gérard changed to the most lenient sentencing option (p.a.i.). The three who had originally opined for the *bagne* also shifted to that option. In strict terms, life incarceration in the *bagne* was not a sentence applicable to Gérard: He had already escaped the *bagne* and come to live clandestinely and

575

illegally in Paris. By the royal edict of March 1724, such persons, when convicted of a crime subject to afflictive or capital penalties, were subject to the death sentence.

By a final vote of eight to five, the verdict of the Châtelet was *plus amplement informé* during one year in prison against Gérard, and during one year at liberty against Méclet and Thibault. The record of judgment does not relate the argumentation that undoubtedly occurred among the thirteen judges. The two ostensibly extreme positions in judgment of Gérard were those of Bachois de Villefort (death) and Boucher d'Argis (p.a.i.). But only ostensibly: Bachois de Villefort declared Gérard probably guilty ("strongly suspected") of Kerse's murder but not proven guilty of that murder by the evidence of the case, and he voted the death sentence essentially for particularly treacherous theft compounded by a felonious record and character; Boucher d'Argis also contested the proof of the murder charge against Gérard when he opined for p.a.i. with prison. The central issue in the Gérard case was not penology: It was proof.

The Châtelet prosecutor immediately appealed *a minima* to the Tournelle of the Parlement. The Tournelle judged the case on February 3 and vindicated the prosecutor's appeal. The Parlement convicted Gérard of premeditated murder and robbery and condemned him to the *question préalable* and to breaking on the Grève. And the Tournelle issued a quite minimal *retentum:* Gérard was to receive all of the blows and to be strangled on the wheel only after remaining exposed for three long hours. Judgment of Thibault and Méclet was suspended until after the execution. Their fate would hinge largely on Gérard's statements during the *question préalable* and in a possible death testament at the site of execution. Such extraordinary power over accomplices inhered to those events.

Sentence was executed against Gérard on February 6, one month less one day from the inception of the case. Early that morning he was notified of the Parlement's judgment and put to the *question* at the Châtelet. The *question* was administered by Bachois de Villefort and Degouve de Vitry. Leg braces were the instrument of torture. The following is the text of his *question préalable* in its sequence of three interrogations:

Ques: Did you murder Kerse, who had given you hospitality, and after having murdered him, did you remove most of his furniture and belongings, with the help of Méclet and Thibault?
Ans: I am innocent of Kerse's death. By the love of God, I will die innocent.
Ques: Were you tried a first time under the name of Castel, and a second time under the name of Villemain, and then convicted and branded?
Ans: I was condemned to the *bagne* for three years and branded *GAL* by judgment at Dôle for poaching game.
Ques: Do you persist in denying that you were ever a hairdresser?
Ans: Yes. I never did that work.

He was then seated, and the braces were tied around his legs. The magistrates repeated the questions just listed, in different order, for the interrogation under duress. Gérard refused to answer most of them.

At the first wedge: I told you the truth during my trial. I cannot speak falsely now and risk damnation of my soul. You can drive in ten thousand wedges, and I will not say more than this. [He did not cry out or groan.]

At the second wedge: [In a firm voice and without any groan or sigh] I have nothing to say but the truth, and I have said it.

At the third wedge: I have told the truth. I will die innocent.

At the fourth wedge: He refused to answer.

At the fifth wedge: He said nothing.

At the sixth wedge: He said nothing.

At the seventh wedge: He said nothing.

At the eighth and final wedge: He still refused to speak or answer.

The two judges and recording secretary attested that Gérard did not cry out once during questioning with the leg braces. He was untied, placed on the mattress, and given a brief period of rest. Then Bachois and Degouve asked their final questions.

Ques: What is your name, surname, age, occupation, birthplace, and domicile?
Ans: I am Nicolas Gérard, age thirty-six. I was born in a village of the Franche-Comté or Burgundy, whose name I do not know. I am a masonry laborer by trade. I live on the rue de Cléry.
Ques: Do you persist in what you have said previously, and in denying that you murdered Kerse?
Ans: I do persist. I am not guilty of his murder. I know that I am going to die today, but I can only speak the truth. I believe that the Lord will have pity on my soul.
Ques: Were Méclet and Thibault your accomplices in the murder of Kerse?
Ans: No. I had nothing to do with his murder, so I could not have had any accomplices. I do not know who killed Kerse. I do not fear the justice of men, only the justice of the Lord.

The minutes of the *question* were read to Gérard; he was asked if his statements were true and if he wished to detract from or add to those statements. He affirmed them as true, neither adding nor detracting. The *question préalable* was completed. The ritual of execution was then commenced.

S. P. Hardy recorded the execution of Gérard; his sources were the magistrates of the Châtelet and Parlement who were in attendance. Hardy's account was of intensely agonistic behavior:

Nicolas Gérard was executed soon after the cortege arrived at the Grève, for he refused to make any death testament [the final statements that the condemned were urged to make by the confessor and magistrates]. He remained alive on the wheel for about one hour. It is said that this wretch had the audacity to speak with great insolence to his judges at the Tournelle. Far from manifesting any sign of anguish or repentance at the Châtelet before execution, when the prison chaplain announced to him the arrival of the priest–confessor he said, "Voltaire and Rousseau died without a confessor, and I can do without one just as well as them." He endured all wedges of the *brodequins* without the slightest avowal of guilt or accomplices. . . . When the executioner tied his hands, he said, "You can tie as tightly as you wish without any fear of hurting me, because I feel strong now." He stubbornly persisted in denying guilt up to his last gasp at the Grève.[22]

On March 3, the Tournelle sentenced Méclet to *plus amplement informé* for a period of one year with imprisonment; Thibault received the same but at liberty with assigned residence in Paris. On March 6, 1782, Méclet was released from prison with sentence of indefinite *plus amplement informé* at liberty. The case was closed.[23]

The Châtelet decided that the evidence against Gérard did not prove his guilt of Kerse's murder. The Parlement of Paris decided that it did. The only sentences possible for both courts were *plus amplement informé* or death, for the *question préparatoire* had been abolished in 1780.[24] This radical divergence in judgment of the Gérard case may have derived partially from concerns beyond the case. By 1780–1, the Parlement of Paris was progressively restricting the death penalty to crimes of murderous violence or robberies accompanied by assault. It was bending royal penology of other capital offenses to the breaking point by not rendering death sentences. The compensation for this silent defiance of royal edicts was implacability toward murderers and armed robbers. The magistrates of the Tournelle envisioned the immense geographic jurisdiction for which they were responsible. The magistrates of the Châtelet envisioned Paris, or the immediacy of the Grève and its audiences. Breakings were the most agonistic of executions, therefore the most heroic and subversive in potential for the victims. During 1780, there had been twelve executions in

---

[22] "Mes Loisirs, ou Journel d'événemens tels qui'ils parviennent à ma connoissance," B.N. ms. français, 6683, fols. 405–6 (entry for February 6, 1781). Gérard's alleged statement about Voltaire and Rousseau is plausible. Both died in 1778, and their refusals of confession and last rites of the Church were widely known. Voltaire returned to Paris to die in February. On instructions from the archbishop of Paris, several priests entreated him to confess in letters and visits to the Quai des Théatins. He consistently and publicly refused. He was followed by acclaiming crowds during his final visits to the Academy and Comédie-Française and died with almost equal publicity on May 30, 1778 (Theodore Besterman, *Voltaire* (Oxford: Blackwell, 1976, pp. 574–7). During the 1770s and 1780s it was not uncommon for the condemned to refuse the ministrations of confessors and to refuse to make death testaments at the site of execution. Agonistic subversion of the executionary ritual reached its apogee during those decades, as I shall demonstrate in Volume 2.

[23] Inventory 450, 1780–90, vols. H–Z.

[24] The mandatory penalty for premeditated murder for men was death on the wheel. Furthermore, a royal edict of March 1724 stipulated the following for former *bagnards:* "Ceux qui seront condamnés aux galères à temps ou à perpétuité pour quelque crime que ce puisse être, seront flétris avant d'y être conduits, des trois lettres GAL *pour, en cas de récidive en crime qui mérite peine afflictive, être punis de mort* [italics mine]. (Isambert, vol. 21, p. 261). The Parlement of Paris did not always apply this draconian provision to former *bagnards* who were convicted of crimes that carried only afflictive penalties. It applied the provision to those convicted of capital offenses (particularly if the offenses were violent) and to escapees of the *bagne* convicted of serious crimes. The case of Etienne Olagnier illustrates that practice. He was a two-time escapee of the *bagnes* who was convicted of at least four assaults with injury on villagers in the region of Lyons, where he lived. None of the assaults were lethal or accompanied by thefts, but one was with a knife. All were in drunken rampages. The Lyon presidial sentenced him to death by hanging; the Parlement of Paris upheld that judgment in December 1786 (A.N. AD III 17). Gérard was accused of a far more serious crime.

Paris, and this was many; four of them had been in December. Seven of the condemned had been executed for crimes of violence.

But the dissention between and within the two courts over the Gérard case also expressed one of the most controversial and liminal issues within eighteenth-century criminal justice: the issue of the probative value of sheer material, circumstantial, and character evidence, or *indicia*, in capital cases, especially in cases where conviction meant the noose, stake, or wheel.[25] Could *indicia* alone, however extensive, establish proof of guilt sufficient for the death sentence? Could such evidence of guilt intellectually and morally substitute, in judgment, for the authority of first-person truth (confession by the defendant) and the authority of direct sense perception (testimony by ocular witnesses to the criminal act)? The criteria for classification and evaluation of evidence in all forms were clear and rigorous in Old Regime jurisprudence. As I shall demonstrate, the formal *indicia* of Gérard's guilt were various in nature, numerous, and convergent. Their force was not diminished by contrary evidence. They established strong probability of his guilt. But there were only *indicia* against Gérard; there was no eyewitness to the murder and no confession. At the Châtelet and the Parlement, the decisive issue was probably not the specific *indicia* of guilt in the case; it was most likely the general probative value of *indicia* in a mandatory death offense.

In its orthodox and pure meaning (and not in its penal significance), a sentence of *plus amplement informé* declared that evidence for guilt in the case was far stronger than evidence for innocence, but that proof of guilt was not complete; it declared probability of guilt, but a probability short of proof. In pronouncing that sentence against Gérard, the Châtelet was adhering to the traditional logic of Roman–canonical jurisprudence wherein proof of guilt in a death case must be "more clear than the light of day," a clarity deemed impossible without either confession or at least one irreproachable eyewitness. In convicting Gérard, the Tournelle was reasoning at the modernistic frontiers of the 1670 ordinance. It was also responding pragmatically to the extreme rarity of confessions in capital offenses, the general rarity of eyewitnesses in clandestine murder cases, and the notorious atrocity of such crimes.

In the *Traité*, Jousse provided the most comprehensive and balanced eighteenth-century account of *indicia* in relation to proof and punishment, and

---

[25] *Indicia* (Latin) or *indices* (French) were the generic terms for elements of material, circumstantial, and character evidence; an element of such evidence was an *indice*. The word is closer in meaning to "indication," "sign," or "clue" than to "evidence" in the Anglo-American legal sense. They were fourth and last in the hierarchy of categories of proof. *Preuve* in the singular signified proof, but *preuves* signified all forms of what is denoted by the term "evidence" in Anglo-American usage, including confession and eyewitness testimony. This usage of *preuves* for all forms of "evidence" is illustrated by the following passage from Jousse's *Traité*: "La règle générale qu'il faut observer à cet égard, est qu'un accusé ne doit point être condamné sans avoir contre lui des preuves claires & évidentes, qui soient fondées ou sur son aveu; ou sur des titres non contredits [incriminating writing in his hand]; ou sur des témoins sans reproches; ou sur des indices indubitables & plus clairs que le jour" (vol. 1, p. 825). For economy of expression, I have used the term *indicia* to refer only to material, circumstantial, or character evidence.

of the controversy. The tensile importance of the issue was expressed by a textual fact: Of the 283 folio pages that Jousse devoted to *preuves* in jurisprudence and practice, almost half (137) were devoted to the fourth and traditionally least conclusive form of proof, *indicia*. He affirmed that *indicia*, however indubitable and numerous, could not establish "perfect proof," for that could emerge only from confession and ocular witness, supported by *indicia*. *Indicia* alone could establish, at best, "conjectural" (or ratiocinative) proof. But necessity to solve crimes otherwise insoluble and punish criminals otherwise unpunishable dictated that conjectural proof from *indicia* be permitted and utilized.[26] But in each case, the *indicia* of guilt were to be rigorously evaluated: They had to bear directly on the crime and the suspect; their meaning had to be evident; they had to be numerous and mutually supportive; their pattern had logically to exclude other explanations of the crime. But even in forming a rational proof of guilt, *indicia* could not form a perfect proof. Only with reluctance did Jousse accept probability of guilt in final judgment. Serpillon refused to accept probability as legitimate proof of guilt in capital cases.[27]

[26] "Ainsi, à proprement parler, on ne doit chercher des preuves parfaites que dans les actes mêmes qui contiennent le fait principal dont on cherche la preuve, soit dans la confession de l'accué, soit dans la déposition de ceux qui ont été les témoins directs & immédiats du fait: les indices, quelque indubitables qu'ils soient, ne formant presque jamais qu'une preuve imparfaite. Mais la nécessité ou l'on est de trouver des preuves pour punir les auteurs des crimes a fait adopter l'usage de la preuve conjecturale ou indirecte, *lorsqu'on n'en peut avoir d'autre* [italics mine]. On n'est pas toujours, en effet, dans le cas d'avoir la déposition de deux témoins qui ont vu l'accusé commettre le crime dont il est prévenu; au contraire, cela n'arrive presque jamais par la précaution que prennent les criminels de se cacher lorsqu'ils commettent quelque mauvaise action. Ainsi il arrive le plus souvent qu'on n'a qu'un témoin *de visu*, et quelque fois même point du tout; de manière qu'on est alors obligé d'avoir recours à cette autre espèce de preuve, qui est fondée sur le raisonnement, & sur la connoissance d'autre faits qu'on appelle *indices*, par le moyen desquels on peut parvenir à la connoissance du fait principal. . . . C'est pourquoi on a toujours mis la preuve par arguments au nombre des preuves legitimes. . . . Quoiqu'il soit vrai de dire, en général, que la preuve par conjectures, & qui n'est fondée que sur des indices, soit une preuve incertaine; néamoins il peut arriver qu'il y ait un si grand nombre d'indices dans un même procès, & que plusieurs de ces indices aient une liaison si intime & si nécessaire avec le fait principal [the crime], que cela forme alors une preuve complette, & qui équivaut à une démonstration. La certitude, ou force de la preuve par argument, ou par indices, dépend principalement de trois choses: (1) de la liaison nécessaire, ou du moins très prochaine, des indices au fait principal; (2) de leur grand nombre; (3) de leur accord ou conformité, c'est-à-dire, de la liaison qu'ils ont les uns avec les autres" (ibid., pp. 752–3). Claude-Louis Ferrière, dean of the Law Faculty of the University of Paris, expressed the negative and more traditional position on the probative value of *indicia:* "Les indices ne sont pas, à proprement parler, des preuves, & le Juge ne peut pas condamner un accusé sur des indices; mais ils font naître des soupçons; de sorte que plusieurs indices qui concourrent de différens parts, font un commencement de preuve qui porte quelquefois le Juge à condamner l'accusé à la question, si le crime est capital; mais il est de la prudence du Juge de ne rien ordonner à cet égard qu'après beaucoup de réflexions" (vol. 2, p. 20). Title XXV, Article 5, of the ordinance had simply authorized *indicia* as elements of proof; it did not state whether or not they were sufficient for conviction by themselves.

[27] Execution was absolute and irreparable. It should not be decided from imperfect proof (*indicia* alone), however "considerable." He accepted that such proof could be sufficient for conviction and condemnation, but only to penalties other than death. His acceptance was from pragmatic necessity, and not from principle. Serpillon's position of principle was based on the following distinction between probable and certain *science:* "Il est vrai qu'il y a des indices si pressantes

Conjectural proof represented a great conundrum in eighteenth-century criminal justice. Most of the crimes that required such proof for their solution were both clandestine and capital: premeditated murders, rapes, nocturnal burglaries, and highway or street robberies.[28] Such crimes rarely generated either confessions or eyewitnesses. And the penalty for conviction was death. To convict from "conjectural proof" was to execute from imperfect proof, from probability and not certainty of guilt.[29] The conundrum was simultaneously epistemological and moral.

Why was conjectural proof unsatisfying, and regarded as potentially treacherous by many eighteenth-century jurists and magistrates? Proof by *indicia* was unsatisfying precisely because it was ratiocinative, and thus interpretative. The magistrate was obliged to create that proof by inducing a pattern from the *indices.* They could not exist independently of the magistrate's critical reasoning, and thus of his intelligence, experience, and subjectivity. This dynamic intellectual enterprise made him liable to errors in judgment, and with a life at stake. *Indicia* and their combinations were variable; the quality of proof that could be derived from them was also variable, and ultimately fragile.[30] In

qu'ils paroissent capables de former une conviction; parce qu'ils concluent par une conséquence si nécessaire, qu'elle produit la science; mais la science des Juges ne suffit pas pour condamner; il y a deux sortes de science, celle qui produit une certitude morale, & celle qui produit une certitude physique; la science morale est celle qui dépend du raisonnement, comme celle qui n'est fondée que sur des indices; la science qui produit une certitude physique, est celle qui dépend immédiatement des sens, telle qu'est celle qui dépend des témoins qui ont vu commettre le crime; ces deux espèces de science forment les deux differentes espèces de conviction morale ou physique; mais les convictions morales ne sont pas suffisantes en matière criminelle, ou il ne s'agit que du fait; les questions du fait ne sont pas de la morale, mais seulement de la pure connoissance de la physique" (Serpillon, vol. 3, p. 1073).

28 "La preuve par indices ou présomptions est admise principallment dans les grands crimes, & dans ceux dont il est très difficile d'avoir la preuve; comme sont tous les délits cachés & qui se commettent en sécret, ou pendant la nuit" (Jousse, *Traité,* vol. 1, p. 828).

29 "Il y a plus à difficulté de scavoir si sur une preuve de cette espèce, qui n'est fondée que sur des présomptions, on peut condamner un accusé à la mort. Cette question est une des plus importantes qu'on puisse agiter en matière criminelle" (ibid., p. 830). But he affirmed (citing sixteenth- and seventeenth-century judgments of the Parlement of Paris) that in cases of premeditated murder, clandestine in nature, "il n'est pas nécessaire . . . d'avoir des témoins *de visu* pour pouvoir condamner l'accusé: la preuve conjecturale y est aussi admise; & lorsque les présomptions sont violentes, elles suffisent pour faire condamner l'accusé à la question, ou à une autre peine capitale" (ibid., vol. 3, p. 253). In both the *Institutes au droit criminel* (1757) and the *Loix criminelles de France dans leur ordre naturel* (1783), Muyart de Vouglans was equivocal on this issue. In the latter work he argued that strong or compelling *indices* joined with other less compelling *indices* could justify conviction and the death penalty. But for murder cases he offered only two such compelling *indices.* Two or more witnesses saw the defendant leaving the building in which the murder occurred and in which the corpse was found, with a bloody sword or knife in his hand and at the time of the murder; doctors ascertained that the mortal wound was caused by such a weapon. A corpse found in the cellar of a hostelry and recognized by two or more witnesses as that of someone who lodged there; the hotel-keeper (and defendant) denied in interrogation ever having known or lodged the victim (*Loix criminelles,* p. 805). His general position was that *indicia* alone in capital cases justified either the *question* or *plus amplement informé.*

30 "Il est difficile de déterminer quel doit être le nombre & la qualité des indices nécessaires pour former une preuve complette: cela dépend uniquement de la prudence & des lumières du Juge, qui doit, dans tous ces cas, examiner la force de chaque indice en particulier, & la conséquence qui résulte de la comparaison de ces indices, & de leur liaison avec le fait principal" (Jousse,

contrast, confession of guilt existed independently of the magistrate's reasoning, even though it had been elicited by his questions, and it had to be carefully evaluated. So too did the testimony of an eyewitness to the crime, which was also subject to evaluation. Confessions and eyewitness depositions were regarded as intrinsically objective forms of evidence.

The conundrum was rooted in the 1670 ordinance and was aggravated by the decline in use of the *question préparatoire*. The ordinance had dethroned confession as the queen of proof and elevated testimony to a comparable probative status. But the consequences of that enlargement and enhancement of testimonial evidence were paradoxical. Few witnesses were eyewitnesses to crimes. Most were sources of *indicia*, more witnesses meant greater quantity of material, circumstantial, and character *indices*. Eyewitness depositions would have increased arithmetically after 1670; depositions that provided *indicia* would consequently have increased geometrically. Greater efficiency in policing, and therefore in the scope of summonses, amplified the paradox.

Eighteenth-century jurists and magistrates, like their seventeenth-century forebears and the authors of the ordinance, still believed in certainty while understanding the idea – especially the limits – of probability. They were heirs to that Cartesian duality. They desired certainty, not probability, in criminal judgment. Certainty did not exist without either first-person avowal or eyewitness depositions. In practice, the greater the number of witnesses available to them, the more they had to contend with judging from probability. Certainty in judgment of capital cases remained an epistemological and moral goal, but that pristine goal became increasingly elusive for eighteenth-century magistrates. That is why Jousse devoted almost half of his discussion of proof to *indicia*.

Jousse listed twenty-six *indices* of guilt common to most crimes; essentially the same list was given by other eighteenth-century jurists and the sixteenth-century "criminalists." Seven specific *indicia* were particular to judgment of murder cases (1) if the defendant was seen with bloodstained clothes or weapons during the period of the murder; (2) if he had appropriated, sold, given, or still possessed any belongings of the victim; (3) if he had been seen at night in or near the victim's dwelling, or if he had gone there at any undue time; (4) if there had been any serious quarrel or manifest enmity between him and the victim; (5) if any object belonging to him, or fragment of clothing, was found near the victim's body; (6) accusation by the victim on the verge of death; (7) if at least two witnesses saw him leaving the murder site "pale, trembling, in an emotional

---

Traité, vol. 1, p. 829). And Muyart: "Mais comme cette Loi [the ordinance] ne s'explique point, ni sur le nombre, ni sur la qualité des circonstances & présomptions qui doivent servir à former cette preuve, elle a voulu sans doute par-là s'en rapporter à la prudence des Juges; parce qu'en effet, comme ces circonstances peuvent varier à l'infini, & même se croiser entr'elles de manière que, tandis que les unes vont à la décharge de l'Accusé, les autres tendent au contraire à le convaincre de son crime, il n'étoit pas possible de donner des Règles bien sûres pour pourvoir discerner les cas particuliers où les indices peuvent former une preuve, de ceux ou ils n'en peuvent former aucune" (*Loix criminelles*, p. 803).

state," or carrying a weapon.[31] Murder by premeditation was determined from the following *indices:* (1) the nature of the weapon and the exact wound inflicted, especially if both were unquestionably lethal; (2) the moral character of the defendant, particularly if he was a former offender or had a history of violence; (3) if the site of the murder was private, interior, and concealed from view; (4) the time of the murder, especially if late at night; (5) strong enmity between the defendant and the victim; (6) if the defendant took actions that were precautionary, such as acquiring or preparing weapons, hiding his possessions beforehand, or arranging escape and refuge; (7) flight from the area of the murder soon after it was committed.[32] Let us return to the conviction of Nicolas Gérard by the Parlement of Paris, a conviction from *indicia.*

Gérard was not simply a *répris de justice.* He was a multiple offender, a *bagnard,* and an escapee. His criminal history was not violent, but the last conviction was for theft from a home where he had the status of guest – a theft in betrayal of trust. Character evidence of guilt was reinforced by the classic traits of a *gen sans aveu:* no definite employment or respectable economic means; dissimulation of identity; generally furtive and illicit behavior. His past and present social being suggested a capacity for murder to larcenous ends. Such "character" was one of the most powerful single *indices* of guilt in law. The wound that killed Kerse was most probably a razor slash; its depth and regularity suggested that it was given from behind, either while the victim was asleep or while he was being held. Gérard's razor looked as if it had been used on cartilage or bone, and its sheath was stained red. The pillow on which he had slept was also stained with blood. The murder was nocturnal (on the fifth/sixth); Gérard admitted to having occupied the room during that evening, night, and morning and was seen to have been there. Medical examination of the corpse, his admission, and depositions placed him at the site of the murder during the time of the murder. It would have been difficult and dangerous for him, or anyone, to have attempted to carry and hide the corpse outside the room, for the building and the streets were trafficked and watched at all hours. He had appropriated most of the victim's belongings, before and after the murder. The body was most probably concealed in the room while most of the belongings were removed. When he was discovered Saturday evening, he immediately fled the building and the street. The fact that he did not flee the Quarter on Sunday was evidence of material desperation, not of innocence: He had prearranged to get the 15 livres from Bazin in the tavern on the rue des Filles-Dieu that morning.

Nine of the thirteen distinct and major *indices* of guilt for premeditated murder existed against Nicolas Gérard. Their number and pattern constituted strong probability that he had murdered Kerse to accomplish the robbery of Kerse. In addition, there were three lesser *indicia* against him: cohabitation with

---

[31] Jousse, *Traité,* vol. 3, pp. 552–3.
[32] Ibid., pp. 480–1. See also Guyot, vol. 8, p. 508.

the victim; general denunciation as a suspect (by several witnesses); variations and inconsistencies in his statements during interrogations and confrontations. This was a full combination of character, material, and circumstantial evidence of guilt. It was derived from documentation, statements by Gérard, and many concordant depositions. The only possible alternative explanation for those *indicia* was the logically fragile story and allegations of Gérard. But his story and allegations were not supported by any exterior or independent evidence. Both the general and detailed juristic criteria for conviction by "conjectural proof" were met in the Gérard case.

Why, then, were most of the thirteen Châtelet judges not convinced by that "proof"? All judges heard defendants in double voice: They listened for confession, even partial, but they usually heard denial; they listened beyond the denial for responses that indicated guilt, such as distress, evasiveness, inconsistencies, and contradictions. From Gérard they heard a voluble, generally implausible, but not altogether impossible account. It had inconsistencies of detail and a contrived quality. He had been tried at least twice before and was thus familiar with judicial procedure. But they also heard constant, passionate, and adamantine denial of guilt. They could not use the *question préparatoire* with retention of evidence to test Gérard's denial. Such adamantine denial could not persuade of innocence. But it could instill doubt of guilt, and thus indecision, when proof of guilt was based solely on *indicia*. The judicial expression of that doubt and indecision was *plus amplement informé*. Such caution in judgment of capital cases belonged to a venerable tradition of jurisprudence.[33] And the caution gave considerable potency to guilty defendants.

The Gérard case also illustrates a deep and paradoxical inequality within Old Regime criminal law and justice. Study of both eighteenth-century jurisprudence and trials reveals that the criteria for proof of guilt were more exacting in capital cases, and thus for the conviction of hard and socially dangerous criminals, than in cases subject only to afflictive or defaming penalties, and thus for the conviction of comparatively anodyne first offenders in less serious crimes (in further refutation of the "black legend"). And one might argue that the system of trial and judgment accorded greater importance to protecting defendants from the noose, wheel and *bagne* than to protecting French society from those defendants.

The Châtelet and the Parlement essentially concurred in their judgments of Thibault and Méclet; the differences were in the form of *plus amplement informé* against Méclet. By their sheer actions, both were objectively agents of Gérard in his robbery of Kerse, although there was no evidence that they aided or participated in the murder of Kerse. Yet they were not convicted of complicity in

---

[33] "Mais une maxime que les Juges doivent toujours avoir devant les yeux c'est que dans l'incertitude, ils doivent prononcer en faveur de l'accusé. C'est pourquoi les Juges qui sont éclairés, ne peuvent être trop réservés à se déterminer quand il s'agit de punir; & principalement lorsqu'il s'agit d'imposer une peine capitale. . . . Si le preuve du crime n'est pas convainquant, ils doivent en réserver la punition à Dieu" (Jousse, *Traité*, vol. 1, p. 833–4).

the robbery of Kerse. Both groups of magistrates followed a leading and binding principle of Old Regime criminal law in not convicting them: Complicity in a crime had to be knowing, and thus intentional, to be subject to conviction and penal sanction; it had to be subjective, not merely objective.[34] For conviction of agents or participants to ensue, their criminal foreknowledge or intent had to be established from either evidence or confession. Their cases were individualized in trial and judgment, so that judges could determine the exact nature of their involvement in the crime and whether that involvement was culpable by knowledge and intent. Defendants who were convicted of complicity received lesser penalties than principal authors, unless they had directly assisted in the act or unless the crime was extremely serious (such as premeditated murder). These provisions gave systemic protection to defendants accused of complicity, particularly in serious crimes.

Neither Thibault nor Méclet were *mal-famés*, legally or by local reputation. Gérard disculpated both in the *question préalable*. Their statements during interrogations and confrontations were generally consistent (although in his first interrogation Thibault said that he had known Méclet for two years, and in his final interrogation that it was for six months). Evidence of complicity with Gérard was extremely fragmentary in the case of Thibault, who had participated in the removal of Kerse's belongings through the mediation of Méclet. There were three strong *indices* against Méclet: He was in Kerse's room (at least briefly) on two occasions while the corpse was hidden there; he had found a buyer for the mirror and chest and stored Kerse's other belongings in his room; he had run away when he saw that Thibault and Gérard were arrested. In addition, two witnesses (Legoy and Bazin) stated that Méclet was present when Gérard falsely claimed ownership of the furniture and belongings. He vehemently denied that he had heard such claims. Kerse's body was genuinely hidden; conceivably he did not see it. His panic when he saw Thibault and Gérard under arrest was suggestive, but not conclusive, evidence of complicity in robbery. Finally, he gave an unvarying and plausible explanation for aiding Gérard in the removal, sale, and storage of Kerse's furniture and belongings. Both defendants insisted that they had acted in "good faith" and ignorance of criminality, from friendship with each other and through trust in Gérard. They were accorded the benefit of the doubt: Their sentences of *plus amplement informé* expressed inadequacy of evidence for conviction as accomplices in robbery, deferment of final judgment, and mild punishment.

Even if one concludes that Thibault and Méclet were probably innocent of any design to rob Kerse and to share in the fruits of that robbery, as the Châtelet and the Parlement concluded, the question of their awareness remained problematical. The question has social and moral depth. They were not rustics

---

[34] "Il faut pour que le complice puisse être puni, qu'il ait coopéré au crime sciémment & en connoissance de cause; car s'il l'avoit fait de bonne foi, & sans scavoir ce dont il s'agit, il cesseroit d'être punissable" (ibid., p. 24).

but native Parisians who had lived most of their lives in the city. Because of their urban and plebeian experience, it is not likely that they were unaware of possible criminality in Gérard's project to move and sell Kerse's goods. And they had known him only for a short time. In questioning them, Bachois de Villefort insisted – cogently, repeatedly, and with mounting exasperation – that they could not have been unaware of such possible criminality. When they responded with equal insistence that they had trusted and believed Gérard, they were admitting that they had chosen to trust and believe him. But that choice was undoubtedly far from simple in nature. Choosing to believe Gérard was choosing to preserve their relations with him and with each other, for Méclet had become dependent on Gérard, just as Thibault was dependent on Méclet. Why were those relations important to them?

We may approach that question by examining the individual social beings of Méclet and Thibault. The former was a journeyman cabinet-maker, sporadically employed (and probably unemployed at the time of the case), who shared a small furnished room with a seamstress, and prowled the local taverns. The latter was a former locksmith, part-time soldier, and sometime public letter writer at a few sous each missive, who shared Méclet's lodgings and rent. Their individual social beings were most precarious. They survived through alliances, dodges, and hustles.

The "big man," the "gregarious stranger," the "skillful talker": Gérard wielded plebeian charisma – sordid, magnetic, and effective. Commodities and services circulated around and through him. He was adept at creating social and economic credit for himself and his companions, and credit meant small but extensible opportunities for self-aggrandizement. Taverns were citadels of conviviality and alliances, for plebeians like Méclet and Thibault. Gérard's capacity to generate credit and exchanges in the taverns gave him power over such companions. Méclet was a beneficiary of that power, before he and Thibault became its victims. They were trapped into trust by their need, by the actuality and promise of reciprocities with Gérard, by a symbiotic web of which he was the temporary center.

Gérard was even more profoundly entrapped. His condition of branded former convict and escapee from the *bagne* forced him to be motile and to navigate interstices of Parisian society. But the motility and navigation were conspicuous. That quality was registered in his dress: the leather apron of a stonemason, worn over a long frock coat (a bourgeois garment); a wig (but unkempt and unpowdered), surmounted by a shabby hat. This was social indeterminacy. Even the aliases were conspicuous by their number: François, Bourguignon, Lionnais. An authentic laborer or journeyman who was not trying to conceal his identity used only two names in public: his family patronymic; his trade sobriquet. In deploying three or four names, Gérard provoked suspicion. Finally, there was the inevitable ostentation of his charisma, especially to the gaze of the local tavern-keepers.

Silent and intelligent surveillance of Gérard by denizens of the Quarter and the building made possible the expeditious prosecution of Gérard. The depositions that completed his conviction were expressions of that surveillance; they were local memory of suspect detail translated into legal witness. And this was one of the most cruel paradoxes of eighteenth-century Paris: The great city lured the fugitive and the desperate; its immensity and swarm gave them the illusion of refuge, concealment, even freedom; but in reality, that immensity dissolved into Quarters with observers and arbiters, in whose eyes such persons were marked by their strangeness and defined by their social indefinability.[35]

The fifteen protagonists of this case (excluding police and magistrates) formed almost a social microcosm of petty bourgeois and popular inner Paris.[36] Although they defy classification in the nomenclature of modern sociology, they may be placed in a rough social hierarchy: the master artisan Bazin and the tavern owners; Pain, locksmith and building superintendent; Kerse, self-employed tailor who worked at his domicile; Méclet, journeyman cabinet-maker; the tavern-keepers and salaried servingmen; and the others, who worked at various and occasional menial tasks. At the top of the hierarchy (Bazin and the tavern owners), there was the lowest level of bourgeois status, in eighteenth-century Parisian terms: independent mastery of a shop or ownership of a business, and employment of labor. At the large base of the hierarchy, there were characteristic figures from the "populace." Among them, only Legoy and Méclet may be described, even remotely, as "proletarian." The others either did not produce commodities and capital or did so only sporadically. All of them were plebeians. Several of them were parasitic in various ways. Some of their occupations were undoubtedly more putative than real; a laundress, cleaning woman, or cook who was mainly a prostitute did not identify herself as a prostitute in deposition.

Taverns and wineshops were at the center of relations between the male protagonists. This was characteristic in eighteenth-century Paris. The tavern was a nuclear site of popular and petty-bourgeois friendship, conviviality, neighborliness, sexuality, gambling, commerce, work relations, rumor, strikes, riots, and criminality. Passages from cramped and poorly heated tenement rooms and apartments, or from ateliers and shops, to the local taverns and back were osmotic and constant. Alcohol, frequently consumed in great quantities and to drunkenness, lubricated this sociability and its exchanges. In the taverns, those who were domiciled mingled with the legions of those who drifted. Generalized

---

35 The close "mesh" of the Parisian Quarter was pithily expressed by Daniel Roche: "De la maison à la rue pas de coupure, le voisinage déborde aux maisons proches, aux ateliers, aux boutiques, aux cabarets peu distants. Pour chacun, un quartier se dessine fait de relations quotidiennes, et de réputations changeants," *Le peuple de Paris*, p. 255. See also Garrioch, *Neighbourhood and Community*, pp. 16–56.

36 Among them, only Antoinette Liébaut, Louise Orry, and Jean-Baptiste Riau could not sign their names.

social promiscuity created general opportunity.[37] Gérard had undoubtedly met Kerse in a tavern near the rue de Cléry.

Tavern owners and their servingmen wielded fundamental power within an economy and society where cash was scarce. The mechanics of that power are revealed by the Gérard case. They could grant or refuse credit for drink and food. Customers were not required to pay when served: They were usually allowed to drink to surfeit and then settle their bill when they left or the tavern closed. Bills were often large, and very many customers could not pay. The practice created indebtedness, the necessity for credit, and empowerment of the tavern-keeper. In collateral for credit, in pledge of payment, tavern-keepers accepted commodities: clothing, bedding, watches, buckles, razors, virtually any object with sale or barter value. Those objects were currency in the popular and tavern economies. The tavern-keeper was simultaneously banker, pawnbroker, and fence. He was a beneficiary of generalized theft and a principal agent in "recycling" stolen goods into the economy of popular consumption; those goods accepted in "pledge of payment" for drink and not redeemed with cash became his to barter or sell. For such sales, there was a plethora of ambulant street pedlars and junk, old-clothes, fabric, and jewelry shops throughout the city.[38] This creditor–debtor relationship was symbiotic. Credit with the tavern-keeper had ultimately to be redeemed, either by cash payment or sacrifice of the commodities pledged. But since wine and food were also currency, such credit could be used by its recipient to create greater value, to create friend-ships, alliances, and dependencies among drinking companions. Such credit was the material source of Gérard's charisma in the taverns with plebeians like Thibault and Méclet. And it seems that by the time of Kerse's murder, Gérard was running out of pledgeable or salable possessions.

Clothing, bedding, and fabric were the bulk of the commodities taken from Nicolas Kerse, and they were among the most common objects stolen in

[37] On the abundance of social exchanges in taverns and wineshops, see Brennan, *Public Drinking;* Roche, *Le peuple de Paris*, pp. 262–8; Garrioch, *Neighbourhood and Community*, pp. 180–90, Benabou, *La prostitution*, pp. 195–205. In 1780, there were approximately 2,000 taverns and wine-shops and 2,800 cafés (that sold beer and liquor) in Paris; this meant 1 drinking establishment for every 150 to 200 persons. They were clustered most thickly along and near the great axes of traffic: the rues and portes Saint-Denis and Saint-Martin; the rue Montmartre; the Halles; the river docks; the rue du faubourg Saint-Antoine–rue Saint-Antoine; the rue du faubourg Saint-Jacques–rue Saint-Jacques. Most were open seven days a week, from dawn until 10:00 or 11:00 P.M. (Roche, *Le peuple de Paris*, p. 258). Garrioch has examined the clientele of taverns and wineshops in five Quarters of the city, at midcentury and in 1788: master merchant artisans and all social types below that level were habitués; bourgeois of more elevated status and nobles were rare (*Neighbourhood and Community*, pp. 185–6).

[38] Profit in these operations required accurate estimates of value and thus close knowledge of the popular economy. Gérard's gold watch illustrates these transactions. Chatillon, keeper of the "Drum" on the rue Nôtre-Dame de Bonne-Nouvelle, initially gave Gérard 4 or 5 livres' credit before he demanded payment; he thereby made Gérard indebted to him. He then redeemed the watch from the grocer Decoffe and kept it as collateral for Gérard. On the strength of that collateral, Gérard's continuing drink bill had risen to the large sum of 149 livres by the time of his arrest. The watch had a value of 5 to 7 gold louis, or 200 to 240 livres. Chatillon and his employer would undoubtedly have become its owners.

eighteenth-century Paris. They were valuable because they were the most malleable and negotiable objects in the popular economy of consumption.[39] They could be pledged in payment for drink and food, sold to haberdashers, old-clothes dealers and tailors, altered or fashioned for personal wear, adornment, and disguise, or bartered for sex and other services. Gérard would have been considerably aggrandized by Kerse's stock of commodities. Nicolas Kerse was archetypal urban prey: possessed of negotiable goods; foreign, and deficient in French; frail, solitary, and probably lonely.

[39] For inventories of clothing worn by the living and the dead, and on changing styles, colors, fabrics, and values in popular dress during the eighteenth century, see Roche, *Le peuple de Paris*, pp. 165–203, and R. C. Cobb, *Death in Paris: The Records of the "Basse-Geôle" of the Seine October 1795 – September 1801* (Oxford: Oxford University Press, 1978).

Conclusion: Judgment: knowledge or power?

These three cases illustrate permutations of intent, confession, and denial in Old Regime criminal law. Trial procedure was organized to illuminate those elements of each case in *grand criminel*. Testimonial, material, and character evidence were the fundamental and common epistemes in the system of trial and judgment. They served as the instruments for either substantiating confession or determining the veracity of denial. And it was primarily from those epistemes that criminal intent, or its absence, was inferred. The cases also illuminate a governing principle of criminal law and justice: the individuation of each defendant in trial and judgment.

Old Regime criminal justice was a world of voices and artifacts that were carefully transcribed or described. To enumerate only the voices: There were a total of nine defendants in our three cases; a total of twenty-five witnesses were heard. It was an ethnography. But it was not transparent. Witnesses could not be interrogated by magistrates when they made depositions. They could not lie with impunity, but they could select their emphases and their silences. In large measure, they were protected by the law from their own truth or its traces. Often, as in the Gérard case, their depositions suggested or even disclosed their own ambient illegality or criminality, but without liability: serving liquor after legal closing hour; prostitution and pimping; trafficking in stolen goods. Similarly, the artifacts of a case were frequently problematic in judicial and social meanings. They had to be studied by magistrates, inductively and critically.

Most of the judges and prosecutors who tried and decided these three cases were magistrates of considerable experience.[1] Each possessed a mental archive

---

[1] The three cases were judged by a total of twenty-six judges and three criminal lieutenants of the Châtelet. We know the tenure in office for twenty-seven of those magistrates. The following are their names and the number of years each had served on the bench at the time when they judged the cases: *Loyer, Caignote, et al.* (May 1749): Negre, criminal lieutenant (14); Lejuge (2); Hurel (4); Guerey de Voisins de Marivaux (7); Roger de Bonlieu (10); Pitoin (11); Roger de Montheuchet (14); Lugat (40); Tarrade (54). *Gosset and Legrand* (March 1762): Lenoir, criminal lieutenant (10); Huerne (2); Millon (11); Dufresnoy (19); Defontaine (23); Pillet (35); Couvreur (43). *Gerard, Méclet, Thibault* (January 1781): Bachois de Villefort, criminal lieutenant (19); Nau de Champlouis (6 months); Baron (1); Baron (2); Devin de Fontenay (2); Garnier (3); Combault de Canthère (6); Boucher d'Argis (9); Bellanger (18); Phélippe de la Marnière (26); Pelletier (36); Avril (40); Fosseyeux (43). The average among the twenty-six judges was twelve years on the bench before judgment of the case.

of criminal justice. The archive would have been arranged in memory by type of crime and type of defendant, just as criminal justice was ordered in law and practice. The longer the experience of a magistrate, the larger his mental archive. Each archive was a fund of knowledge, empirically developed. It was both science and wisdom. But what power over defendants could judges derive from their mental archives?

An entire hermeneutic tradition, one that extends from the works of Francis Bacon to those of Michel Foucault, insists that expert knowledge in human affairs endows the possessor with power in human affairs. From the vantage of that tradition, no form of knowledge as power could be more indubitable than expert knowledge of criminal law combined with authority to judge. But was the eighteenth-century French magistrate's archive of knowledge an instrument of power, or was it instead an intellectual acquisition of little political value?

We may answer the question by examining the relations between a magistrate's mental archive and his permissible judicial acts. Our hypothetical judge of the Châtelet has tried sixty cases of burglary during his ten years on the bench. Forty of those cases resulted in convictions. The principal characteristics of those forty burglaries and their convicted authors were, in fact and in our judge's memory, far more similar than they were different. They shared a strong pattern of characteristics, a pattern that could indicate probability of guilt in future burglary cases. Our judge was aware of that pattern and its projective value. He was confronted with his sixty-first burglary case and its defendant. During preparatory instruction of the case, it transpired that several characteristics of this burglary and this defendant matched the pattern of the forty cases of convicted burglars. The judge was rationally justified in presuming the guilt of the defendant, or in believing that the defendant was probably guilty of the burglary. His guilt became a reasonable hypothesis. That power to presume rationally was based on the judge's mental archive. But it was no more than a power of tentative classification. The judge could not decide the fate of the defendant on the basis of presumption or hypothesis, however rational. He and his colleagues had to obey criminal procedure.

Procedure, the fixed sequence of investigative and trial actions, made the judge start afresh intellectually with each burglary before him. It forced him to shelve most of his rich mental archive of burglaries. The guilt or innocence of the present defendant could not be decided from similarities or dissimilarities between him and forty previously convicted burglars. Procedure required that it be decided from the full and discreet evidence that emerged from investigation and trial of the specific case. That evidence had to satisfy the rules for proof of guilt in capital cases, if the defendant was to be convicted.[2] If the evidence that

---

[2] Because magistrates were forbidden by the ordinance to question witnesses (and I have found no trace, in the records of the Châtelet, of their violating that injunction), they were powerless to shape testimony into evidence. Judges could only react analytically to depositions. When trying accomplices to crimes, magistrates had the burden of proving criminal intent, and thus penal liability, from evidence. Otherwise, they could not convict.

emerged from complete trial did not satisfy those rules, the defendant could not be convicted of burglary, even if there were comprehensive resemblances between him and forty previously convicted burglars. In such a case, our judge was obliged to adopt the following attitude: "I suspect that he is guilty, but I cannot find him guilty, for I must obey the rules of proof." At most, he could opine for longer detention under *plus amplement informé*. We should recognize the intellectual and emotional discipline, even self-abnegation, inherent to that position.

The Public Ministry, without partiality and without passion, demands nothing of defendants except under the hypothesis of a factual truth; and if the hypothesis that presents someone as guilty is found to be false, the cause of that Defendant and of the Public Ministry immediately become one and the same cause. So long as the truth of the hypothesis remains uncertain, one searches for elucidation of the still unknown truth of the crime, and the inclination of public authority is rather in the Defendant's favor insofar as it can justifiably incline in one or the other direction.[3]

But when those rules for proof of guilt were satisfied, there could be little margin for rational doubt of guilt among judges. They were obliged to convict, even if they felt strong compassion for the defendant. Once convicted according to those rules, this sixty-first burglary defendant became another pure specimen of burglar to be filed in the judge's mental archive. Our judge thereby acquired an increment to his scientific knowledge of burglary. Yet that enhanced knowledge would be of quite limited power for him in the next trial of a burglary defendant. It could aid him in asking more penetrating questions in interrogations and in evaluating general evidence with more perspicacity. But it could not form the basis for judgment, and thereby give him transcendent power over the defendant.

The judge's mental archive and criminal procedure were in subtle dialectical relation. Procedural rules were fixed, but they were intricate. The greater the experience of the judge, and thus his archive, the greater his capacity to follow those rules with exactitude. In each case, the judicial result of exactitude would be a higher quality of evidence, whether for guilt or for innocence. The by-product of that judicial result would be accurate classification of the defendant in the judge's mental archive, and thus an increase in his almost purely scientific knowledge of burglaries.

Experience and its mental archive were indeed the intellectual power of Old Regime French magistrates. But the system of trial, proof, and judgment prevented them from translating that intellectual power into political power over defendants. Judges, not defendants, were subjugated by the rigidity of criminal procedure. The system required them to recreate their knowledge with each case, and each case therefore resembled a laboratory experiment whose final outcome and meaning could not be known until the end. The system did generate science. But it generated power only indirectly and inadequately.

[3] L'Averdy, *Code pénal*, p. xxxi.

Conclusion to Volume 1

Now, the true means by which kings can and should conserve, perpetuate, and augment the love binding them and their subjects consists in justice and in peace: in justice, by causing it to be dispensed and administered pure, good, equal, and succinct, without exception of any persons, and without stain or suspicion of greed toward our subjects: in peace, without and within the realm; in peace intrinsic, by making it possible for the common man to live under the shelter and protection of his king, in good, sure, and loving peace, to eat his bread and live on his possessions tranquilly, without being harassed, beaten, pillaged, tormented, or molested . . . , which is the greatest benefaction, contentment, and treasure that a king can accord to his people, and by which the people become more inclined to bless and obey their prince. . . . For these reasons, we have loved, honored, and empowered justice, commanded and ordered that it be duly and virtuously dispensed.[1]

From the late fifteenth century to the eighteenth, French kings and their Chancellors gradually created an objective and comprehensive legal system for the government of France. In creating rule by law, each reign built on foundations laid by predecessors.

The royal system was based on empowerment of cohesive families and kinship groups through venal and then hereditary offices, a process that brought into being what was virtually a distinct and self-perpetuating Estate from highly disparate social elements. Because offices were made transmissible private property (in 1604) and ennoblements by superior offices were made hereditary (after 1644), the kings of France promoted dynasticism, not individualism, in career service to the state, just as they promoted a vocational sense of identity, as against a traditional Estate identity, among all families engaged in officialdom. Superior and ennobling offices were made a theoretical possibility for those families, even for those of modest means in lesser offices. From the Valois through the Bourbons, monarchs signified to families within and without officialdom, "The service you perform is necessary and honorable, even in lesser offices. That service defines you for us. Your property, authority, and privileges in and through civil offices will be assured, so long as you perform your duties. Through persisting and maturing in public service, you may eventually advance

---

[1] Francis I, preamble to the September 1523 edict against banditry, in Isambert, vol. 12, p. 127.

to major and ennobling offices of state." Those propositions remained valid to the end of the Old Regime, despite episodes of intense conflict between kings and magistrates, when certain offices were abolished but then usually reinstated. They demarcated the broadest avenue of upward social and political mobility in early modern and Old Regime France, the avenue that most families of the eighteenth-century Parisian themistocracy had traveled.

During that long process, the monarchy was not a "superstructure," or a mere instrument for the rule of a social class that controlled the means of production. It was the most independently and profoundly creative force in the social and political history of France. Yet by developing a legalistic state with new social foundations, monarchs incrementally alienated much of their power, behind the linguistic disguise of delegation, and their sovereignty gradually acquired a mythical quality. One might say, in brutal simplification, that the Valois and Bourbon kings sold the state to several thousand families, while strictly codifying the manner in which those families were to accede to judicial and administrative offices and to exercise state power. From Louis XII to Louis XVI, monarchs did so with the objective of creating a governing elite that would be uniform, stable, disciplined, professionally competent, dedicated, and just. But they also did so with the contradictory purpose of raising money (from the original sale of offices and then fees collected when they were resold) to make war. Justice and war were the great priorities of French kings, but war was their greatest expenditure, from Francis I to Louis XVI. The great expansionist reigns – Francis I (1515–47), Louis XIII (1622–43), Louis XIV (1661–1715) – were also those most creative in criminal and civil law.

The sums raised by the Treasury from venal-hereditary offices never compensated for the permanent loss of tax revenue from the families of officials. Because of its militarism, the French monarchy lived in a penumbra of bankruptcy. The royal objective of a nomistic, professional governing class was attained, but at the price of a double royal weakness: minimal power over the quotidian government of France; a chronically indebted Treasury in the richest kingdom of Europe, indebtedness that was compounded and entrenched by the practice of borrowing money from the world of venal-hereditary officialdom.

The inevitable result of the system was the maturation of constitutionalist ideas of the state within the body of the state, and by an intellectual evolution that corresponded to actual political evolution. As themistocracy became indispensable, self-replicating, and quasi-autonomous, it became easy for superior magistrates who were proprietary and dynastic to develop the conviction, during the seventeenth and early eighteenth centuries, that they represented and protected the "fundamental laws of the realm." Most of those laws regarding the privileges and powers of corporations, institutions, communities, and Estates were royal in their origins, but in the mind of *parlementaires* they formed a binding tradition that kings could not alter on their solitary authority. In the name of fundamental laws, superior magistrates defied major royal policies during the second half of the eighteenth century, asserting that they, and not the king and his ministers, represented the general interests of French civil society. As conflict deepened, Louis XV and then Louis XVI forcefully and unsuccessfully asserted sovereignty over the state and the realm:

As if it were permissible to ignore that sovereign power resides in my person alone, whose essential character is the spirit of counsel, justice, and reason. That it is from me alone that the courts have their existence and authority. That the plenitude of that authority, which they exercise in my name, always remains with me, and that its usage can never be turned against me. That it is to me alone that legislative power belongs, without any contingency or sharing. . . . That the public order, in its entirety, emanates from me, and that I am its supreme guardian. That my people is one with me and in my person, and that the rights and interests of the "nation" – which some have dared to describe as an entity separate from the monarch – are indissolubly united with my own, and remain in my hands only.[2]

The Estates-General of 1789 was the result of that paralytic conflict of legal wills. Politically, 1789 was as much culmination as rupture in the tensile relationship of monarchy and magistracy.

The outcome was profoundly ironic. It was not simply, or even essentially, the dramatic ending of both monarchy and themistocracy. Through archprofessionalism strongly alloyed with caste, venal-hereditary officialdom – the world exemplified by the magistrates of the Châtelet and Parlement of Paris – created the conditions necessary for its coherent supplantation by a new political regime. Those conditions were a widespread ethos and language of public authority and constitutionalism; recognition of law and recourse to its tribunals among all groups of civil society; clearly defined vocations and techniques for legalistic, as against personal, governance; tens of thousands of men and families educated and experienced in judicial and administrative tasks. The Revolutionary, and especially republican, concept of public "careers open to talent" was, dialectically, an outgrowth of public careers monopolized by families of merit. The linkage was incarnated by deputies in the Constituent Assembly and by executive personnel in major organs of the Revolutionary state during the years 1792 to 1799. (The latter will be examined in Volume 2, in the conclusion to this work).

Those men, and their analogs and successors, were not the only creativity, and modernity, of the old system. The long history of incrimination in France has not been written. During about two hundred years, from the 1530s to the 1750s, kings and chancellors developed a statutory criminal law for the entire realm. It consisted in definitions and penalties for serious offenses; mandatory codes for trial and judgment; definition of the jurisdictional powers of various royal and seigneurial courts; a magistracy constituted, invested, and regulated by the monarchy. Royal statutes penalized most forms of treason, rebellion and sedition; slander and libel; private violence; fraud, theft, and depredation on

---

[2] Louis XV addressing the Parlement of Paris on March 3, 1766, in J. Flammermont and M. Tourneux, *Remonstrances du Parlement de Paris aux XVIII siècle* (Paris, 1895), vol. 2, pp. 557–8.

property; and offenses to religion, public morals, marriage, and the family. Their great prehension expressed the ideology of monarchical sovereignty, as well as the enlarged conception of social order and discipline that issued from 'the seventeenth-century Counter-Reformation. Those statutes will be examined in the context of their enforcement by the Châtelet and Parlement from 1736 to 1789. Their legacy was powerful. Most crimes defined in the Revolutionary Penal Code of 1791 had been defined originally by royal legislation during the period 1530 to 1750, although the authors of the Penal Code refused to acknowledge their heritage.

Since the promulgation of the Ordinance of Blois by Louis XII in March 1498, lawcourts, both superior and subaltern, were bound to apply, interpret, or (when necessary), reason from analogy with royal statutes. Parlements and other superior appeals courts were obliged to enforce that adherence in lower courts, and Chancellors to enforce it over Parlements. Royal criminal law was binding on jurisdictions in every province, unless exceptions were specified (which was rarely done from the mid-sixteenth century to the Revolution). It applied to all subjects of the Crown: clerics and laymen, peers of the realm and plebeians. It was exclusive of all other laws: "The judgments rendered and contracts or obligations agreed to in foreign realms and sovereignties, for whatever cause, will have no authority or execution in France."[3] Its language was exclusively French: "We wish that all decrees and all procedures, whether of sovereign or subaltern and inferior courts, whether in registers, inquests, contracts, commissions, sentences, testaments, and all other actions and writs of justice, be henceforth pronounced, registered, and delivered to all parties involved in the maternal French language, and in no other."[4]

Royal law – criminal, civil, and administrative – was one of the most important instruments for the political and cultural unification of France. It laid foundations for a "nation."

Any dichotomy of a judicial Old Regime based on public corporal punishments and a modern, or post-Enlightenment and post-Revolutionary, justice based on imprisonment at labor and therapeutic reformation of felons is false, for Old Regime penology deployed, and frequently combined, both categories of action. The scale was evenly gradated. Incarcerations – *plus amplement informé*, the *hôpital-général*, the galleys and *bagnes* – filled its broad middle range. The development of carceral punishments after 1670 had the following long-term effects: It further refined and rarefied the death penalty; it reduced the frequency of sentences to banishment; it gave magistrates greater opportunity for equity in selecting punishment for juvenile offenders and for all accomplices in serious crimes. When royal statutes gave judges discretion in sentencing, the rules that governed their selection of penalty, especially in appellate decision, were biased to moderation or leniency and prevented them from making indis-

---

[3] Ordinance of Louis XIII, Article 121 (January 1629), in Isambert, vol. 16, p. 262.
[4] Ordinance of Francis I at Villers-Cotterets (August 1539), Article 111, in Isambert, vol. 12, pp. 622–3.

criminate use of *hôpitaux* and *bagnes*. During the second half of the eighteenth century, the judges of the Châtelet and Parlement, operating within the parameters of the 1670 ordinance and against a dramatic escalation of crime, gradually shifted penal emphasis from banishment and death to incarceration. This development culminated in the prison-ridden Penal Code of 1791, although the culmination was hidden beneath new terminology, institutions, and implacability.

Spectacles of punishment were integral to the system of criminal justice, but they were one of its weakest components. For someone who was inclined to a criminal act to be deterred from the act by a spectacle of punishment, the following conditions would have had to be met. (1) He would have to imagine himself in the place of the punished. If, for whatever reason (differences of gender, social condition, *pays*, even personal appearance), he did not do so, he would not vicariously undergo the punishment. It would then be an alien event, perhaps even an occasion for sadistic amusement. (2) The specific punishment would have to inspire a fear and aversion greater than the anticipated gain from the crime, such that he would say to himself, "The gain I expect is not worth even the risk of that experience." (3) He would have to believe that if he committed the crime he would probably (a) be caught, (b) be convicted, (c) receive that punishment or worse. (4) He had to be in a situation of choice, not one of imperious need. All of those conditions – identification, fear, probabilities, freedom of choice – had to be met for spectacle alone to deter the spectator. Old Regime criminal justice could only exceptionally produce the conditions necessary for deterrence by punitive example. It contained, within its system, great obstacles to deterrence.

Punishment was a warning and a threat. But it was not a promise. Too many contingencies separated the criminal from punishment for there to be promise: (1) the fortuitousness of arrest; (2) strict rules for proof of guilt that governed trial and judgment; (3) assessments of criminal intent and responsibility that determined penal liability; (4) rules for sentencing that were weighted to moderation in punishment. The contingencies were compounded by the fact that the socioeconomic self-interest of high-ranking magistrates was not threatened by most crimes. Their private life-style (which included footmen who doubled as bodyguards) and source of wealth (rentier capital and real estate, instead of money and commercial properties) insulated them. They had both the professional duty and the social luxury of impartiality, procedural scrupulosity, and measure in judgment and punishment. Many, if not all, of those contingencies belonged to public knowledge, and thus to criminal awareness. The spectacle of a hanging or of a chain gang on its way to the *bagnes* was not likely to produce empathetic terror of such punishment among the criminally inclined. It was more likely to provoke the idea that the victims were among the unlucky or clumsy minority of killers, thieves, or rioters who were caught and convicted.

For deterrence to be achieved, the contingencies would have to be eliminated or drastically reduced. The legislators of Revolutionary criminal justice would attempt to eliminate them – by vastly increased policing, mandatory and comparatively severe penalties, expeditive trial procedure, and judgment by jurors who were largely drawn from social groups that suffered crimes of violence and theft, jurors who were freed from Old Regime rules of proof.

In the name of equity, royal justice apportioned penalties to crimes in a way that was both measured and diffuse: measured because the hierarchy of penalties corresponded to the hierarchy in gravity of crimes, such that lesser crimes (the majority committed) were punished by penalties that were often transient experiences for transient persons; diffuse because several penal forms (such as public whipping and display in stocks, banishment from the locality for three or five years, or comparable sentences to the galleys) engulfed a host of very different crimes (pilferage, fraud, injurious assault, sacrilege). Most of those convicted were punished in ways that could not terrify either them or their audience, for most punishments were too momentary, familiar, irrelevant, or surmountable to inspire decisive fear among the populace.

The capacity of the penal system to produce moral or spiritual change in most of the punished was also dubious. The Châtelet and Parlement judged increasing numbers of recidivists, who wore the brand, in the course of the century. Criminals who did not believe that their acts were immoral, who maintained that disbelief during the long trial process, who obstinately denied guilt in the face of compelling evidence, or who did not fear damnation of their souls were not likely to be morally converted by the experience of punishment, despite the public shaming inherent to the experience. Very many of them translated that obstinacy into active defiance at the site of punishment.

The 1670 ordinance and its jurisprudence formed a sophisticated and holistic system for determining the truth of crimes and their suspects, within the limits of reason. Its principles and practice were almost the opposite of its representation in the black legend. As a system of power over the potentially and actually criminal, it was chronically weak, because of its self-restraints, rationality, and equity. Those qualities were sources for the great crisis of criminal justice that developed during the second half of the eighteenth century.

The silent premise of the ordinance was that serious crimes were neither frequent in local jurisdictions nor prevalently collective in nature. That premise probably reflected the France of 1670 – a realm of some 18 million, of which at least 85 percent were country people in hamlets and villages. There were few cities. The artisanate was small in numbers, generally domiciled, and regimented by guild masters. Villages and market towns were the essential units of social life. Those communities were mostly walled, endogamous in social structure, inhabited by people who knew each other, and self-disciplining. The seigneury was still a microsovereignty within rural civilization, a framework for production and order. The Church enjoyed great potency in moral policing through the fine grid of its parishes, schools, and entitlements.

But that was no longer the France of the mid-eighteenth century, in most provinces. Demographic expansion (especially in the numbers of the young), severe economic fluctuations, and extensive migrations combined to erode traditional structures of discipline and to swell towns and cities with the desperate, the anonymous, and the embittered.

It is certain that the provinces depopulate themselves every day in order to swell the population of the Capital, and that it is almost always the dregs of the provinces that abandon them; the immense abyss of the Capital is the repair for the vices of the provinces. Who are the instruments of these public calamities [rioting and crimes]? They are always persons whose names and residences are unknown, individuals who seem foreign to the very city that provides their subsistence; creatures who live only for the moment and who disappear with the same ease with which they appear; men who belong to nothing, who have no property, and who flee with the speed of lightning to avoid judicial pursuit. . . . The majority of laborers, hod-carriers, messengers, and porters exist in a kind of anarchy and dangerous license in the midst of a civilized Capital. . . . Bound by no ties to the city, their emigration is as rapid as it is obscure.[5]

Vagabondage, begging, and robbery were indeed pervasive on main roads. In the metropolis and its region, property crimes steadily increased in volume, as did collective offenses by plebeians. From the 1760s onward in Paris and its hinterlands, the procedural system was overburdened with crimes, and with criminals who were actuated by powerful needs, who rejected the moral norms of the criminal law, who resisted inculpation and refused contrition from the moment of arrest through the experience of punishment. Those realities and their impact will be closely examined in Volume 2.

And yet, successive monarchs, chancellors, and themistocrats remained loyal to the fastidious and majestic 1670 ordinance until the 1780s, for they ventured no significant changes in trial and judgment until the end of that decade. Their loyalty was not to social control and repression. It was to conceptions of truth and justice.

[5] Nicolas Des Essarts, *Dictionnaire universel de police* (Paris, 1783), vol. 7, pp. 460–1.

Index

abduction, 47–8
absolutism, royal, 156, 201–3, 239–40, 271
Acquinas, Thomas, 245, 246
advocates, royal, 55, 59
alterity, 178–93, 202, 255
ambition, 266
amende honorable, see punishment, legal
ancestry, 204
    of Châtelet judges and executive officers,
        103–41
    of *parlementaires*, 157–71
Angran family, 122, 126, 128, 129
antiaristocratic sentiment, 178
Argouges family, 117, 122–5, 150, 167
aristocracy
    military, 182, 185–97, 204
    pluralism of, 176–7, 188–9, 237
    split between two main segments, 176,
        178–93, 200–1, 204, 229–30
    traditional social model of, 269
    see also elites; nobility
aristocratic reaction, 156, 193–7, 202
Aristotle, 245, 246, 264, 289
Arnauld, Antoine, 245
arrest, arbitrary, 39, 42
artisans, 3, 8, 14–19, 30–1, 50, 66–7, 141–3,
    203–4, 535, 598
assault, 519–35
Assemblée de Police, 33
Assembly of Notables, 1787, 156
attroupements, 38–40
Aubert, Léon-Urbain, 207, 211–12, 233, 239
authority, 43–4, 302, 305
    of craft guilds, 8, 142, 203
    ecclesiastical, 497–8
    familial, 46–9, 235–6, 238, 269–70
    judicial, 55, 276, 302, 305, 453, 497–8, 591
    moral and intellectual competence for, 273
    of office, 252
    public, 42–3, 236, 595

    of robe over sword, 41, 192–3
    rule-bound, 494
    of service in high offices of state, 173,
        272–3
    venal-hereditary officialdom and, 45–51,
        239, 593–5
    of vocation, 69, 272
Avocat-Général (Parlement of Paris), 91

Bachois de Villefort, Charles-Simon, 121,
    559–71, 574–6
Bacon, Francis, 591
bagnes, see incarceration; punishment, legal
banishment, *see* punishment, legal
banking, 46
Bastille, 270, 374
Beccaria, Cesare, 283, 326
beggars, 15, 17, 19, 21–2, 33, 34, 277–8,
    345, 411, 465, 502, 535, 599
Benabou, Erica-Marie, 349–51
Bentham, Jeremy, 326
Bergeret family, 219–21, 229–31, 234–5
Beteille, André, 238
Bicêtre, pp. 358–74; *see also* incarceration;
    punishment, legal
Bien, David, 194
"black legend," 420, 598
Black Musketeers, 38–9, 185, 192
Bluche, François, 122, 137, 156–7, 167
Bosher, John, 214
bourgeois militia, 31
bourgeoisie, 46, 66, 137, 141–2, 144, 173,
    194, 268
    antiaristocratic sentiment, 178
    demarcation of themistocracy from, 102,
        141, 204–5
    increase in ennoblements, 1715–89, 177
    mercantile, 50
    upper strata, 155
    values of, 269

Index

Index

Lieutenant criminal, 60
Lieutenant Generalcy of Police, 32–4, 40–2, 350, 351, 367, 368, 369, 370, 410
Lieutenants particuliers, 60–1
lineage property, stable conveyance of, 47–51, 231–2, 276
lits de justice, 88
logic, study of , 244–6

magistrates, 28–9, 42–4, 50–1, 55
of the Châtelet, 28, 32, 34, 42, 55, 59, 103–41, 249–63
oath of office, 251
see also themistocracy
maîtres de requêtes, 25, 179, 398, 408
marc d'or, 67, 223
marriage, 46–51, 98, 139, 234–5, 276, 299–300, 307, 596
of Châtelet judges and executive officers, 133–41
among elites, 178–9
of high ranking military officers, 185–8, 191
of Intendants, 180–2, 191
of parlementaires, 158–63, 164
Marseilles, 14, 316–30
Maussion family, 137, 206–40, 256
Mer, Louis-Bernard, 490–1
merchants, 50, 133, 137, 141, 178
Mercier, Louis-Sébastien, 16, 20, 351, 358, 388
mercy, royal, 293, 394–408, 548
merit, 192, 202, 275
meritocracy, of families, 137, 139, 202, 275, 276, 595
Michau family, 256–7
military, 26, 31, 37–41, 44, 50, 70, 179, 229, 520
high-ranking, 182, 185–91, 198
nobility, 50, 137, 150, 179, 182, 185–92, 204, 268
subordination to civil and judicial authority, 39–43, 192–3
militia, 31, 33
misconduct, professional, 269–70
Molière, Jean-Baptiste, 154
monarchy, 2, 20–1, 23, 25, 27–8, 37–47, 81, 305, 394–408, 548
confrontation with the 3rd Estate, 88, 144, 201
and corporate democracy, 271–2
as primary creative force in the development of rule by law, 28, 42, 43–4, 417–18, 593–6

properties of, 2, 25, 232
and themistocracy, 55, 239–40, 256–7, 273, 594–5
see also absolutism, royal; kings of France
Montaigne, Michel de, 204–5
Moreau family, 117, 127, 130–3, 141
Mousnier, Roland, 45, 144
Muyart de Vouglans, Pierre-François, 248, 250, 285, 287, 289, 298, 300–1, 307, 384–5, 444, 533

National Assembly (1789–90), 201
négociants, 141–2, 155
nepotism, 89, 165, 172, 275, 276
Nicole, Pierre, 245
nobility, 10, 25, 40, 44–5, 81, 141, 498
abolition of, 202
affinities of themistocrats with, 174
avenues to, 177–8
defined, 175–7, 191, 272
five criteria, 272
robe, 144–56, 174, 191, 194, 197–205, 268
sword, 50, 137, 150, 179, 182, 185–205, 269
values of, 196–7, 269
noblesse d'épée, see nobility, sword
noblesse de robe, see nobility, robe
notaries of the Châtelet, 112–13
Nouët family, 150–2

office, venal-hereditary, 45–51, 65, 69, 127, 147, 272, 275, 593–5
costs of, 55, 65–7, 98, 102, 233
privileges, revenues, rewards of, 55, 65–9, 98, 145, 156, 173, 176, 236, 264, 266, 273
officialdom, royal, 202–3
Oratorians, 273
order
corporate, 202–3
and criminal law, 302
crime as disruption of, 298
general principles of, 21, 203
protection of, 69, 299, 504
recurrent crises of, 21–2, 275
public, 203, 275, 298–9, 302, 498
superordination as essence of, 259–60

Palais de Justice, 22–3, 26
pardon, see mercy, royal
Paris
crime, incidence of, 9, 500–1
eighteenth-century, 1–22

Index